ISBN: 9781290810029

Published by:
HardPress Publishing
8345 NW 66TH ST #2561
MIAMI FL 33166-2626

Email: info@hardpress.net
Web: http://www.hardpress.net

FAVORITE SONGS AND HYMNS

FOR

SCHOOL AND HOME

CONTAINING

FOUR HUNDRED AND FIFTY OF THE WORLD'S BEST SONGS AND HYMNS,
INCLUDING NATIONAL SONGS AND MANY SONGS OF DAYS; ALSO, THE ELEMENTS OF
MUSIC AND TWENTY-FIVE RESPONSIVE SCRIPTURAL READINGS.

EDITED BY

J. P. McCASKEY,

Compiler of the "Franklin Square Song Collection."

> Music softens and subdues the rebellious disposition, refines and soothes the wayward, turbulent passions, nerves the heart to deeds of valor and heroism, gives joy and consolation in the hour of affliction, carries the soul captive across the rough and stormy sea of life, and stands beyond the vale of Time to welcome with angelic voice the wandering spirit to its final home.—*John Hall.*

NEW YORK ∴ CINCINNATI ∴ CHICAGO

AMERICAN BOOK COMPANY

Time wrecks the proudest piles we raise,
The towers, the domes, the temples fall;
The fortress crumbles and decays,
One breath of song outlasts them all.

Oliver Wendell Holmes.

To Rev. S. F. Smith, Author of "My Country, 'Tis of Thee."

One of my keenest musical impressions is connected with that marvellous show, the first World's Fair, held in London, and known as the Crystal Palace Exhibition. I shall never see such another. As I stood in the gallery of the great crystal transept and looked down upon a spectacle such as has been witnessed since, but had never before been seen, a feeling of intoxication—there is no other word for it—came over me. I remember perfectly well falling into a kind of dream as I leaned over the painted iron balcony and looked down on the splendid vista. The silver-bell-like tones of an Erard—it was the 1000-guinea piano—pierced through the human hum and noise of splashing waters, but it was a long way off. Suddenly, in the adjoining gallery, the large organ broke out with a blare of trumpets that thrilled and riveted me with an inconceivable emotion. I knew not then what those opening bars were. Evidently something martial, festal, jubilant and full of triumph. I listened and held my breath to hear Mendelssohn's "Wedding March" for the first time, and not know it! To hear it when half the people present had never heard of Mendelssohn, three years after his death, and when not one in a hundred could have told me what was being played, that is an experience I shall never forget. As successive waves of fresh inexhaustible inspiration flowed on, vibrating through the building without a check or a pause, the peculiar Mendelssohnian spaces of cantabile melody alternating as they do in that march with the passionate and almost fierce decision of the chief processional theme, I stood riveted, bathed in the sound as in an element. I felt ready to melt into those harmonious yet turbulent waves and float away upon the tides of "Music's golden sea setting toward Eternity." The angel of Tennyson's Vision might have stood by me whispering, "And thou listenest the lordly music flowing from the illimitable years." Some one called me, so I was told afterward, but I did not hear. They supposed that I was following; they went on, and were soon lost in the crowd. Presently one came back and touched me, but I did not feel. I could not be roused, my soul was living apart from my body. When the music ceased the spell slowly dissolved, and I was led away still half in dreamland. For long years afterward the "Wedding March" affected me strangely.—*Haweis' Musical Memories.*

⁂ The Franklin Square Song Collection, comprising Eight numbers, has sold its hundreds of thousands. The present Supplementary Number, which is more than twice the size of any that has preceded it, is issued in response to the wish of many who have enjoyed the series. Our purpose has been to make this final number the best book of its kind in the world. It is made up from all that have preceded it; and contains some favorite songs not found in any of them. In its 400 pages there are 450 songs and hymns, with much additional matter of interest and value. When we consider the influence of a song or hymn sung by generations and beloved of millions, the pleasure it has afforded, the hope it has inspired, the love it has breathed, the courage it has aroused, stirring the depths of feeling and enriching life with experiences and memories; when we think of hundreds of such heart-songs of home and country, each with its history of deepest interest, could it be written; when we know that the Franklin Square Collection, made up largely of such songs, is a book known and prized, used and enjoyed, in perhaps a hundred thousand schools and homes in and beyond the United States,—when we consider all this, and what it means, we are almost ready to say that nothing has been published within a generation, either in America or in Europe, that we would rather have given to the world. These books reach so many people of fine sensibility; are referred to with pleased interest so often and so widely; are enjoyed, alone and with others, by day and by night, on land and sea, with voice and musical instruments of every kind; and grow in favor, as they become better known, with young and old, rich and poor, learned and unlearned. Blessings on the dear old songs and those who made them! All the merit of the book is theirs. The Compiler is simply glad and grateful that it has been his privilege to contribute to the enjoyment of so many good people, so widely scattered, yet everywhere recognizing the "one touch of nature" that "makes the whole world kin." To Prof. Carl Matz, and to publishers who have kindly permitted the use of their copyrighted songs, he is under special obligations.

Table of Contents.

A Spring Song,	C. Pinsuti.	277
A Soldier in the Village Street,	W. Hutchinson.	218
A Song for the Oak,	H. F. Chorley.	251
A Song for Our Banner,	W. V. Wallace.	293
Abide with Me,	Wm. H. Monk.	121
Adeste Fideles,	Anonymous.	125
After,	Louis Diehl.	236
A Greenness Light and Tender,	Folksong.	266
Ah! For Wings to Soar,	Jullien.	99
Ah! I Have Sighed to Rest Me,	G. Verdi.	226
Ah! 'Tis a Dream,	E. Lassen.	193
A Hundred Years to Come,	W. C. Brown.	108
A Life on the Ocean Wave,	Henry Russell.	146
A Little Word in Kindness Said,	Anonymous.	267
Alice, Where Art Thou?	J. Ascher.	370
All Among the Barley,	Elizabeth Stirling.	315
All Hail the Power of Jesus' Name,	E. Perronet.	19
All's Well,	J. Braham.	115
All the Saints Adore Thee,	J. B. Dykes.	294
All Together,	Geo. F. Root.	138
All is Still, in Sweetest Rest,	F. Küchen.	78
Alleluia! Alleluia!	Easter Carol.	96
Alpine Horn, The,	E. J. Loder.	81
America,	T. Dwight.	133
Amid the Greenwood,	Thalberg.	203
Andreas Hofer,	Folksong.	241
Angelic Songs are Swelling,	F. W. Faber.	186
Angry Words,	Anonymous.	130
Annie Laurie,	Lady John Scott.	128
Anvil Chorus, The,	G. Verdi.	152
Ark of Freedom, Glory's Dwelling,	J. Haydn.	133
Art Thou Weary?	St. Stephanos.	97
As a Little Child,	C. M. Von Weber.	69
As the Wind Blows,	Richard Genee.	242
Ask Me Not Why My Heart,	Charles Jeffrey.	224
At Dawn Aurora Gaily Breaks,	Wm. Jones.	37
At Evening Time,	M. J. Sporle.	215
Auld Lang Syne,	Robert Burns.	256
Aunt Jemima's Plaster,	Anonymous.	346
Autumn Leaves,	Charles Dickens.	147
Away, Away,	D. F. E. Auber.	318
Ave Sanctissima,	Felicia Hemans.	213
Awake, My Soul, and With the Sun,	Thos. Ken.	305
Away with Melancholy,	W. Mozart.	149
Baby Bye, Here's a Fly,	Theodore Tilton.	148
Baby is a Sailor Boy,	George Cooper.	231
Baby's Night,	Anonymous.	225
Baloo, Baloo, My Wee, Wee Thing,	Lullaby.	362
Battle Hymn of Republic,	Julia Ward Howe.	105
Beautiful Bells,	E. O. Lyte.	85
Beautiful Day, The,	D. Hime.	280
Beautiful Faces,	David Swing.	285
Beautiful Spring Time,	Guiseppe Verdi.	254
Believe Me if All Those Endearing,	T. Moore.	350
Ben Bolt,	T. D. English.	299
Be Thou, O God, Exalted High,	W. Franc.	61
Beulah Land,	J. R. Sweeny.	19
Birdie Sweet,	Childhood Songs.	147
Bird's Nest, The,	Helen Thomas.	287
Birds Are in the Woodland,	Anonymous.	35
Birds Sleeping Gently, The,	J. Ascher.	370
Bloom On, My Roses,	F. H. Cowen.	129
Blossom Time,	Mary E. Dodge.	137
Blue Alsatian Mountains,	Stephen Adams.	45
Blushing Maple Tree,	Hamilton Aide.	139
Boatman's Return, The,	M. J. Sporle.	249
Boat Song,	C. M. Von Weber.	127
Bonnie Banks of Loch Lomond,	Anonymous.	342
Bonnie Charlie,	Lady Nairne.	364
Bonnie Doon,	Robert Burns.	248
Brave Old Oak,	E. J. Loder.	251
Bridal Chorus,	R. Wagner.	268
Bride Bells, The,	J. L. Roeckel.	232
Brightly,	Michael Haydn.	16
Bright, Rosy Morning,	Anonymous.	114
Buttercup Test,	Childhood Songs.	185
Buy My Strawberries,	C. Howard.	136
By Killarney's Lakes and Fells,	Wm. B. Bradbury.	88
Call John,	Wm. B. Bradbury.	88
Calm Was the Night,	Arthur Sullivan.	273
Carol, Brothers, Carol,	W. A. Muhlenberg.	263
Castles in Spain,	V. Bellini.	94
Chapel, The,	Uhland.	62
Chatterbox, The,	Jane Taylor.	302
Cheer, Boys, Cheer,	Charles Mackay.	54
Cheerily the Bugle Sounds,	J. H. Hewitt.	247
Chide Mildly the Erring,	W. H. Bradbury.	124
Child, is Life Bright Alone,	W. H. Emra.	48
Child of Earth with Golden Hair,	C. E. Horn.	66
Child of the Regiment,	G. Donizetti.	224
Children's Songs,		135, 271, 301
Chime Again, Beautiful Bells,	H. R. Bishop.	174
Christ is Born in Bethlehem,	Anonymous.	159
Christ is Born of Maiden Fair,	Gauntlet.	253
Christmas As It Comes,	Anonymous.	195
Christmas Carol,	Thomas Helmore.	262
Christmas Hymn,	Henry Dielman.	267
Christmas is Coming,	J. P. McCaskey.	329
Christmas is Here,	W. M. Thackeray.	324
Christmasse of Olde,	Anonymous.	198
Christmas Song,	A. Adam.	27
Christmas Time is Come Again,	Anonymous.	158
Christ was Born on Christmas Day,	J. M. Neale.	262
Church Militant,	H. S. Cutler.	107
Columbia, God Preserve Thee Free,	J. Haydn.	133
Columbia, the Gem of the Ocean,	D. T. Shaw.	155
Come, All Ye Faithful,	J. Reading.	125
Come, Boys, and Sound Your A,	W. Wetmore.	90
Come, Cheerful Companions,	French Air.	58
Come, Come Quickly Away,	Anonymous.	272
Come, let us Join in Merry Chorus,	Offenbach.	283
Come, let us Learn to Sing,	Anonymous.	301
Come, My Gallant Soldier,	H. R. Bishop.	239
Come, Oh, Come With Me,	Italian Air.	64
Come Out, 'tis Now September,	E. Sterling.	315
Come, Swell the Strain,	Charles Jarvis.	337
Come to the Old Oak Tree,	English.	131
Come to the Sparkling Fountain,	Anonymous.	109
Come, Thou Almighty King,	Charles Wesley.	305
Come Where Flowers are Flinging,	Von Flotow.	252
Come with the Gipsy Bride,	M. W. Balfe.	246
Come, Ye Disconsolate,	Samuel Webbe.	142
Corn Song, The,	Godfrey Marks.	316
Coronation,	Oliver Holden.	19
Cousin Jedediah,	H. S. Thompson.	250
Cradle Hymn,	J. J. Rousseau.	118
Cradle Song of Soldier's Wife,	T. T. Barker.	285
Cradle Song of Virgin,	Joseph Barnby.	199
Dawn of Day, The,	Samuel Reay.	349
Dearest Native Land,	H. Proch.	154
Dearest Spot, The,	W. T. Wrighton.	156
Dear Father, Drink No More,	Temperance.	60
Deck the Hall,	Welsh Air.	300
Deserted by the Waning Moon,	J. Braham.	115

Ding, Dong, I Love the Song, . *Poniatowski.* 100
Dip, Boys, Dip the Oar, . . *F. Sarona.* 203
Distant Drum, The, . . *Anonymous.* 313
Down in a Coal Mine, . *J. P. Geoghegan.* 87
Down the Stream So Cheerily, . *Anonymous.* 291
—Do They Think of Me at Home? *C. W. Glover.* 36
⹀Dream Faces, . . . *W. M. Hutchinson.* 326
Drift, My Bark, . . . *F. Kucken.* 170
Ehren on the Rhine, *Wm. M. Hutchinson.* 218
Elements of Music, One Hundred Points, . 372
Emmanuel, ... *W. C. Dix.* 336
Ere the Twilight Bat was Flitting, *B. Covert.* 103
Evening Hymn, . . *Felicia Hemans.* 213
Evening Hymn, . . *F. Mendelssohn.* 305
—Ever of Thee, . . . *Foley Hall.* 49
Ever to the Right,. . . *Anonymous.* 179
Eve's Lamentation, . . *M. P. King.* 77
Fade, Fade, Each Earthly Joy, . *H. Bonar.* 275
Fading, Still Fading, . . *Portuguese.* 145
Fair Luna, . . . *J. Barnby.* 240
Faithful Little Bird, . *D. M. Craik.* 176
—Far Away, . . . *M. Lindsay.* 32
Far Out on Desolate Billow, *R. W. Raymond.* 275
⹀Farewell is a Lonely Sound, *J. C. Englebrecht.* 297
Farewell to the Woods, . *German.* 200
Farmer, The, . . *Kindergarten.* 125
Father Joe, . . *F. Von Flotow.* 264
Fisherman's Chorus, . *D. F. E. Auber.* 157
Flag of Our Union Forever, . *Geo. P. Morris.* 293
—Flag of the Free, . . *J. P. McCaskey.* 295
+—Flee As a Bird, . *Mary S. B. Dana.* 50
—Flow Gently, Sweet Afton, . *Robert Burns.* 53
Flowrets Blooming, . . *F. Schubert.* 327
—Flowers for the Brave, . *E. W. Chapman.* 144
Flow, Rio Verde, . . *Anonymous.* 13
Follow Me, Full of Glee, . *Movement Song.* 270
Forever and Forever, . *C. C. Converse.* 169
⹀Fourth of July Hymn, . *T. Hastings.* 267
Fox and Goose, . . *Childhood Song.* 303
Freedom's Flag, . . *John J. Hood.* 46
—Gentle Annie, . . *Stephen C. Foster.* 140
German Lullaby, . . *Slumber Song.* 320
Give Me Jesus, . . *Slave Hymn.* 309
+ ⹀Gloria Patri, . . *Anonymous.* 97
Glory and Love to the Men of Old, *C. F. Gounod.* 368
God Bless Our Native Land, . *T. Dwight.* 133
God Rest You, Chrysten Gentilmen, *Swiss Air.* 198
God Shall Charge His Angel Legions, . 29
Golden Rule, . . . *Anonymous.* 187
Golden Slumbers Kiss Your Eyes, . *Lullaby.* 225
Golden Stars for Me are Shining, . *H. Proch.* 154
Good-Bye . . *J. C. Engelbrecht.* 297
Good Cheer, . . . *Anonymous.* 211
Good Night, . . . *Franz Abt.* 211
Good Night (Round), . . *Anonymous.* 249
Good Night, Ladies, . . *Serenade.* 85
Good Three Bells, . . *Charles Jarvis.* 337
—Go to Sleep, Lena Darling, . *J. K. Emmet.* 172
⹀Greenwood Tree, The, . *Sidney Nelson.* 141
Guadeamus Igitur, . . *College Song.* 237
+ ⹀Guide Me, Great Jehovah, . *F. Herold.* 273
⹀Hail and Farewell, . *Mrs. C. Barnard.* 259
—Hail Columbia, . . *F. Hopkinson.* 153
Hail Columbia, New, . . *O. W. Holmes.* 371
Hail to the Brightness, . *Thos. Hastings.* 351
Hail, Thou Most Sacred One, *Felicia Hemans.* 213
Hallelujah Chorus, . . *G. F. Handel.* 112
Happy and Light, . . *M. W. Balfe.* 180
Happy Are We To-night, . *M. S. Pike.* 221
Hard Times, Come Again No More, *S. C. Foster.* 342
—Hark! I Hear an Angel Sing, *R. G. Shrival.* 101

Hark! the Herald Angels Sing, *Chas. Wesley.* 304
Hark! the Vesper Hymn is Stealing, *T. Moore.* 25
⊢Harp that Once through Tara's Halls, *T. Moore.* 83
Heart Bowed Down, The, . *M. W. Balfe.* 177
Hearts and Homes, . . *John Blockley.* 231
Heaven is My Home, . *A. S. Sullivan.* 339
⹀Heavens Are Telling, The, . *L. Beethoven.* 28 +
Heavily Wears the Day, . . *German* 212
Heirs of Unending Life, . *B. Beddome.* 119
—Herdsman's Mountain Home, . *Volkslied.* 122
Here under the Leafy Greenwood Tree, *Nelson.* 141
He's the Lily of Valley, . *Slave Hymn.* 311
Ho, Ho, Vacation Days are Here, *J.C.Johnson.* 332
⹀Holy, Holy, Holy, . . *J. B. Dykes.* 294 +
Holy Night (Heilige Nacht) . *Michael Haydn.* 173
⹀Home Again, . . . *M. S. Pike.* 9
Home, Can I Forget Thee?. . *German.* 333
⹀Home of the Soul, . . *Philip Phillips.* 120 +
Home's Not Merely Four Square Walls, *Rossini.* 62
⹀Home, Sweet Home, . *John Howard Payne.* 12
How Dear to My Heart, . *S. Woodworth.* 206
⹀How Gentle God's Commands, *H. G. Nageli.* 119 +
Humpty Dumpty, . . *Mother Goose.* 321
Hush, My Babe, Lie Still and Slumber, *Watts.* 118
I Have Fruit, I Have Flowers, . *J. A. Wade.* 192
I Have Heard the Mavis Singing, . *S. Nelson.* 42
I Have Roamed Over Mountain, *W. Bradbury.* 288
I Know a Bank, . . *Charles E. Horn.* 98
I Love the Merry Sunshine, . *Stephen Glover.* 75
⊣I Love Thy Kingdom, Lord, . *T. Dwight.* 245 +
I Sat Beneath the Maples Old, . *C. Pinsuti.* 277
I Want Forty Dozen of Fine Waxen Dolls, . 329
If Ever I See, on Bush or Tree, . *Little Folks.* 261
Image of the Rose, . . *G. Reichardt.* 354
I'm a Forester Free, . . *E. Reyloff.* 91
I'm a Shepherd of the Valley, . *F. G. Klaner.* 182
I'm Glad I am a Farmer, . *Anonymous.* 135
In Excelsis Gloria, . . *Welsh Air.* 132
In Flakes of a Feathery White, *W. O. Bourne.* 352
In Heavenly Love Abiding, . *F. Mendelssohn.* 26
In Merry Chorus, . . *J. Offenbach.* 283
In Shadowland, . . . *C. Pinsuti.* 265
In the Quarries Should You Toil, . *Anonymous.* 55
In the Starlight, . . *Stephen Glover.* 292
In the West the Sun Declining, . *Franz Abt.* 211
In the Wild Chamois Track, . *Malibran.* 81
Ingleside, The, . . *T. F. Weisenthal.* 83
Innisfail, . . . *E. C. Phelps.* 106
Integer Vitæ, . . . *College Song.* 237
Into the Woods My Master Went, . *S. Lanier.* 360
It's Rare to See the Morning Bleeze, *H. Ainslee.* 83
It is Better to Laugh than Be Sighing, *Donizetti.* 257
I've Been Roaming, . . *Charles E. Horn.* 52
I've Reached the Land of Corn and Wine, . 19
—Ivy Green, The, . . *Henry Russell.* 319
I Will Sing You a Song, . *G. H. Gates.* 120
I Would That My Love, . *F. Mendelssohn.* 189
—Jamie's on the Stormy Sea, . *Bernard Covert.* 103
Jem, the Carter Lad,. . . *J. S. Baker.* 86
⹀Jerusalem the Golden, . *Alexander Ewing.* 358 +
Jerusalem, My Happy Home, . *Latin Hymn.* 143
—Jesus is Mine, . . . *Horatius Bonar.* 275 +
Jesus Lives, . . . *C. F. Gellert.* 121
⊣Jesus, the Very Thought of Thee, . *G. Rossini.* 341 +
Jeannette and Jaennot, . *Charles W. Glover.* 348
Johnny Schmoker, . . . *German.* 222
Jolly Old St. Nicholas, . . *Anonymous.* 300
Joy, Joy, Freedom To-day, . . *Anonymous.* 184
Joy to the World, . . . *Isaac Watts.* 72
⊣Juanita, ... *Caroline Norton.* 44
Kathleen, ... *W. Williams.* 194

—Kathleen Mavourneen,	*F. W. N. Crouch.*	70
—Killarney,	*M. W. Balfe.*	43
—Kind Words Can Never Die,	*Abby Hutchinson.*	344
Landing of the Pilgrims,	*F. Hemans.*	245
Last Rose of Summer, The,	*Thomas Moore.*	322
Laughing Glee,	*Martini.*	286
Lead, Kindly Light,	*J. H. Newman.*	29
Leaves Around Me Falling,	*Greek Air.*	31
Let Erin Remember,	*Thomas Moore.*	160
Let the Palms Wave,	*J. Faure.*	190
Let us Pause in Life's Pleasures,	*S. C. Foster.*	342
Life is but a Fleeting Dream,	*C. J. Dunphy.*	351
Life Let Us Cherish,	*H. G. Nageli.*	25
Lightly Row,	*Spanish Melody.*	261
Listen to the Mocking Bird,	*Alice Hawthorne.*	65
Little Bird, The,	*Anonymous.*	301
Little Boy Blue,	*Eugene Field.*	366
Little by Little,	*C. Barnard.*	174
Little Cherry Blossom,	*Anonymous.*	185
Little Girl, Don't You Cry,	*German.*	92
Loch Lomond,	*Old Scotch.*	342
Longing for Spring,	*German.*	123
Long, Long Ago,	*T. H. Bayly.*	345
Long, Weary Day, The,	*Suabian Volkslied.*	76
Look Our Ransomed Shores Around,	*Holmes.*	371
Lord, Dismiss us with Thy Blessing,	*W. Shirley.*	340
Lord's Prayer, The,	*S. J. Hale.*	59
Look Not upon the Wine,	*R. S. Willis.*	60
Lord, in this Thy Mercy's Day,	*W. H. Monk.*	359
Love and Mirth,	*J. Strauss.*	126
Loving Voices,	*Charles W. Glover.*	258
Lovely May,	*Little Folks.*	261
Love's Golden Dream,	*Lindsay Lennox.*	334
Love Thy Mother, Little One,	*Russian.*	201
Mahogany Tree, The,	*W. M. Thackeray.*	324
Maid of the Mill, The,	*Hamilton Aide.*	367
Make the Best of It,	*C. J. Dunphy.*	351
Make Your Mark,	*Anonymous.*	55
Mandolin Song, The,	*Spanish.*	228
Many Thousand Gone,	*Slave Hymn.*	311
Marching Song,	*German.*	74
Marseilles Hymn,	*Rouget de Lisle.*	323
Mary of Argyle,	*Sidney Nelson.*	42
Maxwelton's Braes are Bonnie,	*Lady John Scott.*	128
Massa's in the Cold Ground,	*S. C. Foster.*	162
May Queen, The,	*Alfred Tennyson.*	296
May the Grace of Christ, Our Saviour,	*Doxology.*	79
Mellow Horn, The,	*Wm. Jones.*	37
Melodies of Many Lands,	*C. W. Glover.*	10
Merrily Every Bosom Boundeth,	*German Air.*	67
Mermaid's Evening Song,	*Stephen Glover.*	196
Methought the Stars Were Blinking Bright,		208
Midshipmite, The,	*F. E. Weatherly.*	39
Miller of the Dee, The,	*Charles Mackay.*	150
Miller's Daughter, The,	*Bohemian Air.*	291
Mill May,	*Anonymous.*	68
Mill Wheel, The,	*Anonymous.*	353
Mine Eyes Have Seen the Glory,	*Julia W. Howe.*	105
Minstrel Boy, The,	*Thomas Moore.*	202
Monarch of the Woods,	*J. W. Cherry.*	269
Moon is Beaming o'er the Lake,	*John Blockley.*	57
Morning's Ruddy Beam,	*G. Linley.*	93
Mountain Bugle, The,	*J. H. Hewitt.*	247
Mountain Maid's Invitation,	*H. Werner.*	361
Mower's Song, The,	*Anonymous.*	353
Murmur, Gentle Lyre,	*Anonymous.*	221
Musical Alphabet,	*Anonymous.*	249
Musical Scale, The,	*Anonymous.*	301
Music on the Waves,	*C. W. Glover.*	307
Must I Leave Thee, Paradise,	*M. P. King.*	77
Must I Then, Must I Then,	*Folksong.*	84
My Bonnie is Over the Ocean,	*Anonymous.*	175
My Country, 'Tis of Thee,	*S. F. Smith.*	293
My Native Land, Again Mine Eye,	*E. Lassen.*	193
My Normandy,	*Frederic Berat.*	23
My Old Kentucky Home,	*Stephen C. Foster.*	167
My Own Native Land,	*W. B. Bradbury.*	288
National Hymn,	*S. F. Smith.*	293
Nearer, My God, to Thee,	*Sarah F. Adams.*	119
Never Alone,	*R. W. Raymond.*	275
Never Say Fail,	*Anonymous.*	123
New Hail Columbia,	*O. W. Holmes.*	371
Ninety and Nine,	*Ira D. Sankey.*	244
Nobody Knows the Trouble I've Seen,	*Slave.*	310
None Can Tell,	*G. B. Allen.*	48
Noontide Ray, The,	*D. F. E. Auber.*	233
Not in Halls of Regal Splendor,	*Welsh.*	132
Now All the Bells,	*Easter Carol.*	96
Now I Lay Me Down to Sleep,	*H. F. Allen.*	274
Now Thank We All Our God,	*Martin Rinkart.*	71
Nursery Songs,	302, 303,	321
Nymphs of Air and Sea,	*Henry Smart.*	188
O Come, Come Away,	*W. E. Hickson.*	356
O Could Our Thoughts,	*Anne Steele.*	255
O Fair Dove, O Fond Dove,	*Jean Ingelow.*	208
O I'm a Happy Creature,	*Spanish.*	228
O That I Never More Might See,	*G. Donizetti.*	205
O Thou Joyful Day,	*Johannes Falk.*	336
O What Can You Tell,	*R. W. Raymond.*	278
Oft in Danger, Oft in Woe,	*H. K. White.*	31
Oft in the Stilly Night,	*John Stevenson.*	168
Oh, Boys, Carry Me 'Long,	*Stephen C. Foster.*	163
Oh, For a Thousand Tongues,	*Charles Wesley.*	97
Oh, Gladly Now We Hail Thee,	*V. Bellini.*	161
Oh, How Cold the Winter Weather,	*Anonymous.*	123
Oh, Lord, Keep Me from Sinking Down,	*Slave.*	311
Oh, Mary, Call the Cattle Home,	*Chas. Kingsley.*	306
Oh, My Bravest and Best,	*V. Bellini.*	284
Oh, the Sports of Childhood,	*O. R. Barrowes.*	223
Oh, Wert Thou in the Cauld Blast,	*Robert Burns.*	205
Oh, What is the Matter with Robin?	*Little Folks.*	317
Old Cottage Clock, The,	*J. L. Molloy.*	314
Old Dog Tray,	*Stephen C. Foster.*	165
Old Easy Chair by the Fire,	*Jas. C. Beckel.*	343
Old Familiar Place, The,	*C. W. Glover.*	69
Old Folks at Home,	*Stephen C. Foster.*	166
Old Gaelic Lullaby,	*J. G. Whittier.*	320
Old Hundred,	*W. Frane.*	61
Old Kentucky Home,	*Stephen C. Foster.*	167
Old Oaken Bucket,	*Samuel Woodworth.*	206
Old Santa Claus,	*John Read.*	365
One by One the Sands are Flowing,	*V. Bellini.*	214
Once Again the Flowers We Gather,	*Chapman.*	144
One Summer Eve, in Pensive Thought,	*Cherry.*	14
On Yonder Rock Reclining,	*D. F. E. Auber.*	243
On the Mountain Steep and Hoary,	*Anonymous.*	122
Our Country's Flag, O Emblem Dear,	*J. J. Hood.*	46
Our Father in Heaven,	*S. J. Hale.*	59
Our Flag O'er Us Waving,	*C. Verdi.*	152
Our Songs of Joy and Gladness,	*Meyerbeer.*	178
Out in a Beautiful Field,	*Anonymous.*	149
Out of the Window,	*J. Norton.*	281
Over the Dark Blue Sea,	*Swiss Air.*	238
Over There,	*T. C. O'Kane.*	21
Over the Stars There is Rest,	*Franz Abt.*	210
Over the Summer Sea,	*G. Verdi.*	220
Palms, The,	*J. Faure.*	190
Peace on Earth,	*G. Donizetti.*	283
Playtime Songs,	*Little Folks.*	330, 331
Pleasure Climbs to Every Mountain,	*Gollmick.*	260
Poor Tho' My Cot May Be,	*G. Donizetti.*	357
Praise God from Whom All Blessings Flow,		61

Praise Ye Jehovah's Name,	*Anonymous.*	305
Praise to God,	*Sebastian Bach.*	51
Prayer from Freischutz,	*C. M. Von Weber.*	359
Pretty Pear Tree,	*Anonymous.*	149
Pull Away, Brave Boys,	*G. Rossini.*	47
Rain upon the Roof,	*G. Clifford.*	33
Raise Your Hands,	*Anonymous.*	187
Rise, Crowned with Light,	*A. Lyoff.*	51
Robinson Crusoe,	*Rogue's March.*	56
Rosy Crown, The,	*C. M. Von Weber.*	63
Row, Row, Cheerily Row,	*D. M. Muloch.*	38
Sands o' Dee, The,	*Francis Booth.*	306
Saw Ye Never in the Twilight,	*C. F. Alexander.*	198
Scenes That Are Brightest,	*W. V. Wallace.*	143
Scout, The,	*Fabio Campana.*	234
Scotch Cradle Song,	*Old Lullaby.*	362
Sea Gulls, The,	*Anonymous.*	241
Search Thro' the Wide World,	*G. Donizetti.*	217
See At Your Feet,	*M. W. Balfe.*	104
See the Proud Banner of Liberty,	*G. Verdi.*	152
See the Sun's First Gleam,	*German.*	328
See Yon Chapel on the Hill,	*Uhland.*	62
Shall We Meet Beyond the River,	*E. S. Rice.*	79
She Wore a Wreath of Roses,	*T. H. Bayly.*	82
Shells of Ocean,	*J. W. Cherry.*	14
Should Auld Acquaintance,	*Robert Burns.*	256
Shout the Glad Tidings,	*W. A. Muhlenberg.*	73
Silent Night,	*Michael Haydn.*	173
Silently Falling Snow,	*Wm. O. Bourne.*	352
Silver Chimes,	*Mrs. C. Barnard.*	22
Sing Glad Songs for Him,	*J. P. McCaskey.*	134
Sing, Smile, Slumber,	*C. F. Gounod.*	95
Slave Hymns,	*Anonymous.*	311
Sleep, Sleep, My Darling,	*Lullaby.*	320
Slumber, Dearest,	*C. M. Von Flotow.*	229
Slumber Song, The,	*F. Kücken.*	78
Slumber Songs,	*Anonymous.*	320
Snow Bird, The,	*F. C. Woodworth.*	347
Softly Now the Light of Day,	*G. W. Doane.*	107
Soft Music is Stealing,	*M. S. B. Dana.*	127
Soft O'er the Fountain,	*Caroline Norton.*	44
Soldiers' Chorus ("Faust")	*C. F. Gounod.*	368
Soldiers' Farewell,	*J. Kinkel.*	355
Somewhere,	*F. Campana.*	24
Song of Night,	*German.*	209
Song of Parting,	*F. Abt.*	229
Songs, Revealing Sacred Feeling,	*Von Weber.*	359
Sons of Men, Behold From Far,	*Chas. Wesley.*	173
Sound Our Voices Long and Sweet.	*Bohemian.*	17
Sound Your A,	*W. B. Bradbury.*	90
Sparkling and Bright,	*Chas. F. Hoffman.*	61
Speed Away,	*I. B. Woodbury.*	298
Speak Gently,	*W. V. Wallace.*	20
Spider and the Fly,	*O. H. Normino.*	279
Spring, Gentle Spring,	*J. Riviere.*	15
Spring Song, A,	*Ciro Pinsuti.*	277
Spring Time Once Again,	*John Logan.*	312
Star Spangled Banner,	*Francis S. Key.*	151
Stars Trembling O'er Us,	*D. M. Muloch.*	35
Steal Away,	*Slave Hymn.*	308
Stranger Star, The,	*C. F. Alexander.*	198
Strawberries Grow in the Mowing,	*Anonymous.*	68
Strike the Cymbal,	*Pucitta.*	363
Summer Days are Coming,	*Charles Jeffreys.*	40
Sweet and Low,	*J. Barnby.*	34
Sweeter than the Breath of Morning,	*Meyerbeer.*	191
Swing, Cradle, Swing,	*George Cooper.*	231
Swinging 'Neath the Old Apple Tree,	*Barrowes.*	223
Swing Low, Sweet Chariot,	*Slave Hymn.*	309
Tara's Harp,	*Thomas Moore.*	83
Tea in the Arbor,	*J. Beuler.*	110

Tell Me, Beautiful Maiden,	*Charles Gounod.*	207
The Morn of Life is Past,	*S. C. Foster.*	165
The Son of God Goes Forth to War,	*R. Heber.*	107
The World is Full of Beauty,	*G. Donizetti.*	230
Then You'll Remember Me,	*M. W. Balfe.*	334
There is a Happy Land,	*Andrew Young.*	333
There is Beauty in the Forest,	*G. Donizetti.*	230
There's a Wedding in Orchard,	*M. E. Dodge.*	137
Thine Eyes so Blue and Dreaming,	*E. Lassen.*	216
Those Endearing Young Charms,	*T. Moore.*	350
Thou 'rt Like Unto a Flower,	*A. Rubinstein.*	282
Thou Wilt Come No More,	*S. C. Foster.*	140
Thoughts of Wonder,	*Anonymous.*	339
Three Children Sliding,	*Old Ditty.*	63
Three Fishers,	*Charles Kingsley.*	204
Three Kings of Orient,	*Old Carol.*	195
Time of the Singing of Birds,	*Geo. Barker.*	276
Touch Not the Cup,	*Jas. H. Aikman.*	338
Touch us Gently, Time,	*Barry Cornwall.*	80
Trees and the Master,	*Sidney Lanier.*	360
'Twas in Fifty-five, on a Winter's Night,	*Adams.*	39
Twickenham Ferry,	*Theo. Marzials.*	41
Twilight is Falling,	*B. C. Unseld.*	59
Twinkle Brightly, Stars of Night,	*Anonymous.*	225
Under the Shade of the Trees,	*M. J. Preston.*	30
Upon the Height,	*Folksong.*	181
Verdant Grove, Farewell to Thee,	*Folksong.*	200
Vesper Hymn,	*Thomas Moore.*	25
Waking or Sleeping,	*J. V. Blake.*	109
Watch and Ward,	*J. Montgomery.*	29
Watch on the Rhine,	*Carl Wilhelm.*	290
Way Down upon the Swanee River,	*S. C. Foster.*	166
Wear a Bright Smile,	*G. Verdi.*	102
We are Happy and Free,	*Anonymous.*	238
We'd Better Bide a Wee,	*Claribel.*	335
We May Roam the Wide World Over,	*Glover.*	69
Welcome, Pretty Primrose,	*Ciro Pinsuti.*	183
Welcome to Morning,	*J. Offenbach.*	117
What is Home?	*Charles Swain.*	62
What Fairy Like Music,	*Jos. De Pinna.*	116
What Means This Glory,	*G. Donizetti.*	283
What Pleasure Folks Feel,	*J. Beuler.*	110
What Will You Do, Love?	*Samuel Lover.*	111
What Song Does the Cricket Sing,	*J. Strauss.*	126
When All the World is Young,	*C. Kingsley.*	89
When at Twilight So Softly,	*Victor Hugo.*	95
When I was a Beggarly Boy,	*J. R. Lowell.*	94
When I Come,	*Folksong.*	84
When I was a Lad,	*Anonymous.*	56
When Shall We Meet Again?	*Lowell Mason.*	341
When the Green Leaves,	*Anonymous.*	103
When the Humid Showers Gather,	*G. Clifford.*	33
When on the World's First Harvest Day,	*Aidi.*	139
When the Swallows Homeward Fly,	*F. Abt.*	11
Where is Now the Merry Party,	*M. Lindsay.*	32
Where Will Be the Birds that Sing,	*W. Brown.*	108
While the Morning Bells.	*Sicilian Hymn.*	79
Who is He Plants for Days to Come,	*Gounod.*	134
Who is Sylvia?	*Franz Schubert.*	104
Why Do Summer Roses Fade?	*George Barker.*	18
Will You Walk into My Parlor?	*O. Normino.*	279
Willie, We Have Missed You,	*S. C. Foster.*	164
Winkum, Winkum,	*Nursery Song.*	271
With this Humble Stock in Store,	*C. Howard.*	136
Woodman, Spare That Tree,	*Geo. P. Morris.*	227
Yankee Doodle,	*Anonymous.*	289
Ye Banks and Braes,	*Robert Burns.*	248
Ye Sons of France, Awake to Glory,	*De Lisle.*	323
Yeoman's Wedding Song,	*Poniatowski.*	100
You are Going Far Away,	*Charles Jeffreys.*	248

114   48B.   28ₓ

National Songs.

America,	*T. Dwight.*	133
Andreas Hofer,	*Folksong.*	241
Ark of Freedom, Glory's Dwelling,	*J. Haydn.*	133
Battle Hymn of Republic,	*Julia Ward Howe.*	105
By Killarney's Lakes and Fells,	*M. W. Balfe.*	43
Columbia, God Preserve Thee Free,	*J. Haydn.*	133
Columbia, the Gem of the Ocean,	*D. T. Shaw.*	155
Dearest Native Land,	*H. Proch.*	154
Flag of Our Union Forever,	*Geo. P. Morris.*	293
Flag of the Free,	*R. Wagner.*	295
Flowers for the Brave,	*E. W. Chapman.*	144
Fourth of July Hymn,	*T. Hastings.*	267
Freedom's Flag,	*John J. Hood.*	46
God Bless Our Native Land,	*T. Dwight.*	133
Hail Columbia,	*F. Hopkinson.*	153
Let Erin Remember,	*Thomas Moore.*	160
Marseilles Hymn,	*Rouget de Lisle.*	323
My Country, 'Tis of Thee,	*S. F. Smith.*	293
My Normandy,	*Frederic Berat.*	23
My Own Native Land,	*W. B. Bradbury.*	288
National Hymn, The,	*S. F. Smith.*	293
New Hail Columbia,	*O. W. Holmes.*	371
Now Thank We All Our God,	*M. Rinkart.*	71
Our Flag O'er Us Waving,	*G. Verdi.*	152
Star Spangled Banner,	*Francis S. Key.*	151
Soldiers' Chorus,	*C. F. Gounod.*	368
Watch on the Rhine,	*Carl Wilhelm.*	290
Yankee Doodle,	*Anonymous.*	289

Arbor Day Songs.

A Greenness Light and Tender,	*Folksong.*	266
All Among the Barley,	*Elizabeth Stirling.*	315
Amid the Greenwood,	*Thalberg.*	203
Autumn Leaves,	*Charles Dickens.*	147
Beautiful Spring Time,	*G. Verdi.*	254
Bloom On, My Roses,	*F. H. Cowen.*	129
Blossom Time,	*Mary E. Dodge.*	137
Blushing Maple Time,	*Hamilton Aide.*	139
Brave Old Oak, The,	*E. J. Loder.*	251
Brightly Gleam the Sparking Rills,	*M. Haydn.*	16
Bright Rosy Morning,	*Anonymous.*	114
Buy My Strawberries,	*C. Howard.*	136
Come to the Old Oak Tree,	*Anonymous.*	131
Come Where Flowers are Flinging,	*Von Flotow.*	252
Day on the Mountain, Beautiful Day,	*D. Hime.*	280
Farewell to the Woods,	*German.*	200
Flowrets Blooming,	*F. Schubert.*	327
Greenwood Tree,	*Sidney Nelson.*	141
Hark! I Hear an Angel Sing,	*R. G. Shrival.*	101
I Have Fruit, I Have Flowers,	*J. A. Wade.*	192
I Know a Bank,	*Chas. E. Horn.*	98
I'm a Forester Free,	*E. Reyloff.*	91
I've Been Roaming,	*Charles E. Horn.*	52
Last Rose of Summer,	*Thomas Moore.*	322
Leaves Around Me Falling,	*Greek Air.*	31
Little Cherry Blossom,	*Anonymous.*	185
Longing for Spring,	*German.*	123
Love and Mirth,	*J. Strauss.*	126
Lovely May,	*Little Folks.*	113
May Queen, The,	*A. Tennyson.*	296
Mill May,	*Anonymous.*	68
Monarch of the Woods,	*J. W. Cherry.*	269
Pleasure Climbs to Every Mountain,	*Gollmick.*	260
Pretty Pear Tree,	*Anonymous.*	149
Rosy Crown, The,	*C. M. Von Weber.*	63
Sing Glad Songs for Him,	*C. F. Gounod.*	261
Spring Song, A,	*Ciro Pinsuti.*	277
Spring, Gentle Spring,	*J. Riviere.*	15
Spring Time Once Again,	*John Logan.*	312
Summer Days are Coming,	*Charles Jeffreys.*	40

Swinging 'Neath the Old Apple Tree,	*Barrowes.*	223
Time of the Singing of Birds,	*George Barker.*	276
Verdant Grove, Farewell to Thee,	*Folksong.*	200
Welcome, Pretty Primrose,	*Ciro Pinsuti.*	183
When I Come,	*Suabian Folksong.*	84
When the Green Leaves,	*Anonymous.*	103
When the Swallows Homeward Fly,	*Franz Abt.*	11
Why Do Summer Roses Fade,	*George Barker.*	18
Woodman, Spare that Tree,	*Geo. P. Morris.*	227

Christmas Songs.

Adeste Fideles,	*Anonymous.*	125
Baby's Night,	*Anonymous.*	225
Calm was the Night,	*A. Sullivan.*	273
Carol, Brothers, Carol,	*W. A. Muhlenberg.*	263
Christ is Born in Bethlehem,	*Anonymous.*	159
Christ is Born of Maiden Fair,	*Gauntlet.*	253
Christmas as it Comes,	*Anonymous.*	195
Christmas Carol,	*Thomas Helmore.*	262
Christmas Hymn,	*Henry Deilman.*	267
Christmas is Coming,	*J. P. McCaskey.*	329
Christmasse of Olde,	*Anonymous.*	198
Christmas Song,	*A. Adam.*	27
Christmas Time is Come Again,	*Anonymous.*	158
Christ was Born on Christmas Day,	*J. M. Neale.*	262
Come, All Ye Faithful,	*J. Reading.*	125
Cradle Song of Virgin,	*Joseph Barnby.*	199
Deck the Hall with Boughs of Holly,	*Welsh.*	300
Emmanuel,	*W. C. Dix.*	336
In Excelsis Gloria,	*Welsh Air.*	132
Jolly Old St. Nicholas,	*Anonymous.*	300
Joy to the World,	*Isaac Watts.*	72
Mahogany Tree, The,	*W. M. Thackeray.*	324
O Thou Joyful Day,	*German.*	336
Peace on Earth,	*G. Donizetti.*	283
Saw Ye Never in the Twilight,	*C. F. Alexander.*	198
Silent Night! Holy Night!	*Michael Haydn.*	173
Three Kings of Orient,	*Old Carol.*	195

Children's Songs.

A, B, C, D, E, F, G,	*Alphabet Song.*	303
Ah, Why will My Child be So Cross?		302
Baby Bye, Here's a Fly,	*Theodore Tilton.*	148
Baby is a Sailor Boy,	*George Cooper.*	231
Beautiful Sea, Foaming and Free,		135
Children Go to and fro, in a Merry, Pretty Row,		270
Cricket: Chirp, Chirp, Chirp,		271
Ding, Dong, Bell, Pussy's in the Well,		321
Gay Dances Bibabutzaman,		303
Hare and Hunter: As the Moon Shone Bright,		287
Here Cometh Rosalind Chasing the Bee,		135
Hobby Horse: Hop, Hop, Nimble as a Top,		361
Humpty Dumpty Sat on a Wall,		321
I'm Glad I Am a Farmer,		135
Johnny had a Little Dog, Bingo was His Name,		331
Little Busy Bee Abroad Doth Roam,		271
Little Jack Horner Sat in a Corner,		321
Little Miss Muffet Sat on a Tuffet,		321
Out of the Window, Over the Way,		281
O Pretty Polly, Don't You Cry,		331
O Wild is thy Joy, My Affectionate Boy,		301
Ring around a Rosy, Sit upon a Posy,		330
There is a Happy Land,	*Andrew Young.*	333
There was One, Little Jack,	*Jane Taylor.*	302
Twinkle Brightly, Stars of Night,		225
Wake, Happy Children, in the Dewy Morn,		109
We Come to See Miss Jennie Jones,		330
Wiegenlied: Brother, Thou and I,		320
What Care We for Gold or Silver?		331
Which Way Does the Wind Blow?		135
Winkum, Winkum, Shut Your Eye,		271

Abide with Me,	*Wm. H. Monk.*	121
Adeste Fideles,	*Anonymous.*	125
All Hail the Power of Jesus' Name,	*E. Perronet.*	19
All the Saints Adore Thee,	*J. B. Dykes.*	294
Alleluia! Alleluia!	*Easter Carol.*	96
Angelic Songs are Swelling,	*F. W. Faber.*	186
Art Thou Weary?	*St. Stephanos.*	97
As a Little Child,	*C. M. Von Weber.*	69
Ave Sanctissima,	*Felicia Hemans.*	213
Awake, My Soul, and With the Sun,	*Thos. Ken.*	305
Battle Hymn of Republic,	*Julia Ward Howe.*	105
Be Thou, O God, Exalted High,	*W. Franc.*	61
Beulah Land,	*J. R. Sweeny.*	19
Calm Was the Night,	*Arthur Sullivan.*	273
Carol, Brothers, Carol,	*W. A. Muhlenberg.*	263
Christ is Born in Bethlehem,	*Anonymous.*	159
Christ is Born of Maiden Fair,	*Gauntlet.*	253
Christmas Carol,	*Thomas Helmore.*	262
Christmas Hymn,	*Henry Dielman.*	267
Christmas Song,	*A. Adam.*	27
Christmas Time is Come Again,	*Anonymous.*	158
Christ was Born on Christmas Day,	*J. M. Neale.*	262
Church Militant,	*H. S. Cutler.*	107
Columbia, God Preserve Thee Free,	*J. Haydn.*	133
Come, All Ye Faithful,	*J. Reading.*	125
Come, Thou Almighty King,	*Charles Wesley.*	305
Come, Ye Disconsolate,	*Samuel Webbe.*	142
Coronation,	*Oliver Holden.*	19
Cradle Hymn,	*J. J. Rousseau.*	118
Cradle Song of Virgin,	*Joseph Barnby.*	199
Evening Hymn,	*Felicia Hemans.*	213
Evening Hymn,	*F. Mendelssohn.*	305
Fade, Fade, Each Earthly Joy,	*H. Bonar.*	275
Fading, Still Fading,	*Portuguese.*	145
Flee As a Bird,	*Mary S. B. Dana.*	50
Fourth of July Hymn,	*T. Hastings.*	267
Give Me Jesus,	*Slave Hymn.*	309
Gloria Patri,	*Anonymous.*	97
God Bless Our Native Land,	*T. Dwight.*	133
God Shall Charge His Angel Legions,		29
Guide Me, O Thou Great Jehovah,	*F. Herold.*	273
Hail to the Brightness,	*Thos. Hastings.*	351
Hail, Thou Most Sacred One,	*Felicia Hemans.*	213
Hallelujah Chorus,	*G. F. Handel.*	112
Hark! the Herald Angels Sing,	*Chas. Wesley.*	304
Hark! the Vesper Hymn is Stealing,	*T. Moore.*	25
Heaven is My Home,	*A. S. Sullivan.*	339
Heavens Are Telling, The,	*L. Beethoven.*	28
He's the Lily of the Valley,	*Slave Hymn.*	311
Holy, Holy, Holy,	*J. B. Dykes.*	294
Home of the Soul,	*Philip Phillips.*	120
How Gentle God's Commands,	*H. G. Nageli.*	119
Hush, My Babe, Lie Still and Slumber,	*Watts.*	118
I Love Thy Kingdom, Lord,	*T. Dwight.*	245
In Excelsis Gloria,	*Welsh Air.*	132
In Heavenly Love Abiding,	*F. Mendelssohn.*	26
Jerusalem the Golden,	*Alexander Ewing.*	358
Jerusalem, My Happy Home,	*Latin Hymn.*	143
Jesus is Mine,	*Horatius Bonar.*	275
Jesus Lives,	*C. F. Gellert.*	121
Jesus, the Very Thought of Thee,	*G. Rossini.*	341
Joy to the World,	*Isaac Watts.*	72
Lead, Kindly Light,	*J. H. Newman.*	29
Lord, Dismiss us with Thy Blessing,	*W. Shirley.*	340
Lord's Prayer, The,	*S. J. Hale.*	59
Lord, in this Thy Mercy's Day,	*W. H. Monk.*	359
Many Thousand Gone,	*Slave Hymn.*	311
May the Grace of Christ, Our Saviour,	*Doxology.*	79
Mine Eyes Have Seen the Glory,	*Julia W. Howe.*	105
My Country, 'Tis of Thee,	*S. F. Smith.*	293
Nearer, My God, to Thee,	*Sarah F. Adams.*	119
Never Alone,	*R. W. Raymond.*	275
Ninety and Nine,	*Ira D. Sankey.*	244
Nobody Knows the Trouble I've Seen,	*Slave.*	310
Not in Halls of Regal Splendor,	*Welsh.*	132
Now All the Bells,	*Easter Carol.*	96
Now Thank We All Our God,	*Martin Rinkert.*	71
O Could Our Thoughts,	*Anne Steele.*	255
O Thou Joyful Day,	*Johannes Falk.*	336
Oft in Danger, Oft in Woe,	*H. K. White.*	31
Oh, For a Thousand Tongues,	*Charles Wesley.*	97
Old Hundred,	*W. Franc.*	61
Our Father in Heaven,	*S. J. Hale.*	59
Over There,	*T. C. O'Kane.*	21
Palms, The,	*J. Faure.*	190
Peace on Earth,	*G. Donizetti.*	283
Praise God from Whom All Blessings Flow,		61
Praise Ye Jehovah's Name,	*Anonymous.*	305
Praise to God,	*Sebastian Bach.*	51
Prayer from Freischutz,	*C. M. Von Weber.*	359
Rise, Crowned with Light,	*A. Lyoff.*	51
Saw Ye Never in the Twilight,	*C. F. Alexander.*	198
Shall We Meet Beyond the River,	*E. S. Rice.*	79
Shout the Glad Tidings,	*W. A. Muhlenberg.*	73
Silent Night, Holy Night,	*Michael Haydn.*	173
Slave Hymns,	*Anonymous.*	311
Softly Now the Light of Day,	*G. W. Doane.*	107
Songs, Revealing Sacred Feeling,	*Von Weber.*	359
Sons of Men, Beheld From Far,	*Chas. Wesley.*	173
Steal Away,	*Slave Hymn.*	308
Stranger Star, The,	*C. F. Alexander.*	198
Strike the Cymbal,	*Pucitta.*	363
Swing Low, Sweet Chariot,	*Slave Hymn.*	309
The Son of God Goes Forth to War,	*R. Heber.*	107
There is a Happy Land,	*Andrew Young.*	333
Trees and the Master,	*Sidney Lanier.*	360
Twilight is Falling,	*B. C. Unseld.*	59
Vesper Hymn,	*Thomas Moore.*	25
What Means This Glory,	*G. Donizetti.*	283
When Shall We Meet Again?	*Lowell Mason.*	341

THE SONG COLLECTION.

HOME AGAIN.

MARSHALL S. PIKE.
Per. OLIVER DITSON & Co.

1. Home a-gain, home a-gain, From a for-eign shore! And oh, it fills my soul with
2. Hap-py hearts, hap-py hearts, With mine have laughed in glee, But oh, the friends I loved in
3. Mu-sic sweet, mu-sic soft, Lin-gers round the place, And oh, I feel the childhood

joy, To meet my friends once more. Here I dropped the parting tear, To cross the o-cean's
youth Seem hap-pi-er to me; And if my guide should be the fate, Which bids me longer
charm That time cannot ef-face. Then give me but my homestead roof, I'll ask no pal-ace

foam, But now I'm once again with those Who kindly greet me home. Home again, Home again,
roam, But death a-lone can break the tie That binds my heart to home. Home again, Home again,
dome, For I can live a hap-py life With those I love at home. Home again, Home again,

from a foreign shore, And oh, it fills my soul with joy, To meet my friends once more.
from a foreign shore, And oh, it fills my soul with joy, To meet my friends once more.
from a foreign shore, And oh, it fills my soul with joy, To meet my friends once more.

MUSIC AT HOME.—We have great faith in the humanizing power of music, and especially of music in the house and the home. Even in a moral point of view it is thoroughly harmonizing in its influence. To see a family grouped round the piano-forte in an evening, blending their voices together in the strains of Haydn or Mozart, or in the better known and loved melodies of our native land, is a beautiful sight—a graceful and joyous picture of domestic happiness. The mother takes the piano-forte accompaniment, the father leads with a violin or flute, or supports the melody with the bass, while the young group furnish the soprano and alto parts. What is more likely to make home attractive, or to cause children to grow up in love with domestic life, than such a practice as this? The young ought to be sedulously taught music, so that, when they grow up, no youth, no operative, no man, nor woman, may be without the solace of song. Let a taste for home music be cultivated in the rising generation, and we shall answer for the good effects.

MELODIES OF MANY LANDS.

C. W. GLOVER.

1. The mel - o - dies of ma - ny lands Ere-while have charmed mine ear, Yet
2. Its words I well re - mem-ber now, Were fraught with precepts old, And
3. It told me in the hour of need To seek a sol - ace there, Where

there's but one a - mong them all Which still my heart holds dear; I heard it first from
ev - 'ry line a max - im held, Of far more worth than gold; A les - son 'twas, though
on - ly strick - en hearts could find Sweet answer to their prayer; Ah! much I owe that

lips I loved, My tears it then be - guiled, It was the song my moth-er sang When
simply taught, That can-not pass a - way; It is my guid - ing star by night, My
gentle voice, Whose words my tears beguiled, That song of songs my moth-er sang, When

I was but a child, It was the song my mother sang, When I was but a child.
comfort in the day; It is my guid-ing star by night, My comfort in the day.
I was but a child; That song of songs my mother sang When I was but a child.

"But I have no voice," says one; "I have no ear for music," says another. Could you read before you learned to do so? Could you write without traveling the crooked path of pot-hooks? You can speak, because you learned to do so. And you can sing, provided you learn how. But you can no more sing without learning than the Irishman could play the fiddle who had "never tried." Every human being possesses the faculty of music to a greater or less extent, but the gift must be cultivated, and not allowed to "rust in us unused." It was doubtless conferred on man for a wise purpose; and, like all our other faculties, intended to be exercised for our pleasure and well-being. In our schemes of education, this divine gift of song has been almost entirely overlooked. Very rarely, indeed, does the school-master dream of the necessity for cultivating it, and so the gift lies waste. In Germany music and singing form a part of the school education of almost every child; hence the homes of Germany are musical and temperate.

Sound.—Sound is occasioned by the vibration of some sonorous body which is communicated to the air. This motion of the air is transferred to the tympanum of the ear, and thence, by means of most exquisite mechanical contrivances, through the auditory nerve to the brain. A wave of sound goes out from the sonorous centre in a spherical form, consisting of alternate condensations and rarefactions, something in the same way as a wave of water goes out from the the centre of disturbance in a circular form, consisting of alternate ridges and depressions. The difference between a sound and a musical note is not a difference *per se:* any sound repeated with equal force, at very minute intervals, will produce a musical note, the pitch of the note produced depending solely upon the frequency of the repetition; the more frequent the vibrations become the higher will be the pitch. A single sonorous impulse, or such successive impulses as are irregular in their character, produce noise. Perfectly-timed impulses produce a musical note. Intensity is due to the amount of disturbance in the medium, to the amplitude of the excursion which

WHEN THE SWALLOWS HOMEWARD FLY.

Franz Abt.

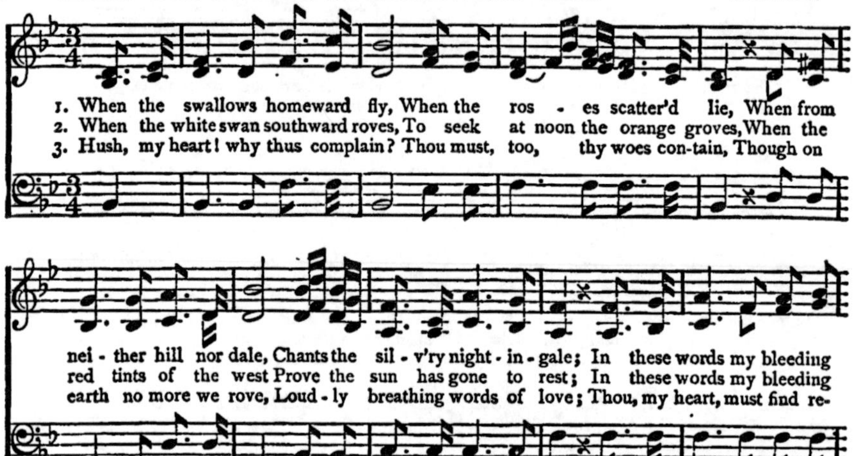
1. When the swallows homeward fly, When the ros - es scatter'd lie, When from
2. When the white swan southward roves, To seek at noon the orange groves, When the
3. Hush, my heart! why thus complain? Thou must, too, thy woes con-tain, Though on
nei - ther hill nor dale, Chants the sil - v'ry night - in - gale; In these words my bleeding
red tints of the west Prove the sun has gone to rest; In these words my bleeding
earth no more we rove, Loud - ly breathing words of love; Thou, my heart, must find re-
heart Would to thee its grief im - part, When I thus thy im - age lose,
heart Would to thee its grief im - part, When I thus thy im - age lose,
lief, Yield - ing to these words be - lief; I shall see thy form a - gain,
Can I, ah, can I e'er know re-pose, Can I, ah, can I e'er know re - pose?
Can I, ah, can I e'er know re-pose, Can I, ah, can I e'er know re - pose?
Though to - day we part a - gain, Though to - day . . we part a - gain.

every little molecule makes back and forth in delivering up its motion and coming to rest. Every note corresponds to a fixed rate of vibration, and harmony is due to the existence of a simple ratio between the rates of vibration of the two notes struck simultaneously. The ratio of the octave is $\frac{2}{1}$, of the fifth is $\frac{3}{2}$, of the fourth $\frac{4}{3}$, of the third $\frac{5}{4}$, and of the minor third $\frac{6}{5}$; that is to say, the number of vibrations of the higher note in the chord corresponds with the numerator of the fraction, and of the lower note with its denominator. When the ratio becomes more complex than $\frac{6}{5}$ the combination is unpleasant to the human ear, as well as to some animals, and is called discordant.

Under the influence of music we are all deluded in some way. We imagine that the performers must dwell in the regions to which they lift their hearers. We are reluctant to admit that a man may blow the most soul-animating strains from his trumpet and yet be a coward; or melt an audience to tears with his violin, and yet be a heartless profligate.—*Hilliard.*

THE old-time singing-master undoubtedly did good in his own day and generation, but he has wrought harm in ours, in having left the impression that a thorough practical knowledge of music can only be acquired by those who possess the gifts of musical genius. The error in this idea has, however, been fully demonstrated; and he who would know what can be accomplished when correct methods are applied to the teaching of music need only go where music is placed on the proper basis and is taught according to correct educational principles. Indeed, it is now conclusively shown that the proportion of children who can not, with proper instruction, learn to sing, is no greater than that of those who can not learn mathematics or language; and that the best teachers in other branches become, even with little knowledge of music, the most successful teachers of this subject, when once properly started. This fact clearly shows that the regular teachers, under proper supervision, will eventually become the teachers of music. It is true that special aptitude may give one pupil the advantage over another in music as in other branches, but the fact remains that *all* can learn something of music, and nearly all can become proficient. Had

HOME, SWEET HOME.

JOHN HOWARD PAYNE.

1. 'Mid pleas - ures and pal - a - ces though we may roam, Be it ev - er so
2. I gaze on the moon as I tread the drear wild, And feel that my
3. An ex - ile from home, splendor daz - zles in vain; Oh, give me my

hum - ble, there's no place like home; A charm from the skies seems to hal - low us
moth - er .now thinks of her child; As she looks on that moon from our own cot - tage
low - ly thatch'd cot - tage a - gain; The birds sing - ing gaily, that came at my

there, Which, seek thro' the world, is ne'er met with elsewhere. Home, home,
door, Thro' the wood-bine whose fragrance shall cheer me no more. Home, home,
call; Give me them, and that peace of mind, dear - er than all. Home, home,

sweet, sweet home, There's no place like home, Oh, there's no place like home.

reading or mathematics been as superficially taught in the past as music, the results would have been no better. Happily, however, the value of a musical training is now recognized by our best educators, and music is being placed on a correct basis. Among large cities, the schools of Boston have already become justly famous for results in this direction, and other cities are turning their attention to this important matter.

THREE VERSES.—We insert this best of songs as a sweet-voiced mother sang it, more than fifty years ago, by fireside and cradle. It is not Home, Sweet Home to us without the familiar second verse which, as a friend says, "belongs there." The homeless author, John Howard Payne, needs nothing besides to rescue his name from oblivion. To have written this little song, which the world has taken to its heart because of its simplicity and tenderness, is infinitely more worthy a human being than to have wielded the sceptre of Augustus Cæsar or of the first Napoleon! An old book lies before us, in which the song appears in five stanzas. It may have originally been so written, the author afterwards retaining but two of the favorite verses; at all events our mothers sang it thus when "Home, Sweet Home" was new, so many years ago.

THE Quakers as a sect, it is known, do not favor music; they think it to be a profitless amusement, indulged in by the world's people. George Thompson, the famous English abolitionist, while lecturing in England on the abolition of slavery in the British Provinces, stopped one night with a Quaker family. He was a great lover of music, and at that time was a good singer. During the evening he sang "Oft in the Stilly Night," which was listened to with the closest attention. In the morning the lady of the house, after Mr. Thompson came from his room, appeared quite uneasy. She wanted to hear the song again, but it would hardly do for her, a Quakeress, to request its repetition. At last, so goes the pleasant little story, her desire getting the better of her, she ventured to say: "George, will thee repeat the words of last evening in thy usual manner?"

THERE can be no doubt that music has a great influence in imparting those delightful sensations which tend to sweeten and prolong life. That this fact is often recognized is testified by the immense number of those who devote themselves entirely to the manufacture and sale of musical instruments. It is, however, ac-

FLOW, RIO VERDE.

1. Flow, Ri-o Ver-de, in mel-o-dy flow; Win her that weep-eth to slum-ber from woe. Bid thy wave's mu-sic roll thro' her dreams, Grief ev-er lov-eth the kind voice of streams; Flow, Ri-o Ver-de, in mel-o-dy flow, Win her that weep-eth to slum-ber from woe!

2. Bear her lone spir-it a-far on the sound, Back to her childhood, her life's fairy ground. Pass like the whis-per of love that is gone, Pass like the whis-per of love that is gone. Flow, Ri-o Ver-de, soft-ly flow on, Flow, Ri-o Ver-de, soft-ly flow on.

3. Dark, glassy wa-ter, so crim-soned of yore, Voi-ces of sor-row are known to thy shore. Thou shouldst have echoes for grief's deepest tone, Thou shouldst have ech-oes for grief's deep-est tone. Flow, Ri-o Ver-de, soft-ly flow on.

* Ree-o *Vare-day.*

knowledged throughout the world, that the human voice has no equal for the production of sweet, elevating, enchanting sounds that delight the ear and give tone and coloring to the words of the poet. Hence, of all kinds of music, vocal music should claim the especial attention of all earnest and progressive educators, for singing is known to improve the enunciation, refine the taste, elevate the morals, confirm the health, strengthen the social feeling, and add much to the pleasure of all. The consideration of health is one to which too much attention cannot be given. Singing is beneficial, indirectly, by increasing the flow of spirits, and dispelling weariness and despondency; and directly by the exercise which it gives to the lungs and the vital organs. We cannot sing without increased action of the lungs, and this causes the heart and all the organs of digestion and nutrition to act with renewed vigor. The singer brings a greater quantity of air into contact with the blood, and hence the blood is better purified and vitalized. Healthful and highly oxygenized blood gives energy to the brain, and thus the mind as well as the body shares the benefit of this delightful exercise.

HANDEL was one of the most humorous of mortals, and at the same time one of the most irritable. His best jokes were perpetrated frequently during his most violent bursts of passion. Having occasion to bring out one of his oratorios in a provincial town of England, he began to look about for such material to complete his orchestra and chorus as the place might afford. One and another was recommended, as usual, as being a splendid singer, a great player, and so on. After a while these were gathered together in a room, and, after preliminaries, Handel made his appearance, puffing, both arms full of manuscripts. "Gentlemen," quoth he, "you all read manuscripts?" "Yes, yes." responded from all parts of the room. "We play in the church," added an old man behind a violoncello. "Very well, play dis," said Handel, distributing the parts. This done, and a few explanations delivered, Handel retired to a distant part of the room to enjoy the effect. The stumbling, fumbling and blundering that ensued is said to have been indescribable. Handel's sensitive ear and impetuous spirit could not long brook the insult, and clapping his hands to his ears, he ran to the old gentleman of the violoncello, and shaking his fist furiously at the terrified man and the instrument, said, "You blay in de church!—very well— you may blay in de church—for we read, De Lord is long suffering, of great kindness, forgiving iniquity, transgression and sin; you sal blay in de church, but you sal not blay for me!" and snatching together his manuscripts, he rushed out of the room, leaving his astonished performers to draw their own conclusions.

SHELLS OF OCEAN.

J. W. CHERRY.   C. MATZ ARR.

1. One sum-mer eve, with pen-sive thought, I wan-der'd on the sea-beat shore, Where oft, in heed-less in-fant sport, I gather'd shells in days be-fore, I gath-er'd shells in days be-fore: The plashing waves like mus-ic fell, Re-spon-sive to my fan-cy wild; A dream came o'er me like a spell, I thought I was a-gain a child, A dream came o'er me like a spell, I thought I was a-gain, a-gain a child.

2. I stoop'd up-on the peb-bly strand, To cull the toys that round me lay, But, as I took them in my hand, I threw them one by one a-way, I threw them one by one a-way: Oh, thus, I said, in ev-'ry stage, By toys our fan-cy is be-guiled; We gather shells from youth to age, And then we leave them, like a child, We gath-er shells from youth to age, And then we leave them, leave them, like a child.

SPRING, GENTLE SPRING.

J. Riviere.
J. R. Planche.

1. Spring! Spring! gen - tle Spring! Young-est sea - son of the year, Hith - er
2. Spring! Spring! gen - tle Spring! Gust - y March be - fore thee flies, Gloom - y

haste, and with thee bring A - pril with her smile and tear; Hand in hand with
Win - ter ban - ish - ing; Clear - ing for thy path the skies. Flocks and herds, and

joc - und May, Bent on keep - ing ho - li - day. With thy dai - sy di - a -
meads and bow'rs, For thy gra - cious pres-ence long! Come and fill the fields with

dem, And thy robe of bright-est green,— We will wel - come thee and them,
flow'rs, Come and fill the woods with song.— We will wel - come thee and them,

cres.

As ye've ev - er welcomed been. Spring! Spring! gen - tle Spring! Young-est sea - son

of the year, Life and joy to na - ture bring! Na - ture's dar - ling, haste thee here.

NURSERY RHYMES.—Many of these productions have a very curious history, but cannot always be fully traced. Some of them probably owe their origin to names distinguished in our literature; as Oliver Goldsmith, for instance, is believed in his earlier days to have written such compositions. Dr. E. F. Rimbault gives us the following particulars as to some well-known favorites: "Sing a Song of Six-pence" is as old as the sixteenth century. "Three Blind Mice" is found in a music-book dated 1609. "The Frog and the Mouse" was licensed in 1580. "Three Children Sliding on the Ice" dates from 1633. "London Bridge is Broken Down" is of unfathomed antiquity. "Girls and Boys, Come out to Play" is certainly as old as the reign of Charles II.; as is also "Lucy Locket lost her Pocket," to the tune of which the American song of "Yankee Doodle" was written. "Pussy Cat, Pussy Cat, where have you been?" is of the age of Queen Bess. "Little Jonny Horner" is older than the seventeenth century. "The Old Woman Tossed in a Blanket" is of the reign of James II., to whom it is supposed to allude.

WESLEY saw a difference between loud talking and screaming. To a screamer he once said: "Scream no more at the peril of your soul. God now warns you by me, whom he has set over you. Speak as earnestly as you can, but do not scream. Speak with all your heart, but with a moderate voice. It was said of our Lord, 'He shall not cry:' the word properly translated means, 'He shall not scream.'"

BRIGHTLY.

HAYDN'S "SEASONS."

1. Bright - ly, bright - ly gleam the sparkling rills; Sum - mer, sum - mer
2. O - dors, o - dors load the sum - mer air, Mus - ic, mus - ic
3. Faint - ly, faint - ly sounds the dis - tant fall; Light - ly, light - ly

sleeps on ver - dant hills, A - mid the shades we ram - bling stray, Where cooling fountains
sweet - ly ech - oes there; And bright-est maids, with soft - est glance, Then join the song and
wood - land ech - oes call, And in their voice we seem to hear The tones of friends once

Chorus.

sport - ive play.
lead the dance. } Peal - ing, peal - ing come the laugh and shout; While
gay and dear.

gai - ly we sing till the old for - ests ring, While gai - ly we sing till the

old for-ests ring With the joy of our mer - ry rout, With the joy of our mer - ry rout.

SOUND OUR VOICES LONG AND SWEET.

BOHEMIAN MELODY.

1. Sound our voices long and sweet, And roll the stirring drum; Friends and neighbors round us meet, And
2. Now the ro - sy morn is come, Of merry, gladsome May, With birds that carol, bees that hum—A

to our greeting come: Come where music float - eth oft, On soft and balmy air:
welcome, hap-py day. Wild flowers now in fair - y nooks are shedding sweet per-fume, The

Ye whose hearts by grief are stirred, And ye whose skies are fair. } Tra la la la la la la
Spring makes glad the mossy brooks, And all the meadows bloom. }

la la la la la la la la, Tra la la la la la la la la lo la la.

Sound our voices long and sweet, And roll the stirring drum; Friends and neighbors round us meet, And

to our greeting glad-ly come, To our greeting glad-ly come, To our greeting come.

2

THE EAR.—The sound-wave passes first into the auditory canal, about an inch in length, and striking against the tympanum, or ear-drum, which closes the orifice of the external ear, it throws this membrane into vibration. Next, a series of small bones, called respectively, from their peculiar form, the *hammer, anvil,* and *stirrup,* conduct to the inner ear, which is termed, from its complicated stucture, the *labyrinth.* This is filled with liquid, and contains semi-circular canals, and the cochlea (snail-shell) which receive the vibrations and transmit them to the auditory nerve, the fine filaments of which are spread out to catch every pulsation of the sound-wave. The middle ear, which contains the chain of small bones, is a simple cavity about half an inch in diameter, filled with air. It communicates with the mouth by means of the Eustachian tube. Within the labyrinth are also fine, elastic hair-bristles and crystalline particles among the nerve-fibres, wonderfully fitted, the one to receive and the other to prolong the vibrations; and lastly, a lute of 3,000 microscopic strings, so stretched as to vibrate in uni-

WHY DO SUMMER ROSES FADE?

GEORGE BARKER

Why do sum-mer ros-es fade? If not to show how fleet-ing,
Then while sum-mer ros-es last, Oh, let's be friends to-geth-er,
But though sum-mer ros-es die, And love gives place to rea-son,

All things bright and fair are made, To bloom awhile as half a-fraid To join our sum-mer
Sum-mer time will soon be past, With au-tumn leaves around us cast, And then comes win-try
Friendship pass without a sigh, And all on earth pass coldly by; 'Tis but a win-try

greet-ing? Or do they on-ly bloom to tell, How brief a sea-son
weath-er. Sure-ly as the sum-mer's day, Friend-ship, too, will
sea-son, And friendship, love and ros-es too, The spring-time shall a-

love may dwell, Or do they on-ly bloom to tell, How brief a sea-son love may dwell?
pass a-way, Sure-ly as the sum-mer's day, Friendship too will pass a-way.
gain re-new, And friendship, love and ros-es too, The spring-time shall a-gain re-new,

son with any sound. The Eustachian tube is generally closed, thus cutting off the air in the inner cavity from the external air. If at any time the pressure of the atmosphere without becomes greater or less than that within, the tympanum feels the strain. A forcible blow upon the ear may produce in this way temporary deafness. In the act of swallowing, the tube is opened and the equilibrium restored. We may force air into the cavity of the ear by closing our mouth and nose, and forcibly expiring the air from our lungs. This will render us insensible to low sounds, while we can hear the higher ones as usual.—*Steele.*

A tired bee hums in E; while in pursuit of honey it hums contentedly in A. The common horse-fly, when held captive, moves its wings 335 times a second; a honey-bee, 190 times. Youmans says it is marvelous how slight an impulse throws a vast amount of air into motion. We can easily hear the song of a bird 500 feet above us. For its melody to reach us it must have filled with wave-pulsations a sphere of air, one thousand feet in diameter, or set in motion eighteen tons of the atmosphere.

BEULAH LAND.

EDGAR PAGE.
J. R. SWENEY, by per.

1. I've reached the land of corn and wine, And all its rich-es freely mine; Here shines undimm'd one
2. The Saviour comes and walks with me, And sweet communion here have we; He gent-ly leads me
3. A sweet per-fume up-on the breeze Is borne from ever-ver-nal trees, And flow'rs that never
4. The zephyrs seem to float to me, Sweet sounds of heaven's mel-o-dy, As an-gels with the

bliss-ful day, For all my night has pass'd a-way.
with His hand, For this is Heaven's bor-der land.
fad-ing grow Where streams of life for-ev-er flow.
white-robed throng, Join in the sweet redemption song.
} Oh, Beu-lah land, sweet Beulah land, As

on thy highest mount I stand, I look a-way a-cross the sea, Where mansions are pre-

pared for me, And view the shin-ing glo-ry shore, My heav'n, my home, for-ev-er-more.

ALL HAIL THE POWER OF JESUS' NAME.

E. PERRONET, 1780.
O. HOLDEN, 1793. "CORONATION."

1. All hail the power of Je-sus' name! Let angels prostrate fall; Bring forth the royal di-a-dem, And
2. Sinners, whose love can ne'er forget The wormwood and the gall, Go, spread your trophies at His feet, And
3. Let ev'ry kindred, ev'ry tribe, On this ter-res-trial ball, To Him all ma-jes-ty as-cribe, And

crown Him Lord of all; Bring forth the royal di-a-dem, And crown Him Lord of all.
crown Him Lord of all; Go, spread your trophies at His feet, And crown Him Lord of all.
crown Him Lord of all; To Him all ma-jes-ty as-cribe And crown Him Lord of all.

MUSICAL HEREDITY.—Heredity shows itself more markedly, it would seem, in the arts than in the sciences. Taking music we find some remarkable instances. The Bach family, which took its rise about 1550 and became extinct in 1800, presents an unbroken series of musicians for nearly two centuries. The head of the family was a baker of Presburg, his two sons were the first who were musicians by profession. Their descendants "overran Thuringia, Saxony, and Franconia," says Papillon. "They were all organists, church singers, or what is called in Germany, 'city musicians.' When they became too numerous to live all together, and the members of this family were scattered abroad, they resolved to meet once a year, on a stated day, with a view to maintaining a sort of patriarchal bond of union. This custom was kept up until nearly the middle of the eighteenth century, and oftentimes more than a 100 persons bearing the name of Bach—men, women, and children—were to be seen assembled. In the family are reckoned twenty-nine eminent musicians, and twenty-eight of a lower grade." Rossini's family

SPEAK GENTLY.

WALLACE. BATES.

1. Speak gen-tly—it is bet-ter far To rule by love than fear; Speak
2. Speak gen-tly to the young—for they Will have e-nough to bear; Pass
3. Speak gen-tly to the err-ing, know They must have toiled in vain; Per-

gen-tly—let no harsh word mar The good we may do here. Speak gen-tly to the
through this life as best they may, 'Tis full of anx-ious care. Speak gen-tly to the
chance unkindness made them so; Oh, win them back a-gain. Speak gen-tly, 'tis a

lit-tle child! Its love be sure to gain; Teach it in ac-cents soft and mild, It
ag-ed one, Grieve not the care-worn heart, Whose sands of life are near-ly run; Let
lit-tle thing Dropped in the heart's deep well; The good, the joy, that it may bring, E-

rit.

may not long re-main, Teach it in accents soft and mild, It may not long re-main.
such in peace de-part, Whose sands of life are nearly run, Let such in peace de-part.
ter-ni-ty shall tell, The good, the joy, that it may bring, E-ter-ni-ty shall tell.

often played music at fairs; Beethoven's father and grandfather were musicians; Mozart's father was Capellmeister to the Bishop of Saltzburg.—*Cornhill.*

IT is night now, and here is home. Gathered under the quiet roof, elders and children lie, alike at rest. In the midst of a great calm the stars look out from the heavens. The silence is peopled with the past—sorrowful remorse for sins and short-comings, memories of passionate joys and griefs rise out of their graves, both now alike calm and sad. Eyes, as I shut mine, look at me that have long since ceased to shine. The town and the fair landscape sleep under the starlight, wreathed under the Autumn mist. Twinkling among the houses, a light keeps watch here and there, in what may be a sick chamber or two. The clock tolls sweetly in the silent air. Here is night and rest. An awful sense of thanks makes the heart swell and the head bow, as I pass to my room through the sleeping house, and feel as though a hushed blessing were upon it.—*Thackeray.*

THE skill of the painter and sculptor, which comes in aid of the memory and imagination, is, in its highest degree, one of the rarest, as it is one of the most exquisite, accomplishments within our attainment. In its perfection it is as seldom witnessed as in speech or music. The plastic hand must be moved by the same ethereal instinct as the eloquent lips or the recording pen. The number of those who can discern the finished statue in the heart of the shapeless block, and bid it start into artistic life—who are endowed with the exquisite gift of moulding the rigid bronze or the lifeless marble into graceful, majestic, and expressive forms—is not greater than the number of those who are able with equal majesty, grace and expressiveness to make the spiritual essence, the finest shades of thought and feeling, sensible to the mind through the eye and the ear in the mysterious embodiment of the written and the spoken word. If Athens in her palmiest days had but one Pericles, she had also but one Phidias.—*Everett.*

OVER THERE.

D. W. C. HUNTINGTON.
T. C. O'KANE, by per.

1. Oh, think of a home o - ver there, By the side of the riv - er of light, Where the saints all im - mor - tal and fair, Are o - ver there, robed in their gar - ments of white.

2. Oh, think of the friends o - ver there, Who be - fore us the jour - ney have trod, Of the songs that they breathe on the air, In their home in the pal - ace of God.

3. I'll soon be at home o - ver there, For the end of my jour - ney I see; Ma - ny dear to my heart o - ver there, Are watch - ing and wait - ing for me.

Chorus.

O - ver there, o - ver there, o - ver there, o - ver there, Oh, think of a home o - ver there, o - ver there; O - ver there, o - ver there, o - ver there, o - ver there, Oh, think of a home o - ver there.

SILVER CHIMES.

CLARIBEL.

They are chiming gai - ly now, as they chimed so long a - go, Sil - ver tones that we loved so

well; And what is it that they say To our in - ner thoughts to - day? And

what is the tale that they tell?

{ 1. They   whisper first of all,   In that qui - et e - ven
  2. Of a   waking up to life,   Of a long and bit - ter
  3. Of a   peaceful life at last,   Of a sense of per - il }

fall,   Of the   hap - py days of   childhood that we   passed;   When each
strife, Of a   rest - less spir - it   fret - ting in its   pain;   Of a
past,   Of a   fu - ture left in   saf - er hands than   ours;   Of a

gar - land that we made, Seem'd too beau - ti - ful to fade; And each but - ter - fly   more
sea - son when the bells On - ly racked us with their spells, On - ly mocked us with   old
sweet, re - fresh - ing dew, Fall - ing on our lives a - new, As the rain - drops fall and

D.S. After last stanza.

ra - diant than   the   last,   the   last.
mem - o - ries   a - gain, a - gain.   } They are chiming gai - ly now, As they
sat - is - fy   the flowers, the   flowers.

chimed so long a - go, Sil - ver tones that we loved so well. Like a

sto - ry that is told, Seem those memories of old, Haunting still with a mag-ic spell, magic spell.

MY NORMANDY.

FREDERIC BERAT.

Andante.

1. When hope her cheering smile supplies, And win - ter flies far, far a - way; Be -
2. I've seen Hel - ve - tia's flow-ery fields, Its cot-tag - es, its i - cy hills; And
3. There is an age in all our lives, When ev - 'ry dream must lose its spell; An

neath, dear France, thy beauteous skies, When spring becomes more sweet and gay; When
I - ta - ly, thy sky so clear! And Ven - ice, with her gon - do - lier. In
age in which the soul re - calls The scenes o'er which it loved to dwell; When

na - ture's dressed a - gain in green, The swal - low to re - turn is seen; I
greet-ing thus each for - eign part, There's still one land most near my heart, A
e'en my muse shall si - lent prove, Per - haps de - spise these songs of love,— 'Tis

love a - gain the land to see, Which gave me, gave me birth, my Nor-man-dy.
land most cherished, loved by me, My na - tive, na - tive land, my Nor-man-dy.
then I hope the land to see, Which gave me, gave me birth, my Nor-man-dy.

THE training of the voice and the study of elementary principles should be commenced in early youth. After one has reached maturity his inclinations lead usually to that which directly contributes to his business or his favorite pursuits He soon tires of the essentials in learning to sing, and if nature has not endowed him with a voice fully equipped and ready to meet practical demands on short notice, he is quite apt to give up the undertaking before it is fairly begun. The public school can be made to furnish an elementary musical and singing practice to the rich and poor alike, and with very little expense in money or time. What a grand thing it would be for us all, as a people, if the children could grow up in the atmosphere of song in the school-room! It would enable many a heart to attune itself to love, duty, hope and benevolence, that must otherwise be listless and dumb. The wonderful utility and influence for good that well-regulated music has in the school-room is not usually understood by school boards and the public. Its sanitary effects, its softening influence, its recreative tendencies, its power to quicken the inertia of the school, are things understood only by wise teachers and others whose privilege it is to observe carefully the bearings and results of school work.—*W. T. Giffe.*

SOMEWHERE.

F. CAMPANA.
ALFRED C. SHAW.

LIFE LET US CHERISH.

Life let us cher - ish While yet the ta - per glows, And the fresh flow - 'ret

Pluck ere it close. Why are we fond of toil and care, Why choose the rank - ling
Pluck ere it close. When clouds ob - scure the atmosphere, And fork - ed light - nings
Pluck ere it close. The gen - ial sea - sons soon are o'er; Then let us, ere we
Pluck ere it close. A - way with ev - 'ry toil and care, And cease the rank - ling

thorn to wear, And heed - less by the lil - y stray, Which blossoms on our way?
rend the air, The sun resumes his sil - ver crest, And smiles a - dorn the west.
quit this shore, Contentment seek; it is life's zest, The sun - shine of the breast.
thorn to wear, With man - ful hearts life's conflict meet, Till death sounds the re - treat.

VESPER HYMN.

THOMAS MOORE.

1. Hark! the ves-per hymn is steal-ing O'er the wa - ters, soft and clear; Near-er yet and
2. Now like moonlight waves retreat-ing To the shore, it dies a - long; Now, like an - gry

near - er peal-ing, Soft it breaks up - on the ear, Ju - bi - la - te, Ju - bi - la - te,
surg - es meet-ing, Breaks the mingled tide of song. Ju - bi - la - te, Ju - bi - la - te,

Ju - bi - la - te, A - men. Far-ther now, now farther stealing, Soft it fades up - on the ear.
Ju - bi - la - te, A - men. Hark! again, like waves retreating To the shore, it dies a - long.

* Pronounce as in *la* or *fa-ther*.

It was the great organ uttering the low first notes of the closing hymn. The music began soft and faint. It rose and swelled into a wave of tender melody. Then it died away, soon the sound poured from the church again, swelling, rolling, then sinking to a sigh. When it came again voices were mingled with it, chanting a hymn. At its fullness the blended harmony seemed to fill the whole air—to drop from the leaves, from the mysterious stars. The solemn roll of the organ, the clear, tender chanting of the voices, swelled into a billow of peace and resignation. There was grief in it—the chastened grief of perfect faith. There was joy in it also—the exalted joy of adoration. It touched the girl like a hand of love; it thrilled her like the voice of hope. As she listened she trembled, and her head slowly sank until her hands covered her face, she sobbed so that her whole frame shook; and the music, now faint, now deep and strong, poured a balm of melody upon her wounds. And as it soothed and comforted her, she lifted her face to the stars whence this hymn of peace seemed to come. She made the sign of the cross upon her breast and her lips moved. Soon she was crying again, but softly. When the last note of the hymn trembled and ceased, she arose and went slowly away. Her head was bent, but in her step was to be seen the firmness of hope.

IN HEAVENLY LOVE ABIDING.

FELIX MENDELSSOHN.

1. In heavenly love a - bid - ing, No change my heart shall fear, And safe in such con-fid - ing, For noth - ing changes here. The storm may roar with - out me, My heart may low be laid, But God is round a - bout me, And can I be dis-mayed? But God is round a - bout me, And can I be dismayed?

2. Wher - ever He may guide me, No want shall turn me back; My Shepherd is be-side me, And noth - ing can I lack. His wis - dom ev - er wak - eth, His sight is nev - er dim; He knows the way He tak - eth, And I will walk with him; He knows the way He tak - eth, And I will walk with Him.

3. Green pastures are be - fore me, Which yet I have not seen; Bright skies will soon be o'er me, Where darkest clouds have been. My hope I can - not meas - ure, My path to life is free, My Saviour has my treas - ure, And He will walk with me; My Saviour has my treas - ure, And He will walk with me.

CHRISTMAS SONG.

A. ADAM.
"CANTIQUE DE NOEL."

Andante Maestoso.

1. Oh, sol - emn hour! when hearts were lowly bending, And all the world seem'd enshrouded in
2. Oh, love - ly hour! when light first faintly gleaming, And hearts were fill'd with a rapture di -
3. Oh, what delight! to hearts bowed down with sorrow, When cheering words o'er our sad spirits

night; When pleading prayers to Heaven were as - cend - ing, Above the gloom smiled a spir-it of
vine; Led by the star whose rays were brightly beam - ing, Came eastern sa - ges round that ho-ly
fall; Tho' dark the night, still comes a bright to - mor-row, When trusting hearts on their dear Saviour

pp

light; 'Twas Hope's bright form they saw so bright-ly shin - ing In robes un - fad - ing
shrine; While there they saw the King of Glo - ry sleep - ing, Our Friend, Pro - tec - tor,
call; Then let each voice in grate - ful notes as-cend - ing, Ex - tol His name, the

f

greet their tearful eyes; Beau - ti - ful Hope! no lon - ger hearts re-pin - ing, As
in a manger laid; Their hearts were glad, and sad eyes ceased their weeping, For
bond, the slave, the free, All shout His praise, in love and concord blending, In

love and joy on wings of faith a - rise, As love and joy on wings of faith a - rise.
Faith was twin - ing wreaths that never fade, For Faith was twin - ing wreaths that never fade.
songs of faith and im - mor-tal - i - ty! In songs of faith and im - mor-tal - i - ty!

The pupil accustomed to reading from the treble or G clef staff will of course need more or less practice to become familiar with the bass staff; somewhat for the same reason many find it a little confusing at first to keep the mind fixed upon the key-tone, or Tonic's place, when changing into the different keys. We find but little trouble, provided pupils are not kept too long reading in any one key. When drilling upon letter names of degrees of both staffs we sometimes use this plan, viz: Draw a staff of eleven long lines; let the class look at it a few moments, to see how cumbersome it is; tell them the first lower line is named G, second B, and so on to the eleventh, inclusive, space below F, etc. Then erase the middle (sixth) line, except a short portion in the middle of it, when we see the two staffs, with the C (middle C) line half way be-

tween—no letter names changed. Pupils may be told that when they read from the bass staff, they are merely working in the lower part of what was once (for a few moments) our eleven-line or "great staff," also, that the first line of bass staff bears the same name as the second line of treble, second same as third; spaces same way. Repeated practice does the chief important work. Little devices attract and interest the younger pupils; such as building an "eleven board fence" and finding it too much work to climb; "cut it down, about half," or build a log house, give each log a name, etc. It pays to interest. We find no success without it. If you can thoroughly interest your younger pupils without the aid of any devices, well and good. If you belong to that class, who consider themselves "above such trifling things," so much the worse for your pupils.

THE HEAVENS ARE TELLING.

The heav'ns are tell-ing His praise with de-vo-tion; Their voice proclaims for-e'er the Lord: He's prais'd by the earth and prais'd by the o-cean; Re-ceive, O man, their god-like word. Who holds the heavens' in-num-'ra-ble stars? Who leads the sun its path a-long? It comes all smil-ing and lights them from far And runs its course a he-ro strong, And runs its course a he-ro strong.

LEAD KINDLY LIGHT.

Rev. J. R. Dykes.
John Henry Newman, 1833.

1. Lead, kindly Light, amid th'encircling gloom, Lead Thou me on; The night is
2. I was not ev-er thus, nor pray'd that Thou Shouldst lead me on; I lov'd to
3. So long Thy pow'r has blest me, sure it still Will lead me on O'er moor and

dark, and I am far from home, Lead Thou me on. Keep Thou my feet; I
choose and see my path; but now Lead Thou me on. I lov'd the gar-ish
fen, o'er crag and torrent, till The night is gone, And with the morn those

do not ask to see The dis-tant scene; one step e-nough for me.
day; and, spite of fears, Pride rul'd my will: remember not past years.
an-gel fac-es smile, Which I have lov'd long since, and lost a-while.

WATCH AND WARD.

J. Montgomery.
Mendelssohn, "Trust."

1. God shall charge His an-gel le-gions Watch and ward o'er thee to keep;
2. On the li-on vain-ly roar-ing, On his young, thy foot shall tread;
3. Since, with pure and firm af-fec-tion, Thou on God hast set thy love,
4. Thou shalt call on Him in trou-ble, He will heark-en, He will save;

Though thou walk through hos-tile re-gions, Though in des-ert wilds thou sleep.
And, the drag-on's den ex-plor-ing, Thou shalt bruise the ser-pent's head.
With the wings of His pro-tec-tion He will shield thee from a-bove.
Here for grief re-ward thee dou-ble, Crown with life be-yond the grave. A-men.

In the plaza at St. Augustine, Florida, there stands a monument erected to the memory of the Confederate soldiers of that place who fell during the late war. Their names are given, mostly Spanish names. But it was the inscription, so unusual and so beautiful, that stayed our steps, and took us back again to the place to make sure that there might be no mistake in recalling it. We had never seen or heard it, and did not know it to be an adaptation of the last words of "Stonewall" Jackson as he sank to death on the field of Chancellorsville: "They have crossed over the river and rest under the shade of the trees." We were simply impressed and attracted by its beauty and appropriateness. A brief extract from Sarah Nicholas Ran-

dolph's life of Gen. Thomas J. Jackson ("Stonewall" Jackson) published in 1876, will be read with interest in this connection: "A few minutes before he died, he cried out in his delirium, 'Order A. P. Hill to prepare for action; pass the infantry to the front; tell Major Hawks—' then stopped, leaving the sentence unfinished. Presently a smile of ineffable sweetness spread itself over his pale face, and he said, quietly and with an expression as of relief, 'Let us cross over the river and rest under the shade of the trees.' And then, without pain or the least struggle, his spirit passed from earth to the God who gave it." A foot-note upon the page states that the account here given of the death of this distinguished officer was written by Dr. McGuire,

UNDER THE SHADE OF THE TREES.

E. O. LYTE.
M. J. PRESTON.

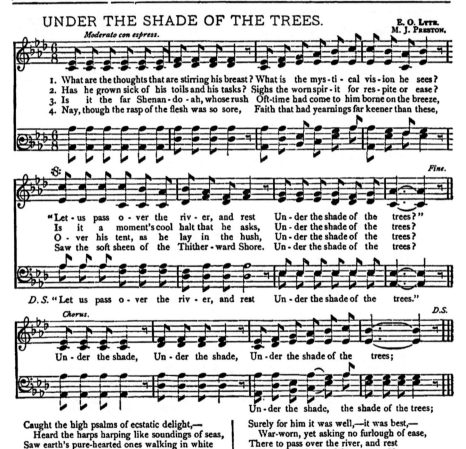

Moderato con espress.

1. What are the thoughts that are stirring his breast? What is the mys-ti-cal vis-ion he sees?
2. Has he grown sick of his toils and his tasks? Sighs the worn spir-it for res-pite or ease?
3. Is it the far Shenan-do-ah, whose rush Oft-time had come to him borne on the breeze,
4. Nay, though the rasp of the flesh was so sore, Faith that had yearnings far keener than these,

Fine.

"Let-us pass o-ver the riv-er, and rest Un-der the shade of the trees?"
Is it a moment's cool halt that he asks, Un-der the shade of the trees?
O-ver his tent, as he lay in the hush, Un-der the shade of the trees?
Saw the soft sheen of the Thither-ward Shore. Un-der the shade of the trees?

D. S. "Let us pass o-ver the riv-er, and rest Un-der the shade of the trees."

Chorus.   *D.S.*

Un-der the shade, Un-der the shade, Un-der the shade of the trees;

Un-der the shade, the shade of the trees;

Caught the high psalms of ecstatic delight,—
Heard the harps harping like soundings of seas,
Saw earth's pure-hearted ones walking in white
Under the shade of the trees.—*Cho.*

Surely for him it was well,—it was best,—
War-worn, yet asking no furlough of ease,
There to pass over the river, and rest
Under the shade of the trees.—*Cho.*

and is taken from the "Battle-Fields of Virginia." The beautiful lines which are here set to music are from an ode written by Mrs. Margaret J. Preston, of Lexington, Virginia, at the request of the authorities of the Virginia Military Institute, to celebrate its semi-centennial anniversary. This lady is one of the noted female writers of America. Though written by request this ode is far from being written to order. It is full of genuine inspiration; and these verses, their burden the dying words of a heroic soul passing from the storm of battle into a dream of sylvan rest, fasten themselves upon the memory and linger like music in our ears. There are tears in them but they are not tears born of despair.

THE aching head may well cease to throb when laid upon that softest pillow for human pain—"God knows!" The sleep that falls like heavenly dew to the music of the lullaby—"All things work together for good to them that love God," and "Fear not! I am with thee!" brings strength and renewal of youth, with balm for present ills. Your "shadowy future" is definite and distinct to Him. Whatever of seeming disaster it may hold for you be assured that it is only in seeming; that His purposes toward you must, from the necessities of His own nature, be all love and goodness. Be patient, yet hopeful, in awaiting the development of His will.—*Marion Harland*

LEAVES AROUND ME FALLING.

GREEK MELODY.

1. The leaves a-round me fall - ing, Are preaching of de - cay; The hol-low winds are
2. The light my path surround - ing, The loves to which I cling, The hopes within me
3. The friends, gone there before me, Are call-ing from on high; And joy-ous an-gels
4. I hear the in - vi - ta - tion, And fain would rise and come, A sin - ner to sal -

call - ing, "Come, pil-grim, come a - way!" The day, in night de - clin - ing, Says
bound - ing; The joys that round me wing,— All melt, like stars of ev - en, Be-
o'er me Tempt sweetly to the sky. "Why wait," they say, "and with - er 'Mid
va - tion, An ex - ile to his home; But, while I here must lin - ger, Thus,

I must, too, de - cline; The year, its life re - sign - ing,—Its lot foreshadows mine.
fore the morning's ray,— Pass up-ward in - to heav - en, And chide at my de - lay.
scenes of death and sin? Oh, rise to glo - ry, hith - er, And find true life be - gin."
thus let all I see Point on, with faithful fin - ger, To heaven, O Lord, and Thee.

OFT IN DANGER, OFT IN WOE.

H. K. WHITE, 1806.

1. Oft in dan - ger, oft in woe, On - ward, Chris-tians, on - ward go;
2. On - ward, Chris- tians, on - ward go, Join the war, and face the foe;
3. Let your droop - ing hearts be glad; March in heaven - ly ar - mor clad;

Fight the fight, main - tain the strife, Strengthen'd with the bread of life.
Will ye flee in dan - ger's hour? Know ye not your Cap - tain's power?
Fight, nor think the bat - tle long, Vict'ry soon shall tune your song.

4. Let not sorrow dim your eye,
   Soon shall every tear be dry;
   Let not tears your course impede,
   Great your strength, if great your need.

5. Onward then in battle move,
   More than conquerors ye shall prove;
   Though opposed by many a foe,
   Christian soldiers, onward go.

EARLY STEPS.—There will be found in all districts some persons not friendly to instruction in music in the schools, and one or more that are bitterly opposed to it. These persons should be handled with gloves; reasoned with and persuaded. As among bad boys, if one is won to the teacher's cause, he will do much toward making the others behave; so by making an ally of one of the original opponents of music, the others may be weakened in their opposition. At any rate, let not the teacher who loves music and desires to have its refining influence in his school—let not such be afraid to approach the enemies of musical instruction, whether the hostility has its origin in penuriousness or prejudice. The blacksmith instructs his apprentice to keep close to the horse to avoid being hurt in the event of an accident. It will surely not be denied that if tact and persuasion are the only instruments, "the end justifies the means." Begin by getting an opinion in favor of music from the patrons; proceed by getting a similar opinion from the school. When singing has been introduced, make it as general as possible,

FAR AWAY.

M. LINDSAY.

1. Where is now the mer-ry par-ty, I remem-ber long a-go; Laughing round the Christmas fire-side, Brighten'd by its rud-dy glow: Or in summer's balm-y eve-nings, In the field up-on the hay? They have all dispers'd, and wander'd Far a-way, .. far a-way, They have all dispers'd, and wander'd Far a-way, far a-way.

2. Some have gone to lands far dis-tant, And with strangers made their home; Some upon the world of wa-ters All their lives are forced to roam; Some are gone from us for-ev-er, Longer here they might not stay,—They have reached a fair-er re-gion Far a-way, .. far a-way, They have reached a fairer re-gion Far a-way, far a-way.

3. There are still some few re-main-ing, Who remind us of the past, But they change as all things change here, Nothing in this world can last; Years roll on and pass for-ev-er, What is coming, who can say? Ere this clos-es ma-ny may be Far a-way, .. far a-way, Ere this clos-es ma-ny may be Far a-way, far a-way.

but, should a pupil desire not to sing (make it impossible for him to *refuse*), let him be excused on apparently good grounds. Let not boys from twelve to sixteen be urged to sing. If their voices are rough, or breaking, advise them not to sing; and if pupils cannot sing in tune, do not permit them to sing—at least, not with the more tuneful children. Children with chronic sore-throat, or bad colds, and young ladies who say it tires them, should not be urged to sing, since great care should be taken of the voices of children. What children shall study is not generally in the power of the teacher to decide, the directors usually claiming that authority. Let music be treated in the same manner. Give all a chance to join in the exercise, but because a few refuse to take part, do not give up in despair. To bring about the introduction of music, do not call a town-meeting. Such a course gives rise to a division of opinion and argument contrary to the movement on foot, and when a person has once taken a stand publicly on a measure, he seldom leaves the position chosen. Look, therefore, to early steps.—*Blackman.*

RAIN UPON THE ROOF.

G. CLIFFORD, from "SONG CROWN."
Per. F. J. HUNTINGDON.

NOTE.—Instead of singing the "la la" accompaniment and chorus, the words only may be sung, repeating, with expression, the last four lines of each verse. It is usually sung without this accompaniment and is always a favorite with schools.

MUSIC IN SCHOOLS.—Controversy in reference to the introduction of the study of music in public schools is not uncommon. Those who oppose, hold that music is a specialty, that there is no general necessity for its culture, because its use is only for the few. A little observation will show the opposite of this to be the truth. What, indeed, is more common than music? It follows us from the cradle to the grave. The infant is cradled with a lullaby. Every ingleside blossoms with song. Every service of the sanctuary is strengthened by it. Every emotion of our human nature utters itself through it. Every convention is enlivened by it. Almost every town has its band, and every hamlet its instrument, and every hedge and grove their warblers. It is common almost as the air we breathe. The very fact of its use makes it useful, and shows its need. But it is said, How can a science so difficult and so hard

7 SWEET AND LOW.

J. BARNBY.
ALFRED TENNYSON.

1. Sweet and low, sweet and low, Wind of the western sea; Low, low, breathe and blow, Wind of the western sea; O-ver the rolling waters go, Come from the dying moon and blow, Blow him a-gain to me, While my lit-tle one, while my pret-ty one sleeps.........

2. Sleep and rest, sleep and rest, Fa-ther will come to thee soon; Rest, rest on moth-er's breast, Fa-ther will come to thee soon; Fa-ther will come to his babe in the nest, Sil-ver sails all out of the west, Un-der the sil-ver moon Sleep, my lit-tle one, sleep, my pret-ty one, sleep.........

to master, be introduced into our common schools? No one expects the science to be mastered in the common schools. We have grammar; but who supposes that the common schools will exhaust the study, and send out accomplished philologists? We have reading and writing; but who supposes that the common schools are to turn out finished scholars in belles-lettres? What is desired is simply this,—that the presence and power of music shall be felt in the common schools. That the children shall be able to sing. That the teachers shall so far master the fundamental principles of the science, as to be able to guide the children in the culture of this department of art. The mother needs it in the family. Our manhood needs its refining and hallowing power. Our churches demand it. Our very nature by divine providence craves it, and no primary or secondary instruction can be complete without it.—*E. E. Higbee.*

STARS TREMBLING O'ER US.

1. Stars trembling o'er us, And sun-set be-fore us, Moun-tain in shad-ow and
2. Come not, pale Sor-row, Flee, flee till to-mor-row, Rest soft-ly fall-ing o'er
3. As the waves cov-er The depths we glide o-ver, So let the past in for-
4. Heav'n shines a-bove us, Bless all that love us,— All that we love, in thy

for-est a-sleep,
eye-lids that weep;
get-ful-ness sleep,
ten-der-ness keep,
} Down the dim riv-er We float on for-ev-er, Speak not, ah,

breathe not! there's peace on the deep, Speak not, ah, breathe not! there's peace on the deep.

BIRDS ARE IN THE WOODLAND.

1. Birds are in the wood-land, birds are on the tree, Mer-ry Spring is com-ing,
2. Fruits are ripe in Au-tumn, leaves are sere and red, Then we glean the corn-fields.

glad of heart are we, Then come sport-ive breez-es, fields with flow'rs are gay,
thank-ing God for bread, Then at last comes Win-ter, fields are cold and lorn,

In the woods we're singing, thro' the Summer day, In the woods we're singing, thro' the Summer day.
But there's happy Christmas, when our Lord was born, Then there's happy Christmas, when our Lord was
[born.

CARE OF THE VOICE.—Mr. Eichberg, Supervisor of Music in the public schools of Boston, gave the following caution, which is well worth heeding. He says: The age of most of the pupils in the high schools renders extreme caution in the treatment of their voices a duty and a sacred obligation. The common belief that boys' voices alone require especial care during the period of transition has led to much loss of voice and of health. Just as important, if less striking, changes occur in the nature and 'timbre' of the female voice. I am convinced that the voice of a girl from twelve to seventeen years of age requires all the more careful management from the very fact that, not suffering, like a boy, from an almost absolute impossibility to sing, she is likely to over-exert herself, to the lasting injury of both health and voice. When teachers are better acquainted with these physiological facts, they will understand the necessity of not sacrificing such young—such temporarily "diseased" voices—to the

DO THEY THINK OF ME AT HOME?

J. E. CARPENTER.
CHAS. W. GLOVER.

Do they think of me at home, Do they ev-er think of me? I who
Do they think of me at eve? Of the songs I used to sing? Is the
Do they think of how I loved In my hap-py, ear-ly days? Do they

shared their ev-'ry grief, I who min-gled in their glee? Have their hearts grown cold and
harp I struck untouch'd, Does a stranger wake the string? Will no kind for-giv-ing
think of him who came, But could nev-er win their praise? I am hap-py by his

strange To the one now doom'd to roam, I would give the world to know,—"Do they
word Come a-cross the rag-ing foam? Shall I nev-er cease to sigh,— "Do they
side, And from mine he'll nev-er roam, But my heart will sad-ly ask,— "Do they

think of me at home?" I would give the world to know, "Do they think of me at home?"
think of me at home?" Shall I nev-er cease to sigh, "Do they think of me at home?"
think of me at home?" But my heart will sad-ly ask, "Do they think of me at home?"

desire of exhibiting and showing off their classes. Another frightful cause of injury proceeds from the desire of many female pupils always to sing the highest part—the first soprano. It is with them "*Aut Cæsar, aut nullus.*" Periodical examination of the pupils' voices, by the teacher, has seemed to me the only safe course in order to remedy this evil. In Jenny Lind's younger days, it is related that she applied for instructions to Garcia, the great teacher of vocal music in Paris. He heard her sing, and then told her her voice was gone, that she must not sing a note for a year, and return to him at the end of that time, and in the meantime improve her health. She faithfully complied with these directions, and came back to Garcia at the appointed time. Rest at a critical period, had restored her voice, to her own delight and to the gratification of her master. From that moment a grand career was open before her, which has made her name a "household word" in two continents.

THE MELLOW HORN.

WM. JONES.

1. At dawn Aurora gaily breaks, In all her proud attire, Majestic o'er the glassy lake, Reflecting liquid fire; All nature smiles to usher in The blushing queen of morn, And huntsmen with the day begin To wind the mellow horn. The mellow horn, The mellow, mellow horn; The mellow horn, The mellow, mellow horn; And huntsmen with the day begin To wind the mellow horn. The mellow, mellow horn, The mellow, mellow horn.

2. At eve when gloomy shades obscure The tranquil shepherd's cot, When tinkling bells are heard no more, And daily toil forgot, 'Tis then the sweet enchanting note On zephyrs gently borne, With witching cadence seems to float Around the mellow horn. The mellow horn, The mellow, mellow horn; The mellow horn, The mellow, mellow horn; 'Tis then the sweet enchanting note On zephyrs gently borne: With witching cadence seems to float Around the mellow horn. The mellow, mellow horn, The mellow, mellow horn.

* An Echo can be made by Soprano and Alto humming these two bars to this note, with lips closed and teeth apart.

I𝐅 the voice be not of the best, it is of small conse-quence. The full-voiced sound will absorb all indi-viduality of voice. Each will be aggregated with all. The little separate waves will go to form an entire ocean of sound, a multitudinous oneness and massive whole, without any prominent individualizing. Es-pecially is this true when the voices are under the controlling and assimilating influence of a powerful, and well-played organ; and, in congregational sing-ing, the organ should have the largest liberty of ut-terance, the foundation-stops being alone employed. So then it may be taken as a fact that, in the people's music of the church, the control and use of the voice require little artistic training, but only so much mus-ical endowment as almost everybody naturally has, and so much musical memory as to remember such simple melodies as form the staple of tunes adapted to general use. All the better, to be sure, if prelim-inary training has been secured, with some knowledge of the elementary rules of music. This were best done in early life, and while at school; and we hesitate not to say that it is a great mistake whenever in any school, public or private, instruction in music and singing is omitted for what is thought more practical.

ROW, ROW, CHEERLY ROW.

D. M. Mulock.
"Emigrants' Song."

Steady Time.

1. Pull, brave boys, pull on to-geth-er, Row, row, cheer-ly row,
2. On through vir-gin for-ests go-ing, Row, row, cheer-ly row,
3. Build the hut and clear the for-est, Row, row, cheer-ly row,

Hand to hand thro' wind and weath-er, Row, row, cheer-ly row. O'er the smooth, deep
Where the might-y riv-er's flow-ing, Row, row, cheer-ly row, With the old land
Help will come when need is sor-est, Row, row, cheer-ly row, Nev-er let our

wa-ters glid-ing, Row, row, cheer-ly row, Or the ra-pids dark di-vid-ing,
far be-hind us, Row, row, cheer-ly row, Where the new-land home shall find us,
cour-age fail us, Row, row, cheer-ly row, Nev-er let one friend be-wail us,

Chorus.

Row, row, cheer-ly row. Pull, my boys, pull on to-geth-er, Row, row,

cheer-ly row, Hand to hand thro' wind and weath-er, Row, row, cheer-ly row.

THE MIDSHIPMITE.

Stephen Adams.
Fred. E. Weatherly.

1. 'Twas in fif-ty-five, on a winter's night, Cheerily, my lads yo-ho! We'd got the Rooshan
2. We launch'd the cutter and shoved her out, Cheerily, my lads yo-ho! The lubbers might ha'
3. "I 'm done for now; good-bye!" says he, Steadily, my lads, yo-ho! "You make for the boat, never

lines in sight, When up comes a lit-tle Mid-ship-mite, Cheerily, my lads, yo-
heard us shout, As the Middy cried, "Now, my lads, put about." Cheerily, my lads, yo-
mind for me!" "We 'll take 'ee ... back, sir, or die," says we, Cheerily, my lads, yo-

ho! "Who 'll go ashore to-night," says he, "An' spike their guns a-long wi' me?" "Why,
ho! "We made for the guns, an' we ramm'd them tight, But the musket shots came left and right, An'
ho! "So we hoisted him in, in a terrible plight, An' we pull'd, ev'ry man with all his might, An'

bless 'ee, sir, come along!" says we, Cheerily, my lads, yo-ho! Cheer-i-ly, my
down drops the poor little Midshipmite, Cheerily, my lads, yo-ho! Cheer-i-ly, my
sav'd the poor little Midshipmite, Cheerily, my lads, yo-ho! Cheer-i-ly, my

lads, yo-ho! . . . With a long, long pull, An' a strong, strong pull, Gaily, boys, make her

go! An' we 'll drink to-night To the Midshipmite, Singing cheer-i-ly, lads, yo-ho!

MUSICAL TRASH.—I wish to express my unfeigned disgust at the flood of musical trash that is annually poured from our music publishing houses in the shape of new tune-books. Every fresh book must contain new and original music. The old tunes must be mangled past recognition, and the compiler must rack his brains to invent new and more dreadful abortions, labeled with astounding names, and called tunes. If all the organists in the country were to meet in convention, and then vote on the best and most useful chorals, they would blot out of existence nine-tenths of these tunes, and give us a list of not over one hundred congregational tunes of real merit. There are at least twenty-four hundred pages of new tunes published every year. Of these how many are worth the paper they are printed upon? Perhaps a dozen tunes. Taking all the civilized people in the world together, it is found that only one man in a million is a musical composer of real genius. Plenty of people can pick out a tune on the piano. They are not composers. We have in the United States a few men, like Zundel and Tuckerman, who can write a choral. The music they give us will live. As for the rest, to the trunk-maker with it! A poor tune-book will make good kindling. To the fire with the rubbish, and let the smoke rise as incense to pure art.—*Barnard.*

SUMMER DAYS ARE COMING.

CHARLES JEFFREYS.

1. The sum-mer days are com-ing, The blos-soms deck the bough, The bees are gai-ly humming, And the birds are sing-ing now. We've had our May-day gar-lands, We have crown'd our May-day queen With a cor-o-net of ro-ses Set in leaves of bright-est green, But her reign is al-most o-ver, The spring is on the wane, Oh, haste thee, gen-tle Sum-mer, To our pleas-ant land a-gain.

2. The min-strel of the moon-light, The love-lorn night-in-gale, 'Hath sung his month of mu-sic, To the rose queen of the vale; And what though he be si-lent? As the night comes slowly on, We will trip a-long the green-sward To sweet mu-sic of our own. Oh, the sum-mer days are com-ing, And sum-mer nights more dear; Oh, haste thee, gen-tle Sum-mer, For there's joy when thou art near.

3. We'll rise and hail thee ear-ly, Be-fore the sun hath dried The dewdrops that will spar-kle On the green hedge by our side; And when the blaze of noonday Shines up-on the thirst-y flowers, We will seek the wel-come cov-ert Of our jas-mine shad-ed bowers. Oh, the sum-mer days are com-ing, The spring is on the wane; Oh, haste thee, gen-tle Sum-mer, To our pleas-ant land a-gain.

TWICKENHAM FERRY.

THEO. MARZIALS. CARL MATZ Arr.

Not too fast.

1. O - hoi - yeho, Hoyeho, Who's for the ferry? The briar's in the bud, and the sun's going down, And I'll
2. O - hoi - ye-ho, Hoyeho, "I'm for the ferry, The briar's in the bud, and the sun's going down, And it's
3. Ohoiyeho, Ho! you're too late for the ferry, The briar's in the bud, and the sun's going down, And he's

row ye so quick, and I'll row ye so steady, And 'tis but a penny to Twickenham town. The
late as it is, and I have-n't a penny, And how shall I get me to Twickenham town?" She'd
not rowing quick and he's not rowing steady, You'd think 'twas a journey to Twickenham town. "O -

ferryman's slim and he ferryman's young, And he's just a soft twang in the turn of his tongue, And he's
a rose in her bonnet, and oh! she look'd sweet As the little pink flower that grows in the wheat, With her
hoi, and O - ho," you may call as you will, The moon is a-ris-ing on Petersham Hill, And with

fresh as a pip - pin and brown as a berry, And 'tis but a pen - ny to Twick - en - ham town.
cheeks like a rose and her lips like a cherry, "And sure and you're welcome to Twickenham town."
love like a rose in the stern of the wherry, There's danger in cross-ing to Twick - en - ham town.

Chorus.

The ferryman's slim, and the ferryman's young, and he's just a soft twang in the turn of his tongue; And he's
[fresh as a pippin, and

CODA. After last verse. *rall.*

brown as a berry, And 'tis but a penny to Twickenham town. Ohoiyeho, Hoyeho, Ho- ye-ho, Ho!

EARLY GENIUS.—Gounod, the musical composer, early manifested his talent. How he secured liberty to follow the bent of his genius, is told in the following incident: It seems that when a boy at college, every effort was made to destroy his musical genius. His professor, M. Poirson, was in despair. His parents intended him for the *ecole normale*. On its being announced to him that he was to go up for the necessary examination, the boy burst into tears, and steadily refused to continue his classical studies. His mother appealed to M. Poirson, and implored him to recall her boy to what she considered to be his duty. The stern professor accordingly sent for him, and, in a tone more threatening than encouraging, said to him: "So you wish to be a musician?" "Yes, sir," replied the terrified boy. "But that is not a profession." "What, sir; the profession of Beethoven, of Mozart, of Gluck, is not a profession?" "But, remember that Mozart at your age had composed music worth publishing, whereas you have only scribbled notes on paper. However, here is your last chance; if you really are a musician, you can set words to music." The old man copied out the poem, "Joseph," "A peine au sortir de l'en France." The boy hurried to his school desk, and after studying the subject, wrote an air and accompaniment, which he brought

MARY OF ARGYLE.

S. NELSON.

Moderato.

1. I have heard the mavis singing His love-song to the morn; I have seen the dew-drops clinging To the
2. Though thy voice may lose its sweetness, And thine eye its brightness, too, Though thy step may lack its
[fleetness, And thy

rose just new-ly born; But a sweeter song has cheer'd me At the evening's gentle close, And I've
hair its sun-ny hue, Still to me wilt thou be dearer Than all the world shall own; I have

seen an eye still brighter Than the dew-drop on the rose; 'Twas thy voice, my gentle Mary, And thine
loved thee for thy beauty, But not for that a-lone. I have watch'd thy heart, dear Mary, And its

art-less, winning smile, That made this world an E - den, Bon - ny Ma - ry of Ar-gyle.
goodness was the wile That has made thee mine forever, Bon - ny Ma - ry of Ar-gyle.

back to his professor, and showed to him, pale with emotion. He felt that on his judgment his future career depended. He sang it to the old man, who listened in amazement, and led him to his drawing room, where he made him play the accompaniment on a piano. Those present were enraptured by the beauty of the composition, and it was at once decided that young Gounod must follow the bent of the undoubted genius with which he was gifted.

PASSING by one of the city schools yesterday, we listened to the scholars singing: "Oh, how I love my teacher dear!" There was one boy, with a voice like a tornado, who was so enthusiastic that he emphasized every word, and roared "Oh, how I love my teacher dear!" with a vim that left no possible doubt of his affection. Ten minutes later, that boy had been compelled to stand on the floor for putting shoemaker's wax on his teacher's chair, got three demerit marks for drawing a picture of her with red chalk on the back of an atlas, been well shaken for putting a bent pin on another boy's chair, scolded for whistling out loud, sentenced to stay after school for drawing ink moustaches on his face, and blacking the end of another boy's nose, and soundly whipped for throwing nine spit-balls against the ceiling. You can't believe more than half a boy says when he sings.—*Hawkeye*.

KILLARNEY.

M. W. BALFE'S LAST SONG.

Moderato.

1. By Kil-lar - ney's lakes and fells, Em'-rald isles and wind-ing bays, Mountain paths and
2. In - nis-fal - len's ruin - ed shrine May suggest a pass-ing sigh; But man's faith can
3. No place else can charm the eye With such bright and va - ried tints, Ev' - ry rock that
4. Mu - sic there for e - cho dwells, Makes each sound a har - mo - ny; Ma - ny-voiced the

woodland dells, Mem-'ry ev - er fond - ly strays, Boun-teous na-ture loves all lands,
ne'er de - cline Such God's wond - ers float - ing by; Cas - tle Lough and Glena bay;
you pass by, Ver-dure broid - ers or besprints, Vir - gin there the green grass grows,
cho - rus swells, 'Till it faints in ec - sta - sy. With the charmful tints be - low,

Beau - ty wan - ders ev - 'ry - where, Foot-prints leaves on ma - ny strands,
Moun - tains Tore and Ea - gle's Nest; Still at Mu - cross you must pray
Ev - 'ry morn springs na - tal day, Bright-hued ber - ries daff the snows,
Seems the heav'n a - bove to vie, All rich col - ors that we know,

rall.　　　　　dim. *pp* a tempo.

But her home is sure - ly there! An - gels fold their wings and rest, In that E - den
Tho' the monks are now at rest. An - gels won - der not that man There would fain pro-
Smil - ing win - ter's frown a - way. An - gels oft - en pausing there, Doubt if E - den
Tinge the cloud-wreaths in that sky. Wings of an - gels so might shine, Glancing back soft

cres.　　　　　*f*

of the West, Beau - ty's home, Kil - lar - - ney, Ev - er fair Kil - lar - ney.
long life's span, Beau - ty's home, Kil - lar - - ney, Ev - er fair Kil - lar - ney.
were more fair, Beau - ty's home, Kil - lar - - ney, Ev - er fair Kil - lar - ney.
light di - vine, Beau - ty's home, Kil - lar - - ney, Ev - er fair Kil - lar - ney.

LIFE-SOUNDS.—We think for a moment of life-sounds, of which there are so many around us. Do you know why we hear a buzzing, as the gnat, the bee, or the cockchafer fly past? Not by the beating of their wings against the air, as many people imagine, and as is really the case with humming birds, but by the scraping of the under-part of their hard wings against the edges of their hind-legs, which are toothed like a saw. The more rapidly their wings are put in motion the stronger this grating sound becomes. Some insects, like the drone-fly, force the air through the tiny air-passages in their sides, and as these passages are closed by little plates, the plates vibrate to and fro and make sound-waves. All these life-sounds are made by creatures which do not sing or speak; but the sweetest sounds of all in the woods are the voices of the birds. All voice-sounds are made by two elastic bands or cushions, called vocal chords, stretched across the end of the tube or windpipe through which we breathe, and as we send the air through them we tighten or loosen them as we will, and so make them vibrate quickly or slowly and make sound-waves of different lengths. But if you will try some day in the woods you will find that a bird can

JUANITA.

SPANISH MELODY.
Words by MRS. NORTON.

mf

1. Soft o'er the fountain, Ling'ring falls the south-ern moon; Far o'er the mountain
2. When in thy dreaming, Moons like these shall shine a-gain, And daylight beaming,

Breaks the day too soon! In thy dark eye's splendor, Where the warm light loves to dwell,
Prove thy dreams are vain. Wilt thou not, re - lent-ing, For thine ab - sent lov-er sigh,

Slower. *A tempo.*

p *mf*

Wea - ry looks, yet ten - der, Speak their fond fare - well! Ni - ta! Jua - ni - ta! *
In thy heart con - sent - ing, To a prayer gone by? Ni - ta! Jua - ni - ta!

Tenderly. rit.

p

Ask thy soul if we should part! Ni - ta! Jua - ni - ta! Lean thou on my heart.
Let me lin - ger by thy side! Ni - ta! Jua - ni - ta! Be my own fair bride!

* Wah-ne-ta.

surpass you over and over again in the length of his note; when you are out of breath and forced to stop he will go on with his merry trill as fresh and clear as if he had only just begun. This is because birds can draw air into the whole of their body, and they have a large stock laid up in the folds of their windpipe, and besides this the air-chamber behind their elastic bands or vocal chords has two compartments where we have only one, and the second compartment has special muscles by which they can open and shut it, and so prolong the trill. Only think what a rapid succession of waves must quiver through the air as a tiny bird agitates his little throat and pours forth a volume of song! The next time you can do so, spend half-an-hour listening to him, or to the canary bird as he swings in his cage, and try to picture to yourself how that little being is moving all the atmosphere around him. Then dream for a little while about Sound, what it is, how marvelously it works outside in the world, and inside in your ear and brain; and then, when you go back to work again, you will hardly deny that it is well worth while to listen sometimes to the voices of Nature and ponder how it is that we hear them.—*Miss A. R. Buckley.*

BLUE ALSATIAN MOUNTAINS.

STEPHEN ADAMS.
CLARIBEL. C. MATZ, ARR.

Not too slow.

1. By the blue Al-sa-tian mountains Dwelt a maiden young and fair, Like the careless-flow-ing
2. By the blue Al-sa-tian mountains Came a stranger in the Spring, And he lin-ger'd by the
3. By the blue Al-sa-tian mountains Many spring-times bloom'd and pass'd, And the maiden by the

foun-tains Were the rip-ples of her hair, Were the rip-ples of her hair; An-gel
foun-tains Just to hear the maid-en sing, Just to hear the maid-en sing; Just to
foun-tains, Saw she lost her hopes at last, She lost her hopes at last. And she

mild her eyes so win-ning, Angel bright her hap-py smile, When be-neath the fountains spin-
whis-per in the moonlight, Words the sweetest she had known, Just to charm a-way the hours,
withered like a flow-er That is wait-ing for the rain, She will never see the stranger,

ning, You could hear her song the while. A-dé, A-dé, A-dé, Such songs will pass away,
Till her heart was all his own. A-dé, A-dé, A-dé, Such dreams may pass away,
Where the fountains fall a-gain. A-dé, A-dé, A-dé, The years have passed away,

Chorus.

Tho' the blue Al-sa-tian moun-tains Seem to watch and wait alway. }
But the blue Al-sa-tian moun-tains Seem to watch and wait alway. } A-dé, A-dé, A-dé,
But the blue Al-sa-tian moun-tains Seem to watch and wait alway. } [A-day,]

Such songs will pass away, Tho' the blue Alsa-tian mountains Seem to watch and wait alway.

AMERICA, it is said, is the only country where the music in divine worship is committed exclusively to two men, two women, and an organist in the gallery. The rector of each church should insist upon the congregation taking part in the music. He should adopt a book, drill the congregation in simple hymns and chants, and have the choir lead the singing, instead of monopolizing it. If this were done, there would soon be a great change in the character of church music, and the Psalmist's injunction would be carried out, "Let all the people praise thee, O God." There should also be musical instruction in the divinity schools; a little time might profitably be taken from the Calvinistic and Arminian controversy, and like theological subtleties, and given to teaching the candidate for holy orders how to read, how to preach, and how to sing. Music is among the most powerful of religious influences, and, in the past and present, has done much to carry forward all great religious movements by heartily rousing the multitude.

FREEDOM'S FLAG.

ADAM GEIBEL.
JOHN J. HOOD, by per.

Allegro maestoso.

1. Our country's flag! O em-blem dear Of all the soul loves best, What glo - ries in thy
2. Beneath thy rays our fa - thers bled In freedom's ho - ly cause; Where'er to heav'n thy
3. Proud banner of the no - ble free! Emblazon'd from on high! Long may thy folds un-

folds ap-pear Let no - ble deeds at - test: Thy pres-ence on the field of strife En-
folds outspread, Pre - vail sweet Freedom's laws. Prosper - i - ty has marked thy course O'er
soil'd re - flect The glo - ries of the sky! Long may thy land be Free-dom's land, Thy

kin-dles val - or's flame; A-round thee, in the hour of peace, We twine our nation's fame.
all the land and sea; Thy favor'd sons in dis-tant climes, Still fondly look to thee.
homes with vir - tue bright, Thy sons a brave, u - ni-ted band, For God, for Truth, and Right!

ff Chorus.

Then hur-rah, hur - rah, for Free-dom's Flag! We hail, with ring - ing cheers, Its

glow - ing bars and clus - t'ring stars, That have braved a hun - dred years.

PULL AWAY, BRAVE BOYS.

Rossini.
" William Tell."

1. Pull a - way, pull a - way, pull a - way, brave boys, Pull a - way, pull a - way, our hearts are
2. Pull a - way, pull a - way, pull a - way, brave boys, Pull a - way, pull a - way, to the bending

gay; Pull a - way, pull a - way thro' the dash - ing spray, On this glo - rious sum - mer day.
oar; Pull a - way, pull a - way, let us heed no more, The mu - sic from the shore.

Pull a - way, pull a - way, while with joy we're singing, And our hearts beat high with glee; Pull a -
Pull a - way, pull a - way, while our pulse is danc - ing, And our hearts are light and free; Pull a -

way, pull a - way, while our songs are ring - ing, Gay - ly o'er the sound - ing sea.
way, pull a - way, thro' the wa - ters glanc - ing, Swift we go o'er the sound - ing sea.

O'er the sea, o'er the sea, re - sound - ing, re - sound - ing, re - sound - ing, O'er the

the sound - ir 3ea, the sea re - sound - ing.

sea, o'er the sea, re - sound - ing, re - sound - ing, re - sound - ing, Pull a -

the sound - ing sea, the sound - ing sea.

THE MOONLIGHT SONATA.—The *Wide-Awake Magazine* tells a pretty story of the way that Beethoven composed this beautiful piece of music. He was going by a small house one evening and heard some one playing his Symphony in F on the Piano. He stopped to listen, and heard a voice say: "What would I not give to hear that piece played by some one who could do it justice." The great composer opened the door and entered. "Pardon me," said Beethoven, somewhat embarrassed; "pardon me, but I heard music, and was tempted to enter. I am a musician!" The girl blushed, and the young man assumed a grave, almost severe manner. "I heard also some of your words," continued Beethoven. "You wish to hear, that is, you would like—in short, would you like me to play to you?" There was something so strange, so comical in the whole affair, and something so agreeable and eccentric in Beethoven's manner, that we all involuntarily smiled. "Thank you," said the young shoemaker; "but our piano is bad, and then we have no music." "No music?" repeated Beethoven, "how, then, did mademoiselle—." He stopped and colored, for the young girl had just turned towards him, and by her sad, veiled eyes he saw that she was blind. "I entreat you to pardon me," stammered he: "but I did not remark at first. You play, then, from memory?" "Entirely!" "And where have you heard this music before?" "Never, excepting the music in the streets." She seemed frightened, so Beethoven did not

NONE CAN TELL.

W. H. EMRA, G. B. ALLEN.

1. Child, is life bright a - lone? None can tell. Al - ways laugh-ter, nev - er moan? None can tell. Will spring flow'rets bloom as sweet, Un - der care-less rov - ing feet, Or lie with-er'd with the heat? None can tell, None can tell.

2. Youth, is she tru - ly thine? None can tell. Will love's light e - ter - nal shine? None can tell. Will the sun make glad thy day, Or will black clouds hide his ray, And love's ten - der beams de - cay? None can tell, None can tell.

3. Bride, is there joy for thee? None can tell. Or will blue skies cloud-ed be? None can tell. Will the bright dream ne'er depart, Or will grief, with last - ing smart, Keep a dull grasp on thy heart? None can tell, None can tell.

add another word, but seated himself at the instrument and began to play. He had not touched many notes when I guessed, says the narrator, who accompanied him, what would follow, and how sublime he would be that evening. I was not deceived. Never, during the many years I knew him, did I hear him play as on this occasion for the blind girl and her brother on that old dilapidated piano. At last the shoemaker rose, approached him, and said in a low voice: "Wonderful man, who are you then?" Beethoven raised his head, as if he had not comprehended. The young man repeated the question. The composer smiled as only he could smile. "Listen," said he; and he played the first movement in the F Symphony. A cry of joy escaped from the lips of the brother and sister. They recognized the player and cried: "You are, then, Beethoven!" He rose to go, but they detained him. "Play for us once more, just once more," they said. He allowed himself to be led back to the instrument. The brilliant rays of the moon entered the curtainless windows and lighted up his broad, earnest, and expressive forehead. "I am going to improvise a sonata to the moonlight," he said, playfully. He contemplated for some moments the sky sparkling with stars; then his fingers rested on the piano, and he began to play in a low, sad, but wondrously sweet strain. The harmony issued from the instrument as sweet and even as the bright rays of the beautiful moonlight spread over the shadows on the ground.

EVER OF THEE.

G. LINLEY.
FOLEY HALL.

Moderato.

1. Ev - er of thee I'm fond - ly dream - ing. Thy gen - tle voice my
2. Ev - er of thee, when sad and lone - ly, Wand -'ring a - far my

spir - it can cheer; Thou art the star that, mild - ly beam - ing, Shone o'er my path when
soul joy'd to dwell; Ah! then I felt I loved thee on - ly, All seemed to fade be -

all was dark and drear: Still in my heart thy form I cher - ish,
fore af - fec - tion's spell; Years have not chill'd the love I cher - ish,

Ev -'ry kind tho't like a bird flies to thee. Ah! nev - er till life and mem -'ry per - ish,
True as the stars hath my heart been to thee. Ah! nev - er till life and mem -'ry per - ish,

Can I for-get how dear thou art to me: Morn, noon and night, where'er I may be,
Can I for-get how dear thou art to me: Morn, noon and night, where'er I may be,

ad lib.

Fond - ly I'm dream-ing ev - er of thee; Fond - ly I'm dream-ing ev - er of thee.
Fond - ly I'm dream-ing ev - er of thee; Fond - ly I'm dream-ing ev - er of thee.

4

HYMN WRITERS.—We have sought for hymns in the books of every denomination of Christians. There are certain hymns of the sacrifice of Christ, of utter and almost soul-dissolving yearning for the benefits of His mediation, which none could write so well as a devout Roman Catholic. Some of the most touching and truly evangelical hymns in the Plymouth Collection we have gathered from this source. We have obtained many exquisite hymns from the Moravian collections, developing the most tender and loving views of Christ, of His personal presence, and gentle companionship. We know of no hymn-writers that equal their faith and fervor for Christ as present with his people. Nor can any one conversant with these fail to recognize the fountain in which the incomparable Charles Wesley was baptized. His hymns are only Moravian hymns re-sung. Not alone are the favorite expressions used and the epithets which they loved, but, like them, he beholds all Christian truths through the medium of confiding love. The *love-element* of this school has never been surpassed. To say that we have sought for hymns expressing the deepest religious feeling, and particularly the sentiments of love, and trust, and divine courage, and

FLEE AS A BIRD.

SPANISH MELODY.
MARY S. B. DANA, 1840.

Expression.

1. Flee as a bird to your moun - tain, Thou who art wea - ry of sin; . . .
2. He will protect thee for - ev - er, Wipe ev - e-ry fall - ing tear; . . .

Go to the clear-flowing foun - tain, Where you may wash and be clean; Fly, for th' a-venger is
He will forsake thee, Oh, nev - er, Sheltered so ten-der- ly there! Haste then, the hours are

near thee, Call, and the Sav - iour will hear thee, He on His bo - som will
fly - ing, Spend not the mo - ments in sigh - ing, Cease from your sor - row and

bear thee; Oh, thou who art wea - ry of sin, Oh, thou who art wea - ry of sin.
cry - ing, The Sav-iour will wipe ev - 'ry tear, The Sav-iour will wipe ev - 'ry tear,

hopefulness, is only to say that we have drawn largely from the best Methodist hymns. The contributions of the Wesleys to hymnology have been so rich as to leave the Christian world under an obligation which cannot be paid as long as there is a struggling Christian brotherhood to sing and be comforted amid the trials of this world. Charles Wesley was peculiarly happy in making the Scriptures illustrate Christian experience, and personal experience throw light upon the deep places of the Bible. Some of his effusions have never been surpassed. Nor are there any hymns that could more nobly express the whole ecstasy of the apostolic writings in view of death and heaven. Cowper, Stennet, Newton, Doddridge, and many other familiar authors, will be found in every collection that aspires to usefulness. With whatever partiality to Dr. Watts we may have begun our work, a comparison of his psalms and hymns with the best effusions of the best hymn-writers has only served to increase our admiration, and our conviction that he stands above all other English writers. Nor do we believe any other man, in any department, has contributed so great a share of enjoyment, edification, and inspiration to struggling Christians as Dr. Watts.—*H. W. Beecher.*

PRAISE TO GOD.

ANNA L. BARBAULD, 1773.
SEBASTIAN BACH. "NUREMBERG."

1. Praise to God, im - mor - tal praise, For the love that crowns our days;
2. Flocks that whit - en all the plain, Yel - low sheaves of ri - pened grain,
3. All that spring, with boun-teous hand, Scat - ters o'er the smil - ing land;
4. Lord, for these our souls shall raise Grate - ful vows and sol - emn praise:

Boun - teous source of ev - 'ry joy! Let Thy praise our tongues em - ploy.
Clouds that drop their fattening dews, Suns that tem - perate warmth dif - fuse.
All that lib - eral au - tumn pours From her rich, o'er - flow - ing stores:
And, when ev - 'ry bles - sing's flown, Love Thee for Thy - self a - lone.

RISE, CROWNED WITH LIGHT.

ALEXANDER POPE.
ALEXIS LVOFF. "RUSSIAN HYMN."

1. Rise, crown'd with light, . . im - pe - rial Sa - lem, rise; Ex - alt thy
2. See a long race . . . thy spa - cious courts a - dorn, See fu - ture
3. See barbarous na - . . tions at thy gates at - tend, Walk in thy
4. The seas shall waste, . . the skies to smoke de - cay, Rocks fall to

tow'r - ing head and lift thine eyes; See Heav'n its spark - ling por - tals
sons, and daugh-ters yet un - born, In crowding ranks on ev - 'ry
light, and in thy tem - ple bend: See thy bright al - tars throng'd with
dust, and mountains melt a - way; But fix'd His word, His sav - ing

wide . . . dis - play, And break up - on thee in a flood of day.
side . . . a - rise, De - mand-ing life, im - pa - tient for the skies.
pros - trate kings, While ev - 'ry land its joy - ous tri - bute brings.
pow'r . . . re - mains, Thy realm shall last, thy own Mes - si - ah reign.

INFLUENCE OF MUSIC.—Man is as much a child of the beautiful as he is of wisdom or genius, Nature never drives us if she can avoid it; she prefers to allure us. She makes all things charming. She paints the fields and the woods that we may go to them, led by affection. She makes the face of youth beautiful, throws color on the cheek, and makes the lines of smiles and laughter come and go, and she sends the soul into the eyes, that young years may build up everlasting frienship. Yielding to his Divine Master's guidance, man follows the beautiful, and to the idea of home or temple or garden or city, he comes with both hands full of ornament. He claims for his house and his dress what God gives to the peach, or the leaf, or the rose. In this deep philosophy music comes as the decoration of a thought. Man submits his truths to several steps of this ennobling work. He found them in prose and he asks Milton or Dante, or Tennyson or Longfellow to frame them into poetry, but not yet satisfied

I'VE BEEN ROAMING.

CHAS. E. HORN.

Lively.

1. I've been roam-ing, I've been roam-ing Where the mea-dow dew is sweet;
2. I've been roam-ing, I've been roam-ing By the rose and lil-y fair;
3. I've been roam-ing, I've been roam-ing Where the hon-ey-suc-kle creeps;
4. I've been roam-ing, I've been roam-ing O-ver hill and o-ver plain;

And I'm com-ing, and I'm com-ing With its pearls up-on my feet,}
And I'm com-ing, and I'm com-ing With their blos-soms in my hair,} I've been
And I'm com-ing, and I'm com-ing With its greet-ing on my lips,}
And I'm com-ing, and I'm com-ing To my bow-er back a-gain, O-ver

roam-ing, I've been roam-ing Where the mea-dow dew is sweet,
(4) hill, and o-ver plain, To my bow-er back a-gain,

And I'm com-ing, and I'm com-ing With its pearls up-on my feet.
(4) And I'm com-ing, and I'm com-ing To my bow-er back a-gain.

he takes the thought to the great musician and asks Mozart or Weber or Schubert to pour still more color on the blessed thought. It was not enough for the Greeks that some of their truth took the poetic form of the drama, it must also be sung on the stage, so that between the uplifted hands of both Poetry and Music all might see how sorrowful was Œdipus or how sweet Antigone. Thus all through its history, music has ever been the final decoration of a sentiment. Poetry has done much when it has gathered up some of the pensive meditations of man when he draws near his long home and has called this rhythmical arrangement a poem. Even read to us, its flow of harmonious feet is impressive; but when Mozart goes further, and wreathes those words with his composition into a requiem, then is the cup of our realization full, and all the pomp and splendor of earth sink like the summer sun.—*Swing.*

FLOW GENTLY, SWEET AFTON.

J. E. SPILMAN.
Words by ROBERT BURNS.

1. Flow gent-ly, sweet Af - ton, a - mang thy green braes; Flow gent-ly, I'll sing thee a
2. How loft-ty, sweet Af - ton, thy neighbor-ing hills, Far marked with the courses of
3. Thy crys-tal stream, Af - ton, how love - ly it glides, And winds by the cot where my

song in thy praise; My Ma-ry's a - sleep by thy murmur-ing stream, Flow gent-ly, sweet
clear-winding rills; There dai - ly I wan-der, as morn ris - es high, My flocks and my
Ma - ry re - sides! How wan-ton thy wa-ters her snow-y feet lave, As gath'ring sweet

Af - ton, dis - turb not her dream. Thou stock-dove, whose e - cho re - sounds from the
Ma - ry's sweet cot in my eye. How pleas - ant thy banks and green val - leys be -
flowerets, she stems thy clear wave! Flow gent - ly, sweet Af - ton, a - mang thy green

hill, Ye wild whistling black-birds in yon thorn-y den, Thou green-crest - ed
low, Where wild in the woodlands the prim-ros - es blow! There oft, as mild
braes, Flow gent-ly, sweet riv - er, the theme of my lays: My Ma - ry's a -

lap-wing, thy screaming for - bear, I charge you, dis-turb not my slum-ber - ing fair.
evening creeps o - ver the lea, The sweet-scented birk shades my Ma - ry and me.
sleep by thy mur-mur-ing stream, Flow gent-ly, sweet Af - ton, dis - turb not her dream.

CHEER, BOYS, CHEER.

H. Russell.
Charles Mackay.

1. Cheer, boys, cheer, no more of i - dle sor - row, Courage! true hearts shall
2. Cheer, boys, cheer, the stead - y breeze is blow - ing, To float us free - ly

bear us on our way; Hope points be - fore and shows the bright to - mor - row;
o'er the o - cean's breast; The world shall fol - low in the track we're go - ing,

Let us for - get the dark - ness of to - day. So fare - well, England,
The star of Em - pire glit - ters in the West. Here we had toil and

much as we a - dore thee, We'll dry the tears that we have shed be - fore;
lit - tle to re - ward it, But there shall plen - ty smile up - on our pain;

Why should we weep to sail in search of for tune? So fare - well, England! fare -
And ours shall be the prai - rie and the for - est, And bound - less meadows ripe,

well for - ev - er - more. Cheer, boys, cheer for coun - try, moth - er coun - try,
ripe with gol - den grain. Cheer, boys, cheer for England, moth - er Eng - land,

Cheer, boys, cheer the will-ing strong right hand, Cheer, boys, cheer, there's
Cheer, boys, cheer, u-nit-ed heart and hand, Cheer, boys, cheer, there's

wealth for hon-est la-bor, Cheer, boys, cheer for the new and hap-py land!

MAKE YOUR MARK.

Firmly.

1. In the quar-ries should you toil, Make your mark! Make your mark! Do you delve up-
2. Would you seek for treasures rare, Make your mark! Make your mark! Wealth that will with
3. Life is fleet-ing as a shade, Make your mark! Make your mark! Marks of some kind

on the soil, Make your mark! Make your mark! In what-ev-er path you go,
gold com-pare, Make your mark! Make your mark! While the light is in thine eye,
must be made, Make your mark! Make your mark! Make it while the arm is strong,

In what-ev-er place you stand, Mov-ing swift or mov-ing slow, With a firm and
While the bloom is on thy cheek, Ere the toils and cares of life, Make the res-o-
In the gol-den hours of youth, Nev-er, nev-er make it wrong, Make it with the

hon-est hand, Make your mark, Make your mark, Make, make your mark!
lu-tion weak, Make your mark, Make your mark, Make, make your mark!
stamp of truth, Make your mark, Make your mark, Make, make your mark!

GOOD TEACHERS.—Not every one who is a good player is for that reason a good teacher. The best player may be the poorest teacher. To be a good musician is one thing, to be a good teacher is another. There are many who possess a great amount of information, but who can impart little or nothing. There are others who attempt to be guides, but who do not know the road. There are not a few who attempt to teach, who were never properly taught. Teachers are not made, they are born. It is difficult to judge of a good teacher. Inquire before you engage one. The fact that parents have no full appreciation of the importance of a child's education, accounts for the indifference which they show in the selection of teachers. Many parents engage poor teachers for beginners. A sadder mistake was never made in the process of education. As well may you lay a foundation of soft brick, consoling yourself with the idea that you will finish the house with grey stone. The first teacher is very likely the one who will make or mar the musical future of your child.—*Merz.*

Music is the only one of the fine arts in which both man and all other animals have a common property —mice and elephants, spiders and birds.—*Richter.*

ROBINSON CRUSOE.

Air—"ROGUE'S MARCH."

1. When I was a lad, I had cause to be sad, A ver-y good friend I did lose, O! I war-rant you, Dan, you have heard of this man, His name it was Rob-in-son Cru-soe. Oh, Rob-in-son Cru-soe! Oh, poor Robin-son Cru-soe! He went off to sea and be-tween you and me, Old Neptune wreck'd Robinson Cru-soe.

2. But he saved from a-board an old gun and a sword, And another odd mat-ter or two, so That by dint of his thrift he just managed to shift, And keep a-live Rob-in-son Cru-soe. Oh, Rob-in-son Cru-soe! Oh, poor Robin-son Cru-soe! Whether tempest or Turk, or wild man or work, No mat-ter to Rob-in-son Cru-soe.

3. His hut was a match for um-brel-la of thatch, And his clothes were too old to be new, so That his parrot at last would cry out as he passed, "Hurrah for old Rob-in-son Cru-soe. Oh, Rob-in-son Cru-soe! Oh, poor Robin-son Cru-soe! His par-rot is dead, and his goats have all fled The home of old Rob-in-son Cru-soe.

The cannibals came to his island one day,
   To feast, for all cannibals do so,
But Friday, their man, jumped out of the pan,
   And ran off to Robinson Crusoe.
Oh, Robinson Crusoe! Oh, poor Robinson Crusoe!
He fired off his gun, and then there was fun
   For lonely old Robinson Crusoe.

But he never lost hope, and he never would mope,
   And he always had faith, as should you, so
That come as it might, it always was right
   With honest old Robinson Crusoe.
Oh, Robinson Crusoe! Good old Robinson Crusoe!
Where can school-boy be found to stop at a round
   "Hurrah for old Robinson Crusoe!"

THE MOON IS BEAMING O'ER THE LAKE.

JOHN BLOCKLEY.

1. The moon is beam-ing o'er the lake, Come sail in our light ca-noe; Sweet
2. The ves-per bell is peal-ing, From yon-der lone-ly tower; Its

sounds of mu-sic we'll a-wake, As we glide o'er the wa-ters blue. In our
tones now gen-tly steal-ing, Pro-claim the ves-per hour. Sweet

light ca-noe, As mer-ry we row, O-ver the rip-pling sil-ver tide; While
sounds a-rise, To the tran-quil skies, Like one of earth's sweetest mel-o-dies; Now

free from care, Our spir-its are, As a-way we mer-ri-ly glide, ... The
sad, now gay, As it floats a-way, On the wings of the summer breeze, ... The

moon is beam-ing o'er the lake, Come sail in our light ca-noe; Sweet
moon is beam-ing o'er the lake, Come sail in our light ca-noe; Sweet

sounds of mu-sic we'll a-wake, As we glide o'er the wa-ters blue.
sounds of mu-sic we'll a-wake, As we glide o'er the wa-ters blue.

THE following tribute to the memory of the late Matthew Arbuckle, whose magic cornet made his name a household word with millions, will doubtless waken a responsive echo in the heart of every one who was privileged to know that brilliant artist and kindly, courteous gentleman: "Half-a-dozen years ago," writes a lady, one of his pupils, "an old cornet hung upon the wall of my home, and it somehow happened that I tried it 'to see how it would go.' By a little persistence I got a tone, and finally became fascinated with the noise I could produce, and, working away as much as the neighborhood would endure without complaints to the police, I got some mastery.

The performance was horrible, of course, but one April day I appeared at Mr. Arbuckle's door in New York, a petitioner for lessons. I remember how kindly he received me; how he gave me courage at once by commending my poor attempt at 'Robin Adair,' so that he could know what I could do and where to begin with me. I remember the next three months of his helpfulness, his patience, his encouragement, his hopefulness; how he put no limit to the 'hour's lesson' we had bargained for, and often entertained and helped me a whole afternoon, sometimes taking his cornet, and, forgetting all the world else, giving me his wonderful rendering of delightful airs and ballads. I re-

COME, CHEERFUL COMPANIONS.

VIVE LA COMPAGNIE.

1. Come, cheerful companions, u - nite in our song, Here's to the friends we love!
2. And first, the dear pa-rents who watch o'er our youth, They are the friends we love!
3. Next, think of the ab-sent to all of us dear, They are the friends we love!
4. And here's to the good, and the wise, and the true, They are the friends we love!

May boun-ti-ful Heav-en their sweet lives prolong! Here's to the friends we love!
And next are the teachers who tell us of truth, They are the friends we love!
Oh, would they were with us, we would they were here! They are the friends we love!
Their beau-ti-ful lives are for me and for you, They are the friends we love!

Oh, sym-pa-thy deepens whenev-er we sing; Friendship's the mys-ti-cal word in our ring;

Here's to our friends! Here's to our friends! Here's to the friends we love!

member, too, his comical running to the corner of the room and hiding his face when I had my lesson poorly, and how he would look over his shoulder laughing at me and shouting: 'Try it again,' and when the work was done to his satisfaction, how proud and glad and happy he seemed. He was every inch a gentleman; in every fibre a musician. He gave me music arranged by his own hand; he selected and tested a cornet for me, and all the 'crooks' and 'mutes' and mouthpieces, and every other appliance of a cornetist's outfit, and there was nothing he could do, by instruction and advice, that he left undone. A country girl of fourteen, alone in the great city so far as kindred were concerned,

he bade me welcome to his home. His wife was almost a mother to me, his daughter a friend indeed. I want to say how good he was, how true to his art, how kind, sweet-tempered, big-hearted—a noble man in every thing.

CHRISTOPHER NORTH, a lover of nature, never said a truer or a wiser thing than this, in his Soliloquy on the Seasons: "Turn from the oracles of man, still dim even in their clearest response—to the oracles of God, which are never dark. Bury all your books when you feel the night of skepticism gathering around you; bury them all, powerful though you may have deemed their spell to illuminate the unfathomable; open your Bible, and all the spiritual world will be as bright as the day."

TWILIGHT IS FALLING.

A. S. KIEFFER. B. C. UNSELD.
From "TEMPLE STAR."

1. Twi - light is steal - ing O - ver the sea; Shad-ows are fall - ing Dark on the lea;
2. Voic - es of lov'd ones! Songs of the past! Still lin - ger round me, While life shall last;
3. Come in the twi - light, Come, come to me! Bring-ing some mes-sage, O - ver the sea,

Borne on the night winds, Voi - ces of yore, Come from the far - off shore.
Lone - ly I wan - der, Sad - ly I roam, Seek - ing that far - off home.
Cheer - ing my path - way, While here I roam, Seek - ing that far - off home.

D. S. Gleameth a man - sion fill'd with de - light, Sweet, hap - py home so bright.

CHORUS. *D.S.*

Far a - way be - yond the star - lit skies, Where the love-light nev - er, nev - er dies.

THE LORD'S PRAYER.

MRS. S. J. HALE.

1. Our Fa - ther in Hea - ven, we hal - low Thy name; May Thy Kingdom, all
2. For - give our trans-gres-sions, and teach us to know That hum-ble com-

ho - ly, on earth be the same: O give to us dai - ly our
pas sion that par - dons each foe: Save us from temp - ta - tion, from

por - tion of bread; It is from Thy boun - ty that all must be fed.
weakness and sin; And Thine be the glo - ry, for - ev - er A - MEN.

LOOK NOT UPON THE WINE.

R. S. WILLIS.

1. Look not upon the wine when it Is red with-in the cup! Stay not for pleasure when she fills Her tempt-ing beak-er up! Though clear its depths, and rich its glow A spell of mad-ness lurks below; Tho' clear its depths and rich its glow, There's madness lurks below.

2. They say 'tis pleasant on the lip, And mer-ry on the brain; They say it stirs the sluggish blood, And dulls the tooth of pain. Ay! but with-in its glow-ing deeps A dead-ly ser-pent unseen sleeps; Ay! but within its glowing deeps A dead-ly ser-pent sleeps.

3. Its ros-y light will turn to fire, Its cool-ness change to thirst; And, by its mirth, up-on the brain, A sleep-less worm is nursed. There's not a bub-ble at the brim That does not car-ry food to him; There's not a bub-ble at the brim But car-ries food to him.

4. Then dash the brimming cup aside, Quaff not its pur-ple wine; Take not its madness to thy lip—Let not its curse be thine. 'Tis red and rich, but grief and woe Are in those ro-sy depths below; 'Tis red and rich, but grief and woe Are in those depths below.

DEAR FATHER, DRINK NO MORE.

Slow.

1. Dear fath-er! drink no more, I pray, It makes you look so sad, Come home, and drink no more, I say, 'Twill make dear moth-er glad.

2. Dear fath-er! think how sick you've been, What aches and pains you know! Oh! drink no more, and then you'll find A home where'er you go.

3. Dear fath-er! think of moth-er's tears, How oft and sad they flow, Oh! drink no more, then will her grief No long-er rack her so.

4. Dear fath-er! think what would become Of me, were you to die! With-out a fath-er friend or home, Be-neath the chil-ly sky.

Dear father, drink no more, I pray,
    It makes you look so sad,
Come home, and drink no more, I say,
    'Twill make that home so glad.

Thus spake, in tenderness, the child,
    The drunkard's heart was moved,
He signed the pledge; he wept, he smiled,
    And kissed the boy he loved.

SPARKLING AND BRIGHT.

TEMPERANCE SONG.

1. Sparkling and bright, in its li - quid light, Is the wa - ter in our glass - es;
2. Bet - ter than gold is the wa - ter cold, From the crys - tal foun - tain flow - ing;
3. Sor - row has fled from hearts that bled, Of the weep - ing wife and moth - er,

'Twill give you health, 'Twill give you wealth, Ye lads and ro - sy lass - es!
A calm de - light, both day and night, To hap - py homes be - stow - ing:
They have given up the poi - son'd cup, Son, hus - band, daughter, broth - er.

Chorus.

Oh, then re - sign your ru - by wine, Each smil - ing son and daugh - ter,

There's noth-ing so good for the youth-ful blood, Or sweet as the sparkling wa - ter.

OLD HUNDRED.

W. FRANC, 1543.

1. Be Thou, O God, ex - alt - ed high, And as thy glo - ry fills the sky,
2. With one con - sent let all the earth To God their cheer - ful voi - ces raise;
3. For He's the Lord, su - preme - ly good; His mer - cy is for - ev - er sure;

Doxology: Praise God, from whom all bless-ings flow, Praise Him, all crea-tures here be - low;

So let it be on earth dis-played, Till Thou art here, as there, o - beyed.
Glad hom - age pay with aw - ful mirth, And sing be - fore Him songs of praise.
His truth, which al - ways firm - ly stood, To end - less a - ges shall en - dure.

Praise Him a - bove, ye heavenly host; Praise Fa - ther, Son, and Ho - ly Ghost.

WHAT IS HOME?

CHAS. SWAIN.
AIR FROM ROSSINI.

1. Home's not mere-ly four square walls, Though with pic-tures hung and gild-ed;
2. Home's not mere-ly roof and room, Needs it some-thing to en-dear it;

Home is where af-fec-tion calls—Filled with shrines the heart hath build-ed.
Home is where the heart can bloom; Where there's some kind lip to cheer it.

Home!—go, watch the faith-ful dove, Sail-ing 'neath the heaven a-bove us;
What is home with none to meet? None to wel-come—none to greet us?

Home is where there's one to love, Home is where there's one to love us.
Home is sweet—and on-ly sweet—Where there's one we love to meet us.

Home is where there's one to love, Home is where there's one to love us.
Home is sweet—and on-ly sweet—Where there's one we love, to meet us.

THE CHAPEL.

Words by UHLAND.

1. See yon chap-el on the hill, Calm it looks o'er all the plain;
2. Sad-ly chants the choir a-long; Sad-ly sounds the chap-el bell;
3. Those who once had smiled in joy, To the bur-ial there they bring;

Cheer-ful-ly by mead and rill, Sings the shep-herd boy his strain.
Hush'd is now the shep-herd's song, And he lis-tens in the dell.
Shep-herd boy! Oh, shep-herd boy! O'er thee too they yet will sing.

THE ROSY CROWN.

C. M. Von Weber.

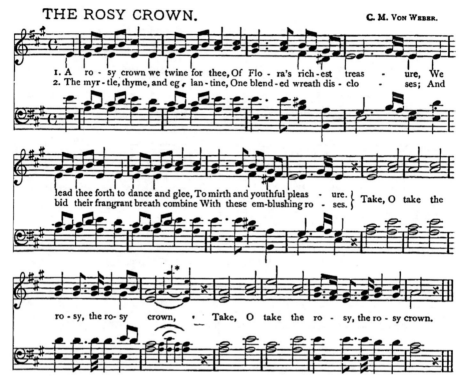

1. A ro - sy crown we twine for thee, Of Flo - ra's rich - est treas - ure, We
2. The myr - tle, thyme, and eg - lan - tine, One blend - ed wreath dis - clo - ses; And

lead thee forth to dance and glee, To mirth and youthful pleas - ure.
bid their frangrant breath combine With these em-blushing ro - ses.
Take, O take the

ro - sy, the ro - sy crown, Take, O take the ro - sy, the ro - sy crown.

We bade the fairest flowers that grow,
Their varied tribute render,
To shine above that brow of snow,
In all their sunny splendor.
Take, O take, etc.

Then deign to wear the wreath we twine,
Thy beauteous ringlets shading;
And be its charms a type of thine,
In all except their fading.
Take, O take, etc.

THREE CHILDREN SLIDING.

A. D. 1633.

mf

Not too Fast.

1. Three child - ren slid - ing on the ice, All on a sum - mer's day, As
2. Now had these chil - dren been at home, Or slid - ing on dry ground, Ten
3. You pa - rents all that chil - dren have, And you, too, that have none, If

rit.

it fell out they all fell in, The rest they ran a - way
thous - and pounds to pen - ny one, They had not all been drown'd
you would have them safe a - broad, Pray keep them safe at home.

* Grace notes in Chorus are the original music in opera of "Der Freischutz," from which this is taken.

EDUCATION.—When a boy I was very fond of music, and am so now; and it so happened that I had the opportunity of hearing much good music. Among other things I had abundant opportunities of hearing that great old master, Sebastian Bach. I remember perfectly well—though I knew nothing about music then, and, I may add, know nothing whatever about it now—the intense satisfaction and delight which I had in listening by the hour together to Bach's fugues. It is a pleasure which remains with me, I am glad to think, but of late years I have tried to find out the why and wherefore, and it has often occurred to me that the pleasure in musical compositions of this kind is essentially of the same nature as that which is derived from pursuits which are commonly regarded as purely intellectual. I mean that the source of pleasure is exactly the same as in most of my problems in morphology—that you have the theme in one of the old master's works followed out in all its endless variations, always appearing and always reminding you of unity in variety. So in painting; what is called truth to nature is the intellectual element coming in, and truth to nature depends entirely upon the intellectual culture of the person to whom art is addressed. If you are in Australia, you may get the credit for being a good artist—I mean among the natives—if you can draw a kangaroo after a fashion. But among men of higher civilization the intellectual knowledge we possess brings its criticism into our appreciation of works of art, and we are obliged to satisfy it as well as the mere sense of beauty

COME, OH, COME WITH ME.

ITALIAN MELODY.

1. Come, O come with me, the moon is beam-ing, Come, O come with me; the stars are gleam-ing; All a-round, a-bove, with beau-ty teem-ing; Moon-light hours have joys for me. Tra la la la la la la la la la, Tra la la la la la la la la.

2. My skiff is by the shore, she's light and free, To ply the feather'd oar is joy to me; And while we glide a-long, o'er the dark blue sea, We'll sing our sweet-est mel-o-dy. Tra la la la

in color and in outline. And so the higher the culture and information of those whom art addresses, the more exact and precise must be what we call its "truth to nature." If we turn to literature the same thing is true, and you find works of literature which may be said to be pure art. A little song of Shakespeare or of Goethe is pure art, although its intellectual content may be nothing. A series of pictures is made to pass before your minds by the meaning of words, and the effect is a melody of ideas. And if you will let me for a moment speak of the very highest forms of literature, do we not regard them as highest simply because the more we know the truer they seem, and the more competent we are to appreciate beauty the more beautiful they are? No man ever understands Shakespeare until he is old, though the youngest may admire him; the reason being that he satisfies the artistic instinct of the youngest and harmonizes with the ripest and richest experience of the oldest. It is not a question whether one order of study or another should predominate, but rather of what topics of education you shall select, combining all the needful elements in such due proportion as to give the greatest amount of food and support and encouragement to those faculties which enable us to appreciate truth, and to profit by those sources of innocent happiness which are open to us, and at the same time to avoid that which is bad and coarse and ugly, and to keep clear of the multitude of pitfalls and dangers which beset those who break through the natural or moral laws.—*Thos. H. Huxley.*

LISTEN TO THE MOCKING BIRD.

ALICE HAWTHORNE.

1. I'm dreaming now of Hal-lie,   sweet Hal-lie,   sweet Hal-lie,   I'm dreaming now of
2. Ah! well I yet re-mem-ber,   re-mem-ber,   re-mem-ber,   Ah! well I yet re-
3. When the charms of spring awaken,   a-wak-en,   a-waken, When the charms of spring a-

Hal-lie,   For the thought of her is one that nev-er dies;   She's sleep-ing in the
mem-ber,   When we gathered in the cot-ton side by side;   'Twas in the mild Sep-
wak-en,   And the mocking bird is sing-ing on the bough,   I feel like one for-

val-ley,   the val-ley,   the val-ley,   She's sleeping in the val-ley, And the
tem-ber,   Sep-tem-ber,   Sep-tem-ber,   'Twas in the mild Sep-tem-ber, And the
sak-en,   for-sak-en,   for-sak-en,   I feel like one for-sak-en, Since my

Chorus.

mocking bird is singing where she lies.   Listen to the mocking bird,   Listen to the
mocking bird was singing far and wide.   Listen to the mocking bird,   Listen to the
Hal-lie is no longer with me now.   Listen to the mocking bird,   Listen to the

mock-ing bird,   The mock-ing bird still sing-ing o'er her grave;   Lis-ten to the

mocking bird, Listen to the mocking bird, Still singing where the weeping willows wave.

CHILD OF EARTH.

CHAS. E. HORN.

Allegro con anima.

1. Child of earth with the gold - en hair, Thy soul's too pure and thy
2. I'll rob of its sweets the hon - ey bee, I'll crush the wine from the

face too fair, To dwell with the crea - tures of mor - tal mould, Whose
cow - slip tree, I'll pull thee ber - ries, I'll heap thy bed Of

lips are warm as their hearts are cold. Roam, roam to our fai - ry home.
down - y moss and the pop - pies red. Roam, roam to our fai - ry home.

Child of earth with the gold - en hair, Thou shalt dance with the fai - ry queen Thro'
Child of earth with the gold - en hair, Dim sleep shall woo thee, dar - ling boy, In her

sum - mer nights on the moon - lit green, To mu - sic mur - mur - ing sweet - er
mild - est mood, with dreams of joy, And when with the morn - ing ends her

far Than ev - er was heard 'neath the morn - ing star.
reign, Pleas - ure shall bid thee wel - - come a - gain.

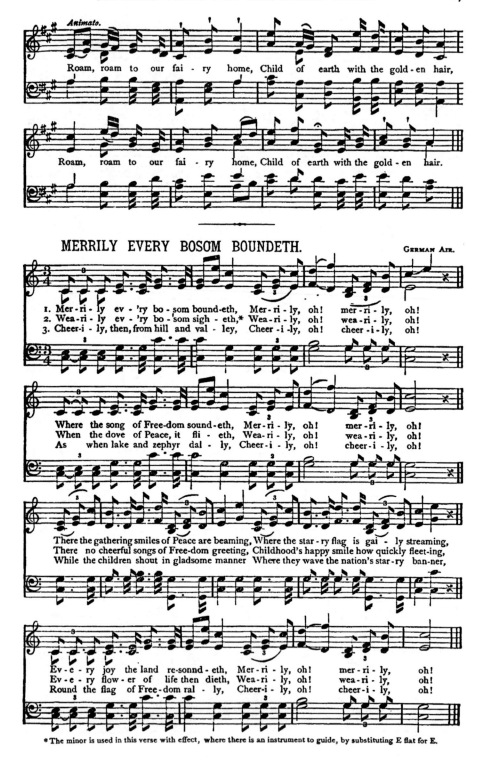

MERRILY EVERY BOSOM BOUNDETH.

GERMAN AIR.

1. Mer - ri - ly ev - 'ry bo - som bound-eth, Mer - ri - ly, oh! mer - ri - ly, oh!
2. Wea - ri - ly ev - 'ry bo - som sigh - eth,* Wea - ri - ly, oh! wea - ri - ly, oh!
3. Cheer-i - ly, then, from hill and val - ley, Cheer -i -ly, oh! cheer-i - ly, oh!

Where the song of Free-dom sound-eth, Mer - ri - ly, oh! mer - ri - ly, oh!
When the dove of Peace, it fli - eth, Wea - ri - ly, oh! wea - ri - ly, oh!
As when lake and zephyr dal - ly, Cheer-i - ly, oh! cheer-i - i - ly, oh!

There the gathering smiles of Peace are beaming, Where the star - ry flag is gai - ly streaming,
There no cheerful songs of Free-dom greeting, Childhood's happy smile how quickly fleet-ing,
While the children shout in gladsome manner Where they wave the nation's star-ry ban-ner,

Ev - e - ry joy the land re-sonnd - eth, Mer - ri - ly, oh! mer - ri - ly, oh!
Ev - e - ry flow - er of life then dieth, Wea - ri - ly, oh! wea - ri - ly, oh!
Round the flag of Free-dom ral - ly, Cheer-i - ly, oh! cheer-i - ly, oh!

*The minor is used in this verse with effect, where there is an instrument to guide, by substituting E flat for E.

The very worst specimens of musical incompetency which may be heard in drawing-rooms are due to the want of perception and the vanity of those who exhibit them. There are many men and women who might sing or play agreeably if they would confine themselves to things within their powers; but vaulting ambition carries them pell-mell into the dangers of difficult music which can only be encountered successfully after years of study and practice, and makes of the struggles, which, it is to be hoped, are more painful to their hearers than themselves, a terrible warning. When one has been present at one or two performances of this kind, he can understand the feelings of a professor of music who was gifted with a very tender conscience besides a great talent, and, being asked the reason of an unusual fit of gloom, replied: "Well I am just thinking whether I ought to go on teaching these amateurs. They come and learn, but they understand nothing; and they mostly have voices not unlike little cats." No less dreadful than the amateur who has no talent for music is he who has a good deal of talent and so much enthusiasm that his mind is incapable of taking thought for anything else that is excellent. For him the big world has nothing at all outside of music.

MILL MAY.

Rapidly.

"First Steps in Music."
Per. Ivison, Blakeman, Taylor & Co.

1. The straw-ber-ries grow in the mowing, Mill May, And the bob-o-link sings on the
2. Come, come ere the sea-son is o-ver, Mill May, To the fields where the strawberries
3. The sun slant-ing un-der your bon-net, Mill May, Will soon bring a soft glow to your

tree; On the knolls the red clo-ver is grow-ing, Mill May; Then
grow; While the thick-grow-ing stems and the clo-ver, Mill May, Shall
face; And your lip— the straw-ber-ries leave on it, Mill May, A

CHORUS.

come to the meadow with me. Yes, come, the ripe clusters a-mong the thick grass, We'll
meet us wher-ev-er we go. Yes, come, the ripe clusters a-mong the thick grass, We'll
tint that the sea-shell would grace. Yes, come, the ripe clusters a-mong the thick grass, We'll

pick in the mowing, Mill May, Mill May; And the long afternoon to-gether we'll pass, Where the

clo-ver is growing, Mill May, Mill May; Where the clover is growing, Mill May.

OLD FAMILIAR PLACE.

C. W. GLOVER.

1. We may rove the wide world o'er, But we ne'er shall find a trace Of the home we loved of
2. We may sail o'er ev-ery sea, But we still shall fail to find An-y spot so dear to

yore, Of the old fa-mil-iar place; Other scenes may be as bright, But we miss, 'neath alien
be As the one we left be-hind; Words of comfort we may hear, But they can-not touch the

rall. *a tempo.*

skies, Both the welcome and the light Of the old, kind, loving eyes. Home is home, of this be-
heart, Like the tones to memory dear, Of the friends from whom we part. Home is home, the wanderer

rall.

reft, Mem'ry loves a-gain to trace All the forms of those we left In the old fa-mil-iar place.
longs All the scenes of youth to trace, And to hear the old home songs In the old fa-mil-iar place.

AS A LITTLE CHILD.

C. M. VON WEBER.

Moderato.

1. As a lit-tle child re-lies On a care be-yond its own,
2. So let me, a child, re-ceive What to-day Thou shalt pro-vide,
3. Qui-et, Lord, my fro-ward heart, Make me lov-ing, meek and mild;

Knows be-neath its fa-ther's eyes It is nev-er left a-lone,—
Calm-ly to Thy wis-dom leave What to-mor-row may be-tide,
Up-right, sim-ple, free from art, Make me as a lit-tle child.

KATHLEEN MAVOURNEEN.

F. W. N. CROUCH.

1. Kath-leen Mavourneen, the grey dawn is break-ing The horn of the hun-ter is
2. Kath-leen Mavourneen, a-wake from thy slum-bers; The blue mountains glow in the

Small notes to be sung to the 2nd verse.

heard   on the hill; The lark from her light wing the bright   dew is shak - ing;
sun's   golden light; Ah! where is the spell that once hung   on my num - bers? A-

Kathleen   Ma-vour-neen, what! slum-b'ring still?   Kath - leen Ma-
rise in   thy beau-ty,   thou star of my night; A - rise   in thy

con amore affette.

vourneen,   what! slum - b'ring still! Or hast thou for-got-ten   how
beau - ty,   thou star of my night! Ma - vour-neen, Ma-vour-neen, my

soon   we must sev - er? Oh! hast thou for-got-ten   this   day   we must
sad   tears are falling, To think that from E - rin   and   thee   I must

part?   It may be for years, and it may be for - ev - er; Then why   art thou
part!   It may be for years, and it may be for - ev - er; Then why   art thou

si - lent, thou voice of my heart? It may be for years, and it

may be for - ev - er; Then why art thou si - lent, Kathleen Mavourneen?

NOW THANK WE ALL OUR GOD.
[NUN DANKET ALLE GOTT.]

MARTIN RINKART, 1644.
C. WINKWORTH, *Tr.* 1858. J. CRÜGER.

1. Now thank we all our God, With heart and hands and voi - ces.
2. O may this bounteous God, Through all our life be near us,
3. All praise and thanks to God, The Fa - ther, now be giv - en,

Who wondrous things hath done, In whom His earth re - joi - ces:
With ev - er joy - ful hearts, And bless - ed peace to cheer us,
The Son and Him who reigns, With them in high - est Heav - en;

Who from our moth - ers' arms Hath blessed us on our way
And keep us in His grace And guide us when per - plexed,
The one e - ter - nal God, Whom earth and Heav - en adore;

With count - less gifts of love, And still is ours to - day.
And free us from all ills, In this world and the next.
For thus it was, is now, And shall be ev - er - more!

In his very valuable work upon the authorship and history of English hymns, Rev. Samuel W. Duffield makes special mention of no less than one hundred and fifteen hymns and metrical versions of psalms by Isaac Watts. This voluminous hymn-writer came of sturdy stock. He was the grandson of Thomas Watts, a naval officer, who blew up his ship during the Dutch War in 1656, perishing with all on board. His father, Isaac Watts, inherited the family traits of courage and resolute purpose. He was a deacon in a Congregational Church at Southampton, in what were stormy days for the nonconformists. During this time of agitation his son Isaac, the oldest of nine children, was born July 17, 1674. The deacon and his pastor were imprisoned for nonconformity, and the child, then a babe at the breast, was often taken by his mother to the jail door, where she was accustomed to sit upon a stone near the entrance, with him in her arms. In 1683, his father was again imprisoned for six months for the old offence, and on his release was forced to "live privately in London for two years." Meanwhile Isaac had gone on with his studies. About this time he had the opportunity of a free education if he would give up nonconformity but, being a staunch little Dissenter, he declined the offer, and went to London where he continued his studies under Mr. Thomas Rowe until 1694. Here he became attached to Miss Elizabeth Singer and proposed marriage, which she declined. This lady afterwards married his instructor, Mr. Rowe. He always remained a bachelor. His earliest hymn was occasioned

JOY TO THE WORLD.

ISAAC WATTS, 1709.
G. F. HANDEL. "ANTIOCH."

1. Joy to the world, the Lord is come! Let earth re-ceive her King; Let
2. Joy to the world, the Sav-iour reigns, Let men their songs em-ploy; While

ev - 'ry heart pre-pare Him room, And Heav'n and nature sing, And
fields and floods—rocks, hills and plains Re-peat the sounding joy, Re-

And Heav'n and na-ture
Re - peat the sounding

Heav'n and na-ture sing, And Heav'n and na - ture sing.
peat the sounding joy, Re - peat the sound - ing joy.
sing,
joy,

sing, And Heav'n and na - ture sing.
joy, Re - peat the sounding joy.

3.
No more let sin and sorrow grow,
Nor thorns infest the ground;
He comes to make His blessings flow
Far as the curse is found.

4.
He rules the world with truth and grace,
And makes the nations prove
The glories of His righteousness,
And wonders of His love.

by a dislike of the verses sung in the meeting-house at Southampton. In 1696, he became tutor in a family at Newington. Here, for the children, he wrote of the "little busy bee," "the dogs that delight to bark and bite," "the voice of the sluggard," as well as that best of cradle-songs, "Hush, my dear, lie still and slumber." It was at this time that he wrote the "Divine and Moral Songs." He entered the ministry in 1698, preaching his first sermon at Mark Lane, London, but physical infirmity interfered much with this work. In 1713, after one of his distressing attacks of fever and neuralgia, Sir Thomas Abney took him to his own home. Long afterwards he said to Lady Huntingdon: "This day thirty years I came hither to the house of my good friend, Sir Thomas Abney, intending to spend but one single week under his friendly roof, and I have extended my visit to the length of exactly thirty years." He published his hymns and psalms from time to time, in book form, and so widely known are many of them in the Christian Church that they are to be found in almost every hymn book. He died Nov. 25, 1748, at the age of seventy-five. In person Dr. Watts was of spare habit, and hardly more than five feet in stature, so that he was known as "the little doctor." He was an able writer and a good speaker, with an unusually fine voice. If it be a greater thing to write a noble hymn, that is sung throughout the world, than to rule a nation wisely, then is he one of the world's great benefactors!

FROM the time when medical knowledge was first embodied in rules of practice, and probably from a much earlier period, music has held a recognized place in the treatment of disease. In no class of diseases, however, are we likely to derive so much benefit from the use of so pleasant a remedy as in those affecting the mind itself. In melancholia and allied states of depression its value is generally admitted in our own day. Ancient practitioners were also cognizant of its usefulness in this respect. We must all have felt how suitable is its infinite variety and facility of expression to the changing moods of the sane, and it is therefore the less difficult to understand how straying minds are pleased and settled by its charm. Certain it is that its beneficial effect is in this case considerable, and our readers, though possibly unable to acquire a knowledge of the art, should at least possess, and, if needful, assert in practice, a sense of its therapeutic value.—*Lancet.*

The poets and sages are no more agreed in their answers to the question, "What is music?" than they were, and are, on Pilate's pathetic question, "What is truth?" or on that which has been asked almost as frequently, "What is time?" Plato, with godlike calm, says, "The whole universe is music, for everything in it is order and harmony." Fuller holds that music is the poetry of sounds, as poetry is the music of words. According to Wagner's theory, it is the art of singing words, and of speaking in sounds which express that which is otherwise inexpressible. Schopenhauer's definition is unique: "Music is arithmetic come to life."

SHOUT THE GLAD TIDINGS.

W. A. MUHLENBURG, 1823.

AN OLD SINGER.—It is in his translation of the Gospel of St. John, completed A. D. 735, that the venerable Bede appears to us as the first writer of English vernacular prose. The story of the writing of this first prose book in the English language, as related by Cuthbert, one of Bede's pupils, is full of pathetic interest: As the season of Easter was drawing near, the zealous scholar and teacher began to feel symptoms of approaching death. But he continued faithfully the performance of his daily duties, and suffered nothing to distract his attention from his accustomed labor or to abate his usual cheerfulness and good humor. Now and then, while in the midst of his labors, with his pupils all around him, he would sing some verses of an English song—"rude rhymes that told how before the need-fare, Death's stern 'must go,' none can enough bethink him what is to be his doom for good or ill. We never read without weeping," writes Cuthbert. And so the anxious days passed, and Ascension week drew near, and both master and pupils toiled with increased zeal to finish, if possible, the work in hand—the translation of St. John's Gospel. "Learn with what speed you may," said the dying man; "for I know not how long I may last. I do not want my scholars to read a lie or to work to no purpose when I am gone." The last day came, and his pupils stood around him. "There

MARCHING SONG.

From the GERMAN.

1. March on, March on, our way a-long, While gai-ly beats the drum, dum di dum!
2. March on, March on, my comrades brave, With mus-kets flash-ing bright, dum di dum!
3. March on, March on, our steps are light, Our hearts from fear are free, dum di dum!

With stead-y tramp and ring-ing song The way will short be-come, dum di dum!
The stars and stripes a-bove us wave, And flaunt the morn-ing light, dum di dum!
For free-dom's sa-cred cause we fight, For law and li-ber-ty, dum di dum!

Tra la la la la dum! Tra la la la la dum! La la la la la la la, dum di dum!

With stead-y tramp and ring-ing song The way will short be-come, dum di dum!

is still one chapter wanting," said the scribe, seeing the master's increased weakness. "It is easily done," said Bede; "take thy pen and write quickly." They wrote until eventide drew on. Then the scribe spoke again: "There is yet but one sentence to be written, dear master." "Write it quickly," was the response of the dying man. "It is finished now," at length said the youth. "Thou hast well said," faintly replied the master, "all is finished now." The sorrowing pupils supported him tenderly in their arms while he chanted the solemn "Glory to God," and with the last words of the song his breathing ceased. Such is the story of the beginning of our literature. The humble translation of the Gospel of St. John, completed under circumstances of such painful anxiety, and amid the gathering shadows of death, was the vanguard, so to speak, of that long procession of noble works which, for a thousand years, has been contributing to the development and glory of the English nation.—Baldwin.

MUSIC is too often looked upon as nothing but a mere passing enjoyment—something only for the moment, to be heard and perhaps little regarded—as simply a concord of sounds agreeable to the ear: but true art occupies a much higher sphere than this; and to be able to truly appreciate and enjoy it, we must know something of the laws by which it is governed.

I LOVE THE MERRY SUNSHINE.

J. W. Lake.
Stephen Glover.

1. I love the mer-ry, mer-ry sunshine, It makes the heart so gay, To hear the sweet birds
2. I love the mer-ry, mer-ry sunshine, Thro' the dewy morning's show'r, With its ro-sy smiles ad -

sing-ing On their summer hol-i-day, With their wild-wood notes of du-ty, From
vanc-ing, Like a beau-ty from her bower! It charms the soul in sad-ness, It

hawthorn bush and tree; Oh, the sunshine is all beau-ty, Oh, the mer-ry, mer-ry sun for
sets the spir-it free; Oh, the sunshine is all gladness, Oh, the mer-ry, mer-ry sun for

me. I love the mer-ry, mer-ry sunshine, It makes the heart so gay, To hear the sweet birds

sing-ing On their summer hol-i-day, The mer-ry, mer-ry sun, the mer-ry, mer-ry,

merry, merry sun for me, The merry, merry sun, the merry sun, The mer-ry, mer-ry sun for me.

THE influence of music upon a pure mind cannot be understood in this life, much less expressed. The teacher who introduces music into the school as a regular exercise, will have better discipline and will himself be better. It quickens thought in the students and relieves the monotony of routine, Teach the student to read by note, if possible. If you have no books, use the fingers for notes. Take a given pitch—as C, as a standard. Tell your pupils that to sing they must put into action a vocal reed organ, with lungs as bellows, the wind-pipe as pipe, vocal chords as reeds, tongue as the bridge, the roof of the mouth as sounding board. Ask them to define a tone, allowing them to express their own ideas. Illustrate by means of a piece of rubber stretched and vibrated; thus teach them that sound is vibration collected and reflected from anything that produces sound. Illustrate lines, spaces, rests, and so on through the fundamental principles. Inform yourselves thoroughly here. Be not like soldiers on a long march with rations for only a few days. Be true to your calling. It is said that Michael Angelo, while at his work, wore fastened to the forepiece of his artist's cap a lighted candle that no shadow of himself might fall upon his work. This custom spoke a more eloquent lesson than he knew. How often the shadows fall upon our work—falling from ourselves!—*Russel*.

THE LONG WEARY DAY.

(DEN LIEBEN LANGEN TAG.)

SUABIAN VOLKSLIED.

1. The long, long wea-ry day, In tears is passed a-way, The long, long weary day, In tears is passed a-way, Yet still at even-ing I am weeping, As from my window's height, I look out on the night; I still am weep-ing, My lone watch keep-ing; As from my window's height, I look out on the night; I still am weep-ing, My lone watch keep-ing.

2. For oh! my love is dead; To Heav'n his soul is sped. For oh! my love is dead; To Heav'n his soul is sped. For him, with heart and soul I'm weeping; To see him nev-er more, It grieves my heart so sore! I still am weep-ing, My lone watch keep-ing, To see him nev-ermore, It grieves my heart so sore! I still am weep-ing, My lone watch keep-ing.

3. When I, his truth to prove, Would trifle with his love, When I, his truth to prove, Would trifle with his love, He'd say, "Thou shalt for me be weeping Up-on some fu-ture day, When I am far a-way, Thou shalt be weep-ing, Thy lone watch keep-ing; Up-on some fu-ture day, When I am far a-way, Thou shalt be weep-ing, Thy lone watch keep-ing."

4. Had naught but land or sea
Parted my love from me,
I should not now sad tears be weeping;
But hope he'd come once more,
And love me as of yore,
And say, "Cease weeping,
Thy lone watch keeping,"

5. Now comes he nevermore!
It grieves me, ah! so sore!
And still at evening am I weeping;
When the stars above appear,
I see his eyes so clear;
My lone watch keeping,
I still am weeping.

EVE'S LAMENTATION.

M. P. KING.

Andante affettuoso.

Must I leave thee, must I leave thee, must I leave thee, Par - a - dise? Thus

leave thee, leave thee, na - tive soil; these hap - py, hap - py walks, these walks and shades!

Yet must I leave thee, must I leave thee, must I leave thee, Par - a - dise? O

flow'rs that nev - er will in oth - er climate grow, Who now shall rear ye to the sun?

From thee, from thee how shall I part, how shall I part? Yet must I leave thee,

must I leave thee, must I leave thee, Par - a - dise, must leave thee, Par - a - dise?

GRADUALLY, in Italy, singing became an art. What we mean by singing when we speak of it as a source of pleasure of the higher kind, is really an Italian art, which has been diffused over the civilized world; and the Italian school of singing is still the great school,—others, in so far as they differ from that school, being inferior. The first distinctive characteristic of the Italian school of singing is the delivery of the voice, the mode of uttering a single note. Italians generally (for singing in this way has become a second nature to the whole people) use their voices in quite a different way from the generality of other people. They naturally utter their notes with a purity and a freedom rarely heard from untaught persons of other races. The delivery of the voice is the foundation of their excellence as singers. Indeed, it may almost be said to constitute that excellence; for not only is there no great singing without it, but the chief aim of Italian vocal discipline is to attain execution united with this free vocal utterance.

THE SLUMBER SONG.

F. KÜCHEN.

1. { All is still in sweet-est rest, / Al - les still in süs - ser Ruh!
   Be thy sleep se - rene-ly blest! / D'rum mein Kind so schlaf auch du!
2. { Close each lit - tle, lov - ing eye, / Schlies-se dei - ne Aeu - ge-lein,
   Let them like two rose - lets lie; / Lass sie wie zwei Knos-pen sein!

Winds are moan - ing o'er the wild, / Draus-sen säu - selt nur der Wind,
And when pur - pling morn shall glow, / Mor - gen wenn die Sonn' er - glüht,
Lul - la - by, sleep on, my child; / Su, su, su! schlaf ein, mein Kind:
Still as rose - lets fresh - ly blow, / Sind sie wie die Blum' er - blüht,

Lul - la - by, sleep on, my child, La, lul - la - by, sleep on, my
Su, su, su! schlaf ein, mein Kind; Su, su, su, su! schlaf ein, mein
Still as rose - lets fresh - ly blow; La, lul - la - by, sleep on, my
Sind sie wie die Blum' er - blüht, Su, su, su, su! schlaf ein, mein

child; May an - gel gleams Per - vade thy dreams! . . . . .
Kind: Su, su, su, su! In gu - ter Ruh'! . . . . . .

There are singers who have voices of remarkable power, range and flexibility, who can never be great because, either by nature or from bad and ineradicable habit, they cannot attain this pure and free delivery of the voice. Their tone is guttural, or it is nasal, or it is rough, or it is unsteady, or something else; it may be merely constrained; in any case, the fault is more or less destructive. There may be great singing without great power, without remarkable flexibility, without the ability to execute a roulade or trill; but there can be no singing really great without this free, pure delivery of the voice. A singer who can go through the whole range of his voice, from low to high, swelling out the tone and diminishing it with the vowel sound of broad *a* (ah), preserving that sound pure, and uniting with it perfect intonation through crescendo and diminuendo, has conquered much more than half the difficulties of the art of vocalization. All the rest, almost without exception, are mere "limbs and outward flourishes."

SHALL WE MEET BEYOND THE RIVER?

H. L. HASTINGS.
ELIHU S. RICE, 1866.

1. Shall we meet be-yond the riv-er, Where the sur-ges cease to roll?
2. Shall we meet in that blest har-bor, When our storm-y voyage is o'er
3. Shall we meet in yon-der ci-ty, Where the tow'rs of crys-tal shine?
4. Shall we meet with Christ, our Sav-iour, When He comes to claim His own?

Where, in all the bright for-ev-er, Sor-row ne'er shall press the soul?
Shall we meet and cast the an-chor By the fair ce-les-tial shore?
Where the walls are all of jas-per, Built by work-man-ship di-vine?
Shall we know His bless-ed fa-vor, And sit down up-on His throne?

Cho.—Shall we meet, shall we meet, Shall we meet be-yond the riv-er?

Shall we meet be-yond the riv-er, Where the sur-ges cease to roll?

WHILE THE MORNING BELLS.

"SICILIAN HYMN."

1. While the morn-ing bells are ring-ing, We to Thee our songs would raise,
2. When the night was fold-ed o'er us, Heav-y dark-ness shut us in;
3. Thanks to Thee, O heaven-ly Fath-er, For Thine all-pro-tect-ing arm;

Thanking Thee for Thy pro-tec-tion, Lift-ing to Thee notes of praise.
But we slept in peace-ful qui-et, Thou our night-ly guard hast been.
Thro' the day, we pray thee, keep us Free from e-vil, safe from harm.

DOXOLOGY.

May the grace of Christ, our Saviour,
And the Father's boundless love,
With the Holy Spirit's favor,
Rest upon us from above!

Thus may we abide in union
With each other and the Lord,
And possess, in sweet communion,
Joys that earth can ne'er afford.

THE popular ballad, "Listen to the Mocking Bird," was written and first published in 1855, by Septimus Winner, of Philadelphia, under the *nom de plume* of "Alice Hawthorne," his mother's maiden name. It was suggested incidentally by listening to a colored man, Dick Milburn, known as "Whistling Dick," who wandered about the city whistling in imitation of a mocking bird, at the same time strumming an accompaniment upon a guitar. Struck by his remarkable performance as a warbler, Mr. W. said to him one day, half in jest, "Dick, I'll write you a song for your mocking bird." The compass of the negro's voice was hardly an octave, and, as will be observed, the melody was made very simple, so as not to be beyond his reach. The words, "Listen to the Mocking Bird," which run higher, were to be spoken by him, not sung, except where they came within his compass, followed by the whistler's marvelous imitation of the bird. The man was a very good-natured fellow, but of so little intellectual capacity that, though he came to Mr. Winner's music store night after night to learn the words of the song, he was never able to master more than one verse of it. Such, however, was his sense of the comic, and such his facility in improvising lines to the music, suggesting ridiculous fancies to attract the laughing crowd, that his "Mocking Bird" soon added greatly to Dick's local reputation. The song was published in ballad form and at once became very popular, and such is its hold upon the public fancy that, although it has been sung and whistled and played the country over for an average lifetime, it still retains its place as a song of national reputation. It was sold by Mr. Winner to the firm of Lee and Walker for a trifling sum. The profits from its sale have exceeded one hundred thousand dollars, perhaps the largest

TOUCH US GENTLY, TIME.

BRYAN WALLER PROCTER.
(BARRY CORNWALL.)

1. Touch us gen - tly, gently, Time! Let us glide a - down thy stream. Gently as we sometimes
2. Touch us gen - tly, gently, Time! We've not proud nor soaring wings; Our am - bi - tion, our con -

glide Thro' a quiet, quiet dream; Humble voyagers are we, Husband, wife, and children three, One is
tent, Lies in simple, simple things; Humble voyagers are we O'er life's dim, unsounded sea, Seeking

lost—an an - gel fled   To the a - zure overhead, Touch us gently, O gentle Time!
on - ly some calm clime;   Touch us gen - tly, gentle Time, Touch us gently, O gentle Time!

amount ever realized from any musical composition of its class. There have been published upwards of fifty different arrangements, with variations, each differing from every other in some musical peculiarity, making it one of the most widely known of all airs and ballads; and yet the composer, during the twenty-eight years of the first copyright, never received upon the song anything beyond the price at which it was originally sold. This song at once gave him a reputation which opened the market everywhere to his efforts. It was followed, as it had been preceded, by others in different veins, humorous and pathetic. His first song, "How Sweet are the Roses," was published in 1850; his last, a merry "Party at the Zoo," a tuneful bit of humor, has just appeared (1888) in one of the magazines. Between these dates he has written a hundred or more songs, both words and music, many of which have sold by tens of thousands and are very widely known, among them, "What is Home without a Mother?" "Let us Live with a Hope," "I'll Sail the Seas over," etc., besides a large number of instruction books upon different instruments. Some of these songs which, at the time of writing them, he sold for a few dollars each, have netted their publishers full as many thousands, and he laughs pleasantly as he recalls the mistake of these low figures. His songs have had a very large sale also in Great Britain, more than sixty of them having been republished in England. His numerous instruction books have been published under his own name, but his songs under various *noms de plume*, among them "Alice Hawthorne," the most familiar, giving name to the "Hawthorne ballads"; "Aspley Street," from the street in which he lived; "Mark Mason," a degree of the Masonic order to which he belongs, and others.

THE ALPINE HORN.

MALIBRAN.

1. In the wild chamois track, At the breaking of morn, With the hunter's pride, O'er the mountain side,
2. I have cross'd the proud Alps, I have sail'd down the Rhone, And there is no spot Like the simple cot,

We are led by the sound of the Al-pine horn, Trala la la la la la la la la.
And the hill and the val-ley I call my own, Trala la la la la la la la la.

O that voice to me is a voice of glee, Where-ev-er my footsteps roam; And I
There the skies are bright, and our hearts are light, Our bosoms without a fear; For our

long to bound, When I hear that sound, Again to my mountain home, In the wild chamois track, at the
toil is play, And our sport, the fray With the mountain roe or deer.

breaking of morn, With a hunter's pride, O'er the mountain side, We are led by the sound of the

Al-pine horn; Trala la la la la la la la la, Tra la la la la la la la la la.

6

A WRITER in a late art journal says: "How many composers in the country, native or foreign born, can, without the aid of an instrument, sit down at their home or while riding in the cars, or while walking along the street, and write out such musical ideas as they may, in inspired moments, conceive; and more, how many Americans can write an acceptable harmony to these melodic ideas either with or without the aid of an instrument? A composer must be able to realize the effect of chord connection, inversions, suspensions, sequences, doubling or omitting of notes according to circumstances, progression of individual parts, nature and characteristic peculiarities of the voices or instruments to be employed, etc.,—all this in his head clearly, besides a practical conception of the effect of the legato and staccato, in any kind of phrase or passage in the duophonic, triphonic, tetraphonic, or polyphonic arrangements. Then he must be a person of originality, both in melodic and harmonic ideas. The music must be correct in every particular, which means perfection

SHE WORE A WREATH OF ROSES.

T. H. BAYLY.
JOS. P. KNIGHT.

1. She wore a wreath of ro - ses 'The first time that we met, Her lovely face was smiling Be-
2. A wreath of orange blossoms When next we met she wore; The look upon her features Was more
3. And once again I see that brow, No bridal wreath is there, The widow's sombre cap conceals Her

neath her curls of jet, Her foot-step had the light - ness, Her voice the joyous tone, The
thoughtful than before; And standing by her side was one Who strove, and not in vain, To
once lux - uriant hair; She weeps in si - lent sol - itude, And there is no one near, To

to - kens of a youthful heart Where sorrow is unknown; I saw her but a moment, Yet me-
soothe her leaving that dear home She ne'er might view again; I saw her but a moment, Yet me-
press her hand within his own, And wipe a-way the tear; I see her broken - hearted! Yet me-

thinks I see her now, With the wreath of summer flowers Up - on her snowy brow.
thinks I see her now, With the wreath of orange blossoms Up - on her snowy brow.
thinks I see her now, In the pride of youth and beauty, With a garland on her brow!

in form, phrasing, counterpoint, proper distribution of expression marks, proper marking of the tempos, good taste in the use of any of the embellishments, such as the tirata, direct, inverted or full turn, also the turn after any kind of note or dotted note, the prepared or unprepared trill, spring or mordent, simple or compound appoggiaturas, after-notes and harmonics, and withal an eye for the fitness of things for which the composition is intended, as well as a good knowledge of dramatic effect. Now, sir, I hope that any American who thinks he can compose according to the above conditions, will quietly set to work for his own satisfaction, and each year compose an overture, sonata, concerto, symphony, song without words, fugue, poetry, and music enough for a half hour's performance. Study harmony at least three months each year at the end of two or more years to revise these pieces, and those which are as good in his estimation as when written to be played over before intimate friends; if they are satisfied with them other folks will be; if not, the compositions should be destroyed."

THE INGLE SIDE.

HEW AINSLEE.
T. F. WEISENTHAL, 1836.

1. It's rare to see the morning bleeze, Like a bonfire frae the sea; It's fair to see the
2. Glens may be gilt wi' gowans rare, The birds may fill the tree, And meadows hae the

bur - nie kiss The lip o' the flow'ry lea; An' fine it is on green hillside,Where
scented ware That sim - mer growth can gie; But the canty hearth where cronies meet, An' th'

hums the bonnie bee, But rarer, fairer, fin - er far Is the In - gle side for me.
dar - ling o' our e'e, That makes to us a warl' complete, O, the In - gle side for me.

TARA'S HARP.

With Feeling.

MOORE'S MELODIES.

1. The harp that once thro' Ta-ra's halls The soul of mu - sic shed; Now hangs as mute on
2. No more to chiefs and ladies bright The harp of Ta - ra swells; The chord a - lone that

Ta - ra's walls As tho' that soul were fled. So sleeps the pride of former days, So
breaks at night Its tale of ru - in tells. Thus Free-dom now so seldom wakes; The

glo-ry's thrill is o'er, And hearts that once beat high for praise Now feel that pulse no more.
on - ly throb she gives Is when some heart, in-dignant, breaks, To show that still she lives.

I REMEMBER once asking a distinguished Polish lady, herself a notable musician and pupil of the great Chopin, whether she ever played Hungarian music. "No," she answered, "I cannot play it; there is something in that music which I have not got—something which is wanting in me." What was wanting I came to understand later, when I became familiar with Hungarian music as rendered by the Tzigane players. It was the training of a gipsy's whole life which was wanting here—a training which alone teaches the secret of deciphering those wild strains which seem borrowed from the voice of the tempest or stolen from whispering reeds. In order to have played the Hungarian music aright she would have required to have slept on mountain tops during a score of years, to have been awakened by fallen dews, to have shared the food of eagles and squirrels, and have been on equally familiar terms with stags and creeping things —conditions which unfortunately lie altogether out of the reach of delicate Polish ladies.—*Blackwood.*

WHEN I COME.

1. Must I then, must I then leave my hap-py lit-tle town, hap-py lit-tle town, And
2. Ah, thy tears! ah, thy tears! they are fall-ing like the rain, fall-ing like the rain, Sweet
3. In a year, in a year, when the lit-tle ber-ries ripe, lit-tle ber-ries ripe, I'll

1. Muss I denn, muss I denn zum Städ-te-le 'naus, Städ-te-le 'naus, Und

thou, my love, bide here? When I come, when I come, when I come back again, come back again, Then with
love, so dear to me; In the world, in the world, there are many fair beside, many fair beside, But
come a-gain to thee, And if then, oh, if then thou dost truly love me still, truly love me still, My

du mein Schatz bleibst hier? Wenn I komm, wenn I komm, wenn I wiedrum komm, wiedrum komm, Kehr' I

thee I'll stay, my dear. If now with thee I cannot re-main, My love for thee's the same. When I
I'll be true to thee! Think not an-oth-er when I see, This heart will faithless be. In the
dar-ling wife thou'lt be. In that brief year I'll have served my time, And thou canst call me thine! And if

ein, mein Schatz, bei dir. Kann I gleich nit all-weil bei dir sein, Han I doch mein' Freud' an dir; Wenn I

come, when I come, when I come back again, come back again, Then with thee I'll stay, my dear!
world, in the world, there are many fair beside, many fair beside, But I'll be true to thee.
then, oh, if then thou dost truly love me still, truly love me still, My darling wife thou'lt be.

komm, wenn I komm, wenn I wiedrum komm, wiedrum komm, Kehr' I ein, mein Schatz, bei dir.

2.
Wie du weinst, wie du weinst, dass I |: wandere muss :|
  Wie wenn d' Lieb' jetzt wär' vorbei;
Sind au drauss, sind au drauss der |: Mädele viel :|
  Lieber Schätz, I bleib' ich treu.
  Denk' du net, wenn I 'ne And're seh',
  No sei mei Lieb' vorbei:
Sind au drauss, sind au drauss der |: Mädele viel, :|
  Lieber Schatz, I bleib' dir treu.

3.
Uebers Jahr, übers Jahr wenn me |: Träubele schneidt, :|
  Stell' I hier mi wiedrum ein;
Bin I dann, bin I dann dein |: Schätzele noch, :|
  So soll die Hochzeit sein.
  Uebers Jahr da ist mein' Zeit vorbei,
  Do g'hör I mein und dein;
Bin I dann, bin I dann dein |: Schätzele noch, :||
  So soll die Hochzeit sein.

BEAUTIFUL BELLS.

E. O. LYTE.

1. 2. Ring a - gain, Ring a - gain, Beauti - ful bells, beau - ti - ful bells;

Ring - ing, Ring - ing, Ring - ing, Ring - ing,

Ring a - gain, Ring a - gain, Beau - ti - ful bells, beau - ti - ful bells.

Ring - ing, Ring - ing, Ring - ing, Ring - ing.

1. On the breeze of ev' - ning steal - ing, Hark! the bells are slow - ly peal - ing, Wak - ing
2. As the toil of day is end - ing, Thro' the vales the bells are send - ing Tones with

ev - 'ry ten - der feel - ing, Beautiful bells, beauti - ful bells, bells, beautiful bells.
ev - 'ry mur - mur blending, Beautiful bells, beauti - ful bells, bells, beautiful bells.

GOOD-NIGHT, LADIES.

Sostenuto.

1. Good-night, la - dies! Good-night, la - dies! Good-night, la - dies! We're going to leave you now.
2. Fare - well, la - dies! Fare - well, la - dies! Fare - well, la - dies! We're going to leave you now.
3. Sweet dreams, ladies! Sweet dreams, ladies! Sweet dreams, ladies! We're going to leave you now.

Allegro. *Repeat pp.*

Mer - ri - ly we roll along, roll along, roll along, Mer - ri - ly we roll along, Over the dark blue sea.

There was a well-fed, prosperous looking woman of strident voice on one of the suburban trains the other morning, and above its roar and rattle her accents could be distinguished telling the story of the friend who was visiting her. "You remember Lou, of course," she said "Well, she's been staying with me since last week. And, you know! the funniest thing has happened. Lou—that's her name—always has a way of adopting other people's habits easily. Adaptability, I suppose, some people call it. For instance, if she was with a gay crowd she was gay, and with sober people she was sober. She hadn't been in our house three days before she got to talking as loud as if some one was deaf. And when I spoke to her about it—half joking, you know—she said she supposed from my talking so loud that Robert was deaf, and so she had spoken above her ordinary tone. Now, what I'd like to know, Kate, is if my voice is unusually loud. Tell me the truth." The car listened breathlessly. When Kate did the kind-hearted thing, sacrificing her desire to be honest in her instinct to be kindly, and said that she never thought so, the lady with the voice said decidedly: "There, I was sure of it! Something's the matter with Lou, and I shall advise her to consult an aurist."

JEM, THE CARTER LAD.

J. S. BAKER.

1. My name is Jem, the Car-ter lad, A jol-ly chap am I,   I always am content-ed, Be the
2. My fa-ther was a car-ri-er, Long years ere I was born, He used to rise at day-break, To
3. I sel-dom think of pol-i-tics, Nor dream of being great, I care not for their high-bred talk A-
4. I think I will conclude my song, 'Tis time I was a-way, My horses know the round they go, I

weather wet or dry. I snap my fin-ger at the snow, And whistle at the rain, I've braved the storm for
go his rounds each morn. He'd sometimes take me with him, And in the balmy spring, I loved to sit up-
bout the chair of state, I act uprightly man to man, And that's what makes me glad, You'll find there beats an
can no longer stay, Tho' many weary miles we've gone, It's happy days we've had, For none can treat a

Chorus.

many a year, And can do so a-gain.   Crack, crack, goes my whip, I whistle and I sing, I
on the cart, And hear my fa-ther sing.   Crack, crack, goes my whip, I whistle and I sing, I
honest heart In Jem, the Car-ter lad.   Crack, crack, goes my whip, I whistle and I sing, I
horse more kind Than Jem, the Carter lad.   Crack, crack, goes my whip, I whistle and I sing, I

sit up-on my wag-on, I'm as hap-py as a king. My hor-ses al-way will-ing, For

me, I'm nev-er sad, For none can lead a jol-lier life Than Jem, the Car-ter lad.

DOWN IN A COAL MINE.

J. B. Geoghegan.

With Spirit.

1. I am a jo-vial col-lier lad, and blithe as blithe can be, Then let the times be
2. My hands are horn-y, hard and black, with working in the vein, And, like the clothes up-
3. At ev-'ry shift, be't soon or .late, I haste my bread to earn, And anx-ious-ly my
4. How lit-tle do the great ones care, who sit at home se-cure, What hid-den dan-gers
5. Then cheer up, lads, and make ye much of ev-'ry joy ye can, But let your mirth be

good or bad, they're all the same to me; 'Tis lit-tle of the world I know, and,
on my back, my speech is rough and plain; Well, if I stum-ble with my tongue, I've
kin-dred wait and watch for my re-turn; For Death, that lev-els all a-like what-
col-liers dare, what hard-ships they en-dure; The ve-ry fires their mansions boast, to
al-ways such as best becomes a man; How-ev-er For-tune turns a-bout, ours

care-less of its ways, Down where the bright stars nev-er glow I wear a-way my days.
but one thing to say, 'Tis not the col-lier's heart that's wrong, his head but goes astray.
e'er their rank may be, A-mid the fire and damp may strike, and fling his dart at me.
cheer themselves and wives, Mayhap were kindled at the cost of jo-vial col-liers' lives.
still the jo-vial soul, What would our country be with-out the lads that mine for coal?

Chorus.

Down in a coal mine, underneath the ground, Where a gleam of sunshine never can be found;

Digging dusky diamonds all the season round, Down in a coal mine, underneath the ground.

"CALL JOHN."   Wm. B. Bradbury.

John - ny, John - ny, can you tell us, Tell us how to sing this song? Ha, ha, ha, ha,
Johnny can John, John, John!

No, no, no, no, no, no, no, no, no, no, no, no, no, Never will I teach you how to sing, no,

ha! Ha, ha, ha, ha, ha, ha, ha, ha! John, John, John, John! we have learned this song.

no! Such a set of blunderheads, Such a set of blunderheads never'll learn to sing.

WHEN ALL THE WORLD IS YOUNG.

CHARLES KINGSLEY.
MRS. CHAS. BARNARD.

Allegretto.

1. When all the world is young, lad, And all the trees are green, And ev - 'ry goose a
2. When all the world is old, lad, And all the trees are brown, And all the sport is

mf

swan, lad, And ev - 'ry lass a queen; Then hey for boot and sad - dle, lad! And
stale, lad, And all the wheels run down; Creep home, and take your place there, The

round the world a - way; Young blood must have its course, lad, And ev - 'ry dog his day. Young
spent and maimed a - mong; God grant you find one face there You loved when all was young. God

1st verse. *2d verse.*

blood must have its course lad, And ev - 'ry dog his day. *rit.*
grant you find one face there You loved when...................... all was young.

Sing 2d verse more slowly and tenderly.

There is no mere earthly immortality I envy so much as the poet's. If your name is to live at all, it is so much more to have it live in people's hearts than only in their brains! I don't know that one's eyes fill with tears when he thinks of the famous inventor of logarithms; but a song of Burns' or a hymn of Charles Wesley's goes straight to your heart, and you can't help loving both of them, the sinner as well as the saint. The works of other men live, but their personality dies out of their labors; the poet who reproduces himself in his creation, as no other artist does or can, goes down to posterity with his personality blended with whatever is imperishable in his song.—*Holmes.*

In its physical effects alone music is worth far more than all it costs in the pupil's study or teaching force, in its influence upon mental and physical health, and the resultant energy of effort to grasp and master the daily tasks assigned. The earnest efforts to give forth school songs with spirit and emphasis quickens the brain, expands the lungs, vitalizes the blood, quiets nervous irritability, chases away the blues, and warms up the whole human organism into the best condition and the happiest mood for the exercises of the day. Thus more work, and better work, can be done in six hours by the wide-awake teacher with music as an auxiliary to his work than in twelve hours without it.—*Hickok.*

SOUND YOUR A.

W. J. WETMORE.
W. B. BRADBURY.

I'M A FORESTER FREE.

Allegro con spirito.

E. REYLOFF.

1. I'm a For-es-ter free and bold, And hunt the wild wolf to his hold, I care for nei-ther
monarch's board has bet-ter fare, A fat deer's haunch each day is there, And costs me noth-ing,

heat nor cold, I've rent and tax-es free, I've rent and tax-es, I've rent and tax-es
I de-clare; No pay they get from me, No pay they get, No pay they get from

free. At morning light I track the roe, Thro' brier and brake in chase I go, Of rag-ing
me. I laugh at those who toil for gold, Their freedom's bought, their hearts are sold, So I'll be

storms no fear I know; At morning light, I track the roe, Thro' brier and brake in chase I go, Of
king of the greenwood bold, I laugh at those, who toil for gold, their freedom's bought, their hearts are sold, So

rag-ing storms no fear I know. A For-ester's life for me, A Forester's life for
I'll be king of the greenwood bold. A For-ester's life for me, A Forester's life for

me, A For-es-ter's life for me, A For-es-ter's life for me. 2. No
me, A For-es-ter's life for me, A For-es-ter's life for me.

A curious account of the effect of various kinds of music on different animals is given by a writer in *The Spectator.* The general order of the experiments, based upon the supposition that animal nerves are not unlike our own, was so arranged that the attention of the animals should be first arrested by a low and gradually increasing volume of sound, in those melodious minor keys which experience showed them to prefer. The piccolo was then to follow in shrill and high-pitched contrast; after which the flute was to be played to soothe the feelings ruffled by that instrument. Pleasure and dislike were often most strongly shown where least expected; and the last experiment indicated stronger dislikes, if not stronger preferences, in the musical scale, in the tiger than in the most intelligent anthropoid apes. With "Jack," a six-months-old red orang-outang, "as the sounds of the violin began, he suspended himself against the bars, and then, with one hand above his head dropped the other to his side and listened with grave attention. He then crept away on all fours, looking back over his shoulder, like a frightened baby," and covered himself with his piece of carpet. Then his fear gave place to pleasure, and he sat down, with smoothed hair and listened to the music. The piccolo at first frightened him, but he soon held out his hand for the instrument and was allowed to examine it. "The flute did not interest him, but the bagpipe, reproduced on the violin, achieved a triumph." The capuchins were busy eating their breakfast; "but the violin soon attracted an audience. They dropped their food and clung to the bars, listening, with their heads on one side, with great attention. At the first sounds of the flute the macaques ran away; and the piccolo excited loud and angry screams from all sides." When the flute was played to the elephant, he stood listening with deep attention, one foot raised

LITTLE GIRL, DON'T YOU CRY.

Andante con espress.   GERMAN.

Tenderly.

1. Ah, lit-tle girl, don't you cry, don't you cry! Bro-ken your doll is I know, yes, I know.
2. Ah, lit-tle girl, don't you cry, don't you cry! Bro-ken your slate is I know, yes, I know.
3. Ah, lit-tle girl, don't you cry, don't you cry! Bro-ken your heart is I know, yes, I know.

Gone is your playhouse, your playmates gone too, None left to play now but me, dear, and you.
Gone your old schoolmates, your school days all o'er, Glad, wild or sad, they will come back no more.
Gone the bright vision of girlhood's sweet dreams, Fad-ed ere nightfall your sun's golden beams.

Ba-by-hood's sorrows will soon pass you by, Ah, lit-tle girl, don't you cry, don't you cry!
Youth, life and love, dear, full soon you will try, Ah, lit-tle girl, don't you cry, don't you cry!
Heav'n holdeth all for which now, dear, you sigh, Ah, lit-tle girl, don't you cry, don't you cry!

from the ground and the whole body still. "But the change to the piccolo was resented. After the first bar the elephant twisted round and stood with its back to the performers, whistling and snorting and stamping its feet. The violin was disliked, and the signs of disapproval were unmistakable." The deer were strongly attracted by the violin, and showed equal pleasure at the tones of the flute. The ostrich seemed to enjoy the violin and the flute, though it showed marked dislike for the piccolo. "The ibexes were startled at the piccolo, first rushing forward to listen, and then taking refuge on a pile of rock, from which, however, the softer music of the flute brought them down to listen at the railing. The wild asses and zebras left the hay with which their racks had just been filled; and even the tapir which lives next door, got up to listen to the violin; while the flute set the Indian wild ass kicking with excitement. But the piccolo had no charms for any of them and they all returned to their interrupted breakfasts." A sleeping tiger was awakened by the soft playing of the violin near its cage, listened to the music for a time in a very fine attitude, then purred, lay down again and dozed. At the first notes of the piccolo, it "sprang to its feet and rushed up and down the cage, shaking its head and ears, and lashing its tail from side to side. As the notes became still louder and more piercing, the tiger bounded across the den, reared on its hind feet, and exhibited the most ludicrous contrast to the calm dignity and repose with which it had listened to the violin. With the flute which followed, the tiger became quiet, the leaps subsided to a gentle walk, and coming to the bars and standing still and quiet once more, the animal listened with pleasure to the music."

MORNING'S RUDDY BEAM.

G. Lesse.

Allegro.

1. { Morning's ruddy beam tints the eastern sky,
   { Let the sluggard sleep, we must slumber shun,

   Up, comrades, climb the mountain high;
   Ere night-fall

2. { Evening's gentle ray gilds the glowing west,
   { Hap-py in his toil, roaming blithe and free,

   Each hunt-er sighs for home and rest;
   O hunt-er,

hon-or must be won. { Haste, haste, haste, haste, the mer-ry bu-gle sounding, Chides our de-
                    { Haste, haste, haste, haste, o'er rock and glacier bounding, Soon each gallant

thine's the life for me. { Haste, haste, haste, haste, with spoils in plenty la-den, Each one is
                         { Haste, haste, haste, haste, fond wife or anxious maiden, Waits her gallant

lay, chides our de-lay. } { Morning's ruddy beam tints the eastern sky,
hunter will single out his prey. } { Let the sluggard sleep, we must slumber shun,
stored, each one is stored. } { Evening's gentle ray gilds the glowing west,
hunter around the humble board. } { Hap-py in each toil, roaming blithe and free,

1st time. *2nd time.* *1st time f, 2nd time pp.*

Up, comrades, climb the mountain high;
Ere night-fall
Each hunt-er sighs for home and rest.
Oh, hunt-er,

hon-or must be won. Tra la la la la la
thine's the life for me. Tra la la la la la

Repeat pp.

la, la la la la la, la, Tra la la la la la, la, la la la la la.
Tra la la la la la la, la, la, Tra la la la la la, la, la.

THERE are clear indications that up to the time of the Reformation music was in continual progress in England. But, unfortunately, the Wars of the Roses and the ruthless destruction which accompanied the suppression of the monasteries, the only homes of art of all kinds in those rough, savage days, have obliterated all but the rarest indications. But it is certain, not only from the treatises and compositions of the fourteenth and fifteenth centuries that have survived, but from the splendor of the English school, when we again encounter it about 1520, that in the interval our music had been growing and flourishing, as everything in England grows and flourishes when it really seizes hold of the English people. Palestrina (from 1550 to 1600) no doubt wrote more nobly than any of his contemporaries, including our own Tallis and Byrd; but it is not too much to say that the English predecessors of Tallis and Byrd— Edwards, Redford, Shepperd, Tye, White, Johnson and Marbecke, who date from 1500 to 1550, were much in advance of any of the predecessors of Palestrina on the Continent. For they were their equals in science and they far surpass them in tunefulness and what I may call the common sense of their music. Their compositions display a "sweet

CASTLES IN SPAIN.
[ALADDIN.]

V. BELLINI.
JAMES RUSSELL LOWELL.

1. When I was a beg-gar-ly boy, And lived in a cel-lar damp, I had not a friend, nor a toy, But I had Al-lad'-din's lamp; When I could not sleep for cold, I had fire e-nough in my brain And builded, with roofs of gold, My beau-ti-ful cas-tles in Spain!

2. Since then I have toiled day and night, I have mon-ey and power, a good store, But I'd give all my lamps sil-ver bright, For one that is mine no more; Take, Fortune, whatev-er you choose, You gave and may snatch it a-gain; I have nothing 'twould pain me to lose, For I own no more cas-tles in Spain!

reasonableness," a human feeling, a suitability to the words and a determination to be something more than a mere scientific and mechanical puzzle, which few, if any, of the Continental composers before 1550 can be said to exhibit. I have only to mention the familiar title of the charming madrigal, "In going to my lonely bed," to convince many of this truth. Such was our position in the first half of the sixteenth century; and the half century following is the splendid time of English music, in which the illustrious names of Morley, Weekes, Wilbye, Ford, Dowland and Orlando Gibbons shine like stars. These names may be unknown to some of you, but the men existed and their works live—live not alone by reason of their science, their pure part-writing and rich harmonies, but by the stream of beautiful melody which flows through all their works—melody which is ear-haunting even to our modern and jaded natures and which has no parallel elsewhere. Those of you who have heard such works as the "Silver Swan," by Gibbons, and "Since first I saw your face," by Ford, will, I am sure, endorse my favorable opinion.—*Arthur Sullivan.*

SING, SMILE, SLUMBER.
[CANTI, RIDI, DORMI.]

Victor Hugo.
Charles Gounod.

1. When at twi-light so softly thy voice breaks into song,
2. When the smile on thy lip chases doubt far from my breast,
3. In the silence of night when mine eye, vigil doth keep,
1. Quand tu chan-tes ber-cé-e Le soir entre mes bras,

Can'st thou tell the sweet mem'ries of
All my gloom is dispelled and for-
And thy lips murmur softly of
Entends tu ma pen-se-e Qui

old that round me throng,
ev - er in light I rest,
love, e'en in thy sleep,
te repond tout bas.

All the dear happy days then return to me, hallowed by thee.
In thy sweet smile confiding, 'tis innocence only I see.
Ah! the sight of thy beauty my soul with rapture doth fill.
Ton doux chant me rappelle les plus beaux de mes jours;

Ah! then sing, ah! sing for - ev - er, then sing, ah! sing to me, Then sing, ah! sing for-
Ah! then smile, ah! smile forev - er, then smile, ah! smile on me, Then smile, ah! smile for-
Ah! then slumber on my fair one, ah! slumber, slumber still, Then slum - ber fair one,
Ah! Chantez, chantez, ma bel - le, chantez, chantez tou-jours, chantez, chantez, ma

ever, sing still to me. Ah! sing for - ev - er, still sing to me.
ever, smile still on me. Ah! smile for - ev - er, still smile on me.
slum - ber, slumber still, Then
belle, chantez tou - jours, chan - tez, ma belle, chan - tez tou - jours.

slumber, my fair one, ah! slum - ber, slum - ber still.

St. Stephanos, the Sabaite, was a monk of the monastery of Sabas, where he was placed by his uncle, St. John Damascene. Here he found St. Cosmas, who contributed not a little to form his style—a thing not difficult, for Stephen entered the monastery as a boy of ten. He remained within these walls fifty-nine years. Dr. Neale speaks of the Latin stanzas of "Art Thou Weary" as being "very sweet"—but his own rendering is quite free. The original is of the eighth century. Stephen was born in 725 and died in 794, and this is the finest of his hymns. Miss Sally Pratt McLean has used this familiar hymn in her story of "Cape Cod Folks." It is the duet which George Olver and Benny Cradlebow sing together as they are mending the boat just before Cradlebow's heroic death. Captain Arkell tells of it thus: "By and by, him and George Olver struck up a song. I've heern 'em sing it before, them two. As nigh as I calc'late, it's about findin' rest in Jesus, and one a askin' questions, all f'ar and squar', to know the way and whether it's a goin' to lead thar straight or not, and the other answerin'. And *he*—he was a tinkerin', 'way up on the foremast. George Olver and the

NOW ALL THE BELLS.

EASTER CAROL.

1. Al-le-lu-ia! Al-le-lu-ia! Al-le-lu-ia! Now all the bells are ring-ing,
2. Al-le-lu-ia! Al-le-lu-ia! Al-le-lu-ia! O has-ten we to meet him,
3. Al-le-lu-ia! Al-le-lu-ia! Al-le-lu-ia! Still, Je-sus! we a-dore thee

To welcome Easter Day, And we with joy are sing-ing Our car-ol sweet and gay,
With our companions dear, With love and awe to greet him, As he is draw-ing near;
With faith which may not fail; Still as we kneel be-fore thee, We hear thee say "All hail!"

For Je-sus hath a-ris-en From Joseph's rocky cave, Hath burst his three days' pris-on,
Of old his friends were bidden To haste to Gal-i-lee: Still in his Church, all glo-rious,
Thou, who art now de-scending To raise us up to thee, An East-er-tide un-end-ing

And triumphed o'er the grave. Al-le-lu-ia! Al-le-lu-ia! Al-le-lu-ia!
Our ris-en Lord will be. Al-le-lu-ia! Al-le-lu-ia! Al-le-lu-ia!
Grant us in heaven to see. Al-le-lu-ia! Al-le-lu-ia! Al-le-lu-ia!

rest of us was astern, and I'll hear to my dyin' day how his voice came a floatin' down to us thar—chantin' like it was—cl'ar and fearless and slow. So he asks, for findin' Jesus, ef ther's any marks to foller by; and George, he answers about them bleedin' nail-prints, and the great one in his side. So then that voice comes down agin', askin' ef thar's any crown, like other kings, to tell him by; and George, he answers straight about that crown o' thorns. Then says that other voice, floatin' so strong and cl'ar, and ef he gin up all and follered, what should he have—what now? So George, he sings deep o' the trial and the sorrowin'. But that other voice never shook, a askin' and what if he held to him to the end, what then should it be—what then? George Olver answers, 'Forevermore, the sorrowin' ended—Death gone over.' Then he sings out, like his mind was all made up. And if he undertook it, would he likely be turned away?' 'An' it's likelier,' George answers him, 'that heaven and earth shall pass.' So I'll hear it to my dyin' day—his voice a floatin' down from above thar, askin' them questions that nobody could ever answer like, so soon he answered 'em for himself."

OH, FOR A THOUSAND TONGUES.

CHARLES WESLEY.
CARL G. GLASER. "AZMON."

1. Oh, for a thou-sand tongues, to sing   My dear Re-deem-er's praise;
2. My gra-cious Mas-ter and my God,   As-sist me to pro-claim,
3. Je-sus! the name that charms our fears,   That bids our sor-rows cease;

The glo-ries of my God-and King,   The tri-umphs of His grace!
To spread thro' all the earth a-broad,   The hon-ors of Thy name.
'Tis mu-sic in the sin-ner's ears,   'Tis life, and health, and peace.

He breaks the power of reigning sin,
He sets the prisoner free;
His blood can make the foulest clean;
His blood availed for me.

Hear Him, ye deaf; His praise, ye dumb,
Your loosened tongues employ;
Ye blind, behold your Saviour come;
And leap, ye lame, for joy.

ART THOU WEARY?

ST. STEPHANOS, 780.
J. H. HOPKINS. "NEALE."

1. Art thou wea-ry, art thou lan-guid, Art thou sore dis-tressed?
2. Hath He marks to lead me to Him, If He be my Guide?
3. Is there di-a-dem, as Mon-arch, That His brow a-dorns?

After last verse.

"Come to Me," saith One, "and com-ing, Be at rest."   A-men.
"In His feet and hands are wound-prints, And His side."
"Yea, a crown, in ve-ry sure-ty, But of thorns."

If I find Him, if I follow,
What His guerdon here?
"Many a sorrow, many a labor,
Many a tear."
If I still hold closely to Him,
What hath He at last?
"Sorrow vanquished, labor ended,
Jordan passed."

If I ask Him to receive me,
Will He say me nay?
"Not till earth, and not till Heaven
Pass away."
Finding, following, keeping, struggling,
Is He sure to bless?
"Saints, apostles, prophets, martyrs,
Answer, Yes." Amen.

GLORIA PATRI.

Glory to be to the Father, and   to the Son, And to the Ho-ly Ghost;
As it was in the beginning, is now, and ev-er shall be, World without end, A-men.

I KNOW A BANK.

SHAKSPEARE.
CHAS. E. HORN.

1. I know a bank whereon the wild thyme grows, I know a bank whereon the wild thyme grows, Where
2. I know a bank whereon the wild thyme grows, With sweet musk roses and with eglantine; There

ox - lips, and   the nodding violet blows, Where ox-lips and the nodding vio-let blows, I
Sleeps Ti - tan - ia sometime of the night, Lulled in these flow'rs with dances and delight, I

know a bank whereon the wild thyme grows, The wild thyme grows. There sleeps the fairy queen,

La, la,   la, la, la, la, la, la,

There sleeps sometime of the night, Lulled   in their flowers   With dances and de -

la, la, la, la, la, la,   la,   La, la, la, la, la,   la, la, la, la, la,   la,   la,

light.   There sleeps the fai - ry   queen,   There sleeps sometime of the night,

la, la, la, la, la,   la,   la,   la,   la,   la, la, la, la, la,   la, la,   la,   la,   la,

With

Lulled   in   their flowers, With dances and de - light.   With dan - ces and de -

la,   la,   la,   la,   la,   la,   la, la, la, la, la,

AH, FOR WINGS TO SOAR.

JULLIEN.
PRIMA DONNA WALTZ.

Espression.

1. Ah! for wings to soar   O'er the dark blue sea,   Speed-ing from this
2. Ah! for one sweet word,   Whispered in mine ear,   Stir - ring, as it
3. Ah! for one bright smile,   Full of love's sweet art,   Strong to cheer and

ex - ile shore, To live in peace with thee. The years seem bright when hope's soft star Shone
oft hath stirred, My heart with mem'ries dear. The years roll on, and hope once strong Grows
charmed to wile Each sor - row from the heart. No stranger's words can comfort bring, No

out in light a-cross our way, And ev-'ry hill and vale a - far Was gladden'd by its ray.
faint and wea-ry with de-lay Ah, me! how earnest-ly I long To thee to fly a-way!
stranger's smile give joy to me; Oh! for some sea-bird's buoyant wing To bear me home to thee!

YEOMAN'S WEDDING SONG.

PRINCE PONIATOWSKI.
Words by MARIA X. HAYES.

Allegretto giojoso.

1. Ding dong, ding dong, ding dong, I love the song, For it is my wedding morn - ing,
2. Ding dong, ding dong, ding dong, my steed, hie on, For the church will soon be fill - ing, They

And the bride so gay in fine ar - ray, For the day will be now a-
must not wait, they must not wait, For were we late, they'd deem the groom un-

con brio.

dorn . . . ing. Tho' I've little wealth but sov'reign health,
will . . ing. The sun is high in the morning sky, And the

And am but a yeoman free, When heart joins hand, there's none in the
lark o'er our heads doth sing, A bri - dal song as we gal - lop a-

land Can be rich - er in joys than we. Ding dong, ding dong, we'll gallop a-
long, Keep-ing time to the bells as they ring. Ding dong, ding dong, we'll gallop a-

long. All fears and doubting scorning, Ding dong, we'll gallop along, All fears and doubting

scorning; Thro' the valley we'll haste, for we've no time to waste, As this

is my wed-ding morn - ing. wed-ding morn - ing.

HARK! I HEAR AN ANGEL SING.

W. C. BAKER.
R. G. SHRIVAL.

1. Hark! I hear an angel sing, Angels now are on the wing, And their voices ringing clear,
2. Just beyond yon cliff of snow, Sil - ver rivers brightly flow; Smiling woods and fields are seen,
3. Look! oh, look, the southern sky Mirrors flow'rs of ev'ry dye, Children tripping o'er the plain,

Tell us that the Spring is near. Dost thou hear them, gentle one, Dost thou see the glorious sun
Mantled in a robe of green; Birds and bees and brooks and flow'rs, Tell us all of vernal hours;
Spring is coming back again, Spring is coming, shouts of glee, Singing birds on bush and tree,

Ris - ing higher in the sky. As each day, as each day it passes by? Hark! I hear an angel sing,
There the birds are weaving lays For the happy, the happy Springtime days. Just beyond yon cliff of snow,
And the bee it merry hums, For the Springtime comes, it comes, it comes. Hark! I hear an angel sing,

Angels now are on the wing, And their voices singing clear, Tell us that the Spring is near.
Sil - ver rivers brightly flow, Smiling woods and fields are seen, Mantled in a robe of green.
Angels now are on the wing, And their voices singing clear, Tell us that the Spring is near,

By permission Oliver Ditson Company, owners of copyright. An Arbor Day Song.

WHY are certain violins of more value than others? Accurate judgment is a matter which depends on the union of so many qualities that it is rare indeed to find two opinions completely alike. Nevertheless there are a few instruments which, by universal consent, have become the standard of taste. An appeal to these famous violins must decide what is that tone which confers the immense value which some violins have realized, the distinguishing characteristics of tone of the violins made by Nicholas Amati, Stradivarius, and Guarnerius, the Raphaels, Titians, and Claudes of the musical world. In some violins there is apparent power under the ear, arising from coarseness. This is a species of power which is observable chiefly by the player. The listener, especially if at a little distance, does not hear this power. The tone is clogged and thickened with the resinous particles that have remained in the wood, and which, perhaps, from its nature, may never leave it altogether, and the vibration is not therefore perfect. Another cause of false power is a certain imperfect build wherein the parts are not properly calculated, as in the fine Cremona instruments. What is real power? It is simply musical tone, divested of all adventitious qualities. When tone of this class is heard near, the effect is charming to the ear. When heard afar off, it seems to swell out, becoming grand, glorious! Who that has heard a great player on a fine instrument, has not been astonished at the immense quantity of tone which arises from this exceedingly fine quality?—*Pearce.*

WEAR A BRIGHT SMILE.

G. VERDI.

Wear a bright smile, tho' the dark cloud of sorrow Dim for a while Hope's bright, sunny ray;

Wear a bright smile, for per-haps by to-mor-row, The grief that oppresses will van-ish a - way.

1. Wear a bright smile, forget grief and sighing, Ban - ish each canker that preys on the heart:
2. Wear a bright smile, for sad - ness is o - ver, Let us en-joy ev - 'ry mo-ment that flies,

Hope, smiling hope, tho' the moments are fly-ing, O'er fading dreams will a ha - lo im - part;
Hearts will not al - ter but e'er will dis-cov-er A charm in the rose though it withers and dies;

Hope, smiling hope, tho' the moments are fly-ing, O'er fading dreams will a ha - lo im-part.
Love will not al - ter, but e'er will dis-cov-er A charm in the rose though it withers and dies.

JAMIE'S ON THE STORMY SEA.

BERNARD COVERT.

1. Ere the twilight bat was flitting, In the sun-set, at her knitting, Sang a lone-ly
2. Warmly shone the sunset glowing; Sweetly breath'd the young flow'rs blowing; Earth with beauty
3. Cur-few bells re-motely ringing Mingled with that sweet voice singing, And the last red
4. How could I but list, and lin-ger, To the song, and near the sin-ger, Sweetly woo-ing

maid-en, sit-ting Un-derneath her threshold tree; And, ere daylight died be-fore us,
o-ver-flow-ing, Seemed the home of love to be, As those an-gel tones as-cending,
ray seemed clinging, Lin-geringly to tower and tree; Near-er as I came, and nearer,
Heav'n to bring her Ja-mie from the storm-y sea; And while yet her lips did name me,

And the vesper stars shone o'er us, Fit-ful rose her tender chorus, "Jamie's on the stormy sea."
With the scene and season blending, Ever had the same low ending, "Jamie's on the stormy sea."
Finer rose the notes, and clearer! Oh! 'twas Heaven itself to hear her, "Jamie's on the stormy sea!"
Forth I sprang, my heart o'ercame me; "Grieve no more, love, I am Jamie, Home returned to love and thee,"

WHEN THE GREEN LEAVES.

1. When the green leaves come again, my love, When the green leaves come again, Why put on a dark and
2. Ah! the spring will still be like the last, Of its prom-ise false and vain, And the summer die in
3. So the seasons pass, and so our lives, Yet I nev-er will complain; But I sigh, while yet I

cloud-y face, When the green leaves, When the green leaves, When the green leaves come again?
win-ter's arms, Ere the green leaves, Ere the green leaves, Ere the green leaves come a-gain.
know not why, When the green leaves, When the green leaves, When the green leaves come again.

Nay, lift up your thankful eyes, my love!
  Thinking less of grief or pain;
For as long as hill and vale shall last,
  Will the green leaves come again.

Sure as earth lives under winter's snow,
  Sure as love lives under pain,—
It is good to sing with every thing,
  When the green leaves come again.

SEE AT YOUR FEET.

M. W. Balfe.
From "Bohemian Girl."

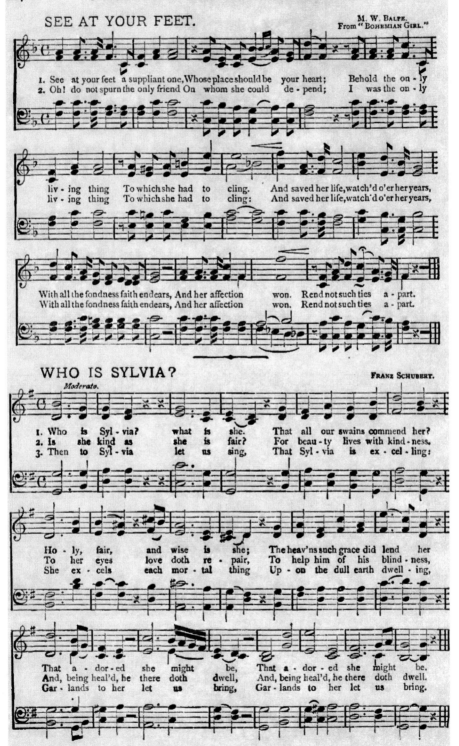

1. See at your feet a suppliant one, Whose place should be your heart; Behold the on - ly
2. Oh! do not spurn the only friend On whom she could de - pend; I was the on - ly

liv - ing thing To which she had to cling. And saved her life, watch'd o'er her years,
liv - ing thing To which she had to cling: And saved her life, watch'd o'er her years,

With all the fondness faith endears, And her affection won. Rend not such ties a - part.
With all the fondness faith endears, And her affection won. Rend not such ties a - part.

WHO IS SYLVIA?

Franz Schubert.

Moderato.

1. Who is Syl - via? what is she. That all our swains commend her?
2. Is she kind as she is fair? For beau - ty lives with kind - ness.
3. Then to Syl - via let us sing, That Syl - via is ex - cel - ling:

Ho - ly, fair, and wise is she; The heav'ns such grace did lend her
To her eyes love doth re - pair, To help him of his blind - ness,
She ex - cels each mor - tal thing Up - on the dull earth dwell - ing,

That a - dor - ed she might be, That a - dor - ed she might be.
And, being heal'd, he there doth dwell, And, being heal'd, he there doth dwell.
Gar - lands to her let us bring, Gar - lands to her let us bring.

BATTLE-HYMN OF REPUBLIC.

JULIA WARD HOWE.

Allegretto.

1. Mine eyes have seen the glo - ry of the com - ing of the Lord; He is
2. I have seen Him in the watch-fires of a hun - dred cir - cling camps; They have
3. I have read a fie - ry gos - pel, writ in bur - nished rows of steel; "As ye
4. He has sound-ed forth the trum - pet that shall nev - er call re - treat; He is
5. In the beau - ty of the lil - ies, Christ was born a - cross the sea, With a

tramp - ling out the vin - tage where the grapes of wrath are stored; He hath
build - ed Him an al - tar in the eve - ning dews and damps; I can
deal with my con - tem - ners, so with you my grace shall deal; Let the
sift - ing out the hearts of men be - fore his judg - ment seat; Oh, be
glo - ry in his bos - om that trans - fig - ures you and me; As He

loosed the fate - ful light-ning of His ter - ri - ble swift sword. His truth is marching on.
read His righteous sen - tence by the dim and flar - ing lamps. His day is marching on.
He - ro, born of wom - an, crush the ser - pent with his heel, Since God is marching on."
swift, my soul, to an - swer Him! be ju - bi - lant, my feet! Our God is marching on.
died to make men ho - ly, let us die to make men free, While God is marching on.

Chorus.

Glo - ry! glo - ry! Hal - le - lu - jah! Glo - ry! glo - ry! Hal - le - lu - jah!

Glo - ry! glo - ry! Hal - le - lu - jah! His truth is march - ing on.

THE most favorable period in the whole school life for laying a solid foundation for the intelligent rendering of music is the first three years, and here is where we must make a more sensible and intelligent beginning. We need first to appreciate the ability of the little child to learn the elements of music. This we shall never know till we learn better how to present these elements in their simplicity, in accordance with the mental laws, by which the mind acquires a knowledge of all subjects. The supposition has been that little children could not be taught to read music intelligently, simply because it had not been generally and successfully accomplished. The failure has not been on account of inability on the part of the children to learn music, nor on account of the notation by which it is represented, as some would have us to believe, but on account of a lack of knowledge among those employed in the teaching of this subject.—*Holt.*

INNISFAIL.

E. C. PHELPS.
THOMAS C. LATTO.

Andante con moto espress.

1. O land of saints, of streams and song, And sorrow wild as Benshee's wail, The hundred harps of
2. The glo-ry of a thousand years Is not to van-ish like a dream, We swear it by the

Ta - ra long To swell the cry of In - nis-fail, Whose modest maidens watch and pray For
quenchless tears That o'er the grave of Emmet stream; Green flag be foremost as of yore; Thy

help that comes from Heav'n alone; Whose stalwart sons sus-tain the sway In ev - 'ry em - pire
pri - mal strength, lov'd isle, renew; Thy honors bright'ning more and more, Long as a shamrock

Chorus.

save their own. O In - nis-fail, my own dear isle, Tho' ling'ring years of wrong be thine, The
drinks the dew. O In - nis-fail, my own dear isle, Tho' ling'ring years of wrong be thine, The

cres.

sunburst thro' the storm shall smile; The day has dawn'd, thy light shall shine. O Innisfail! O Innisfail!

CHURCH MILITANT.

REGINALD HEBER, 1827
H. S. CUTLER. "ALL SAINTS."

1. The Son of God goes forth to war, A kingly crown to gain; His blood-red banner
2. The mar - tyr first, whose eagle eye Could pierce beyond the grave, Who saw his Master
3. A glorious band, the chos - en few, On whom the Spirit came: Twelve valiant saints, their
4. A no - ble army, men and boys, The matron and the maid, Around the Saviour's

streams a - far, Who follows in His train? Who best can drink his cup of woe, Tri-
in the sky, And called on Him to save: Like Him, with pardon on his tongue, In
hope they knew, And mocked the cross and flame: They met the tyrant's brandished steel, The
throne rejoice, In robes of light ar - rayed: They climbed the steep ascent of Heav'n Thro'

umphant o - ver pain; Who pa - tient bears his cross below, He follows in His train.
midst of mor - tal pain, He prayed for them that did the wrong: Who follows in His train?
li - on's go - ry mane; They bowed their necks the death to feel: Who follows in their train?
per - il, toil, and pain: O God! to us may grace be given To follow in their train!

SOFTLY NOW THE LIGHT OF DAY.

DONIZETTI.

p

1. Soft - ly now the light of day Fades up - on my sight a - way; Free from care, from
2. Soon for me the light of day Shall for - ev - er pass a - way; Then, from sin and

la - bor free, Lord, I would commune with Thee. Thou, whose all - per - va - ding eye
sor - row free, Take me, Lord, to dwell with Thee. Thou who, sin - less, yet hast known

cres.

Naught escapes, without, within, Pardon each in - firm - i - ty, O - pen fault, and se - cret sin.
All of man's in - firm - i - ty, Then, from Thine e - ter - nal throne, Jesus, look with pitying eye.

PRESENTLY George came to the door of the sick room, and begged her to go down and sing to him. Of course, in the house of a dean's widow no music except sacred must be heard on a Sunday; but to have Helen sing it, George would condescend even to a hymn tune; and there was Handel, for whom he professed a great admiration! . . . Although she had often sung from Handel for his pleasure, content to reproduce the bare sounds which both they and the words represented, she positively refused this evening to gratify him. She would sing from "The Creation" if he liked, but nothing out of "The Messiah" would she or could she sing. Perhaps she could herself hardly have told why, but George perceived the lingering influence of the morning's sermon, and, more vexed than he had ever yet been with her, for he could not endure her to cherish the least prejudice in favor of what he despised, he said he would overtake his aunt, and left the house. The moment he was gone, she went to the piano, and began to sing "Comfort ye." When she came to "Come unto me," she broke down. But with sudden resolution she rose, and having opened every door between it

A HUNDRED YEARS TO COME.

W. C. BROWN.

1. Where, where will be the birds that sing, A hun-dred years to come? The
2. Who'll press for gold this crowd-ed street, A hun-dred years to come? Who'll
3. We all with-in our graves shall sleep, A hun-dred years to come! No

flowers that now in beau-ty spring, A hun-dred years to come? The ro-sy lip, the
tread yon church with will-ing feet, A hun-dred years to come? Pale, trembling age, and
liv-ing soul for us will weep, A hun-dred years to come! But oth-er men our

lof-ty brow, The heart that beats so gai-ly now? Oh, where will be love's
fie-ry youth, And child-hood with its heart of truth, The rich, the poor, on
lands will till, And oth-ers then our streets will fill; While oth-er birds will

beam-ing eye, Joy's pleas-ant smile, and sor-row's sigh, A hun-dred years to come?
land and sea, Where will the might-y mil-lions be, A hun-dred years to come?
sing as gay, As bright the sun shine as to-day, A hun-dred years to come!

and her brother, raised the top of the piano, and then sang "Come unto me" as she had never sung in her life, nor did she stop there. At the distance of six of the wide standing houses, her aunt and cousin heard her singing "Thou didst not leave," with the tone and expression of a prophetess—of a Mænad, George said. She was still singing when he opened the door, but when they reached the drawing-room she was gone. She was kneeling beside her brother.—*Macdonald.*

THE profane never hear music; the holy ever hear it. It is God's voice, the divine breath audible. When it is heard then is a Sabbath. It is omnipotent. All things obey music as they obey virtue. . . . Woe to him who wants a companion, for he is unfit to be a companion even of himself. We inspire friendship in our fellow-men when we have contracted friendship with the gods. . . . The wood-thrush launches forth his evening strain from the midst of the pines. I admire the moderation of this master. There is nothing tumultuous in his song. There is as great an interval between the thrasher and the wood-thrush as between Thomson's "Seasons" and Homer.—*H. D. Thoreau.*

COME TO THE SPARKLING FOUNTAIN.

CHILDHOOD SONGS.

1. Come, oh, come with me where the sparkling fountain Flows at the foot of for-est-clad
2. Come, oh, come, the stream is gushing free, Drink where wa-ter gleams, so cool to
3. Come, oh, come with me to springs the fair-est, Drink, oh, drink with me of nec-tar

mountain; While we dwell be-low our song shall be "Pure, bright water, no drink but thee!"
see; Hill and val-ley through, the glens a-round, Bless-ings glad on water a-bound.
rar-est; Nev-er shall it cause thee woe or wailing, Ev-er a blessing un-fail-ing.

Tra la la la la la la la la la, Tra la la la la la la la la.

WAKING OR SLEEPING.

J. V. BLAKE.

Solo.

1. Wake, hap-py children, In the dew-y morn, Wake when the birds sing For the ro-sy
2. Play, hap-py children, In the gold-en noon, Soon day is end-ed And the night comes
3. Sleep, hap-py children, In the ho-ly night, Gone is the day-beam, But the stars are
4. Morn, noon and night-time, God your soul shall keep, Wak-ing or play-ing, Or in qui-et

Solo. wake wake *Chorus.* *cres.* *rit.*

Chorus.

dawn. Wake at dawn, wake at dawn. Oh,.............. wake in the rosy dawn, Starry night is gone.
soon. Play at noon, play at noon. Oh,.............. play in the golden noon, It will fade too soon.
bright. Sleep at night, sleep at night. Oh,.............. sleep in the holy night, When the stars are bright.
sleep, Safe shall keep, safe shall keep. Oh,.............. waking or sleep-ing, God our souls shall keep.

TEA IN THE ARBOR.

Andante non troppo.

J. BEULER.

1. What pleasure folks feel, when they live out of town, In the culture of turnips and
2. I de-cline as I can, when oft they in - vite, For of ru - ral de-lights I'm no
3. I had on thin shoes and the grav-el was damp, The thought of it made me quite
4. Of lit - tle green flies on my dress came a host, And a bee put me all in a

flow - ers, And getting a friend, now and then, to come down To look at their walks and their
lov - er; Of insects and rep-tiles I can't bear the sight, They make me to shudder all
ner - vous, From a cold, or a fit of the gout, or the cramp, I said to myself, "Oh! pre-
flut - ter; A great dad-dy-long-legs stuck fast on my toast, And left one of his limbs in the

bow - ers, And such is the taste of some dear friends of mine, Mister, Mistress, and Miss Ma - ry
o - ver. How - ever, last Monday I went there to dine: "I am glad you are come," said Miss
serve us!" And when we got there a great frog made me jump, Which was excellent fun to Miss
but - ter. In rath - er bad temper I homeward did jog, And next morning I wrote to Miss

Bar - ber, Who will oft have me come to their vil - la to dine, And then to take tea in the
Bar - ber, "I know you will like it, the weather's so fine, And we all will take tea in the
Bar - ber; Then there was a long cat-er - pil - lar fell plump In my first cup of tea in the
Bar - ber, That here in my pock-et, I found the great frog, Which frighten'd me first in the

ar - bor; Where there are sweet willies and daf-fy-down-dil-lies, Per-fumes like the shop of a
ar - bor." Sweet lillies and willies and daf-fy-down-dil-lies, Per-fumes like the shop of a
ar - bor. Sweet lil-lies and willies and daf-fy-down-dil-lies, Per-fumes like the shop of a
ar - bor. "And though there be lillies and daf-fy-down-dil-lies," Said I, in my note to Miss

bar-ber, And ro-ses and posies to scent up your noses; Then come and take tea in the ar-bor.
bar-ber, And ro-ses and posies to scent up your noses; Then come and take tea in the ar-bor.
bar-ber, And ro-ses and posies to scent up your noses; Did you ever take tea in the ar-bor?
Barber,"And ro-ses perfuming, excuse from com-ing A-gain to take tea in the ar-bor!

WHAT WILL YOU DO, LOVE?

SAMUEL LOVER, 1842.

Not too Fast.

1. "What will you do, love, when I am go-ing, With white sail flow-ing, the seas be-
2. "What will you do, love, if distant tid-ings Thy fond con-fid-ings should un-der-
3. "What would you do, love, when home re-turn-ing, With high hopes burning, with wealth for

yond? What will you do, love, when waves divide us, And friends may chide us for be-ing
mine; And I a-bid-ing 'neath sultry skies, Should think other eyes more bright than
you, If my bark, which bounded o'er foreign foam, Were lost near home, ah! what would you

fond?" "Tho' waves divide us, and friends be chiding, In faith a-bid-ing, I'll still be true;
thine?" "Oh, name it not, tho' brand of shame Were on thy name, I'd still be true;
do?" "So thou wert spared, I'd bless the mor-row, In want and sor-row, that left me you;

And I'll pray for thee on the stormy o-cean, In deep de-vo-tion; that's what I'll do."
But that heart of thine, should an-oth-er share it, I could not bear it,—what would I do?"
And I'd welcome thee from the wasting billow, This heart thy pillow; that's what I'd do."

HALLELUJAH CHORUS.

G. F. Handel.

Hal-le-lu-jah! Hal-le-lu-jah! Halle-lu-jah! Halle-lu-jah! Hal-le - lu-jah! Hal-le-lu-jah!

Hal - le-lu-jah! Halle-lu-jah! Halle-lu-jah! Hal-le - lu - jah! For the Lord God Omnipotent

reigneth! Hal-le - lu-jah! Halle-lujah! Halle - lu-jah! Halle - lu-jah! For the Lord God Omnipotent

reign - eth! Hal-le - lu-jah! Halle-lu-jah! Halle - lu - jah! Hal-le-lu - jah!   The

kingdom of this world   is be - come the kingdom of our Lord, and of his Christ, and of his

Christ; and he shall reign for ever and ever, King of kings................   Halle-lu-jah! Halle

for-ev-er and ev-er,

THE HUMAN EAR.—How do the vibrations of the air speak to your brain? First, I want you to notice how beautifully the outside shell of the ear, or *concha*, as it is called, is curved so that any movement of the air coming to it from the front is caught in it and at once reflected into the opening of the ear. When the air-waves from any quarter have passed in at the opening of your ear, they move all the air in the passage which is called the auditory, or hearing, canal. This canal is lined with little hairs to keep out insects and dust, and the wax which collects in it serves the same purpose. But if too much wax collects, it prevents the air from playing well upon the drum, and therefore makes you deaf. Across the end of this canal a membrane, partly called the *tympanum*, is stretched, like the parchment over the head of a drum, and it is this membrane which moves to and fro as the air-waves strike on it. A violent blow on the ear will sometimes break this delicate membrane, or injure it, and therefore it is very wrong to hit a person violently on the ear. On the other side of this membrane, *inside* the ear, there is air, which fills the whole of the inner chamber and the tube which runs down into the throat. Now, as the drum of the ear is driven to and fro by the sound-waves, it naturally moves the air in the cavity behind it, and also sets in motion here three most curious little bones. The first of these bones is fastened to the middle of the drumhead so that it moves to and fro every time this membrane quivers. The head of this bone fits into a hole in the next bone, the anvil, and is fastened to it by muscles, so as to drag it along with it; but, the muscles being elastic, it can draw back a little from the anvil, and thus give it a blow each time it comes back. This anvil is, in its turn, very firmly fixed to the little bone shaped like a

BRIGHT, ROSY MORNING.

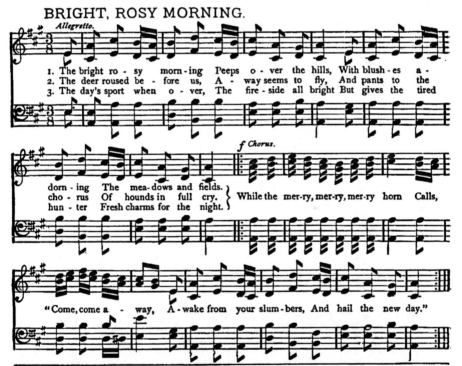

1. The bright ro - sy morn-ing Peeps o - ver the hills, With blush - es a -
2. The deer roused be - fore us, A - way seems to fly, And pants to the
3. The day's sport when o - ver, The fire - side all bright But gives the tired

dorn - ing The mea-dows and fields.)
cho - rus Of hounds in full cry. } While the mer-ry, mer-ry, mer-ry horn Calls,
hun - ter Fresh charms for the night.)

"Come, come a - way, A - wake from your slum-bers, And hail the new day."

stirrup at the end of the chain. This stirrup rests upon a curious body, which looks like a snail-shell with tubes coming out of it. This body, which is called the *labyrinth*, is made of bone, but it has two little windows in it, one covered only by a membrane, while the other has the head of the stirrup resting upon it. Now you will readily understand that when the air in the auditory canal shakes the drumhead to and fro, this membrane must drag the hammer, the anvil, and the stirrup. Each time the drum goes in, the hammer will hit the anvil, and drive the stirrup against the little window; every time it goes out it will draw the hammer, the anvil, and the stirrup out again, ready for another blow. Thus the stirrup is always playing upon this little window. Meanwhile, inside the bony labyrinth there is a fluid like water, and along the little passages are very fine hairs, which wave to and fro like reeds; and whenever the stirrup hits at the little window, the fluid moves these hairs to and fro, and they irritate the ends of a nerve, and this nerve carries the message to the brain. There are also some curious little stones called otoliths, lying in some parts of this fluid, and they, by their rolling to and fro, probably keep up the motion and prolong the sound. You must not imagine we have explained here the many intricacies which occur in the ear. We can only hope to give you a faint idea of it, so that you may picture to yourselves the air-waves moving backwards and forward in the canal of your ear, then the tympanum vibrating to and fro. the hammer hitting the anvil, the stirrup knocking at the little window, the fluid waving the fine hairs and rolling the tiny stones, the end of the nerve quivering, and then in some marvelous way (*how we know not*) the brain hearing the message.—*Buckley.*

ALL'S WELL.

J. BRAHAM.

1. De-sert-ed by the wa-ning moon, When skies proclaim night's cheerless noon On
2. Or sail-ing on the mid-night deep, While wea-ry messmates soundly sleep, The

tow-er, fort, or tented ground, The sentry walks his lonely round, The sen - try walks his
careful watch patrols the deck, To guard the ship from foes or wreck, To guard the ship from

lone - ly round, The sen - try walks his lone - ly round. And should a footstep
foes or wreck, To guard the ship from foes or wreck. And while his thoughts oft

haply stray Where caution marks the guarded way, Where caution marks the guarded way, the guarded way, [Who goes
homeward veer, Some friendly voice salutes his ear, Some well-known voice salutes his ear, salutes his ear, [What

there? Stranger, quickly tell! A friend. The word? Good-night. All's .. well, All's...
cheer? Brother, quickly tell! A-bove. Be - low? Good-night. All's .. well, All's...

well. The word, Good-night? All, all's well. well, A - bove, Be - low, All, all's well

The effect is better when the voices answer each other in duet in the last braces as indicated.

ABOUT the worst use a congregation can make of a choir is to leave it to do the singing for the people. To say nothing of human worship by proxy, the congregation which leaves the choir to do all the singing misses many advantages. Yet this is too often the case, and in some quarters increasingly so. In too many places of worship the work of the choir is becoming a separate and independent performance, and the body of the congregation look on with indifference or listen with interest, as the case may be. You may call it a Sunday concert in the House of God, but never call it congregational worship when the people pay little heed to the singing, and take little personal part in it. Either the congregations should take more part and interest in the vocal worship, or leave it to the choir altogether, merely following their programme in hand, as at an oratorio. Few congregations are prepared for such a decision as would exclude them altogether from the singing part of worship except as listeners. Then, if they would not give up their right to sing, let them show their appreciation of the privilege by more skillful and hearty singing. Good congregational singing is not to be had without toil and cost. If it could come by merely wishing for it, then many congregations would sing much better than they do. They need to inform themselves what really is good congregational singing, and then lay themselves out for it accordingly. A

WHAT FAIRY-LIKE MUSIC.

Jos. DePinna.

1. What fai-ry-like mu-sic steals o-ver the sea, En-tran-cing the
2. The winds are all hush'd, and the wa-ters at rest; They sleep like the

sen-ses with charm'd mel-o-dy? 'Tis the voice of the mer-maid, that floats o'er the
passions in in-fan-cy's breast; Till storms shall un-chain them from out their dark

main, As she min-gles her song with the gon-do-lier's strain! 'Tis the voice of the
cave, And break the re-pose of the shore and the wave. Till storms shall un-

mermaid, that floats o'er the main, As she mingles her song with the gon-do-lier's strain.
chain them from out their dark cave, And break the re-pose of the shore and the wave.

minister cannot from the pulpit give much advice about singing. The congregation needs at times to be called together apart from worship, and solely for practice and instruction in the vocal art. A skillful and judicious teacher can soon point out the usual faults and lead them on by intelligent practice to better work. Occasional practice in congregational singing is indispensable, and there is no first-class work done without it. The exercises for the production of the voice should be gone through, as also exercises in the different intervals and through various keys. A month's practice of this kind will be of more use for improvement than the singing of a hundred tunes. Those who take part in the psalmody of the congregation should be encouraged to practice the exercises at home. The unison practice has many advantages, but it does not supersede private practice. The defects of the voice may be pointed out very clearly in the singing class, where more or less individual instruction may be given, but they can be most effectually corrected by private practice; and those who will persevere in private for only half an hour a day will soon be able to make a better public contribution to the general worship of song.

WELCOME TO MORNING.

J. OFFENBACH.

1. The sun is ris-ing o'er the o - cean, The smil-ing wa-ters greet the day,
2. The birds flit o'er the dew - y mead-ows; They car - ol sweet in branches high:
3. Oh, come, let clouds of grief and sad - ness, Fly swift as shades of night a - way;

And joy - ous winds to danc - ing mo - tion, Wake the bil - lows of the day.
While down the vales the fright-ed shad - ows Hast - en from the dawn to day.
Let all our hearts, like birds of glad - ness, Wel - come in the glad new day,

Trio.

See, where the clouds roll up the moun-tains; Night has her mis - ty ban - ner furled;
Rocked on the wa-ter's pla - cid bo - som, Pure - ly the wa - ter - lil - ies gleam,
Bright flow'rs, and streams, and birds of heaven, In - cense and prais - es waft a - bove;

And spring-ing from a thousand fountains, Light and joy o'er - flow the world.
While willow branch and bending blos-som, Bid good-mor - row to the stream.
From hearts and voic - es now be giv - en, Songs of praise, and joy, and love.

Full Chorus.

Sunbeams of splendor the world are a-dorn-ing, Join in the chorus, the earth and ocean sing,

Welcome the glory, the sunlight, the morning, And make the joyous, joyous echoes ring.

LULLABIES.—A recent writer, says: The subject of lullabies, or "sleep songs," as my little ones are fond of calling them, is by no means a common one, and until my attention was called to it by an article entitled, "Wanted—A Lullaby." I imagined there could be no lack of them in the English language. Having a number of these "sleep" or dream songs in my collection in French and German, as well as in the English language, I have never been at a loss for one to soothe a restless child, or comfort a fretful babe. To me the perfection of a slumber song, or lullaby, is the "Cradle Hymn," by good old Dr. Watts. The tune, as well as the words, has descended to me, being the same to which my weary eyes responded in baby sleep, and by which my fretful distress was soothed in restlessness or pain. I have ever used it with my children, and no matter what may be sung at the commencement of the sleepy-time concert, the last of all is sure to be, "Hush; my dear, lie still and slumber." When in my own early childhood, the last lines of the second verse were sung, the impression made upon my almost infant mind, as

CRADLE HYMN.

ISAAC WATTS.
J. J. ROUSSEAU.

1. Hush, my babe, lie still and slum-ber, Ho-ly an-gels guard thy bed.
2. Soft and ea-sy is thy cra-dle, Coarse and hard thy Sa-viour lay:
3. Hush, my child, I did not chide thee, Though my song may seem so hard:

Heav'n-ly bless-ings with-out num-ber, Gent-ly fall-ing on thy head.
When His birthplace was a sta-ble And his soft-est bed was hay.
'Tis thy moth-er sits be-side thee, And her arms shall be thy guard,

How much bet-ter thou'rt at-tend-ed, Than the Son of God could be;
Oh, to tell the won-drous sto-ry, How his foes a-bused their King;
May'st thou learn to know and fear Him, Love and serve Him all thy days;

When from heav-en He de-scend-ed, And be-came a child like thee.
How they killed the Lord of glo-ry, Makes me an-gry while I sing.
Then to dwell for-ev-er near Him, Tell his love and sing His praise.

I lay in my little trundle bed, was one that can never be effaced. Often I was so affected as to beg that they should be sung softly, and that the next verse should be more loud and clear, to dispel in a degree this feeling of sadness. The closing lines of the last verse have ever seemed a blessing descending on the youthful head. The air to which this "song of songs" to myself and children is wedded, is a soft and plaintive one, well adapted to the words. It has long been a favorite lullaby in English-speaking homes the wide world over. Next to this, which is sacred to me from association, and the appropriateness of the words as the evening song of a Christian mother to her babe and younger children, is that gem of Gottschalk's "Slumber on, baby dear." In the German we have the "Schlummerlied" of Kucken, in which the lullaby, as a refrain, has a solemn, impressive sound which, combined with the beauty of the words in the original, makes it a favorite wherever heard. In the Italian and Spanish there are several of these cradle-songs.

NEARER, MY GOD, TO THEE.

LOWELL MASON.—" BETHANY."
SARAH F. ADAMS, 1848.

1. Near - er, my God, to Thee, Near - er to Thee\ E'en though a cross it be
2. Though like a wan-der-er, The sun gone down, Dark-ness be o - ver me,

D.S. Near - er, my God, to Thee,

That rais-eth me, Still all my song shall be,\ Near -er, my God, to Thee,
My rest a stone; Yet in my dreams I'd be /

Near - er to Thee!

There let the way appear	Then with my waking thoughts	Or if on joyful wing,
Steps unto heaven;	Bright with Thy praise,	Cleaving the sky,
All that Thou sendest me,	Out of my stony griefs	Sun, moon, and stars forgot,
In mercy given;	Bethel I'll raise;	Upward I fly,
Angels to beckon me	So by my woes to be	Still all my song shall be,
|: Nearer, my God, to Thee, :|	|: Nearer, my God, to Thee, :|	': Nearer, my God, to Thee, :|
Nearer to Thee!	Nearer to Thee!	Nearer to Thee.

HOW GENTLE GOD'S COMMANDS.

Slow and Soft.

H. G. NÄGELI—" DENNIS."

1. How gen - tle God's com - mands! How kind His pre - cepts are!
2. Be - neath His watch - ful eye, His saints se - cure - ly dwell:
3. Why should this anx - ious load Press down your wea - ry mind?
4. His good - ness stands ap - proved Through each suc - ceed - ing day;

Come, cast your bur - dens on the Lord, And trust His con - stant care.
That hand which bears cre - a - tion up, Shall guard His chil - dren well.
Haste to your Heavenly Fa - ther's throne, And sweet re - fresh - ment find.
I'll drop my bur - den at His feet And bear a song a - way.

[Or this Hymn.]

Heirs of unending life,	God will support our hearts	'Tis He that works to will,
While yet we sojourn here,	With might before unknown;	'Tis He that works to do;
O let us our salvation work	The work to be performed is ours,	His is the power by which we act,
With trembling and with fear.	The strength is all His own.	His be the glory too.

Beddome, 1795.

HOME OF THE SOUL.—"Now, I saw in my dream, that these two men went in at the gate; and, lo! as they entered, they were transfigured, and they had raiment put on that shone like gold. There was also that met them with harps and crowns, and gave them to them; the harps to praise withal, and the crowns in token of honour. Then I heard in my dream, that all the bells in the city rang again for joy, and that it was said unto them, 'Enter ye into the joy of your Lord.' I also heard the men themselves, that they sang with a loud voice, saying, 'Blessing, and honour, and glory, and power, be unto Him that sitteth upon the throne, and unto the Lamb, for ever and ever.' Now, just as the gates were opened to let in the men, I looked in after them, and, behold, the city shone like the sun; the streets also were paved with gold; and in them walked many men, with crowns on their heads, palms in their hands, and golden harps to sing praises withal. There were also of them that had wings, and they answered one another without intermission, saying, 'Holy, holy, holy is the Lord!' And after these things they shut up the gates of the city; which, when I had seen, I wished myself among them."—*Pilgrim's Progress.*

HOME OF THE SOUL.

From "SINGING PILGRIM."
Mrs. G. H. GATES. Per. PHILIP PHILLIPS.

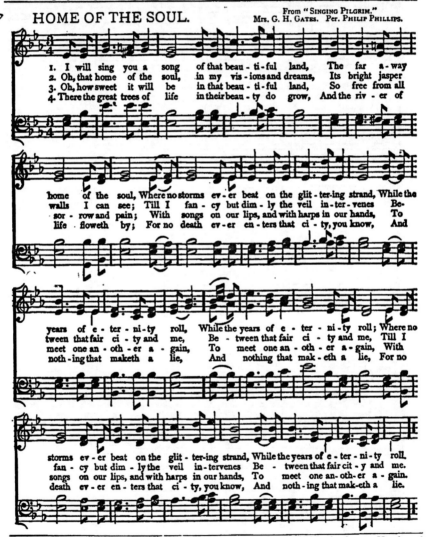

1. I will sing you a song of that beau-ti-ful land, The far a-way home of the soul, Where no storms ev-er beat on the glit-ter-ing strand, While the years of e-ter-ni-ty roll, While the years of e-ter-ni-ty roll; Where no storms ev-er beat on the glit-ter-ing strand, While the years of e-ter-ni-ty roll.

2. Oh, that home of the soul, in my vis-ions and dreams, Its bright jasper walls I can see; Till I fan-cy but dim-ly the veil in-ter-venes Be-tween that fair ci-ty and me, Be-tween that fair ci-ty and me, Till I fan-cy but dim-ly the veil in-tervenes Be-tween that fair cit-y and me.

3. Oh, how sweet it will be in that beau-ti-ful land, So free from all sor-row and pain; With songs on our lips, and with harps in our hands, To meet one an-oth-er a-gain, To meet one an-oth-er a-gain, With songs on our lips, and with harps in our hands, To meet one an-oth-er a-gain.

4. There the great trees of life in their beau-ty do grow, And the riv-er of life floweth by; For no death ev-er en-ters that ci-ty, you know, And noth-ing that maketh a lie, And nothing that mak-eth a lie, For no death ev-er en-ters that ci-ty, you know, And noth-ing that mak-eth a lie.

THE building of the wall of it was of jasper, and the city was pure gold like unto clear glass—God shall wipe away all tears from their eyes, and there shall be no more death, neither sorrow nor crying, neither shall there be any more pain : for the former things are passed away—And I heard the voice of harpers harping with their harps, and they sang, as it were a new song before the throne—He shewed me a pure river of water of life, clear as crystal. In the street of it, and on either side of the river was the tree of life, and the leaves of the tree were for the healing of the nations—There shall in no wise enter into it anything that defileth, neither whatsoever worketh abomination, or maketh a lie.—*Revelations.*

ABIDE WITH ME.

W. H. MONK. J. F. LYTE.

Reverently.

1. A - bide with me, fast falls the ev - en - tide; The dark-ness
2. Swift to its close ebbs out life's lit - tle day; Earth's joys grow
3. I need Thy pres - ence ev' - ry pass - ing hour; What but Thy
4. Hold thou Thy cross be - fore my clos - ing eyes; Shine through the

deep - ens; Lord, with me a - bide; When oth - er help - ers
dim, its glo - ries pass a - way; Change and de - cay in
grace can foil the tempt - er's power? Who, like Thy - self, my
gloom, and point me to the skies; Heav'n's morn - ing breaks, and

fail, and com - forts flee, Help of the help - less, oh, a - bide with me.
all a - round I see; Oh, Thou who chang - est not, a - bide with me.
guide and stay can be? Thro' cloud and sun - shine, Lord, a - bide with me.
earth's vain shad - ows flee; In life, in death, O Lord, a - bide with me.

JESUS LIVES.

F. E. COX *tr.* "ST. ALBINUS."
CH. FURCHTEGOTT GELLERT, 1757.

1. Jesus lives! no lon - ger now Can thy terrors, Death, ap - pall us; Je - sus lives! by
2. Jesus lives! henceforth is death But the gate of life im - mor - tal; This shall calm our
3. Jesus lives! for us He died; Then, alone to Je - sus liv - ing, Pure in heart may
4. Jesus lives! to Him the throne O - ver all the world is giv - en: May we go where

this we know Thou, O Grave, canst not enthrall us. Al - le - lu - ia!
trembling breath, When we pass its gloomy por - tal. Al - le - lu - ia!
we a - bide, Glo - ry to our Saviour giv - ing. Al - le - lu - ia!
He is gone, Rest and reign with Him in Heav - en. Al - le - lu - ia! A - men.

I **HAVE** often seen piano-forte players and singers make such strange motions over instrument or song book, that I have wanted to laugh at them. "Where did our friend pick up these fine ecstatic airs?" I would say to myself. Then I would remember my lady in "marriage a la mode," and amuse myself thinking an affectation was the same thing in Hogarth's time as in our own. But one day I bought me a canary bird and hung it up in a cage at my window. By-and-by he found himself at home, and began to pipe his little tunes; and there he was, sure enough, swimming and waving about, with all the droopings and liftings, languishing side-turnings of the head that I had laughed at. And now I should like to ask who taught him all this?—and me, through him, that the foolish head was not the one swinging itself from side to side and bowing and nodding over the music, but that other which was passing its shallow and self-satisfied judgment on a creature made of finer clay than the stalwart frame which has so very long

HERDSMAN'S MOUNTAIN HOME.
(DER SCHWEIZERBUE.)

CARL MATZ Arr.

1. On the mountain, steep and hoary, Sounds the herdsman's evening song; Where the clouds, in golden
2. Where the Alpine rose is blowing, Where the herdsman builds his home; From his couch at morning

glo - ry, Float the am-bient tide a - long, Where the clouds, in gold-en glo - ry, Float the
go - ing, With the lark he loves to roam! From his couch at morning go - ing, With the

ambient tide a - long. La la la   la la la la la la la   la la   la   la
lark he loves to roam! La la la   la la la la la la la la   la la   la   la

carried that same critical head upon its shoulders?

YOUR former conversation has made me think repeatedly what a number of beautiful words there are of which we never think of estimating the value, as there are of blessings. How carelessly, for example, do we (not we, but people) say "I am delighted to *hear from you*." No other language has this beautiful expression, which, like some of the most lovely flowers, loses its charm for want of close inspection. When I consider the deep sense of these very simple and very common words, I seem to hear a voice coming from afar through the air, intrusted to the care of the elements, for the nurture of my sympathy.—*Landor.*

WE often hear that this or that "is not worth an old song." Alas! how few things are! What precious recollections do some of them awaken! What pleasurable tears do they excite! They purify the streams of life; they can delay it in its shelves and rapids; they can turn it back again to the soft cool moss amidst which its sources issue.—*Landor.*

NEVER SAY FAIL.

SCHOOL-DAY SINGER.

1. Keep work-ing, 'tis wis - er than sit-ting a - side; Nev - er, oh, nev - er say fail!
2. In life's ros - y morn-ing, in manhood's fair pride, Nev, oh, nev - er say fail!

And dreaming, and sigh-ing, and wait-ing the tide; Nev - er, oh, nev - er say fail!
Let this be your mot-to, your foot-steps to guide, Nev - er, oh, nev - er say fail!

In life's earn-est bat - tle they on - ly pre - vail, Who dai - ly march on-ward and
In storm and in sun-shine what-ev - er as - sail, Push on-ward and con - quer, and

nev-er say fail! Nev-er say fail! Nev-er say fail! Nev-er, oh, nev-er say fail!
nev-er say fail! Nev-er say fail! Nev-er say fail! Nev-er, oh, nev-er say fail!

LONGING FOR SPRING.

GERMAN. CARL MATZ, *arr*,

1. Oh, how cold the Win - ter weath - er, All is sor - row - ful and
2. Could I hast - en to the moun - tains, Could I see the val - ley
3. Quick-ly come in all thy beau - ty, Love - ly Spring - time, come a-
4. Yes, O Spring, we love thee tru - ly, Come in all thy bright ar -

drear, And the North wind whistles rude - ly, No bright sun - beam shin - eth near.
green, I would lie down 'mid the flow - ers, While the sun peep'd in be - tween.
gain! Bring us flow - ers, shade, and sing - ing, Brighten ev' - ry hill and plain.
ray; Bring us soon thy love and glo - ry, Song and pleas - ure, dance and play.

THE BLACKBOARD.—Lessons in music written on the blackboard the moment they are wanted are always more interesting to pupils than such as are contained in a book. The teacher should accustom himself to write with ease and rapidity, and should depend more upon the blackboard lessons than upon any others. The board should have the lines of the staff painted upon it, so as to save the time of the teacher. The staff, without clefs, should also be so cut into the slates of the pupils that it may always be ready for use when they are called upon to write what is sung, as well as to sing what is written. The time which is occupied in writing a lesson is not lost in a well-regulated school, for the pupils will watch the movements of the teacher with interest, and will examine each note and character as it is written. It may also at times be desirable for the teacher to have his pupils name the tones as he writes them. No written lessons can possibly do away with the necessity for the blackboard. If all the teachers in the world should set themselves to writing lessons, and all the printers in the world should be employed to print them, and all the shops should be full of the books containing them, and all the pupils in the world should have all the money in the world with which to purchase all the books of printed lessons in the world, and every pupil should be furnished with a copy of every book that was ever printed, still the necessity for the blackboard would remain. It might indeed be superseded in part by a sufficiency of printed lessons, so far as practical vocal exercises are concerned; but yet for these it can never be given up by a good teacher; but even if it were given up for these, it would still be needed constantly for the illustration of such subjects as will be constantly coming up in teaching. The idea of giving up the black-

CHIDE MILDLY THE ERRING.

W. B. BRADBURY.

1. Chide mildly the erring, Kind language endears, Grief follows the sinful, Add not to their tears;
2. Chide mildly the err-ing, Jeer not at their fall, If strength be but human, How weak were we all!
3. Chide mildly the erring, Entreat them with care, Their natures are mortal, They need not despair,

A-void with re-proach-es Fresh pain to be-stow, The heart which is stricken
What mar-vel that foot-steps Should wan-der a-stray, When tempests so shadow
We all have some frail-ty, We all are un-wise, The grace which redeems us

Needs never a blow; The heart which is stricken Needs never a blow.
Life's wearisome way? When tempests so shadow Life's wearisome way.
Must come from the skies; The grace which re-deems us Must come from the skies.

board is preposterous; and any one who entertains the thought of doing without one, proves almost conclusively that he cannot be a good practical teacher. Perhaps our language on this point may appear to be strong, but surely there is no subject on which we feel a greater degree of certainty than this. That the black-board is an indispensable requisite in every well-furnished school-room, whatever be the subject taught, is the concurrent testimony of all good teachers in all parts of the world, in all departments of school-teaching. It is needed, too, from the beginning to the end of a course; it is not to be used for a few of the first lessons, and then to be given up; its use is never to be wholly discontinued.—*T. F. Seward.*

DON'T DRAG.—How should the congregation sing? With animation and pleasure, as if they liked it. Let the tune be announced in a clear, emphatic, and perhaps lively manner, and let the people take it up boldly and quickly. "Push things." There is more danger of dying of dullness than galloping into an unseemly canter. In a plain choral the time may be quite rapid, if the last note of each line is held slightly. Most people cannot hold a long breath, and unless they sing fast cannot sing at all. Rather than drag the psalm out into the dreary funeral-procession pace commonly heard, we had better be a little too gay. It is the slow and heavy style of performance that has brought church music into certain disrepute that it does not deserve.

COME, ALL YE FAITHFUL.

J. READING, d. 1692.

1. O come, all ye faith - ful, Joy - ful and tri - umphant, O come ye, O come ye to
2. Sing al - le - lu - ia, All ye choirs of an - gels; O sing, all ye bliss - ful ones of
3. Yea, Lord, we greet Thee, Born this hap - py morning; Je - sus, to Thee be the

A - des - te, fi - de - les, Læ - ti tri - um-phan - tes, Ve - ni - te, ve - ni - te in

Beth - le - hem.   Come and be - hold Him, Mon - arch of   An - gels! O come, let us a -
Heav'n a - bove.   Glo - ry to God   In the highest,   glo - ry! O come, let us a -
glo - ry giv'n;   Word of the Fa - ther, Now in flesh ap - pear - ing, O come, let us a -

Beth - le - hem,   Na - tum vi - de - te,   Regem an - ge - lo - rum, Ve - ni - te, a - do -

dore Him, O come, let us a - dore Him, O come, let us a - dore   Him, Christ the Lord.

re - mus, Ve - ni - te, a - do - re - mus, Ve - ni - te, a - do - re - mus   Do - mi - num.

THE FARMER.

KINDERGARTEN.

1. Shall I show you how the farmer, shall I show you how the farmer, Shall I show you how the

farm - er *sows his** bar - ley and wheat? Look, 'tis so, so that the farm - er, look, 'tis

so, so that the farm - er, Look, 'tis so, so that the farm - er *sows his** bar - ley and wheat.

*For 2d verse, sing—"mows his"; 3d, "brings in"; 4th, "threshes"—thus making four verses.

MEMORY BELLS.—On the fifth day of my journey across the Syrian desert the air above lay dead, and all the whole earth that I could reach with my utmost sight and keenest listening was still and lifeless as some dispeopled and forgotten world that rolls round and round in the heavens through wasted floods of light. The sun, growing fiercer, shone down more mightily now than ever on me he shone before, and as I drooped my head under his fire and, closing my eyes against the glare that surrounded me, slowly fell asleep, for how many minutes or moments, I cannot tell, but after awhile I was gently awakened by a peal of church bells—my native bells—the innocent bells of Marlen, that never before sent forth their music beyond the Blaygon hills! My first idea naturally was, that I still remained fast under the power of a dream. I roused myself, and drew aside the silk that covered my eyes, and plunged my bare face into the light. Then at least I was well enough wakened, but still those old Marlen bells rang on, not ringing for joy, but properly,

LOVE AND MIRTH.

J. STRAUSS.
BADEN POLKA.

Allegretto.

1. What song doth the crick-et sing? What news doth the swal-low bring?
2. Mark the morn when first she springs Up-ward on her gold-en wings;
3. With the leaves the ap-ples wres-tle, In the grass the dai-sies nes-tle,
4. Is it mirth? then why will man Mar the sweet song all he can?

What doth laughing child-hood tell? What calls out the marriage bell?
Hark! the soar-ing, soar-ing lark, And the echo-ing for-est—hark!
And the sun smiles on the wall, Tell us, What's the cause of all?
Bid him rath-er aye re-joice, With a kind and mer-ry voice,

What say all? "Love and mirth, In the air and in the earth;
What say they? "Love and mirth, In the air and in the earth;
"Mirth and love, Love and mirth, In the air and in the earth;
Bid him sing, "Love and mirth, In the air and in the earth;

Ver-y, ver-y soft and mer-ry is the glad-some song of earth."

prosily, steadily, merrily ringing for "church." After a while the sound died away slowly; it happened that neither I nor any of my party had a watch by which to measure the exact time of its lasting, but it seemed to me that about ten minutes had passed before the bells ceased. I attributed the effect to the great heat of the sun, the perfect dryness of the clear air through which I moved, and the deep stillness of all around me; it seemed to me that these causes, by occasioning a great tension, and consequent susceptibility of the hearing organs, had rendered them liable to tingle under the passing touch of some mere memory, that must have swept across my brain in a moment of sleep. Since my return to England, it has been told me that like sounds have been heard at sea, and that a sailor becalmed under a vertical sun, in the midst of the wide ocean, has listened in trembling wonder to the chime of his own village bells—*Kinglake's Eothen.*

THE BOAT SONG.

C. M. Von Weber.

Moderato.

1. On we are float - ing in sun - shine and shad - ow, Soft are the
2. Light - ly our boat on the wa - ter is swing - ing, On - ward she
3. Com - rades, sing on, while the ech - oes, a - wak - ing, Join in your
4. Soon will the man - tle of ev' - ning fall o'er us, Soon will the

rip - ples that sing as we go, Soft - ly they break on the
floats while the swift oars we ply, Gay are our hearts as the
mu - sic with hap - 'py re - frain, Sing while the waves on the
day - light fade out from the sky, Then with the thought of a

edge of the mea - dow, Woo - ing the grass - es with mel - o - dies low.
songs we are sing - ing, Bright are our hopes as the ra - di - ant sky.
sun - ny banks break - ing, An - swer your ca - dence with mu - sic a - gain.
wel - come be - fore us, Back thro' the twi - light we'll cheer - ful - ly hie.

SOFT MUSIC IS STEALING.

German Air.
Mary S. B. Dana.

Andante.

1. Soft, soft mu - sic is steal - ing, Sweet, sweet lingers the strain: Loud, loud now it is
2. Join, join, children of sad - ness, Send, send sor - row a - way; Now, now changing to
3. Sweet, sweet mel - o - dy's num - bers, Hark! hark! gently they swell, Deep, deep, wak - ing from

peal - ing, Waking the ech - oes a - gain. { Yes, yes, yes, yes, } Waking the echoes a - gain.
glad - ness, War - ble a beau - ti - ful lay. } Warble a beau - ti - ful lay.
slumbers Thoughts in the bosom that dwell. } Thoughts in the bosom that dwell.

EARLY VOCAL TRAINING.—It is a good sign of the times that the study of music is slowly creeping into our schools, and being recognized by teachers and school committees. Still, the movement in this direction is halting and feeble. The cultivation of singing among children will, it is believed, insure a rich, resonant chest-tone, will break the shrill head-tone, will banish the nasal twang, and make our national speech melodious. To do this implies, of course, that the exercise of singing shall not be crowded into a mere fraction of a school session, but that, like reading and spelling, it be brought into the front and made honorable. Practical men can understand the advantage of this; men who do not care for music can see this thing as clearly as the best trained musi-cians; and we ask them to think of it and act upon it. Another point: All children sing. They sing al-most as surely as they talk. The want of "ear" may make here and there an exception, but it will be so rarely found that it need not be estimated Not all adults sing, can sing, or can be taught to sing Dis-use of the vocal chords in childhood will, doubtless, incapacitate an adult for singing, and his throat will be like a withered arm, beyond recovery for actual use.

MEMORY.—The sight of a faded flower pressed in a book brings back, with a little shock of feeling, the hand that gathered it, or the distant hills upon which it once bloomed years ago. The touch of satin or fine hair is also capable of reviving the recollec-tion of scenes, and places, and persons. But for

ANNIE LAURIE.

Tenderly.   LADY JOHN SCOTT.

1. Max - welton's braes are bon-nie, Where ear-ly fa's the dew, And 'twas there that An-nie
2. Her brow is like the snawdrift, Her throat is like the swan; Her face it is the
3. Like dew on th' gowan ly - ing Is th' fa' o' her fairy feet, And like winds in summer

Lau-rie Gave me her promise true, Gave me her promise true, Which ne'er for-got will
fair - est That e'er the sun shone on, That e'er the sun shone on, And dark blue is her
sigh-ing, Her voice is low and sweet, Her voice is low and sweet, And she's a' the world to

be, }
e'e, }   And for bon-nie An - nie Lau - rie, I'd lay me down and dee.
me, }

freshness and suddenness, and power over memory, all the senses must yield to the sense of hearing. When memory is concerned, music is no longer it-self; it ceases to have any proper plane of feeling; it surrenders itself wholly, with all its rights, to memory, to be the patient, stern and terrible exponent of that recording angel. What is it? Only a few trivial bars of an old piano-forte piece, "Murmures du Rhone" or "Pluie des Perles." The drawing-room window is open, the children are playing on the lawn, the warm morning air is charged with the scent of the lilac blossoms. Then the ring at the bell, the confusion in the hall. The girl at the piano stops, and one is lifted in dying or dead. Years, years ago! but passing through the streets, a bar or two of the "Murmures du Rhone" brings the whole scene up before the girl, now no longer a girl but a middle aged woman look-ing back to one fatal summer morning. The enthu-siastic old men, who invariably turned up when Madame Grisi was advertised to sing in her last days, seemed always deeply affected. Yet it could hardly be at what they actually heard—no, the few notes recalled the most superb soprano of the age in her best days; recalled also the scenes of youth quenched in the grey mists of the dull, declining years. It was worth any money to hear even the hollow echo of a voice which had power to bring back, if only for a moment, the "tender grace of a day that was dead."—*Haweis.*

BLOOM ON, MY ROSES.

F. H. COWEN.
R. E. FRANCILLON.

1. Bloom on, bloom on, my roses, more brightly than be-fore, For un-to you, my ros-es, Re-turn I nev-er more. I go, the rose to gath-er Whose fra-grance fills the skies, That fades not e'en in win-ter, Nor dies when summer dies, Nor dies when summer dies. Bloom on, bloom on, my ros-es, More brightly than be-fore, For un-to you, my ros-es, Re-turn I nev-er-more, Return I nev-er-more, Return, . . re-turn I nev-er-more. Bloom on, bloom on, Bloom on, bloom on, bloom on, bloom on, bloom on, . . bloom on. . . . .

2. I go to flower in sun-shine More bright than summer weaves, To drink of pur-er dew-drops Than glit-ter on your leaves, To float on gales more fragrant Than e'en the ros-es move, To pluck the rose of Heaven, That blooms on earth as love, That blooms on earth as love. Bloom on, bloom on, my ros-es, More brightly than be-fore, Bloom on, bloom on, my ros-es, I need your bloom no more, I need your bloom no more, Your bloom, your bloom, your bloom no more.

THE school-room with its inmates is like an organ with many stops and keys, and he who plays it must decide what the music of its pipes shall be. If his hand is skillful and his ear well-trained, the psalm with which the day begins, will lose none of its sweetness or of its strength as the hours advance. Conscious of the importance of his mission and the responsibility reposed in him, there will steal from under his tuneful fingers a strain of such wondrous melody, that they who hear can never resist its power. Still will the keys be pressed, still will the harmony go on, and still from every stop and key there will come its unpretending part, always in its own good time and always bearing upon its bars the purest lessons which government can teach. Sometimes, indeed, a discord will be heard, sometimes a note be struck not quite in tune, but the heedful ear of the master will detect the complaining key, the firm hand will gently remove the hidden cause, and the harshness be soon forgotten in the sweeter song that follows. These influences are never lost. They may seem to be unheard, uncared-for and unknown; but by-and-by they will come softly back, and the echoes, faintly though they call, still tell that they were listened to and loved, still tell that the gentleness and affection which are carried away from pleasant school-rooms do sometimes live long after the days of school are dead, do sometimes— oftentimes—carry with them the burden of a song that will never be hushed again, and furnish with their dying cadences convincing proof that only that school-room government which springs from genuine affection will stand the test of time.—*R. M. Streeter.*

IF you ask me wherefore song was made a part of worship, the answer must be because music is the fit

ANGRY WORDS.

CHILDHOOD SONGS.

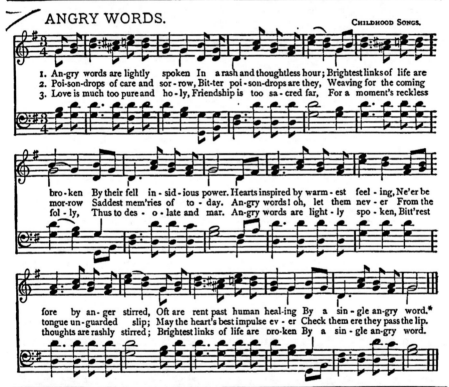

1. An-gry words are lightly spoken In a rash and thoughtless hour; Brightest links of life are bro-ken By their fell in-sid-ious power. Hearts inspired by warm-est feel-ing, Ne'er be fore by an-ger stirred, Oft are rent past human heal-ing By a sin-gle an-gry word.*

2. Poi-son-drops of care and sor-row, Bit-ter poi-son-drops are they, Weaving for the coming mor-row Saddest mem'ries of to-day. An-gry words! oh, let them nev-er From the tongue un-guarded slip; May the heart's best impulse ev-er Check them ere they pass the lip.

3. Love is much too pure and ho-ly, Friendship is too sa-cred far, For a moment's reckless fol-ly, Thus to des-o-late and mar. An-gry words are light-ly spo-ken, Bitt'rest thoughts are rashly stirred; Brightest links of life are oro-ken By a sin-gle an-gry word.

language of a service of love. No man sings when he is angry. The notes of accordant voices speak of amity and fellowship. As music is said to consist of the harmony of sweet sounds, and as sounds without harmony become mere noise, so the strains of the psalm or hymn are at once the type and sign of the communion of saints. Where there is heard no music that souls are met who are without variance. They are the signal of the presence of the peace of Christ and of God. And as the chords of human hearts should thrill together in glad unison when they come before God, whenever they find expression in such singing they tend to do so. Music is the tamer of evil passions. We cannot hate each other when we sing together. The fable of Orpheus charming the beasts with his lyre represents a reality; and the Christians of the catacombs were right when they chose Orpheus as an emblem of Christ, and carved him over their tombs. Among all the numberless things men can do with their varied faculties, song is asked of them, to be offered before God, that they may stand before His mercy-seat in unity, and turn from His presence better prepared to live in charity and peace.—*Swinnerton.*

* A clergyman, whose family was noted for amiability and mutual affection, was asked the secret of his successful training. "I call," said he, "the influence of music to my aid. If I see any of my little ones seeming to be angry, I say, 'Sing, children, sing!' and before the strain is ended every unpleasant feeling disappears, and harmony again prevails." May it not be well for parents and teachers to profit by this hint? The above melody, to the accompanying words, has been suggested by one who has often seen its happy influence in the school-room among the children.

COME TO THE OLD OAK TREE.

1. Come to the old oak-tree, By the light of the pale moon's glance; O
2. Spring, with its ear-ly leaves, And the Sum-mer, with all its flowers, Here

come with a foot-step free,—— And join in the gyp-sies' dance.
Art in her beau-ty weaves— Bright wreaths in fair Na-ture's bowers.

DUET OR SEMI-CHORUS.

A - round us, a - bove us, Pure mel - o - dy floats, And voi - ces that
No storm - clouds are dark-ling The haunts of the free, But all here is

CHORUS.

love us Re - peat the soft notes. Then come to the old oak-tree, By the
sparkling In beau - ty for thee. Then come to the old oak-tree, By the

light of the pale moon's glance, Oh, come with a foot-step free, And join in the gyp-sies'

dance; Then dance, then dance where the light-est of light feet dance!

IN EXCELSIS GLORIA.

WELSH AIR.

Allegretto.

1. Not in halls of reg-al splendor, Not to princes of the earth, Did the her-ald
2. Not by world-ly wealth or wisdom, Not by power of law or sword, But by ser-vice
3. Bid the new-born Monarch welcome; Pay him homage, ev-'ry heart! Hal-le-lu-jah!

an-gels ren-der Tid-ings of His birth.   Not to statesman, priest, or sage,
to win freedom, Ser-vice of the Lord.   Born to pov-er-ty and pain,
let His kingdom Come and ne'er de-part.   Jus-tice hath on Mer-cy smiled,

They proclaimed the golden age 'Twas the poor man's heritage! In ex-cel-sis glo-ri-a!
Born to die and thus to reign, Freeing men from death's domain, In excel-sis glo-ri-a!
God and men are recon-ciled Thro' Emmanuel, wondrous Child. In excel-sis glo-ri-a!

For on shepherds low-ly   Burst the an-them ho-ly!   In ex-cel-sis
Lo! from earth as Heaven   Praise shall aye be giv-en: In ex-cel-sis
Blend we then our voices,   Earth with Heaven rejoic-es,   In ex-cel-sis

glo-ri-a!   War and blood-shed cease,   Selfishness its slaves re-lease,

Love shall reign and white-robed Peace! In excelsis glo-ri-a! In ex-cel-sis glo-ri-a!

COLUMBIA, GOD PRESERVE THEE FREE!

Joseph Haydn.

1. Ark of Free-dom! Glo-ry's dwelling! Columbia, God pre-serve thee free! When the
2. Land of high, he-ro-ic glo-ry: Land whose touch bids slav'ry flee: Land whose
3. Vain-ly 'gainst thine arm con-tend-ing, Ty-rants know thy might, and flee. Free-dom's

storms are round thee swelling, Let thy heart be strong in thee, God is with thee, wrong re-
name is writ in sto-ry, Rock and ref-uge of the free: Ours thy greatness—ours thy
cause on earth de-fend-ing, Man has set his hope on thee; Widening glo-ry—peace un-

pell-ing: He a-lone thy champion be.
glo-ry; We will e'er be true to thee. } Ark of Free-dom! Glo-ry's dwelling! Columbia,
end-ing—Thy re-ward and por-tion be.

God preserve thee free! Ark of Freedom! Glory's dwelling! Columbia, God preserve thee free!

AMERICA.

T. Dwight.

1. God bless our na-tive land! Firm may she ever stand, Through storm and night; When the wild
2. For her our pray'rs shall rise To God a-bove the skies, On him we wait; Thou who art

tempests rave, Rul-er of wind and wave, Do Thou our coun-try save By Thy great might!
ev-er nigh, Guarding with watchful eye, To Thee a-loud we cry, God save the State!

It would be a good test of the breadth and richness of the faith of any sect to manifest how much of the whole amplitude of the organ, from its rumbling ground-tier of pipes to the softest lute-vibrations it would call into play. No sect can command the whole chromatic gamut which the Gospel sweeps. Here is the continual call for charity and humility and joy in the comprehensiveness of Christianity. It needs the full choir of churches for its expression. It cannot spare any stop in the organ-growth of history. Each new sect that endures is a new range of pipes taking up a slighted sentiment, or working up some more delicate tone or elaborate variation into the symphony of grace. We shall drop our intellectual differences about trinity and unity, free-will and constraining grace, when we reach Heaven. But we shall still be ranged, there as here, by the sentiments we most naturally give utterance to. We shall see then, doubtless, what need there is of the utmost power of every party to celebrate the circle of the Divine glory, how deep is the justice, how high the love, how wide the providence, that are twined into the pure harmony of the heavenly hallelujah.—*Starr King.*

SING GLAD SONGS FOR HIM.

C. F. Gounod.
Clara Morton.

CHILDREN'S SONGS.

Which way does the wind blow, And where does he go? He rides o'er the water, And over the snow!
O'er wood and o'er valley, And over the height, Where goats cannot traverse, He tak - eth his flight.
He rages and tosses When bare is the tree, As, when you look upwards, You plainly may see.
But whither he cometh, Or whither he goes, There's no one can tell you, There's no one that knows.

BEAUTIFUL SEA.
Allegretto.

Beau - ti - ful sea, beau - ti - ful sea, Oh, how I love on thy bo - som to roam,
Foaming and free, foaming and free, There is my rest - ing-place, there is my home.
O - ver the deep stormy winds sweep, Fly - ing a - way o'er the foam - crested wave.
O - ver the deep fierce - ly they leap, But in our good ship the dan - ger we'll brave.

ROSALIND.

Here cometh Ros - a - lind, chasing the bee, Bright as the sunshine up - on the blue sea.
"Ros - a - lind, Ros - a - lind, where have you been?" "O - ver the meadow, and over the green."
"Whom are your flowers for? where did they grow? Some like the blue sky, and some like the snow."
"Down by the merry brook, there's where they grew; And I have brought them, dear sister, for you."

OH, BROAD LAND.
Maestoso.

Oh, broad land, oh, fair land, Oh, land that gave us birth, Oh, near land, oh, dear land, Our home of all the earth;
We honor and praise thee, Oh realm enrich'd by heav'n, We love thee, we bless thee, For priceless blessings giv'n.
For freedom, for knowledge, Alike to great and small, For care and protection, And equal rights to all.

THE FARMER.

I'm glad I am a farmer, the sturdy plough to wield, Or reap and bind the ripen'd grain that waves in yonder field.
I'm glad I am a farmer, his heart is always gay As merrily his song rings out amid the new-mown hay.
O happy is the farmer, for when the day is o'er, The ev'ning shadows gather round, that he may work no more.
How peacefully around him, soft sleep her curtain throws, There's nothing half so tranquil as the laborer's re-
[pose.

BOOK OF NATURE.—All children should settle in their own minds whether they will be Eyes or No Eyes; whether they will see for themselves, or let other people look for them, or pretend to look and dupe them and lead them about—the blind leading the blind, till both fall into the ditch. God has given you eyes and it is your duty to use them. If your parents tried to teach you in the most agreeable way by beautiful picture-books, would it not be ungrateful and wrong to shut your eyes and refuse to learn? Then is it not altogether wrong to refuse to learn from your Father in Heaven, the great God, who made all things, when he offers to teach you all day long by the most beautiful and wonderful of all picture-books, which is simply all things that you can see, hear and touch, from the sun and stars above your head to the mosses and insects at your feet? It is your duty to learn His lessons. God's Book, which is the Universe, and the reading of God's Book, which is Science, can do nothing but good, and teach you nothing but truth and wisdom. God did not put this wondrous world about your young souls to tempt or mislead them. So, use your eyes, your senses and your brains, and learn what God is trying to teach you by them. I do not mean that you must stop there and learn nothing more. There are things which neither your senses nor your brains can tell you; and they are not only more glorious, but actually more true and more real than any things which you can see or touch. But you must begin at the beginning, and the more you try to understand *things* the more you will be able hereafter to understand men, and that which is above men. You begin to find out that truly Divine mystery that you have a mother on earth, simply by lying soft and warm upon her bosom: and so it is by watching the common

BUY MY STRAWBERRIES.

Allegretto.   HOWARD.

1. With this hum-ble stock in store,   Which is not mine own,   I your pa-tron-age im-plore, For the sad and lone; List to lit-tle Ju-lia's cry, Buy my ber-ries, come and buy; List to lit-tle Ju-lia's cry, Buy my ber-ries, come and buy!
2. Cheered by wo-man's kind-ly face,   Aid-ed by her hand,   In the bus-y market-place, Here pray let me stand, And beseech those pass-ing nigh, Flow'rs and ber-ries, come and buy; And beseech those passing nigh, Flow'rs and ber-ries, come and buy.
3. Let a lit-tle maid-en's prayer,   Void of an-y art,   Reach the sym-pa-thet-ic ear, Move the friend-ly heart; List to lit-tle Ju-lia's cry, Buy my ber-ries, come and buy; List to lit-tle Ju-lia's cry, Buy my ber-ries, come and buy.

natural things around you, and considering the lilies how they grow, that you will *begin* at least to learn that far Diviner mystery—that you have a Father in Heaven. So you will be delivered out of the tyranny of darkness and fear, into God's free kingdom of light and faith and love; and will be safe from the venom of that tree which was planted long ago, and grows in all lands and climes, whose name is the Tree of Unreason, whose roots are conceit and ignorance and its juices folly and death. It drops its venom into the finest brains, making them call sense nonsense. It drops its venom into tenderest hearts, and makes them call wrong right, and love cruelty; but any little child who will use the faculties God has given him, may find an antidote to all its poison in the meanest herb beneath his feet.—*Charles Kingsley.*

MOZART and Haydn being at a party, the former laid a wager with the latter that he could not play at sight a piece of music which he (Mozart) would compose. Haydn accepted the challenge, and Mozart speedily wrote down a few notes and presented them to Haydn, who, having played a prelude, exclaimed, : "How do you think I can play that? My hands are at each extremity of the piano, and there is at the same time a note in the middle." "Does that stop you?" said Mozart; "well, you shall see me do it." On coming to the difficult passage, Mozart, without stopping, struck the note in the middle of the piano with his nose; and every one naturally burst out laughing. What made the act more ridiculous was that Haydn had a flat nose, while that of Mozart was prominent, well adapted for such notes.

BLOSSOM TIME.

MARY E. DODGE.

Lively.

1. There's a wedding in the orchard, dear, I know it by the flowers; They're wreathed on ev'ry
2. While whispers rang a - mong the boughs of prom - is - es and praise, And play - ful, lov - ing

bough and branch, or falling down in showers. The air is in a mist, I think, and scarce knows which to
mes - sages sped through the leaf-lit ways. And just beyond the wreathed aisles that end against the

be— Wheth - er all fragrance, cling-ing close, or bird - song, wild and free. And
blue, The rai - ment of the wedding-choir and priest came shi - ning through. And

count-less wedding jew - els shine, and gold - en gifts of grace; I nev - er saw such
though I saw no wedding-guest, nor groom, nor gen - tle bride, I know that ho - ly

wealth of sun in an - y sha - dy place. It seemed I heard the flutt'ring robes of
things were asked, and holy love re - plied. And something thro' the sunlight said: "Let

Cho.—There's a wed-ding in the orchard, dear, I

maidens clad in white, The clasp-ing of a thousand hands in ten - der - est de - light.
all who love be blest! The earth is wedded to the spring, and God, He knoweth best."

know it by the flowers; They're wreathed on ev'ry bough and branch, or falling down in showers.

WORDS AND MUSIC.—In the teaching of music, great attention should be given not only to the reading of exercises at sight, but also to the manner and method of singing songs. It should never be forgotten that music is a mighty power for good or evil, and for that reason the character of the music, as well as the words, is a matter of the highest importance. Profanity, sometimes blasphemy, is encouraged by the setting of sacred words to music that is most frivolous. What Herder, the great German philosopher, has said, in speaking of the influence of poetry upon the mind of a child is equally applicable here: "How dry and sterile some men imagine the human mind, the child's mind, to be! And what a great, excellent ideal world it would be to me, if

I ever should attempt to write songs for it! To fill the whole youthful, child-like soul; to put songs into it, which will generally remain in it through life and give it its tone; which will be to it lasting voices, encouraging to generous deeds and noble fame, to virtue and consolation, like the heroic ballads and stirring war songs of the ancient nations; what a great aim, what a glorious work would this be!"

THE DOXOLOGY.—Wherever the English language is spoken, the stanza most frequently on the lips of Christian congregations, is the long-metre doxology. It was written by Thomas Ken, a celebrated English prelate, born in 1637. He was a man of devoted piety, broad and generous benevolence, and great firmness and loftiness of character, united with ten-

ALL TOGETHER.

GEORGE F. ROOT.
Permission JOHN CHURCH & COMPANY.

derness of spirit. He was one of the seven Bishops committed to the Tower for disobedience by James II., but proved his loyalty by refusing to take the oaths to William and Mary. and was consequently deprived of his bishopric. He was regarded with the highest esteem even by his enemies, and Queen Anne, upon her accession to the throne granted him a pension. He was the author of several volumes of elaborate sermons, and of many poetical productions of a religious character. His morning and evening hymns are still repeated in thousands of English families. The doxology is the closing stanza of a morning hymn beginning with the familiar line,

"Awake, my soul, and with the sun."

We owe a debt of gratitude to any man who has put the thought and aspirations of humanity into words that linger in our memories or voice themselves in the popular heart, and we cannot but feel that we are rearing a monument of song in honor to the author of our peerless doxology every time we join in the grand and solemn hymn of praise,

Praise God from whom all blessings flow,
Praise him all creatures here below,
Praise him above, ye heavenly host,
Praise Father, Son and Holy Ghost.

THE effect of good music is not caused by its novelty. On the contrary, it strikes us all the more forcibly the more familiar we are with it.—*Goethe.*

THE BLUSHING MAPLE TREE.

HAMILTON AIDÉ.

1. When on the world's first har - vest day, The for - est trees be - fore the Lord Laid
2. There ran thro' all the leaf - y wood A mur - mur and a scorn - ful smile, But
3. And there be - fore the for - est trees, All blushing, pale, by turns she stood; In

down their au - tumn of - fer - ings Of fruit in sun - shine stored, The Ma - ple
si - lent still the Ma - ple stood, And looked to God the while. And then, while
ev - 'ry leaf, now red and gold, She knew the kiss of God, And still, when

on - ly, of them all, Be - fore the world's great har - vest King, With emp - ty hands and
fell on earth a hush, So great it seemed like death to be, From His white throne the
comes the au - tumn time, And on the hills the har - vest lies, The blushing Ma - ple-

rall. molto.

si - lent stood—She had no of - fer - ing to bring; For . . .
migh - ty Lord Stoop'd down and kissed the Ma - ple - tree; At . . .
tree re - calls Her life's one beau - ti - ful sur - prise; And . . .

calando.

in the ear - ly sum - mer time, While oth - er trees laid by their hoard, The
that swift kiss there sud - den thrilled, In ev - 'ry nerve, thro' ev - 'ry vein, An
still, when comes the au - tumn time, And on the hills the har - vest lies, The

rit.

Ma - ple winged her fruit with love, And sent it dai - ly to the Lord.
ec - sta - cy of joy so great It seemed al - most a - kin to pain.
blush - ing Ma - ple tree re - calls Her life's one beau - ti - ful sur - prise.

Probably no hymn of recent origin has become a greater favorite than " Abide with me; fast falls the eventide." Several years ago, the Rev. James King, of Berwick-upon-Tweed, in England, collected and collated fifty-two representative hymnals used in various branches and by the various parties in the Church of England at home and abroad, and all of them published between 1863 and 1885. These he regarded as a committee, each member of which could, as it were, give one vote for each approved hymn. Thus, if a hymn was found in fifteen hymnals, then it was credited with fifteen votes or marks of approval; if found in twenty hymnals, twenty marks; and so on. The hymns thus found to rank highest were, All praise to Thee, my God, this night, Hark I the herald angels sing, Lo! He comes with clouds descending, Rock of Ages, cleft for me, each of which received fifty-one marks. Then comes Abide with Me, with forty-nine marks, followed by Awake, my soul, and with the sun, Jerusalem the golden, Jesus, lover of my soul, Sun of

GENTLE ANNIE.

Stephen C. Foster.

Andante mosso.

1. Thou wilt come no more, gen-tle An-nie, Like a flower thy spir-it did de-
2. We have roamed in youth 'mid the bow-ers, When thy down-y cheeks were in their
3. Ah! the hours grow sad while I pon-der Near the si-lent spot where thou art

part, Thou art gone, a-las, like the ma-ny That have bloomed in the summer of my
bloom, Now I stand a-lone 'mid the flowers, While they mingle their perfume o'er thy
laid, And my heart bows down when I wander By the stream and the meadows where we

heart. Shall we nev-er more be-hold thee, Never hear thy winning voice a-
tomb. Shall we nev-er more be-hold thee, Never hear thy winning voice a-
strayed. Shall we nev-er more be-hold thee, Never hear thy winning voice a-

gain, When the spring-time comes, gentle Annie, When the wild flo 'rs are scattered o'er the plain?

my soul, Thou Saviour dear, and When I survey the wondrous Cross, with an equal number of marks. Of the origin of Abide with Me, Mr. King gives the following interesting account: "This well-known hymn was composed by Henry Francis Lyte, born in 1793, at Ednam, near Kelso, the birthplace of James Thomson, author of *The Seasons*. He took holy orders, and in 1823, when thirty years of age, was appointed perpetual curate of Lower Brixham, Devon, where for about a quarter of a century he labored amongst the warm-hearted, rough seafaring population. In the autumn of 1847 his increasing weakness demanded change and repose, and his medical advisers accordingly urged him to pass the coming winter in a more genial clime. Before taking his journey he made an effort to address his flock once more, and with a wasted frame and hectic flush he spoke with deep earnestness. His subject was the Holy Communio , and he impressed upon his people the vital importa ce of close communion with the Saviour: 'O, brethr n, I stand here among you to-

THE GREENWOOD TREE.

SIDNEY NELSON.

Allegretto.

1. Here un-der the leaf-y green-wood tree, I pass the noon-tide hour, And
2. The but-ter-fly sports on gold-en wing, A sing-ing stream runs by; And

hap-pi-er far am I than he Who seeks but the court-ly bow-er; For
ma-ny a bird that hailed the spring, Still greet-eth the sum-mer sky. For

near me grows the wild white rose, A bright sky beams a-bove, And upward springs the
paint-ed halls and pal-ace walls I care not, whilst for me, Fair na-ture yields her

lark who sings The tru-est notes of love. Here un-der the leaf-y
smil-ing fields, And the shade of a greenwood tree. Here un-der the leaf-y

greenwood tree, I pass the noon-tide hour, And hap-pi-er far am I than he Who

seeks but the courtly bow-er. Hith-er quickly come to me! Un-der the leaf-y greenwood tree.

FAMOUS CHOIR.—There is perhaps no choir of music in the world equal to that of the Dom-Kirche, or Cathedral of Berlin. It is very celebrated, and said to be even better than the far-famed choir at Rome. It consists of about fifty singers, the treble and alto parts sung by boys. It is arranged in double chorus, and the music of the old composers, in eight parts, is often performed. The choir is entirely professional—that is, the singers are such by profession; they have learned to sing, and that is their business or calling. The boys who sing the upper parts are trained daily, and are preparing in their turn to be professors, teachers and composers of music, vocalists or instrumentalists here or elsewhere. The parts are, of course, well balanced as to power, and the chorus of men's voices, tenors and bassos singing in unison, as they often do, is peculiarly grand and effective. In addition to the regular choir, there is a preparatory department, consisting of some twenty or thirty fine-looking little boys of from eight to ten years of age. These are candidates for future membership, and form a juvenile choir. They stand in one side of the choir, and lead in the congregational singing, thus affording relief to the regular choir, and giving them time to breathe and recruit. We have said that these boys *stand*. This is equally true of the others, for there are no seats in the organ loft, and the members of the choir all stand during the whole service. The various exercises are distributed between the choir, the people, and the minister, so as to hold the attention and keep all employed. Those parts of the service performed by the choir or people, are sung, and

COME, YE DISCONSOLATE.

SAMUEL WEBBE.
THOMAS MOORE, 1824.

1. Come, ye dis-con-so-late, where-'er ye lan-guish, Come, at the mer-cy seat fer-vent-ly kneel; Here bring your wounded hearts, here tell your an-guish: Earth hath no sor-row that Heav'n can-not heal.
2. Joy of the des-o-late, light of the stray-ing. Hope, when all oth-ers die, fade-less and pure, Here speaks the Com-fort-er, in mer-cy say-ing, Earth hath no sor-row that Heav'n can-not cure.
3. Here see the Bread of Life; see wa-ters flow-ing Forth from the throne of God, pure from a-bove; Come to the feast of love, come, ev-er know-ing Earth hath no sor-row but Heav'n can re-move.

that belonging to the minister is read. The congregational tunes are sung much slower than we heard them in England, and about the time similar tunes are sung in America. There is not an instant during the service that is unoccupied, one exercise following promptly upon another. There are no rubrical directions and the hymns are not read before they are sung. The hymns are known the moment one enters the church, their numbers being suspended on tablets in various parts of the house, so as to be seen by all; and the particular hymn that is about to be sung, or that is being sung, is known by the tablet in front of the organ loft, which contains the number of that only, so that any one coming in after the service has been commenced, has only to look to the choir tablet, and he knows at once where to find his place. The organ is not played when the choir sing, but is used only for voluntaries, interludes, and responses, and for accompanying the congregation.—*Lowell Mason.*

Cowper's Wreck of the Royal George, and his Lines on Receipt of My Mother's Picture, will ever keep his memory warm; but his hymns are more than magnificent. What power there is in the lines, "Oh, for a closer walk with God," and "God moves in a mysterious way!" I have sometimes thought that to be the author of a hymn like "Nearer, my God, to Thee," and some others I could name, is the highest achievement of human fame, one that angels themselves might envy. Yet Cowper died doubting about the hereafter, though after his last breath had passed his face changed; a look of surprise overspread it, as that of one who had unexpectedly passed into everlasting rest.—*J. T. Fields.*

SCENES THAT ARE BRIGHTEST.

"MARITANA."
W. V. WALLACE.

Tenderly.

1. Scenes that are brightest may charm for a - while   Hearts that are light - est and
2. Words can-not scat - ter the   thoughts we   fear,   For though they flat - ter they

dim.   *f*   *p*

eyes that   smile; Yet o'er   them, a - bove us, though na - ture beam, With none to
mock the   eat; Hopes will still de - ceive us   with   tear - ful cost,   And when they

love us, how   sad   they   seem!   With none to love us, how   sad   they seem!
leave us the   heart   is   lost!   And when they leave us the   heart   is   lost.

JERUSALEM, MY HAPPY HOME.

LATIN, A. D. 900.

1. Je - ru - sa - lem,   my hap - py home, Name ev - er   dear   to   me,
2. When shall these eyes   thy heav'n built walls, And pearl - y   gates be - hold?
3. There hap - pier bow - ers than Eden's bloom, Nor   sin nor   sor - row know;

When shall my   la - bors have an   end   In joy and peace and   thee?
Thy bulworks with sal - va - tion strong, Thy streets of shin - ing   gold?
Blest seats! through rude and storm - y scenes   I   on - ward press to   you.

Why should I shrink from pain or woe,
Or feel at death dismay?
I've Canaan's goodly land in view,
And realms of endless day.

Jerusalem, my happy home,
My soul still pants for thee;
Then shall my labors have an end,
When I thy joys shall see.

THE beautlful custom of decorating the graves of the soldiers should have its lessons for the schools. Decoration day committees may secure an ample supply of bouquets if they will adopt the plan of certain Grand Army Posts in the larger cities. Instead of requesting donations of flowers from the citizens at large, all the schools of the village, town, or city, may be enlisted in the good work of providing them, representatives of the committees visiting the various schools some days before the flowers are wanted, and speaking of the propriety of the children's doing what they can to furnish them. The boys and girls will at once be interested. The bouquets may be brought to the schools on the afternoon preceding Decoration Day, to be called for by local committees. Thousands of bouquets may thus be obtained. The entire locality is laid under contribution for flowers, and in the most effective way possible. The children—each boy or girl—has done something, or has decided that he or she can do nothing, for the observance of the day—and thus has come into *personal* contact with the thought of gratitude due, and honor paid, to the patriotic dead. The teachers call the attention of their schools to the meaning of the day, under circumstances most favorable to producing a lasting impression. The story of the war is retold; the meaning of the great struggle is taught as the lesson of the hour; and in every way the result is profitable to all. "What we would have in the community we must put into the schools."

FLOWERS FOR THE BRAVE.

E. W. CHAPMAN.
BELLINI. "NORMA."

1. Once a - gain the flowers we gath - er On these sa - cred mounds to lay; O'er the tombs of fall - en he - roes Float the stars and stripes to - day. From the mountain, hill, and val - ley, Is - sued forth a no - ble throng, With he - ro - ic val - or fight - ing Till was heard the vic - tor's song. With he - ro - ic val - or fighting Till was heard the vic - tor's song.

2. But these brave men now are sleeping While their deeds in memo - ry live, And the trib - ute we are bringing 'Tis the na - tion's joy to give. Bring we here the gold and pur - ple, Scarlet, blue, and lil - y white, Tas - sels from the sil - ver birch - es And the tu - lips gay and bright. Tas - sels from the sil - ver birches And the tu - lips gay and bright.

3. Swords no more are bright - ly flashing, Foes no more our land mo - lest; Slumb'ring in the green - clad val - ley, Low and peace - ful is their rest. Earth to them was full of promise, Home and friends and life were dear, But when loud the war - cry ech - oed; Quick the war - cry echoed, Quick the answer, "We are here."

4. Swift - ly now the years are roll - ing, While the hon - or and the fame Of the val - iant brave in - creases, And more dear each no - ble name. Bring the flow'rs the grave to garland, Let the sweetest mu - sic rise, Let the stars and stripes be wav - ing, O'er their gen'rous sac - ri - fice. Let the stars and stripes be waving O'er their gen'rous sac - ri - fice.

CHARM OF VOICE.—Amidst the gay life, the beautiful forms, the brilliant colors of an Athenian multitude, and an Athenian street, the repulsive features, the unwieldy figure, the naked feet, the rough threadbare attire of the philosopher Socrates must have excited every sentiment of astonishment and ridicule which strong contrast can produce. It was (so his disciples described it) as if one of the marble satyrs, which sat in grotesque attitudes with pipe or flute in the sculptors' shops of Athens, had left his seat of stone and walked into the plane-tree avenue or the gymnastic colonnade. ·Gradually the crowd gathered round him. At first he spoke of those plying their trades about him; and they shouted with laughter as he poured forth his homely jokes. But soon the magic charm of his voice made itself felt. The peculiar sweetness of its tone had an effect which even the thunder of Pericles failed to produce. The laughter ceased—the crowd thickened—the gay youth, whom nothing else could tame, stood transfixed and awestruck in his presence—there was a solemn thrill in his words, such as his hearers could compare to nothing but the mysterious sensation produced by the clash of drum and cymbal in the worship of the great mother of the gods: the head swam—the heart leaped at the sound—tears rushed from their eyes, and they felt that, unless they tore themselves speedily away from that fascinated circle, they should ere long sit down at his feet and grow old in listening to the marvelous music of this second Marsyas.—*Athenæum.*

FADING, STILL FADING.

PORTUGUESE.

1. Fad-ing, still fad-ing, the last beam is shi-ning, Fa-ther in heav-en! the day is de-clin-ing, Safe-ty and in-no-cence fly with the light, Temp-ta-tion and dan-ger walk forth with the night: From the fall of the shade till the morning-bells chime, Shield me from danger, save me from crime. Fa-ther, have mer-cy, Fa-ther, have mer-cy, Fa-ther, have mer-cy, through Jesus Christ our Lord.

2. Fa-ther in heav-en! oh, hear when we call! Hear, for Christ's sake, who is Sav-iour of all; Fee-ble and faint-ing we trust in Thy might, In doubting and dark-ness Thy love be our light; Let us sleep on Thy breast while the night ta-per burns, Wake in Thy arms when morn-ing re-turns. Fa-ther, have mer-cy, Fa-ther, have mer-cy, Fa-ther, have mer-cy, through Jesus Christ our Lord. A-men.

A LIFE ON THE OCEAN WAVE.

Epes Sargent.
Henry Russell.

1. A life on the o-cean wave, A home on the roll-ing deep, Where the scattered waters
2. Once more on the deck I stand Of my own swift-gliding craft, Set sail! fare-well to the
3. The land is no longer in view, The clouds have begun to frown, But with a stout vessel and

rave, And the winds their rev-els keep! Like an ea-gle caged, I pine On this
land, The gale fol-lows far a-baft: We shoot thro' the sparkling foam, Like an
crew, We'll say, let the storm come down! And the song of our heart shall be, While the

dull, unchanging shore; Oh, give me the flashing brine, The spray and the tempest roar! A
o-cean bird set free; Like the o-cean bird, our home We'll find far out on the sea! A
winds and the waters rave, A life on the heaving sea, A home on the bounding wave! A

life on the o-cean wave, A home on the roll-ing deep! Where the scattered wa-ters

rave; And the winds their rev-els keep! The winds, the winds, the

winds their revels keep, the winds, the winds, the winds their revels keep.

* The part after asterisk, frequently omitted, is sung after each verse, after last verse, or not at all, as preferred.

AUTUMN LEAVES.

Andante affettuoso. CHARLES DICKENS.

1. Au-tumn leaves, autumn leaves Lie strewn around me here; Autumn leaves, autumn leaves, How
2. Withered leaves, withered leaves, That fly be-fore the gale; Withered leaves, withered leaves, To

sad, how cold, how drear! How like the hopes of childhood's day, Thick-clust'ring on the bough; How
tell a mournful tale Of love once true, and friends once kind, And happy moments fled, Dis -

like those hopes is their decay, How faded are they now! Au-tumn leaves, autumn leaves Lie
pelled by every breath of wind, For - got-ten, changed, or dead. Au-tumn leaves, autumn leaves Lie

strewn a-round me here; Au-tumn leaves, autumn leaves, How sad, how cold, how drear!

BIRDIE SWEET.

Allegretto. cres. CHILDHOOD SONGS.

1. Birdie sweet, birdie sweet, Where may you be going? From the North, hasten South, Autumn winds are
2. Birdie sweet, birdie sweet, When you are returning, Fly to me, let me see What new songs you're learning.

[blowing.

cres.

Haste along, haste along, Soon 'twill be cold weather, Should you stay you may be Frozen limb and feather.
Come again, come again, Soon 'twill be spring weather, Chirp for me songs so free, Bird of golden feather.

There is a common but also a very erroneous impression that only a favored few can learn music. In the schools of New Haven, "two hundred and forty-eight children out of six thousand were found unable to sing the scale, and one hundred and forty of these belonged to the primary grades;" that is, out of this multitude, only one hundred and eight above the primary grade could not sing. The superintendent says: "A systematic course of training the voices of the little ones in the primary rooms has been commenced. Thus far the experiment has been a complete success. Children from five to eight years of age readily sing the scale, both singly and in concert, and read from the blackboard notes on the staff by numerals and syllables with as little hesitation as they call the letters and words of their reading lessons." In the Hancock School, of Boston, of about one thousand girls, less than a dozen were unfitted from all causes for attaining to a fair degree of success in singing. The U. S. Commissioner of Education, when visiting the schools at New Haven, was surprised and gratified at hearing children in the primary schools sing at sight exercises marked on the blackboard by the teacher: "The exercises are placed on the blackboard in the presence of the scholars, and they are required to sing them once through without the aid of teacher or instrument, and are marked accordingly." In primary schools, gymnastic exercises often accompany the singing. When children are trained to erect posture, and the right use of the vocal organs, speaking, reading, and singing are most invigorating exercises; expanding the chest, promoting deep breathing, quickening the circulation, and arousing both the physical and mental energies.

BABY BYE, HERE'S A FLY.

THEODORE TILTON.
G. B. LOOMIS.

1. Ba - by bye, here's a fly, We will watch him, you and I. How he
2. Spots of red dot his head; Rain-bows on his wings are spread! That small

crawls up the walls, Yet he nev - er falls! I be-lieve, with those six legs,
speck is his neck, See him nod and beck! I can show you, if you choose,

You and I could walk on eggs! There he goes, on his toes, Tick-ling ba - by's nose.
Where to look to find his shoes; Three small pairs, made of hairs, These he always wears.

Black and brown is his gown,
He can wear it upside down!
It is laced round his waist,
I admire his taste!
Pretty as his clothes are made,
He will spoil them, I'm afraid,
If to-night he gets sight
Of the candle-light.

In the sun webs are spun,
What if he gets into one?
When it rains he complains
On the window panes.
Tongues to talk have you and I,
God has given the little fly
No such things; so he sings
With his buzzing wings.

He can eat bread and meat,
See his mouth between his feet!
On his back is a sack
Like a peddler's pack.
Does the baby understand?
Then the fly shall kiss her hand;
Put a crumb on her thumb,
May be he will come.

Round and round on the ground,
On the ceiling he is found;
Catch him? No. Let him go.
Never hurt him so!
Now you see his wings of silk
Drabbled in the Baby's milk;
Fie! oh fie! foolish fly!
How will you get dry?

All wet flies twist their thighs;
So they wipe their head and eyes,
Cats, you know, wash just so;
Then their whiskers grow!
Flies have hair too small to comb;
Flies go all bareheaded home;
But the gnat wears a hat:
Do you laugh at that?

Flies can see more than we,
So how bright their eyes must be!
Little fly, mind your eye,
Spiders are near by.
For a secret I can tell,
Spiders will not treat you well;
Haste away, do not stay,
Little fly, good day!

AWAY WITH MELANCHOLY.

W. MOZART.

1. A-- way with mel-an-chol-y! Nor dole-ful changes ring On life and human
2. Then what's the use of sighing, While time is on the wing; Can we prevent his
3. The rose will bloom re - fuse If plucked not in the spring; Life soon its fragrance

fol - ly, But mer-ri-ly, mer-ri-ly sing Fa la. Come on, ye ro - sy hours, Gay,
fly - ing? We'll merri-ly, mer-ri-ly sing Fa la. If griefs, like A-pril showers, A
lose, Then merri-ly, mer-ri-ly sing Fa la. Come then, ye ro - sy hours, Gay,

smiling moments bring; We'll strew the way with flowers, And merri-ly, merri-ly sing Fa la.
moment's sadness bring, Joy soon succeeds like flowers, Then cheerily, cheeri-ly sing Fa la.
smiling moments l ring; We'll strew the way with flowers, And merri-ly, merri-ly sing Fa la.

PRETTY PEAR TREE.

FINE.

1. Out in a beau-ti-ful field, There stands a pretty pear tree, Pretty pear tree with leaves.

1st Voice or Semi-Chorus.　　2nd Voice or Semi-Chorus.　　Chorus.　D.C.

What is there on that tree? A ve-ry pret-ty branch. { Branch on the tree, Tree in the ground. }

2. What is there on the branch?
　　　　A very pretty bough.
Cho. Bough on the branch,
　　Branch on the tree,
　　Tree in the ground. Out in, &c.
3. What is there on the bough?
　　　　A very pretty nest.
Cho. Nest on the bough,
　　Bough on the branch,
　　Branch on the tree,
　　Tree in the ground. Out in, &c.
4. What is there in the nest?
　　　　A very pretty egg.

Cho. Egg in the nest,
　　Nest on the bough,
　　Bough on the branch,
　　Branch on the tree,
　　Tree in the ground. Out in, &c.

5. What is there in the egg?
　　　　A very pretty bird.
Cho. Bird in the egg,
　　Egg in the nest,
　　Nest on the bough,
　　Bough on the branch,
　　Branch on the tree,
　　Tree in the ground. Out in, &c.

STAR-SPANGLED BANNER.—This beautiful and patriotic national song was composed by Francis Scott Key, of Baltimore, at the time of the bombardment of Fort McHenry, in 1814, when that stronghold was successfully defended from the attack of the British fleet. "The scene which he describes," says Chief Justice Taney, "and the warm spirit of patriotism which breathes in the song, were not the offspring of mere fancy or poetic imagination. He tells us what he actually saw, what he felt while witnessing the conflict, and what he felt when the battle was over and the victory won by his countrymen. Every word came warm from his heart, and for that reason, even more than from its poetical merit, it never fails to find a response in the hearts of those who hear it." By authority of President Madison, Mr. Key had gone to the British fleet under a flag of truce to secure the release of his friend, Dr. Beanes, who had been captured by the enemy and was detained on board the flagship, on the charge of violating his parole. He met General Ross and Admirals Cockburn and Cochrane, and with difficulty secured from them a promise of the gentleman's release, but was at the same time informed that they would not be permitted to leave the fleet until after the proposed attack on Fort McHenry, which the admiral boasted he would carry in a few hours. The ship on which himself, his friend and the commissioner who accompanied the flag of truce, were detained, came up the bay and was anchored at the mouth of the Patapsco, within full view of Fort McHenry. They watched the flag of the fort through the entire day with an

THE MILLER OF THE DEE.

CHAS. MACKAY.

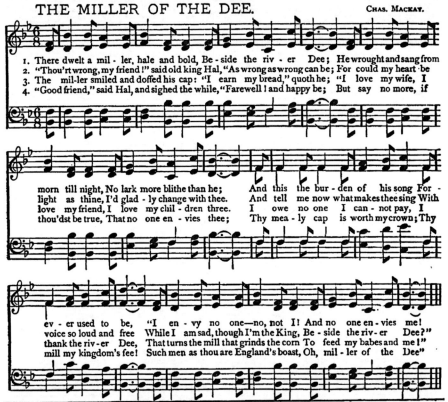

1. There dwelt a mil - ler, hale and bold, Be - side the riv - er Dee; He wrought and sang from morn till night, No lark more blithe than he; And this the bur - den of his song For ev - er used to be, "I en - vy no one—no, not I! And no one en - vies me!

2. "Thou'rt wrong, my friend!" said old king Hal, "As wrong as wrong can be; For could my heart be light as thine, I'd glad - ly change with thee. And tell me now what makes thee sing With voice so loud and free While I am sad, though I'm the King, Be - side the riv - er Dee?"

3. The mil - ler smiled and doffed his cap: "I earn my bread," quoth he; "I love my wife, I love my friend, I love my chil - dren three. I owe no one I can - not pay, I thank the riv - er Dee, That turns the mill that grinds the corn To feed my babes and me!"

4. "Good friend," said Hal, and sighed the while, "Farewell! and happy be; But say no more, if thou'dst be true, That no one en - vies thee; Thy mea - ly cap is worth my crown; Thy mill my kingdom's fee! Such men as thou are England's boast, Oh, mil - ler of the Dee"

anxiety that can better be felt than described, until night prevented them from seeing it. During the night they remained on deck, noting every shell from the moment it was fired until it fell. While the bombardment continued, it was evidence that the fort had not surrendered, but it suddenly ceased some time before day, and, as they had no communication with any of the enemy's ships, they did not know whether the fort had surrendered or the attack been abandoned. They paced the deck for the rest of the night in painful suspense, watching with intense anxiety for the return of the day. As soon as it dawned, their glasses were turned to the fort, and, with a thrill of delight, they saw that "our flag was still there!" The song was begun on the deck of the vessel, in the fervor of the moment when he saw the enemy hastily retreating to their ships, and looked upon the proud flag he had watched for so anxiously as the morning opened. He had written, on the back of a letter, some lines, or brief notes that would aid him in recalling them, and for some of the lines as he proceeded he had to rely on his memory. He finished it in the boat on his way to the shore, and wrote it out as it now stands immediately upon reaching Baltimore. In an hour after it was placed in the hands of the printer, it was on the streets hailed with enthusiasm, and at once took its place as a national song. The music of the Star Spangled Banner, to which it was at once adapted, is an old French air, long known in England as "Anacreon," and afterwards in America as "Adams and Liberty." Mr. Key died in 1846. At San Francisco, a monument costing $150,000 has been erected to his memory.

STAR-SPANGLED BANNER.

FRANCIS SCOTT KEY. 1814.

Solo or Quartette.

1. Oh, say, can you see, by the dawn's early light, What so proudly we hail'd at the
2. On the shore dim-ly seen thro' the mists of the deep, Where the foe's haughty host in dread
3. And where is that band who so vauntingly swore, That the hav-oc of war and the
4. Oh, thus be it ev-er when freemen shall stand Be-tween their loved home and wild

twilight's last gleaming, Whose broad stripes and bright stars, thro' the perilous fight, O'er the ramparts we
si - lence re - pos-es, What is that which the breeze, o'er the tower-ing steep, As it fit - ful-ly
bat - tle's con-fu-sion, A . . home and a country should leave us no more? Their blood has wash'd
war's des - o-lation; Blest with vict'ry and peace, may the heav'n-rescued land Praise the pow'r that hath

watch'd, were so gal-lant-ly streaming? And the rockets' red glare, the bombs bursting in air, Gave
blows, half conceals, half dis- clos- es? Now it catches the gleam of the morning's first beam, In full
out their foul footsteps' pol- lu-tion. No re-fuge could save the hireling and slave From the
made and preserv'd us a nation! Then conquer we must, when our cause it is just, And

Chorus. *ff*

proof thro' the night that our flag was still there. Oh, . . say, does that star- span - gled
glo - ry re - flect - ed, now shines on the stream: 'Tis the star-span - gled ban - ner: oh,
ter - ror of flight or the gloom of the grave: And the star-span - gled ban - ner in
this be our mot - to: "In God is our trust!" And the star-span - gled ban - ner in

cres. *ff*

ban - ner yet wave
long may it wave
tri - umph doth wave   } O'er the land of the free and the home of the brave.
tri umph shall wave

AN extraordinary feature of the musical world of the present day is the enormous orchestras which can be produced on special occasions. A chorus of several thousand voices supported by hundreds of instruments may now be heard, rendering the immortal compositions of the greatest masters of the divine art, in the People's Palace at Sydenham and elsewhere. These orchestras are chiefly selected from the ranks of the people, of whom the artisan is the chief element. The reduction in the cost of instruments and the adoption of what may be called the joint-stock principle are tending still further to enlarge the boundaries of the practical musical world. At any time and for any purpose it is now easy to secure a band and chorus sufficient in numbers and executive power to render in an efficient and powerful manner, the glorious productions of Beethoven, Mozart, Handel, and other great masters. On all these occasions, the violin bears a most important part. It is the leading instrument in these great performances, as it is, after the voice, the most powerful medium of expression in solo. It is also the people's instrument. The labors of many eminent violin-makers, following in the steps of the great masters, have so immensely improved the art, that a good instrument may now be possessed by any one. And it may be said that with its improvement has arisen also the extensive and wide-spread practice of music generally. An ear accustomed to the fine tone of a good violin will not now tolerate a bad piano forte.

OUR FLAG O'ER US WAVING.

G. VERDI.
Air—Anvil Chorus "Il Trovatore."

Spirited.

1. See   the proud banner of Lib-er-ty streaming, Its bright starry folds o'er us ra-diant-ly
2. Bright starry ban-ner! thy fame we will cher-ish, And shield thee and save thee, or no-bly   we'll

gleaming; Hear the loud trumpet its war note re-peating, The roll of the drums where brave armies are
per-ish: Proudly our ea-gles are floating a-bove thee, Columbia, for ev-er we bless thee and

meet-ing, brave armies meeting,   are meeting!   On, on to glo-ry's field, our proud flag o'er us
love thee! bless thee and love thee, and love thee!   On, on to vic-to-ry! our country now and

wav-ing! Marching to conquest, ev-'ry dan-ger no-bly brav-ing. March, march, march on to
ev-er,   Palsied the trai-tor hand our Union that would sever: Hail! hail! hail!   land of

tutta forza.

vic-to-ry! March on! March on! on! March on! March on! on! March on to victo-ry!
Lib-er-ty!   Hail! noble land, hail! Hail! noble land, hail! Hail! land of lib-er-ty!

HAIL COLUMBIA.

F. HOPKINSON, 1798.
Tune—"PRESIDENT'S MARCH."

With energy.

1. Hail, Co-lum-bia ! hap-py land, Hail, ye heroes, heav'n-born band, Who fought and bled in
2. Immortal patriots, rise once more, Defend your rights, defend your shore ! Let no rude foe, with
3. Behold the chief who now commands, Once more to serve his country stands The rock on which the

freedom's cause, Who fought and bled in freedom's cause, And when the storm of war was gone En-
im - pious hand, Let no rude foe, with impious hand, Invade the shrine where sacred lies Of
storm will beat, The rock on which the storm will beat, But armed in vir-tue. firm and true, His

joy'd the peace your val-or won. Let in - de-pendence be our boast, Ev - er mind-ful
toil and blood, the well-earn'd prize. While off'ring peace, sincere and just, In Heav'n we place a
hopes are fixed on Heav'n and you. When hope was sinking in dismay, When glooms obscur'd Co-

what it cost; Ev - er grate-ful for the prize, Let its al-tar reach the skies.
man-ly trust, That truth and jus-tice will pre-vail, And ev' - ry scheme of bondage fail.
lumbia's day, His stead-y mind, from chan-ges free, Resolved on death or lib - er - ty.

Chorus.

Firm, u - ni - ted, let us be, Ral - ly - ing round our lib - er - ty,

As a band of broth-ers join'd, Peace and safe-ty we shall find.

It is stated that the late Dr. Ray Palmer originally wrote his most famous hymn on a leaf of a pocket diary. There it remained for a year and a half. Its author then met Dr. Mason on the street in Boston. The existence of the hymn was discovered by Dr. Mason's inquiry for new materials for a hymn and tune book which he was then compiling. He took the hymn and in a few days returned it with the tune "Olivet," which he had composed for it. His sagacious judgment of it was expressed in saying to the author, "You may live many years and do many good things. But I think you will be best known to posterity as the author of 'My faith looks up to Thee.'" It was one of those fleeting conjunctions of circumstances and of men by which God often sets forward to their fulfillment his eternal decrees. The doctor of music and the future doctor of theology are thrown together in the roaring thoroughfare of commerce for a brief interview, scarcely more than enough for a morning salutation, and the blessed result to mankind is the publication of a Christian lyric which is to be sung around the world.

Music stands nearest to divinity. I would not give the little I know for all the treasures of the world! It is my shield in combat and adversity, my friend and companion in moments of joy, my comforter and refuge in those of despondency and solitude.—*Martin Luther.*

DEAREST NATIVE LAND.

H. PROCH.

1. Gold-en stars for me are shin-ing Here by zephyrs fanned; But for thee, dear land, I'm
2. On a for-eign shore I languish Weary and a-lone, Where no friend can soothe mine

pin-ing, Dear-est native land! Comes the tho't of those who love me In my na-tive home,
anguish, None can heed its moan! Oh, the deep, the ardent longings, In my breast that burn,

What hath power alike to move me, Now a-far I roam? What hath power a-
As my thoughts with heart o'erflowing, Back to thee re-turn,

like to move me, Now a-far I roam? Golden stars for me are shin-ing,
heart o'er-flow-ing, Back to thee re-turn. Golden stars for me are shin-ing,

Here by zephyrs fanned, But for thee, dear land, I'm pining, Dear-est na-tive land.

COLUMBIA, GEM OF THE OCEAN.

D. T. Shaw.

Spirited.

1. Oh, Co-lum-bia, the gem of the ocean, The home of the brave and the free, The
2. When war wing'd its wide des-o-la-tion, And threaten'd the land to de-form, The
3. The star-spangled banner bring hither, O'er Columbia's true sons let it wave; May the

shrine of each pa-triot's de-vo-tion, A world of-fers hom-age to thee, Thy
ark then of freedom's foun-da-tion, Co-lum-bia, rode safe thro' the storm: With the
wreaths they have won nev-er wither, Nor its stars cease to shine on the brave. May the

mandates make he-roes as-sem-ble, When Lib-er-ty's form stands in view; Thy
garlands of vic-t'ry a-round her, When so proudly she bore her brave crew, With her
ser-vice u-ni-ted ne'er sev-er, But hold to their colors so true; The

banners make tyr-an-ny tremble, When borne by the red, white and blue, When
flag proudly float-ing be-fore her, The boast of the red, white and blue, The
ar-my and na-vy for-ev-er, Three cheers for the red, white and blue, Three

borne by the red, white and blue, When borne by the red, white and blue, Thy
boast of the red, white and blue, The boast of the red, white and blue, With her
cheers for the red, white and blue, Three cheers for the red, white and blue, The

banners make tyr-an-ny tremble, When borne by the red, white and blue.
flag proud-ly floating be-fore her, The boast of the red, white and blue.
ar-my and na-vy for-ev-er, Three cheers for the red, white and blue.

EVENINGS AT HOME.—There is nothing that contributes more to the pleasure of evenings at home than music in families. To cultivate a love of music among children, creates and fosters a refined sentiment that is not forgotten when they arrive at maturity. Music engenders and promotes good feeling. The blending of the voices of parents and children in song strengthens the ties that bind them together, and the love that centres about the home fireside. It renders home attractive, interesting, and beautiful; and in every home circle where it is tolerated and cultivated, there will be found a greater freedom from all those discords and inharmonious contentions, that render so many parents miserable and their children anxious to find a more congenial atmosphere elsewhere. Music is not an unmanly or effeminate way of spending one's time, as many unrefined parents aver when they proscribe even the coveted fiddle their sons enjoy scraping in the attic. Every home should have a musical instrument in it that can be used as an accompaniment to the family voices. It will give employment and amusement to the children in their otherwise unoccupied hours. It will keep them at home, and very often out of bad influences elsewhere.

THE DEAREST SPOT.

W. T. WRIGHTON.

The dear-est spot of earth to me, Is home, sweet home, The fairy land I've longed to see, Is
I've taught my heart the way to prize My home, sweet home, I've learned to look with lover's eyes, On

home, sweet home. There how charmed the : ase of hearing, There where hearts are so endearing,
home, sweet home. There where vows are truly plighted, There where hearts are so u - ni - ted,

All the world is not so cheer - ing, As home, sweet home.   The dear - est spot of
All the world be sides I've slighted, For home, sweet home,   The dear - est spot of

earth to me, is home, sweet home; The fair - y land I've longed to see, Is home, sweet home.

What an auxiliary is music to the teacher, brightening up dull faces, inspiring cheerfulness that becomes an impetus to labor, softening and soothing nervous irritation often so difficult to contend against, which has been excited by the crowded school impatient under the restraint and monotony of position and occupation! Think, too, of each child frequently going home at night, like the honey-laden bee, with a gay little song to charm the work-wearied father's heart; a lullaby which, sung over the baby's cradle, shall soothe the mother's spirit while it closes baby's eyes; holy hymns that shall make the very roof tree a better shelter for the hearts beneath it. Thus the influence of the public school goes out blessing and blest; and we gather sheaves of joy to hold close to humble hearts, thankful that we may be permitted to aid in making the world happier and better, as well as wiser; that we, too, amid the silent, unseen influences, are serving our country and our God, and at the same time learning the useful lesson of how to labor and to wait.

THE wonder of the English skylark's song is its copiousness and sustained strength. There is no theme, no beginning or end, like most of the best bird-songs, and a perfect swarm of notes pouring out like bees from a hive. We have many more melodious songsters; the bobolink in the meadows, the vesper sparrow in the pastures, the purple finch in the groves, the winter wren, or any of the thrushes in the woods, or the wood wagtail. But our birds all stop where the English skylark has only just begun. Away he goes on quivering wing, inflating his throat fuller and fuller, mounting and mounting, and turning to all points of the compass as if to embrace the whole landscape in his song, the notes still raining upon you as distinct as ever, after you have left him far behind. The English skylark also sings long after all the other birds are silent—as if he had perpetual spring in his heart.—*John Burroughs.*

IT would, of course, be more amusing to recite connected than unconnected words, as it is more amusing to sing passages than single notes; but as no singing voice ever yet was formed by the exclusive utterance of anything that could be called music, so no speaking voice will ever be formed by the exclusive utterance of anything that can be spoken of as literature.—*Hullah.*

FISHERMEN'S CHORUS.

D. F. E. AUBER.
From "MASANIELLO."

1. Be - hold how brightly breaks the morning, Tho' bleak our lot . . our hearts are warm,
2. A - way, no cloud is lowering o'er us, Free - ly now . . . we'll stem the wave,

To toil inured, all dan - ger scorn - ing, We'll hail the breeze or
Hoist, hoist all sail, while full be - fore us, Hope's beacon shines to

brave the storm, Put off, put off, our course we know; Take heed, whisper low; Look out and spread your
cheer the brave, Put off, put off, our course we know; Take heed, whisper low; Look out and spread your

net with care; Take heed, whisper low; The prey we seek we'll soon, we'll soon en - snare; The

prey we seek we'll soon, we'll soon ensnare; Take heed, whisper low; take heed, whisper low.

FORM.—Nothing is more common than to hear it said that Mozart is a great master of form; that Beethoven's form is at times obscure, and so forth. Of course what is meant is, that in the arrangement and development of the musical phrases, there is a greater or less fitness of proportion, producing an effect of unity or incoherence as the case may be. But the idea of musical form can be made intelligible to any one who will take the trouble to glance at so simple a melody as " The Blue Bells of Scotland." That air consists of four phrases, each of which is divided into an elation and depression. The first two phrases are repeated; the third and fourth occur in the middle; and the first two recur at the close. Thus music appears visibly to the eye to possess all the essential properties of emotion. May we not, therefore, say that the secret of its power consists in this, that it alone is capable of giving to the simplest, the subtlest, and the most complex emotions alike, that full and satisfactory expression through sound, which hitherto it has been found impossible to give to many of them in any other way ?—*Music and Morals.*

CHRISTMAS TIME IS COME AGAIN.

Not too Slow.   CHRISTMAS CAROL.

1. Christ - mas time is come a - gain, Christ-mas plea - sures bring-ing;
2. An - gels sang, let men re - ply, And chil-dren join their voi - ces;

Let us join our voic - es now, And Christmas songs be singing. Years a - go, one
Raise the cho - rus loud and high, Earth and heav'n re - joic - es. When we reach that

star - ry night, Thus the sto - ry's giv - en, An - gel bands o'er Bethlehem's plains,
hap-py place Joy - ous prais - es bringing, Then, be - fore our Father's face,

Chorus.

Sang the songs of heaven. } Glo - ry be to God on high! Peace, goodwill to
We shall still be singing. }

mor-tals! Christ, the Lord, is born to-night, Heav'n throws wide its por - tals.

CHRIST IS BORN IN BETHLEHEM.

CHRISTMAS ANTHEM.

1 Lo! descending, the heavens rending, Messengers from God to men, Angels winging, tidings
2. Dearest Saviour, grant Thy fa-vor, While in these Thy courts we stay, Thy rich blessing on us

bringing, Christ is born in Beth-le-hem; Come with gladness, and ban-ish sadness, Children,
rest-ing, On this hap-py fes-tive day, Bells are ring-ing, and birds are sing-ing, Woods and

sweet-ly tune your voices, Sing a-loud while Heaven rejoices; Hal-le-lu-jah! Hal-le-
fields their trib-ute bringing, Back the hills the ech-o flinging; Let our voi-ces, swell the

lu-jah! "Peace on earth, good will to men." Lift aloud a loft-y strain, God is reconciled to man:
chorus In a grateful song of praise; Joyful come before Him now, Humbly in His presence bow,

Glo-ry to our Sav-iour King, Heaven and earth with glory ring. Praise Him, praise Him, the
Now to Him our trib-ute bring, Lord of lords and King of Kings. Praise Him, praise Him, ye

Lord Je-ho-vah praise. Praise Him, praise Him, the Lord Jehovah praise. Hosanna! Ho-san-na!
grateful children, praise. Praise Him, praise Him, ye grateful children, praise. Hosan-na! Hosanna!

Two easily distinguishable mental influences seem to belong to music, according as it is heard by those of musical sensibility who really appreciate it, or by others who are unable to do so. To the former it opens a book of poetry which they follow, word for word, after the performer, as if he read it to them; thinking the thoughts of the composer in succession with scarcely greater uncertainty or vagueness than if they were expressed in verbal language of a slightly mystical description. To the latter the book is closed; but though the listener's own thoughts unroll themselves uninterrupted by the composer's ideas, they are very considerably colored thereby. "I delight in music," said once a great man of science; "I am always able to think out my work better while it is going on." As a matter of fact he resumed at the moment a disquisition concerning the date of the glacial period at the precise point at which it had been interrupted by the performance of a symphony of Beethoven, having evidently mastered in the interval an intricate astronomical knot. To ordinary mortals, with similar deficiency of musical sense, harmonious sound seems to spread a halo like that of light, causing every subject of contemplation to

LET ERIN REMEMBER.

T. MOORE.
Arranged by BALFE.

1. Let E-rin remember the days of old, Ere her faithless sons be-tray'd her; When
2. On Lough Neagh's bank as the fisherman strays, When the clear cold eve's declin-ing, He

Ma-lachi wore the col-lar of gold, Which he won from the proud in-va-der; When her
sees the round towers of oth-er days, In the wave be-neath him shin-ing, Thus shall

kings, with standard of green unfurl'd, Led the Red-Branch Knights to dan-ger; Ere the
mem'ry oft-en, in dreams sublime, Catch a glimpse of the days that are o-ver; Thus,

em'rald gem of the west-ern world Was set in the brow of a stran-ger.
sighing, look thro' the waves of time, For the long-faded glo-ries they cov-er.

seem glorified as a landscape appears in a dewy sunrise. Old memories rise to the mind and seem infinitely more affecting than at other times; still living affections grow doubly tender; new beauties appear in the picture or the landscape before our eyes, and passages of remembered prose or poetry float through our brain in majestic cadence. In a word, the sense of the beautiful, the tender, the sublime, is vividly aroused, and the atmosphere of familiarity and commonplace, wherewith the real beauty and sweetness of life are too often veiled, is lifted for the hour. As in a camera-obscura, or mirror, the very trees and grass which we had looked on a thousand times are seen to possess unexpected loveliness. But all this can only happen to the non-musical soul when the harmony to which it listens is really harmonious, and when it comes at an appropriate time, when the surrounding conditions permit and incline the man to surrender himself to its influences; in a word, when nothing else demands his attention.

An excellent mother, who had learned the lesson of life, writing to her son on the birth of his eldest child, says: "Give him education, that his life may be useful; teach him religion that his death may be happy."

OH! GLADLY NOW WE HAIL THEE.

V. BELLINI.

1. Oh! glad - ly now we hail thee, Dear friends of ear - ly time!
2. The trees a - round our dwell - ing, Where ear - ly friendships met,

The same old love we cher - ish As in our ear - ly prime;
The riv - er and the fount - ain, Our hearts can ne'er for - get:

As na - ture nev - er chang - es Our hearts are still the same,
There hearts and homes were lov - ing, And round the hearth at even,

And still on friend-ship's al - tar As bright-ly burns love's flame.
Our hum - ble prayers as - cend - ed On wings of love to heaven.

Oh! glad - ly now we hail thee, Dear friends of ear - ly time!

The same old love we cher - ish As in our ear - ly prime,

Stephen Collins Foster was born in Allegheny, Pennsylvania, on the 4th of July, 1826. He was the youngest child of William B. Foster, a merchant of Pittsburg, and mayor of his native city, member of the State legislature, and a Federal officer under President Buchanan. His sister was the wife of Rev. Edward Y. Buchanan, a brother of the President. The compiler of the Franklin Square Collection recalls his keen enjoyment of the organ of the Episcopal church at Paradise, a country parish in Lancaster county, Pennsyl-vania, of which Mr. Buchanan was for many years the rector. Mrs. Buchanan always played at the Sunday morning service, and since we have learned to enjoy the songs of her brother, none of which had then been written, we seem to understand more the spell under which the music of this gentle, gifted lady brought and held us as a child. She too had inherited "a double portion of the divine gift of music." For the facts in the sketch here given we are indebted to an article by Mr. Robert P. Nevin, of Pittsburg, who says: The

MASSA'S IN THE COLD GROUND.

STEPHEN C. FOSTER.

Rather Slow, with Feeling.

1. Round de meadows am a-ring-ing, De darkies' mournful song, While de mocking-bird am singing,
2. When de autumn leaves are fall-ing, When de days are cold, 'Twas hard to hear old massa call-ing,
3. Mas-sa make de darkeys love him, Cayse he was so kind, Now, dey sadly weep a-bove him,

Hap-py as de day am long. Where de i-vy am a-creep-ing O'er the grassy mound,
Cayse he was so weak and old. Now de orange trees am blooming On de sand-y shore,
Mourning cayse he leave dem behind. I can-not work before to-morrow, Cayse de tear-drop flow, I

Chorus, 1st and 2nd Voices 1st time.

Dare old massa am a-sleep-ing, Sleeping in de cold, cold ground.
Now de summer days am com-ing, Massa nebber calls no more. } Down in de corn-field,
try to drive away my sor-row, Pickin' on de old ban-jo.

Hear dat mournful sound: All de darkies am a-weep-ing, Massa's in de cold, cold ground.

evidences of a musical capacity of no common order were apparent in Stephen at an early period. Going into a shop one day, when about seven years old, he picked up a flageolet, the first he had ever seen, and comprehending, after an experiment or two, the order of the scale on the instrument, was able in a few minutes, uninstructed, to play any of the simple tunes within the octave with which he was acquainted. He was a boy of delicate constitution, not addicted to the active sports or any of the more vigorous habits of boys. A recluse, owning and soliciting no guidance but that of his text-book, in the quiet of the woods, or, if that were inaccessible, the retirement of his chamber, he devoted himself to music. At the age of seventeen he went to Cincinnati into the office of his brother, discharging the duties of his place with faithfulness and ability. His spare hours were still devoted to his favorite pursuit, although his productions were chiefly preserved in manuscript, and kept for the private entertainment of his friends. At that time a Mr. Andrews, of Pittsburg, offered a silver cup for the best original negro song, Mr. Morrison Foster sent to his brother Stephen a copy of the advertisement announcing the fact, with a letter urging him to become a competitor for the prize. He finally yielded, and in due time forwarded a melody entitled, "Way down South, whar de Corn grows." When the eventful night came, the various pieces in competiton were rendered to the audience by Nelson Kneass to his own accompaniment on the piano. The audience expressed by their applause a decided preference for Stephen's melody; but the committee decided in favor of some one else. This experiment of Foster's served a profitable purpose, for it led him to a critical investigation of the school of music to which it belonged. This had been, and was yet, unquestionably popular. To what, then, was it indebted for its captivating points? It was to its truth to Nature in her simplest and most childlike mood. Settled as to

7 OH, BOYS, CARRY ME 'LONG.

Stephen C. Foster.

theory, Foster applied himself to its exemplification. The Presidential campaign of 1844 was distinguished by political song-singing. Clubs for that purpose were organized in all the cities and towns and hamlets. So enthusiastic became the popular feeling in this direction, that, when the November crisis was come and gone, these clubs lived on. Among them was one, composed of a half-dozen young men, Foster—home again, and a link once more in the circle of his intimates—at its head. One night he laid before them a song entitled "Louisiana Belle." It elicited unanimous applause, and in the course of a few nights the song was sung very widely in Pittsburg. Foster then brought to light his portfolio specimens, since universally known as "Uncle Ned" and "O Susanna!" The favor with which these latter were received far surpassed even that of "Louisiana Belle." Their fame spread far and wide, until from the drawing-rooms of

Cincinnati they were introduced into its concert halls, and there became known to W. C. Peters, who at once requested copies for publication. These were cheerfully furnished by the author. He did not look for remuneration. For " Uncle Ned," which appeared in 1847, he received none; "O Susanna!" soon followed, and "imagine my delight," he writes, "in receiving one hundred dollars in cash! Though this song was not successful," he continues; "yet the two fifty-dollar bills I received for it had the effect of starting me on my present vocation of song-writer." In pursuance of this decision, he set himself to work, and began to pour out his productions with astonishing rapidity. Out of the list, embracing about one hundred and fifty of his songs, the most flatteringly received among his negro melodies were those already enumerated, followed by "Nelly was a Lady," in 1849; "My Old Kentucky Home," and "Camptown Races," in 1850; "Old Folks at Home" in 1851; "Massa's in the Cold Ground," in 1852; "Oh, Boys, Carry me 'long," in

WILLIE, WE HAVE MISSED YOU.

STEPHEN C. FOSTER.

Moderato.

1. Oh! Wil-lie, is it you, dear, Safe, safe at home? They did not tell me true, dear; They
2. We've longed to see you night-ly, But this night of all; The fire was blazing bright-ly And
3. The days were sad without you, The nights long and drear; My dreams have been about you. Oh!

said you would not come, I heard you at the gate, And it made my heart rejoice; For I
lights were in the hall. The lit-tle ones were up 'Till 'twas ten o'clock and past, Then their
wel-come, Wil-lie dear! Last night I wept and watched By the moonlight's cheerless ray, 'Till I

knew that welcome footstep And that dear, fa-mil-iar voice, Making music on my ear In the
eyes began to twinkle, And they've gone to sleep at last; But they listened for your voice Till they
thought I heard your footstep, Then I wiped my tears a-way; But my heart grew sad again When I

lone-ly mid-night gloom: Oh! Wil-lie, we have missed you; Wel-come, wel-come home!
thought you'd never come;—Oh! Wil-lie, we have missed you; Wel-come, wel-come home!
found you had not come;—Oh! Wil-lie, we have missed you; Wel-come, wel-come home!

1853; "Hard Times come again no more," in 1854; "Old Black Joe," in 1860. In all these compositions Foster adheres scrupulously to his theory adopted at the outset. His verses are distinguished by a *naïveté* characteristic and appropriate, but consistent at the same time with common sense. Enough of the negro dialect is retained to preserve distinction, but not to offend. The sentiment is given in plain phrase, under homely illustration; but it is a sentiment nevertheless. The melodies are of twin birth, literally with the verses, for Foster thought in tune as he traced in rhyme, and traced in rhyme as he thought in tune. That he had struck upon the true way to the common heart, the successes attending his efforts surely demonstrate. His songs had an unparalled circulation. Artists of the highest distinction favored him with their friendship. Herz and Sivori, Ole Bull and Thalberg, were alike ready to approve his genius, and to testify that approval in the choice of his melodies as themes about which to weave their witcheries of embellishment. Complimentary letters from men of literary note poured in upon him; among others, one full of generous encouragement from Washington Irving, dearly prized and carefully treasured to the day of Foster's death. Similar missives reached him from across the seas—from strangers and from travellers in lands far remote; and he learned that, while "O Susanna," was the familiar song of the cottager of the Clyde, "Uncle Ned" was known to the dweller in tents among the Pyramids. Of his sentimental songs, "Maggie by my Side," "Jennie with the Light-brown Hair," "Willie, we have missed you," "Come where my love lies dreaming," and others, are among the leading favorites. The verses to most of these airs were all of his own composition. Indeed, he could seldom satisfy himself in his "settings" of the stanzas of others. The last three years of his life he passed in New York. During all that time his efforts, with perhaps one exception, were limited to the production of songs of a pensive character. He died after a brief illness, January 13th, 1864. His

7 OLD DOG TRAY.

STEPHEN C. FOSTER.

1. The morn of life is past, And ev-'ning comes at last, It brings me a dream of a
2. The forms I called my own, Have vanished one by one, The loved ones, the dear ones have
3. When thoughts recall the past, His eyes are on me cast; I know that he feels what my

once hap-py day, Of mer-ry forms I've seen Up-on the vil-lage green,
all passed a-way, Their hap-py smiles have flown, Their gen-tle voic-es gone; I've
break-ing heart would say: Although he can-not speak, I'll vain-ly, vain-ly seek, A

Chorus.

Sport-ing with my old dog Tray.
noth-ing left but old dog Tray.
bet-ter friend than old dog Tray.

Old dog Tray's ev-er faith-ful, Grief cannot drive him a-

way, He's gen-tle, he is kind; I'll nev-er, nev-er find A bet-ter friend than old dog Tray.

remains reached Pittsburg a few days later, and were conveyed to Trinity Church, where, on the day following, in the presence of a large assembly, appropriate and impressive ceremonies took place, the choral services being sustained by a company of his former friends and associates. His body was then carried to the Allegheny Cemetery, and, to the music of "Old Folks at Home," finally committed to the grave. Mr. Foster was below medium height, and of slight, well-proportioned frame. His shoulders were marked by a slight droop—the result of a habit of walking with his eyes upon the ground a pace or two in advance of his feet. He nearly always when he went out, which was not often, walked alone. Arrived at the street-crossings, he would frequently pause, raise himself, cast a glance at the surroundings, and if he saw an acquaintance nod to him in token of recognition, and then, relapsing into the old posture, resume his way. For his study he selected a room in the topmost story of his house, farthest removed from the street, and was careful to have the floor of the apartment and the avenues of approach to it thickly carpeted, to exclude as effectually as possible all noises, inside as well as outside of his own premises. The furniture of this room consisted of a chair, a lounge, a table, a music-rack, and a piano. From the sanctum so chosen, seldom opened to others, and never allowed upon any pretence to be disarranged, came his choicest compositions. If Mr. Foster's art embodied no higher idea than the vulgar notion of the negro as a man-monkey—then it might have proved a tolerable catch-penny affair, and commanded an admiration among the boys of various growths until its novelty wore off. But the art in his hands teemed with a nobler significance. It dealt, in its simplicity, with universal sympathies, and taught us all to feel with the slaves the lowly joys and sorrows it celebrated. May the time be far in the future ere the lips fail to move to its music, or sympathetic hearts to respond to its influence; and may we, who owe him so much, preserve gratefully the memory of the rare master, Stephen Collins Foster.

OLD FOLKS AT HOME.

STEPHEN C. FOSTER.

Con espressione.

1. 'Way down up-on de Sv-nee river, Far, far a-way, Dere's wha my heart is turning ev-er, Dere's wha de old folks stay. All up and down de whole crea-tion, Sad-ly I roam, Still longing for de old planta-tion, And for de old folks at home.

2. All roun' de lit-tle farm I wandered When I was young, Den ma-ny hap-py days I squander'd, Ma-ny de songs I sung. When I was playing with my brother, Hap-py was I, Oh! take me to my kind old mother, There let me live and die.

3. One lit-tle hut among de bushes, One that I love, Still sad-ly to my mem'ry rushes, No mat-ter where I rove. When will I see de bees a-humming, All roun' de comb? When will I hear de banjo tumming, Down in my good old home?

Chorus.

All de world is sad and drea-ry, Ev-'ry where I roam, Oh! darkies, how my heart grows wea-ry, Far from de old folks at home.

MY OLD KENTUCKY HOME.

Stephen C. Foster.

Rather slow.

1. The sun shines bright in the old Kentucky home, 'Tis summer, the darkies are gay; The
2. They hunt no more for the possum and the coon, On the meadow, the hill, and the shore, They
3. The head must bow and the back will have to bend, Wher - ev - er the darkey may go; A

corn top's ripe and the meadow's in the bloom, While the birds make music all the
sing no more by the glimmer of the moon, On the . . . . bench by the old cabin
few more days, and the trouble all will end In the . . . .

day. The young folks roll on the lit - tle cab - in floor, All
door. The day goes by like a shadow o'er the heart, With
field where the su - gar-canes grow; A few more days for to tote the wea - ry load, No

mer - ry, all happy and bright, By'm-by, hard times comes a knocking at the door, Then, my
sorrow where all was de - light; The time has come when the darkies have to part, Then, my
matter, 'twill never be light, A few more days till we tot - ter on the road, Then, my

Chorus.

old Kentucky home, good night! Weep no more, my la - dy, Oh! weep no more to-day! We will

sing one song for the old Kentucky home, For the old Kentucky home, far a - way.

Echo was a very beautiful nymph, fond of the woods and hills, where she devoted herself to woodland sports. She was a favorite of Diana, and attended her in the chase. But Echo had one failing; she was fond of talking, and, whether in chat or argument, would have the last word. Juno, having discovered that some deception had been practiced by Echo, passed sentence upon her in these words : "You shall forfeit the use of that tongue with which you have cheated me, except for the one purpose you are so fond of—reply. You shall still have the last word, but no power to speak first." This nymph saw Narcissus, a beautiful youth, as he pursued the chase upon the mountains. How she longed to address him in the softest accents, and win him to conversation, but it was not in her power. She waited with impatience for him to speak first, and had her answer ready. One day, the youth, being separated from his companions, shouted aloud, "Who's here?" Echo replied, "Here." Narcissus, looking around but seeing no one, called

OFT IN THE STILLY NIGHT.

STEVENSON.
MOORE'S MELODIES.

1. Oft in the still-y night, ere slum-ber's chain hath bound me,
2. When I re-mem-ber all the friends so link'd to-geth-er

D.C. Thus, in the still-y night, ere slum-ber's chain hath bound me,

Fond mem'-ry brings the light of oth-er days a-round me,—
I've seen a-round me fall, like leaves in win-try wea-ther,

Sad mem'-ry brings the light of oth-er days a-round me.

The smiles, the tears of childhood's years, the words of love then spok-en, The
I feel like one who treads a-lone some ban-quet hall de-sert-ed, Whose

eyes that shone, now dimm'd and gone, the cheer-ful hearts now bro-ken:
lights are fled, whose gar-lands dead, and all but him de-part-ed.

out, "Come." Echo answered, "Come." As no one came, Narcissus called again, "Why do you shun me?" Echo asked the same question. "Let us join one another," said the youth. The maid answered with all her heart in the same words, and hastened to the spot. He started back, exclaiming, "Hands off? I would rather die than you should have me." "Have me," said she, but it was all in vain. He left her, and she went to hide her blushes in the recesses of the woods. From that time forth she lived in caves and among mountain cliffs. Her form faded with grief, till, at last, all her flesh had shrunk away, her bones had changed into rocks, and there was nothing left of her but her voice. With that she is still ready to reply to any one who calls her, and always keeps up her old habit of having the last word.—*Age of Fable.*

There is something in the very shape of harps, as though they had been made by music.—*Bailey.*

It is well to remember, in connection with the symbolism of the organ, that only those elements of the faith and life of every church which can pass up into noble anthems, chants, and hymns, which can be set to music, are its worthy and enduring elements. You can not put proofs of the trinity or controversial supports of the unity of God, the arguments of Bishop Bull, or the arguments of Professor Norton, into hymns. You can not chant rubrics, and thirty-nine articles, and damnatory clauses of the Athanasian formula. But reverence for God, devout prostration before the law which "the Father" represents, love for the pity and sacrifice which "the Son" interprets, joy in the ever-present grace, and prayer for the quickening life, which "the Spirit" symbolizes, adoration of Infinite holiness, submission to Infinite sovereignty, grateful trust in Infinite love—sentiments in which Trinitarian and Unitarian, Calvinist and Arminian, Partialist and Universalist, come at once into fellowship—these fly to music for expression.—*Starr King.*

FOREVER AND FOREVER.

CHAS. C. CONVERSE.

1. A maid reclined beside a stream At fall of summer day, And half awake, and half a-dream, She watch'd the rip-ples play, She mark'd the wa-ters fall and heave, The deep'ning shadows throng, And heard, as darken'd down the eve, The riv-er's babbling song. And thus it sung with tink-ling tongue, That rip-pling, shad-'wy riv-er, "Youth's bright-est day will fade a-way, For-ev-er and for-ev-er."

2. The twilight past, the moon at last Rose broadly o'er the night; Each ripple gleams beneath her beams As, wrought in sil-ver bright, The heav-ing wa-ters glide a-long, The mingling with their voice, The nightingale now pours his song, And makes the shades rejoice. And thus he sung with tune-ful tongue, That bird be-side the riv-er, "When youth is gone, true love shines on, For-ev-er and for-ev-er."

DRIFT, MY BARK.

F. KÜCKEN.
W. J. WETMORE.

1. Drift, my bark, while stars are beaming In the cloudless evening sky;   Rock me while my love lies
D.C. bark, my bark, while stars are beaming In the cloudless evening sky;   Rock me while my love lies

O'er the wave sweet music

dreaming,   Sparkling billows, peacefully.   O'er the wave sweet mu - sic floats, Sweet as
dreaming,

floats,   Sweet as siren's   witching notes,   O'er the wave the witching notes, the siren's witching

si - ren's   witching notes, O'er   the wave sweet music floats,   sweet as siren's, as the siren's

notes, Drift my   Sparkling billows, peace-ful-ly. O'er   the wave sweet music floats, O'er   the

si - ren's   witching notes,

wave sweet   mu - sic floats,   As the si - ren's witching notes, As the si - ren's witching

notes.   Drifting onward, swift we're glid-ing, Lov-ing friends   to meet once

GO TO SLEEP, LENA DARLING.

J. K. EMMET.
LULLABY IN "FRITZ."

1. Close your eyes, Le - na, my darling, While I sing your lul - la - by; Fear thou no danger, Lena,
2. Bright be de morn-ing, my darling, Ven you ope your eyes Sunbeams glow all 'round you, Lena,

Move not, dear Le - na, my dar-ling, For your brooder watches nigh you, Le - na dear.
Peace be with thee, love, my dar-ling, Blue and cloudless be the sky for Le - na dear.

Angels guide thee, Lena dear, my darling, Noth-ing e - vil can come near; Brightest flow - ers
Birds sing their bright songs for thee, my darling, Full of sweetest mel - o - dy. An-gels ev - er

blow for thee, Dar - ling sis - ter, dear to me. Go to sleep, go to sleep, my
hov - er near, Dar - ling sis - ter, dear to me. Go to sleep, go to sleep, my

ba - by, my ba - by, my ba - by; Go to sleep, my ba - by,

ba - by, oh, by, Go to sleep, Le - na, sleep.

SILENT NIGHT.

MICHAEL HAYDN.

1. Si - lent night! Ho - ly night! All is calm, all is bright
2. Si - lent night! Ho - ly night! Shep - herds quake at the sight!
3. Si - lent night! Ho - ly night! Son of God, love's pure light,

Round yon vir - gin moth - er and Child! Ho - ly In - fant, so ten - der and mild,
Glo - ries stream from Heav - en a - far, Heav'n - ly hosts sing Al - le - lu - ia,
Ra - diant beams from Thy ho - ly face, With the dawn of re - deem - ing grace,

Sleep in heav - en - ly peace, Sleep in heav - en - ly peace.
Christ, the Sav - iour, is born! Christ, the Sav - iour, is born!
Je - sus, Lord, at Thy birth, Je - sus, Lord, at Thy birth.

SONS OF MEN, BEHOLD.

THIBAUT, 1254.
CHARLES WESLEY, 1739.

1. Sons of men, be - hold from far, Hail the long ex - pect - ed Star;
2. Mild it shines on all be - neath, Pierc - ing thro' the shades of death,
3. Na - tions all, re - mote and near, Haste to see your God ap - pear;

Ja - cob's Star that gilds the night Guides be - wil - dered na - ture right.
Scat - t'ring er - ror's wide - spread night, Kind - ling dark - ness in - to light.
Haste, for Him your hearts pre - pare, Meet Him man - i - fest - ed there.

There behold the Day-Spring rise,
Pouring light upon your eyes;
See it chase the shades away,
Shining to the perfect day.

Sing, ye morning stars, again,
God descends on earth to reign,
Deigns for man His life t'employ:
Shout, ye sons of God, for joy.

LITTLE BY LITTLE.

Mrs. Chas. Barnard.

1. Lit - tle by lit - tle the day goes by, The day so dark or fair;
2. Lit - tle by lit - tle the skies grow clear, Spring-buds come smil - ing out;
3. Lit - tle by lit - tle the world grows strong, Up - borne by the good in men,

Short if you sing thro' it, long if you sigh, With its gladness, or toil and care, The years are the full
Lit - tle by lit - tle the sun shines near, The brighter for pain and doubt,—A bloom of ra - di - ant
Fighting the bat - tle of right against wrong, Seen far beyond mor-tal ken; Brave souls ne'er are

sheaves We bear to the Master's door, The treasures we bring, or the leaves that we fling On the
beauty, That bridal or shrine might know, Which, gone with the May that has vanished away, To
wanting, Full arm'd for the deadly strife, What tho' demons may rage, as the contest they wage, The

Mas - ter's thresh - ing floor, On the Mas - ter's thresh - ing floor.
fruitage most rare may grow, To fruitage most rare may grow.
crown is im - mor - tal life, The crown is im - mor - tal . life.

CHIME AGAIN, BEAUTIFUL BELLS.

H. R. Bishop.

Andante.

1. Chime again, chime again, beau-ti - ful bells, Now thy soft mel - o - dy floats on the wind,
2. Chime again, chime again, beau-ti - ful bells, Lin - ger a-while o'er the deep, dusk-y bay,

Bursting at in - ter-vals o - ver the sails, Leaving a train of re - flec-tion be-hind;
Faint-er and faint - er thy mel - o - dy swells, Fast fades the land and thy sounds die away; The

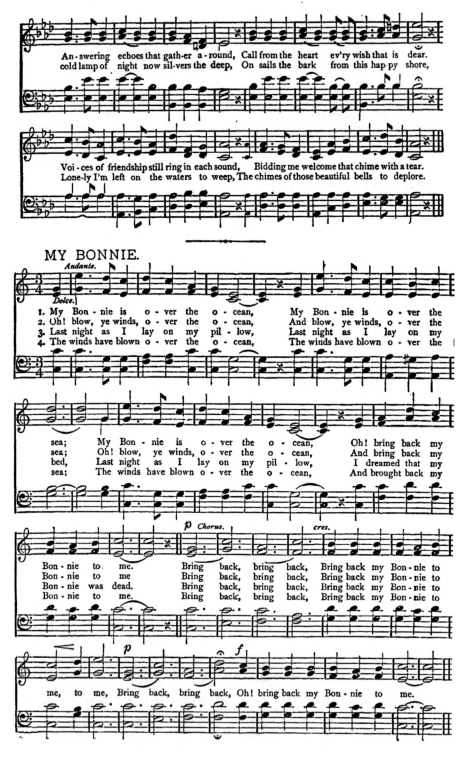

An-swering echoes that gath-er a-round, Call from the heart ev'ry wish that is dear.
cold lamp of night now sil-vers the deep, On sails the bark from this hap-py shore,

Voi-ces of friendship still ring in each sound, Bidding me welcome that chime with a tear.
Lone-ly I'm left on the waters to weep, The chimes of those beautiful bells to deplore.

MY BONNIE.

Andante.

Dolce.

1. My Bon-nie is o-ver the o-cean,   My Bon-nie is o-ver the
2. Oh! blow, ye winds, o-ver the o-cean,   And blow, ye winds, o-ver the
3. Last night as I lay on my pil-low,   Last night as I lay on my
4. The winds have blown o-ver the o-cean,   The winds have blown o-ver the

sea;   My Bon-nie is o-ver the o-cean,   Oh! bring back my
sea;   Oh! blow, ye winds, o-ver the o-cean,   And bring back my
bed,   Last night as I lay on my pil-low,   I dreamed that my
sea;   The winds have blown o-ver the o-cean,   And brought back my

p Chorus. *cres.*

Bon-nie to me.   Bring back, bring back, Bring back my Bon-nie to
Bon-nie to me   Bring back, bring back, Bring back my Bon-nie to
Bon-nie was dead.   Bring back, bring back, Bring back my Bon-nie to
Bon-nie to me.   Bring back, bring back, Bring back my Bon-nie to

p *f*

me, to me, Bring back, bring back, Oh! bring back my Bon-nie to me.

Music stands alone among the arts as the creation of man's intellect. It is the sole aim of the painter and of the sculptor to reproduce in idealized forms what he sees around him, and of the poet to give form and color to what he sees within as well as without him. In each case the artist seeks to express by means of his art that which already existed for him. The painter gazes out upon a world of color and form; he sees before him all that his art would reproduce. It is only as he sees nature truly and reproduces her conscientiously that he is great. It is impossible to see truly without imagination, or to produce faithfully without technical skill, and it is necessary, in order to be a worthy interpreter of God, that a man should be honest, earnest, and reverent. If he seek to imitate even nature servilely, he must fail. In purely human creations it is only the man who catches the fire, essence, and beauty of another man's thought who can truly translate his work. A mere rendering of word for word is not translation. In just the same way the spirit of that beauty which has been spread so lavishly over the world must be taken into the artist's soul; it must be assimilated and made part of his very being, and then given out again as a living

FAITHFUL LITTLE BIRD

From "Songs of Our Youth."
Miss Muloch. Carl Matz *arr.*

1. I had a bird, a little bird, My garden groves a-mong; It sang, but scarce its note I heard, It had been there so long. I never listened to its lay, A-mid my bow'r of ros-es gay, Yet all day long, be-side my door, The lit-tle bird sang ev-er-more; All sum-mer long, be-side my door, The lit-tle bird sang ev-er-more.

2. But autumn came, the roses passed, The happy time was gone; Yet still, amid the win-try blast, The lit-tle bird sang on. And when I droop'd with grief oppressed, The lit-tle bird flew in my breast; Now all day long, be-side my door, The lit-tle bird sings ev-er-more; All win-ter long, be-side my door, The lit-tle bird sings ev-er-more.

work, re-created by the love which has given form to the thought in its first inception, and developed under the brooding meditation and patient study by which every thought worth the having is perfected. But even here the work is not creative. We see the painter reaching forth, by his genius, taking the evanescent beauty which is lying around him, and making it permanent, bringing this far-away loveliness down to our household and every-day uses. The sculptor, too, crystallizes by his art into permanent forms the fleeting beauty around him. Poetry, which is more nearly akin to music than any other of the arts, and which undoubtedly stands higher in the scale, differs from it widely in this respect. The world of imagination from which the poet draws must be present to him in order that he may reproduce it, or he will be a versifier, not a poet. But music stands apart from these; it seems a distinct creation, for it really reproduces nothing which previously existed either in the world of sense or of thought.—*Mrs. Herrick.*

HELMHOLTZ fixes the lowest limit of musical sounds at sixteen vibrations per second, and the highest at 38,000. Below this number the pulsations cease to link themselves together, and become distinct sounds. The range of the ear is thus about eleven octaves. The practical range of music is, however, only about seven octaves. The capacity to hear the higher tones varies in different persons. A sound which is entirely audible to one may be utter silence to another. Some ears cannot distinguish the squeak of a bat or the chirp of a cricket, while others are acutely sensitive to these shrill sounds. Indeed, the auditory nerve seems generally more alive to the short, quick vibrations than to the long, slow ones. The whirr of a locust is much more noticeable than the sighing of the wind through the trees. A continuous blast of air has no effect to produce sound. The rush of the grand aërial rivers above us we never hear. They flow on ceaselessly but silently in the upper regions of the air. A whirlwind is noiseless. Let, however, the great billows strike a tree and wrench it violently from the ground, and we can hear the secondary shorter waves which set out from the struggling limbs and from the tossing leaves.

THE HEART BOWED DOWN.

M. W. BALFE
From "BOHEMIAN GIRL".

1. The heart-bow'd down by weight of woe, To weak-est hopes will cling, To
2. The mind will in its worst de-spair. Still pon-der o'er the past, On

thought and im-pulse while they flow, That can no com - fort bring, that can, that
mo-ments of de-light that were Too beau-ti-ful to last, that were too

can no com-fort bring; To those ex-cit-ing scenes will blend, O'er
beau-ti-ful to last; To long de-part-ed years ex-tend, Its

pleasure's path-way thrown; But mem'ry is the on-ly friend That grief can call its
vis-ions with them flown; For mem'ry is the on-ly friend That grief can call its

own, That grief can call its own............., That grief can call its own.

OUR SONGS OF JOY AND GLADNESS.

MEYERBEER.

Con spirito.

1. Our songs of joy, our songs of joy and glad-ness, We'll sing, we'll sing, we'll sing in cheerful
2. Awake, awake! awake sweet notes of pleasure, In song, in song, in full and joyous

lay, No note of pain, no note of pain or sad - ness Shall greet, shall
song, Move on, move on, move on in grace - ful meas - ure, To speed, to

greet, shall greet this joyous day, Yes, then hail this joy - ous day.
speed, to speed the hours along, Speed the hours, the hours a - long.

Yes, then hail, this joy - ous
Speed the hours, the hours a -

Our songs of joy, our songs of joy and gladness, We'll sing, we'll sing, we'll sing in cheerful
Awake, awake! awake sweet notes of pleasure, In song, in song, in full and joyous

day.
long.

lay; No note of pain, no note of pain or sadness Shall greet, shall greet shall greet this joyous
song; Move on, move on, move on in graceful measure, To speed, to speed, to speed the hours a -

day. This joy - ous day, All hail this joy-ous day, All hail, all hail, all hail this joy - ous
long. This joy - ous day, All hail this joy-ous day, All hail, all hail, all hail this joy - ous

day, all hail this day, all hail this day, this mer - ry,mer - ry, mer - ry,
day, all hail this day, all hail this day, this hap - py,hap - py, hap - py,

mer - ry, mer - ry mer - ry, mer - ry, day. Our songs, our songs, our songs of joy and
hap py, hap - py hap - py, hap - py, day. Awake, awake! awake, sweet notes of

glad - ness, We 'll sing, we 'll sing, we 'll sing in cheer - ful lay; No note of
pleas - ure, In full, in full, in full and joy - ous song, Move on, move

pain, no note of pain or sadness, Shall greet, shall greet, shall greet this happy day.
on, move on, in graceful measure, To speed, to speed, to speed the hours along.

EVER TO THE RIGHT.

1. Ev - er to the right, boys, Ev - er to the right! Give a ready hand and true
2. Ev - er to the right, boys, Ev - er to the right; Nev - er let your teach - er say,
3. Ev - er to the right, boys, Ev - er to the right; To ev - 'ry stu - dy well at - tend, To

To the work you have to do, Ev - er to the right, Ev - er to the right.
"Why my wish - es dis - o - bey?" Ev - er to the right, Ev - er to the right.
ev - 'ry schoolmate be a friend: Ev - er to the right, Ev - er to the right.

HAPPY AND LIGHT.

M. W. Balfe.
From "Bohemian Girl."

Happy and light of heart are those, Yes, Happy and light of heart are those who in each other faith repose,

er faith repose, Hap - py and light, and light of heart are those,

Who faith re - pose, in each oth - er faith repose, ah, Hap - py and light of

heart are those, who in each oth - er faith repose. Who in each oth - er, Who in each

other, Who in each oth - er faith re - pose, Happy and light of heart are those, Who

in each oth - er faith repose, Who in each oth - er faith repose, repose, yes, Hap - py and

light of heart are those, Who in each oth - er faith repose, Happy and light, Happy and

light, Who in each oth - - - - er faith re - pose, Their faith re - pose.

UPON THE HEIGHT.

GERMAN FOLK-SONG.

1. Up - on the height I stood, The sun be - gan to set, I
2. The lit - tle flow - ers close Their eye - lids by de - grees, And
3. And in re - pose they lie, Who call a cot their own, They

saw how o'er the wood Hung evening's gold - en net. The dew from Heaven
ev - 'ry bil - low flows, Un - ruf - fled by the breeze. The golden bee - tle
dream of home and sigh, Who rove the world a - lone. A long - ing fills my

fell, Peace o'er the earth a - rose, With sound of eve - ning bell Sank
rocks Its cra - dle is the rose, The shepherd and his flocks Re -
breast, Oh, how I fain would fly, And seek e - ter - nal rest, In

Na - ture to re - pose, Sank Na - ture to re - pose.
tir - ing to re - pose, Re - tir - ing to re - pose.
yon far home on high, In yon far home on high.

A choir of twenty or thirty full-voiced singers concentrating their vocal energies mainly upon the melody, and singing with clear, distinct articulation, with bold, commanding tone, and with firm, steady movement, may set before the congregation such a plain and inviting path of song, and inspire with such confidence all who have ability to sing, that the result will be a successful, and even admirable illustration of the people's chorus. A hundred little rivulets, no one of which could find its way to the sea alone, may join the river that passes near them, and be wafted safely to the ocean; but the stream that conveys them owes much of its grandeur to these little tributaries. In the production of this great, melodic chorus, a strong lead of men's voices upon the "air" is indispensable. Men's voices are valuable for dignity and impressiveness; but in the chorus of which we speak, their chief value is their strength.—*Furber.*

I'M A SHEPHERD OF THE VALLEY.

GERMAN SONG.

1. I'm a shep-herd of the val-ley, La la la la la, La la la la la;
2. In the fresh and dew-y morn-ing, La la la la la, La la la la la;
3. Free from en-vy ev-er liv-ing, La la la la la, La la la la la;

With my sheep I wan-der dai-ly, La la la la la, La la la la la;
When the first gray light is dawn-ing, La la la la la, La la la la la;
Nev-er with a broth-er striv-ing, La la la la la, La la la la la;

Where the ten-der grass is grow-ing, Where the laugh-ing wa-ters play;
Wak-ing from my peace-ful slum-ber, Loud re-sounds my cheer-ful song;
Though the shep-herd's lot be low-ly, Yet con-tent I well may be;

Where the ver-nal winds are blow-ing, With my flock I love to stray.
Up the moun-tain then I clam-ber, With my sheep, a hap-py throng.
If my store in-crease but slow-ly, Ev'-ry day has joys for me.

La la la la la, La la la la la, With my flock I love to stray.
La la la la la, La la la la la, With my sheep, a hap-py throng.
La la la la la, La la la la la, Ev'-ry day has joys for me.

WELCOME, PRETTY PRIMROSE.

Ciro Pinsuti.

1. Welcome, pretty primrose flow'r, That comes when sunshine comes, When rainbows arch the sil-ver
2. Gaz-ing on the ear-ly flow'r, I seem to hear the spring That calls the sunshine ev-'ry

shower Of ev-'ry cloud that roams, Of ev-'ry cloud that roams. I joy to see thy
hour, And tells the bird to sing, And tells the bird to sing. And as I dream, my

promise bloom, That tells of spring's new day! And in my thoughts a-far I roam, O'er
dream is rife With thoughts a-kin to thee; Of glad spring-life, a sweet spring-life, That's

sun-ny haunts a-way! Welcome! Welcome! Welcome! primrose flow'r! Welcome, pretty
ver-y dear to me! Welcome! Welcome! Welcome! primrose flow'r! Welcome, pretty

primrose flow'r, To me thy coming, seems To wake again the springtime hour, With sunshine in its dreams.

Ah! ... Ah! . Welcome, pretty, pretty, pretty, pretty primrose flower, With sunshine in its dreams!

If to be effective the work of education must have regard to all the powers of the human soul, it should not neglect the imagination, or phantasy, which most certainly enters into the activities of will and intelligence in our earliest youth as well as in our ripened age. The world of art is no less real than the world of thought. While truth is searched often by a process of analytic thought, demanding on this account a thorough discipline of the intellect; the beautiful is grasped by an æsthetic intuition, demanding for this purpose a careful culture of the phantasy. In the one case we have the process of science; in the other, the process of art. Why neglect either, when their source is the same? For when, by the phantasy, we see through and beneath the build of things, the primordial form governing all and in all manifesting its presence, what is this but the same truth in form which we reach through the analysis of thought? The same glory is in it after all, in the one case authenticating itself as truth through the activities of intellect; in the other case, looking out through the form, and revealing itself therein as the beautiful, through the intuitive glance of the phantasy. To the sphere of art, thus briefly characterized, music belongs, and addresses itself to that soul power which realizes the beautiful. The form material here in which the idea enshrines itself, and

JOY! JOY! FREEDOM TO-DAY.

1. Joy! Joy! freedom to-day! Care! care! drive it away! Youth, health and vigor our senses o'er-power;
2. Ring! ring! merrily, bells! Swing! swing! onward your swells! Telling of hope, love and joy to the world.

Trouble! count it for naught! Banish, banish the thought. Pleasure and mirth shall rule o'er this hour.
Triumph proud ye proclaim! Freedom! what can we name Fairer than Fatherland flag here unfurled?

Joy to-day! joy, joy to-day! and care, care, drive it far a-way! Joy to-day! joy,

joy to-day! and care, care, drive it far a-way!   away, away!   away, a-way!

through which it is made to reach in upon the soul, is in itself almost spiritual—viz., sound; and this is the chief medium through which the infinitude and indefiniteness of feeling can come to an expression. Therefore, we may say, in brief, that music is the utterance, under sound forms of sense, of the beautiful in those sentiments and aspirations which fill the heart, and thence gush forth like crystal waters from deep hidden springs. It is the outflowing of the feeling heart. While giving body to emotion and sentiment, with their power made tangible, as it were, it penetrates the soul, awakening depths of feeling and affection slumbering there, and leading the whole engrasped spirit into sad or joyful communings with itself, or into wondrous and visionary excursions into the vast past of its hopes, and loves, or into the vaster future that lies before it like a far-off landscape in the evening twilight.—*E. E. Higbee.*

Let us meet our gracious God with cheerful songs. Give him warm welcome to our hearts and homes. Yield him, O yield him, the honors due to his holy name. Praise him for His goodness, now and forever—in time, as you are able; in eternity, with sweet-voiced, perfect praise. "Blessed be the Lord God of Israel; for He hath visited and redeemed His people."

LITTLE CHERRY BLOSSOM.

LITTLE ONES.

1. Lit - tle Cher - ry Blos - som   Lived up in a tree,   And a ve - ry
2. But one sun - ny morn - ing,   Think - ing it was May,   "I'll not wear," said
3. Blossom would not lis - ten,   For the sky was bright,   And she wished to
4. Bye - and - bye the sun - shine   Fad - ed from her view;   How poor Blossom
5. Ah! poor Cher - ry Blos - som!   She in fool - ish pride   Changed her proper

hap - py   Lit - tle thing was she.   Clad all thro' the win - ter
Blos - som,   "This old dress to - day."   Mis - ter Breeze this hear - ing,
glis - ten   In her robe of white.   So she let the brown one
shivered   As it cold - er grew;   Oh, for that warm wrap - per
clothing,   Took a cold and died.   All ye lit - tle Blossoms,

In a dress of brown,   Warm she was tho' liv - ing   In a northern town.
Ve - ry kindly said,   "Do be careful, Blossom,   Win - ter is not fled."
Drop and blow a - way,   Leaving her the white one   All so fine and gay.
Ly - ing on the ground: Now Jack Frost will nip her—   He is prowling round.
Hear me and take care,—   Go not clad too lightly,   And of pride be - ware.

THE BUTTERCUP TEST.

mf   ECHOES OF CHILDHOOD.

Allegretto.

1. Butter - cups ev - 'ry one Bright like the summer sun, Looking and smiling so bon - ny,
2. If I can slip you in, Close under Johnny's chin; If you can there shine so clear - ly,
3. Chasing the dragon - fly, Johnny with shout and cry Tramples the fair meadows o - ver,
4. Stirring you thro' and thro', How the winds play with you, Putting you all in a flut - ter;

Some of you come with me, Something I want to see, Want to find out about John - ny.
Tho' he may own it not, We shall the truth have got, Johnny loves butter most dear - ly.
While I string lilac bells, Or in the grassy dells, Hunt for the four-leav - ed clo - ver.
Tell me, oh, butter - cup! Thro' the grass peeping up, Tell me, does Johnny like but - ter?

Music as written is divided into small, equal por-tions, called measures. These may be indicated to the ear by counting the parts as "one, two;" "one, two;" or to the eye, by motions of the hand, called beats, or beating time. Measures are represented by spaces between perpendicular lines across the staff. The lines dividing music into measures are called bars. There may be different kinds of notes in the measure, but there must be an equal amount in every measure, that is, one measure must contain as much in the aggregate as any other. Parts of measures are represented by notes and rests. Four kinds of measure are in general use, viz.: Double, composed of two parts and indicated by two counts or beats; Triple, indicated by three beats; Quadruple, four

beats; and Sextuple, six counts or beats. Figures at the beginning of the music indicate these measures.

INFLUENCE.—Music, in its capacity of doing good, comes next to the sacred influence of the pulpit. Its power is as yet a thing undeveloped. Consider, for instance, what the general impression was as to the availability of music in the Sunday-school thirty or forty years ago, and compare the Sunday-schools of to-day with those of that period. What would these schools be if we should drop the music out of them bodily? They would almost dissolve and vanish. It is the invisible chain which holds them together and animates them. There is, besides, a power in music to reach, to direct, to comfort the Christian's heart, which is, comparatively speaking, yet undreamed of.

ANGELIC SONGS ARE SWELLING.

REV. F W. FABER, 1850.
J M. ARMSTRONG *arr.*

1. Hark! hark! my soul, an - gel - ic songs are swell-ing O'er earth's green fields and
2. On - ward we go, for still we hear them sing-ing, "Come wea - ry souls, for
3. Far, far a - way, like bells at ev' - ning peal-ing, The voice of Je - sus

o-cean's wave-beat shore. How sweet the truth those bless-ed strains are tell - ing
Je - sus bids you come!" And, through the dark, its ech-oes sweet -ly ring-ing,
sounds o'er land and sea; And la - den souls by thou-sands meek-ly steal-ing,

Of that new life when sin shall be no more.] *Chorus.*
The mu - sic of the gos - pel leads us home. } An - gels of Je - sus,
Kind Shep-herd, turn their wea-ry steps to thee.]

An - gels of light, Sing-ing to wel - come the pil - grims of the night.

Rest comes at length; tho' life be long and dreary,
　The day must dawn, and darksome night be past;
All journeys end in welcome to the weary,
　And heaven, the heart's true home, will come at last.

Angels, sing on! your faithful watches keeping;
　Sing us sweet fragments of the songs above;
Till morning's joy shall end the night of weeping,
　And life's long shadows break in cloudless love.

RAISE YOUR HANDS.

1. Raise your hands, if they are clean, By your teacher to be seen; Hands and faces, clean and bright,
2. Al - most see the pur - ple tide All a - long our fingers glide; Oh, how healthy we must be,
3. Brush your clothes, and comb your hair, Wash your face and hands with care; Sparkle, sparkle, water pure,

How they will our hearts de - light! Raise them high, and turn them so; Oh, they're almost
When the blood can flow so free! Hid with dirt we should not know There are pret - ty
Dirt - y hands we can't en - dure. Washing's pleasant, we are sure; Spar-kle, sparkle,

white as snow! Hold them ve - ry still a - gain— Teacher, don't you see each vein?
veins be - lov; All that glad - ly come to school, All must learn the clean - ly rule.
wa - ter pure; Washing's pleas - ant, we are sure, Spar - kle, sparkle, wa - ter pure!

THE GOLDEN RULE.

1. To do to others as I would That they should do to me, Will make me honest, kind and good, As
2. We never should behave amiss, Nor need be doubtful long; As we may always tell by this, If
3. I know I should not steal, or use The smallest thing I see, Which I should never like to lose, If

children ought to be, Will make me hon - est, kind and good, As children ought to be.
things are right or wrong, As we may al - ways tell by this, If things are right or wrong.
it be - longed to me, Which I should never like to lose, If it belonged to me.

4.	5.	6.
Nor others should I treat with spite,	But any kindness they may need,	Then let me ne'er at home, at school,
Or strike an angry blow;	I'll do, whate'er it be;	In action or in word,
Because I would not think it right,	As I am very glad, indeed,	Appear not to have learned this rule,
If they should serve me so.	When they are kind to me.	Of the dear Christ, the Lord.

Archbishop Whately cured a person of shyness by saying: "You are shy because you are thinking of the impression you are making. Think only of the pleasure you can give to others and not of yourself." In speaking of bashfulness he says: "Let both the extemporary speaker and the reader of his own compositions study to avoid, as far as possible, all thoughts of self, earnestly fixing the mind on the matter of what is delivered; and the one will feel the less of that embarassment which arises from the thought of what opinion the hearers will form of him, while the other will appear to be speaking, because he actually will be speaking, the sentiments, not indeed which at that time first arise in his own mind, but which are then really present to his mind, and occupy his thought."

The quickness of perception with regard to all sounds, but those especially which are faint or distant, is much improved by exercise or culture.—*Hervey.*

NYMPHS OF AIR AND SEA.

1. Nymphs of air and ancient sea, Such the gifts we bring to thee; Lo! these plumes of
2. Take these shells, approach them near; They shall murmur in thine ear— Tunes that lull the

rich de-vice, Plucked from birds of Par-a-dise. Lo! these drops of essence
slumb'ring sea More than mermaid's har-mo-ny. Take these pearls, no diving

rare, Shook from wand'ring me-teor's hair.
slave Drags their like from o-cean's cave.

hair. Nymphs of an-cient sea, Such the gifts we bring to thee; Nymphs of
cave. Nymphs of an-cient sea, Such the gifts we bring to thee; Nymphs of

air and an-cient sea, Such the gifts we bring to thee.

I WOULD THAT MY LOVE.

MENDELSSOHN.

Allegretto con moto.

1. I would that my love could si-lent-ly flow in a sin-gle word; I'd
2. To thee on their wings, my fairest, that soul-felt word they would bear, Should'st

give it the merry breezes, They'd waft it away in sport, I'd give it the merry breezes, They'd
hear it at ev'ry moment, And hear it ev'ry where, Should'st hear it at ev'ry moment, And

waft it away in sport, away in sport, away in sport, they'd waft it away in sport. 3. At
hear it ev'ry where, and ev'ry where, and ev'ry-where, and hear it ev'ry-where.

night, when thine eyelids in slumber have closed those bright heav'nly beams, Still there, my love, it will

haunt thee, e'en in thy deepest dreams, Still there, my love, it will haunt thee, e'en in thy deepest

dreams, e'en in thy deepest, thy deepest dreams, E'en in thy deepest, deep-est dreams.

This Charming Song of Mendelssohn's may be sung as a Duet, as in the original.

My chief interest is in the music of the Bible. The Bible, like a great harp with innumerable strings, swept, by the fingers of inspiration, trembles with it. So far back as the fourth chapter of Genesis you find the first organist and harper, Jubal. So far back as the thirty-first chapter of Genesis you find the first choir. All up and down the Bible you find sacred music—at weddings, at inaugurations, at the treading of the wine-press. Can you imagine the harmony when those white-robed Levites, before the symbols of God's presence, and by the smoking altars, and the candlesticks that sprang upward and branched out like trees of gold, and under the wings of the cherubim, chanted the one hundred and thirty-ninth Psalm of David? You know how it was done. One part of that great choir stood up and chanted, "Oh! give thanks unto the Lord, for He is good!" Then the other part of the choir, standing in some other part of the temple, would come in with the response: "For His mercy endureth forever." Then the first part would take up the song again, and say, "Unto Him who only doeth great wonders." The other

THE PALMS.

J. FAURE.

1. Let the palms wave on this most happy day! Greetings they bear to us of joy and gladness.
2. His gentle voice pervades the mighty throng. 'Tis He who freedom gives o'er land and sea;
3. Rejoice, rejoice, Je-ru-sa-lem the holy! Loud let thy joyous notes in praise ascending.

Je-sus is come to take all grief a-way, He comes to banish gloom and sad-ness.
'Tis He who gives in darkest night a song, Gives light, O Lord, that we may come to Thee!
Laud Him, the Child of Bethlehem the lowly, All hearts a-flame, in song all voices blending.

People and tongues shall chant His praise; Tune every voice, His name be glad-ly singing. Ho-

san-na! Glory to God! Glory to Him who comes bringing sal-va - - tion!

part of the choir would come in with the overwhelming response, "For His mercy endureth forever," until in the latter part of the song, the music floating backward and forward, harmony in accord with harmony, every trumpet sounding. every bosom heaving, one part of this great white-robed choir would lift the anthem, "Oh! give thanks unto the God of heaven," and the other part of the Levite choir would come in with the response: "For His mercy endureth forever." How are we to decide what is appropriate, especially for church music? There may be a great many differences of opinion. In some of the churches they prefer a trained choir; in others, the old style precentor. In some places they prefer the melodeon, the harp, the cornet, the organ; in other places they think these things are the invention of the devil. Some would have a musical instrument played so loud you cannot stand it, others would have it played so low you cannot hear it. But, while there may be great varieties of opinion in regard to music, it seems to me that the general spirit of the Word of God indicates what ought to be the great characteristic of church music.—*Talmage.*

SWEETER THAN THE BREATH OF MORNING.

MEYERBEER.
From "HUGUENOTS."

1. Sweet-er than the breath of morn-ing,
1. *No - bil don-na e tan-to o - ne - sta,*
2. When a-round some joys de - cay - ing,

Fresh-wing'd from the balmy west, Or
Che far lie-to un re po - tria,
Tint - ed by the clouds of years,

lil - y with the gold-en dawn - ing,
Messagie-re qui m'in - vi - ta,
Let thy smile be o'er it play - ing,

Blush-ing o'er its snow-white breast;
Ca - va - lier, per un di voi,
Grief will then for-get its tears.

Thy look is sun - shine, and ev - er seems Like fai - ry vis - ions we form in
Sen - za no mor - lo, si renda d'o - nor a chi fu de - gno di tanto a -
Of all the mu - sic youth ev - er made Thy faint-est mur - mur far sweeter

dreams. Tho' time may steal the leaves from gladness, Hope's bright wings may clouded be, Oh!
mor. No-bil donna e tan-to o - ne - sta, Che far lie - to un re po - tria, A
play'd. Oh! light as zephyrs wing'd with glad - ness, May thy path of sun - shine be! Oh!

life should leave all free from sad - ness, Days all bright and fair for
me cre - de - te, Mai niun si - - gnor. A tanta gloria fu e - letto an -
life should leave all free from sad - ness,— Days all bright and fair for

thee, all bright for thee, all bright for thee.
cor, a tan - ta glo - ria, e - let - to an - cor.
thee, all fair for tnee, all fair for thee.

I HAVE FRUIT, I HAVE FLOWERS.

J. A. WADE.

I have fruit, I have flowers, That were gathered in the bowers, Amid the blooming hills so

high, so high, I have fruit, I have flowers, The daughters of the showers, Of the

dews and the rills, Will you buy? I've a young nightingale That by moonlight in the vale So

fondly to a rose his love did sigh, I stole within their bower, Caught the silly bird and flower, Will you

buy the pretty lovers? Will you buy? Will you buy? Will you buy, buy, buy? Will you

buy? Will you buy, buy, buy? I have fruit, I have flowers, The daughters of the showers, Of the

dews and the rills, Will you buy?   I have fruit,   I have flowers, Will you buy? Will you

buy?   Will you buy? Will you buy? Will you buy?   I have fruit,   I have flowers.

Will you buy? Will you, will, ... will   you

buy? Will you buy? Will you buy, buy, buy? Will you buy? Will you buy? Will you buy?

AH, 'TIS A DREAM.

Andante espressione.

E. LASSEN.

1. My na - tive land a - gain it meets mine   eye,   The old oaks raise their boughs on
2. I   feel the kiss that was in youth   so   dear,   The words, "I love!" fall on   mine
3. And now when far   in dis - tant lands   I   roam   My heart will wan - der to   my

high,   The   vi - o - lets greet - ing   seem,   Ah! 'tis a dream.
ear,   I   see   thine eyes' soft   beam!   Ah! 'tis a dream.
home,   But   while   these fan - cies   teem,   Ah! 'tis a dream.

13

It is all very well to analyze vocalization, and to school and develop the organs of speech; but if the expression be lifeless, or hypocritical, there exists a want that no skill whatsoever can supply. We express ourselves in our actions; but there is no tell-tale of the soul like the voice. Encourage sweetness of temper, and the voice will catch the cadences of persuasiveness. The laugh is very expressive. It may be merry, scornful, encouraging, or the reverse. It may be empty, or very full of significance; hearty or affected. Explosive, loud laughter, like all inordinate laughter, in fact, is proof of no very good breeding. A spirit that has been long subjected to ennobling occupations, when merriment is in order, is not overpowered by the sudden emotion. Those who "burst out laughing" on slight provocation should school their inclinations, and certainly not laugh in a repulsive voice. It is not affectation to improve the tone of the voice. It is the simplicity of good nature. So also of speech. Who is willing to offend? No one who is worthy of respect; no one who respects himself. As social beings, we are under obligation to make ourselves as agreeable as possible to those around us, and as few things are more annoying to a sensitive ear than an unpleasant voice either in laughter, in speech, or in singing, all should endeavor to use this marvelous organ in its best tones.

KATHLEEN.

W. WILLIAMS.

1. Oh! leave not your Kathleen, there's no one can cheer her; A-lone in the wide world un-
2. Oh! leave not the land, the sweet land of your childhood, Where joyous-ly passed the first

pit-ied she'll sigh; And scenes that were loveliest when thou wert but near her, Re-call the sad
days of our youth! Where gai-ly we wandered 'mid val-ley and wildwood, Oh! those were the

vis-ion of days long gone by. 'Tis vain that you tell me you'll never for-get me, To the
bright days of in-no-cent truth. 'Tis vain that you tell me you'll never for-get me, To the

land of the sham-rock you'll ne'er re-turn more; Far a-way from your

sight you will cease to re-gret me, You'll soon for-get Kathleen and E-rin-go-Bragh.

THREE KINGS OF ORIENT.

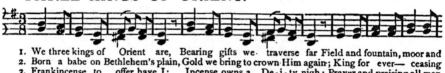

1. We three kings of Orient are, Bearing gifts we. traverse far Field and fountain, moor and
2. Born a babe on Bethlehem's plain, Gold we bring to crown Him again; King for ever— ceasing
3. Frankincense to   offer have I;   Incense owns a . De-i-ty nigh; Prayer and praising all men
4. Myrrh is mine; its bitter perfume Breathes a life of gath'ring gloom; Sorrowing, sighing, bleeding,
5. Glorious now behold Him rise, King and God and   Sac - rifice; Heaven sings "Hallelujah!"

Chorus.

mountain, Following yonder Star.   Oh,   star of wonder, star of might, Star with roy - al
never— Over us all to reign.   Oh,   star of wonder, star of might, Star with roy - al
raising, Worship Him, God on high.   Oh,   star of wonder, star of might, Star with roy - al
dying, Seal'd in the stone-cold tomb.   Oh,   star of wonder, star of might, Star with roy - al
"Hal-le-lu-jah!" earth replies,   Oh,   star of wonder, star· of might, Star with roy - al

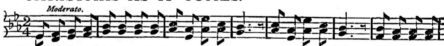

beau - ty bright, Westward lead - ing, still proceed - ing, Guide us to   the   perfect light.

The last three verses may be sung each by a different voice, to represent the Wise Men.

CHRISTMAS AS IT COMES.

Moderato.

1. Hail, all hail, each happy season, Christmas as it comes, Christmas as it comes! Bringing with it
2. Friends that have for long been parted, Christmas brings again, Christmas brings again; Each to oth - er
3. Old men with their locks of silver, Young men in their prime, Young men in their prime; Mothers, children,
4. Birth - days of our friends are honored, Days we greet with zest, Days we greet with zest ; But that birthday

deeper gladness To our happy homes; Bringing with it deeper gladness To our happy homes.
tells his sto - ry, Be it joy or pain; Each to oth-er tells his sto - ry, Be it joy or   pain.
all expectant, Welcome Christmas time; Mothers, children, all expectant, Welcome Christmas time.
in Ju - de - a Is of all days best,   But that birthday in Ju - de - a Is of all days best.

MERMAID'S EVENING SONG.

Stephen Glover.

Moderato.

Hark! what mystic sounds are those, Stealing soft-ly o'er the sea? Whence that music soft and low

D. C. List, a-gain the sound draws near, Falling sweetly on the ear; Borne up-on the breeze along,

cres.

Sound-ing as the billows flow? 'Tis the Mermaid's song, 'Tis the Mermaid's song, Borne upon the breeze a-

'Tis the Mermaid's evening song, 'Tis the Mermaid's song, 'Tis the Mermaid's song, Borne upon the breeze a-

Hark! hark!   Hark! hark!   'Tis   the

cres.   f

long,   'Tis the Mermaid's song, 'Tis the Mermaid's song, 'Tis the Mermaid's evening song.

Mermaid's song,   Hark! hark!   Hark! hark! 'Tis the Mermaid's evening song.

1st time. Allegro.

Who would not a Mermaid be, Dwelling 'neath the restless sea! Down among its mystic forms, Cradled by the

dim.

rising storms, Where the dolphins play and leap, In a coral cave to sleep! In a coral cave, In a

cres.   rall.   D. C. Chorus.

coral cave, In a coral cave to sleep! In a coral cave, In a coral cave, In a coral cave to sleep!

CHRISTMASSE OF OLDE.

SWISS AIR.
EUGENE FIELD.

1. God rest you, Chrysten gen - til men, Wher- ev - er you may be, wher - ev - er
2. Last night ye shepherds in ye east Saw many a wondrous thing, saw many a
3. God rest you, Chrysten gen - til men, Far - ing where'er you may, far - ing wher-
4. But thinking on ye gen - til Lord That died up - on ye tree, that died up-

you may be, God rest you all in fielde or hall, Or on ye stormy
wondrous thing; Ye sky last night flamed passing bright Whiles that ye stars did
e'er you may; In noblesse court do thou no sport, In tour - nament no
on ye tree, Let troublings cease and deeds of peace A - bound in Chrystan-

sea; For on this morn, this morn, our Chryst is born, That saveth you and me, that saveth, saveth,
sing, And angels came to bless, to bless ye name Of Jesus Chryst, our Kyng, our Kyng, Of Jesus
playe, In Paynim land hyld thou thy hand, thy hand, From bloudy works this daye, this daye, From bloudy
tie— For on this morn, this morn, ye Chryst is born, That saveth you and me, that saveth, saveth,

you and me, For on this morn our Chryst was born, That sav - eth you and me.
Chryst, our Kyng, For on this morn our Chryst was born, That sav - eth you and me.
works this daye, For on this morn our Chryst was born, That sav - eth you and me.
you and me, For on this morn our Chryst was born, That sav - eth you and me.

THE STRANGER STAR.

C. F. ALEXANDER.

1. Saw ye nev - er in the twi - light, When the sun had left the skies,
2. Heard ye nev - er of the sto - ry, How they crossed the des - ert wild,
3. Know ye not that low - ly Ba - by Was the bright and Morn - ing Star,

Up in heaven the clear stars shin-ing Thro' the gloom like lov-ing eyes?
Journeyed on by plain and mountain, Till they found the Ho-ly Child?
He who came to light the Gen-tiles, And the darkened isles a-far?

So of old the wise men, watch-ing, Saw a blaz-ing stran-ger star,
How they o-pen'd all their treas-ure, Kneel-ing to that In-fant King,
And we too may seek His cra-dle, There our hearts' best treas-ures bring,

And they knew the King was giv-en, And they fol-lowed it from far.
Gave the gold and fra-grant in-cense, Gave the myrrh in of-fer-ing?
Love and faith and true de-vo-tion, For our Sa-viour, God, and King.

CRADLE SONG OF VIRGIN.

Allegretto non troppo.

JOSEPH BARNBY.
Words from OLD LATIN.

1. The Virgin stills the crying Of Jesus sleepless ly-ing; And singing for His pleas-ure Thus
2. O Lamb, my love in-vit-ing, O Star, my soul delighting, O Flower of mine own bear-ing, O
3. My Child, of might indwelling, My Sweet, all sweets excelling, Of Bliss the Fountain flow-ing, The
4. Say, would'st Thou heavenly sweetness, Or love of answering meetness? Or is fit music wanting? Ho!

più lento.

calls upon her Treas-ure, My Darling, do not weep, My Je-su,* sleep!
Jew-el past com-par-ing! My Darling, do not weep, My Je-su, sleep!
Day-spring ever glow-ing. My Darling, do not weep, My Je-su, sleep!
Angels, raise your chant-ing! My Darling, do not weep, My Je-su, sleep!

*Je-zoo, a beautiful use of the Latin vocative, for English nominative.

MENDELSSOHN, Bartholdy Felix, was the son of a rich merchant and banker of Hamburg, and was born in that city A. D. 1809. The early development of the musical faculty in him forces him into comparison with the precocious Mozart, but his more fortunate position saved him from the premature drudgery of public display. His earliest musical instructor was the natural guardian of his infancy, his mother. At eight years of age he was esteemed a prodigy, and not without reason. He could then play at sight the most intricate scores of Bach, and, without premeditation, transpose most difficult exercises into all sorts of keys. He also evinced a wonderful faculty in extemporizing upon a given theme. At this period he was put under the care of the severe but methodical Zelter, a man not disposed to give way to fervid impressions, yet warmly devoted to his "glorious boy." Zelter, writing to Goethe, in 1821, tells him, "I desire to show your face to my favorite pupil before I die." Upon the circle which surrounded Goethe as its centre, the young musician made a profound impression, winning, at the same time, the affection of all. Before his father would allow him to devote himself to music as his profession, he took him to Paris to consult the then aged Cherubini. The ordeal proposed by that consummate musician to test the proficiency of the aspirant was the composition of a *Kyrie* for chorus and full orchestra, which was accomplished to the

FAREWELL TO THE WOODS.

Moderate Time.   GERMAN AIR.

1. Ver - dant grove, farewell to thee,   Clad in ver - nal beauty; Thine my parting
2. What   delight   to   lin - ger here,   'Mid the sha - dy bowers; From the sil - ver
3. But   the night for- bids my stay,   I   must leave   in   sor - row; To   your rest, ye

song shall be,   'Tis a   sa - cred du - ty; Let thy warbler's tuneful throng
foun - tain clear,   Cull-ing fra - grant flow-ers; Would I might with garlands crowned,
birds, a - way,   And dream of   the mor-row. Fare   ye well, ye sha - dy bow'rs,

Bear the echoes of my song,   Far o'er hill and val - ley,   Far o'er hill and valley.
Breathing odors sweet around,   Tar - ry with thee long - er,   Tar - ry with thee longer.
With your blooming, fragrant flow'rs, Till an-oth - er meet - ing,   Till an-oth-er meeting.

perfect satisfaction of the renowned judge. Throughout the period of his celebrity, he was not only distinguished for his composition, but still more as a performer. Language was exhausted in the attempt to describe his excellence as a pianist, and the churches were invaded by crowds, who always thronged the aisles when he was expected to play on the organ. In a word, the only thing he could not do on the organ was to "play the people out." The more effectively he played, the more fixed the congregation remained, and an instance is on record how once at St. Paul's cathedral, the vergers managed to check the energy of the performer by stopping the bellows of the instrument. In 1846, he completed, and himself conducted, at Birmingham, the oratorio of Elijah, the reception of which left his warmest admirers nothing to desire, but it was in the decrees of that unsearchable Providence which often shows us the highly gifted

"——To mock our fond pursuits,
And teach our humbled hopes that life is vain,"

that this star, the cynosure of all observers, should sink to the horizon before it had reached its culminating point. The honors which accumulated upon him were oppressive to the constant sense of fatigue that possessed him. To a young friend who begged him to play after the triumphant conclusion of the Birmingham festival, he replied mournfully that he could not. The abiding shadow of the unseen world was settling upon him. In 1837, he had accepted the post of director of the concerts at Leipsic. In this city he continued to reside till his death, which happened in 1847, at the age of thirty-eight years.

LOVE THY MOTHER, LITTLE ONE.

Air: "To Alexis."

Allegretto grazioso.

1. Love thy Moth-er, lit-tle one, Kiss and clasp her neck a-gain, Thou may'st
2. Press her lips the while they glow With the love they've never told; Thou may'st

one day be a son, That shall mourn her loss in vain. }
one day press in woe. Kissing till thine own are cold. } Ah, the love thy Mother

bears! Till Death divide she will ca-ress thee, And night and morn her

lov-ing arms shall press thee. Mir-ror then her love for thee, Gazing in her tender

eyes; Thou one day wilt, sad-ly sigh-ing, Have no an-swer to thy

cry-ing, Have no an-swer to thy cry-ing; Love thy Mother, lit-tle one!

The teacher while he is giving instruction in vocal music, should be careful to avoid singing too much with his pupils. When they sing he should usually listen, and when he sings they should listen; this will enable them to imitate his example, and him the better to observe their faults. His example is of the utmost importance in singing, as in all other things, and good taste or good style can here be communicated in no other way. When he wishes to correct a fault, let him give an illustration of it, or contrast a bad example with a better one. The bad example may perhaps be caricatured, to render the contrast stronger, in which case it may safely be left to the pupils to choose which of the two examples they should imitate. It is the duty of the teacher to correct faults from the beginning. In speaking to his pupils he should be careful to distinguish between the tones themselves, the names of the tones, the syllables that are applied to tones, and the notes representing the tones. Also, between singing by syllables, by words, by rote, and by note. We sing by rote when we catch the tone by ear; we sing by

THE MINSTREL BOY.

T. MOORE.
Arranged by BALFE.

Lively.

1. The min-strel boy   to the   war is gone, In the ranks   of   death you'll
2. The min-strel fell,   but the   foe-man's chain Could not bring   that proud   soul

find   him; His fa-ther's sword he hath gird-ed on, And his wild harp slung   be-
un - der; The harp   he loved ne'er   spoke a-gain, For he   tore its   chords a-

hind   him.   "Land of song!" said the   war-rior bard, "Tho' all   the world be-
sun - der, And said, "No chain   shall   sul-ly thee, Thou soul of love and

trays thee, One sword at least thy rights shall guard, One   faithful harp   shall praise thee."
bra-very! Thy songs were made for the pure and free, They shall never sound in sla-very."

note when we interpret the notes, or sing from the written characters. Taste, style, and appropriate expression, both as relates to tones and words, should always receive careful attention. Never introduce into a children's class, or any other class, low, doggerel verse. Let the words selected be mainly of a cheerful character, always such as will interest, and often such as must elevate the tone of the pupil's thought. Shut out entirely from the school all that partakes of buffoonery, waggery, and low, vulgar merriment.

One Sunday, after the choir at Oberlin College had sung without distinctly pronouncing the words, President Finney, in his prayer, alluded to their work as follows: "O Lord, we have sung an anthem to Thy praise. Thou knowest the words but we do not. We do pray Thee that those that lead us may open their mouths, that we may know what they say, that we may join in Thy praise. May they not sing to be heard of men; nor mock Thee, and offend Thy people or the house of God, by displaying themselves."

AMID THE GREENWOOD.

THALBERG.

Andante, with expression.

1. A - mid the green-wood smiling, Once stood a love - ly cot: A huntsman's blooming
2. The huntsman hath de - part - ed, The maid - en, too, is gone, The cot, in ru - ins

daughter Gave beau - ty to the spot; And when a-broad she wander'd, Then
fall - ing, Is des - o - late and lone; A wil - low shall be plant - ed Up-

I was ev - er nigh; When friendly I address'd her, Full sweet was her re - ply.
on this orphan ground. Oh, tree! may'st thou still flourish, Shed bloom and freshness round !

DIP, BOYS, DIP THE OAR.

SARONA.

Allegretto.

1. 'Tis moonlight on the sea, boys, Our boat is on the strand; She
2. The zeph - yrs woo the spray, boys, Their laugh-ter fills the air; We'll
3. What tho' the dark rocks frown, boys, Their home is on the shore; When

Chorus.

bids us all be free, boys, And seek a fair - er land.
bid them wake our song, boys, And steal a - way our care.
fair - er lands ap - pear, boys, Our dangers will be o'er.

Dip, boys, dip the oar,

Bid farewell to the dusk-y shore; Free - dom ours shall be, As we cross the deep blue sea.

WHILE word-music appeals to our intellect through its force of representation, instrumental music appeals directly to the emotions. The former appears clad in shadowy generalities, and the latter arises in its primitive life-giving power. Music is of a lyrical nature, and therefore remains all-powerful where the expression of poetry ceases. Music can be an aid to poetry and can increase its effect on the ear and heart by means of melody, but it can also act independently, forming its theme from its own resources. In the former case it is hampered by the text and must conform itself to the pace of the stream of words. Its compass of tone is prescribed and its liberty restricted thereby. Instrumental music stands alone in its unapproachable sovereignty. In its lyric nature it unfolds the most tender, mysterious feelings hidden in the inmost depths of the human heart. The orchestral instruments are the highest means through which the composer expresses his genius, as well as the purest utterances of his soul in tender or powerful strains, representing the same in the form of a symphony. While in the opera the combination of song,

THREE FISHERS.

JOHN HULLAH.
CHARLES KINGSLEY.

poetry, decoration, acting, costumes, and orchestral effects produce an impression on the listener, and through their union take possession of the senses by their representations of the outer world, it is the sphere of pure instrumental music, of the symphony itself, to enter the recesses of the heart, and find an echo there where love, joy, friendship, sorrow, hope, and earnest striving reign supreme.—*M. Steinhert.*

THE author of "Three Fishers" was a noted poet, preacher and novelist of England. He was professor of modern history at Cambridge, afterwards Canon of Westminster and chaplain to the Queen. He died in 1875. During his boyhood his father was rector of a small parish on the sea-coast, from which he had often seen the herring fleet put out to sea. On these occasions it was customary to hold a short but impressive religious service on the quay, at which not only the fishermen, but also their wives, sweethearts and children were present. Recalling this scene vividly, at the close of a weary day, he wrote this touching poem, whose beauty is enhanced by the plaintive air to which it has been set by John Hullah, an English composer of reputation.

OH, WERT THOU IN THE CAULD BLAST.

ROBERT BURNS.
F. MENDELSSOHN.

1. Oh, wert thou in the cauld blast, On yonder lea, On yonder lea, My plai-die to the an-gry
2. Oh, were I in the wildest waste, Sae black and bare, Sae black and bare, The desert were a Para -

airt, I'd shel-ter thee, I'd shel-ter thee. Or did mis-for-tune's bit-ter storms A-
dise, If thou wert there, If thou wert there, Or were I mon-arch of the globe, With

round thee blaw, A-round thee blaw, Thy shield should be my bosom, To share it a', To share it a'.
thee to reign, With thee to reign, The brightest jewel in my crown Wad be my queen, Wad be my queen.

OH! THAT I NEVER MORE MIGHT SEE.

DONIZETTI.
"ANNA BOLENA."

1. O that I never more might see The smile that hides a sor - row, Better 'twould be that mise-ry
2. He who beholds thee pensively, Thinks of thy maiden pleas-ure, And gazing alone, alone on thee,

From tears some poor relief might bor - row. Tears, like refreshing show-ers, Falling on drooping
Beholds so near his heart's fond trea - sure. O that for empty splendor, Hearts should their peace sur-

a piacere. *a tempo.*

flow - ers, Bear from the lone heart half its pain, Bidding it bloom a - gain.
ren - der! Poor is the triumph pomp may claim O'er ruined heart and blighted fame.

IN some communities the want of an appreciation of music is made very apparent. Selfishness, impoliteness and clownishness, are often manifested to an unpardonable degree when a young lady is called to the piano. The first note struck is taken by the rest of the company as a signal for loud conversation and uproarious laughter. When she has finished, it would often be difficult for many of the company to tell whether she had played the "Danube Waltzes" or "Yankee Doodle." Common civility should, in the parlor or in the concert hall, require at least respectful attention. We are aware that the number of third and even tenth-rate musicians in the world is large. Many young ladies who consider themselves adepts in the art of music seem to regard a discord as satisfactory as a chord. How many "proficients" in music would be speechless from ignorance if called upon to define gamut! how many would almost swoon if called upon to run it! And yet, notwithstanding all this, impoliteness or rudeness is quite inexcusable.

THE difference in musical taste is sometimes due to a peculiarly nervous constitution, or to the depressed or elated condition of the mind. Grief is often soonest solaced by a lively air; hilarity best controlled by a plaintive one. But, after all, that which influences musical taste, or any kind of taste, most is education. Teach children to admire the sublime and the beautiful in nature. At the home fireside and in the school-room, everywhere, children should be instructed in music. Correct taste in music flings wide the gate to the highway of all that is beautiful, noble and good. Among the fine arts it stands foremost.

THE OLD OAKEN BUCKET.

E. KAILLMARK.
SAMUEL WOODWORTH.

1. How dear to my heart are the scenes of my childhood, When fond recol-
The or-chard, the mead-ow, the deep-tangled wildwood, And ev-'ry loved

lec-tion pre-sents them to view! The wide-spreading pond, and the mill that stood
spot which my in-fan-cy knew, The cot of my fa-ther, the dai-ry-house

by it, The bridge and the rock where the cat-a-ract fell. The old oak-en
nigh it, And e'en the rude buck-et that hung in the well,

buck-et; the i-ron-bound bucket, The moss-covered buck-et that hung in the well.

That moss-covered bucket I hailed as a treasure,
  For often at noon, when returned from the field,
I found it the source of an exquisite pleasure,
  The purest and sweetest that nature can yield.
How ardent I seized it, with hands that were glowing,
  And quick to the white-pebbled bottom it fell,
Then soon, with the emblem of truth overflowing,
  And dripping with coolness, it rose from the well.
The old oaken bucket, the iron-bound bucket,
  The moss-covered bucket arose from the well.

How sweet from the green, mossy brim to receive it,
  As, poised on the curb, it inclined to my lips!
Not a full-blushing goblet could tempt me to leave it,
  Tho' filled with the nectar that Jupiter sips.
And now, far removed from the loved habitation,
  The tear of regret will intrusively swell,
As fancy reverts to my father's plantation,
  And sighs for the bucket that hung in the well;
The old oaken bucket, the iron-bound bucket,
  The moss-covered bucket which hangs in the well.

TELL ME, BEAUTIFUL MAIDEN.

[BARCAROLLE.]

Charles Gounod.

Movimento di Barcarola.

Tell me, beautiful maiden, Tell me, where will you go? Fair sails o-ver us swaying,
Di - tes, la jeune bel - le, Où voulezvous al - ler? La voile ou-vre son ai - le,

Lightly the breezes blow, ... Light - ly the breezes blow.
La bri-se va souf - fler, ... La bri-se va souf - fler.

1. At our prow Hope is smiling, Fond hearts gently beguiling Far o'er the crys-tal bay,—
2. To the South-land fast flying Ere yon fair moon be dying, Tell me, love, shall we go?
3. "Let us go," said the maiden, "To that glorious Aidenn, Where love, true love, never dies!
1. L'a - vi-ronest d'i-voi - re, Le pavillon de moi - re, Le gouver - nail d'or fin,

D.S.

Silken sail softly fall - ing, Sea-nymphs tenderly calling, "Come away, love, a - way!"
Or with speed of the wind, love. 'Till our Eden we find, love, Tell me, love, shall we go?
Of that land and its glo - ry, Few, ah! few tell the sto - ry! Few, ah! few find the prize!
J'ai pour lest une oran - ge, Pour voile une aile d'an - ge, Pour mousse un sé-ra - phin.

After last verse.

Tell me, beautiful maiden, Tell me, where will you go? Fair sails o-ver us swaying,
Di - tes, la jeune belle, où voulezvous al - ler? La voile ou-vre son ai - le,

Lightly the breezes blow, ... Light - ly, light - ly blow.
La brise va souf - fler, ... La brise va souf - fler.

O FAIR DOVE, O FOND DOVE.

JEAN INGELOW.
A. S. GATTY. C. MATZ *arr.*

Allegro moderato.

1. Me - thought the stars were blink - ing bright, And the old brig-sails un - furled: I
2. My true-love fares on this great hill, Feed - ing his sheep for - aye: I

said I will sail to my love this night, At the oth - er side of the world. I
look'd in his hut, but all was still, My love was gone a - way. I

cres. *mf*

stepp'd a - board, we sail'd so fast, The sun shot up from the bourne; But a
went to gaze in the for - est creek, And the dove mourned on a - pace; No

Poco lento con molto espress.

dove that perch'd up - on the mast Did mourn, and mourn, and mourn. O fair dove! O
flame did flash, nor fair blue reek Rose up to show me his place. O last love! O

fond dove! And dove with the white, white breast! Let me a-lone, the dream is my own, And the
first love! My love with the true, true heart! To think I have come to this your home, And

pp rall. *mf*

heart is full of rest. }
yet we are a - part. } 3. My love, he stood at my right hand, His eyes were grave and sweet, Me -

thought he said, In this far land, O is it thus we meet? Ah, maid most dear, I

am not here, I have no place, no part, No dwelling more, by sea or shore, But

on - ly in thy heart, O fair dove! O fond dove! till night rose o - ver the

bourne The dove on the mast, as we sail'd fast, Did mourn, and mourn, and mourn.......

SONG OF NIGHT.

GERMAN.

Slowly.

1. Now night's dark shades ap - pear—*(dark shades appear,) I to my couch re - pair;
And safe in qui - et rest— (in qui - et rest,) My dreamings all are blest.
2. Yes, while I sleep and dream— (I sleep and dream,) Bright forms around me gleam;
To guard my slumbers still— (my slumbers still,) From all approach of ill.

There an - gels are keep - ing Their watch while I'm sleep - ing,
From Heav'n they're de - scend - ing, And o'er me are bend - ing,

*The small notes may be played or sung as an echo.

No other form of stage performance is so thoroughly unnatural as the average opera. It is conceived and executed from a standpoint as purely imaginary as a fairy tale. To begin with, we have the chorus. The idea of a party of male and female individuals shouting their unanimous opinions and expressions in four-part music is essentially absurd. Then we have the chorus brought on in the queerest and most impossible situations. A party of conspirators will steal upon an unsuspecting victim, singing their threats and intentions in tones loud enough to warn him even if he were the inmate of a deaf and dumb asylum, while the aforesaid victim announces, in a lusty tenor, that he has not the least idea of the impending calamity. In Fra Diavolo we have two or three villains about to attack a young girl. They sing from their place of concealment; but she is temporarily deaf and does not hear them. In Lucia and Hamlet the heroines go mad and sing their most brilliant numbers under the influence of their delirium. In Lucia also, while the unhappy heroine is getting more and more hopelessly insane under the influence of her own vocal pyrotechnics, the male chorus, clad as Scotchmen, stand around in a semi-circle and sing an acccompaniment to her crazy act, instead of sending for the doctor. In Faust, when Valentine dies, the soldiers and villagers sing him to death most inconsiderately. Margaret gets off her sick bed to sing a trio with Faust and Mephistophiles, and the chorus is very noisy while paralyzing Mephisto with the hilts of their swords in the form of a cross.

OVER THE STARS THERE IS REST.

FRANZ ABT.
T. T. BARKER.

GOOD NIGHT.

FRANZ ABT.

1. In the west the sun de-clin-ing, Sinks beneath the mountain height, Tints the clouds with
2. Bleak-er winds the flow'rs be-numbing, On the hearth the crick-et sings; Home the la-den
3. In the wind the grass is bending, Flow'rs now slumber in the shade; Birds to seek their
4. Man now seeks his peace-ful dwelling, Cir-cles round the rud-dy blaze; Of the sweets of

gold-en lin-ing, Sets the hills with ru-bies shining, Then bids all the world good night.
bee flies humming, And the drow-sy bat is coming, Dart-ing on his leath-ern wings.
nests are wending, Flocks in fold the shepherds tending, Homeward flies the mountain maid.
la-bor tell-ing, Till his heart with rapture swelling, Grate-ful gives his Mak-er praise.

Good night, Good night! Good night, Good night! Good night, Good night!

GOOD CHEER.

Lively.

1. There's much good cheer in youth-ful days, When fair-y scenes the heart en-gage,
2. The Sum-mer's smile we ev-er greet, We love its ber-ries fresh and sweet,

When all is sun-ny, clear, and bright, And pleas-ures reign from morn till night.
And Au-tumn comes with welcome glee, O yes, its fruits we long to see.

Oh, who like us is free from care? Oh, who in sports has
And all the year 'tis filled with good, To us who sail on

half our share? We bound like roe-bucks o'er the plain, And ev-er fresh and free re-main.
youth's bright flood, We let our pleasures take the wing, And ev-er, ev-er, ev-er sing.

1st. 2nd.

La la la la la la la la la la la la la la la la la la la.

CABINET ORGAN.—The piano now has a rival in the United States in that fine instrument which has grown from the melodeon into the cabinet organ. It seems to us peculiarly the instrument for *men*. We trust the time is at hand when it will be seen that it is not less desirable for boys to learn to play upon an instrument; and how much more a little skill in performing may do for a man than for a woman! A boy can hardly be a perfect savage, nor a man a mere money-maker, who has acquired sufficient command of an instrument to play upon it with pleasure. How often, when we have been listening to the swelling music of the cabinet organs at the warerooms of Mason and Hamlin, in Broadway, have we desired to put one of those instruments into every clerk's boarding-house room, and tell him to take all the ennui, and half the peril, out of his life by learning to play upon it! No business man who works as intensely as we do, can keep alive the celestial harmonies within him,—no, nor the early wrinkles from his face,—without some such pleasant mingling of bodily rest and mental exercise as playing upon an instrument. The simplicity of the means by which music is produced from the cabinet organ is truly remarkable. It is called a "reed" instrument; which leads many to suppose that the canebrake is despoiled to procure its sound-giving apparatus. Not so. The reed employed is nothing but a thin strip of brass with a tongue slit in it, the vibration of which causes the musical sound. One of the reeds, though it produces a volume of sound only surpassed by the pipes of an organ, weighs about an ounce, and can be carried in a vest-pocket. In fact, a cabinet organ is simply an accordion of immense power and improved

HEAVILY WEARS THE DAY.

GERMAN AIR.

1. Heav-i-ly wears the day in sighs and tears away, Heavily wears the day in sighs and tears away; With
2. Oft did he tell me so, when I would bid him go, Oft did he tell me so, when I would bid him go,— My
3. Oh, that it could be so! Yes, I would let him go; Oh, that it could be so! Yes, I would let him go, And

weeping I am weary, weary, When at the door I stand, seeing the darken'd land all still and dreary, I am so
trifling never made him weary: "When I am far away, over the bounding spray, You will be dreary, dear one, and
of my weeping never weary, Only to have him come back to his own lov'd home, To hear his cheery "Do not be

weary; When at the door I stand, seeing the darken'd land, All still and dreary, I am so weary.
weary; When I am far away, over the bounding spray, You will be dreary, dear one, and weary."
dreary;" Only to have him come back to his own lov'd home, To hear his cheery "Do not be dreary."

mechanism. Twenty years ago, one of our melodeon-makers chanced to observe that the accordion produced a better tone when it was drawn out than when it was pushed in; and this fact suggested the first great improvement in the melodeon. Before that time, the wind from the bellows, in all melodeons, was forced thro' the reeds. At this point of development, the instrument was taken up and covered with improvements, making it one of the most pleasing musical instruments in the possession of mankind. When we remarked above, that the American piano is the best in the world, we expressed only the opinion of others, but now that we assert the superiority of American cabinet organs over similar instruments made in London and Paris, we are communicating knowledge of our own. Indeed, the superiority is so marked that it is apparent to the merest tyro in music. In the new towns of the great West, the cabinet organ is usually the first instrument of music to arrive, and, of late years, it takes its place with the piano in the fashionable drawing-rooms of the Atlantic States.—*James Parton.*

THE first effect of culture in its most popular form—scientific knowledge—is sometimes to unsettle faith and unchurch the souls of men. The remedy for this moral and religious unsettling lies, not in a cowardly retreat from knowledge, but in a manful advance into a larger knowledge. The higher up in the scale of humanity a people stands, the profounder its homage to the moral law. Fire the poet or painter or musician with the passion of patriotism, the enthusiasm of humanity, the worship of the infinite and eternal God, and you will get the work which shall prove immortal.—*R. H. Newton.*

EVENING HYMN.

Ave, Sanctissima.

1. Hail, thou most sa - cred One, We lift our souls to Thee; Hear Thou our
2. Je - sus, most gra-cious One, We trust Thy ten - der care; We give our

even - ing song, 'Tis night - fall on the sea. Watch us while shad - ows lie
hearts to Thee, Hear Thou our hum - ble prayer. Oh, Thou whose love doth shine

Far o'er the wa - ters spread, Hear Thou the heart's lone sigh, Thine too hath
Match - less for ev - er - more, Come and each thought re - fine, Come, we im-

ril.

bled. Thou who hast tast - ed death, Aid us when death is near, Whis-per of
plore. Save Thou our souls from ill, Guard Thou our lives from fear; Our hearts with

a tempo.

heav'n to faith, Blest Sa - viour, Blest Sa - viour, hear. Sa - viour, most gra - cious, Oh,
com - fort fill, Blest Sa - viour, Blest Sa - viour, hear. Sa - viour, most gra - cious, Oh,

take us to thy care. Je - sus, we be - seech Thee, Hear Thou our prayer.
take us to thy care. Je - sus, we be - seech Thee, Hear Thou our prayer.

rall.

ONE BY ONE.

Allegro Moderato.

Vincenzo Bellini.
Adelaide Anne Proctor.

1. One by one the sands are flow - ing, One by one the mo - ments fall; Some are
2. Ev - 'ry hour that fleets so slow - ly, Has its task to do or bear: Lu - mi -

com-ing, some are go - ing, Do not strive, ah! do not strive to grasp them all! One by
nous the crown and ho - ly, If thou set each, if thou set each gem with care. Do not

one thy du - ties wait thee, Let thy whole strength go to each; Let no
look at life's long sor - row, See how small each mo - ment's pain; God will

[gifts from
fu - ture dreams elate thee, Learn thou first what these can teach, what these can teach, One by one, bright
help thee for to - morrow, Ev - 'ry day be - gin a - gain, be-gin a - gain, Do not linger with re -

Lento.

Heaven, Joys are sent thee here below; Take them readily when given, Ready too to let them go.
gretting, Or for passion's hour despond; Nor, the daily toil forgetting, Look too eagerly be-yond.

Rall. un poco.

One by one thy griefs shall meet thee, Do not fear an arm - ed band; One will fade while others
Hours are golden links, God's token, Reaching Heav'n, but one by one Take them lest the chain be

greet thee, Shadows passing thro' the land. One by one thy griefs shall meet thee, Do not fear an armed
brok - en Ere the pilgrimage be done. Hours are golden links, God's token, Reaching Heav'n, but one by

Lento.

band; One will fade while others greet thee, Shadows passing thro' the land; One will fade
one, Take them lest the chain be brok-en Ere the pil-grim-age be done; Hours are gold -

while oth - ers meet thee, Shadows pass - ing thro' the land, One by one.
en links, God's tok - en, Reaching Heav-en one by one, One by one.

AT EVENING-TIME.

SPORLE.
C. M. STEADMAN.

Allegretto.

1. The lights fade out of calm-ed sea, Dark shadows seam its breast; Flush'd like to pet - al
2. Rest comes at last! o'er pur-ple hills The sheep-bell tin - kles clear. And slow the low-ing
3. Rest comes at last! oh, wea-ry heart, Fever'd and faint with care, And toil-ing 'neath thine

ad lib.

of a flow'r, The sail fades in the west. Far o'er the blue the weary winds Have gone, and swells no
kine descend The paths, and on the ear Ring joy-ous ech-oes from a - far, The sic-kles keen laid
earthly cross, Too great for man to bear: Take courage, faint not, but endure! Soon shall the day be

more The waves' sad mu - sic, or the break Of rip - ples on the shore.
by; Then all sound dies, and earth and sea Sleep calm 'neath si - lent sky.
past! At ev - en -tide the end shall come, And bring thee rest at last.

The hymn, "From all that dwell below the skies," is Isaac Watts's version of the one hundred and seventeenth psalm. It is a brief rendering of the shortest chapter in the Bible, yet it is full of force and fervor. There is a charm in poetry and music which can never be exhausted, but by some it is not even realized. "An instance of this was witnessed," says G. J. Stevenson, "in a large school of poor children located at Lambeth Green, London. The day's work was done, the usual singing and prayer were over, and three hundred boys were expecting in a moment to be free from authority and at play. This psalm by Dr. Watts had been sung to the tune of the 'Portuguese Hymn.' The master made a few remarks about the pleasure music produces and asked the children to try to sing the hymn again. They did so; it was done with care and much feeling. Again the request was preferred—would they like to sing it again? The reply from hundreds of voices was a simultaneous 'Yes.' It was repeated, if possible with increased delight to the boys. Then followed a few remarks about the music of Heaven, and how sweet it must be there, and the boys were asked if they had not felt more happy in that singing than if they had been at play. Another unanimous 'Yes,' and again they repeated the song until hymn and tune may have been fixed in their memories for life."

THINE EYES SO BLUE AND DREAMING.

E. LASSEN.
RICHARD FIELD *tr.*

SEARCH THRO' THE WIDE WORLD.

DONIZETTI.
"DAUGHTER OF REGIMENT."

1. Search thro' the wide world, Where can ye find He - roes so dar - ing, Com - rades so
2. Brave sons of bat - tle, Hear the de - cree, Live ye but long enough, Gen'rals ye'll

kind? Pocket full or pen - ni - less, Go where ye may, All are proud to
be. Heed - less of dan - ger, On - ward ye go, Loved by the

serve ye well, Heedless of pay, Men look with en - vy, Ladies with de - light, On the corps re-
beau - ti - ful, Fear'd by the foe, Show but your col-ors, All do own their sway, Yours it is to

sist - less in love as in fight. Matchless in fame, Foremost in glo - ry. In the camp, in the
conquer, and theirs to o - bey! Matchless in fame, Foremost in glo - ry. In the camp, in the

grave, on the field of war, There is not in the world such a gallant corps, There is not such a gal - lant

corps! War sounds the trump, to your standard ye fly, Vic - to - ry's wreath must be yours, or ye die!

EHREN ON THE RHINE.

Wm. M. Hutchinson.

Tempo di Marcia.

mf

1. A sol - dier stood in the vil - lage street, And bade his love a - dieu, His
2. They march'd a - way, down the vil - lage street, The ban - ners float - ing gay. The

gun and knap - sack at his feet, His com - pa - ny in view. With tears she kiss'd him
children cheer'd for the tramping feet, That went to war a - way. But one a - mong them

dim. *pp* *p cres.*

once a - gain, Then turn'd a - way her head, He could but whis - per in his pain, And
turn'd him round, To look but once a - gain. And tho' his lips gave out no sound, His

pp rall. *p Allegro.*

this is what he said: "Oh, love, dear love, be true, This heart is on - ly thine, When the
heart sigh'd this refrain: "Oh, love, dear love, be true, This heart is on - ly thine, When the

war is o'er We'll part no more At Eh - ren on the Rhine, Oh, love, dear love, be true, This
[A - ren.]

heart is on - ly thine, When the war is o'er, We'll part no more, At Eh - ren on the Rhine."

EARLY BEGINNINGS.—Nearly all the great masters were precocious in their abilities. Haydn began his career at the age of eight. When fifteen he had already developed much of the skill and independence for which he became famous. At that age he happened to hear of a vacancy in the choir of the church at Tell, and circumstances made him anxious to obtain the post. The choir-master, however, on receiving his application, refused to allow him to join the choir. Nevertheless, on the following Sunday, Haydn managed to smuggle himself into the choir, and sit next to the principal soloist. Just as this soloist rose to deliver himself of the solo, Haydn snatched the music from his hand, and at once began to sing it himself at sight. The church authorities were so electrified that they gave him a good sum of money as soon as the service was over. Beethoven, at fifteen, was one of the chief musicians under the Elector of Cologne. At four, Mozart could play freely on the harpsichord; at six he not only composed, but began to travel as a *virtuoso.* The Archbishop of Salzburg, a few years afterwards, would not believe that a child so young could of himself accomplish all he was accredited with. Accordingly, he shut him up in a cell with

OVER THE SUMMER SEA.

VERDI.

Allegretto.

1. O - ver the sum-mer sea, With light hearts gay and free, Join'd by glad minstrel - sy,
2. List, to my roun-de - lay As we glide on our way; Ne'er will my love de - cay,
3. Hark, there's a bird on high, Far in yon a - zure sky, Fling-ing sweet mel - o - dy,

Gay - ly we're roam - ing; Swift flows the rippling tide; Light - ly the zephyrs glide;
Ne'er will I leave thee; While o'er the wa - ters deep; Now our oars gai - ly sweep,
Each heart to glad - den; And its song seems to say, "Ban - ish dull care a - way;

Round us, on ev' - ry side, Bright crests are foam - ing. Fond hearts, en - twin - ing,
True in the time they keep, What can grieve thee? Fond hearts, en - twin - ing,
Nev - er let sor - row stay, Brief joys to sad - den." Fond hearts, en - twin - ing,

cres.

Cease all re - pin - ing; Near us is shin - ing Beau - ty's bright smile.

pen, ink, paper, and the words for a mass. Within a week the young prisoner produced a complete score for the inspection of the incredulous archbishop. The result of its performance was that the mass became a stock piece at the Salzburg Cathedral, while Mozart became the prelate's *consert-meister,* at the age of twelve. Mendelssohn was a noted improviser on the pianoforte at the age of eight. Schumann, as a school-boy, could at any time gather a knot of companions, who eagerly listened as he described their characters on the piano. Chopin did a still more wonderful thing, when a boy in his father's school. Sonntag thought him such a miracle at ten, that she gave him a valuable gold watch as a token of admiration. At nine he was asked to assist at a public concert for the poor. He selected as his subject a difficult concerto, and was dressed by his mother like a little dandy for the occasion. After a great success, he went home to his mother, who asked him as she embraced him, what the public liked best. "Oh, mamma," said the unconscious young genius, "nobody could look at anything but my collar!"

HAPPY ARE WE TO-NIGHT.

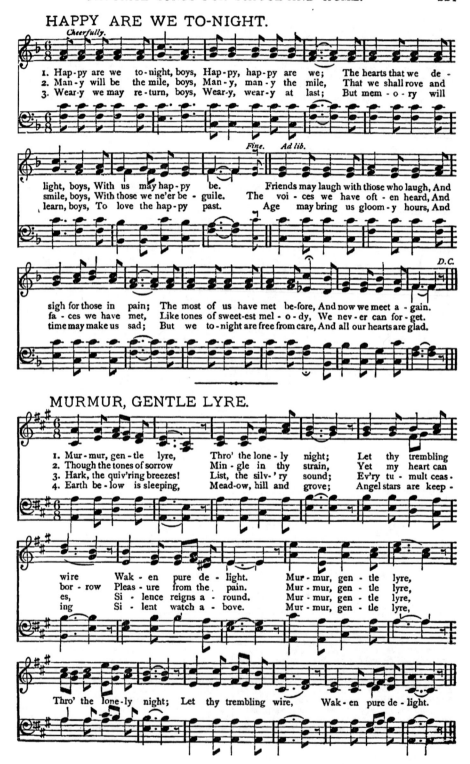

1. Hap-py are we to-night, boys, Hap-py, hap-py are we; The hearts that we de-
2. Man-y will be the mile, boys, Man-y, man-y the mile, That we shall rove and
3. Wear-y we may re-turn, boys, Wear-y, wear-y at last; But mem-o-ry will

light, boys, With us may hap-py be. Friends may laugh with those who laugh, And
smile, boys, With those we ne'er be- guile. The voi-ces we have oft-en heard, And
learn, boys, To love the hap-py past. Age may bring us gloom-y hours, And

sigh for those in pain; The most of us have met be-fore, And now we meet a-gain.
fa-ces we have met, Like tones of sweet-est mel-o-dy, We nev-er can for-get.
time may make us sad; But we to-night are free from care, And all our hearts are glad.

MURMUR, GENTLE LYRE.

1. Mur-mur, gen-tle lyre, Thro' the lone-ly night; Let thy trembling
2. Though the tones of sorrow Min-gle in thy strain, Yet my heart can
3. Hark, the quiv'ring breezes! List, the silv-'ry sound; Ev'ry tu-mult ceas-
4. Earth be-low is sleeping, Mead-ow, hill and grove; Angel stars are keep-

wire Wak-en pure de-light. Mur-mur, gen-tle lyre,
bor-row Pleas-ure from the pain. Mur-mur, gen-tle lyre,
es, Si-lence reigns a-round. Mur-mur, gen-tle lyre,
ing Si-lent watch a-bove. Mur-mur, gen-tle lyre,

Thro' the lone-ly night; Let thy trembling wire, Wak-en pure de-light.

We heard from a bright woman the other day the expression "a musical snob," and asked what it meant. "A musical snob, my dear, is one of the most insufferable of all snobs. I mean by it an imperfectly-educated amateur, a person who can perhaps play fairly well on some musical instrument, or can possibly sing without serious faults the ordinary run of songs one hears in the parlor or at an amateur concert. When such meagerly educated musicians claim 'to know all,' though they really know little more than nothing; when they profess to have no interest in 'popular music,' but dote on 'the classical;' when such self-satisfied persons criticise every musician, affect to discover faults where others more competent to give an opinion are free to award credit—why, they are musical snobs, my dear, and the laughing stock of everybody who loves music. Such shallow frauds find fault with the programmes at the summer concerts because they are too light; such meretricious musicians affect to dislike Gericke, to sneer at Thomas, and to dote on Seidl. They can't bear to hear an Italian opera; they must have 'Varkner' or nothing. They like Von Bulow, but 'can't bear' Krebs, and regard Carreno as a mere 'amateur.' They are wild

JOHNNY SCHMOKER.

Johnny Schmoker, Johnny Schmoker, kann'st du sin-gen? Kann'st du spielen? Ich kann spielen auf der Trom-mel. Rub a dub a dub, das ist die Trommel. Fi-fey.

Witty witty wink, das ist die Fi-fey. Rub a dub a dub, das ist die Trommel, Mein

Rub a dub a dub, Mein wit-ty wit-ty wink, das ist die Fi-fey. Triangle.

3d time.—Triangle.
p ‖: Ting ting ting, das ist Triangle. :‖
p Witty witty wink, das ist die Fifey.
f Rub a dub a dub, das ist die Trommel.
f Mein rub a dub a dub, mein witty witty wink,
p Mein ting ting ting, das ist Triangle.

(*D. C.* Johnny Schmoker, for 4th time.)

4th time.—Trombone.
f ‖: Boom boom boom, das ist die Trombone. :‖
5th time.—Cymbal.
‖: Zim zim zim, das ist die Cymbal. :‖
6th time.—Viol.
p ‖: Voom voom voom, das ist die Viol. :‖
7th time.—Doodelsack. (Bagpipe.)
‖: Twack twack twack, das ist der Doodelsack. :‖

about the 'chello.' If they hear the 'crowd' praising a singer they immediately pounce on his or her 'style,' or 'phrasing,' or 'tones'—anything at all to make precious little knowledge pass as the dictum of an artist, a critic, or a lover of the 'best music.' A musical snob, my dear, is one of the most repulsive of its species, for it persists in pushing its snobbishness upon the sight and hearing of an abused and disgusted public. Be patient with the creature; may be it can't help it."

In the old humorous song here given, sing to first *D. C.* then repeat from the beginning, omitting the part marked 1st time, passing to part marked 2d time, continue on to *D. C.* of this (second part) then repeat again from the beginning, omitting both first and second time parts, passing to third time, or new part, and so on. Observe that the motions are made only when the words describing the instruments are sung, as for example, at "Rub-a-dub," the roll of the drum is imitated, before and after which the arms and hands are motionless. At every *D. C.* let the arms fall. It represents a lively old fellow, a German musician, who is telling his friend Johnny Schmoker about the instruments upon which he can play, describing them by motions while he sings. When performed by a chorus, especially of men, the movements being in exact time and all together, the effect produced is unique and entertaining. The motions are made only when the words describing the instruments are sung, as for example at "Rub-a-dub-a-dub" the roll of the drum is imitated, beginning in the case of all the instruments with the first and ending exactly with the last word; of "Witty witty wink," the hands are placed as if playing the fife and the fingers only move; of "Ting ting ting," the right hand strikes three times under the left as if playing the triangle; of "Boom boom boom," the hand is moved forward and back as if playing the trombone; and so on to the last, which is imitated by crooking both arms and striking with them against the sides as if playing the bagpipe. Observe that the singing in the case of some of the instruments is loud and of others soft; also, that the phrase where each instrument is first mentioned is repeated, and that the first movement which is sung when each instrument is introduced is (to save room) printed but once. The effect of this song with a company of children is highly amusing and greatly enjoyed.

SWINGING 'NEATH THE APPLE-TREE.

O. R. BARROWES.
Per. BIGLOW & MAIN.

1. Oh, the sports of child - hood! Roaming thro' the wild - wood, Running o'er the mead - ows,
2. Swaying in the sun - beams, Floating in the shad - ow, Sail - ing on the breez - es,
3. Oh, the sports of child - hood! Roaming thro' the wild - wood, Sing - ing o'er the mead - ows,

hap - py and free; But my heart's a - beat - ing For the old time greet - ing,
hap - py and free; Chas - ing all our sad - ness, Shout - ing in our glad - ness,
hap - py and free; How my heart's a - beat - ing, Think - ing of the greet - ing,

Chorus.

Swing - ing 'neath the old ap - ple tree. Swing - ing, swing - ing,
Swing - ing 'neath the old ap - ple tree. Swing - ing, swing - ing,
Swing - ing 'neath the old ap - ple tree. Swing - ing, swing - ing,

Swing - ing,

Swing - ing, swing - ing, Lull - ing care to rest 'neath the old ap - ple tree,

Swing - ing, Swing - ing 'neath the old ap - ple tree,

Swinging, swinging, swinging, swinging, swing - ing 'neath the old ap - ple tree.

Swing - ing, Swing - ing, Swing - ing 'neath the old ap - ple tree.

CHILD OF THE REGIMENT.

DONIZETTI.
CHAS. JEFFERYS.

Andante con moto.

1. Ask me not why my heart with fond e - mo - tion Beats for the brave companions of my
2. Chide me no more! Were I de-void of feel-ing, Would my in - grat-i-tude not wake thy

youth! Had they not tend-ed me with love's devotion, I had not lived, a - las, to prove my
fears? Worthless would be this moment's fond reveal-ing, If I could cast a-side the ties of long, long

truth: A help-less babe   up - on the field I lay,   And but for
years.   Thou hast my love;   thine is a mother's claim;   To them for-

them my life had passed a - way,   My life had passed   a - way: Ere I for-
get   not that thou ow'st the name,   My mother, my moth - er   dear, Ere I can

get them, all their loving kindness, Bring o'er my heart   ob-livion of the past: But when you
cease to think of all their kindness, Bring o'er my heart   ob-livion of the past: But when you

win for me that fa - tal blindness, In mer-cy let that moment, that moment, be my last.

GOLDEN SLUMBERS.

LULLABY OF 17TH CENTURY.

Smoothly.

1. Gold - en slum - bers kiss your eyes, Smiles a - wake you when you rise;
2. Care is heav - y, there - fore sleep; You are care, and care must keep;

Sleep, pret - ty wan - tons, do not cry, And I will sing a lul - la - by,
Sleep, pret - ty wan - tons, do not cry, And I will sing a lul - la - by,

Lul - la - by, lul - la - by, lul - la - by.

BABY'S NIGHT.

1. Twin - kle bright - ly, stars of light, Christ - mas Eve is Ba - by's night;
2. Dar - ling, raise your soft blue eyes, To the brill - iance of the skies;
3. You, so near, in robe of white, To the spir - its clothed in light;
4. Ah, my prec - ious! I can see Ser - aphs look - ing out at me,

rit.

Sweet my dar - ling, God is good, Thus to hon - or ba - by - hood.
Can you see the an - gel-throng? Can you hear their won - drous song?
You whose gen - tle soul might be Tuned to high - est min - strel - sy.
Ev - ery time the im - pulse bids Ba - by lift its droop - ing lids.

Heavenly music I can hear
Falling on my raptured ear,
When my baby's cooing voice,
Makes the mother's heart rejoice.

Since the Lord of Glory shares
Such a form as baby wears,
Every little child should be
Vested with new sanctity.

Twinkle brightly, stars of light,
Christmas Eve is Baby's night;
Sweet my darling, God is good,
Thus to honor babyhood.

15

AH! I HAVE SIGHED TO REST ME.

G. VERDI.
"IL TROVATORE."

Andante Sostenuto.

dolce.

1. Ah! I have sighed to rest............ me Deep in the qui - et
2. Out of the love I bear............. thee, Yield I my life for

grave,— sigh'd to rest me, But all in vain I crave. O fare thee
thee; Wilt thou not think, Wilt thou not think of me? O think of

1 well, my Le - o - no - ra, fare - thee - well! Ah! I have sigh'd for rest, Yet all in vain do I

sf

crave, O fare - thee - well, my Le - o - no - ra, fare - thee - well!

2 *a tempo.*

me, my Le - o - no - ra, fare - thee - well! Out of the love I

bear thee, Yield I my life for thee. Ah! think of me,* ah! think of

* *Non ti scordar di me!*

me, my Le - o - no - ra, fare-thee-well! Tho' I no more be - hold thee,

Yet is thy name a spell, Yet is thy name, yet is thy name a spell,

cres - - cen - - do.

Cheering my last lone hour, Le - o - no - ra, fare - well!

WOODMAN, SPARE THAT TREE.

HENRY RUSSELL.
GEORGE P. MORRIS.

1. Wood - man, spare that tree! Touch not a sin - gle bough; In youth it shel - tered
2. That old fa - mil - iar tree, Its glo - ry and re - nown Are spread o'er land and
3. When but an i - dle boy, I sought its grateful shade; In all their gush - ing
4. My heart-strings round thee cling, Close as thy bark, old friend! Here shall the wild - bird

me, And I'll pro - tect it now; 'Twas my fore - fa - ther's hand, That
sea, And would'st thou hew it down? Woodman, for - bear thy stroke! Cut
joy, Here, too, my sis - ters played; My moth - er kissed me here; My
sing, And still thy branches bend. Old tree, the storm thou'lt brave, And,

placed it near his cot, There, woodman, let it stand, Thy axe shall harm it not!
not its earth-bound ties; Oh! spare that a - ged oak, Now tow - 'ring to the skies.
fa - ther pressed my hand, For - give this fool - ish tear, But let that old oak stand!
woodman, leave the spot; While I've a hand to save, Thy axe shall harm it not.

It is stated on what seems very good authority that stringed instruments were unknown among the American Indians and among the ancient Mexicans. The mandolin, which was introduced here by the Tipaldis a few years ago, has taken firm hold upon the affections of music-loving people of some localities, and many amateur clubs have been formed for the purpose of becoming efficient performers on this beautiful little instrument. Many people regard it as a very inferior instrument, but Beethoven did not think it beneath him to compose music for it. Only two varieties of mandolins have as yet been brought to this country, the Milanese and the Neapolitan, having eight strings, although they are also made in Germany. The strings are of wire and are twanged with a plectrum, or pick, or tortoise shell, and it is said that it is not difficult to learn to play well on this instrument. The guitar seems to stand between the wooden sounds of the banjo and the tinkling of the mandolin, while its sweet sadness suggests more than any other instrument its appropriateness as an accompaniment while the voice sings love songs. The mandolin "craze" is regarded as a passing fancy, but the demand for guitars is constant and steady, and to-day, as it was nearly fifty years

THE MANDOLIN SONG.

SPANISH.
"MANDOLINATA."

1. O I'm a hap-py crea-ture, Merry from morn till night; I love a gay and
2. Tho' cloudy be the morn-ing, Sunny may be the noon; But mu-sic ne'er can
3. I wish there were no fight-ing, Never a speck of war, That weak and strong could

joy-ous day, And song is my de-light: The world is all be-fore me, Nev-er a care I
charm the ear, If strings be out of tune. Then sing in cheerful measure, Mer-ri-ly all the
right all wrong Without a wound or scar; I wish there were no sor-row, Nev-er a cause of

know, Then why should I despond or sigh, When pleasures freely flow? O sing in cheerful measure,
day; And with a smile for-get awhile Your sorrows while you may. O sing in cheerful measure,
woe, If on-ly men could all agree, How glad the days would go! O sing in cheerful measure,

Mer-ri-ly all the day, And with a smile for-get awhile Your sorrows while you may.

ago, the best instruction book is that written by Carulli. Another excellent one is by Carcassi, these two being the best published. The zither is fast becoming a dangerous rival to the above-named stringed instruments. Not so difficult as the harp, perhaps, but more difficult to play well than the banjo, mandolin, or guitar, the zither is so delightful when well played that the performer feels more than repaid for the time spent in practicing. This instrument was formerly supposed to have been invented by the ancient Greeks, but it is now generally conceded that it originated in the Tyrolese Alps or else in Southern Germany, where it is very common. The name cithara has been applied to several stringed instruments of various forms, and was known as early as the ninth century in Germany. In its present form it is shaped not unlike a harp, has from thirty-one to forty-four strings, and, being laid on a properly constructed table, is played with both hands, a shield being worn on the thumb of the right hand. The zither embraces almost six octaves, and consequently is nearly equal to the piano in scope. The instrument which has forty-four strings is generally preferred by professional players, while amateurs use those having a less number.—*Karl Merz.*

SONG OF PARTING.

Andante sostenuto.

FRANZ ABT.
FOR GRADUATION DAY.

1. Sweet songs our voices blending, Make glad this promised day, But minor strains as-cend-ing Our
2. When years are onward go - ing We'll backward look to thee, O Al - ma Ma-ter, show-ing Our
3. Our part-ing trib-ute rais-ing, We turn at last a - way, Down future vis-tas gaz - ing Where

part-ing still de - lay, In time to come will meet-ing Bring with it earn-est greet-ing: With
hearts can grateful be, While thro' the wel-kin ring- ing Comes Mem'ry treasure bringing: With
Hope, in fair ar - ray, Shows ra-diant light il - lum-ing The am - a-ranth's fair blooming: With

ar - dor true our band, Rove we o'er sea, o'er land, Join hand in hand, Join hand in hand.

SLUMBER, DEAREST.

C. M. VON FLOTOW.

1. Slumber, dearest, while a-bove thee, Angel eyes are bending now; And their starry pinions waving,
2. Deep-er now the mid-night shadows Gather in the val-ley fair; Softly thro' the lat - tice stealing,

Lightly fan thy placid brow; All is hushed and still around thee, While my lonely watch I keep;
Comes the cool, refreshing air; Till the ro - sy light of morn-ing Spangles o'er the crystal deep,

Thou art dreaming, sweetly dreaming, Sleep on, darling, peaceful sleep, Darling, peaceful be thy sleep.
Till the birds their songs a - wak-en, Sleep on, darling, peaceful sleep, Darling, peaceful be thy sleep.

MENDELSSOHN delighted in the open air and beautiful scenery. When he was twenty, he staid some time at Chester, in England. He loved afterward to tell of the charm which the meadow and brook, the trees and grass, had for him there. He spent much time sketching and painting; but his head was full of music, and everything suggested a musical idea to him. He was very fond of carnations, and he set a bunch of them to music in the album of a daughter of his host, with a drawing of the flowers over the notes; not forgetting to set some delicate arpeggia in the music for the scent of the flowers. On seeing the younger sister with some bell-shaped flowers in her hair, he said that the fairies might dance on the trumpets, and he set them to a capriccio. He never tired of merry-making, and one afternoon towards dusk, he, with a number of young people, was one of a happy young company that was picnicking in a thicket. Some one gaily proposed a fire; and all began to drag the boughs and twigs into place,

THE WORLD IS FULL OF BEAUTY.

G. DONIZETTI.

1. There is beau-ty in the for-est, Where the trees are green and fair;
2. There is beau-ty in the foun-tain, Toss-ing gai-ly in its play,
3. There is beau-ty in the moon-light When it falls up-on the sea,
4. There is beau-ty in the bright-ness Beam-ing from a lov-ing eye,

There is beau-ty in the mead-ow Where wild flowers scent the air;
While the rain-bow hues are glit-t'ring On its sil-v'ry-shin-ing spray.
While the blue foam-crest-ed bil-lows Dance and frol-ic joyous-ly;
In the warm blush of af-fec-tion, In the tear of sym-pa-thy!

There is beau-ty in the sun-light, And the soft blue beams a-bove.
There is beau-ty in the stream-let, Murm'ring soft-ly through the grove.
There is beau-ty in the light'ning gleam That fit-ful shines a-bove.
In the sweet low voice whose ac-cents The spir-it's glad-ness prove.

Oh! the world is full of beau-ty, When the heart is full, the heart is full of love.

so that they soon had a fine bonfire. While still lingering around it, Mendelssohn began to ask for some music, but nothing could be found save a worn-out fiddle of the gardener's. Mendelssohn, all undismayed, began to play, shouting with laughter at his performance; but soon there was a hush in the chat and sport, and the whole party sat spell-bound at the music which he drew from even that despised fiddle. He would sit for hours improvising dance-tunes, and liked nothing better than to entertain his friends with his music. He always looked back on this visit to Chester as one of the brightest spots in a bright life.

IMMORTALITY! This master thought which should be most in our minds, ever present with us, is one to which millions seem never to give a passing moment of serious reflection. They are as their dogs and their horses. Of all human beings, the clergy not excepted, those in the educational work should ponder most this sublime truth, and make it familiar as their native air to the youth who are passing through the schools.

HEARTS AND HOMES.

J. BLOCKLEY.

1. Hearts and homes, sweet words of pleas-ure, Mus - ic breath - ing as ye fall; Mak - ing
2. Hearts and homes, sweet words re - veal-ing, All most good and fair to see; Fit - ting

each the oth - er's trea - sure, Once di - vid - ed, los - ing all. Homes, ye
shrines for pur - est feel - ing, Tem - ples meet to bend the knee. In - fant

may be high or low - ly, Hearts a - lone can make you ho - ly; Be the
hands bright gar - lands wreathing, Hap - py voi - ces in - cense breathing, Em - blems

dwell-ing e'er so small, Hav - ing love, it boast - eth all.
fair of realms a - bove, For love is heav'n, and heav'n is love.

SWING, CRADLE, SWING.

GEORGE COOPER.

Smoothly.

1. Ba - by is a sail - or boy, Swing, cradle, swing; Sailing is the sailor's joy, Swing, cradle,
2. Snowy sails and precious freight, Swing, cradle, swing; Baby's captain, mother's mate, Swing, cradle,
3. Never fear, the watch is set, Swing, cradle, swing; Stormy gales are never met, Swing, cradle,
4. Little eyelids downward creep, Swing, cradle, swing; Now he's in the cove of sleep, Swing, cradle,

swing. Swing, cradle, Swing, cradle, Swing, cradle, swing; Swing, cradle, Swing, cradle, Swing, cradle,
[swing.

THE BRIDE BELLS.

Joseph L. Roeckel.

Allegretto.

1. Maid El - sie roams by lane and lea, Her heart beats low and sad, Her thoughts are far a-
3. A   year by seas, a year by lands, A year since then has died, And El - sie at the

way   at sea, With her bon - nie sai - lor   lad, With her bon - nie   sai - lor   lad. But
al - tar stands, Her   sai - lor at her   side, Her sai - lor   at   her   side, While

Kling,   lang,   ling,   She seems to hear her bride bells ring, Kling, lang, ling,
Kling,   lang,   ling,   Their bonnie bride bells gai - ly ring, Kling, lang, ling,

pp   *cres.*   *f* 1st.   FINE.

Kling, lang,   ling,   She seems to hear her bride bells ring, her bride bells   ring!
Kling, lang,   ling,   Their bon - nie bride bells gai - ly ring, their bride bells   ring!

piu lento.

2. That night her   lov - er's good ship rode The   fu - rious Bis - cay

foam,   And   as   the stream - ing   deck he   trod.   He

thought of her at home, He thought of her at
home; While Kling, lang, ling, He seem'd to hear his home bells ring! Kling, lang,
ling, Kling, lang, ling, He seem'd to hear his home bells ring, his home bells ring!

THE NOONTIDE RAY.

AUBER.
FAIRIES' SONG.

1. The mid-day sun is pour-ing His scorching beams a - long the sky, No more the birds are
2. The herds in shade are panting, The leaves hang drooping on the bough; No more her sweet song
3. The wa-ters bright are shining, Re - flect-ing back the noon - tide ray; The vales and hills seem

soar - ing, The flow'rets droop and die. Fly, then, sis - ter spir - its,
chant - ing, The thrush is si - lent now. Hide, then, sis - ter spir - its,
pin - ing Be - neath the burning day. Rest, then, sis - ter spir - its,

fly, The mid-day sun is pour - ing His beams a - long the sky.
hide, The herds in shade are pant - ing, The leaves droop on the bough.
rest, The wa - ters bright are shin - ing, Be - neath the noon-tide ray.

THE SCOUT.

H. B. FARNIE.
FABIO CAMPANA.

Come! boor, your "Little blue."*   I war not, friend, with you!   'Twas for this can a bold Uhlan* His

bri-dle drew: Merely a pet-rel   I,   Telling the storm is nigh.   Clink we a glass, so

may it pass Your homestead by!   Lurking in brake by day,   Reading by stars my   way,

Clattering fast thro' hamlet old, O'er lonely wold, Maidens pale at my glance, Peasants cow'r 'neath my

lance.   Mis-er-ly souls hide fast their gold From Uh-lan   bold!   Yet his the risk, not theirs.

Thousand and more to   one,   Lit-tle for odds he   cares, Rather too many than none! Ha! ha! ha!

*"Petit blue"—Small country wine.   *Uh-*lan*, light cavalry, of Tartar origin, armed with lance, pistol and sabre.

Come, boor, your "Little blue!" I war not, friend, with you. 'Twas for this can a bold Uhlan His bridle drew.

Merely a petrel I, Telling the storm is nigh, Clink we a glass, so may it pass Your homestead by.

Such a home I've left far a - way, Lov'd ones there for me now are sighing.

I càn see the moon's placid ray On roof and tree and pale face ly-ing!

Ah! Give thy hand, good peasant, to me, Hearts are hearts the weary world all over.

Peace still dwell with thine and thee! So now pray-eth the war-worn ro-ver!

If we take this central image of Song, and ask why it is used to describe Heaven, the future of regenerated humanity, the answer would be—because of its fitness. If this final condition were defined in bare words, it would be as follows: Obedience, Sympathy, Feeling or Emotion, and Adoration. These, in a sense, constitute Heaven, or the state of regenerated humanity. By the consent of all ages, Heaven has been represented under a conception of music, and will be in all ages to come. It is subjected to many sneers, but the sneer is very shallow. The human mind must have some form under which it can think of its destiny. It is not content to leave it in vagueness.

It is a real world we are in, and we are real men and women in it. We dwell in mystery and within limitations, but over and above the mystery and the limitation is an indestructible sense of reality. I am, and I know that I am. Standing on this solid rock, I find reality about me, nor can I be persuaded that other beings and things are dreams or shadows. It is in my very nature to believe in reality, and so I demand definite conceptions, nor can I rest in vagueness or be content with formless visions and their abstractions. Thus the human mind has always worked and thus it always will work—leaving behind it the logicians and plodders in science, in the free exercise of the logic

AFTER.

LOUIS DIEHL.

Andante con express.

1. Af - ter showers, the tran - quil sun; Af - ter snow, the em - 'rald leaves; Sil - ver
2. Af - ter knell, the wed - ding bells; Af - ter bud, the ra - diant rose; Joy - ful

stars when day is done; Af - ter har - vest, gold - en sheaves; Af - ter clouds, the
greet - ings from fare - wells; Af - ter weep - ing, sweet re - pose; Af - ter bur - den,

vio - let sky; Af - ter tem - pest, lull of waves; Qui - et woods when
bliss - ful meed; Af - ter flight, the down - y nest; Af - ter fur - row,

winds go by; Af - ter bat - tle, peaceful graves; Af - ter bat - tle, peaceful graves.
wak - ing seed; Af - ter shadowy riv - er— rest, Af - ter shadowy riv - er— rest.

of human nature. I do not absolutely know what sort of a world this will be when it is regenerated, but I must have some conception of it. I do not absolutely know what Heaven is like—it will be like only to itself—but if I think of it at all, I must do so under some present definite conception. The highest forms under which we can now think are art-forms—the proportion of statuary and architecture, color of painting, and music. The former are limited and address a mere sense of beauty, but music addresses the heart and has its vocation amongst the feelings and covers their whole range. Hence music has been

chosen to hold and express our conception of moral perfection. Nor is it an arbitrary choice, but it is made for the reasons that music is the utterance of the heart, it is an expression of morality, and it is an infinite language. Before the sneer at Heaven as a place of endless song can prevail, it must undo all this stout logic of the human heart. We so represent it because when we frame our conception of Heaven or moral perfection, we find certain things, and when we look into the nature and operations of music, we find again the same things, namely: Obedience, Sympathy, Emotion, Adoration.—*Rev. T. T. Munger.*

GAUDEAMUS IGITUR.

COLLEGE SONG.

1. Gau - de - a - mus i - gi - tur, Ju - ve - nes dum su - mus; Gau - de - a - mus i - gi - tur,
2. U - bi sunt qui an - te nos In mundo fu - e - re? U - bi sunt qui an - te nos
3. Vi - ta no - stra bre - vis est, Bre - vi fi - ni - e - tur, Vi - ta no - stra bre - vis est,

Ju - ve - nes dum su - mus; Post ju - cun - dam ju - ven - tu - tem, Post mo - les - tam
In mun - do fu - e - re? Va - di - te ad su - pe - ros, Tran - si - te ad
Bre - vi fi - ni - e - tur, Ve - nit mors ve - lo - ci - ter, Ra - pit nos a -

se - nec - tu - tem, Nos ha - be - bit hu - mus, Nos ha - be - bit hu - mus.
in - fe - ros, U - bi jam fu - e - re, U - bi jam fu - e - re.
tro - ci - ter, Ne - mi - ni par - ce - tur, Ne - mi - ni par - ce - tur.

Vivat academia,	Quis confluxus hodie	Alma mater floreat,	Vivat et respublica
Vivant professores,	Academicorum?	Quæ nos educavit,	Et qui illam regit,
Vivat membrum quodlibet,	E longinquo convenerunt	Caros et commilitones,	Vivat nostra civitas,
Vivant membra quælibet,	Protinusque successerunt	Dissitas in regiones	Mæcenatum caritas,
Semper sint in flore.	In commune forum.	Sparsos, congregavit.	Quæ nos hic protegit.

INTEGER VITAE.

ODE OF HORACE,
FOR MALE QUARTETTE.

Andante.

1. In - te - ger vi - tæ sce - le - ris - que pu - rus non e - get Mau - ris jac - u - lis nec
2. Si - ve per Syr - tes i - ter æs - tu - o - sas, Si - ve fac - tu - rus per in - hos - pi -
3. Po - ne me, pi - gris u - bi nul - la cam - pis Ar - bor æs - ti - va re - cre - a - tur
4. Po - ne sub cur - ru nim - i - um pro - pin - quo So - lis, in ter - ra dom - i - bus ne -

ar - cu, nec ve - ne - na - tis gra - vi - da sa - git - tis, Fus - ce, pha - re - tra;
ta - lem Cau - ca - sum vel quæ lo - ca fab - u - lo - sus Lam - bit Hy - das - pes.
au - ra; Quod la - tus mun - di ne - bu - læ ma - lus - que Ju - pi - ter ur - get.
ga - ta; Dul - ce ri - den - tem La - la - gen a - ma - bo, Dul - ce lo - quen - tem.

OVER THE DARK BLUE SEA.

C. Matz Arr.
Alpine Melody.

1. We are hap-py and free   as a crew can   be,   While our
2. Come a-way then with me,   o'er the dark blue   sea,   And a
3. On our ves-sel we'll ride   with the wind and the   tide,   O'er the

la la la la   la   la la la la   la

bark is sail - ing o'er the   sea;   Our   sails we heave   at the call of the
gal-lant sail - or you shall   be;   I'll   leave my home   on the waters to
heaving o - cean swift-ly   glide;   Should   wild winds roar,   with each man to his

la la la la   la   la la la la   la   la la la la   la

brave,   For   we   love the home   of the o - cean wave.
roam,   For   I   love to bound   o'er the sparkling foam.
oar,   We   will safe-ly land   on our des-tined shore.

Bass Solo.

la la la la   la   la la la la   la   la la la la   O our   la
                                                         O what
                                                         Then from

O   our hearts   do burn with glee,   As we sail
O   what joy   it is   to me,   Thus to sail
Then, from toils   and per-ils free,   And the dan -

hearts   do burn with glee,   As we   sail   o'er the rolling
joy   it is   to   me,   Thus to   sail   o'er the rolling
toils   and per - ils   free,   And the   dan - - gers of the

o'er the rolling sea;   Let us all   unite in love,   Trusting in
o'er the rolling sea;   Loud we'll raise   our merry strain,   As we sail
gers of the sea.   We will all   unite in love,   Praising him

sea;   Let us all   unite in love,   Trusting in   the God a -
sea;   Loud we'll raise   our merry strain,   As we sail   o'er the foaming
sea,   We will all   unite in love,   Praising Him   who rules a -

the God a-bove.
the foaming main.
who rules above.
} Mer-ri-ly now we row a-long, row a-long, row a-long,

bove.
main.
bove.
} Mer-ri-ly now we row a-long, row a-long, row a-long,

Mer-ri-ly now we row a-long, O-ver the dark blue sea.

COME, MY GALLANT SOLDIER, COME.

Allegretto marzial.

H. R. Bishop.

1. Come, my gal-lant soldier, come, Leave the proud embattled field, Shrilly fife and rolling drum,
2. In thy na-tive val-ley find, Far away from pomp and pow'r, Constant love and peace of mind,

All the pleasures war can yield, Quickly come again, behold the happy land Where thou wert born, And
Here in bright affection's bow'r, Quickly come again, behold the happy land Where thou wert born, And

la la la la

hear its mu-sic sweet and wild, The mer-ry mountain horn. La la la la la la la la

la la la la la la la.

la la la la la la la la la la la la la, The mer-ry mountain horn.

Hymns are the exponents of the inmost piety of the Church. They are crystalline tears, or blossoms of joy, or holy prayers, or incarnated raptures. They are the jewels which the church has worn, the precious stones formed into amulets, more potent against sorrow and sadness than the most famous charms of wizard and magician, and he who knows the way that hymns flowed knows where the blood of piety ran. I do not know of any steps now left on earth by which one may so soon rise above trouble or weariness as the verses and music of a hymn; and if the angels that Jacob saw sang when they appeared, then I know that the ladder he beheld·was but the scale of divine music let down from Heaven to the earth.—*H. W. Beecher.*

FAIR LUNA.

ANDREAS HOFER.

Moderato.

1. In Man-tu-a in fet-ters, The faithful Hofer lay, In Man-tu-a the hostile hordes Took
2. With hands fast bound behind him, He marched with steady pace; With courage still unflinching To
3. The drummer now no long-er His faithful drum doth beat, As Andreas Hofer march-es Be-

his brave life a-way, With grief his comrades' tears now flow, All Germany is plunged in woe, And
meet death face to face, From I-selberg he oft had sent That winged death to which he went In
neath the gloomy gate; Although in fetters he is free, Up-on the bastion form is be, The

mourn'd the loving hand, Thro'out his Tyrol-land, And mourn'd the loving hand, Thro'out his Tyrol-land.
his own Ty-rol-land, His faithful Tyrol-land, In his own Tyrol-land, His faithful Tyrol-land.
man of Ty-rol-land, The man of Tyrol-land, The man of Tyrol-land, The man of Tyrol-land.

THE SEA GULLS.

ECHOES OF CHILDHOOD.

Not too slow.

1. Far a-bove the deep blue sea, On the breez-es fresh and free, Sea-gulls float-ing,
2. Would that I could al-so fly, O-ver cliffs so dark and high, Up-ward to the
3. Fall-ing now, a-gain they rise, Fill the air with startling cries, Dart-ing downward

With varied expression·

one, two, three, Flap their white wings laz-i-ly, Flap their white wings laz-i-ly.
bright blue sky, In the sun-shine dreami-ly, In the sun-shine dream-i-ly.
on a prize, Has-ten homeward speed-i-ly, Has-ten homeward speed-i-ly.

To the bare and rocky home, | "Hark!" the old birds say, "beware, | When the smoke has cleared away,
Where, above the wavelets' foam, | For we think there's danger near." | "Are our darlings safe?" they say.
While the old birds seaward roam, | Smoke and thunder fill the air, | "Ah, not one is hurt to-day!"
Live the young gulls merrily. | And the gulls cry piteously. | Cry the sea-gulls joyously.

AS THE WIND BLOWS.

RICHARD GENÉE.

1. The wind blows north, the wind blows south, The wind blows east and west; No matter how the free wind
2. "Oh, wind," I said, "why dost thou blow, And out to ocean roar, When I would steer my little bark

Some ship will find it best. Out on the wide sea, the wide sea, the wide sea,
To-ward some pleasant shore?" "Out on the deep sea, the deep sea, the deep sea,

One shouts with happy air, "Trim all the sails, the wind is blow - ing fair." One ship is sail-ing a-
Op-pose my will no more; When I blow shoreward, turn thou to the shore, Yet if thy will with

down the west While winds are fair, and waves at rest, See. all her white sails are gai - ly set; Home -
mine must strive, Against my might set all thy skill; Do thou the best that a mor-tal can, And

speed-ing bark, Hope smil-eth yet! One ship is toil-ing far to the east, With masts all bare, thro'
fight me brave-ly like a man; Stand by thy wheel, and on-ward go, Keep watch around, a-

foam-ing yeast, Strug-gle all fierce, and stern, and wild, By wind and wave op-pressed.
bove, be-low; Such hearts will make the ports they seek What-ev-er wind may blow."

ON YONDER ROCK RECLINING.

From "Fra Diavolo."

1. On yon-der rock re-clin-ing, That fierce and swarthy form behold! Fast his hands his
2. On strength and skill re-ly-ing, He's fearless of the treach'rous dart, From his face, with

carbine hold, 'Tis his best friend of old! This way his steps in-clining, His scarlet plume waves
hurried steps, Dangerous foes de-part. But to the kind and gentle, A milder spir-it

o'er his brow, And his vel-vet cloak hangs low, Playing in grace-ful flow!
doth he know, From his lips, in man-ly tones, Tender-est ac-cents flow.

Trem-ble! E'en while the storm is beat-ing, A-far hear ech-o re-peat-ing His

name, Di-a-vo-lo! Trem-ble! E'en while the storm is

beat-ing, A-far hear ech-o re-peat-ing His name, Di-a-vo-lo!

ANOTHER grand voice of nature is the thunder. Ignorant people often have a vague idea that thunder is produced by the clouds knocking together, which is very absurd, if you remember that clouds are but water-dust. The most probable explanation of thunder is much more beautiful than this. Heat forces the air-atoms apart. Now, when a flash of lightning crosses the sky, it suddenly expands the air all round it as it passes, so that globe after globe of sound-waves is formed at every point across which the lightning travels. Light travels so rapidly (192,000 miles in a second) that a flash of lightning is seen by us and is over in a second, even when it is two or three miles long. But sound comes slowly, taking five seconds to travel a mile, and so all the sound-waves at each point of the two or three miles fall on our ear one after the other, and make the rolling thunder. Sometimes the roll is made even longer by the echo, as the sound-waves are reflected to and fro by the clouds on their way; and in the mountains we know how the peals echo and re-echo until they die away.

THE NINETY AND NINE.

IRA D. SANKEY.
ELIZABETH C. CLEPHANE, 1868.

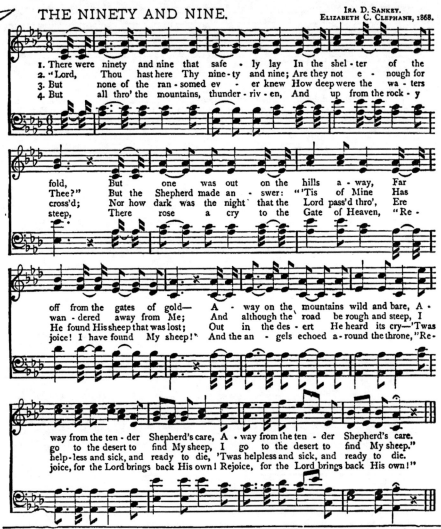

1. There were ninety and nine that safe - ly lay In the shel - ter of the
2. "Lord, Thou hast here Thy nine - ty and nine; Are they not e - nough for
3. But none of the ran - somed ev - er knew How deep were the wa - ters
4. But all thro' the mountains, thunder - riv - en, And up from the rock - y

fold, But one was out on the hills a - way, Far
Thee?" But the Shepherd made an - swer: "'Tis of Mine Has
cross'd; Nor how dark was the night that the Lord pass'd thro', Ere
steep, There rose a cry to the Gate of Heaven, "Re -

off from the gates of gold— A - way on the mountains wild and bare, A -
wan - dered away from Me; And although the road be rough and steep, I
He found His sheep that was lost; Out in the des - ert He heard its cry—'Twas
joice! I have found My sheep!" And the an - gels echoed a - round the throne, "Re -

way from the ten - der Shepherd's care, A - way from the ten - der Shepherd's care.
go to the desert to find My sheep, I go to the desert to find My sheep."
help - less and sick, and ready to die, 'Twas helpless and sick, and ready to die.
joice, for the Lord brings back His own! Rejoice, for the Lord brings back His own!"

"WE have selected music," says Rev. Henry Ward Beecher, in his preface to the Plymouth Collection, "with reference to the wants of families, of social meetings, and of the lecture-room, as well as of the great congregation. But the tunes are chiefly for congregational singing. We have gathered up whatever we could find of merit, in old or new music, that seemed fitted for this end. Not the least excellent are the popular revival melodies, which, though they have been often excluded from classic collections of music, have never been driven out from among the people. These have been gathered up, and fitly arranged, having already performed most excellent service. They are now set forth with the best of all testimonials—the affection and admiration of thousands who have experienced their inspiration. Because they are home-bred and popular, rather than foreign and stately, we like them none the less. And we cannot doubt that many of them will carry up to heaven the devout fervor of God's people until the millennial day."

LANDING OF THE PILGRIMS.

FELICIA HEMANS.

1. The breaking waves dashed high On a stern and rock-bound coast, And the woods against a
2. Not   as   the conqueror comes, They,   the   true-heart-ed,   came;   Not   with the roll of
3. A - midst the storm they sang, And the stars heard, and the   sea! And the sounding aisles of the
4. What sought they thus a - far?   Bright jew - els of   the   mine?   The wealth of the seas, the

storm-y sky   Their   gi - ant branches tossed; And the heav-y night hung dark   The
stir - ring drums, And the trumpet that sings of fame;   Not   as   the   fly - ing   come,   In
dim woods rang To the an - them of   the   free.   The   o - cean ea - gle soared From his
spoils of war? They sought a faith's pure shrine;   Ay,   call   it   ho - ly   ground,   The

hills and wa - ters o'er,   When a band of exiles moored their bark On the wild New England shore.
si - lence and in   fear;   They shook the depths of the desert gloom With their hymns of lofty cheer.
nest by the white wave's foam, And the rocking pines of the forest roared, This was their welcome home!
soil where first they trod!   They have left unstained what there they found, Freedom to worship God.

I LOVE THY KINGDOM, LORD.

TIMOTHY DWIGHT.
G. F. HANDEL. "ST. THOMAS."

1. I   love   Thy   king - dom,   Lord,   The   house   of   Thine   a - bode,
2. I   love   Thy   church,   O   God!   Her   walls   be - fore   Thee   stand,

The Church our   blest   Re - deem - er   saved With   His   own   pre - cious blood.
Dear   as   the   ap - ple   of   Thine   eye,   And   grav - en   on   Thy   hand.

For her my tears shall fall,	Beyond my highest joy,	Sure as Thy truth shall last,
For her my prayers ascend;	I prize her heavenly ways,	To Zion shall be given
To her my cares and toils be given,	Her sweet communion, solemn vows,	The brightest glories earth can yield,
Till toils and cares shall end.	Her hymns of love and praise.	And brighter bliss of Heaven.

COME WITH THE GIPSY BRIDE.

M. W. BALFE.
From "BOHEMIAN GIRL."

1st & 2d times *f*, 3d time *p*.

Come with the Gip - sy bride, And re - pair to the fair,

Where the ma - zy dance Will the hours en - trance.

FINE.

DUET.

Love is the first thing to clasp, But if he es - cape your grasp. Friendship will then be at

SOLO.

hand, In the young rogue's place to stand; Hope, then, will be nothing loath To point out the way to

cres. *f* D.C.

both; Hope, then, will be nothing loath To point out the way to both.......................

ff

In the Gipsy's life you read............... The life that all would like to lead;.........

In the Gipsy's life you read The life that all would like to lead. D.C.

THE MOUNTAIN BUGLE.

J. H. Hewitt.

1. Cheer-i-ly the bu-gle sounds, When home returning o'er the lake; Mer-ri-ly my bo-som
2. Fear-lessly thy footsteps roam, Where snows hang on the diz-zy steep, Driv-ing from its rocky

bounds, As each clear sound bids echo wake; Joy-ous-ly I wing the note, To tell thee that thy
home The ech-o of the hol-low deep. Mer-ri-ly the wild stag bounds, A-lert he knows the

hun-ter's near; Mer-ri-ly I speed my boat To-wards the home by thee made dear.
hun-ter near; Cheer-i-ly the glen resounds With cho-rus and the hun-ter's cheer.

Dearest, for thee, thee on-ly, These mountain wilds are sweet to me; Each crag and val-ley
Dearest, for thee, thee on-ly, These mountain wilds are sweet to me; Each crag and val-ley

lone-ly, Is blest because 'tis loved by thee. Sound, sound, sound, sound the
lone-ly, Is blest because 'tis loved by thee. Sound, sound, sound, sound the

mer-ry, mer-ry mountain horn, At eve-ning's close and morning's ear-ly dawn.
mer-ry, mer-ry mountain horn, At eve-ning's close and morning's ear-ly dawn.

The music of church bells has become a matter of poetry. I remember, though somewhat imperfectly, a touching story connected with the church bells of a town in Italy, which had become famous all over Europe for their peculiar solemnity and sweetness. They were made by a young Italian artisan, and were his heart's pride. During the war, the place was sacked, and the bells carried off no one knew whither. After the tumult was over, the poor fellow again returned to his work; but it had been the solace of his life to wander about at evening, and listen to the chimes of his bells; and he grew dispirited and sick, and pined for them till he could no longer bear it, and left his home, determined to hear them once again before he died. He went from land to land, stopping in every village, till the hope that alone sustained him began to falter, and he knew, at last, that he was dying. He lay, one evening, in a boat that was slowly floating down the Rhine, almost insensible, and scarce expecting to see the sun rise again, that was now set-

BONNIE DOON.

ROBERT BURNS.

Ye banks and braes of bon-nie Doon, How can ye bloom sae fresh and fair, How
Oft have I strayed by bon-nie Doon, To see the rose and woodbine twine; Where

can ye sing, ye lit-tle birds, And I sae wea-ry, full of care? You'll
il-ka bird sang of his love, And fond-ly sae did I o' mine, With

break my heart, ye lit-tle birds, That wan-ton through the flow'ring thorn; Ye
light-some heart I pulled a rose, Full sweet up-on its thorn-y tree; But

mind me of de-part-ed joys, De-part-ed, nev-er to re-turn,
my false lov-er stole the rose, And left the thorn be-hind to me.

ting gloriously over the vine-covered hills of Germany. Presently, the vesper bells of a distant village began to ring, and as the chimes stole faintly over the river with the evening breeze, he started from his lethargy. He was not mistaken. It was the deep, solemn, heavenly music of his own bells; and the sounds that he had been thirsting for years to hear, were melting over the water. He leaned from the boat, with his ear close to the calm surface of the river, and listened. They rung out their hymn, and ceased; and he still lay motionless in his painful posture. His companion spoke to him, but he gave no answer; his spirit, in the glad requiem of the beloved bells, had followed the last sound of the vesper chime.—*Willis.*

Harmonious words render ordinary ideas acceptable; less ordinary, pleasant; novel and ingenious ones, delightful. As pictures and statues, and living beauty too, show better by music-light, so is poetry irradiated, vivified, glorified, and raised into immortal life by the influence of harmony.—*Landor.*

BOATMAN'S RETURN.

M. J. SPORLE.

1. Row! row! homeward we steer, Twilight falls o'er us; Hark! hark! soft mu-sic is near,
2. Row! row! sing as we go, Na-ture re-joic-es; Hark! how the hills as we flow
3. Row! row! lo, in the west, Lights dimly burn-ing; Friends in yon har-bor of rest

Friends glide be-fore us! Song lightens our la-bor, Sing as on-ward we go,
Ech-o our voi-ces; Still o'er the dark wa-ters, Far a-way we must roam,
Wait our re-turn-ing! See, now they burn clear-er, Keep time with the oar;

Keep each with his neigh-bor Time as we flow. Row! row! homeward we go,
Ere It-a-ly's daughters Wel-come us home. Row! row! homeward we go,
Now, now we are near-er That hap-py shore. Row! row! homeward we go,

Twi-light falls o'er us; Row! row! Sing as we flow, Day flies be-fore us.

MUSICAL ALPHABET.

CHILDHOOD SONGS.

Come, dear mother, hear me say What I can of A B C: A B C D E F G,
Now, my Al-pha-bet is through, Will you hear dear sis-ter too? A B C D E F G,

H I J K L M N O P; Q R S and T U V, W (dou-ble-you) and
She has said them all to me; Q R S and T U V, W (dou-ble-you) and

X Y Z. Now you've heard my A B C, Tell me what you think of me.
X Y Z. Now we've said our A B C, Let us have a kiss from thee.

1 (ROUND.) 2 3 4

Good night, Slum-ber sound, In peace profound, 'Till morning's light.

THERE is no subject taught to which the principles of objective teaching can be more easily or more success-fully applied than that of music. The actual objects of thought are always at hand. Sounds must be as clearly presented and named to the mind as colors. Music stands sadly in need of teaching-power. In our schools music should be taught in its simplicity as an art, and not in its complexity as a science. It can be so simplified and symmetrically arranged that the teaching ability of the regular teacher, who knows little of it as a science, can be employed; but while music is regarded as a special study, to be taught only by spe-cial teachers, the best results will not be obtained. In training children to think sounds in pitch, we must work with the *real sounds* continually. If we would train children to sing in time, we must first teach them to *think* and *feel* the rhythm accurately. The real ob-jects of thought in rhythm are pulsations or accents that must be felt and cannot be conveyed to the mind thro' the eye. Pulsations and the different combinations of lengths of sounds must be indicated to the mind thro' the senses of hearing and feeling, and there is no other way. The quality of musical food given to children to develop a true musical taste is important. They should become familiar with all harmonies by singing them.

COUSIN JEDEDIAH.

H. S. THOMPSON.

Solo or Chorus.

1. Oh! Ja-cob, get the cows home and put them in the pen, For the cousins are a-com-ing to
2. Now, O-bed wash your face, boy, and tallow up your shoes, While I go to see Aunt Bet-ty, and
3. And, Job, you peel the onions, and wash and fix the 'taters, We'll have them on the table in those
4. Tell Josh to put the colt in the double-seated chaise, Let him just card down the cattle, give

see us all a - gain, The dowdy's in the pan, and the tur-key's on the fire, And we
tell her all the news, And, Kit-ty, slick your hair, and put on your Sunday gown, For
shin-y painted waiters, Put on your bran new boots, and those trousers with the straps, Aunt So-
them a lit-tle hay, I'll wear my nice new bell-crown I bought of old U - ri - ah, And I

all must get read-y   for   Cous-in Jed-e-di-ah.
Cousin Jed-e-di-ah   comes right from Boston town.
phia'll take a shine to you, if you look real slick, per-haps.
guess we'll as-ton-ish   our   Cous-in Jed-e-di-ah.

Cous-in Jed-e-di-ah, There's

Repeat.

And Azariah, And Aunt Sophia.   All coming here to tea, Oh! won't we have a

Lively.

Hez-e-kiah,   And Jed-e-di-ah,

jol-ly time, Oh! won't we have a jol-ly time! Je-ru-sha, put the ket-tle on, We'll all take tea.

THE BRAVE OLD OAK.

E. J. LODER.
H. F. CHORLEY.

Maestoso.

1. A song for the oak, the brave old oak, Who hath ruled in the greenwood long, Here's
2. He saw the rare times, when the Christmas chimes Were a mer - ry sound to hear, And the

health and re-nown to his broad green crown, And his fif - ty arms so strong.
squire's wide hall, and the cot - tage small, Were full of Christmas cheer.

There is fear in his frown when the sun goes down, And the fire in the west fades out; And he
And all the day to the re - beck gay, They carol'd with gladsome swains. They are

show - eth his might on a wild midnight, When the storms through his branches shout. Then
gone, they are dead, in the church-yard laid, But the brave tree, he still re - mains. Then

sing to the oak, the brave old oak, Who hath stood in his pride so long; And

still flour - ish he, a hale green tree, When a hun - dred years are gone.

COME WHERE FLOWERS ARE FLINGING.

Von Flotow.
From "Martha."

Come where flowers are fling-ing Beau - ty o'er the meadows gay, Where glad birds are sing-ing,
Come where skies are smil - ing, Where the mer - ry foun-tains play, Come, thy care be - guil - ing,

Free from care the live - long day. } Where thro' light and shadow, Streamlets gen - tle mur-mur
Keep with na - ture hol - i - day. }

as   they stray, O - ver field and mead - ow Fai - ry foot-steps gai - ly lead the way.

2nd time.

Come, come, thy care be - guil - ing, Keep with na - ture hol - i - day, O } fay Weaves with
Come, come, where pleasure fond - ly lin - gers, Where the gen - tle woodland }

mag - ic fin - gers Wreaths to crown the brow of May, to crown the brow of May, lovely May, love - ly

May. { Then a - way to the woods, where the wild flowers bloom, While the breez - es are
      { With our feet light as   fai - ries, and hearts full of glee, We will sing with the

la - den with sweet - est per-fume.
wild bird, and roam with the } bee, O come a - way, O'er sun-ny bank and meadows

gay, And keep with na - ture hol - i - day, Come where plea - sure lin-gers,

Where the gen - tle woodland fay, Weaves with mag - ic fingers wreaths to crown the brow of May.

Wreaths to crown the brow of May, O come a - way, O come a - way, a - way,

CHRIST IS BORN OF MAIDEN FAIR.

Dr. Gauntlet.

1. Christ is born of maid - en fair; Hark the her - alds in the air, Thus a -
2. Shep-herds saw those an - gels bright, Caroll-ing in glo - ri - ous light; "God the
2. Christ is come to save man-kind; As in ho - ly page we find; There-fore

dor - ing hear them there, "In ex - cel - sis glo - ri - a!"
Son is born to - night, In ex - cel - sis glo - ri - a!"
sing with rev' - rent mind, "In ex - cel - sis glo - ri - a!"

BEAUTIFUL SPRING-TIME.

VERDI.

Expression.

1. Beau - ti - ful Spring-time! bright, blooming ro - ses, When hope with pleas - ure
2. Beau - ti - ful Spring-time! sea - son de - part - ed, When birds were sing - ing

sweet - ly re - po - ses, Dream - ing of glad - ness when day - light clo - ses,
gay and light - heart - ed, Tell - ing of joys when our ear - ly life start - ed,

Dreams of the heart when no sor - row was near, Oh! hap - py days! we can nev - er for -
Oh! how those mo - ments have fad-ed a - way! Oh! blissful hours! we shall ev - er re -

get thee, Life was too sweet, ev - 'ry moment was dear! We wandered at even - ing o'er
mem - ber; Sweet was our young life—too sweet to de - cay! We hear the bells chim - ing, when

val - ley and foun - tain, Thro' for - est and dell, by the swift-gliding stream : We roamed with light
peaceful - ly dreaming Of past hap - py hours— of our loved happy band; Tho' Time spreads his

step to the mur - mur - ing foun-tain,'Twas long, long a - go, but it seems a sweet
pin - ions with ra - di - ant seem-ing, He leads us at last to the beau - ti - ful

OH, COULD OUR THOUGHTS.

GERMAN.
ANNE STEELE, 1764.

1. Oh, could our thoughts and wish - es fly A - bove these gloom-y shades, To
2. Lord, send a beam of light di - vine, To guide our up - ward aim! With

those bright worlds beyond the sky, Which sor - row ne'er in - vades! There joys, un-seen by
one re - viv - ing touch of Thine, Our lan - guid hearts inflame, Then shall, on faith's sub-

mor - tal eyes, Or reason's fee - ble ray, In ev - er - blooming prospect rise, Un-
lim - est wing, Our ardent wishes rise To those bright scenes where pleasures spring, Im-

con - scious of de - cay, Un - con - scious of de - cay.
mor - tal in the skies, Im - mor - tal in the skies.

ORIENTAL MUSIC.—The music of the ancient Egyptians has survived by tradition, as has also their language—many of the words and phrases which are carved in phonetic hieroglyphics still being heard in the mouths of the Copts, and even borrowed by their Arab conquerors. Hebrew music could have no other source than from the music of Egypt. The present practitioners of music in the East have no musical notation, and even express astonishment at the idea of musical notes being represented on paper. They are ignorant, and their profession is held in much discredit. The use of music is forbidden by the Koran, although, as if in defiance of its own precept, the Koran itself is chanted. The history of Arabian music has its marvels and its miracles, like that of all ancient nations. Such is the enthusiasm of the nations of the East for music, that, to give an idea of its power, they have all had recourse to fiction—yet the profession of musician is considered disgraceful amongst the Arabs. Eminent musicians have seized with avidity every opportunity of endeavoring to make themselves practically and experimentally aequainted with the insurmountable difficulties of the Eastern music, and have labored, without much success, to represent it by the intervals of our scale. The singularity of their music consists principally in this, that each note is divided into three parts: that is, the progression is by intervals equal each to about

AULD LANG SYNE.

ROBERT BURNS.

1. Should auld acquaintance be for-got, And nev-er brought to mind? Should auld acquaintance
2. We twa ha'e run a-boot the braes, And pu'd the gow-ans fine; But we've wander'd mony a
3. We twa ha'e sported i' the burn Frae mornin' sun till dine, But seas between us
4. And here's a hand, my trus-ty frien', And gie's a hand o' thine; We'll tak' a cup o'

be for-got, And days of auld lang syne?
wea-ry foot, Sin' auld lang syne.
braid ha'e roared Sin' auld lang syne.
kindness yet, For auld lang syne.

For auld lang syne, my dear, For

auld lang syne; We'll tak' a cup o' kind-ness yet For auld lang syne.

one-third of a diatonic interval in our scale, so that the octave consists of eighteen notes instead of thirteen. The running up their scale has no other effect upon a western ear than that of a slide of the voice, or such an effect as is produced by sliding the finger along a violin string. M. Fétis speaks of the music of the Arabs as the most singular, the least rational, which exists in respect to the formation of the musical scale. A French musician, he tells us, discovered that the disagreeable sensation which he experienced from the song of an Arab proceeded from this cause, namely, that the division of the scale of sounds had no analogy with that to which he was accustomed. This scale, so singular and eccentric to us, so natural to the ear of the inhabitants of a great part of Africa and Asia, is divided into thirds of tones, in such a manner that instead of containing the usual sounds in the extent of an octave, it admits eighteen. It is certain that these people have no idea of harmony; they know nothing whatever beyond the rude melody. "I knew in Paris," says the writer just quoted, "an Arab who was passionately fond of the Marseillaise, and who often asked me to play that air for him on the piano; but when I attempted to play it with its harmony, he stopped my left hand and said, 'No, not that air; only the other;' my bass was to his ear a second air, which prevented his hearing the Marseillaise. Such is the effect of education on the organs of sense."—Moore.

IT IS BETTER TO LAUGH THAN BE SIGHING.

Donizetti.
"Lucrezia Borgia."

1. It is bet-ter to laugh than be sigh - ing, When we think how life's moments are
2. In the world we some be-ings dis-cov - er, Far too frig-id for friend or for

fly - ing; For each sorrow fate ev - er is bring - ing, There's a pleasure in store for us
lov - er; Souls unblest and for-ev-er re - pin - ing, Tho' good fortune around them be

spring-ing. Tho' our joys, like the wave in the sunshine, Gleam a while then be lost to the
shin - ing. It were well if such hearts we could banish To some plan-et far dis-tant from

sight; Yet for each sparkling ray, That so passes a-way, Comes another as brilliant and light.
ours, They're the dark spots we trace On this earth's favor'd space, They are weeds that choke up the
[fair flow'rs

Then 'tis bet-ter to laugh than be sigh - ing, They are wise who resolve to be

gay, When we think how life's moments are fly - ing, Oh! en-joy pleasure's gifts while we may.

ALL true arts are expressive, but they are diversely so. Take music; it is, without contradiction, the most penetrating, the profoundest, the most intimate art. There is, physically and morally, between a sound and the soul a marvellous relation. It seems as though the soul were an echo in which the sound takes a new power. Extraordinary things are recounted of the ancient music, and it must not be believed that the greatness of effect supposes here very complicated means. No, the less noise music makes the more it touches. Give some notes to Pergolese, give him especially some pure and sweet voices, and he returns a celestial charm, bears you away into infinite spaces, plunges you into ineffable reveries. The peculiar power of music is to open to the imagination a limitless career, to lend itself with astonishing facility to all the moods of each one, to arouse or calm, with the sounds of the simplest melody, our accustomed sentiments, our favorite affections. In this respect music is an art without a rival, tho' not the first of arts.—*V. Cousin.*

LOVING VOICES.

CHARLES W. GLOVER.

1. Lov-ing voi-ces sweet-ly min-gle Like the mur-mur of a prayer, In gay childhood's fai-ry fan-cies, In youth's visions rich and rare, There are mel-o-dies of Na-ture Ris-ing o-ver land and sea; But like mu-sic in our dwelling Lov-ing voi-ces are to me, But like mu-sic in our dwelling Lov-ing voi-ces are to me.

2. When the heart is sad and heav-y, Soft-ly as the sum-mer rain, Lov-ing voi-ces low and ten-der, Tell up-on the spir-it's pain, O'er life's pathway clouds may gath-er But the shad-ows ev-er flee; For like sun-light in our dwelling Lov-ing voi-ces are to me, For like sun-light in our dwelling Lov-ing voi-ces are to me.

3. Blest and blessing in all tri-al, Sooth-ing all my griefs and fears, Ev-er near, in joy or sadness, Changeless thro' the lapse of years, Oh! more ho-ly and more ten-der Than of yore they seem to be, Like to an-gels in our dwelling Lov-ing voi-ces are to me, Like to an-gels in our dwelling Lov-ing voi-ces are to me.

MUSIC pays for the immense power that has been given it; it awakens more than any other art the sentiment of the infinite, because it is vague, obscure, indeterminate in its effects. It is just the opposite art to sculpture, which bears less towards the infinite, because everything in it is fixed with the last degree of precision. Such is the force, and at the same time the feebleness, of music, that it expresses everything and expresses nothing in particular. Sculpture, on the contrary, scarcely gives rise to any reverie, for it clearly represents such a thing, and not such another.

Music does not paint; it touches; it puts in motion imagination—not the imagination that reproduces images, but that which makes the heart beat, for it is absurd to limit imagination to the domain of images. The heart, once touched, moves all the rest of our being; thus music, indirectly, and to a certain point, can recall images and ideas; but its direct and natural power is neither on the representative imagination nor is it upon the intelligence; it is on the heart, and that is an advantage sufficiently beautiful.—*Victor Cousin.*

Music, the medicine of the breaking heart.—*Hunt.*

HAIL AND FAREWELL!

PARTING SONG.
MRS. CHAS. BARNARD.

Not too slow.

1. Hail and farewell, dear com-pan - ions, Friends that we know to be true;
2. Then shall our hap-pi - ness, wan - ing, Chill 'neath the shad-ow and cloud?

D. C. Hail and farewell, dear com-pan - ions, Friends that we know to be true;

Fine.

Th'past with its ro - sy to - mor - rows, Days when our sor-rows were few!
Shall the high heart nev - er daunt - ed, Low in the ash - es be bowed?

Th'past with its ro - sy to - mor - rows, Days when our sor-rows were few!

Sweet be the lay of the song - bird, Fragrant the flowers on our way,
Not if Thy words, Divine Mas - ter Ev - er our inmost thought fill;

Lovely the dawn of the morn - ing, Hap-py the hours of our day;
Brief is the life Thou hast giv - en, Love is but do-ing Thy will:

rall.

Crys-tal the skies bend a - bove us, Perfumed the earth and the air —
Kind words are eas - i - ly spok - en, End-less their ech - oes may be;

rit. *lento.*

What can our friends, tho' they love us, Give us than school days more fair!
Kind deeds must ev - er be - tok - en, Hearts that are loy - al to Thee.

Parting Song for Graduation. *D. C.* may be sung by the full school, as may the entire song.

THE one instrument that comes nearest the voice in its ability to interpret musical expression is not the piano, but the violin. The piano is only an improved harp. Heretofore young girls have spent laborious years in learning how to play the piano, an accomplishment difficult to acquire, and requiring incessant practice to retain proficiency. But there has been a change lately that may make the violin as popular among women as the piano has been. Thousands of girls are now learning how to finger the strings. The mastery of the violin is easier to obtain than that of the piano, and does not require so much strength of hand and wrist. The delicate fingering it involves is just what girls can more easily learn. It is no novelty for women, for the painters of the middle ages represented the angels as playing on viols as well as harps.

PLEASURE CLIMBS TO EVERY MOUNTAIN.

GOLLMICK.

Soprano Solo.

1. Pleasure climbs to ev-'ry moun-tain, Waves in ev - 'ry bush and tree, Whispers
2. Ev-'ry blos - som round us spring-ing, Sweet to smell, and fair to see, Seems with

Vocal Accompaniment.

1. Pleasure climbs to ev-'ry moun-tain, Waves in ev - 'ry bush and tree,
2. Ev-'ry blos - som round us springing, Sweet to smell, and fair to see,

in each bubbling foun-tain, O how sweet this world can be! When with ear - liest ray of
fra - grant voices sing - ing, "O how fair this world can be!" E'en in tem - pests wildly

Whispers in each bubbling fountain, O how sweet this world can be. When with earliest
Seems with fragrant voices sing - ing, "O how fair this world can be!" E'en in tem - pests

morn-ing, All things wake to life and glee, Sparkling fresh they hail the dawning, O how
burst - ing, Nature still has charms for me, For my heart securely trusting, Knows whose

ray of morning, All things wake to life and glee, Sparkling fresh they hail the dawning,
wildly bursting, Nature still has charms for me, For my heart se - curely trusting,

bright this world can be! O how bright! O how bright! how bright this world can be!
world this world must be! Knows whose world, Knows whose world, whose world this world must be!

O how bright this world can be! O how bright! O how bright this world can be!
Knows whose world this world must be! Knows whose world, Knows whose world this world must be!

LOVELY MAY.

SPANISH MELODY.

1. Love - ly May, love - ly May, Decks the world with blos-soms gay; "Come ye all,
2. Light - ly pass, light - ly pass, Thro' the nod - ding mead - ow grass, Woodlands bright,

come ye all," Thus the flow-ers call. . Sparkles now the sun - ny dale, Fragrant is the
woodlands bright, Wake from winter's night. Where the sil-ver brooklet flows. Rippling soft - ly

flow - ery vale; Song of bird, song of bird, In the grove is heard.
as it goes, Will we rest, will we rest, In green moss - y nest.

1.

Lightly row! Lightly row!
O'er the glassy waves we go;
Smoothly glide! Smoothly glide!
On the silent tide.
Let the winds and waters be
Mingled with our melody;
Sing and float! Sing and float!
In our little boat.

2.

Far away! Far away!
Echo in the rocks at play,
Calleth not, Calleth not,
To this lonely spot.
Only with the sea-bird's note,
Shall our dying music float!
Lightly row! Lightly row!
Echo's voice is low.

3.

Lightly row! Lightly row!
O'er the glassy waves we go;
Smoothly glide! Smoothly glide
On the silent tide.
Let the winds and waters be
Mingled with our melody;
Sing and float! Sing and float
In our little boat.

IF EVER I SEE.

CHILDHOOD SONGS.

Allegro.

1. If ev - er I see, On bush or tree, Young birds in a pret - ty nest,
2. My moth-er, I know, Would sor - row so, Should I be sto - len a - way:
3. And when they can fly, In the bright blue sky They'll war - ble a song to me;

I must not, in my play, Steal the birds a - way, To grieve their moth-er's breast.
So I'll speak to the birds In my soft - est words, Nor hurt them in my play.
And then if I'm sad, It will make me so glad, . To think they are hap - py and free.

CHRISTMAS CAROL.

J. M. Neale.
Thomas Helmore.

1. Christ was born on Christmas day, Wreathe the holly, twine the bay, Light and life and joy is He, The Babe, the
2. He is born to set us free; He is born our Lord to be; Carol, Christians, joyfully; The God, the Lord, by
3. Let the bright red berries glow Ev'rywhere in goodly show, Light and life and joy is he, The Babe, the Son, the

Holy One of Ma-ry.
all adored for ev-er. Christian men, rejoice and sing; 'Tis the birth-day of our King. Carol, Christians,
Holy One of Ma-ry.

joyfully; The God, the Lord, By all adored For-ev-er. Night of sadness, Morn of gladness Evermore:

Ev-er, Ev-er, Af-ter many troubles sore, Morn of gladness ever-more, and ever-more.

Midnight scarcely passed and over, Drawing to the holy morn; Very early, Very early, Christ was born.

Sing out with bliss, His name is this: Emmanuel! As 'twas foretold, In days of old, By Gabriel.

CAROL, BROTHERS, CAROL.

W. A. Muhlenberg.

Ca - rol, brothers, ca - rol, Ca - rol joy - ful - ly, Ca - rol the good tidings, Ca - rol mer - ri - ly.

Ca - rol, brothers, ca - rol, Ca - rol joy - ful - ly, Ca - rol the good tidings, Ca - rol mer - ri - ly; And

pray a gladsome Christmas For all good Christian men, Carol, brothers, ca - rol, Christmas day a - gain.

1. Ca - rol, but · in glad - ness, Not in songs of earth, On the Saviour's
2. At the mer - ry ta - ble Think of those who've none, The orphan and
3. List-'ning an - gel mu - sic, Dis - cord sure must cease, Who dare hate his
4. Let our hearts re - spond - ing, To the ser - aph band, Wish this morning's

birth - day, Hal - lowed be our mirth; While a thous - and bless - ings
the widow Hun - gry and a - lone; Boun - ti - ful your off - 'rings
broth - er, On this day of peace? While the heav'ns are tell - ing
sun - shine Bright in ev - 'ry land; Word and deed and pray - er

Fill our hearts with glee, Christmas day will keep The feast of char - i - ty.
To the al - tar bring, Let the poor and need - y Christmas ca - rols sing.
To man - kind good-will, On - ly love and kind - ness Ev - 'ry bo - som fill.
Speed the grate - ful sound, Wish - ing " Mer - ry Christmas!" All the world a - round.

Boys and girls, both young and older grown, do not miss this secret of happiness for yourselves and others: Be kind—and show your love now! Do not wait until some late to-morrow; or until the eclipse of death has come to eyes that now beam with a light clear and bright and tender. One day I met my father on the road to town. "I wish you would take this package to the village for me, Jim," he said hesitatingly. Now, I was a boy of twelve, not fond of work, and just out of the hay-field, tired and hungry. It was two miles into town. I wanted to get my supper and to dress for singing class. My first impulse was to refuse and to do it harshly, for I was vexed that he should ask me after my long day's work. If I did refuse, he would go himself. He was a gentle, patient old man. But something stopped me—one of God's good angels, I think. "Of course, father, I'll take it," I said heartily, giving my scythe to one of the men. He gave me the package. "Thank you, Jim," he said; "I was going myself, but somehow I don't feel very strong to-day." He walked with me to the road that turned off to town, and as he left he put his hand on my arm saying, "Thank you, my son. You've always been a good boy to me, Jim." I hurried into town and back again. When I came near the house, I saw a crowd of farm-hands at the door. One of them came to me, the tears rolling down his face. "Your father!" he said. "He fell dead just as he reached the house. The last words he spoke were to you." I am an old man, now, but I have thanked God over and over again, in all the years that have passed since that hour; and those last words were, "You've always been a good boy to me."

"FATHER JOE."

FRIEDRICH VON FLOTOW.

1. Gliding 'mid the poor and low - ly, With his voice so sad and low, On a mission pure and ho - ly
2. Tho' the life ebb fast and fast - er, Tho' the Reaper Death be nigh, Still he whispers of his Mas - ter
3. I have seen him earnest pleading Till his winning voice did fail; And the lost sheep gently leading,
4. I have seen him tired returning Thro' the lonely midnight way, I have known him till the morning

Goes, contented, Father Joe. When the sunbeams gild the river, When the clouds are black with rain,
Ever watching from the sky, And the crown that waits in Heaven—"Come, my brother, ere too late!"
Tho' his cheek was wan and pale. "God shall raise the meek in spirit, He the haughty shall bring low,
Seek and guide, and toil and pray. Oh! God grant that where the fountains Of His mercy ev - er flow,

Sits he by the couch of fever, By the weary bed of pain, By the wea - ry bed of pain.
Till the sin - ner stands forgiven At the bright, eter - nal gate, At the bright, e - ter - nal gate.
And the poor rich joys inherit!" Hear our loving Father Joe, Hear our lov - ing Father Joe.
Far beyond the distant mountains I may meet dear Father Joe, I may meet dear Father Joe.

The hands are such dear hands; they are so full; they turn at our demands so often; they reach out, with trifles scarcely thought about, so many times; they do so very many things for me, for you—if their fond wills mistake we may well bend, not break. They are such fond, frail lips that speak to us. Pray, if love strips them of discretion many times, or if they speak too slow or quick, such things we may pass by; for we may see days not far off when those small words may be held not as slow, or quick, or out of place, but dear, because the lips are no more here. They are such dear, familiar feet that go along the path with ours—feet fast or slow, and trying to keep pace—if they mistake, or tread upon some flower that we would take upon our breast, or bruise some reed or crush poor Hope until it bleed, we may be mute, not turning quickly to impute grave fault: for they and we have such a little way to go—can be together such a little while along the way—we will be patient while we may. So many little faults we find; we see them, for not blind is Love. We see them; but if you and I perhaps remember them some by-and-by they will not be faults then—grave faults— to you and me, but just odd ways—mistakes, or even less—remembrances to bless.

Days change so many things—yes, hours ;
We see so differently in suns and showers.
  Mistaken works to-night
May be so cherished by to-morrow's light,
We may be patient : for we know
There's such a little way to go.

IN SHADOWLAND.

CIRO PINSUTI.

1. She sits alone all thro' the day, And reads or knits her time away, But when the qui-et
2. There's Nellie with her golden hair, Time cannot make her face less fair! And Willie's voice is
3. She thinks they love her still, and wait, As long ago—if she were late—They'd wait and call her

night is nigh, She folds her work and lays it by, And sees a-gain a-round her stand, Her
still as sweet, As when they two so loved to meet, She hears his step, and clasps his hand, Now
by her name, Nor were content until she came, And gladly would she join their band, And

loved and lost in Shadowland, Her loved and lost, her loved and lost in Shadow-land! In
once again in Shadowland, Now once again, now once again in Shadow-land! In
journey on thro' Shadowland, And journey on, and journey on thro' Shadow-land! In

Shadowland, in Shadowland, She meets them all in Shadow-land, In

Sha-dowland, in Shadowland, She meets them all in Sha-dow-land, She

meets them all in Sha-dow—land! meets them all in Shadowland!

A **false** view of life is our radical defect. Our political problems always hinge on some money problem, our educational system looks primarily to the fitting of men for money-getting, for our young men even success means riches, and our very worship implies that the poor are unfit for the kingdom of Heaven. Thus we lose sight of man and think only of money; increase our wealth, while faith and hope and love and intelligence diminish. We build great cities to be inhabited by little men, are keen to drive a bargain and slow to recognize a noble man. We have eyes for bank notes, and move dumb and unraised beneath the starlit heavens. If it were possible that a great philosopher or poet should arise among us, some foreigner would have to point him out to us; but we know our own, our men of boundless wealth, whom we envy and despise. So long as our whole national life-struggle continues to be carried on around this single point of finance, what hope is there of avoiding fatal conflicts? The rich will worship their god Mammon alone, and the poor will plot and scheme to shatter the idol; and mechanical contrivances, such as arbitration boards and legislative enactments, will leave the root of the evil untouched. It is essential that we should know that the real and final test of a government, as of a religion, is the kind of man, and not the amount of money, it produces. We must return to the ideals of our forefathers, who preferred freedom, intelligence and strength to wealth.—*Bishop Spaulding.*

A GREENNESS LIGHT AND TENDER.

German Folk-Song.

A CHRISTMAS HYMN.

"DUANE STREET."
ELEANOR A. HUNTER.

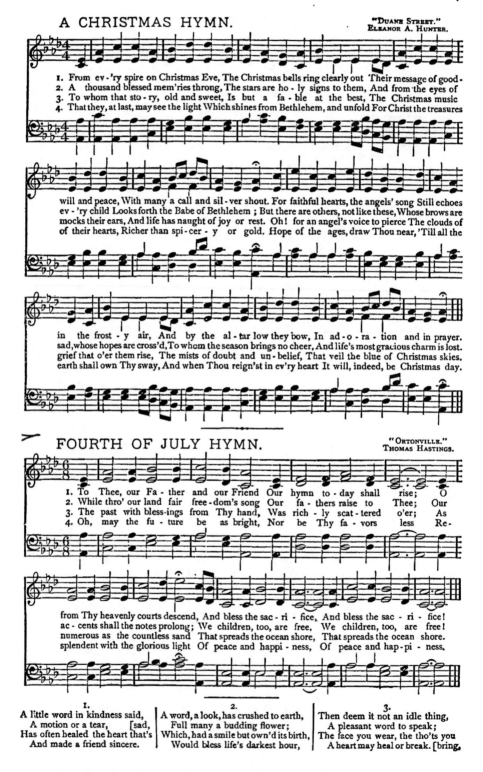

1. From ev-'ry spire on Christmas Eve, The Christmas bells ring clearly out Their message of good-
2. A thousand blessed mem'ries throng, The stars are ho-ly signs to them, And from the eyes of
3. To whom that sto-ry, old and sweet, Is but a fa-ble at the best, The Christmas music
4. That they, at last, may see the light Which shines from Bethlehem, and unfold For Christ the treasures

will and peace, With many a call and sil-ver shout. For faithful hearts, the angels' song Still echoes
ev-'ry child Looks forth the Babe of Bethlehem ; But there are others, not like these, Whose brows are
mocks their ears, And life has naught of joy or rest. Oh! for an angel's voice to pierce The clouds of
of their hearts, Richer than spi-cer-y or gold. Hope of the ages, draw Thou near, 'Till all the

in the frost-y air, And by the al-tar low they bow, In ad-o-ra-tion and in prayer.
sad, whose hopes are cross'd, To whom the season brings no cheer, And life's most gracious charm is lost.
grief that o'er them rise, The mists of doubt and un-belief, That veil the blue of Christmas skies.
earth shall own Thy sway, And when Thou reign'st in ev'ry heart It will, indeed, be Christmas day.

FOURTH OF JULY HYMN.

"ORTONVILLE."
THOMAS HASTINGS.

1. To Thee, our Fa-ther and our Friend Our hymn to-day shall rise; O
2. While thro' our land fair free-dom's song Our fa-thers raise to Thee; Our
3. The past with bless-ings from Thy hand, Was rich-ly scat-tered o'er; As
4. Oh, may the fu-ture be as bright, Nor be Thy fa-vors less Re-

from Thy heavenly courts descend, And bless the sac-ri-fice, And bless the sac-ri-fice!
ac-cents shall the notes prolong; We children, too, are free, We children, too, are free!
numerous as the countless sand That spreads the ocean shore, That spreads the ocean shore.
splendent with the glorious light Of peace and happi-ness, Of peace and hap-pi-ness.

1.	2.	3.
A little word in kindness said, A motion or a tear, [sad, Has often healed the heart that's And made a friend sincere.	A word, a look, has crushed to earth, Full many a budding flower; Which, had a smile but own'd its birth, Would bless life's darkest hour,	Then deem it not an idle thing, A pleasant word to speak; The face you wear, the tho'ts you A heart may heal or break. [bring,

BRIDAL CHORUS.

RICHARD WAGNER.
From "LOHENGRIN."

1. Guid-ed by us, thrice happy pair, Enter this doorway, 'tis love that invites; All that is brave,
2. Home joys divine, home joys so pure, Love ev-er faithful and love ev-er sure; All that is brave,

all that is fair, Love now triumphant forev-er unites. Champion of virtue, boldly advance, Flower of

beau-ty, gen-tly ad-vance; Now the loud mirth of rev'ling is end-ed, Night bringing peace and

bliss has descended, Fann'd by the breath of hap-piness, rest, Clos'd to the world, by love on-ly blest!

Guid-ed by us, thrice happy pair, En-ter this doorway, 'tis love that invites; All that is brave,
Home joys divine, home joys so pure, Love ev-er faithful and love ev-er sure; All that is brave,

all that is fair, Love now triumphant for-ev-er unites, for-ev-er u-nites.

MONARCH OF THE WOODS.

J. W. Cherry.

Bold. *f*

1. Behold the monarch of the woods! The mighty old oak tree; He braves the raging of the
2. How oft the monarch of the woods, Upon a summer's day, Has seen the merry children

storm, On land or roll-ing sea; He waves his branches deck'd with green, In summer's golden
sport, And 'neath its shadow play; From youth to manhood they spring up, And old age comes at

glow, And i - vy clothes his leaf - less form Thro' win - ter's frost and snow: King
last, Then green grass waves up - on their graves, And all life's dreams are past! Yet

Time, the conqueror of all, He bold - ly doth de - fy, For green and hearty will he
stronger grows the mighty tree, In hale and heart - y prime, And stands the monarch of the

Repeat Chorus ad lib.

stand When a - ges have gone by. Green and heart - y, green and heart - y,
woods, De - fy - ing age and time. Stands the mon - arch of the woods, the

heart - y will he stand, When a - ges have gone by, When a - ges have gone by.
mon-arch of the woods, De - fy - ing age and time, De - fy - ing age and time.

EARLY IMPRESSIONS.—Much stress should be laid upon the fact that the youthful memory, being exceedingly tenacious, impressions made upon the child are likely to be indelible. The great incidents in the history of the Israelites were woven into song, and these eucharistic epics were required to be diligently taught to their children. So, in the present day, the simple doctrines and thrilling events of Christianity should be wrought into verse and impressed upon the mind of the teacher by the power of music. Truths thus inculcated will cling to the soul forever. We all know that cherished memories of home and friends are ours with such enduring vividness that the record can never be effaced. But in all the reminiscences of days gone by there is nothing that so haunts the spirit as the songs to which we were accustomed in childhood. The sweet tones of a mother's voice will live and speak in the heart long after the voice has been hushed to silence. The recollection of the hymns which were first heard amid the throng of worshipers in the city, or in the embowered country church, will remain in morning freshness long after the sanctuary has mouldered into ruins. We may cross oceans, and wander in foreign

FOLLOW ME, FULL OF GLEE.   MOVEMENT SONG.

1. Chil-dren go, to and fro, In a mer-ry, pret-ty row: Footsteps light, fa-ces bright,
2. Birds are free, so are we, And we live as hap-pi-ly; Work we do, stud-y, too,
3. Work is done, play's be-gun, Now we have our laugh and fun: Hap-py days, pret-ty plays,

'Tis a hap-py, hap-py sight; Swiftly turn-ing round and round, Do not look up-on the ground;
Learning dai-ly something new; Then we laugh, and dance, and sing, Gay as birds or an-y-thing.
And no naughty, naughty ways. Holding fast each oth-er's hand, We're a hap-py, cheerful band;

Chorus.

Fol-low me, full of glee, Sing-ing mer-ri-ly.
Fol-low me, full of glee, Sing-ing mer-ri-ly. } Sing-ing mer-ri-ly, mer-ri-ly, mer-ri-ly,
Fol-low me, full of glee, Sing-ing mer-ri-ly.

Sing-ing mer-ri-ly, mer-ri-ly, mer-ri-ly, Follow me, full of glee, Sing-ing mer-ri-ly.

climes; the erect frame may be bowed with the weight of years, and raven ringlets may be changed to locks of snowy whiteness; but the old home-songs heard in the distance in the still morning, or sung by ourselves in some calm hour of reflection, or by the home-circle on a winter's evening, will bring around us the friends and the scenes of other days and of far-off lands; and while the dim eye of age sparkles with unwonted brilliancy, the heart will beat with the buoyancy of early youth. It is not at all improbable that the songs learned in the nursery, or around the fireside, will be used by the Holy Spirit in after years as the means of conversion to a better life, it may be, to our final salvation from endless ruin. On the contrary, bacchanalian or ribald songs, which are apt to be learned and used by those who are unaccustomed to religious melodies, are, in the hands of the Destroyer, a potent means of ruin. Shall we quietly allow this tremendous power to pass into the hands of the enemy, or shall we not eagerly seize upon it as our lawful right, and wield it for the good of our race and the glory of our God?—*Service of Song.*

CHILDREN'S SONGS.

1. Winkum, Winkum, shut your eye, Sweet my ba - by, lul - la - by, For the dews are falling soft,
2. Chickens long have gone to rest, Birds lie snug with - in their nest, And my birdie soon will be

Lights are flick'ring up a - loft, And the head-light's peeping over Yonder hill-top capp'd with clover.
Sleeping like a chick - a - dee; For with on - ly half a try, Winkum, Winkum shuts her eye.

THE LITTLE BEE.

1. The lit - tle busy bee Abroad doth roam thro' all the day, On airy wing thro' meadows gay, To
2. Who taught it thus to roam Amid the riches of the field? And from the flowers that sweets do yield, To
3. It learned from God alone, He put the sweets within the flower, He sends the bee to drain its store, And

bring its honey home, To bring its honey home, To bring its hon - ey home.

THE CRICKET.

1. { Chirp, chirp, chirp! Soon as fades the light, } Little cricket In the thicket, Chirp, chirp, chirp!
   { Chirp, chirp, chirp! Thro' the summer night; }
2. { Chirp, chirp, chirp! While I soundly sleep, } Little cricket In the thicket, Chirp, chirp, chirp!
   { Chirp, chirp, chirp! You still waking keep; }

Little cricket In the thicket, Chirp, chirp, chirp, Cricket in the thicket, Chirp, chirp, chirp!

FAITH and hope and love are the only eternal things. These are the three eternal elements of man's being. Cultivate kindness of heart here and there. You must do this in reference to the good time coming. You must always be looking forward to something better. If we do not look forward, we fail in one of the requisites of immortal being. Hope and love and faith must be trained, or no man can come into closer relations with God. We must not keep religion for Sunday, and ignore it the other six days. We must saturate ourselves and our work with religion. God's children we are all the time. You can pull a boat, or practice at a piano, or take the baby to ride, with that same spirit with which an archangel goes to his duties. We should make life a joy, moving and being in God and for God. I have not spoken to you as students, but as children of a common Father, who gives us strength, and leads us, one step at a time, forward if we will, to the empire of perfect life.—*Rev. Edward Everett Hale.*

COME, COME QUICKLY AWAY.

Allegretto e Staccato.

1. Come, come quickly a - way! Soft winds chide our de-lay; Night's call let us o - bey, Come a -
2. All, all, circled in rest, On earth's boun-ti - ful breast, Our soft slumbers be blest, While we
3. Then shall beam on our sight, Morn, morn, dewy and bright, Our hearts, hap-py and light, Hail the

way; Night, night, welcome 'to thee; Our sleep gen-tle shall be; Come, come, hap-py and free,
dream. Shad-ows dark'ning the plain, Moonbeams kissing the main, Till comes morning a-gain,
day! Flow'rs a-dorn-ing the green, No dark cloud intervene, While we're crowning our queen,

Come a - way! Hark! hark! soft-ly and clear, Come a - way! Sweet sounds steal on the ear:
With bright beam. Hark! hark! soft-ly and clear, Come a - way! Sweet sounds steal on the ear:
Queen of May. Hark! hark! soft-ly and clear, Come a - way! Sweet sounds steal on the ear:

Come a - way! Come quickly a - way, quickly a - way, quickly a - way! Come, come

quickly a - way! Soft winds chide our de-lay; Night's call let us o - bey; Come a - way!

GUIDE ME, GREAT JEHOVAH.

F. Herold.
Prayer from "Zampa."

1. Guide me, O Thou great Je - ho - vah! Pil - grim through this bar - ren land:
2. Op - en now the crys - tal fountain, Whence the heal - ing wa - ters flow;
3. When I tread the verge of Jor - dan, Bid my anx - ious fears sub - side;

I am weak, but Thou art might - y, Hold me with Thy power - ful hand:
Let the fier - y, cloud - y pil - lar Lead me all my jour - ney through:
Bear me through the swell - ing cur - rent, Land me safe on Ca - naan's side:

Bread of Heav - en, Bread of Heav - en, Feed me now and ev - er - more.
Strong De - liv - 'rer, Strong De - liv - 'rer, Be Thou still my strength and shield.
Songs of prais - es, Songs of prais - es, I will ev - er give to Thee.

CALM WAS THE NIGHT

A. S. Sullivan.
Charlotte Elliott.

1. Calm was the hallowed night! Dis - cord al - lay'd, Valley and mountain height Slumber'd in shade.
2. Sud - den - ly round them shone, Far thro' the night, Dazzling to look up - on, Splendors of light;

rit.

Roofed by Heav'n's azure fair, Making their flocks their care, Shepherds in open air, Tranquilly stayed.
Then drew an angel near, And to al - lay their fear, Poured on their ravished ear Words of de - light.

Ne'er since the world began	Well might the tidings told,	Well might the Shepherds haste,
Angels of God	Chorus unseen,	Eager as we,
Music so sweet to man	Waken your harps of gold,	Ere yet the night was past,
Sounded abroad;	Wondrous their sheen!	This sight to see;
On that auspicious morn,	Sweet rang your minstrelsy,	Where light the meteor shed,
Changing our state forlorn,	"Glory to God on high!"	Well might the Magi tread,
Christ as a babe was born,	"Peace on earth," amnesty,	Joyful, the path that led,
Jesus the Lord!	"Good-will towards men!"	Saviour, to Thee!

The voice glides on at its own sweet will in speaking, obeying no rule whatever, whilst in song it springs or drops from one tone to the next over strictly measured gaps. In singing, short syllables are lengthened out and cease in fact to be short, and, except in certain kinds of dramatic singing and in recitative, the accent naturally falls on the vowels and not on the consonants. In speaking, only the lower third of the voice is employed as a rule, whilst in singing the greatest effect is generally produced, except in the case of contraltos and basses, by the use of the upper and middle notes. In speech the range of tone, even in the most excitable persons, hardly ever exceeds half an octave; in singing the average compass is two octaves. Singing tends to preserve purity of language, the rules which govern the utterance of every note also affecting the articulate element combined with it and keeping the words cast in fixed forms—a stereotype of sound, if I may venture the metaphor. Speech, on the other hand, like handwriting, is always changing.—*Sir Morell Mackenzie.*

NOW I LAY ME DOWN TO SLEEP.

Andante con molto espressione.

HENRY R. ALLEN.

1. Near the camp-fire's flick'ring light, In my blanket bed I lie, Gazing thro' the shades of
2. Sad - ly sings the whip-poor-will In the boughs of yonder tree, Laughingly the dancing
3. 'Mid those stars one face I see— One the Saviour called away— Moth - er, who in infan-
4. Fainter grows the flick'ring light, As each ember slowly dies; Plain - tively the birds of

piu lento.

night   At the twinkling stars on high.   O'er me spirits   in the air   Si - lent vig - ils
rill   Swells the midnight melo - dy.   Foeman may be lurking near   In   the canyon
cy   Taught my baby lips to   pray.   Her sweet spirit hovers near,   In   the lone - ly
night   Fill the air with sadd'ning cries,   O - ver me they seem to cry: "You may nev - er

rit.

seem   to keep,   As I breathe my childhood's prayer,   "Now I lay me down to sleep."
dark and deep,   Low I breathe in Je - sus' ear: ' "I pray the Lord my soul to   keep."
moun - tain brake,   Take me to her, Saviour dear,   "If I should die before I   wake."
more   a - wake."   Low I lisp: "If I should die,   I pray the Lord my soul to   take."

CODA *(after last verse.) Softly and tenderly.*

"Now   I   lay   me down to sleep,   I pray the Lord   my soul to keep;   If

I   should die be - fore I   wake,   I   pray the Lord   my soul   to   take."

NEVER ALONE.

Ferd. Silcher.
Rossiter W. Raymond, by per.

1. Far out on the des-o-late bil-low, The sail-or sails the sea; Alone with the night and the
2. Far down in the earth's dark bosom, The min-er mines the ore; Death lurks in the dark be-
3. Forth in-to the dread-ful bat-tle The steadfast sol-dier goes; No kiss when he lies a-
4. Lord, grant as we sail life's ocean, Or delve in its mines of woe; Or fight in its ter-ri-ble

Chorus.

temp-est, Where countless dan-gers be; Yet nev-er a-lone is the Christian, Who
hind him, And hides in the rock be-fore; Yet nev-er a-lone is the Christian, Who
dy-ing No hand, his eyes to close; Yet nev-er a-lone is the Christian, Who
con-flict, This com-fort all to know, That nev-er a-lone is the Christian, Who

lives by faith and prayer; For God is a friend un-fail-ing, And God is ev-'ry-where.

JESUS IS MINE.

T. E. Perkins.
Horatius Bonar.

Tenderly.

1. Fade, fade each earthly joy, Je-sus is mine! Break ev-'ry ten-der tie, Je-sus is mine!
2. Tempt not my soul away, Je-sus is mine! Here would I ev-er stay, Je-sus is mine!
3. Farewell, mortal-i-ty, Je-sus is mine! Welcome, e-ter-ni-ty, Je-sus is mine!

Dark is the wilderness, Earth hath no resting place, Je-sus a-lone can bless, Je-sus is mine!
Per-ish-ing things of clay, Born but for one brief day, Pass from my heart away, Je-sus is mine!
Welcome, O loved and blest, Welcome, sweet scenes of rest, Welcome, my Savior's breast, Jesus is mine!

THE Dark Angel of Death was standing outside the musician's door, for little Anita, Maestro Narditti's child, was fading away; no tears, no prayers, could avail, not even Carissima's lovely voice. Carissima's voice was hushed; the Maestro had no heart to take up his dearly-loved violin and play to soothe his sorrow, as he had done many years ago when his wife died and left this little one behind. Heaven had given him the divine gift of genius and had bidden him call aloud to the world. So Carissima and he had played aloud together through sickness, through sorrow and success, and through all the changing scenes of life they had been faithful friends. They had just come back from the crowded hall; the people said that never before had the Maestro played so beautifully, and that never before had the violin's voice sounded so mournful and pathetic. Well, you see, they did not know the reason, but we do; for both were thinking of the little dying girl, and how could their thoughts be anything but sorrowful, or the outward expression of those thoughts be anything but mournful? The father was

THE TIME OF THE SINGING OF BIRDS.

GEORGE BARKER.

1. The time of the sing-ing of birds is come, The trees are robed in green; The
2. A - way in wood - lands wide and deep The shad - owy grass bends low, Be-fore
3. But not o'er meadow and wood a - lone Doth their spell of beau-ty steal; There are

flow'rs un - fold their tints of gold, And the fair pink may be seen; O'er all the land doth a
winds that creep where daisies sleep, And the dainty wind-flow'rs blow. And deep in the heart of the
hu - man hearts whose bit - ter smarts Its smile hath power to heal. The time of the singing of

prom - ise lie, The her - ald of Sum-mer's reign; At the gold - en beat of her
dim old woods The sun - beams fair have strayed; Like shafts of light they have
birds is come, And we pause in our wea - ry way, While the sad hearts thrill and the

3rd verse.

fly - ing feet The old Earth smiles a - gain.
pierced the night By the arch - ing bran - ches made.
sad eyes fill At the - - - - breath of the scented May.

weeping by his child's bedside. But she said, "Do not weep, sing to me—sing me to sleep, for I am so weary, dear father, and the evening has been so long without thee." Then he rose and he played to her, and she closed her eyes and listened happily to Carissima's voice. It sang a song without words—the music alone told the tale—of a pure young life, too pure for earth, and therefore to be taken away to that fair land where only the good and pure and true dwell. Yet it was hard to leave the earth, harder still to leave the dear ones behind, and to know that they would be desolate; and here the violin's voice sobbed and trembled as if from sorrow, and the melody came sadder and softer, as describing the very parting which was soon to take place; then the lingering notes died away, and the Maestro's hand was still. "Is that all?" murmured the child; "oh, play again." Once more, and the air resounded with a psalm of triumph—the same melody, but no longer soft or sad, for the gates of that Fair Land were opened wide,· and amidst this jubilant strain the child had passed away with the Angel of Death.—*Belgravia.*

A SPRING SONG.

CIRO PINSUTI.

1. I sat be-neath the ma-ples old, The meads were shot with green and gold, And
2. The bus - y bab - bling wa-ter-fall Me - lo-dious-ly kept time to all, The
3. O love - ly, love - ly, love - ly spring! O robed in sunbeams! bridegroom, king! Breathe

un - der-neath my feet there rolled The lit - tle sil - v'ry Gad; The cuck-oo and the
rich May mu - sic mys - ti - cal, Toned to the fresh-'ning air; Each rip-'ning bud that
on my heart and bid me sing, Or rath - er praise and pray; For em - blems are these

thrush were sing-ing, singing, singing, The sheep bells on the hills were ringing, ringing,
o - pen, fresh-ly o - pen flies, Seemed gasping with a gay sur-prise, a gay sur-
sun - ny, bright and sunny hours, These golden meads and stream and flow'rs, and stream and

la la | la la
ring-ing, All life was gay and glad, all life was gay and glad, All life was gay and
prise To greet a world so fair, to greet a world so fair, To greet a world so
flowers, Of ev - er-last-ing May, of ev - er-last-ing May, Of ev - er-last-ing

glad! Was gay and glad, all life was gay, was gay and glad!
fair! To greet a world so fair, to greet a world so fair!
May! Of ev - er-last-ing May, of ev - er-last-ing May!

WE are inclined to think that all the great violins of the famous makers are well known. Most of the celebrated instruments are given names of distinction, such as the Yellow Stradivarius, the Blood Red Knight Guarnerius, the De Beriot Magini, the General Kidd Stradivarius Violoncello, the Servais Stradivarius Violoncello, and others. The reason why Italian instruments are so superior to all others must be ascribed to their exquisite make, the careful adjustment of the various thicknesses of wood and the varnish, the secret of which appears gone for ever. Perhaps another reason may be named in the wood being so ripe and dry as to permit free vibration. The Cremonese obtained their color in oil. The moderns get it in spirit, which imparts a hardness to the tone. Compare a Cremona with the German and other imitations. The former is mellow and rich—the latter too often flinty and harsh. This arises no doubt

O WHAT CAN YOU TELL?

J. C. LOWRY, 1820.
ROSSITER W. RAYMOND by per.

1. O what can you tell, lit-tle peb-ble, lit-tle peb-ble, O what can you tell, lit-tle pebble by the sea? The se-cret of your si-lent life, Now whisper it to me!
2. O what can you tell, lit-tle flow-er, lit-tle flow-er, O what can you tell, lit-tle flower on the lea? The se-cret of your sweet perfume, Now whisper it to me!
3. O what can you tell, lit-tle bird, lit-tle bird, O what can you tell, lit-tle bird up-on the tree? The se-cret of your joy-ous song, Now whisper it to me!
4. O what can you tell, lit-tle child, lit-tle child, O what can you tell, lit-tle child upon my knee? The se-cret of your hap-py smile, Now whisper it to me!

Full Chorus.

It is the love of God in Heav'n, The God who made both

D.S. Thus to the love of God in Heav'n, The God who made both

D. S. after last verse.

you and me, And ev'-ry day I think his praise In si-lence by the sea.
you and me, And ev'-ry day I breathe his praise In fragrance on the lea.
you and me, And ev'-ry day I sing his praise Up-on the sum-mer tree.
you and me, And ev'-ry day I seek his face Up-on my bend-ed knee.

you and me, The praise of all things here is giv'n! And ev-er-more shall be!

from the varnish, which, including the color, it seems impossible to imitate. None of the famous makers seem to have adhered to one color only. Now a fine violin appears of a deep, rich yellow, almost approaching orange; another is a fine red, having something of a most lovely light cherry tint; again, these colors are mixed by the best makers with amber varnish of the purest and clearest consistency, and both colors and varnish are perfectly free from that clouded appearance which so often disfigures modern instruments. The effect is that of perfect transparency. You look at a clear, perfect, rich color, as it were, through the purest crystal. This is one of the certain indications of a genuine instrument. The moderns, as has been said, seem unfortunately to have lost the secret of making this lovely, transparent, clear-colored varnish.

THE SPIDER AND THE FLY.

O. H. Normino.

1. "Will you walk in - to my parlor?" said the Spi - der to the Fly, "The
2. "Will you grant me one sweet kiss?" said the Spi - der to the Fly, "To
3. "For the last time, now I ask you, Will you walk in, Mis - ter Fly?" "No!
4. Now all young folks, take warn-ing, by this fool - ish lit - tle Fly, For

pret - tiest lit - tle par - lor that ev - er you did spy;"
taste your charm - ing lips, I've a cu - ri - os - i - ty;"
if I do, may I be shot: I'm off, so now good-bye!"
pleas-ure is the spi - der's web, to catch you it will try;

You have on - ly got to pop your head just in - side of the door, You'll
"But if, perchance, our lips should meet, a wa - ger I would lay, Of
Then up he springs, but both his wings were in the web caught fast; The
And though you may now think that my ad - vice you want no more, You're

see so ma - ny cu - rious things you nev - er saw be - fore."
ten to one, you would not af - ter let them come a - way."
Spi - der laugh'd, "Ha! ha! my boy, I've caught you safe at last!"
lost if you stand par - ley - ing out - side of Pleasure's door.

1. 2. Oh, will you, will you, will you, will you walk in, Mis - ter Fly?
3. 4. Oh, will you, will you, will you, will you walk out, Mis - ter Fly?

Oh, will you, will you, will you, will you walk in, Mis - ter Fly?
Oh, will you, will you, will you, will you keep out, Mis - ter Fly?

THE BEAUTIFUL DAY.

1. Day on the mountain, the beau-ti-ful day! And the tor-rents leap forth in the
2. Day in the val ley, the riv-u-let rolls Cloud-less and calm as the

pride of his ray; The chamois* a-wakes from his wild for-est dream, And
home of our souls; The har-vest is wav-ing, and fountain and flower, Are

bounds in the gladness and life of his beam, And the horn of the hun-ter is
sparkling and sweet as the ra-di-ant hour; And the song of the reap-ers, the

sound-ing a way! Light, light on the hills! 'tis the beau-ti-ful day!
lark's sun-ny lay, Proclaim thro' the val-ley day, beau-ti-ful day! Pro-

Light, light on the hills! 'tis the beau-ti-ful, beautiful day!
claim thro' the val-ley day, beau-ti-ful, beautiful .... day!

Oh, sol-emn and sad his far set-ing ap-pears, When the last ray de-

* *Sham-my.*

clines, and the flowers are in tears, When the sha - dows of eve - ning like death banners

wave, And darkness en - clos - es the world like a grave; Yet the sun like the

soul shall a - rise from de - cay, And again light the world with day, beau - ti - ful

day; And a - gain light the world with day, beau - ti - ful, beautiful day!

OUT OF THE WINDOW.

J. NORTON.
MOTION SONG.

1. Out of the win - dow, o - ver the way, Saw I a cob - bler mending to - day;
2. Out of the win - dow, o - ver the way, Saw I a tail - or sewing to - day;
3. Out of the win - dow, o - ver the way, Saw I the chil - dren in school to - day;
4. Out of the win - dow, o - ver the way, Soon will be clos - ing the gates of the day,

Thump went the hammer on Sal - lie's shoe, "Humph," said the cobbler, "I guess you will do."
How did he do it? Why to and fro, Ran his great nee - dle through the cloth, so.
What were they do - ing? Why, don't you know? Writing straight let - ters on pages of snow.
Then will the children in robes of white, Sleepily mur - mur, "Good-night, all, good-night."

THE matinee programme was made up of quiet things from Schumann, "Songs without words" from Mendelssohn, and like selections. But two names appeared upon it—those of Von Bulow and a singer unknown to us. "Thou'rt like unto a flower" was the one song announced—we can almost see the programme—and when it came it was but a single verse. But what a verse, as Lizzie Cronyn sang it to Von Bulow's accompaniment! Again and again—three times she sang it, until a sense of courtesy compelled the large audience to forbear further calls upon the singer. Twice afterwards we went a long distance to the great pianist's concerts, in the hope of again hearing this one song. Each time she sang it again and again, to the delight of an appreciative audience. It is one of the perfect bits of work we recall, in a long experience of the concert and operatic stage, taking rank—in our enjoyment on first hearing it, and the pleasure with which we have since remembered it—along with Nilsson's "Angels ever bright and fair," Patti's "Home, sweet home," Scalchi's "It is better to laugh than be sighing," "The last rose of summer," as an Italian prima donna once sang it, and some other things, the memory of which is always pleasure unalloyed, a delight pure and simple.

THOU'RT LIKE UNTO A FLOWER.

H. Heine.
Anton Rubinstein.

PEACE ON EARTH.

DONIZETTI.
J. R. LOWELL.

1. "What means this glory round our feet," The Magi mused, "more bright than morn!" And voices chanted
2. 'Tis eighteen hundred years, and more, Since those sweet oracles were dumb; We wait for Him, like
3. All round a-bout our feet shall shine A light like that the wise men saw, If we our lov-ing

clear and sweet, "To-day the Prince of Peace is born!" "What means this star," the shepherds said, "That
them of yore; A-las! He seems so slow to come! But it was said, in words of gold, No
wills in-cline To that sweet Life which is the Law. So shall we learn to un-derstand The

brightens thro' the rocky glen?" And angels answering, overhead, Sang, Peace on earth, good-will to men!
time or sorrow e'er shall dim, That lit-tle children might be bold, In perfect trust to come to Him.
simple faith of shepherds, then, And kindly clasping hand in hand, Sing, Peace on earth, good-will to men!

IN MERRY CHORUS.

J. OFFENBACH.

Lively.
1. Come, let us join in mer-ry cho-rus, Our hearts and voices light and gay; The sun of
2. Oh, there is mu-sic on the mountain, When winds are whistling wild and free; Tho' frozen
3. Now let our hearts, with pleasure beating, Join in our grateful, joy-ous lays; We ev-er

Chorus.

joy shines brightly o'er us, For 'tis the happy Christmas day: Tra la, la, Tra, la, la,
be each stream and fountain, Wide rolls the song from sea to sea. Tra la, la, Tra, la, la,
look for kind-ly greet-ing These glad-return-ing, hap-py days. Tra la, la, Tra, la, la,

cres. 1 2 Fine.

La, la, la, la, la, la, la, la, la, la, la, la, la, la, la, la, la, la, la, la, la.

THE mistake has been made in teaching music, that the names of the characters representing music have been taught first, instead of music itself. To little children, and even to children of a larger growth, it thus becomes dry and uninteresting; but if we reverse the process and teach music first and the names of characters incidentally, the work may be a constant delight and much valuable time will be saved. Mr. Holt does not claim to have invented anything, but simply to have discovered that the educational principles which underlie the true teaching of any other subject can be applied to music. He has discovered a method of presentation according to such principles that any one having teaching ability can successfully lead even the little child of five years to a surprising knowledge of music, provided only that the teacher has at the outset the musical ability to sing the scale. In order to become a musical nation we must have music taught in the public schools, and the daily work must be done by the regular teachers with special supervision at certain intervals. The only rote lesson in the whole course is the first—the teaching of the scale, which is taken

OH, MY BRAVEST AND BEST.

VINCENZO BELLINI.
" MONTECCHI E CAPULETTI."

1. Oh! my brav - est and best, I re - sign thee, My heart will be des - o - late
2. To thy wish had I breathed a de - ni - al, I know thou wouldst meekly o -

now; And the lau - rels that fame will entwine thee, I nev - er shall see on thy
bey; Ah, then think how severe is the tri - al, To her who now sends thee a -

brow; Thou art called, and to pause were an er - ror, Which naught could here-af - ter ef -
way; Had she cherished the thought to re - fuse thee, Few scarcely would ven - ture to

face, Tho' I think of thy danger with terror, Less could I en - dure thy disgrace.
blame, And 'twere better, far bet - ter to lose thee, Than feel I had darkened thy fame.

as the unit of thought in tune. Aside from this there is no imitation. It is a system of much thinking. Time and tune are taught separately, the whole measure being taken as the unit in tune. He has taught what not to teach, and has stripped music of the technicalities and enigmas which have been a bugbear to so many. He has shown—what has been proved in many schools— that it is as easy for children to read in one key as in another. There are no difficulties in the representation of music. One strong point is that practically but one scale is taught in different positions. The syllables are used simply as a means to an end, and are soon dropped. They are valuable in elementary work if used within certain limits. It can only be said that their use is better than none, since they bring up quickly the characteristic quality of the intervals. All music is written upon the basis of tone relation and these syllables aid the mind somewhat to grasp the idea of this relation of sounds.

THE musical tones which can be used with advantage, and have clearly distinguishable pitch, have between forty and four thousand vibrations in a second, extending over a range of seven octaves.—*Helmholtz.*

BEAUTIFUL FACES.

DAVID SWING.

1. Beau - ti - ful fa - ces are those that wear, It mat - ters lit - tle, if dark or fair,
2. Beau - ti - ful eyes are those that show Like crys - tal panes where hearth-fires glow,
3. Beau - ti - ful lips are those whose words Leap from the heart like songs of birds,

Chorus.

Whole-souled hones - ty print - ed there.
Beauti - ful thoughts that burn be - low.
Yet whose ut - t'rance pru - dence girds.
Beau - ti - ful, beau-ti - ful, beau - ti - ful,

Beau - ti - ful, beau - ti - ful, beau - ti - ful, Beau - ti - ful, beau-ti - ful, beau - ti - ful.

Beautiful hands are those that do
Work that's earnest and brave and true.
Moment by moment the long day through.

Beautiful feet are those that go
On kind ministry to and fro,
Down lowliest ways if God wills it so.

Beautiful shoulders are those that bear
Ceaseless burdens of homely care,
With patient grace and daily prayer.

Beautiful lives are those that bless—
Sweet, silent rivers of happiness,
Whose hidden fountains but few may guess.

CRADLE SONG OF SOLDIER'S WIFE.

T. T. BARKER.

1. Ba - by, sleep! shadows creep Down the hill-sides dark and long! Slum - ber soft - ly,
2. Ba - by, sleep! low I weep, Lest I wake thee in my woe! Where the camp-fires
3. Ba - by, sleep! an - gels keep Ho - ly vig - ils o'er thy head! And thy moth - er's

and thy dreaming May perchance have brighter seeming, For thy mother's cra - dle song!
gleam and quiv - er, Far a - way be - side the riv - er, Fa - ther thinks of thee, I know!
life seems sweeter, Griefs grow dim, and joys com-plet - er, Singing by thy cra - dle bed!

Besides indifference there is no doubt that music has had to suffer much from the lofty contempt with which she and her votaries have been treated by those who professed to have a claim to distinction in other walks. True, since the days of that offensive and priggish nobleman, Lord Chesterfield, things have greatly changed. Eton, Harrow, Rugby—all the great schools—have now their masters for music on the same footing as the other instructors. Go into the officers' quarter in barracks, and you will find pianofortes, violins and violoncellos, and lying about there will be *good* music. Amateur societies flourish, which bring rich and poor together. The Duke of Edinburg told me that he had a complete string quartet among the officers on his ship—all these things point a great reaction in the feelings of the professional classes towards music. But much of the old leaven remains, and one of the most objectionable developments is a curious affectation of ignorance on the part of many men of position in the political and scientific world, as if music were too trivial a matter for their lofty intellects to take notice of. At any great meeting on the subject of music, archbishops, judges, politicians, financiers—each one who rises to speak—will deprecate any knowledge of music with a smug satisfaction, like a man disowning poor relations. I am not here to explain why music should be cultivated, nor to apologize to superior-minded persons for its existence, nor to speak humbly and with bated breath of its merits; but I claim for it boldly and proudly its place amongst the great things and the great influences in the world; and can but express pity for those ignorant and stupid enough to deny its importance in the world and in history, and to look upon it as a mere family pastime fit only for women and children.—*Arthur Sullivan.*

LAUGHING GLEE.

MARTINI.

THE BIRD'S NEST.

HELEN THOMAS.

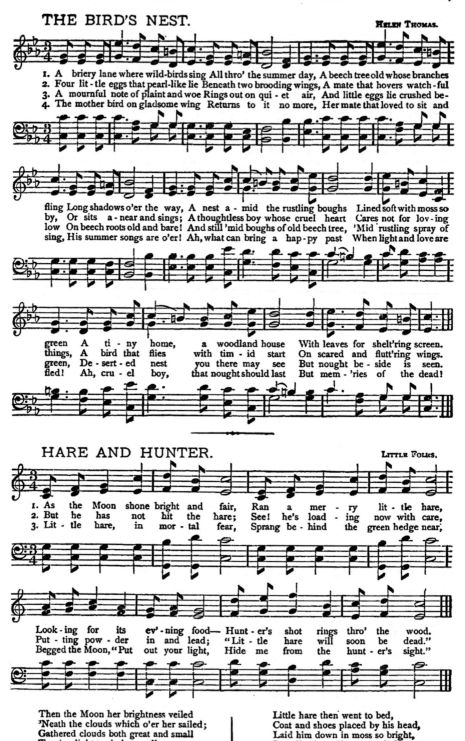

1. A briery lane where wild-birds sing All thro' the summer day, A beech tree old whose branches
2. Four lit-tle eggs that pearl-like lie Beneath two brooding wings, A mate that hovers watch-ful
3. A mournful note of plaint and woe Rings out on qui-et air, And little eggs lie crushed be-
4. The mother bird on gladsome wing Returns to it no more, Her mate that loved to sit and

fling Long shadows o'er the way, A nest a-mid the rustling boughs Lined soft with moss so
by, Or sits a-near and sings; A thoughtless boy whose cruel heart Cares not for lov-ing
low On beech roots old and bare! And still 'mid boughs of old beech tree, 'Mid rustling spray of
sing, His summer songs are o'er! Ah, what can bring a hap-py past When light and love are

green A ti-ny home, a woodland house With leaves for shelt'ring screen.
things, A bird that flies with tim-id start On scared and flutt'ring wings.
green, De-sert-ed nest you there may see But nought be-side is seen.
fied! Ah, cru-el boy, that nought should last But mem-'ries of the dead!

HARE AND HUNTER.

LITTLE FOLKS.

1. As the Moon shone bright and fair, Ran a mer-ry lit-tle hare,
2. But he has not hit the hare; See! he's load-ing now with care,
3. Lit-tle hare, in mor-tal fear, Sprang be-hind the green hedge near,

Look-ing for its ev'-ning food— Hunt-er's shot rings thro' the wood.
Put-ting pow-der in and lead; "Lit-tle hare will soon be dead."
Begged the Moon, "Put out your light, Hide me from the hunt-er's sight."

Then the Moon her brightness veiled
'Neath the clouds which o'er her sailed;
Gathered clouds both great and small
Turning light to darkness all.

Little hare then went to bed,
Coat and shoes placed by his head,
Laid him down in moss so bright,
Soundly slept till morning light.

A GRAND mistake of the old reasoners in their arguing for the goodness of God, was that they tried to prove that in the world there is more evidence of design for happiness than there is of design for pain. Now that position can not be maintained. There is just as much evidence of a design to produce pain as to produce pleasure. For every adaptation of pleasure that you will show me I will undertake to show you one for pain. This life is clearly rudimentary. Men are here to be hammered into something of worth in the next state of existence. Pleasure is to be desired, or expected, but as incidental. Earth is not the place for pleasure. It is the place where men are fashioned for eternity. A piano factory is not the place to go in order to hear music. Suppose a man were to start for some great piano manufactory with the expectation of being enchanted when there by innumerable Thalbergs. He goes along dreaming of the divine harmonies which will greet him when he approaches the place where these sweet-toned instruments are made. He anticipates as much more of delight than Thalberg had given him, as there are more instruments in the factory than were on the boards of the concert hall. "I am going to the place where all those pianos are made," he says, as he hastens on. "They turn out hundreds of them in a day. Oh! how will all sweet, bewildering sounds entrance my senses when I draw near. Hymns and songs of never-wearying melody will sing out to me from every door and window." He comes in sight of the building, and instead of hymns and choral melodies, he hears harsh noises. There are heavy poundings, gratings, sawings, and raspings. There are legs,

MY OWN NATIVE LAND.

WM. B. BRADBURY.

1. I have roamed o-ver mountain, I've crossed o - ver flood, I've traversed the wave-roll'-ing
2. The right hand of friendship how oft have I grasped, And bright eyes have smiled and looked
3. Then hail, dear Co - lum - bia, the land that we love, Where flour-ish - es Lib - er - ty's

strand; Tho' the fields were as green, and the moon shone as bright, Yet it
bland; Yet hap - pi - er far were the hours that I passed In the
tree; 'Tis the birth - place of free - dom, our own na - tive home; 'Tis the

FINE.

was not my own native land. No, no, no, no, no, no. No, no, no, no, no, no.
West, in my own native land. Yes, yes, yes, yes, yes, yes. Yes, yes, yes, yes, yes, yes.
land, 'tis the land of the free. Yes, yes, yes, yes, yes, yes. Yes, yes, yes, yes, yes, yes.

uncouth and clumsy to be worked into proper size and gracefulness. There are strings to be tried, and separate parts to be fitted and knocked together; there are great, heavy packing-boxes to be made, and various other awkward and noisy work to be done. Tools are thumping about; cords and tackling rattling; plenty of confounding noises, but no music. The man stands and sees the workmen ply the hammer, and saw, and file, and punch, and chisel and auger; he sees dust, boards, and shavings flying in all directions. Clatter and clatter surround him. From the windows come broken bits of board, wire and iron; also all the different notes of racket and din; but he hears no sweet melody. Then the man says in astonishment, "Do they call this a piano manufactory—this confused place, full of all jangling noises? No, no; this is no pianoproducing establishment. This is only a dusty and noisy workshop." Yes, it is a workshop, where are being fashioned the instruments which, when touched by skillful fingers, have power to enchant the world. But it is not the platform on which they are to be played. Not there are they to give forth their sweet harmonies. We are in the workshop of humanity. We see evidences of this, turn which way we will. We must feel the mallet and the saw; the punch and the bore. We must be split and ground and worked smooth. The pumice and the sand-paper are for us, also, as well as for the things we fashion; and at last, when we are all set together, polished, and attuned, we shall be played upon by the music-waking influences of Heaven.—Beecher.

IT may be laid down as a general rule that smoking is a bad habit for the singer, male or female—for there *are* females who are proud of being able to smoke cigarettes nowadays! With many instances of great singers before us, who have also been great smokers, it is impossible to say decidedly that singers must not smoke; but the habit is one to be very cautiously indulged in. If smoking in any case induces expectoration, it should at once be given up, for the habit of spitting, to which some smokers allow themselves to give way, is in reality, perhaps the great evil of smoking; it weakens the throat, lungs and chest. Avoid late hours. You require, not only a certain amount of sleep, but to take that sleep before the body and mind are at all overtaxed. From many causes, it is well known, that the human frame is always at its lowest vital energy from about 2 a.m. till 5 a.m. and the nearer you approach these hours in going to bed, the less able are you to derive all the benefit which you require from sleep. Twelve o'clock is late enough for any one. Another reason why late hours are bad is connected not with physical facts so much as with morals. It is true, you may come to no actual harm, or get into no positive evil, by being out late at night, but you place yourself in a position of risk—risk of cold, over-fatigue, inhaling vitiated atmosphere, etc., as well as risk to moral character, which latter, in its way as delicate as the voice, is injured not only by actual violation of right, but by all society, conversation, and literature which tend at all to mar its purity.

YANKEE DOODLE.

NATIONAL AIR.

1. Father and I went down to camp, A-long with Cap-tain Good-'in, And
2. And there we see a thou-sand men, As rich as Squire Da-vid; And
3. And there was Cap-tain Wash-ing-ton Up-on a slap-ping stall-ion, A-
4. And then the feath-ers on his hat, They looked so ver-y fine, ah! I

there we saw the men and boys As thick as has-ty pud-din'.
what they wast-ed ev-'ry day, I wish it could be sav-ed.
giv-ing or-ders to his men; I guess there was a mill-ion.
wan-ted pesk-i-ly to get To give to my Je-mi-ma.

Yan-kee doo-dle keep it up, Yan-kee doo-dle dan-dy,

Mind the mu-sic and the step, And with the girls be han-dy.

And there I see a swamping gun,
  Large as a log of maple,
Upon a mighty little cart;
  A load for father's cattle.

And every time they fired it off,
  It took a horn of powder;
It made a noise like father's gun,
  Only a nation louder.

And there I see a little keg,
  Its heads all made of leather,
They knocked upon't with little [sticks,
  To call the folks together.

And Cap'n Davis had a gun,
  He kind o' clapt his hand on 't,
And stuck a crooked stabbing iron
  Upon the little end on 't.

The troopers, too, would gallop up,
  And fire right in our faces;
It scared me almost half to death
  To see them run such races.

It scared me so I hooked it off,
  Nor stopped, as I remember,
Nor turned about till I got home,
  Locked up in mother's chamber.

10

When American educators visited Europe, some forty years ago, for the purpose of studying school systems, they found that instruction in vocal music was almost universal in the schools of Germany, and some other continental countries. Prior to that time juvenile class instruction in singing was comparatively unknown in this country. It now has its recognized place in the list of studies in the public schools of almost every city in the land. The time approaches when instruction in the elements of vocal music will become very general in our schools. Already school officers are asking candidates for positions as teachers, Can you give instruction in singing? and other qualifications being equal, those who can teach children to sing are preferred to those who cannot.— *Tillinghast.*

It is told of Daniel Webster that he cultivated the eye in reading to such an extent that he would look through a whole printed page while reading aloud one-half of it, and then pronounce the remaining half with the book shut. This habit of *looking ahead* is quite as necessary in the reading of music, and should be cultivated in children from the beginning. It is best acquired by reading from printed music those exercises and songs which are familiar.—*L. W. Mason.*

WATCH ON THE RHINE.

Words by MAX SCHNECKENBURGER.
Music by CARL WILHELM.

With Energy.

1. A voice resounds like thun - der peal, 'Mid dash-ing wave and clang of steel; "The
   Es braust ein Ruf wie Don - ner-hall, Wie Schwertge-klirr und Wo gen-prall: Zum
2. They stand a hun - dred thou - sand strong, Quick to a - venge their country's wrong; With
   Durch Hun-dert-tau - send zuckt es schnell, Und Al - ler Au - gen blit - zen hell; Der

1. Rhine, the Rhine, the German Rhine! Who guards to-day my stream di - vine?"
   Rhein, zum Rhein, zum deutschen Rhein! Wer will des Stro - mes Hu - ter sein?
2. fil - ial love their bo-soms swell; They'll guard the sa - cred land-mark well.
   Deut - sche, bie-der, fromm und stark, Be - schutzt die heil' - ge Lan - des - mark.

Chorus.

Dear Fa - therland! no dan - ger thine, Dear Father-land! no dan - ger thine; Firm stand thy
Lieb Va - derland, magst ru-hig sein, Lieb Va - derland, magst ru-hig sein; Fest steht und

sons to watch, to watch the Rhine, Firm stand thy sons to watch, to watch the Rhine.
treu die Wacht, die Wacht am Rhein! Fest steht und treu die Wacht, die Wacht am Rhein!

3. While flows one drop of German blood,
Or sword remains to guard thy flood,
While rifle rests in patriot's hand,
No foe shall tread thy sacred strand!—*Cho.*

3. So lang' ein Tropfen Blut noch gluht,
Noch eine Faust den Degen zieht,
Und noch ein Arm die Buchse spannt,
Betritt kein Feind hier deinen Strand.—*Cho.*

4. Our oath resounds, the river flows,
In golden light our banner glows,
Our hearts will guard thy stream divine,
The Rhine, the Rhine the German Rhine!—*Cho*

4. Der Schwur erschallt, die Woge rinnt,
Die Fahnen flattern hoch im Wind:
Am Rhein, am Rhein, am deutschen Rhein,
Wir alle wollen Huter sein!—*Cho.*

THE MILLER'S DAUGHTER.

C. Matz, Arr.
Bohemian Melody.

Lively. p

1. Down the stream so cheer - i - ly Be - side the mill we row, Where the echoes mer - ri - ly Their
2. When we call, oh, read - i - ly She answers us a - gain, And stops the wheel right steadily, To
3. Part - ing then, re - gret-ful-ly, We turn the dark'ning hill, With "Pretty maid, adieu," And tic-tac,

play-ful cho - rus throw; Down the stream so cheer - i - ly Be - side the mill we row,
hear our homeward strain, When we call, oh, read - i - ly She answers us a - gain, And
tic - tac goes the mill, Part - ing then, re - gret - ful - ly, We turn the dark'ning hill, With

f

Where the ech-oes mer - ri - ly Their play-ful cho-rus throw. ⎱
stops the wheel right stead-i - ly, To hear our homeward strain. ⎰ Tra la la la, la la la
"Pret - ty maid, a - dieu," And tic-tic, tic-tac goes the mill. ⎰

la la la la la la la la, Tra la la la la la la la la la la la.

f

To the pret - ty Nat - a - lie A pass-ing draught we fill, Sweet-ly sing-ing there, Where

tic - tac, tic - tac goes the mill, tic - tac, tic - tac goes the mill, tic - tac goes the mill.

IN THE STARLIGHT.

Stephen
J. E. Carpenter.   C. Matz, Arr.

1. In the starlight, in the star-light, let us wan-der gay and free, For there's nothing in the
2. In the starlight, in the star-light, at the day-light's dew-y close, When the nightin-gale is

day-light half so dear to you and me. Like the fai-ries in the shad-ow of the
sing-ing his last love-song to the rose; In the calm clear night of summer, when the

woods we'll steal a - long, And our sweetest lays we'll war-ble, for the night was made for
breez-es soft-ly play, From the glit-ter of our dwell-ing we will gen-tly steal a-

song; When none are by to lis-ten, or to chide us in our glee, In the
way Where the silv'ry wa-ters mur-mur, by the mar-gin of the sea, In the

star-light, in the starlight, let us wander gay and free, In the starlight, in the starlight, let us
star-light, in the starlight, we will wander gay and free, In the starlight, in the starlight, we will

wan-der, let us wan-der, In the star-light, in the star-light, let us wander gay and free.
wan-der, we will wander, In the star-light, in the star-light, we will wander gay and free.

THE FLAG OF OUR UNION FOREVER.

GEO. P. MORRIS.
WM. VINCENT WALLACE.

1. A song for our ban-ner, the watch-word re-call, Which gave the Re-pub-lic her
2. What God in His in-fi-nite wis-dom designed, And armed with the weapons of

sta-tion, "U-nit-ed we stand, di-vid-ed we fall," It made and preserved us a
thun-der, Not all the earth's despots or factions combined, Have the power to con-quer or

Chorus.

na-tion. The un-ion of lakes, the un-ion of lands, The un-ion of states none can
sun-der. The un-ion of lakes, the un-ion of lands, The un-ion of states none can

sev-er, The un-ion of hearts, the un-ion of hands, And the flag of our Un-ion for-ev-er.

NATIONAL HYMN.

REV. S. F. SMITH.
"America."—"God Save the King."

1. My country, 'tis of thee, Sweet land of lib-er-ty, Of thee I sing; Land where my
2. My na-tive coun-try thee, Land of the no-ble free, Thy name I love; I love thy
3. Let mu-sic swell the breeze, And ring from all the trees, Sweet freedom's song; Let mor-tal
4. Our fa-thers' God, to thee, Au-thor of lib-er-ty, To thee we sing: Long may our

fath-ers died, Land of the pil-grims' pride, From ev'ry mountain side Let free-dom ring!
rocks and rills, Thy woods and templed hills; My heart with rapture thrills Like that a-bove.
tongues awake; Let all that breathe partake; Let rocks their silence break, The sound pro-long.
land be bright With freedom's ho-ly light; Protect us by thy might, Great God, our King!

Sacred history declares that music and song were very frequently employed among the Hebrews on occasions of solemnity, in both their domestic and religious life. Immense choirs, with their thousand voices, were retained in the Temple to celebrate their feasts and victories, and a great number of books and treatises have been written, but with little satisfaction, upon the music of the Jews. It is not, however, uninteresting to follow out or trace the history of religious song, as found in the sacred record, the Bible, and to notice the musical solemnities of which it makes mention. In Genesis, Jubal is named as being "the father of all such as handle the harp and organ," but not as the inventor of music, as many have supposed or declared. Not until six hundred years after the deluge does the record again speak of music, which is at the time when Jacob is pursued by Laban: "Wherefore didst thou flee away secretly, and steal away from me, and didst not tell me, that I might have sent thee away with mirth, and with songs, with tabret and with harp?" Two hundred and forty-eight years after, at the passage of the Red Sea, the first religious song was intoned by Moses and the Hebrew people: "I will sing unto the Lord, for He hath triumphed glo-

ALL THE SAINTS ADORE THEE.

"NICÆA."
J. B. DYKES.   R. HEBER.

1. Ho-ly, ho-ly, ho-ly! Lord God Al-migh-ty! Ear-ly in the
2. Ho-ly, ho-ly, ho-ly! all the saints a-dore Thee, Cast-ing down their
3. Ho-ly, ho-ly, ho-ly! though the dark-ness hide Thee, Though the eye of
4. Ho-ly, ho-ly, ho-ly! Lord God Al-migh-ty! All thy works shall

morn-ing our song shall rise to Thee. Ho-ly, ho-ly, ho-ly,
golden crowns a-round the glas-sy sea; Cher-u-bim and Sera-phim
sinful man Thy glo-ry may not see, On-ly Thou art ho-ly!
praise Thy name in earth, and sky, and sea. Ho-ly, ho-ly, ho-ly!

mer-ci-ful and migh-ty, God in three per-sons, blessed Trin-i-ty!
fall-ing down be-fore Thee, Which wert, and art, and ev-er-more shalt be.
there is none be-side Thee Per-fect in pow-er, in love, and pu-ri-ty.
mer-ci-ful and migh-ty, God in three per-sons, blessed Trin-i-ty!

riously, the horse and his rider hath he thrown into the sea." Again, in Numbers, it speaks of trumpets, and the manner of blowing them on different occasions, as signals for assembling, departure, or alarm. The schofar, a wind instrument made from the horn of a ram, is reserved for the celebration of the first day of Tischri. After the death of Moses, the sacred writings preserve entire silence upon the subject of music, even to the time of the Judges, when is recorded the second song sung by Deborah and Barak: "Praise the Lord for the avenging of Israel," and a hundred years later occurred the sad and tragic death of the daughter of Jephthah. After this event, even to the time of Samuel, there is no musical record in the sacred writings. He instituted a school of prophets, where song and music were, undoubtedly, an important branch of education. Saul, soon after his coronation, encounters a troop of men inspired by the Holy Spirit, prophesying to the sound of instruments. At their approach he is seized with a divine inspiration and prophesies with them. Subsequently, becoming a prey to melancholy, he calls the youthful David to his side, who, by his inspired songs, dissipates the dark torments that overshadowed his soul.

The words of Hail Columbia were written by Joseph Hopkinson in Philadelphia, in 1798, for the President's March, then a very popular air. The Star Spangled Banner was written in Baltimore in 1814 by Francis Scott Key, and adapted to an old French air long known in England as "Anacreon in Heaven," and later in America as "Adams and Liberty." My Country, tis of Thee, written in Boston in 1832 by Samuel F. Smith, was set by Lowell Mason to the music of the old tune God Save the Queen. The words of Flag of the Free, here given, go well to the Wedding March in Lohengrin. There is always room for a new song that has in it anything to suggest the thought of country, to stir pride in the flag, to quicken the patriotic heart-beat. This music is distinctive in character and known throughout the world, and the song is already sung very widely.

FLAG OF THE FREE.

J. P. McCaskey.
March from Lohengrin.

1. Flag of the Free! fair-est to see! Borne thro' the strife and the thunder of war, Ban-ner so
2. Flag of the Free! all turn to thee,—Golden thy stars in the blue of their sky! Flag of the
3. Flag of the brave, long may it wave! Chosen of God while His might we a-dore, High in the

Cho.—Flag of the Free, all hail to thee! Floating the fair-est on o-cean or shore, Loud ring the

bright with star-ry light, Float ev-er proudly from mountain to shore. [*Final ending.*]
brave! foes let them rave,—Crimson thy bars floating gai-ly on high! . . . .
van, for manhood of man, Symbol of Right thro' the years passing o'er; . . . .

cry, ne'er let it die, "Un-ion and Lib-er-ty [*Omit.* . . . . . .]now, ev-er-more!"

Sa-ges of old thy com-ing fore-saw, Em-pire of jus-tice, em-pire of law;
Splendid thy sto-ry, might-y to save, Matchless thy beau-ty on land or wave,
Flower of the a-ges, promised of yore, Flower of the a-ges, fade nev-er-more!

Flag of our fa-thers! round all the world Blest of the millions wher-ev-er un-furled;
Heroes have borne thee a-loft in the fray, Foemen who scorned thee have all passed a-way;
Emblem of Free-dom, "Ma-ny in One," O'er thee thine ea-gle, bird of the sun;

D.C. for Chorus.

Ter-ror to ty-rants, hope to the slave, Spread thy fair folds to shield and to save,
Pride of our coun-try, hailed from a-far, Ban-ner of Prom-ise, lose not a star,
All hail, "Old Glory!" hearts leap to see How from the nations the world looks to thee.

THE MAY QUEEN.

ALFRED TENNYSON.
WM. R. DEMPSTER, 1845.

1. You must wake and call me ear - ly, call me ear - ly, moth - er dear;   To -
2. Lit - tle Ef - fie shall go with me to-mor - row to the green,   And
3. The night winds come and go, moth - er, up - on the mead - ow grass,   And

mor - row will be the hap - pi - est time of all the glad New Year;   Of
you'll be there too, moth - - er, to see me made the Queen;   The
the hap - py stars a - bove them seem to bright - en as they pass;   There

all the glad New Year, moth - er, the mad - dest, mer - ri - est day: For
shep - herd lads on ev - 'ry side will come from far a - way,   For
will not be a drop o' rain the whole o' the live - long day,   For

I'm to be Queen o' the May, mother, I'm to be Queen o' the May.   I
I'm to be Queen o' the May, mother, I'm to be Queen o' the May.   All
I'm to be Queen o' the May, mother, I'm to be Queen o' the May.   So you must

sleep so sound all night, moth - er, that I shall nev - er a - wake,   If you
the val - ley, moth - er, will be fresh and green and still,   And the
wake and call me ear - ly, call me ear - ly, moth - er dear,   To -

do not call me loud when the day be - gins to break: But
cow - slip and the crow - foot are o - ver all the hill,   The
mor - row'll be the happiest time of all the glad New Year,   To -

GOOD-BYE.

J. C. ENGELBRECHT.

1. Farewell, fare-well is a lone - ly sound And al-ways brings a sigh, But
2. Farewell, fare-well may do for the gay, When pleas-ure's throng is nigh, But

give to me when loved ones part, That sweet old word, "good - bye," That
give to me that bet - ter word, That comes from the heart, "good - bye," That

sweet old word, "good - bye," That sweet old word "good - bye," But
comes from the heart, "good-bye," That comes from the heart, "good-bye," But

give to me, when loved ones part, That sweet old word, "good - bye."
give to me that bet - ter word, That comes from the heart, "good-bye."

Adieu, adieu we hear it oft
  With a tear, perhaps with a sigh,
But the heart feels most when the lips move not,
  And the eye speaks the gentle "good-bye."

Farewell, farewell, is never heard,
  When the tear's in the mother's eye,
Adieu, adieu, she speaks it not,
  But, "My love, good-bye, good-bye."

SPEECH AND SONG.—All boys and girls can sing, if it suits them to do so in the way of play. You never saw little boys and girls "beg off," when they want to sing together. In Germany, it has long been considered certain that all children can sing. They do not admit of exceptions, except in the case of the dumb. They not only argue from the general frequency of singing among children at play, but from the laws of music, as manifested in human language. Speech itself is but a kind of chant, and the voice always moves in musical intervals. The raising of the pitch a third, a fifth, an octave? that is, from *do* to *me,* from *do* to *sol,* and from lower *do* to upper *do?* is by no means confined to singing and recitation; it is what we always do under the influence of the slightest excitement, and when we ask questions. Our voices always go up and down, following the musical intervals. All can sing, therefore; that is, all who can talk, and who raise their voice and let it fall according to the usual laws of speech. And yet we, in this country, assume that many children cannot learn to sing, and they grow up without this great blessing.

SPEED AWAY.

I. B. WOODBURY.

1. Speed a - way! speed a - way! on thine er - rand of light! There's a young heart a-
2. And, oh! wilt thou tell her, blest bird on the wing, That her moth - er hath
3. Go, bird of the sil - ver wing, fet - ter - less now, Stoop not thy bright

wait - ing thy com - ing to - night; She will fon - dle thee close, she will ask for the loved
ev - er a sad song to sing; That she standeth a - lone, in the still qui - et night,
pin - ions on yon mountain's brow; But hie thee a - way, o'er rock, riv - er, and glen,

Who pine up - on earth since the "Day Star" has roved; She will ask if we miss her so
And her fond heart goes forth for the being of light, Who had slept in her bo - som, but
And find our young "Day Star" ere night close again; Up! on - ward! let noth - ing thy

Rit. e Dim.

long is her stay;
who would not stay?   Speed a - way! Speed a - way! Speed a - way!
mis - sion de - lay:

Before leaving Europe we undertook with resolute purpose the study of the English language, and bought one of the famous self-instructors called, "English without a Master; or, English in twelve Lessons." We studied the twelve lessons, but found on our arrival in this country, that our English was poorly calculated to stand the test of familiar conversation. To learn music is, in some respects, much more difficult than to master a language. Should any be tempted to seek help in a "Piano without Master," let us advise them not to do so. They will fail, spending their time and money in vain. While you are alone, your attainments may be satisfactory to yourself, but when you come in contact with musicians you will find, to your mortification, that you know nothing of music, just as we knew nothing of English.—*Karl Merz.*

SPEED AWAY.—It was a beautiful fancy among the Seneca Indians that a white dove let loose, at her grave, by the mother of the lost maiden would seek and find her waiting "Day Star" in the far-off Spirit Land.

BEN BOLT.

Nelson Kneass.
Thomas Dunn English.

Semplice.

1. Oh! don't you remember sweet Alice, Ben Bolt, Sweet Alice whose hair was so brown, Who
2. Un - der the hick-o - ry tree, Ben Bolt, Which stood at the foot of the hill, To -
3. And don't you remember the school, Ben Bolt, With the master so kind and so true, And the
4. There is change in the things I loved, Ben Bolt, They have changed from the old to the new; But I

wept with delight when you gave her a smile, And trembled with fear at your frown? In the
geth-er we've lain in the noon-day shade, And listened to Ap - ple-ton's mill. The mill -
sha - ded nook by the running brook, Where the fairest wild flow'rs grew? Grass
feel in the depths of my spir - it the truth, There never was change in you. Twelve

old church-yard, in the val - ley, Ben Bolt, In a cor-ner ob-scure and a - lone, They have
wheel has fall-en to pieces, Ben Bolt, The raft - ers have tum - bled in, And a
grows on the master's grave, Ben Bolt, The spring of the brook is dry, And of
months twen-ty have past, Ben Bolt, Since first we were friends—yet I hail Thy

fit - ted a slab of the granite so gray, And sweet Alice lies un - der the stone, They have
qui - et that crawls round the walls as you gaze, Has followed the old - en din, And a
all the boys who were schoolmates then, There are on - ly you and I, And of
pres-ence a blessing, thy friendship a truth, Ben Bolt of the salt - sea gale, Thy

ad libitum.

fit - ted a slab of the granite so gray, And sweet Alice lies un - der the stone.
qui - et that crawls round the walls as you gaze, Has fol-lowed the old - en din.
all the boys who were schoolmates then, There are on - ly you and I.
presence a bless-ing, thy friendship a truth, Ben Bolt, of the salt - sea gale!

JOLLY OLD SAINT NICHOLAS.

"SCHOOL CHIMES.
Per. S. BRAINARD'S SONS.

1. Jol - ly old Saint Nich - o - las, Lean your ear this way! Don't you tell a
2. When the clock is strik - ing twelve, When I'm fast a - sleep, Down the chimney,
3. John - ny wants a pair of skates; Su - sy wants a dolly; Nel - ly wants a

sin - gle soul What I'm going to say; Christmas Eve is com - ing soon;
broad and black, With your pack you'll creep; All the stockings you will find
sto - ry - book; She thinks dolls are folly; As for me, my - lit - tle brain.

Now, you dear old man, Whisper what you'll bring to me; Tell me if you can.
Hanging in a row; Mine will be the shortest one; You'll be sure to know.
Is - n't ve - ry bright; Choose for me, Old San - ta Claus, What you think is right.

DECK THE HALL.

WELSH AIR.

1. Deck the hall with boughs of hol - ly,
2. See the blaz - ing yule be - fore us,
3. Fast a - way the old year pass - es,
} Fa la la la la la la la la,

'Tis the sea-son to be jol - ly,
Strike the harp and join the chorus,
Hail the new, ye lads and lasses!
} Fa la la la la la la la la. {
Don we now our
Follow me in
Sing we joy-ous

gay ap-par - el, Troll the ancient Christmas car - ol,
mer - ry measure, While I tell of Christmas treasure,
all to-geth - er, Heedless of the wind and weather.
} Fa la la la la la la la la.

CHILDREN'S SONGS.

LITTLE ONES.

Allegretto.

1. O wild is thy joy, my af - fec - tion-ate boy, What visions of fan - cy come o'er thee? Thy
2. Dost think of a day thou mayst ramble and play, O'er meadows, and forests, and mountains? Or
3. Ah, brief is our mirth, for the visions of earth, Like the shadows of noonday, are fly - ing; But

spir - it so proud, and thy laughter so loud, What transports are glittering be - fore thee?
in the sweet vale, 'mong the lil - ies so pale, By the side of the rills and the foun - tains?
joys that are pure, shall for - ev - er en - dure, Though earth and its transports are dy - ing.

THE LITTLE BIRD.

1. Oh, do not frighten or de - stroy The lit - tle bird with gold - en wing, That
2. See how she nes - tles on the bough, And nour - ish - es her ten - der young; Mark
3. 'Tis cru - el to dis - turb her nest, Or pil - fer to sup - ply a cage; We
4. Then do not frighten or de - stroy The lit - tle bird with gold - en wing, But

car - ols forth the notes of joy To cheer us in the time of spring.
how her warm af - fec - tions flow, And lis - ten to her gen - tle song.
who with lib - er - ty are blest, Should nev - er thus our thoughts en - gage.
oft, like her, thy voice em - ploy, The Au - thor of cre - a - tion sing.

THE SCALE.

1. Come, let us learn to sing, Do re mi fa sol la si do; Loud let our voices ring, Do re mi fa sol la si
2. This is the scale so sweet, Do re mi fa sol la si do; Sing it with accent meet, Do re mi fa sol la si

do; Let us sing with open sound, With our voices full and round, Do si la sol fa mi re do.
do; First ascend in notes so true, Then descend in order too, Do si la sol fa mi re do.

NURSERY SONGS.

JANE TAYLOR.

1. Ah, why will my dear lit - tle child be so cross, And cry, and look sulky and pout?   To
2. If the water is cold and the comb hurts your head, And the soap has got into your eye, Will the
3. It is not to tease you and hurt you, my sweet, But on - ly for kindness and care, That I

lose her sweet smile is a very sad loss: I can't even kiss her without, I can't even kiss her without.
water grow warmer for all that you've said? What good will it do you to cry, What good will it do you to cry?
wash you and dress you and make you look neat, And comb out your tanglesome hair, And comb out your
[tanglesome hair.

THE CHATTERBOX.

JANE TAYLOR.

1. From morn - ing till night it was Lu - cy's de - light, To chat - ter and talk with - out
2. How ve - ry ab - surd! and have you not heard That much tongue and few brains are
3. While Lu - cy was young, if she'd bridled her tongue, With a lit - tle good sense and ex -

stopping; There was not a day but she rat - tled a - way, Like water for - ev - er a - dropping.
connected? That they are supposed to think least who talk most? Their wisdom is always suspected.
er - tion, Who knows but she now might have been our delight, Instead of our jest and aversion!

LITTLE JACK.

JANE TAYLOR.

1. There was one lit - tle Jack, Not very long back, And 'tis said, to his lasting dis - grace, That he
2. His kind friends were much hurt To see so much dirt, And often and well did they scour;   But
3. When to wash he was sent, He reluctantly went With wa - ter to splash himself o'er;   But he

nev - er was seen With his hands at all clean, Nor yet ev - er clean was his   face.
all was in vain, He was dir - ty a - gain Be - fore they had done it an   hour.
left the black streaks All o - ver his cheeks And made them look worse than be - fore.

NURSERY SONGS.

LITTLE ONES.

A, B, C, D, E, F, G, H, I, J, K, L, M, N, O, P, Q, R, S, and T, U, V,

W (double-you), and X, Y, Z. Hap-py, hap-py shall we be, When we've learned our A, B, C.

BIBABUTZEMANN.

Gay dances Bi - ba - butzemann, All in and out and round about; Gay dances Bi - ba - butzemann, Our
Es tanzt ein Bi - ba - butzemann, in unserm Haus, herumdi dum; Es tanzt ein Bi - ba - butzemann, in

house all round about. He whirls himself and twirls himself, And flings his bag behind himself. Gay
un - serm Haus herum. Er rüt - telt sich und schüttelt sich er wirft sein Säckchen hinter sich. Es

FOX AND GOOSE.

Moderato.

1. Fox, you've stolen my grey gander, Better bring him back, Better bring him back! There's a hun - ter
2. Soon he will, his ri - fle showing, Shoot you in the head, Shoot you in the head! Fast the red drops
3. Lit - tle fox, beware, there's danger, Thieving will not do, Thieving will not do! Bet - ter be to

watching yonder, He is on your track, There's a hunter, watching yonder, He is on your track.
will be flowing, You will then be dead, Fast the red drops will be flowing, You will then be dead.
goose a stranger, Mouse is best for you, Bet - ter be to goose a stranger, Mouse is best for you.

1.	2.	3.
Fuchs, du hast die Gans gestohlen,	Seine grosse lange Flinte,	Liebes Füchslein lass dir rathen,
Gieb sie wieder her,	Schiesst auf dich den Schrot,	Sei doch nur kein Dieb:
Sonst wird sie der Jäger holen,	Dass dich färbt die rothe Tinte,	Nimm, du brauchst nicht, Gänse-
Mit dem Schiessgewehr.	Und dann bist du todt.	Mit der Maus fürlieb. [braten

SINCE the Church has been divided into many branches, each has had its sweet singers, whose music has gladdened all the rest. It was Toplady, a severe Calvinist, who gave us "Rock of Ages." Men differ about the atonement; they almost call each other heretics and outcasts in their difference about it; but, when that hymn is sung, every heart rests upon the one Redeemer. It was Charles Wesley, an Arminian, who sang "Jesus, Lover of my Soul." Side by side are Watts and Wesley, Church of England and Dis-senter. F. W. Faber, a devout Catholic, wrote that hymn which breathes the highest spirit of Christian submission, "I worship Thee, sweet Will of God." Madame Guion, an unquestioning Catholic, wrote "O Lord, how full of sweet content!" Francis Xavier, one of the founders of the Jesuit order, wrote "Thou, O my Jesus! Thou didst me upon the Cross embrace." While the Church of England was con-vulsed by the greatest struggle it has known within this century, Keble, closely attached to one of the

HARK! THE HERALD ANGELS SING.

MENDELSSOHN.
CHAS. WESLEY, 1793.

1. Hark! the her-ald an-gels sing, "Glo-ry to the new-born King! Peace on earth, and
2. Christ, by highest heav'n a - dored; Christ, the ev - er - last-ing Lord; Late in time be-
3. Hail! the heav'n-born Prince of peace! Hail! the Son of Righteousness! Light and life to

mer - cy mild,   God and sin - ners re - con-ciled."   Joy - ful, all ye na-tions, rise,
hold him come,   Offspring of the favored one.   Veil'd in flesh, the Godhead see;
all he brings,   Risen with healing in his wings.   Mild he lays his glo - ry by,

Join the triumph of the skies;   With th'angel - ic host proclaim,   "Christ is born in
Hail th'incarnate De - i - ty: Pleased, as man, with men to dwell,   Je - sus, our Im -
Born that man no more may die: Born to raise the sons of earth,   Born to give them

Beth-le - hem."
man-u - el! } Hark! the herald an-gels sing, "Glo - ry to the new-born King!"
se - cond birth.)

contending parties, wrote the Evening Hymn which the whole Church delights to sing. A Unitarian, Sarah F. Adams, gave us "Nearer, my God, to Thee." The controversies over the orthodoxy of that hymn are as dry and cold and dead as the stones Jacob took for his pillow; and, meanwhile, souls mount up by it toward heaven as did the angels on the ladder Jacob saw as he journeyed to Padan-aram.

WE walk here, as it were, in the crypts of life: at times, from the great cathedral above us, we can hear the organ and the chanting choir; we can see the light stream through the open door, when some friend goes out before us; and shall we fear to mount the narrow staircase of the grave that leads us out of this uncertain twilight into eternal light?—*Longfellow.*

WHENEVER I think of God, I can only conceive of him as a Being infinitely great and infinitely good. This last quality of the divine nature inspires me with such confidence and with such joy that I could have written even a Miserere in *tempo allegro.—Haydn.*

COME, THOU ALMIGHTY KING.

CHARLES WESLEY, 1757.
"America."—"God Save the King."

1. Come, Thou Al-might-y King, Help us Thy name to sing, Help us to praise. Fa-ther all
2. Come, Thou e-ter-nal Lord, By Heaven and earth adored, Our prayer at-tend. Come, and Thy
3. Be Thou our com-for-ter; Thy sa-cred wit-ness bear In this glad hour. Om-nip-o-

glo-ri-ous, O'er all vic-to-ri-ous, Come and reign o-ver us, An-cient of days.
children bless; Give Thy good word success; Make Thine own holi-ness On us de-scend.
tent Thou art, O, rule in ev-ery heart, And ne'er from us de-part, Spir-it of power.

1.
Praise ye Jehovah's name;
Praise through His courts proclaim;
Rise and adore.
High o'er the Heavens above,
Sound his great acts of love;
While His rich grace we prove,
Vast as His power.

2.
While His high praise ye sing,
Shake every sounding string;
Sweet the accord!
He vital breath bestows—
Let every breath that flows,
His noblest fame disclose;
Praise ye the Lord.

3.
Now let the trumpet raise
Triumphant sounds of praise,
Wide as His fame!
There let the harps be found,
Organs with solemn sound,
Roll your deep notes around—
Filled with His name.

EVENING HYMN.

SCOTCH TUNE. "WARD."

1. For-give me, Lord, thro' Thy dear Son, The ills that I this day have done;
2. Teach me to live that I may dread The grave as lit-tle as my bed;
3. Be Thou my Guar-dian while I sleep; Thy watch-ful sta-tion near me keep;
4. Lord, let my heart for-ev-er share The bliss of Thy pa-ter-nal care;

That with the world, my-self, and Thee, I, ere I sleep, at peace may be.
Teach me to die that so I may With joy be-hold the judg-ment day.
My heart with love ce-les-tial fill, And guard me from ap-proach of ill.
'Tis heaven on earth, 'tis heaven a-bove, To see Thy face and sing Thy love.

1.
Awake, my soul, and with the sun,
Thy daily stage of duty run;
Shake off dull sloth, and joyful rise,
To pay thy morning sacrifice.

2.
Lord, I my vows to Thee renew—
Scatter my sins like morning dew;
Guard my first springs of thought and [will,
And with Thyself my spirit fill.

3.
Direct, control, suggest, this day,
All I design, or do, or say, [might
That all my powers, with all their
In Thy sole glory may unite.

20

This touching song, "The Sands o' Dee," by Charles Kingsley, occurs in his novel of "Alton Locke." The hero says: "After singing two or three songs, Lillian began fingering the keys, and struck into an old air, wild and plaintive, rising and falling like the swell of an Æolian harp upon a distant breeze. 'Ah! now,' she said, 'if I could get words for that! What an exquisite lament somebody might write to it.' . . My attention was caught by hearing two gentlemen, close to me, discuss a beautiful sketch by Copley Fielding, if I recollect rightly, which hung on the wall—a wild waste of tidal sands, with here and there a line of stake-nets fluttering in the wind—a gray shroud of rain sweeping up from the westward, through which low, red cliffs glowed dimly in the rays of the setting sun —a train of horses and cattle splashing slowly through shallow, desolate pools and creeks, their wet, red and black hides glittering in one long line of level light. One of the gentlemen had seen the spot represented, at the mouth of the Dee, and began telling wild stories of salmon-fishing and wild-fowl shooting—and then a tale of a girl, who, in bringing her father's cattle home across the sands, had been caught by a sudden flow of the tide upon the beach and was found next day a corpse hanging among the stake-nets far below. The tragedy, the art of the picture, the simple, dreary grandeur of the scenery, took possession of me, and I stood gazing a long time, and fancying myself pacing the sands. . . As I lay castle-building, Lillian's wild air still rang in my ears, and combined itself somehow with the picture of the Cheshire Sands, and the story of the drowned girl, till it shaped itself into a song."

THE SANDS O' DEE.

FRANCIS BOOTT.
CHARLES KINGSLEY.

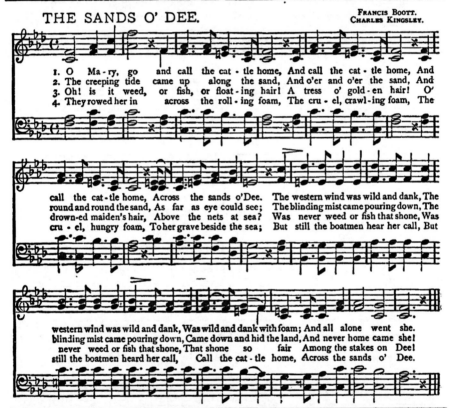

1. O Ma-ry, go and call the cat-tle home, And call the cat-tle home, And
2. The creeping tide came up along the sand, And o'er and o'er the sand, And
3. Oh! is it weed, or fish, or float-ing hair! A tress o' gold-en hair! O'
4. They rowed her in across the roll-ing foam, The cru-el, crawl-ing foam, The

call the cat-tle home, Across the sands o'Dee;
round and round the sand, As far as eye could see;
drown-ed maiden's hair, Above the nets at sea?
cru-el, hungry foam, To her grave beside the sea;

The western wind was wild and dank, The
The blinding mist came pouring down, The
Was never weed or fish that shone, Was
But still the boatmen hear her call, But

western wind was wild and dank, Was wild and dank with foam; And all alone went she.
blinding mist came pouring down, Came down and hid the land, And never home came she!
never weed or fish that shone, That shone so fair Among the stakes on Dee!
still the boatmen heard her call, Call the cat-tle home, Across the sands o' Dee.

Architecture is one of the most fascinating arts, and its study has been to many a man a sublime life-work. Lincoln and York Cathedrals, St. Paul's and St. Peter's, the arch of Titus, Theban temple, Alhambra, and Parthenon, are monuments to the genius of those who built them. But more wonderful than any arch they ever lifted, or any transept window they ever illumined, or any Corinthian column they ever crowned, or any Gothic cloister they ever elaborated, is the human ear. Among the most skillful and assiduous physiologists of our time have been those who have given their time to the examination of the ear, and the studying of its arches, its walls, its floor, its canals, its aqueducts, its galleries, its intricacies, its convolutions, its divine machinery; and yet, it will take another thousand years before the world comes to any adequate appreciation of what God did when He planned and executed the infinite and overmastering architecture of the human ear. The most of it is invisible, and the microscope breaks down in the attempt at exploration. The cartilage which we call the ear is only the storm-door of the great temple clear down out of sight, next door to the immortal soul. Such scientists as Helmholtz, and De Blainville, and Rank, and Buck, have attempted to walk the Appian Way of the human ear, but the mysterious pathway has never been fully trodden but by two feet— the foot of sound and the foot of God.—*Talmage.*

Instruction by the living voice has this advantage over books, that as being more natural, it is also more impressive. Hearing rouses the attention and keeps it alive far more effectually than reading.—*Hamilton.*

MUSIC ON THE WAVES.

J. E. CARPENTER.
CHARLES W. GLOVER.

The winds soft-ly sigh in their mys-ti-cal caves, And the moon gilds the slum-ber-ing seas, The sound of sweet mu-sic comes o-ver the waves Like spir-it-voice borne on the breeze. Faintly and low, soft-ly and slow, Heard o'er the waves as they rip-ple and flow; Faintly and low, soft-ly and slow, Heard o'er the waves as they ripple and flow.

After 1st D.C. pass to Alto Solo.

SOPRANO SOLO.

Is it the song of the si-rens that keep Re-vel be-low in their home of the deep? Or from yon dis-tant ship, far, far o'er the foam, The voice of the ab-sent ones sing-ing of home?

D. C.

ALTO SOLO.

No! 'tis but fan-cy that gives to the breeze The music that steals through the murmuring seas: The sweet song that sounds when the stars shine above, When nature is mu-sic, and mu-sic is love.

D. C. to Soprano Solo.

In the Schools.—No one thing has done more for music in the past twenty years than its introduction as an integral part of our common school education. In the large cities and suburban towns little seems left to desire in that direction. From the time children at the age of five enter the primary school till at the age of sixteen or eighteen they graduate from the high or normal school, music is as much a part of their training as the multiplication table and spelling book. The next generation will see what we foresee, and reap the harvest this generation is so wisely sowing. If, as we contend, music is in itself purifying and elevating, if it can displace and crowd out baser pleasures by giving innocent recreation and excitement to a people that must be amused, a people who must be busy for good or for evil, we can not have too much of it. It can not enter too largely or too deeply into the system of common-school education. In curious juxtaposition in an English paper a short time since was a statement that Dean Stanley had no appreciation of music, and was averse to its introduction into state systems of education; in another column was a report of one of Dean Stanley's addresses on the condi-

STEAL AWAY.

Slave Hymn.

Steal a - way, steal a - way, steal a - way to Je - sus!

Steal a - way, steal a - way home, I've not got long to stay here.

1. My Lord calls me, He calls me by the thun - der; The
2. Green trees are bend - ing, Poor sin - ners stand trem - bling; The
3. My Lord calls me, He calls me by the light - ning; The

trum - pet sounds it in my soul: I've not got long to stay here.

tion of the working classes, lamenting with an evident surprise that while so much had been done within the last twenty years to lessen intemperance among the gentry, so little comparatively had been effected among the laboring class. The inference is natural and not far-fetched which assumes a need among that very working class which had remained unheeded, unsupplied. The gentleman has his elegant home, his intellectual entertainments; an atmosphere of grace and beauty surrounds him, or is easily attainable; his craving for excitement, for a life apart from his labor, is gratified with scarcely an effort on his part. The man less fortunately situated needs recreation and stimulus even more than the other. Warmth, light, companionship, he must have. The gin-palace offers them, ruining body and soul, while it affects to comfort both. Tear down the rum-shop, turn the trades-union into a choral society, bring good music with attractive surroundings before him, educate his children to take part in grand old folk-songs, glees, and madrigals, and in a generation a strange revolution would be wrought.—*Ellis Gray.*

SWING LOW, SWEET CHARIOT.

SLAVE HYMN.

Swing low, sweet char - i - ot, Com - ing for to car - ry me home,

Swing low, sweet char - i - ot, Com - ing for to car - ry me home.

1. I looked o - ver Jor - dan, and what did I see, Com-ing for to car - ry me
2. If you get there be - fore I do, Com-ing for to car - ry me
3. The bright - est day that ev - er I saw, Com-ing for to car - ry me
4. I'm some - times up and some - times down, Com-ing for to car - ry me

home? A band of an - gels coming af - ter me, Com-ing for to car - ry me home.
home, Tell all my friends I'm com - ing too, Com-ing for to car - ry me home.
home, When Je - sus wash'd my sins a - way, Com-ing for to car - ry me home.
home, But still my soul feels heav-en - ly bound, Com-ing for to car - ry me home.

GIVE ME JESUS.

SLAVE HYMN.

1. Oh, when I come to die, Oh, when I come to die, Oh, when I come to die, Give me Je -
2. In the morning when I rise, In the morning when I rise, In the morning when I rise, Give me Je -
3. Dark midnight was my cry, Dark midnight was my cry, Dark midnight was my cry, Give me Je -
4. I heard the mourner say, I heard the mourner say, I heard the mourner say, Give me Je -

sus, Give me Je - sus, Give me Je - sus, You may have all this world, Give me Je - sus.

THE origin of these Slave Songs is unique. They are never "composed" after the manner of ordinary music, but spring into life, ready made, from the white heat of religious fervor during some protracted meeting in church or camp. They come from no musical cultivation whatever, but are the simple, ecstatic utterances of wholly untutored minds. From so unpromising a source we could reasonably expect only such a mass of crudities as would be unendurable to the cultivated ear. On the contrary, however, the cultivated listener confesses to a new charm, and to a power, never before felt, at least in its kind. What can we infer from this but that the child-like, receptive minds of these unfortunates were wrought upon with a true inspiration, and that this gift was bestowed upon them by an ever-watchful Father, to quicken the pulses of life, and to keep them from the state of hopeless apathy into which they were in danger of falling. A technical analysis of these melodies shows some interesting facts. The first peculiarity that strikes the attention is in the rhythm. This is often complicated, and sometimes strikingly original, and it is remarkable that the effects are so satisfactory. Another noticeable feature of the songs is the entire absence of triple time, or three-part measure among them. The reason for this is doubtless to be found in the beating of the foot and the swaying of the body which are such frequent accompaniments of the singing. These motions are in even measure, and in perfect time; and so it will be found that, however broken and seemingly irregular the movement of the music, it is always capable of the most exact measurement. In other words, its irregularities invariably conform to the "higher law" of the perfect rhythmic flow. It is a coincidence worthy of note that more than half the melodies are in the same scale as that in which Scottish music is written; that is, with the fourth and seventh tones omitted. The fact

NOBODY KNOWS THE TROUBLE I'VE SEEN.

SLAVE HYMN.

Slow.

Oh, no-bod-y knows the trou-ble I've seen, No-bod-y knows but Je-sus!

No-bod-y knows the trouble I've seen, Glo-ry Hal-le-lu-jah! { Some-times I'm up, some-
No-bod-y knows the trouble I've seen, Glo-ry Hal-le-lu-jah! { Al-though you see me
     { One day when I was
     { I nev-er shall for-

times I'm down, Oh yes, Lord, Sometimes I'm al-most to the ground, Oh yes, Lord.)
going along so, Oh yes, Lord, I have my tri-als here be-low, Oh yes, Lord. }
walk-ing along, Oh yes, Lord, The element opened, and the Love came down, Oh yes, Lord.)
get that day, Oh yes, Lord, When Je-sus washed my sins a-way, Oh yes, Lord.)

that the music of the ancient Greeks is also said to have been written in this scale, suggests an interesting inquiry as to whether it may not be a peculiar language of nature, or a simpler alphabet than the ordinary diatonic scale, in which the uncultivated mind finds its easiest expression. The variety of forms presented in these songs is truly surprising, when their origin is considered. This diversity is greater than the listener would at first be likely to suppose. The themes are also quite as distinct and varied as in the case of more pretentious compositions. The reader may feel assured that the music as here given is entirely correct. It was taken down from the singing of the Jubilee band, during repeated interviews held for that purpose, and no line or phrase was introduced that did not receive full indorsement from these singers. Some of the phrases and turns in the melodies are so peculiar that the listener might suppose them to be incapable of exact representation by ordinary musical characters. It is found, however, that they all submit to the laws of musical language, and if sung or played exactly as written, all the characteristic effects will be reproduced.— *Theo. F. Seward.*

The song given above, is a favorite on the Sea Islands, off the coast of South Carolina. Once, when ill-feeling was excited and trouble anticipated because of uncertain action of the Government in regard to the confiscated lands on those islands, Gen O. O. Howard was called upon to address the colored people. To prepare them to listen, he requested them to sing. At once an old woman on the outskirts of the meeting began, "Nobody knows the trouble I've seen," and the whole audience joined in. The plaintive melody, and the apt refrain of the rude hymn, produced an effect that can never be forgotten by those who heard it sung.

SLAVE HYMNS.

1. Oh, Lord, Oh, my Lord, Oh, my good Lord! Keep me from sinking down. I tell you what I mean
2. Oh, Lord, Oh, my Lord, Oh, my good Lord! Keep me from sinking down. I look up yonder and what
3. Oh, Lord, Oh, my Lord, Oh, my good Lord! Keep me from sinking down. I bless the Lord I'm going

o do; Keep me from sinking down; I mean to go to Heaven too; Keep me from sinking down.
do I see? Keep me from sinking down; I see the angels beck'ning to me; Keep me from sinking down.
to die; Keep me from sinking down; I'm going to judgment by and by; Keep me from sinking down.

HE'S THE LILY OF THE VALLEY.

He's the li-ly of the val-ley, Oh! my Lord; He's the li-ly of the val-ley, Oh! my Lord.

1. King Je-sus in His chariot rides, Oh! my Lord, With four white horses side by side, Oh! my Lord.
2. What kind of shoes are those you wear, Oh! my Lord, That you can ride upon the air, Oh! my Lord?
3. These shoes I wear are gospel shoes, Oh! my Lord, And you can wear them if you choose, Oh! my Lord.

MANY THOUSAND GONE.

1. No more auction block for me, No more, no more, No more auction block for me, Many thousand gone.

2. No more peck of corn for me, etc. 3. No more driver's lash for me, etc. 4. No more pint of salt for me, etc.

GETTING READY TO DIE.

Getting ready to die, Getting ready to die, Getting ready to die, O Zi-on, Zi-on.

1. When I set out I was but young, Zi-on, Zi-on, But now my race is almost run, Zi-on, Zi-on.
2. Re-ligion's like a blooming rose, Zi-on, Zion, And none but him that feels it knows, Zion, Zi-on.
3. The Lord is waiting to receive, Zi-on, Zi-on, If sinners only would believe, Zi-on, Zi-on.

SPRING-TIME ONCE AGAIN.

JOHN LOGAN.
ARTHUR S. SULLIVAN.

Andante espress.

1. Hail, beauteous stranger of the grove, Thou messen-ger of Spring! Now heaven repairs thy
2. The school-boy wand'ring thro' the wood, To pull the primrose gay, Starts thy thrice-welcome
3. Sweet bird! thy bow'r is ev-er green, Thy sky is ev-er clear; Thou hast no sor-row

ru-ral seat, And woods thy welcome sing. Soon as the daisy decks the green, Thy certain voice we
voice to hear, And im - i-tates thy lay. What time the pea puts on the bloom, Thou fliest thy vocal
in thy song, No win-ter in thy year! Oh, could I fly, I'd fly with thee! We'd make with joyful

hear; Hast thou a star to guide thy path, Or mark the roll-ing year? Glad...............
vale; An annual guest in oth-er lands, An-oth-er Spring to hail. Glad...............
wing; Our annual vis-it o'er the globe, At-tendants on the Spring. Glad...............

spring-time once a-gain, Buds and blooming flowers; Daisies 'mid the greensward, Bird-songs in the

bow'rs; Spring-time once a'-gain; Buds and blooming flow-ers, Daisies 'mid the green-sward,

Bird-songs in the bow'rs; Bird-songs in the bow'rs; Bird - songs, bird-songs in the bow'rs.

THE DISTANT DRUM.

C. MATZ *Arr.*

1. Hark to the sound of the distant drum, Rap tap a ta, rap tap a ta, Beating in time with the pleasant hum
2. Hark to the sound of the distant drum, Rap tap a ta, rap tap a ta, Beating in time with the pleasant hum

That so sweetly fills the air. Come, let us join some melo - dy, Its measured beat to mingle sweet; A-
That so sweetly fills the air. And when these sounds have from us gone, In pleasant cheer t'wards home
[we'll steer, And

non we'll dance right merrily, And keep time with the drum and song. Hark to the sound of the distant drum,
in our dreams repeat the dance, So gaily joined with drum and song. Hark to the sound of the distant drum,

Rap tap a ta, rap tap a ta, Beating in time with the pleasant hum That so sweetly fills the air.

Hark! the trumpet's shrilly note, As its tones toward us float, Tra la la la, Tra la la la, Tra

la la la, Tra la la la la, Tra la la la, Tra la la la, Tra la la la la la la la.

THE OLD COTTAGE CLOCK.

J. L. MOLLOY.
CHARLES SWAIN.

1. That old, old clock of the house-hold stock, Was the bright-est thing and
2. A friend-ly voice was that old, old clock, As it stood in the cor - ner

neat - est: The hands, though old, had a touch of gold, And its chimes sang still the
smil - ing, And blessed the time with a mer - ry chime, All the win-try hours be -

sweet - est, 'Twas a mon - i - tor too, though its words were few, Yet they liv'd thro' na - tions
guil - ing, But a peev-ish old voice had that tiresome clock As it call'd at day - break

al - ter'd, And its voice, still strong, warn'd old and young, When the voice of friendship falter'd.
bold - ly, When the dawn look'd gray o'er the mist-y way, And the air blew ver - y cold - ly.

Chorus.

Tick, tick! it said; Quick, quick to bed! For ten I've giv - en warn - ing, Up
Tick, tick! it said; Quick, out of bed! For five I've giv - en warn - ing, You'll

quick-ly and go, or sure-ly you know, You'll nev-er rise soon in the morn - ing.
nev - er have health, you'll nev-er have wealth, Un - less you're up soon in the morn - ing.

ALL AMONG THE BARLEY.

Elizabeth Sterling.

Cheerfully.

1. Come out, 'tis now September, The hunter's moon's begun, And thro' the wheaten stubble   Is
2. The Spring, she is a young maid, That does not know her mind, The Summer is a ty-rant   Of
3. The wheat is like a rich man, That's sleek and well to do, The oats are like a pack of   girls,

heard the fre-quent gun; Come out, 'tis now September, The hunter's moon's begun, And
most un-right-eous kind, The Spring, she is a young maid, That does not know her mind, The
Laughing and danc-ing too, The wheat is like a rich man, That's sleek and well to do, The

thro' the wheaten stub-ble   Is heard the   frequent gun; The leaves are paling yel-low, Or
Summer is a ty-rant   Of most un-righteous kind; The Autumn is an old friend, That
oats are like a pack of girls, Laughing and dancing too; The rye is like a mi-ser, That's

kindling in-to red, And the ripe and gold-en bar-ley   Is hang-ing down its head.
loves one all he can, And that brings the hap-py bar-ley, To glad the heart of man.
sulk-y, lean, and small, But the free and bearded bar-ley   Is monarch of them all.

All among the bar-ley, Who would not be blithe, When the free and hap-py bar-ley   Is

smil-ing on the scythe? When the free and hap-py bar-ley   Is smil-ing on the scythe?

THE CORN SONG.

Mary Herbert.
Godfrey Marks.

Con Spirito.

1. We sing the plant of prai - ried West, Where men grow strong on a - cres
2. The dog - wood's cup marks plant - ing - time, With finch on bough and blackbird
3. All sum - mer long in bright ar - ray, It rust - ling waves its broad, keen
4. To barns now creak the la - den wains, Whose wealth of treas - ure they must

wide, By plen - ty crown'd, by peace e'er bless'd,—The Corn, the Corn, her gold - en
near, The bee hums loud at bloom's fair prime, And ev' - ry wild-bird's note is
blade, While zephyrs to it find their way, And elves and fays here seek the
hold Safe housed from storm—the far - mer's gains More precious far than Oph - ir's

pride; Ol - ive and grape, fit theme of po - et lays; For thee our harp be strung, oh, royal maize!
clear: Thro' all the land who no - ble empire sways So broad and grand as green and glorious maize?
shade; Oh! glad the hearts of all that on it gaze, Un - til is gathered in the ripened maize.
gold: To Him we raise our grateful song of praise For manna sent from Heav'n, the gen'rous maize.

Chorus.

Then hail to the monarch high! Hail to his wealth of cheer! For we crown him King; no rival need he fear.

Swaying, swaying, billowy sea of maize! The Corn he is King; his sceptre bring; and loud our song of praise;

Swaying, swaying, beautiful, wondrous maize! Blade, tassel and ear with floss so fair, thou born of summer days!

OH, WHAT IS THE MATTER WITH ROBIN?

AUNT CLARA.
From "THE NURSERY."

1. "Oh, what is the matter with Robin, That makes her cry round here all day? I think she must be in great
2. "He carried them home in his pocket; I saw him, from up in this tree: Ah me! how my lit-tle heart
3. "Nor I!" said the birds in a cho-rus: "A cru-el and mischievous boy! I pit-y his fa-ther and

trou-ble," Said Swallow to lit-tle Blue Jay. "I think she must be in great trou-ble, Said
flut-tered For fear he would come and rob me! Ah me! how my lit-tle heart flut-tered For
moth-er; He surely can't give them much joy; I pit-y his fa-ther and moth-er; He

Swallow to litile Blue Jay. "I know why the Robin is cry-ing," Said Wren with a sob in her
fear he would come and rob me! "Oh, what little boy was so wick-ed?" Said Swallow, beginning to
surely can't give them much joy. I guess he forgot what a pleas-ure The dear lit-tle rob-ins all

D.S. "I guess he for-got that the rule is, To do as you would be done

breast, "A naugh-ty bold rob-ber has stol-en, Three lit-tle blue eggs from her
cry; "I wouldn't be guil-ty of rob-bing A dear lit-tle bird's-nest—not
bring, In ear-ly spring-time and in sum-mer, By beau-ti-ful songs that they

by; I guess he for-got that from Heav-en There looks down an All-See-ing

D.S. to last verse only.

nest, A naugh-ty bold rob-ber has stol-en Three lit-tle blue eggs from her nest.
I," I wouldn't be guil-ty of rob-bing A dear lit-tle bird's-nest—not I."
sing, In ear-ly spring-time and in sum-mer, By beau-ti-ful songs that they sing."

Eye, I guess he for-got that from Heav-en There looks down an All-See-ing Eye."

THE MARSEILLAISE.—Richard Grant White, in his work on patriotic national songs, gives a graphic account of the circumstances under which this most stirring of all national airs was written. He says: "This remarkable 'hymn' struck out in the white heat of unconscious inspiration, perfect in all its parts, and in six months adopted by the people, the army, the legislature and the whole nation, is a war-cry, a summons to instant battle. It has no inspiration but glory, and invokes no god but liberty. Rouget de Lisle, its author, was an accomplished officer, an enthusiast for liberty, but no less a champion for just-

ice and an upholder of constitutional monarchy. He was at Strasburg in 1792. One day Deitrich, the Mayor of the town, who knew him well, asked him to write a martial song, to be sung on the departure of six hundred volunteers to the Army of the Rhine. He consented, wrote the song that night—the words sometimes coming before the music, sometimes the music before the words—and gave it to Deitrich the next morning. As is not uncommon with authors, he was at first dissatisfied with the fruit of his sudden inspiration, and, as he handed the manuscript to the Mayor, he said, 'Here is what you asked for, but I

AWAY, AWAY.

D. F. E. AUBER, 1828.

A-way! a-way! the moon and stars are shining; We'll dance o'er hill and flow-'ry green, With laugh-ing eyes and heart that knows no pining; We'll make the night pay homage to our queen. A-way! a-way, a-way, a-way!

The fairy moonlight streaming Up-on the mountain height, } Of mu-sic and de-light.
As if the world were dreaming Of mu-sic and de-light,

fear it is not very good.' But Deitrich looked, and knew better. They went to the harpsichord with Madame and sang it; they gathered the band of the theatre together and rehearsed it; it was sung in the public square, and excited such enthusiasm, that, instead of six hundred volunteers, nine hundred left Strasburg for the army. In the course of a few months it worked its way southward and became a favorite with the Marseillais, who carried it to Paris —where the people, knowing nothing of its name, its author, or its original purpose, spoke of it simply as the 'song of the Marseillais,' and as the Marseillaise

it will be known forever, and forever be the rallying cry of France against tyranny. Its author, soon proscribed as a Royalist, fled from France and took refuge in the Alps. But the echoes of the chord that he had so unwittingly struck pursued him even to the mountain tops of Switzerland. 'What,' said he, to a peasant guide in the upper fastnesses of the border range, 'is this song that I hear—*Allons, enfans de la patrie?*' 'That? That is the Marseillaise.' And thus, suffering from the excesses that he had innocently stimulated, he first learned the name which his countrymen had given to the song he had written."

THE IVY GREEN.

Henry Russell.
Charles Dickens.

Con espressione.

1. A dainty plant is the I - vy green, That creepeth o'er ru - ins old, Of
2. Fast he stealeth, tho' he wears no wings, And a staunch old heart has he, How
3. Whole ages have fled, and their works decayed, And nations have scat - tered been, But the

right choice food are his meals, I ween, In his cell so lone and cold; The wall must be crumbled, the
closely he twineth, how closely he clings To his friend, the huge oak tree! And sly - ly he traileth a -
stout old I - vy shall nev - er fade, From its hale and hearty green; The brave old plant in its

stones decayed, To pleasure his dainty whim, And the moldering dust that years have made Is a
long the ground, And his leaves he gently waves, As he joyously hugs and crowdeth round The
lone - ly days, Shall fatten up - on the past; For the stateliest building man can raise Is the

mer - ry meal for him— Creeping where no life is seen, A rare old plant is the I - vy green,
mold of dead men's graves— Creeping where no life is seen, A rare old plant is the I - vy green,
I - vy's food at last— Creeping where no life is' seen, A rare old plant is the I - vy green,

Creeping where no life is seen, A

Creeping where no life is seen, A rare old plant is the Ivy green,
Creep - ing, creep - ing,
Creep - ing, creep-ing,

rare old plant is the I - vy green, Creeping where no life is seen,

Creeping where no life is seen, Creep - ing, creep - ing, A rare old plant is the Ivy green.

SLUMBER SONGS.

French Lullaby.

1. Sleep, sleep, my darling, Sleep tranquilly. Mother is watching, Praying for thee, May holy an-gels
2. Sleep, sleep, my darling, Sleep tranquilly. Thy heav'nly Father Careth for thee. In thy soft cra-dle

On wings of light, Bring to my ba - by, Dreams fair and bright. Dodo, my darling, peacefully sleep.
Peacefully sleep; While thou dost slumber Watch He will keep. Dodo, my darling, peacefully sleep.

GERMAN LULLABY (WIEGENLIED.)

Not too Slow.

1. Brother, thou and I, Brother, thou and I, We'll sing our lul - la - by. Hush thee, dear, sing
2. Brother, thou and I, Brother, thou and I, We'll sing our lul - la - by. Hush thee, darling,
1. Bru-der, ich und du, Bru-der, ich und du, wir schla - fen im - mer zu. Still und still und

sweet and low, Ba - by now to rest would go; Hush thee, hush thee, Sing-ing soft and low.
have no fear, Lov-ing arms en-fold thee here; Hush thee, hush thee. Mother's watching near.
im - mer still, weil mein Mädchen schlafen will. Stil - le, stil - le, kein Geräusch gemacht.

OLD GAELIC LULLABY.

Whittier's Child Life.

Tenderly.

1. Hush! the waves are roll - ing in, White with foam.— white with
2. Hush! the winds roar hoarse and deep, On they come,— on they
3. Hush! the rain sweeps o'er the knowes, Where they roam,— where they

foam; Fa - ther toils a - mid the din, But ba - by sleeps at home.
come! Broth - er seeks the wand'ring sheep, But ba - by sleeps at home.
roam; Sis - ter goes to seek the cows, But ba - by sleeps at home.

NURSERY SONGS.

MOTHER GOOSE.

Ding, dong, bell, Pussy's in the well; Who put her in? Lit-tle Johnny Green; Who pull'd her out?

Big John Stout. What a naughty boy was that, To drown our lit - tle Pus - sy cat!

2.

1. Lit - tle Jack Hor - ner sat in a cor - ner, Eat-ing a Christmas pie, He

1. Lit - tle Miss Muf - fet Sat on a tuf - fet, Eat-ing some curds and whey, There

put in his thumb, And pulled out a plum, And said, "What a good boy am I."

came a great spider, And sat down beside her, And frighten'd Miss Muffet a - way.

3.

Hump - ty Dump - ty sat on a wall, Hump - ty Dump - ty had a great fall;

All the King's horses and all the King's men, Couldn't put Humpty to - geth - er a - gain.

21

MARSEILLES HYMN.—The authorship of this soul-stirring war song, so often prohibited by despotic rulers, and now the national air of France,—the Marseillaise, as it is called,—has frequently been disputed. In his recent work on Strasburg during the Revolution, M. Seingerlot, an authority upon these historical questions, has brought to light a number of old family papers of this era, from which it appears that Rouget de Lisle, at the time of writing these verses, was an army officer contributing occasionally to the columns of a leading newspaper of Strasburg, owned by the Mayor of the city. The wife of this gentleman, a lady of musical taste, regarded this poem a masterpiece, and urged that it be set to music by the author and published. It accordingly appeared in this form, probably in

April, 1792, entitled, "A war song for the Army of the Rhine." In a letter yet extant, from Madame Deitrich, the Mayor's wife, she says: "The occupation of copying music has enabled me for some days to shut my ears to political wrangles. Politics only are now discussed here. To invent something new for the entertainment of our numerous guests, my husband has hit upon the expedient of having a song composed for the times, which embodies the patriotic feeling of the town. A captain of engineers, Rouget de Lisle, who is a very amiable poet and composer, has rapidly done for him the song and the music. It is spirit-stirring (*entrainment*), and not wanting in originality. It is in the feeling of Gluck, but more lively and alert, and has been performed at our house to the satisfac-

7

THE LAST ROSE OF SUMMER.

THOMAS MOORE.

1. 'Tis the last rose of summer, Left blooming a - lo..; All her lovely com-
2. I'll not leave thee, thou lone one, To pine on the stem, Since the lovely are
3. So soon may I fol-low, When friendships de - cay, And from love's shining

panions Are fad - ed and gone; No flow-er of her kindred, No
sleeping, Go sleep thou with them; Thus kind-ly I scatter Thy
cir-cle The gems drop a - way; When true hearts lie withered, And

rose-bud is nigh, To re-flect back her blushes, Or give sigh for sigh.
leaves o'er the bed, Where thy mates of the garden Lie scent - less and dead.
fond ones are flown, Oh, who would in - hab-it This bleak world a-lone!

tion of all who have heard it." Capt. Rouget de Lisle was asked to draw his inspiration from passing events and the dominant sentiment of the town, which was a frontier stronghold, and no doubt tremendously aroused by the news from Paris and by the declaration of war. Strasburg would probably have to bear the brunt of the invasion, and, in any case, would be the centre of military operations. Political discussion went on, therefore, to the exclusion of other topics. The fact that the Deitrichs kept the harpsichord going, and had Capt. Rouget de Lisle compose this new thing for it to create a diversion amid stirring politics, is a curious example of the power "that shapes our ends, rough-hew them how we will." It would be interesting to know how the song got to Marseilles

without going through Paris. A regimental band may have taken it to the South. The first time it was heard in Paris was the day the Revolutionary deputation of Marseilles, which had come on foot, singing what was ever afterward to be known as their "hymn," entered the capital. It was caught up at once, and spread like wildfire through the nation. The *entrain*, which the Mayor's wife said was one of its characteristics, so roused the Parisians that nothing could withstand their fury. Under the monarchical governments in France, the song has always been held seditious, because of its extraordinary influence · upon the French people. The first time since the Revolution that it was not regarded treasonable by those in authority, was at the opening of the World's Fair, in 1878.

MARSEILLES HYMN.

ROUGET DE LISLE, 1772.

1. Ye sons of France, awake to glo - ry! Hark, hark! what myriads bid you rise! Your children,
2. With lux-u - ry and pride sur - rounded, The vile, in-sa-tiate des-pots dare, Their thirst for
3. Oh, Lib-er - ty! can man resign thee, Once having felt thy gen'rous flame? Can dungeons,

wives, and grand-sires hoary: Behold their tears, and hear their cries, Behold their tears and hear their
gold and pow-er unbounded, To mete and vend the light and air, To mete and vend the light and
bolts and bars con-fine thee? Or whips thy no-ble spir-it tame? Or whips thy no-ble spir-it

cries! Shall hateful tyrants mis-chief breed-ing, With hireling hosts, a ruf-fian band, Af -
air. Like beasts of burden would they load us, Like gods would bid their slaves adore; But
tame? Too long the world has wept be - wail-ing That falsehood's dagger tyrants wield; But

fright and desolate the land, While peace and liberty lie bleeding! To arms, to arms, ye
man is man, and who is more? Then shall they longer lash and goad us? To arms, to arms ye
freedom is our sword and shield, And all their arts are unavailing: To arms, to arms, ye

brave! Th' aveng - ing sword unsheathe! March on, March on,

all hearts re - solved On vic - to-ry or death!

THE MAHOGANY TREE.

W. M. Thackeray.
Fabio Campana.

Cantabile espress e molto accentato.

1. Christ-mas is here; Winds whistle shrill, I - cy and chill, Lit - tle care we;
2. Once on the boughs Birds of rare plume Sang, in its bloom: Night-birds are we;
3. Care, like a dun, Lurks at the gate; Let the dog wait; Hap - py we'll be!

rall.

Lit - tle we fear Weather with-out, Sheltered a - bout The Ma - ho - ga - ny Tree.
Here we carouse, Sing-ing like them, Perched round the stem Of the jol - ly old Tree.
Pile up the coals; While the song rolls Let us for - get, Round the old Tree.

col canto.

a tempo.

Eve-nings we know, Hap - py as this; Fa - ces we miss Pleas-ant to
Here let us sport, Boys, as we sit— Laughter and wit Flash-ing so
Sor - rows, be - gone! Life and its ills, Duns and their bills, Bid we to

see. Kind hearts and true, Gen - tle and just, Peace to your dust!
free. Life is but short, When we are gone, Let them sing on,
flee. Come with the dawn, En - vi - ous sprite; Leave us to - night,

DREAM FACES.

Wm. M. Hutchinson.

Andante.

1. The shad-ows lie a-cross the dim old room, The fire-light glows and fades in-to the
2. Once more I see, a-cross the dis-tant years, A face long gone with all its smiles and

gloom, While mem'ry sails to childhood's distant shore, And dreams, and dreams of days that are no more.
tears; Once more I press a ten-der lov-ing hand, And with my dar-ling 'neath the old oak stand.

p Allegro. Refrain.

Sweet dream-land fa-ces, pass-ing to and fro, Bring back to mem'-ry

days of long a-go, Mur-muring gent-ly thro' a mist of pain, "Hope on, dear

After 3d verse go to Coda.   *p Andante.*

loved one, we shall meet a-gain." 3. But all I loved are gone, And I a-lone in

pp cres . . .

life, To wait, and wait, and wait, Till death shall end the strife; Un-til once more I

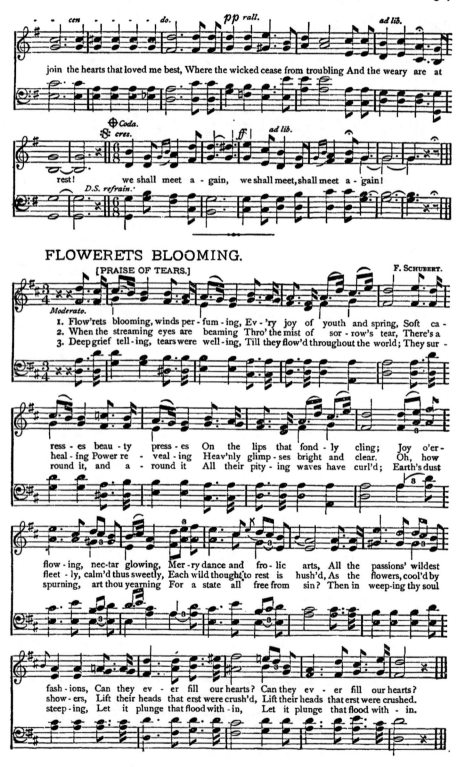

join the hearts that loved me best, Where the wicked cease from troubling And the weary are at

rest! we shall meet a - gain, we shall meet, shall meet a - gain!

FLOWERETS BLOOMING.

[PRAISE OF TEARS.]

F. SCHUBERT.

Moderato.

1. Flow'rets blooming, winds per - fum - ing, Ev - 'ry joy of youth and spring, Soft ca -
2. When the streaming eyes are beaming Thro' the mist of sor - row's tear, There's a
3. Deep grief tell - ing, tears were well - ing, Till they flow'd throughout the world; They sur -

ress - es beau - ty press - es On the lips that fond - ly cling; Joy o'er -
heal - ing Power re - veal - ing Heav'nly glimp - ses bright and clear. Oh, how
round it, and a - round it All their pity - ing waves have curl'd; Earth's dust

flow - ing, nec - tar glowing, Mer - ry dance and fro - lic arts, All the passions' wildest
fleet - ly, calm'd thus sweetly, Each wild thought to rest is hush'd, As the flowers, cool'd by
spurning, art thou yearning For a state all free from sin? Then in weep-ing thy soul

fash - ions, Can they ev - er fill our hearts? Can they ev - er fill our hearts?
show - ers, Lift their heads that erst were crush'd, Lift their heads that erst were crushed.
steep - ing, Let it plunge that flood with - in, Let it plunge that flood with - in.

SINGERS, good and bad, are often troubled with an apparent stoppage in the throat, and this inconvenience seems to be at its worst just at that moment when they wish to sing. To displace or to cure this stoppage, they begin hacking and coughing ("clearing the throat" as it it called,) which proceeding, however, only makes bad worse for the time being, and finally grows into a habit, till at last such people cannot venture to open their mouths without first subjecting the throat to a series of these irritating "hacks." A good master will soon cure this complaint by refusing to continue the lesson whenever the pupil gives way to the bad habit. It is in many cases simply a nervous trick, and if the singer will accustom himself to swallow instead of coughing, whenever he feels the sensation of which we are speaking, he will soon be rid of it. If it result in any case from real weakness of the throat, it may be beneficial to gargle three or four times a day with moderately-strong salt and water, especially before singing. This does not harm the voice, and by bracing and strengthening the muscles of the throat renders them more obedient to the singer's will.

SEE THE SUN'S FIRST GLEAM.

GERMAN.

Allegro.

1. See the sun's first gleam on the mountain stream, Now chant our cho - rus gay, Tra la la, Come,
2. Now the cham-ois fleet we long to meet, With dawn's first blushing ray, Tra la la, With
3. Then at ev - en tide, when the sun doth hide Be - hind yon moun-tain gray, Tra la la, And

com - rades, rouse from the sloth - ful dream, With joy - ous hearts view the morn-ing beam, For we
smil - ing face and with bounding feet, We'll seek him then in his lone re - treat; Then a -
sha - dows veil all the land - scape wide, A - down the rock - y steep we'll glide, Bidding

soon must a-way, must a - way,　　　For we soon must a-way, must a-way, Tra la la, For we
way to the hills, then a - way,　　　Then a - way to the hills, then a-way, Tra la la, Then a -
hail to the close of the day,　　　Bidding hail to the close of the day, Tra la la, Bidding

soon must a - way, must a - way,　　　For we soon must a - way, must a - way.
way to the hills, then a - way,　　　Then a - way to the hills, then a - way.
hail to the close of the day,　　　Bid-ding hail to the close of the day.

THE body should not be kept in a perfectly upright position when singing. The best position is with its chief weight upon the right leg and foot, the head gently leaning forward, the arms and, indeed, the whole carriage disposed in a manner that would indicate to the audience a sort of desire on your part to persuade them and bring them over to your feelings and sentiments. When the right leg begins to tire with the weight of the body, the left can take its turn. A sitting position is a very bad one in which to practice. Singing should always be done in a standing position. Instead of sitting at the pianoforte, and accompanying an exercise or "solfeggio," it is far better to sound the first note of each passage therein, and master the same without any accompaniment. The advantages of this mode of practising must be obvious; but one of the most important is, that the attention is not divided between piano and voice, while it leaves the singer free to give all his attention and care to the production of the notes which he is endeavoring to sing artistically.

CHRISTMAS IS COMING.

1. "I want for-ty doz-en of fine wax-en dolls, And for-ty-four thousand be-
2. "There's Malcolm, and Har-ry, and Clarence, and John, Hope no end of hol-i-day
3. "And wonder-ful pic-tures, books, mu-sic, and flowers, And birds singing gai-ly in

side them; I've a tel-e-phone or-der for good bouncing balls, So ma-ny I nev-er can
treas-ure, Of San-ta Claus' vis-it from evening till dawn They talk or they dream without
ca-ges, Ten thousand good things to make happy the hours Of folks of all sta-tions and

hide them! Toys needed by millions, and trumpets, and drums, With cargoes of candies as-
meas-ure. There's Nellie, and Jennie, and Mary, and Bess, What rare things they'd have me go
a-ges. Move lively, my lads, with full boxes and trays, Kind people will ev-'ry-where

sort-ed, And oranges, almonds, and sweet su-gar plums, Quick pack them or have them im-
hunt-ing! The darlings I love them, and always can guess Silks, ribbons, furs, jewels they're
hail them, The time is fast speeding and it would a-maze If San-ta Claus ev-er should

port-ed.)
want-ing. } For Christmas is coming, a week from to-morrow, And all must be read-y, be-
fail them.)

lieve me; If Santa Claus missed it, ah! there would be sorrow, From blame none could ever relieve me."

PLAY-TIME SONGS.

We come to see Miss Jen-nie Jones, Jen-nie Jones, Jennie Jones, We come to see Miss Jennie Jones,

How is she to day?

1. She's washing:
2. She's ironing:
3. She's sweeping:
4. She's sick:
5. She's dead:

We're right glad to hear it, To
We're right sorry to hear it, To

hear it, to hear it, We're right glad to hear it, And how is she to-day?
hear it, to hear it, We're right sorry to hear it, And how is she to-day?

1. Come, all you young men, in your mer-ry ways, And use well your time in
2. The day is far spent, and the night's com-ing on, So give us your arm and we'll

your youthful days, That you may be happy, That you may be hap-py When you grow old.
jour-ney a-long, That you may be happy, That you may be hap-py When you grow old.

3.

Ring around a ros-y, Sit up-on a pos-y, All the girls in our town Vote for Uncle Jo-sie.

PLAY-TIME SONGS.

LITTLE FOLKS.

THE ROUGH MATERIAL.—In music man does not reproduce any combination of sounds he has ever heard or could hear in the natural world, in the same sense that the painter transfers to his canvas the forms and tints he sees around him. The musicians seizes the rough element of sound and compels it to work his will, and having with infinite pains subjugated and tamed it, he is rewarded by discovering in it the most direct and perfect medium in all Nature for the expression of his emotions. The painter's art lies upon the surface of the world; its secrets are whispered by the yellow cornfields spotted with crimson fire, and the dappled purple of heather upon the hills; but the musician's art lies beneath the surface. His rough material of sound may rather be compared to the dull diamond, earth-incrusted and buried in deep mines; it simply does not exist as a brilliant, and a thing of priceless beauty until it has been refined and made

HO, HO, VACATION DAYS ARE HERE.

J. C. JOHNSON.

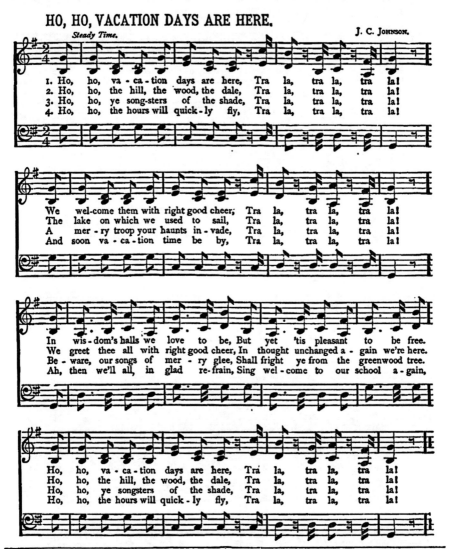

luminous by deliberate arrangement of glittering facets set in the splendor of chaste gold.—*Haweis.*

EARLY DEAD.—In his early death Mendelssohn strikingly resembles Mozart, of whom it cannot be said that he died prematurely. His faculty was developed with amazing rapidity; and from the very early age at which he began to hold a place in public esteem his artistic life was by no means short. Although a painful apprehension to the contrary embittered his last days, yet he lived long enough for fame. Not so Mendelssohn. However extended his mortal span might have been, his fine talent would have continued, in all probability, to unfold and discover fresh beauties as long as his natural faculties were perfect. He died in his thirty-six year, in the period of full promise, withered in the very spring-time of his genius.

BEETHOVEN, born at Bonn, 1770, was equally great in his intellect and his affections. How deep and tender was that noble heart those know who have read his letters to his abandoned nephew whom ne commits so earnestly to "God's holy keeping." There is no stain upon his life. His integrity spotless, his purity unblemished, his generosity boundless, his affections deep and lasting, his piety simple and sincere. "To-

day happens to be Sunday," he writes to a friend in the most unaffected way, "so I will quote you something from the Bible: "See that ye love one another." Beethoven was not only severely moral and deeply religious, but he has this further claim to the admiration and respect of the musical world, that this ideal of art was the highest, and that he was true to his ideal, utterly and disinterestedly true to the end.—*Haweis.*

HOME, CAN I FORGET THEE?

GERMAN MELODY.

Andante.

1. Home, home, can I for - get thee, Dear, dear, dearly loved home? No, no, still I re-
2. Home, home, why did I leave thee? Dear, dear friends, do not mourn. Home, home, once more re-

gret thee, Tho' I may far from thee roam. }
ceive me, Quickly to thee I'll re-turn. } Home, home, home, home, dearest and happiest home.

THERE IS A HAPPY LAND.

HINDOO MELODY.

1. There 'is a hap - py land, Far, far a - way, Where saints in
2. Bright in that hap - py land, Beams ev' - ry eye; Kept by a
3. Come to that hap - py land, Come, come a - way, Why will ye

glo - ry stand, Bright, bright as day; Oh, how they sweet - ly sing,
Fa - ther's hand, Love can - not die. Oh, then, to glo - ry run;
doubt - ing stand, Why still de - lay? Oh, we shall hap - py be,

Wor - thy is our Saviour King, Loud let his prais - es ring, Praise, praise for aye!
Be a crown and kingdom won, And bright a - bove the sun, We'll reign for aye!
When from sin and sor - row free, Lord, we shall live with Thee, Blest, blest for aye!

THEN YOU'LL REMEMBER ME.

M. W. BALFE.

Andante cantabile.

1. When oth-er lips and oth-er hearts Their tales of love shall tell, In
2. When cold-ness or de-ceit shall slight The beau-ty now they prize, And

lan-guage whose ex-cess im-parts The pow'r they feel so well, There
deem it but a fad-ed light Which beams with-in your eyes; When

may, per-haps, in such a scene Some rec-ol-lec-tion be Of days that have as
hol-low hearts shall wear a mask 'Twill break your own to see: In such a moment

hap-py been, And you'll re-member me, And you'll remember, you'll remember me.
I but ask, That you'll re-member me, That you'll remember, you'll remember me.

LOVE'S GOLDEN DREAM.

LINDSAY LENNOX.

dim.

mf

1. I hear to-night the old bells chime Their sweetest, softest strain, They bring to me the olden
2. I look in-to your love-lit eyes, I hear your gen-tle voice, You come to me from Para-

8f

time, In visions once again : Once more across the meadow land, Beside the flowing stream, We wander,
dise, And bid my heart rejoice, Sweet vision fade not from my sight, I would not wake to pain, But dream

[till

Tempo di Valse.

darling, hand in hand, And dream love's golden dream: Love's golden dream is past, Hidden by
at the por - tals bright, I clasp your hand a - gain: Love's golden dream is past, Hidden by

dim.   1st.   2nd.

mists of pain, Yet shall we meet at last, Never to part a - gain.
mists of pain, Yet shall we meet at last, Never to part a - - gain.

WE'D BETTER BIDE A WEE.

CLARIBEL.

1. The puir auld folk at hame, ye mind, Are frail and fail - ing sair, And weel I ken they'd
2. When first we told our sto - ry, lad, Their bless - ing fell sae free, They gave no thought to
3. I fear me, sair, they're failing baith, For when I sit a - part, They'll talk o' Heav'n sae

mf

miss me, lad, Gin I came hame nae mair. The grist is out, the times are hard, The
self at all, They did but think of me, But, lad - die, that's a time a - wa, And
earn - est - ly, It well-nigh breaks my heart! So, lad - die, din - na urge me mair, It

kine are on - ly three,
mith - er's like to dee,   } I can - na leave the auld folk now, We'd bet - ter bide a
sure - ly win - na be,

wee,   I can - na leave the auld folk now, We'd bet - ter bide a wee.

O THOU JOYFUL DAY.
(O DU FRÖHLICHE.)

B. M. SMUCKER, *tr.*

1. O thou joyful day, O thou bless-ed day, Ho - ly, peace - ful Christmas - tide! O thou
2. O thou joyful day, O thou bless-ed day, Ho - ly, peace - ful Christmas - tide! O thou
3. O thou joyful day, O thou bless-ed day, Ho - ly, peace - ful Christmas - tide! O thou

joyful day, O thou bless-ed day, Ho - ly, peace - ful Christmas - tide! Earth's hopes a -
joyful day, O thou bless-ed day, Ho - ly, peace - ful Christmas - tide! Christ's light is
joyful day, O thou bless-ed day, Ho - ly, . peace - ful Christmas - tide! King of all

wak - en, Christ life has tak - en, Laud Him, O laud Him on ev - 'ry side!
beam - ing, Our souls re - deem - ing, Laud Him, O laud Him on ev - 'ry side!
glo - ry, We bow be - fore Thee, Laud Him, O laud Him on ev - 'ry side!

EMMANUEL.

· W. C. DIX.

1. Joy fills our in - most heart to - day, The Roy - al Child is born; The
2. An - gels are thronging round thy bed, Thine in - fant grace to see; The

an - gel hosts in glad ar - ray His ad - vent keep this morn; For
stars are pal - ing o'er Thy head, The Day-spring dawns with Thee; Thou

us the world must lose its charms Be - fore the man - ger shrine; When
art the ver - y light of light, En - light - en us, sweet Child, That

fold - ed in Thy moth - er's arms, Thou sleep - est, Babe Di - vine.
we may keep Thy birth - day bright With ser - vice un - de - filed.

THE GOOD "THREE BELLS."

CHARLES JARVIS.

Spirited. *mf*

1. Come swell the strain, the proud re - frain, That sings of no - ble deeds; How
2. When storms came down with blackest frown, And woke the o - cean's wrath; And
3. They worked by day, they worked al - way, As brave tars on - ly do; When

true men brave on o - cean's wave, Win fame's most worthy meeds! And' high to - day, in
one lost bark in tem - pest dark, Lay in the mad wind's path, Heav'n, pleased to prove how
from the wave they strive to save, A sink - ing ves - sel's crew; A shout rose high, "All

grate - ful lay, 'Mid mu - sic's witching spells, Let ev - 'ry lip bless that good ship, Brave
hu - man love In Al - bi'n bosoms dwells, Turn'd to that wreck, that death-swept deck, Brave
saved!" they cry! Hark how the pæ - an swells! 'Till earth's far bound rings with the sound, "God

Crighton's ship, Three Bells.
Crighton's ship, Three Bells. } Oh! the good ship, Three Bells! Oh! the good ship, Three
bless the ship, Three Bells!"

Three Bells!

Bells! With her stur - dy crew, And her cap - tain true, That man the good Three Bells!

Three Bells!

22

RELIGION is reproached with not being progressive; it makes amends by being imperishable. The enduring element in our humanity is not in the doctrines which we concisely elaborate, but in the faiths which unconsciously dispose of us, and never slumber but to wake again. What treatise on sin, what philosophy of retribution, is as fresh as the fifty-first Psalm? What scientific theory has lasted like the Lord's Prayer? It is an evidence of movement that in a library no books become sooner obsolete than books of science. It is no less a mark of stability that poetry and religious literature survive, and even ultimate philosophies seldom die but to rise again. These, and with them the kindred services of devotion, are the expressions of aspirations and faiths which forever cry out for interpreters and guides. And in proportion as you carry your appeal to those deepest seats of our nature, you not only reach the firmest ground, but touch accordant notes in every human heart, so that, inevitably, the response turns out a harmony.—*Dr. Martineau.*

TOUCH NOT THE CUP.

T. H. BAYLY.
JAMES H. AIKMAN.

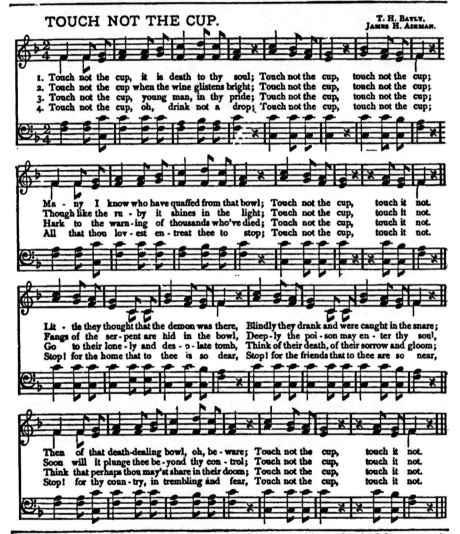

1. Touch not the cup, it is death to thy soul; Touch not the cup, touch not the cup;
2. Touch not the cup when the wine glistens bright; Touch not the cup, touch not the cup;
3. Touch not the cup, young man, in thy pride; Touch not the cup, touch not the cup;
4. Touch not the cup, oh, drink not a drop; Touch not the cup, touch not the cup;

Ma-ny I know who have quaffed from that bowl; Touch not the cup, touch it not.
Though like the ru-in the light, it shines in the light; Touch not the cup, touch it not.
Hark to the warn-ing of thousands who've died; Touch not the cup, touch it not.
All that thou lov-est en-treat thee to stop; Touch not the cup, touch it not.

Lit-tle they thought that the demon was there, Blindly they drank and were caught in the snare;
Fangs of the ser-pent are hid in the bowl, Deep-ly the poi-son may en-ter thy soul,
Go to their lone-ly and des-o-late tomb, Think of their death, of their sorrow and gloom;
Stop! for the home that to thee is so dear, Stop! for the friends that to thee are so near,

Then of that death-dealing bowl, oh, be-ware; Touch not the cup, touch it not.
Soon will it plunge thee be-yond thy con-trol; Touch not the cup, touch it not.
Think that perhaps thou may'st share in their doom; Touch not the cup, touch it not.
Stop! for thy coun-try, in trembling and fear, Touch not the cup, touch it not.

I FEEL sore at heart now. One of the noblest natures that used to sit in these seats, one I loved and who loved me; whose hand was as large in its generosity as a prairie; who had all the prospects of a noble and useful life, who could restrain himself and stop when he'd a mind to. But he has gone down to such a degree in intemperance that his friends have given him up in despair. How many of that kind have I seen; and the time as it passed did not suffice for him, or for them. They say: "To be sure I smoke; but only seven to ten cigars a day; but it is not a necessity for me—I can give it up." Or, "I know I drink a little; but it is not a necessity for me; I can give it up to-day." But they don't; and they don't next year, or the year after; and when they hear the roar of the tide of perdition, over the verge of which they will plunge finally, they can't. The time when men ought to stop is when they first see the peril; when there is time enough for judgment, enough to bring the higher qualities of the mind to sit in judgment over the lower.—*Beecher.*

THOUGHTS OF WONDER.

With spirit.

J. J. ROUSSEAU.

1. Thoughts of won-der! O how migh-ty! How stu-pen-dous! how pro-found!
2. Thous-ands thro' the hours of darkness, Stud the con-cave of the sky:
3. Pause, my thoughts, lo! numerous be-ings Move on ev'-ry plan-et there;

All the stars that spar-kle yon-der, Roll in orbs of vast-ness round.
Thousands, thousands hid from science, Shine un-seen by mor-tal eye.
All for breath, and life, and guidance, Sub-ject to their Mak-er's care.

Thoughts of won-der! O how might-y! How stu-pen-dous! how pro-found!
Thoughts of won-der! O how might-y! How stu-pen-dous! how pro-found!

4. Every world has hills and valleys,
   And His hand formed every flower,
   Every golden-winged insect,
   Sporting in the fragrant bower.—CHO.

5. Every little joy and sorrow,
   Every hope and every fear,
   Follow His supreme direction,
   Fully as some mighty sphere.—CHO.

HEAVEN IS MY HOME.

T. B. TAYLOR.
ARTHUR S. SULLIVAN.

1. I'm but a stranger here, Heaven is my home; Earth is a desert drear, Heaven is my home.
2. What tho' the tempest rage, Heaven is my home; Short is my pilgrimage, Heaven is my home.
3. There at my Saviour's side, Heaven is my home; I shall be glor-i-fied, Heaven is my home.

rit.

Danger and sorrow stand Round me on every hand, Heav'n is my father-land, Heav'n is my home.
Time's cold and wintry blast, Soon will be overpast I shall reach home at last, Heav'n is my home.
There are the good and blest, Those I loved most and best, There, too, I soon shall rest, Heav'n is my home.

HERE in this book which I was reading when you so kindly came to see me, are withered flowers, which I have gathered in my rambles and keep as friends and companions of pleasant places, streams and meadows, and of some who have been with me, and now are not. There is one, this single yellow flower—what is it, that, as I hold it, makes me think of it as I do? Faded flowers have something, to me, miraculous and supernatural about them: though, in fact, it is nothing wonderful that the texture of a flower being dried survives. It is not in the flower, but in our immortal spirit that the miracle is. All these delightful thoughts that come into my mind when I look at this flower—thoughts and fancies, and memories—what are they but the result of the alchemy of the immortal spirit, which takes all the pleasant, fragile things of life, and transmutes them into immortality in our own nature! And if the poor spirit and intellect of man can do this, how much more may the supreme creative intellect mould and form all things, and bring the presence of the supernatural face to face with us in our daily walk! Earth becomes to us, if we thus think, nothing but the garden of the Lord, and every fellow-being we meet and see in it, a beautiful and invited guest; and, as I think, I remember many of the heathen poets, after their manner, have said very fine things about this; that we should rise cheerfully from this life, as a grateful guest rises from an abundant feast; and though doubtless they were very dark and mistaken, yet I confess they always seemed to me to have something of a close and entire fellowship with the wants of men, which I think the Saviour would have approved. If you, sir, can receive this mystery, and go through the honorable path of life which lies before you, looking upon yourself as an immortal spirit walking among supernatural things—for the natural things of this life would be nothing were they not moved and

LORD, DISMISS US WITH THY BLESSING.

W. SHIRLEY, 1774.
"SICILIAN MARINERS' HYMN."

1. Lord, dis - miss us with Thy bless - ing, Fill our hearts with joy and peace; Let us
2. Thanks we give, and ad - o - ra - tion, For the Gos - pel's joy - ful sound; May the

each, Thy love pos - sess - ing, Triumph in re - deem-ing grace: O re -
fruits of Thy sal - va - tion In our hearts and lives a - bound: May Thy

fresh us, O re - fresh us, Trav - eling through this wil - der - ness.
pres - ence, May Thy pres - ence With us ev - er - more be found.

animated by the efficacy of that which is above nature—I think you may find this doctrine a light which will guide your feet in dark places; and it would seem, unless I am mistaken, that this habit of mind is very likely to lead to the blessedness of the Beatific Vision of God, on the quest of which you have happily entered so young; for surely it should lead to that state to which this vision is promised—the state of those who are Pure in Heart. For if it be true, that the reason we see not God is the grossness of this tabernacle wherein the soul is incased, then the more and the oftener we recognize the supernatural in our ordinary life, and not only expect and find it in those rare and short moments of devotion and prayer, the more, surely, the rays of the Divine Light will shine through the dark glass of this eastward form of life, and the more our own spirit will be enlightened and purified by it, until we come to that likeness to the Divine Nature, and that purity of heart to which a share of the Beatific Vision is promised, and which, as some teach, can be attained by being abstract from the body and the bodily life. As we see every day that the supernatural in some men gives a particular brightness of air to the countenance, and makes the face to shine with an inimitable lustre, and if it be true that in the life to come we shall have to see through a body and a glass however transparent, we may well practise our eyes by making this life spiritual, as we shall have also to strive to do in that to which we go. My predecessor, doubtless a very worthy man (for I knew him not), has left it recorded on his tombstone—as I will show you in the church—that he was "full of cares and full of years, of neither weary, but full of hope and of heaven." I should desire that it may be faithfully recorded of me that I was the same!—*"John Inglesant."*

WHEN SHALL WE MEET AGAIN?

SPIRITUAL SONGS.

1. When shall we meet a - gain, Meet ne'er to sev - er? When will peace
2. When shall love free - ly flow Pure as life's riv - er? When shall sweet
3. Up to that world of light Take us, dear Sav - iour; May we all
4. Soon shall we meet a - gain, Meet ne'er to sev - er; Soon shall peace

wreathe her chain Round us for - ev - er? Our hearts will ne'er re - pose, Safe
friend-ship glow Change-less for - ev - er? Where joys ce - les - tial thrill, Where
there u - nite, Bless - ed for - ev - er; Where kin - dred spir - its dwell, There
wreathe her chain Round us for - ev - er; Our hearts will then re - pose Se-

from each blast that blows, In this dark vale of woes, Nev - er— no, nev - er!
bliss each heart shall fill, And fears of part - ing chill Nev - er— no, nev - er!
may our mu - sic swell, And time our joys dis - pel Nev - er— no, nev - er!
cure from world - ly woes; Our songs of praise shall close Nev - er— no, nev - er!

JESUS, THE VERY THOUGHT.

"MANOAH."
BERNARD. ROSSINI.

1. Je - sus, the ve - ry thought of Thee With sweetness fills the breast;
2. Nor voice can sing, nor heart can frame, Nor can the mem - ory find,
3. O Hope of ev' - ry con - trite heart, O Joy of all the meek,

But sweet - er far Thy face to see, And in Thy pres - ence rest.
A sweet - er sound than Je - sus' Name, The Sav - iour of man - kind.
To those who fall, how kind Thou art! How good to those who seek!

4 But what to those who find? Ah! this
   Nor tongue nor pen can show;
   The love of Jesus, what it is
   None but His loved ones know.

5 Jesus, our only joy be Thou,
   As Thou our prize wilt be;
   In Thee be all our glory now,
   And through eternity.

LOCH LOMOND.

OLD SCOTCH SONG.

1. By yon bonnie banks, And by yon bonnie braes, Where the sun shines bright on Loch Lo-mond Where
2. 'Twas then that we parted In yo. shady glen On the steep, steep side of Ben Lo - mond Where
3. The wee birdie sang And the wild flowers spring And in sunshine the waters are sleep-ing, But the

me   and my true love Were ever wont to gae On the bonnie, bonnie banks of Loch Lomond. Oh!
in   pur - ple hue The Highland hills we view And the moon coming out   in the gloaming. Oh!
broken heart it kens Nae second Spring again Tho 'the waeful may cease frae their greet-ing. Oh!

Brisker.

ye'll take the high road and I'll take the low road, And I'll be in Scot-land a - fore   ye, But

me and my true love we'll   never meet again On the bonnie, bonnie banks of Loch Lo - mond.

HARD TIMES.

Moderato.

STEPHEN C. FOSTER.

1. Let   us pause in life's pleasures and count its many tears While we all   sap   sorrow with the
2. While we seek mirth and beauty and music light and gay There are frail   forms fainting at the
3. There's a pale drooping maiden who toils her life away, With a worn heart whose better days are
4. 'Tis a sigh that is wafted across the troubled wave, 'Tis a wail that is heard upon the

poor: There's a song that will linger for - ev er in our ears; Oh! Hard Times, come again no more.
door: Tho'their voices are silent, their pleading looks will say: Oh! Hard Times, come again no more.
o'er: Tho' her voice would be merry, 'tis sighing all the day: Oh! Hard Times, come again no more.
shore, 'Tis a dirge that is murmured around the lowly grave: Oh! Hard Times, come again no more.

'Tis the song, the sigh of the wea-ry; Hard Times, Hard Times, come again no more: Many

days you have lingered around my cabin door, Oh! Hard Times, come again no more.

OLD EASY-CHAIR BY THE FIRE.

JAMES C. BECKEL.

Moderato espressivo.

1. The   days of my youth have all si-lent-ly sped, And my locks are now grown thin and
2. Oh,   she was my guardian and guide all the day, And the angel that watched round my
3. How   ho-ly the place, as we gathered at night Round the al-tar where peace ev-er
4. The   cot-tage is gone which my in-fan-cy knew, And the place is despoiled of its

gray.   My hopes like a dream in the morning have fled, And nothing remains but de-
bed.   Her voice in a murmur of prayer died away For blessings to rest on my
dwelt, To join in an anthem of praise, and unite In thanks which our hearts truly
charms; My friends are all gathered beneath the old yew, And slumber in Death's folded

accel.

cay: Yet I seem but a child as I was long a-go, When I stood by the form of my
head.   Then I thought ne'er an angel that Heaven could know, Tho' trained in its own peerless
felt!   In his sa-cred old seat, with his locks white as snow, Sat the ven-erable form of my
arms;   But oft-en with rapture my bo-som doth glow, As I think of my home and my

a tempo.

sire,   And my dear mother sang, as she rocked to and fro In the old easy-chair by the fire.
choir, Could sing like my mother, who rocked to and fro In the old easy-chair by the fire.
sire,   While my dear mother sang as she rocked to and fro In the old easy-chair by the fire.
sire,   And the dearest of mothers, who sang long ago In an old easy-chair by the fire!

THE CHEERFUL VOICE.—The comfort and happiness of home and home intercourse, let us here say, depend very much upon the kindly and affectionate training of the voice. Trouble, care, and vexation will and must, of course, come; but let them not creep into our voices. Let only our kindly and happier feelings be vocal in our homes. Let them be so, if for no other reason, for the little children's sake. Those sensitive little beings are exceedingly susceptible to the tones. Let us have consideration for them. They hear so much that we have forgotten to hear; for, as we advance in years, our life becomes more interior. We are abstracted from outward scenes and sounds. We think, we reflect, we begin gradually to deal with the past, as we have formerly vividly lived in the present. Our ear grows dull to external sound; it is turned inward and listens chiefly to the echoes of past voices. We catch no more the merry laughter of children. We hear no more the note of the morning bird. The brook that used to prattle so

KIND WORDS CAN NEVER DIE.

ABBY HUTCHINSON.

1. Kind words can nev-er die, Cherished and blest, God knows how deep they lie,
2. Child-hood can nev-er die—Wrecks of the past Float o'er the mem-o-ry,
3. Sweet thoughts can nev-er die, Though, like the flow'rs, Their brightest hues may fly
4. Our souls can nev-er die, Though in the tomb We may all have to lie,

rall. tempo.

Lodged in the breast; Like childhood's sim-ple rhymes, Said o'er a thousand times,
Bright to the last. Man-y a hap-py thing, Man-y a dai-sy spring,
In win-try hours. But when the gen-tle dew Gives them their charms a-new,
Wrapt in its gloom. What though the flesh de-cay, Souls pass in peace a-way,

CHORUS.

Go through all years and climes, The heart to cheer. Kind words can nev-er die,
Floats on time's cease-less wing, Far, far a-way. Child-hood can nev-er die,
With many an add-ed hue, They bloom a-gain. Sweet thoughts can nev-er die,
Live through e-ter-nal day. With Christ a-bove. Our souls can nev-er die,

nev-er die, nev-er die, Kind words can nev-er die, no, nev-er die.
nev-er die, nev-er die, Child-hood can nev-er die, no, nev-er die.
nev-er die, nev-er die, Sweet thoughts can nev-er die, no, nev-er die.
nev-er die, nev-er die, Our souls can nev-er die, no, nev-er die.

gaily to us, rushes by unheeded—we have forgotten to hear such things; but little children, remember, sensitively hear them all. Mark how, at every sound, the young child starts, and turns, and listens; and thus, with equal sensitiveness does it catch the tones of human voices. How were it possible, therefore, that the sharp and hasty word, the fretful and complaining tone, should not startle and pain, even depress the sensitive little being whose harp of life is so newly and delicately strung, vibrating even to the gentle breeze, and thrilling ever to the tones of such voices as sweep across it? Let us be kind and cheerful spoken, then, in our homes.—*Once a Week.*

THE memory of song goes deep. Who is there that, in logical words, can express the effect music has on us? A kind of inarticulate, unfathomable speech, which leads us to the edge of the infinite, and lets us for moments gaze out into that.—*Carlyle.*

THE LIFE OF EMOTION.—It is the life of emotion which music seizes upon and makes objective. We see the character of a nation's heart in its music, as we see the character of its poetry. Italian music is sentimental and superficial; it often sacrifices simplicity to beautiful, to delicate, or to crashing effects; it is intense rather than passionate. French music is sensational and flippant. German music simple, direct, and earnest. We are of course dealing only with the type in every case; no such sweeping criticism can be of universal application. There is one class of music to which these remarks do not apply. In the words of the author of "Music and Morals," "The music of patriotic times and national anthems is always earnest and dignified. In the Marseillaise there is an almost sombre severity, wholly unlike the frivolous, superficial grace and sentimental pathos of the ordinary French school. The men who sing it are not playing at war like fools, nor are they mere children, delighted in its outward pomp and circum-

LONG, LONG AGO.

A. H. BAILEY.

1. Tell me the tales that to me were so dear, Long, long a-go, Long, long a-go;
2. Do you re-mem-ber the path where we met, Long, long a-go, Long, long a-go?
3. Though by your kindness my fond hopes were raised, Long, long ago, Long, long a-go;

Sing me the songs I de-light-ed to hear, Long, long a-go, long a-go.
Ah, yes, you told me you ne'er would forget, Long, long a-go, long a-go.
You, by more el-o-quent lips have been praised, Long, long a-go, long a-go.

Now you are come, all my grief is removed, Let me for-get that so long you have roved,
Then, to all oth-ers my smile you preferr'd, Love, when you spoke, gave a charm to each word,
But by long absence your truth has been tried, Still to your ac-cents I lis-ten with pride,

Let me believe that you love as you loved, Long, long a-go, long a-go.
Still my heart treasures the prais-es I heard, Long, long a-go, long a-go.
Blest as I was when I sat by your side, Long, long a-go, long a-go.

stance. They trudge on, footsore and weary, knowing all the horror and the pain that is in store for them, and still willing to conquer and to die. That is the spirit of the Marseillaise, and in it, as in Garibaldi's Hymn, the seriousness of the crisis had called forth the finest qualities of both the French and Italian characters, and banished for a time what is languishing in the one and frivolous in the other." Poetry, painting, and sculpture reach the emotions indirectly through the intellect. Music reaches them directly, and we should therefore rightly expect to find something in common between the two. We do, in fact, see in both those qualities which would make it possible for the one to be the expression of the other; elation and depression which can be expressed musically by a high or low pitch; intensity and variety, expressed by means of the touch and slight modifications of tune by the player, and change of key by the composer.—*Mrs. Herrick.*

Other things being equal, says a distinguished physician, there is no occupation so conducive to general good health and long living as singing. It does not argue anything that many professional singers die early in life. The hard lives they lead, travelling about from place to place, keeping all kinds of hours, eating all kinds of food, and enduring all kinds of exposure, would break them down even though they had constitutions of steel. In fact, it is only an argument for the truth of my theory that professional singers are able to live as long as they do and be as healthy as they are.

If they stayed in one place, kept regular hours and lived like civilized beings, they would be the longest-lived class of people in the world, and the healthiest, too; though, of course, as long as there were other singers alive, they wouldn't be the happiest. You see if a person is taught to sing properly in the beginning, and then keeps it up regularly, the effect is certain to be very beneficial to all the vital organs. For instance, to begin with, the pupil is taught to breathe as he should, and as very few persons do; that is, by the deep, abdominal method, lifting and lowering the dia-

AUNT JEMIMA'S PLASTER.

Animato.

1. Aunt Je-mi-ma she was old, But very kind and clever; She had a no-tion of her own That she would marry nev-er: She said that she would live in peace, And none should be her master; She made her living day by day In sell-ing of a plaster.

2. She had a sis-ter ve-ry tall, And if she'd kept on growing, She might have been a gi-ant now: In fact, there is no knowing. All of a sud-den she became Of her own height the master, And all because upon each foot Je-mi-ma put a plaster.

3. There was a thief that, night and day, Kept stealing from his neighbors; But none could find the ras-cal out, With all their tricks and labors: She set a trap up-on her step, And caught him with a plaster, The more he tried to get a-way, The more he stuck the faster.

4. Her neighbor had a Thomas cat That ate like an-y glutton; It nev-er caught a mouse or rat, But stole both milk and mutton. To keep it home she tried her best, But ne'er could be the master, Un-til she stuck it to the floor With Aunt Jemima's plaster.

5. Now, if you have a dog or cat, A husband, wife, or lov-er, That you would wish to keep at home, This plaster just dis-cov-er; And if you wish to live in peace, A-void-ing all dis-as-ter, Take my advice, and try the strength Of Aunt Je-mima's plaster.

Chorus.

Sheepskin and beeswax Made this awful plaster, The more you try to get it off The more it sticks the faster.

phragm and filling out the entire lungs below the chest. That develops the lungs, and brings all their surface into action, insures pure blood, and a strong and regular action of the heart. Then the act of singing, by which the lungs are filled to their utmost capacity in the way I have described and then slowly emptied over and over again, is a splendid exercise for those organs. Nothing, in fact, could be better. Then the action of the diaphragm being pressed strongly downward, and of the walls of the stomach being pressed outward,

have a certain effect upon the digestive organs and help to keep them in tone. Added to all this the public singer, if he or she be endowed with the true artistic instinct, has a kind of physical frenzy in singing that throws off a great deal of magnetism. Of course, it often leaves the performer weaker and exhausted at the end of the programme, but it is like the athlete on the bars. The exhaustion is a good sign, if it is not carried too far. After rest and recreation the performer always feels the better for it.

ALL structures, large or small, simple or complex, have a definite rate of vibration depending on their material, size and shape, as the fundamental note of a musical chord. At one time considerable annoyance was experienced in one of the mills in Lowell. Some days the mill was so shaken that a pail of water would be nearly emptied, while on other days all was quiet. Experiment proved it to be only when the machinery was running at a certain rate that the building was disturbed. The simple remedy was in running it slower or faster, so as to put it out of tune with the building. We have here the reason of the rule observed by marching armies when they cross a bridge—viz., stop the music, break step, and open column, lest the measured cadence of a condensed mass of men should cause the bridge to vibrate beyond its sphere of cohesion. The Broughton bridge gave way beneath the measured tramp of only sixty men. Tyndall tells us that the Swiss muleteers tie up the bells of their mules, lest the tinkle bring down an avalanche. The breaking of a drinking glass by the human voice is a well-attested fact, and Chlanni mentions an innkeeper who frequently repeated this interesting experiment for the entertainment of his guests.—*Lovering.*

THE SNOW-BIRD.

Rev. F. C. Woodworth.

1. The ground was all cov-er'd with snow one day, And two lit-tle chil-dren were
2. He had not been sing-ing that tune very long, Ere Em-i-ly heard him, so

bus-y at play, When a snow-bird was sit-ting close by on a tree, And
loud was his song. "Oh, sis-ter! look out of the win-dow," said she; "Here's a

mer-ri-ly sing-ing his chick-a-dee-dee, Chick-a-dee-dee,
dear lit-tle bird sing-ing chick-a-dee-dee, Chick-a-dee-dee,

chick-a-dee-dee, And mer-ri-ly sing-ing his chick-a-dee-dee.
chick-a-dee-dee, Here's a dear lit-tle bird sing-ing chick-a-dee-dee.

"Poor fellow! he walks in the snow and the sleet,
And has neither stockings nor shoes on his feet;
I pity him so! for how cold he must be!
And yet he keeps singing his chick-a-dee-dee.—*Cho.*

"If I were a bare-footed snow-bird, I know
I would not stay out in the cold and the snow,
I wonder what makes him so full of his glee;
He's all the time singing that chick-a-dee-dee.

"O mother! do get him some stockings and shoes,
A frock, with a cloak and a hat, if he choose;
I wish he'd come into the parlor, and see
How warm we would make him, poor chick-a-dee-dee.

The bird had flown down for some crumbs of bread,
And heard every word little Emily said:
"What a figure I'd make in that dress!" thought he,
And he laughed, as he warbled his chick-a-dee-dee.

"I am grateful," he said, "for the wish you express,
But I've no occasion for such a fine dress;
I had rather remain with my limbs all so free,
Than to hobble about, singing chick-a-dee-dee.

"There is One, my dear child, tho' I can not tell who
Has clothed me already, and warm enough too.
Good-morning! O who are so happy as we?"
And away he went, singing his chick-a-dee-dee.

JEANNETTE AND JEANNOT.

Chas. Jeffreys.
Chas. W. Glover.

1. You are go-ing far a-way, Far a-way from poor Jeannette, There is
2. Or when glo-ry leads the way, You'll be mad-ly rush-ing on, Nev-er

no one left to love me now, And you too may for-get; But my
think-ing, if they kill you, that My hap-pi-ness is gone: If you

heart will be with you, Wher-ev-er you may go, Can you
win the day, perhaps, A gen-er-al you'll be, Tho' I'm

look me in the face, And say the same, Jean-not? When you
proud to think of that, What will be-come of me? Oh! if

wear the jack-et red, And the beau-ti-ful cockade, Oh, I fear you will for-
I were Queen of France, Or, still bet-ter, Pope of Rome, I would have no fight-ing

get All the prom-is-es you've made; With your gun up-on your shoulder, And your
men a-broad, No weep-ing maids at home; All the world should be at peace, Or if

bay' - net by your side, You'll be tak - ing some proud la - dy, And be mak-ing her your
kings must show their might, Why, let them who make the quar-rels Be the on-ly men to

bride; You'll be tak - ing some proud la - dy, And be mak - ing her your bride.
fight; Yes, let them who make the quar - rels Be the on - ly men to fight.

THE DAWN OF DAY.

Samuel Reay.

Allegro.

f 1. Come and watch the daylight dawning, O'er the mountain bleak and gray, Come and see the purple
2. Come, thy foot should ne'er be weary, Never tired thy wakeful eye, Earth should ne'er seem dark and
3. Come, the lark has left the meadow, Now he soars beyond our sight, Far away from mist and

Repeat p. *mf* *dim.*

morning Tinge their summits far away. Gaily sounds the voice of gladness O'er the vale and thro' the
dreary, When the morning gilds the sky. Birds shall plume their wings beside thee, Gaily warbling over-
shadow, Singing in a world of light. Come and see what forms of glory Spring to life in morning's

dim. *dim.* *rall.* *pp* *poco cres.*

grove, Here no plaintive note of sadness Tells of aught but peace and love. Tra la la la, tra la la,
head, Sunbeams thro' the green leaves guide thee, Where thy steps may safely tread. Tra la la la, tra la la,
ray, Come and hear the joyful sto - ry Nature tells at dawn of day. Tra la la la, tra la la,

mf *cres.* *ff* *ritard.*

tra la la la, la la, tra la la la, tra la la la, la, la la, tra la.

Music, like other studies taught as a specialty in the schools, must prove unsatisfactory at the best. One or more special teachers of music giving lessons in the different schools of a city at fixed hours, cannot usually do the efficient work that is needed. Rote singing may serve a good purpose in many ways. It disciplines the taste and the voice, and makes many children familiar with pleasant tunes to sing at home. It does not, however, give the pupil any useful ideas that can be applied to self-advancement. To accomplish this, music should be taught as a graded study, on the basis of a uniform system for all schools. Teachers under the direction of competent instructors, who should be required to supervise all instruction, may become very efficient in imparting the elements of music. By this method music in the school can be made of great practical benefit. Music is allied to art by poetical affinity and humanizing power. It is the most elevating of all recreations, while at the same time it forms one of the most available means for the enlivening of toil and care. In teaching drawing, we do not propose to make artists; so in teaching music, it is not proposed to make musicians; but we can make the time devoted to this study of so much practical benefit to the pupil, that he will always feel in it an intelligent personal interest.

THOSE ENDEARING YOUNG CHARMS.

DAVENANT.

1. Be - lieve me, if all those en - dear-ing young charms, Which I gaze on so fond - ly to -
2. It is not while beauty and youth are thine own, And thy cheek's unprofaned by a

day, Were-to change by to - mor-row and fleet from my arms, Like
tear, That the fer - vor and faith of a soul can be known, To which

fair - y gifts fad - ing a - way, Thou wouldst still be a - dored as this
time will but make thee more dear, Oh, the heart that has tru - ly loved,

mo - ment thou art: Let thy love - li - ness fade as it will, And a
nev - er for - gets, But as tru - ly loves on to the close: As the

round the dear ru - in, each wish of my heart, Would entwine it - self ver - dantly still.
sun - flower turns on her god when he sets, The same look that she gave when he rose.

MAKE THE BEST OF IT.

C. J. DUNPHY.

1. Life is but a fleet-ing dream, Care destroys the zest of it; Swift it gli-deth
2. If your friend has e'er a heart, There is something fine in him; Cast a-way his
3. Hap-pi-ness des-pis-es state, Tho''tis no dis-par-agement When the man that's
4. Trust-ing in the Power a-bove, Which, sustaining all of us, In one common

like a stream—Mind you make the best of it Talk not of your wea-ry woes,
dark-er part, Cling to what's di-vine in him; Friendship is our best re-lief,
wise and great Has both joy and mer-ri-ment. Rank is not the spell re-fined,
bond of love Bin-deth great and small of us, Then, what-ev-er may be-fall,

Troubles, or the rest of it, If we have but brief re-pose, Let us make the best of it.
Make no heartless jest of it, It will brighten ev-'ry grief If we make the best of it.
Mon-ey's not the test of it, But a calm, con-tent-ed mind That will make the best of it.
Sor-rows, or the rest of it, We shall o-vercome them all, If we make the best of it.

HAIL TO THE BRIGHTNESS.

THOS. HASTINGS.

1. Hail to the brightness of Zi-on's glad morning! Joy to the lands that in darkness have lain;
2. Hail to the brightness of Zi-on's glad morning! Long by the proph-ets of Is-rael fore-told;
3. Lo! in the des-ert rich flowers are springing, Streams ever co-pious are gliding a-long;
4. See, from all lands, from the isles of the o-cean, Praise to Je-ho-vah as-cending on high;

Hushed be the accents of sor-row and mourning, Zi-on in triumph begins her mild reign.
Hail to the millions from bondage re-turn-ing, Gen-tiles and Jews the blest vis-ion be-hold.
Loud from the mountain-tops echoes are ring-ing, Wastes rise in verdure, and mingle in song.
Fall'n are the engines of war and com-mo-tion, Shouts of sal-va-tion are rend-ing the sky.

Balfe was a good vocalist and a fine composer. He sang in New York in 1834. He acquired such musical reputation as few English singers or composers have ever done. Balfe was born in Ireland, and was first distinguished as a singer. His voice was a barytone of moderate power, but his style was most beautifully finished and full of feeling. He afterwards merged the singer into the composer. His sparkling and effective operas enjoy popularity, as also his arrangement of Moore's melodies and other songs.

Looking at the uses of common sense in the school-room, they are legion. It may be said of teachers what an old Scotch elder said of ministers: "There be three things a mon needs to make him a successful minister, viz.: gude health, religion, and gude sense; if he can have but one o' these, let it be gude sense; for God can gie him health, and God can gie him grace, but naebody can gie him common sense."

Music is the fourth great want of our nature; first food, then raiment, then shelter, then music.—*Bovee.*

SILENTLY FALLING SNOW.

GERMAN AIR.
WM. ORLAND BOURNE.

1. In flakes of a feath-er-y white, 'Tis fall-ing so gent-ly and slow; Oh, pleas-ant to me is the sight, When si-lent-ly fall-ing the snow; Snow, snow, snow, When si-lent-ly fall-ing the snow; Snow, snow, snow, When si-lent-ly fall-ing the snow.

2. The earth is all cov-ered to-day With man-tle of ra-di-ant show; It sparkles and shines in the ray, In crys-tals of glit-ter-ing snow; Snow, snow, snow, In crys-tals of glit-ter-ing snow; Snow, snow, snow, In crys-tals of glit-ter-ing snow.

3. Oh, hap-py the snow-birds I see, While hop-ping and flit-ting they go, They tell of a les-son to me, While feed-ing in beau-ti-ful snow; Snow, snow, snow, While feed-ing in beau-ti-ful snow; Snow, snow, snow. While feed-ing in beau-ti-ful snow.

How spotless it seems, and how pure,
I would that my spirit were so!
Then, long as the soul shall endure,
   More brightly I'd shine than the snow.
   Snow, snow, snow,
More brightly I'd shine than the snow;
   Snow, snow, snow,
More brightly I'd shine than the snow.

But soon with the breath of the spring,
Down streamlets and rivers 'twill flow,
The season of summer will bring
   Bright flowers for silvery snow.
   Snow, snow, snow,
Bright flowers for silvery snow;
   Snow, snow, snow,
Bright flowers for silvery snow.

THE MOWERS' SONG.

German Air.

1. When early morning's ruddy light Bids man to labor go; We haste with scythes all sharp and bright The
2. The cheerful lark sings sweet and clear, The black-bird chirps away, And all is lively, sprightly here Like
3. The maidens come in gladsome train, And skip along their way, Rejoiced to tread the grassy plain And

meadow grass to mow. We mow-ers, dal de ral day, We cut the lil-ies and—
mer-ry, mer-ry May. We mow-ers, dal de ral day, We roll the swaths of green—
toss the new-mown hay. The maid-ens, dal de ral day, They rake the lil-ies and—

ha! ha! ha! ha! ha! ha! Hey, dey, dey, yes, hey, dey, dey, We cut the lil-ies and hay.
ha! ha! ha! ha! ha! ha! Hey, dey, dey, yes, hey, dey, dey, We roll the swaths of green hay.
ha! ha! ha! ha! ha! ha! Hey, dey, dey, yes, hey, dey, dey, They rake the lil-ies and hay.

THE MILL-WHEEL.

Lively.

Kindergarten.

1. The mill-wheels are clapping; the brook turns them round, clip, clap! By day and by night is the
2. How bu-sy the wheels are in turn-ing the stone, clip, clap! And grinding so fine-ly the

grain be-ing ground, clip, clap! The mill-er is jol-ly and ev-er a-lert, That
grain we have grown, clip, clap! The bak-er the flour for the bak-ing will use, And

we may have bread and be glad like a bird, clip, clap, clip, clap, clip, clap!
make us a roll, or a cake if we choose, clip, clap, clip, clap, clip, clap!

THE IMAGE OF THE ROSE.

G. REICHARDT.

Andante con espressione.

1. In yonder val - ley calm - ly blooming, I saw a rose, its leaves un -
2. And thus o'ercome with fond e - mo - tion I lingered, charmed by this sweet
3. In dark and gloomy hours of sad - ness, The form of that dear rose I
1. In ei - nem Tha - le fried - lich stil - le, Sah ei - ne Ro - se ich er -

fold; Endowed with sweeter, brighter beau - ty Than I a - gain can e'er be -
flower; From it my soul a joy re - ceiv - ing, I ne'er had felt un - til that
see, Then quickly grief gives place to gladness, And care and strife de - part from
steh'n; be - gabt mit ho - her, Schönheits Fül - le Wie ich noch kei - ne je ge -

hold, By dew - y fra - grant moss sur - rounded, Shone forth the bud in full - est
hour. Still in my in - most heart re - maineth The cherished im - age of that
me. Yes, Heav'n both weal and woe de - creeing, Con - trols our life with se - cret
seh'n, In duf - tig an - ge - schwell - tem Moo - se, Erschien der Knos - pe vol - le

grace; A fair - er em - blem than this rose Of ho - ly
rose, And ev - er in the dis - tant fu - ture Shall its dear
power, To cheer my lone - li - ness and sor - row To guide and
Pracht, Und schöner als in die - ser Ro - se Hat nie der

f più moto.

vir - tue none shall trace, A fair - er em - blem than this rose Of ho - ly
mem'ry find re - pose, And ev - er in the dis - tant fu - ture Shall its dear
bless me gave this flower, To cheer my lone - li - ness and sor - row, To guide and
Tu - gend Bild ge - lacht. Und schöner als in die - ser Ro - se, Hat nie der

vir - tue none shall trace, Of ho - ly vir - tue none shall trace. Im - age most dear,
mem'ry find re - pose, Shall its dear mem'ry find re - pose. Im - age most dear,
bless me gave this flower, To guide and bless me gave this flower. Im - age most dear,
Tu - gend Bild ge - lacht, Hat nie der Tu - gend Bild ge - lacht. Lieb - li - ches Bild,

stay, O stay! Stay, O stay with me.
Wei - le, O wei - le, Weile, o weile bei mir.

SOLDIER'S FAREWELL.

Andante. J. KINKEL.

1. Ah, love, how can I leave thee? The sad thought deep doth grieve me. But
2. No more shall I be - hold thee, Or to my heart en - fold thee; In
3. I'll think of thee with long - ing, When thoughts with tears come thronging; And
1. Weh' dasz wir schei - den müs - sen! Lasz dich noch ein - mal küs - sen! Ich

know what - e'er be - falls me I go where hon - or calls me. Fare -
war's ar - ray ap - pear - ing, The foe's stern hosts are near - ing. Fare -
on the field, if ly - ing, I'll breathe thy dear name, dy - ing. Fare -
musz an Kai - ser's Sei - ten in's fal - sche Welsch-land rei - ten. Fahr'

tranquillo a molto express.

well, fare - well! My own true love! Farewell, fare - well, My own true love!
wohl, Fahr' wohl, mein ar - mes Lieb, fahr' wohl, fahr' wohl, mein ar - mes Lieb!

Ich werd' auf Maienauen
Dich niemals wiederschauen,
Der Feinde grimme Schaaren
Sie kommen angefahren.

Ich denk' an dich mit Sehnen,
Gedenk' auch mein mit Thränen!
Wenn meine Augen brechen,
Will ich zuletzt noch sprechen:

CHORAL SINGING.—How should a choral be sung, and what tunes shall we select? How shall we know a good tune when we hear it? In answering these questions, I shall try to make myself understood by the unmusical reader. A good tune, fit to be sung by the congregation, must answer Rossini's question: "Will it grind?" For instance, "America" is a very good hand-organ tune. It will grind first-rate. The tune known as Dundee is better still. It contains but two kinds of notes. The figures 1 and 2 represent its character. They are simple numbers, closely related. The tune Arlington has four kinds of notes, that may be represented by the figures 1, 2, 2½, and 4. This, you see, is an irregular arrangement. Tunes containing dotted notes are not the best, because the dotted note destroys that straight-forward, exact, and mechanical character that appeals so directly to the common idea of time and numbers. In brief, the best chorals contain notes related to each other by simple numbers, like Old Hundred, Dundee, Luther's Chant, Missionary Hymn, or related by such numbers as 1, 2, and 3, as Balerma, Dennis, Olmutz, Boylston and others. Of course there are exceptions to this rule. Certain tunes possess a life and animation strong enough to carry them over any ordinary difficulties. Handel's Christmas and the Portuguese Hymn are notable examples. If you take pains to examine the best German chorals, you will find, as a rule, they contain only two kinds of notes—long and short ones, related as 1 to 2. Simple and exact, they are easily caught, and are produced, as we happen to know, with wonderful effect. Having seen that simplicity of form and mechanical exactitude are the standards of a good choral, let us see what more they should have. First comes

O COME, COME AWAY.

W. E. HICKSON.

1. O, come, come a-way, From labor now re-pos-ing, Let bu-sy care a-
2. From toil and from care, On which the day is clos-ing, The hour of eve brings
3. While sweet Phil-o-mel, The weary trav'ler cheer-ing, With evening song her
4. The bright day is gone, The moon and stars ap-pear-ing, With silv'ry light il-

while forbear, O come, come a-way. Come, come, our social joys renew, And
sweet reprieve, O come, come a-way. O come where love will smile on thee, And
notes prolong, O come, come a-way. In answ'ring song of sym-pa-thy, We'll
lume the night, O come, come a-way. We'll join in grateful songs of praise, To

there with trust and friendship, too, Let true hearts welcome you, O come, come a-way.
round the heart will gladness be, And time fly mer-ri-ly, O come, come a-way.
sing in tuneful har-mo-ny, Of hope, joy, lib-er-ty, O come, come a-way.
Him who crowns our peaceful days With health, hope, hap-piness, O come, come a-way.

association. Old Hundred has a rather dry, uninteresting melody; yet it will never die. It has become so bound up with our dearest thoughts, and connected with our most sacred occasions, that we sing it with tearful eyes, and wonder why we love such a dear, stupid old song. Association keeps alive many a psalm that should be happily forgotten. The tunes Mear and Marlow might well be expunged from our books, as too dreary for any cheerful and sensible Christian; yet there they are likely to stay as long as you and I live. Next, the tunes should always be pitched in low keys. I have listened to congregational singing for many years, and I have never heard the people sing above E of the scale with ease. The people—men, women and children—sing the melody, and I find this the limit of their average voices. They can go higher; but it is strained and unpleasant, neither edifying nor agreeable. The tunes should have a simple and flowing movement. The intervals or steps between the notes should not be wide nor unusual. "America" has a remarkably singing melody, confined within seven notes. The tune Ward keeps within six; and Naomi, one of the most beautiful melodies ever written, covers only five notes. Choral music is attracting increased attention every year. It is destined to grow and improve. Let us bid it Godspeed. May the day soon come when we can say: "Yea, let all the people praise the Lord!"—*Barnard.*

POOR THO' MY COT MAY BE.

BETLY.

1. Poor tho' my cot may be, Time pass-es gai-ly; Health, joy, and lib-er-ty Still have been
2. Join then the mountaineer, Leave care and sor-row; Peace and contentment here Kind hearts may

mine; Would you live mer-ri-ly, Fly from the val-ley; Roam-ing the mountain free,
know; Pride must no pal-ace rear, Lest with the mor-row, En-vy be lurk-ing near,

Who can re-pine? Sweet is our song when the day-beam is break-ing, "Speed to the
Pa-rent of woe. Rich-es we need not, we're hap-py with-out them: What could the

mountain top, Hunter, speed on!" "Speed to the mountain top, Hunter, speed on!" Joy-ous the
wealth of the world give us more? What could the wealth of the world give us more? Care, too, so

welcomes at' night-fall a-wak-ing, "Homeward, come homeward, our sports are be-gun."
oft-en will hov-er a-bout them, Bet-ter by far then be hap-py, though poor.

Tra, la, la, la, tra, la, la, la, tra, la, tra, la, la, la, la, la, la, la, la.

It is not uncommon for people more or less intelligent to speak of music and drawing as merely ornamental branches as distinguished from other studies. In looking the world over, what branches do we find more useful or more practical than music and drawing? Into the pleasure of social, or even solitary life, what branch enters so largely as music? If the objective point of education is refinement, what agent or influence is more potent? As to drawing, it enters every branch of industry, from the digging of a ditch to the building of a steamship. The represented line is the beginning of every constructed form. A master workman may have no stronger arm, no more skilful hand, than any of his toiling underlings; but, having an eye for distance and proportion, he is paid well for directing those who boast

JERUSALEM THE GOLDEN.

St. Bernard, a. d. 1150.
Alexander Ewing. Neale *tr.*

1. Je - ru - sa - lem the gold - en! With milk and hon - ey blest,
2. They stand, those halls of Zi - on, All ju - bi - lant with song,
3. And they who with their Lead - er, Have con - quered in the fight,
4. Oh, sweet and bless - ed coun - try, The home of God's e - lect!

Be - neath thy con - tem - pla - tion Sink heart and voice op - press'd.
And bright with many an an - gel, And all the mar - tyr throng.
For - ev - er, and for - ev - er, Are clad in robes of white.
Oh, sweet and bless - ed coun - try, That ea - ger hearts ex - pect!

I know not,— oh, I know not, What joys a - wait me there,
There is the throne of Da - vid, And there from toil re - leas'd,
Oh, land that see'st no sor - row! Oh, state that fear'st no strife!
Je - sus, in mer - cy bring us To that dear land of rest;

What ra - dian - cy of glo - ry, What bliss be - yond com - pare.
The shout of them that tri - umph, The song of them that feast.
Oh, roy - al land of flow - ers! Oh, realm and home of life!
Who art, with God the Fath - er, And Spir - it ev - er blest.

nothing but brawn. Omitting all mention of the artistic or æsthetic value of drawing, its practical utility is enough to place it in the front rank of solid studies. But why not consider, too, its artistic uses? Is it not suggestive that nearly all our best artists and engravers are foreigners? Properly taught, drawing is a most interesting branch to children of any age. Placed against writing as a candidate for popular favor, it wins three-fourths of the hands in any well-regulated school-room. It pleases children in a double manner, for it allows them to *do* and to *learn* at the same time, and to combine these is the secret of the best training in the schools. Let us hear no more of music and drawing not being solid studies.

PRAYER FROM FREISCHUTZ.

Von Weber.

1. Songs, re - veal - ing sa - cred feel - ing, Toward the shin - ing stars float
2. Low - ly bend - ing, Towards thee wend - ing, Lord, who hast no cause nor

steal - ing.   Then out - well - ing, Loud - ly swell - ing,
end - ing!   Still be - friend us; Still de - fend us;

Reach th'e - ter - nal Fa - ther's
Thine e - ter - nal suc - cor

Reach the Fa - ther's dwell - ing, the Fa - ther's dwell - ing.
Thine e - ter - nal suc - cor, thy suc - cor lend us.

LORD, IN THIS THY MERCY'S DAY.

W. H. Monk.

1. Lord, in this Thy mer - cy's day, Ere the time shall pass a - way,
2. Ho - ly Je - sus, grant us tears, Fill us with heart search - ing fears,
3. Lord, on us Thy spir - it pour, Kneel - ing low - ly at Thy door,
4. By Thy night of a - gon - y, By Thy sup - pli - cat - ing cry,

On our knees we fall and pray.
Ere the hour of doom ap - pears.
Ere it close for - ev - er - more.
By Thy will - ing - ness to die,

5. By Thy tears of bitter woe,
For Jerusalem below,
Let us not Thy love forego.

6. Judge and Saviour of our race,
When we see Thee face to face,
Grant us 'neath Thy wings a place.

7. On Thy love we rest alone,
And that love will then be known
By the pardoned round Thy throne.

MUSIC exists for the expression of varied emotion—sadness, longing, hope, triumph, aspirations toward the unobtained or the indefinite, calm fulfilment of an artistic conception of fitness and beauty; and besides these, monotony, long spell of unbroken quiescence, mental perturbation even to a positive sense of physical discomfort, are absolutely essential to relieve and heighten the more ecstatic emotions of pleasure called forth by a musical composition. We cannot always be burning with passion and reciting dramatic duets or heading triumphal processions. We do not do so in real life. This is what the Italians have failed to recognize. Their staggering tenors and palpitating sopranos rave together down by the prompter's box in an almost unintermittent frenzy of passion; a very parody of life bereft of many of its tranquil calms and minor impressions pleasurably painful, each having its own special effect and value by contrast in relation to the rest of our lives. It is not only vivid impressions that are interesting; these heaped up one upon another constitute a plethora of over-strained excitement that will jade and exhaust the most passionate nature. There are countless experiences in life which leave us in a tranquil condition of enjoyment; and since these make up by far the greater portion of our existence, and are the vehicle of the most powerful emotions, are they not worthy of a prominent place in so comprehensive an index of human sentiment as is music?—*Chambers.*

THE TREES AND THE MASTER.

SIDNEY LANIER.

Andantino.

1. In - to the woods my Master went, Clean forspent—for-spent, In - to the woods my
2. Out of the woods my Master went—And He was well con - tent; Out of the woods my

Mas - ter came—Forspent with love and shame, For - spent with love and shame.
Mas - ter came—Content with death and shame, Con - tent with death and shame.

espress.

But the olives they were not blind to Him; The lit - tle gray leaves were kind to Him;
When Death and Shame would woo Him last, From under the trees they drew Him last,

cres. *rall.* *dim.*

The thorn tree had a mind to Him, When in - to the woods He came,
'Twas 'on a tree they slew Him last, When out of the woods He came,

Andante religioso. *rall.*

When in - to the woods He came, When in - to the woods He came.
When out of the woods He came, When out of the woods He came.

MOUNTAIN MAID'S INVITATION.

H. WERNER.
THOMAS POWER.

HOBBY-HORSE.

KINDERGARTEN

"SPEAK GENTLY."—The following reminiscences of a popular song will interest those with whom it is a favorite: David Bates, the author of the poem "Speak Gently," was a Philadelphia broker. He was styled by the board of brokers—it was their custom to nickname each other—"Old Mortality." Prominent literary men of the day frequented his office on Third street. None of his other numerous poems obtained the popularity of "Speak Gently." This was written on the spur of the moment, and was called out by a trivial circumstance. He was writing at his desk, and his wife was sewing in the same room, while his son and a little playmate were having a very spirited romp. The uproar they created greatly disturbed the good lady, and she requested them to be quieter. They subsided for a few moments, but soon there was as much commotion as before, and she reproved them again; but the noise continued. Then she sprang to her feet, and, in no gentle tone, said, "I'll teach you to be quiet!" and both of the boys would have had their ears boxed, but they rushed very quickly for the door, and were out of sight before she could reach them. "Speak gently, wife—speak gently," said Mr. Bates, and turning again to his desk, he took a fresh sheet of paper, and wrote the poem that bears this title. At the supper table that evening he handed it to his wife. She glanced at the title, and thinking it a second reproof, said she did not want to see it, and gave it back to him without reading it. The next day, at his office, one of his literary friends coming in, he showed it to him. "This is a good thing, Bates," said his friend; "you should have it published." And acting upon the suggestion, he sent it with a note to L. A. Godey, editor of *Godey's Magazine*, published

SCOTCH CRADLE-SONG.

OLD LULLABY.

Ba - loo, ba - loo, my wee, wee thing, O saft - ly close thy blink - in' e'e;
Ba - loo, ba - loo, my wee, wee thing, For thou art doub - ly dear to me.

1. Thy fa - ther now is far a - wa', A sail - or lad - die o'er the sea; But
2. Thy face is sim - ple, sweet and mild, Like o - ny sim - mer e'e - nin' fa', Thy
3. O but thy fa - ther's ab - sence lang Might break my dow - ie heart in twa' Wert

hope aye hechts his safe re - turn To you, my bon - nie lamb, an' me.
spark - lin' e'e is bon - nie black, Thy neck is like the moun - tain snaw.
thou na left a daw - tit pledge To steal the ee - rie hours a - wa'.

in Philadelphia. Within a few days he received a check from Mr. Godey for one hundred dollars, with a note complimenting the poem. Mr. Bates looked at the check with amazement, and exclaimed, "Well, this is the biggest one hundred dollars I ever saw!" He kept it locked up in his desk for some time, and would occasionally take it out and look at it. The poem has been translated into many languages, and is greatly admired by foreigners, especially by the cultured Brazilian Emperor. When Rev. J. C. Fletcher, the celebrated American missionary, was in Brazil, he visited Dom Pedro. During the call of the reverend gentleman, the Emperor said, "I have something to show you, and shall be very glad if you can tell me the name of the author." He at once led the way into his private library, where one of the most prominent objects in the room was a large tablet reaching from the floor to the ceiling, on which appeared the familiar poem "Speak Gently," in both the English and the Portuguese languages." "Do you know who wrote this?" asked Dom Pedro. "Yes," replied Mr. Fletcher; "the writer was formerly a fellow-townsman of mine, Mr. David Bates." "I consider it," said the Emperor, "the most beautiful poem of any language that I have ever read. I require all the members of my household to memorize it, and as far as possible, to follow its teachings." Upon Mr. Fletcher's return home, the Emperor sent by him a complimentary letter to the author, expressing his appreciation of the lines and his gratification at learning their authorship. This beautiful little poem, set to very appropriate music—an air from "Maritana," by Wallace—is found in the Franklin Square Song Collection, No. 2, the vocal harmony arranged in four parts.

STRIKE THE CYMBAL.

Chorus. Pucit: A.

Allegro.

Strike the cymbal, roll the tymbal, Let the trump of triumph sound; Powerful slinging! Headlong
From the riv-er, reject-ing quiver, Judah's hero takes the stone. Spread your banners! Shout ho-

bringing Proud Go-li-ath to the ground. } See ad-vances, with songs and dances, All the
sannas! Bat-tle is the Lord's a-lone. }

Chorus.

band of Israel's daughters; Catch the sound, ye hills and waters, Spread your banners! Shout ho-

p Solo.—Slow.

sannas! Bat-tle is the Lord's a-lone. What are haughty monarchs now? Lo! before Jehovah bow!

Faster. *Chorus.*

Pride of princes, strength of kings, To the dust Je-ho-vah brings. Praise him! praise him, ex-

f *ff* *Fine.*

ult-ing nations, praise, Praise him, praise him, ex-ult-ing nations, praise, Hosan-na, Ho-san-na!

A correspondent of one of the leading reviews of Scotland makes a plea for good singing as follows: If the visit to this country of certain Americans interested in the introduction and improvement of church music, were to have no other result, it would still do great good by directing attention to that which should be an integral and important part of the service, the only part of worship in many of our churches in which the people take an audible share. As the old woman excused herself for hearing Dr. Chalmers reading a discourse by saying, "Ay, but it was fell readin' that," so we may say of this, it's "fell" singing. Mr. Sankey has a magnificent voice—clear, sweet and melodious; and his feeling of the truth and beauty and solemnity of what he is singing communicates an indescribable pathos and tenderness to his utterance. Then he has learned what is so carefully attended to in some American schools and so little regarded here, distinct utterance.

BONNIE CHARLIE.

FINLEY DUN.
LADY NAIRNE.

We watched thee in the gloaming hour,
We watched thee in the morning gray,
Tho' thirty thousand pounds they gi'e,
Oh' there's nane that wad betray.—*Cho.*

Sweet's the laverock's note and lang,
Lilting wildly up the glen;
But aye to me he sings a sang,
Will ye no come back again?—*Cho.*

Any prejudice against "singing the gospel" fades away under the spell of his magic voice. Why should there be any prejudice? !For generations most of the Highland ministers—and some of the Lowland ministers, as well—have sung the gospel, sung their sermons, ay, sung their prayers also. The difference is that they sing very badly and he sings very well. He accompanies himself on the organ, it is true, and some of us who belong to the old school can't swallow the kist of whistles yet. But then the American organ "is only a little one." When a deputation from the session waited on Ralph Erskine to remonstrate with him on the enormity of fiddling, he gave them a tune on the violoncello, and they were so charmed that they returned to their constituents with the report that it was all right—"it wasna' ony wee sinful fiddle" that their minister was thus in the habit of operating upon, but a grand instrument, full of grave, sweet melody.

Professor Bain distinguishes sounds considered as sensations into three classes: The first comprises the general effects of sound as determined by quality, intensity, and volume or quantity, to which all ears are sensitive. The second includes musical sounds, for which a susceptibility to pitch is requisite. Lastly, there is the sensibility to the articulateness, distance, and direction of sounds, which are the more intellectual properties. The first and principal difference between sounds experienced by the ear is that between noises and musical tones, every variety of which depends on the rapidity, form, size, and order of succession of the vibrations. In musical tones, the vibrations are periodic, or succeed each other at regular intervals; in noises, they follow each other irregularly. Musical tones begin to be perceived at about thirty vibrations in a second, but a determinate musical pitch is not perceptible till about forty vibrations have been reached.

OLD SANTA CLAUS.

JOHN READ.

Moderato.

1. Old   Santa Claus sat all alone, his pipe up-on his knee,   A   funny look   about his eyes for
2. He   had been busy as a bee, had stuffed his pack with toys; Had gathered worlds of odds and ends, his
3. Of candies too, or clear or striped, he had a bounteous store, And raisins, figs, and prunes, and grapes, but
4. He clapped his specs upon his nose, picked up his rusty pen, And wrote more lines in one short hour than

fun - ny chap he;   His queer old cap was twisted, torn, his wig was all awry; He sat and mused, as
gifts for girls an' boys, Had dolls for girls, and whips for boys, with barrows, horses, drays, Bureaus an' trunks for
wanted something more, "I'm almost ready now," he said, "and Christmas nearly here; But one thing more, I
you could write in ten; Then, Christmas eve and all in bed, Quick down the chimney flew, And left, beside the

lost in thought, while time went flying by.   Santa Claus, who fears no danger, Over all the world a ranger,
Dolly's clothes : all these his pack displays. Santa Claus, who fears no danger, Over all the world a ranger,
need   a book for little folks this year."   Santa Claus, who fears no danger, Over all the world a ranger,
stocking filled, the book he meant for you. Santa Claus, who fears no danger, Over all the world a ranger,

Ev'rywhere a welcome stranger, Speeds afar on Christmas eve!   Santa Claus, who fears no danger,

O - ver all the world a ranger,   Ev'rywhere a welcome stranger, Speeds afar on Christmas eve!

MOTHERS, think less of your furniture and more of the character of your children. A scratch upon the soul of your son is a far greater blemish than a scratch upon your piano. Rather your parlor carpet soiled than the reputation of your child. Let Home compete with club-house or saloon in attractiveness. Let into your windows the broad streams of light during the day, and let there be brightness and cheerfulness at night. Hang pictures on the wall, have flowers, have good books on the table, and musical instruments near by. Let song and the harmony of violin or flute, organ or piano, pleasant converse, innocent games banish the demons of dullness and apathy. Stimulate, by means of the home, a love for the true and the beautiful, a love for higher aims and purer endeavors, and you will do for your children what no time and no circumstances can undo. You have dowered them with life's truest treasures. In that "home" you have fitted them for noble and useful lives. "My office," says a distinguished clergyman, "brings me often to the resting place of the dead, and there are tombstones. many, and many laudatory inscriptions upon them, but

LITTLE BOY BLUE.

J. E. SMITH.
EUGENE FIELD.

1. The lit - tle toy dog   is covered with dust, But   stur-dy and staunch he   stands; And the
2. "Now, don't you go till I   come," he said, "And don't you make an - y   noise!"   So,
3. Ah, faithful to Lit - tle Boy Blue they stand,   Each in the same old   place,   A-

lit - tle toy soldier is   red   with rust, And his musket it moulds in his   hands.   Time
tod - dling off to his   trun - dle bed, He dreamed of the pret - ty   toys: And
waiting the touch of a   lit - tle hand, The   smile of a   lit - tle   face; And they

was when the lit - tle toy   dog   was new, And the soldier was pass - ing   fair,   And
as he was dreaming an   an - gel song A - wakened our Lit - tle Boy   Blue—Oh, the
wonder, as wait - ing these   long years thro' In the dust of that lit - tle   chair,

there was the time when our Lit-tle Boy Blue   Kissed them and put them   there.
years   are ma - ny, the   years   are long, But the   lit   tle toy friends are   true.
What has become of our   Lit - tle Boy Blue, Since he kissed them and put   them   there.

never yet have I read a higher tribute than that which a family of children inscribed upon one of them: 'Our Mother, she always made home happy.' I have little fear for such children. With such a remembrance of such a mother, in such a home, they cannot go wrong. Should they stray, that memory is sufficient to cause them to retrace their steps." A story is told of a num-ber of soldiers during the war, who gave themselves up one night to revelry, loud talk, indecent stories, and songs, of which some, at least, could only be condemned. Among them sat a young man who took no part in their drunken carousal. His comrades taunted him; made sport of his stupidity, as they called it, and at length prevailed on him to give a toast. He arose and said, "Comrades, I give you, 'Our Mothers and our Homes!'" The effect was instantaneous—no more revelry, no more indecent stories, no more ribald song that night. A solemn silence ensued. Tears rolled down many a hardened cheek. One after another they went to their tents, and prayers ascended that night, if never again, from hearts unused to pray. Such is the magic of these simple words.—*Rev. J. Krauskopf.*

THE MAID OF THE MILL.

HAMILTON AIDÉ.
STEPHEN ADAMS.

1. Golden years a-go in a mill beside the sea, There dwelt a lit-tle maid-en, who
2. Leaden years have passed, grey-haired I look around; The earth has no such maidens now, such

plighted her faith to me; The mill-wheel now is si-lent, the maid's eyes clos-ed be; And
mill-wheels turn not round. But whene'er I think of Heav'n, and of what the an-gels be, I

all that now remains of her, are the words she sang to me. "Do not for-get me!
see a-gain that lit-tle maid, and hear her words to me. "Do not for-get me!

Do not for-get me! Think some-times of me still, When the morn breaks,

and the thros-tle a-wakes, Re-mem-ber the maid of the mill!" "Do not for-

get me! Do not for-get me! Re-mem-ber the maid, the maid of the mill!

SOLDIERS' CHORUS.

"FAUST."
C. F. GOUNOD.

Glo - ry and love to the men of old,   Their sons may cop-y their vir-tues bold,

Cour-age in heart and a sword in hand,   Yes, read-y to fight or read-y to die for

Fa - ther-land.   Who needs bidding to dare by a trum-pet blown?

Who lacks pi-ty to spare, when the field is won?   Who would fly from a foe,

if a-lone or last? And boast he was true, as coward might do, when per-il is past?

Glo - ry and love to the men of old,   Their sons may cop-y their vir-tues bold.

Cour - age in heart, and a sword in hand, Read-y to fight for Fa - ther -

land. Now home a - gain, we come, the long and fie - ry strife of bat - tle

o - ver. Rest is pleasant af - ter toil, as hard as ours beneath a stranger

sun. Ma - ny a maid-en fair is wait-ing here to greet her tru - ant sol- dier

lov - er, And many a heart will fail, and brow grow pale to hear the tale of per - il he has

seen. We are at home, we are at home, we are at home, we are at home.

D.C.

24

ALICE, WHERE ART THOU?

J. Ascher.
W. Guernsey.

Andante con espressione.

1. The birds sleeping gen-tly. Sweet Lu-na gleameth bright, Her rays tinge the for-est, And
2. The sil-ver rain fall-ing Just as it fall-eth now; And all things sleep gen-tly! Ah!

all seems glad to-night. The wind sighing by me, Cool-ing my fever'd brow; The
Al-ice, where art thou? I've sought thee by lake-let, I've sought thee on the hill, And

stream flows as ev-er, Yet, Al-ice, where art thou? One year back this e-ven, And
in the pleas-ant wildwood. When winds blew cold and chill; I've sought thee in for-est; I'm

thou wert by my side, And thou wert by my side,
look-ing heav'n-ward now, I'm look-ing heav'nward now,

Vow-ing ... to love me; One year past this e-ven, And
Oh! there 'mid the star-shine,—I've sought thee in for-est, I'a

thou wert by my side, Vow-ing to love me, Al-ice, what-e'er might be-tide.
look-ing heav'nward now, Oh! there a-mid the star-shine, Al-ice, I know, art thou.

NEW HAIL COLUMBIA.

F. HOPKINSON, 1798.
OLIVER WENDELL HOLMES, 1887.

Spirited

1798. Hail, Co-lum-bia! hap-py land, Hail, ye heroes, heav'n-born band, Who fought and bled in
1. Look our ransomed shores around, Peace and safe-ty we have found! Welcome, friends who
2. Graven deep with edge of steel, Crowned with Victory's crimson seal, All the world their
3. Hail, Co-lum-bia! strong and free, Throned in hearts from sea to sea! Thy march tri-umph - ant

freedom's cause, Who fought and bled in freedom's cause, And when the storm of war was gone En-
once were foes! Welcome, friends who once were foes, To all the conquering years have gained,—A
names shall read! All the world their names shall read, Enrolled with his, the Chief that led The
still par-sue! Thy march triumphant still pur-sue With peaceful stride from zone to zone, Till

joy'd the peace your val-or won. Let in-de-pendence be our boast, Ev-er mind-ful
na-tion's rights, a race unchained! Children of the day new-born, Mind-ful of its
hosts, whose blood for us was shed. Pay our sires their children's debt, Love and hon-or,—
Free-dom finds the world her own! Blest in Union's ho-ly ties, Let our grateful

what it cost; Ev-er grate-ful for the prize, Let its al-tar reach the skies.
glorious morn, Let the pledge our Fath-ers signed, Heart to heart for-ev-er bind!
nor for-get On-ly Un-ion's gold-en key Guards the ark of Lib-er-ty!
song a-rise,— Ev-ery voice its trib-ute lend,— All in lov-ing cho-rus blend!

Chorus.

1798. Firm, u-ni-ted, let us be, Ral-ly-ing round our lib-er-ty,
(1-3). While the stars of heaven shall burn, While the o-cean tides re-turn,

As a band of broth-ers join'd, Peace and safe-ty we shall find.
Ev-er may the circ-ling sun Find the Ma-ny still are One!

Written, by request, for Centennial of Constitution of United States at Philadelphia, Sept. 17, 1887.

ELEMENTS OF MUSIC.

1. A Musical Sound is called a **Tone**.

2. Every tone has the three properties of **Length, Pitch, and Power**.

3. There are, therefore, three departments in the Elements of Music:—

    1. **Rhythmics**, treating of the Length of Tones.
    2. **Melod'ics**, treating of the Pitch of Tones.
    3. **Dynam'ics**, treating of the Power of Tones.

The word Rhythmics is derived from the Greek verb "*rheo*," meaning *to flow*, as in the measured movement of poetic lines. Melod'ics is from the Greek "*melod'eo*," to ˏsing harmoniously, or "*melod'ia*," a tune to which lyric poetry is set, a choral song, from "*mel'odos*," musical or melodious. Dynam'ics is from the Greek "*dun'amai*," to be able, or "*dun'amis*," force, energy, power.

Rhythmics comprehends all rhythmic things, or whatever may be derived from the primary fact that tones may be long or short. It includes also the rhythmic structure of phrases, sections and periods. Melodics includes everything that may proceed from the primary distinction of low or high, or from the property of pitch. The word "melody," as commonly used, is of much more limited signification, referring only to a pleasing succession of tones in rhythmic order or to an ordinary tune form. Dynamics embraces not only the mere force of tones, but also their manner or form of delivery.

RHYTHMICS: Length of Tones.

NOTES AND RESTS.

4. **Notes** are characters used to designate two things: By their position on the staff they give the Pitch of the tone, and by their form they indicate its Length.

5. The following are the notes in common use, the relative length of the tones which they represent being indicated by their names.

WHOLE-NOTE. HALF-NOTE. QUARTER. EIGHTH. SIXTEENTH.

A character |♩| called a *Breve*, or *Double-Note*, is sometimes used. It represents a tone twice as long as that represented by a Whole Note.

6. **Rests** are characters used to indicate silence.

7. The following are the Rests in common use; the relative length of the portions of time which they represent, corresponds to that of the notes; it is indicated by their names; the whole rest may also represent a whole *measure* rest without regard to the kind of time:

WHOLE-REST. HALF-REST. QUARTER. EIGHTH. SIXTEENTH.

For brevity and convenience, we shall hereafter speak of the *length of notes*, meaning the length of the *tones represented* by them.

8. A **Dot** placed after a note or a rest increases its length one-half. A dotted whole note is equal to three halves; a dotted half to three quarters. The same is true of Rests. Thus:

9. **Two Dots** placed after a note or a rest increase its length three-fourths, the second dot adding one-half the length of the first. Thus:

10. The **Figure 3** placed above or below three equal notes reduces their length to two of the same kind. Thus, ♩♩♩ equals in length ♩ ♩. Notes written in this manner are called **Triplets**.

11. Two or more notes may represent a single tone by the use of a character called a **Tie**. In vocal music the hooks attached to the notes may be joined for the same purpose, and the notes should be sung to one syllable. The **Slur** is used when the notes differ in pitch, the **Tie** ⌢ when they are of the same pitch.

MEASURES AND PARTS.

12. Music is divided into **Measures and Parts**—into Measures by single bars and into Parts by double bars. The time of each measure is the same as that of every other measure in the part and is determined by the fraction placed at the beginning of each part. If a part is to be repeated, dots, called *Repeating Dots*, precede the double bar.

13. Measures are again divided into certain parts, which may be indicated to the ear by **Counting**, as "one, two," "one two," etc.; or to the eye by motions of the hand, called **Beats**, or *Beating Time*. The length of notes may frequently be estimated, but in complicated movements, it must be indicated as above by some simple method of measurement.

14. A Measure divided into two parts is called *Double Measure*; three parts, *Triple Measure*; four parts, *Quadruple Measure*; six parts, *Sextuple Measure*. Thus:

DOUBLE.   TRIPLE.   QUADRUPLE.   SEXTUPLE MEASURE.

15. Each kind of Measure may have several varieties, depending upon the length of the notes which are expressed by the denominator of the fraction. The following are some of the common varieties:

The pupil should, of course, be taught that a Measure may be filled with other notes than those used in the above examples. Let him fill the measures with notes of different lengths, rests, etc. As will be seen, a piece of music may begin on any part of a measure. When it begins on a fractional part, it ends on a fractional part; and the two parts thus formed equal a complete measure.

16. The **Numerator** of the Fraction at the beginning of the above examples indicates the number of beats into which the measure is divided; the **Denominator** indicates the kind of note which will fill each beat. Thus, ¾ shows that there are three beats in the measure, and that a quarter note will fill each beat.

17. The *limits* or *boundaries* of Measures, as has been said, are marked by light vertical lines, called **Bars**, the end of a Part being marked by a heavy vertical line, or **Double Bar.**

18. The end of a line of poetry in hymnal music is also sometimes indicated by a heavy vertical line, or **Double Bar**, which can have no effect upon the measure.

19. The end of a piece of music is indicated by ‖ a character called a **Close.**

20. Beating Time is designating each part of a Measure by a motion of the hand. In Double Measure, the hand moves *down, up;* Triple Measure, *down, left, up;* Quadruple Measure, *down, left, right, up;* Sextuple Measure, *down, left, left, right, up, up;* or in rapid movement, *down, up.* This may vary according to the taste of the instructor, each having his own method of indicating accent.

21. Counting Time is designating each part of a Measure by a number. In Double Measure, we count *one, two;* Triple Measure, *one, two, three;* Quadruple Measure, *one, two, three, four;* Sextuple Measure, *one, two, three, four, five, six;* or *one, two.* The exercises of beating and counting time are very valuable, and should be practiced frequently. Beating time requires motions of the hand at exactly equal points of time; counting time requires counts at exactly equal points of time. It is common to speak of tones "as so many beats long," or "so many counts long." When the leader tells which way the hand is moving, he is said to be *describing the time.* Select melodies from the book for the purpose of affording variety of practice. Let the class be divided into parts, singing and counting or beating time alternately. Ability to count *inaudibly* should be acquired as soon as possible, for this is essential to success.

22. Accent is a stress given to certain parts of the Measure. In Double Measure, the *first* part is accented; in Triple Measure, the *first* part; in Quadruple Measure, the *first* and *third* parts; in Sextuple Measure, the *first* and *fourth* parts. In measures containing two accents, the *first* is the principal and therefore *louder.* The accents may fall away when followed by a rest, and may be changed when followed by a longer note, this note receiving the accent and being therefore called a Syncopated note. These rules are, however, becoming somewhat obsolete in vocal music, the accented syllables and emphatic words determining the parts to be accented.

23. A Syncopated Note, then, is one that begins on an unaccented part of a measure and continues on an accented part. Thus, in ♩♩♩ the second is a *Syncopated Note*, or a *Syncope*, and should always be accented, that is, expressed forcibly, as if so marked.

24. The length of the beats in each Measure is

indicated by certain Italian words, sometimes modified by other words added thereto, of which the following are the most common:

Adagio—Very slow movement.
Allegretto—Cheerful, not so fast as Allegro.
Allegro—Quick, lively, vivacious.
Andante—Rather slow, gentle, distinct.
Andantino—Somewhat quicker than Andante.
Largo—Very slow and solemn.
Larghetto—Less slow than Largo.
Lento—Slow.
Moderato—Moderate.
Presto—Very quick.
Prestissimo—With greatest rapidity.

MELODICS: Pitch of Tones.

THE STAFF.

25. The **Staff** is used to represent the relative pitch of Tones. It consists of five lines and four spaces, each line and space being called a degree. Thus the staff contains *nine* degrees and the sentence. "Name the degrees on which these notes are found," means "Name the lines and spaces on which these notes are found."

26. Added lines are used to represent tones which are too high or too low to be represented upon the Staff. They may be placed above and below the staff to any extent desired, as they are simply a continuation of the staff, the note immediately above or below the Staff being *in a Space.*

27. The lines and spaces of the Staff are named from the lowest upwards, *1st line, 1st space, 2d line, 2d space,* etc.

28. The added lines and spaces are named from the first line, *space below, 1st line below,* etc.; and from the fifth line, *space above, 1st line above,* etc.

	2d space above.
1st line above.	**1st space above.**
5th line.	
4th line.	**4th space.**
3d line.	**3d space.**
2d line.	**2d space.**
1st line.	**1st space.**
1st line below.	**1st space below.**
	2d space below.

29. Each degree is designated by one of the first seven letters of the alphabet, the position of the letter never changing unless the Clef be changed.

30. Instead of placing a letter on the staff to show the abstract pitch, certain characters are used called **Clefs,** which show how the letters are applied. Thus, the Treble clef marks 𝄞 the position of C on the staff, in the *third* space; and the Bass clef marks the position of C in the *second* space.

31. In four-part songs the Soprano and Alto are written in the **Treble,** and the Tenor and Bass in the **Bass** Clef. There are other clefs used by certain orchestral instruments, as the Alto clef, marking the position of C on the third line (viola), and the Tenor clef, marking the position of C on the fourth line (trombone).

SOPRANO AND ALTO.   TENOR AND BASS.

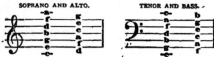

The C on the first line below the Treble Staff, and the C on the first line above the Bass, represent the same tone. It is called *Middle C.* The tones of the

Female voice are an octave higher than those of the Male, hence a Soprano solo sung by a Tenor sounds an octave lower than the notes in which it is written.

32. The different parts are commonly represented in music by two or more staves, united by a **Brace**, and called a **Score.**

33. The **Absolute Pitch** of Tones (the pitch independent of scale relationship), is designated by the letters namiₙg the degrees of the Staff; as, A, B, C, D, E, F, G. The position of these letters is fixed and unchangeable while the other remains unchanged.

34. The difference of pitch between any two tones, as from A to B, from A to E, from C to G, etc., is called an **Interval**. A true knowledge of intervals can only be communicated through the *Ear*. The pupil must listen carefully to tones and compare them constantly. Without this practical acquaintance with the subject, names, definitions and illustrations are of little account.

35. In the *regular succession* of the Natural Tones, there are two kinds of intervals, larger and smaller. The larger intervals are called **Tones** and the smaller **Semi-Tones**. The successive tones of the ꞏₙajor scale, in all the keys, occur in the following order: Between one and two, a *tone;* between two and three, a *tone;* between three and four, a *semi-tone;* between four and five, a *tone;* between

five and six, a *tone;* between six and seven, a *tone;* and between seven and eight, a *semi-tone*. These two half-tones in the octave afford infinite variety in music. Were the eight natural sounds in the octave *equidistant* one from another, there being no semi-tones, the keys would differ only in acuteness and not *in quality*, as now. Choose melodies from the book in the different keys and give the pupils exercise in reading these intervals of tones and semi-tones.

36. Between *any two* tones of the Staff having the interval of a step, another tone may be inserted, dividing the step into two half-steps. Thus, a tone may be inserted between C and D, etc. Some singers of Southern Europe add a certain brilliancy of effect by again dividing the half-step; but ability to do this is not possessed by the people of Centralˀ oꞏ Northern Europe, or of America.

37. The degrees of the Staff represent these inserted tones by the aid of characters called *Sharps* and *Flats*. Thus, a tone inserted between C and D, is named *C sharp*, or *D flat.*

38. A **Sharp**, ♯, placed on a degree, raises the pitch of a tone a half-step; a **Flat**, ♭, placed on it, lowers the pitch of a tone a half-step below that named by the letter.

39. The power of a sharp or a flat may be cancelled by a character called a **Natural**, ♮.

Range of the Human Voice.—The compass of every human voice for singing must fall somewhere within the wide range of notes given herewith. But, of course, no single voice has ever been equal to these thirty-one notes at any one period in life. The boy who sings a high soprano may take nearly all the upper notes, but when grown to manhood his voice "changes," and he has ability to sing only in the three lower octaves. As to the range of notes here found, it requires a phenomenal Bass to reach the lowest (Great Double C), and a Soprano only less remarkable to sing the highest (e″) with confidence and musical effect. If the reader has not learned the compass of his own voice, it will be both interesting and satisfactory to test, with piano or organ, for its highest and lowest notes, as well as for those tones in which it is strong and full, or weak and uncertain. By intelligent practice the compass may be increased and the tones improved.

C D E F G A B C D E F G A B c d e f g a b c' d' e' f' g' a' b' c'' d'' e''

The Staff in the Bass clef extends from **G** to A. Three notes intervene between this and the staff in the Treble, which, as will be seen, may be written in either clef, above the Bass or below the ꞏTreble. Of these, the middle note (**c**) is known as " Middle " C—because midway between the two clefs. The treble clef extends from **e** to f'. All the letters below **G** in the bass and **e** in the treble, occupy places in successive order downwards on the added lines and spaces below the staff; all above A in the bass and f'' in the treble on the added lines above the staff. "Middle C " (c) corresponds to the fourth note on the G string of the violin at ordinary concert pitch, or to Middle C on piano or organ. Great Double C, or Contra C, as it is called, having about thirty-three vibrations to the second, the next higher C doubles that number; and so on, each octave higher doubling the number of vibrations of the octave next below it.

The entire range of the human voice in music—from lowest Bass to highest Soprano—may be reckoned from E♭ below the staff in the bass clef, four octaves, to E♭ above the staff in the treble clef. Vocal sounds lower or higher than this seem to have little power of expression in any sense. Voices are usually considered under three divisions for the male, and four for

the female sex; Bass, Barytone, and Tenor; Contralto, Alto, Mezzo Soprano, and Soprano. The usual range of the Bass is from **F** or **E** below the bass clef, rarely lower, two octaves to **f**; Barytone, from **G**, on first line of bass clef, two octaves, to **g**; Tenor, from C, two octaves, to **c'**; Contralto, the deepest female voice, from F to **c''**, being two and one-half octaves; Alto, two octaves, from F to **f'**; Mezzo Soprano, from A to **a'**; and Soprano from "Middle C" (**c**), two octaves to **c''**, which is also indicated as **c²**. Middle C has about 132 vibrations to the second, and is produced by sound waves from eight to nine feet apart. Waves at half that distance apart, produce a tone one octave higher, half that again the next higher octave, and so on. In large organs, C, an octave below Contra C, with 16½ vibrations per second, is reached, but the effect is imperfect. The piano reaches **a⁴**, with 3,520 vibrations per second, and sometimes **c⁵**, with 4,224 vibrations. The highest note taken in the orchestra is probably **d⁵**, on the piccolo flute, with 4,752 vibrations. The practical range in music is from 40 to 4,000 vibrations per second, embracing seven octaves. The human ear is, however, able to compass eleven octaves, that is to say, it notes vibrations ranging from 16½ up to 38,000 in a single second of time.

40. A Double Sharp, ⅹ, is used on a degree affected by a sharp, to represent a tone a half-step above the one affected by the sharp; its power may be cancelled by a sharp and natural, ♯♮. **A Double Flat,** ♭♭, is used on a degree affected by a flat, to represent a tone a half-step below the one affected by a flat; it may be cancelled by a flat and natural, ♭♮.

41. The **Signature** of a Staff is the part between the clef and the fraction; it is named from the number of sharps or flats which it contains. If there is no signature, the notes correspond with the white keys of piano or organ.

42. A sharp or a flat in the signature applies not only to the degree on which it stands, but also to all others which represent the same pitch.

43. A sharp, a flat, or a natural, placed outside the signature, is called an **Accidental,**—appearing "accidentally" in the measure—and applies only to the degree on which it stands.

44. If not cancelled, as stated above, the signification of a signature extends to the end of the Staff, that of an accidental—whether flat, sharp or natural—extends no farther than the measure in which it appears, except when the last note of a measure is flat or sharp, and the first note of the following measure is the same letter; then, if it is syncopated, the influence of the accidental extends to that note.

THE DIATONIC SCALE.

45. The *Relative Pitch* of tones is indicated by a **Scale**, or Tone Ladder.

46. The **Diatonic Scale,** generally called the *Scale,* consists of a regular succession of intervals from the key-note to the octave, 1st, 2d, 3d, 4th, 5th, 6th, 7th, 8th, or octave, it having been found most agreeable to join to the seven sounds of one group the first of the next higher, making eight in all. The key-note is the first note in the Scale. This Scale is also called the *Major Scale,* to distinguish it from another scale, having its semitones in different order, and called the *Minor Scale.* In the compass of the scale there are five whole tones or degrees and two semi-tones or half-degrees. Commencing on C, that is making C *one* of the scale, these semi-tones are found between the **3d and 4th** and **7th and 8th** degrees. Here we find between the 1st and 3d degrees two whole tones, making a "major" or *greater* third. All music written on the scale when so constructed is said to be in the *major* keys; and this scale can only be formed from the notes in their natural order by commencing on C. There is, however, another series of notes, equally well-fitted for expressing musical ideas, which is formed by commencing on A instead of C, and which, in the natural order of tones, can begin only on A. In this scale the semi-tones always fall between **2 and 3** and **5 and 6.** Here between the 1st and 3d degrees there are not two whole tones, but only a tone and a half, making the "minor" or *lower* third. All music written on the scale when so constructed is said to be in the *minor* keys, which are often most expressive.

47. The tones are named by Numbers and also by Syllables, the latter to afford greater variety of vowel sounds for practice, as well as to form an easy association of degree name and relative pitch of tone—the same syllable being always used in singing the same tone. *Do* is always *one,* *Re* always *two,* and so on. The numbers and syllables are as follows:

By numbers: 1, 2, 3, 4, 5, 6, 7, 8.
By syllables: Do, Re, Mi, Fa, Sol, La, Si, Do.
(Pronounced Doe, Ray, Mee, Fah, Sole, Lah, See, Doe.)

The names of the notes, *Do, Re, Mi,* etc., vibrate throughout the scale, their places depending wholly upon the location of the Key-note. which is always called *Do,* and numbered *one.*

48. There are, as has already been said, two kinds of intervals in the Diatonic scale : *Steps* and *Half-steps,* the intervals between 3 and 4, and 7 and 8, being half-steps, while all the others are steps. The half-steps, or semi-tones, should always be sung "sharp," the voice being slightly pressed or driven above, rather than permitted to fall below the tone indicated by the note upon the staff.

49. In writing the Scale, any tone may be taken as *one,* or *Do;* when this is determined, the others must follow in regular order In the examples below, *one* or *Do* is placed on C, as the intervals of the staff beginning with C, correspond with those of the scale All the steps in the key of C are therefore natural steps. As shown in the following examples, the scale is *extended* upwards, by regarding *eight,* or the octave above one, as *one* of an upper scale, and downwards by regarding *one* as *eight* of a lower scale.

50. The Scale, as written upon the staff, in the key of C, in both clefs, is as follows :—

1, 2, 3, 4, 5, 6, 7, 8 or 1, 2, 3.
Do, re, mi, fa, sol, la, si, do, re, mi.

1, 2, 3, 4, 5, 6, 7, 8 or 1, 5, 3, 1 or 8.
Do, re, mi, fa, sol, la, si, do, sol, mi, do.

THE TONE LADDER.

51 The fact that these Eight Degrees include every possible distance except the *none* and *decime* (ninth and tenth), at which musical tones can be placed from each other, was discovered some centuries ago in Italy. When sung consecutively the thought of ascending or descending a ladder was naturally suggested, and the term "Scale" (Italian word *Scala,* meaning "ladder.") was adopted. The propriety of the name has caused it to be retained by musicians. The order of tones being a "ladder," the distances between them are naturally called *steps.* The tones of the Scale can only be learned by imitation.

The Scale or Tone Ladder may be drawn or neatly painted on the blackboard for permanent use in the form here shown, six or eight inches wide and eighteen high, which will afford spaces three inches in height to represent tone intervals, and one and a-half inch spaces for the semi-tones. Let the scale names and numbers be given as here. The exercises should be written by the side of the scale in **bold figures.** Commas may be used after the figures to indicate short notes, and the dash for notes prolonged. With the pointer, the teacher can direct the work of the class more readily, singing the exercises backwards as well as forwards, by numbers, by syllables, by letters, and by simple vowel sounds.

The following exercises which may be placed upon the board, as well as sung from the page, will afford much variety of useful practice. They may be greatly varied, and supplemented by others to almost any extent. But it is advised that, at first, they be taken in the order here presented, *in short lessons,* so that nothing is passed that is not well learned. Let this drill exercise be pleasantly varied by rote singing—attractive songs and familiar hymns being preferred—

all of which may afterwards be written in the numerals. These figures can be so written as to represent *three* octaves, by placing a dash *above* those that fall below the staff, *below* those that are above the staff, and before and after those *upon* the staff—the dash all the while representing the Staff.

Staff	Syllable	
(8/7	Do / Si	1, 2- 2, 1-
6	La	1, 2, 3- 3, 2, 1-
5	Sol	1, 2, 3, 4- 4, 3, 2, 1-
(4/3	Fa / Mi	1, 2, 3, 4, 5- 5, 4, 3, 2, 1- ·
2	Re	1, 2, 3, 4, 5, 6- 6, 5, 4, 3, 2, 1-
1	Do	1 2 3 4 5 6 7 8 - 8 7 6 5 4 3 2 1-

I.

```
1234   1423   2314   3124   3412   4213
1243   1432   2341   3142   3421   4231
1324   2134   2413   3214   4123   4312
1342   2143   2431   3241   4132   4321
```

II.

```
5678   6578   7568   8567   135
5687   6587   7586   8576   153
5768   6758   7658   8657   315
5786   6785   7685   8675   351
5867   6857   7856   8756   513
5876   6875   7865   8765   531
```

III.

```
1858   1835   3518   5138   5813   8315
1385   1853   3581   5183   5831   8351
1538   3158   3815   5318   8135   8513
1583   3185   3851   5381   8153   8531
```

IV.

```
1468   1846   4618   6148   6814   8416
1486   1864   4681   6184   6841   8461
1648   4168   4816   6418   8146   8614
1684   4186   4861   6481   8164   8641
```

V.

1, 2, 1, 3, 1, 4, 1, 5, 1, 6, 1, 7, 1, 8—
8, 1, 7, 1, 6, 1, 5, 1, 4, 1, 3, 1, 2, 1—
1, 3, 2, 4, 3, 5, 4, 6, 5, 7, 8—
8, 6, 7, 5, 6, 4, 5, 3, 4, 2, 3, 1—

VI.

1, 3, 5, 8, 7, 6, 5—   5, 5, 6, 5, 5, 4, 3—
3, 2, 1, 3, 5, 8, 5—   5, 6, 5, 4, 3, 2, 1—
1, 3, 1, 3, 5, 8, 5—   5, 8, 7, 6, 5, 8, 5—
5, 8, 5, 6, 5, 8, 5—   5, 8, 5, 4, 3, 2, 1—

VII.

8,2,1,3,5,8,5—   1,3,5,8,7,6,5—   1,1,3,3,4,2,1
5,8,5,5,4,3,2—   5,5,6,5,4,3,2—   1,3,5,8,5,4,3
2,3,4,2,3,4,5—   2,3,4,2,3,4,5—   4,3,2,4,3,4,5
5,8,1,4,3,2,1—   5,8,5,1,4,3,2,1—   6,6,5,4,3,2,1

VIII.

2,3,3,2,3,4,5—   1,1,8,8,7,6,5—   8,7,6,5,6,7,8
6,6,6,5,4,3,2—   5,8,1,3,5,4,2—   8,1,2,3,4,3,2
3,3,3,2,3,4,5—   2,5,1,5,6,7,8—   4,2,8,1,4,2,3
·6,7,8,1,3,2,1—   8,1,5,4,3,2,1—   8,8,8,1,5,5,1

MELODIES IN FIGURES.

3,1,6,5,4,3,2— | 1,1,5,5,6,6,5— | 1,3,5,8,6,8,5
3,1,5,5,5,4,5— | 4,4,3,3,2,2,1— | 5,8,6,5,4,3,2
3,2,1,6,5,4,3— | :5,5,4,4,3,8,2: | 4,3,6,5,6,7,8
3,3,5,3,3,2,1— | 1,1,5,6,6,6,5— | 8,6,5,1,8,2,1
  | 4,4,3,1,2,3,1— |

It is of prime importance that there should be a feeling of confidence and prompt readiness—"sure touch"—in passing from one degree of the Scale to another. This can be acquired most readily, as ex-

perience has shown, by frequent exercises upon the numerals, alternating with the names of notes, etc., and hence much of this practice is here condensed into little space. The Scale should be regarded as the *unit* in thinking sounds, and should be taught *as a whole.* The practice of the sounds as relative mental objects, should then form a part of each lesson until these relative sounds are familiar in every ordinary relation to each other.

Simple melodies and familiar tunes may be written on the blackboard in *numerals,* followed by commas or dashes, as the notes are short or long. Pupils may thus be familiarized with the third, fourth, fifth or other intervals, by associating them with like intervals in tunes with which they are perfectly familiar. This will be found a hint of much practical value. No other country gives so much attention to music as Germany, and this, with German teachers, is a favorite method of fixing in the mind certain scale intervals.

Too little attention is directed to developing tone perception in the minds of pupils. The teacher who sings should frequently sound the key-note, then sing *ah* or *la* to any tone or tones in the scale, and have the pupils name the number and syllable, and (when the key is announced), the letter. The same training can be given by sounding the key-note, and having a part of the class sing the tones indicated by the pointer, while the rest of the class, with their backs turned, name the tones that have been sung. To know the name of the note is a very different matter from being able to *sense the tone,* and much less important. This practical knowledge of tones is essential. The teacher should cultivate a soft, distinct, and pleasing quality of tone. A good style of singing can only be acquired by imitation, and that of the teacher should be worthy to be imitated. In these exercises the numerals, or names of the sounds, may be sung first; then the syllables, Do, Re, Mi, etc.; then the letters or the pitch of the sounds, and finally the syllable *ah,* or *la,* for each note. Be careful that every tone is sung with precision. Use D as *one,* throughout the above exercises, afterwards the scale of E♭, E, and C. Be sure that the *pitch* is correct. Test frequently for correct pitch, with tuning fork, pitch-pipe, piano, or organ. The "scale" is sung by the *Syllables;* the names of the successive sound intervals by the *Numerals;* the pitch of the sounds (the key being known) by the *Letters*—a distinction which will be of interest to intelligent pupils. This should be so well known to the class that there can be no mistake as to what is meant when the teacher uses the terms, "*Scale,*" "*Name,*" "*Pitch,*" as words of command during the singing exercise.

Teachers who are not familiar with the scale can, of themselves, by the aid of the organ or piano, readily master the succession of tones found in these exercises. The difficulty is not great, and the pleasure and profit to teacher and school will be positive and lasting—each step forward giving courage for another.

Observe the following directions for singing: 1. Let the body be erect, avoiding stiffness or restraint. 2. Take breath easily and naturally, without raising the shoulders. 3. Let the mouth be well opened, taking care to avoid rigidity of the muscles of the throat and neck. 4. Aim at *purity* of tone, rather than mere power. 5. Practice frequently, singing the vowel *a* (ah), endeavoring to produce the sound in the front part of the mouth. It is recommended to preface the *a* (ah) with the vowels *oo,* *o,* singing them rapidly and uniting them with the *a,* and dwelling upon the *a ;* thus, *oo, o, a.* This prevents the sound from being made too far back in the mouth. 6. Articulate distinctly, but without apparent effort. 7. In singing loud passages, be very careful to avoid shouting.

THE KEY-NOTE.

52. The **Key-note** is *One* of the Scale, and is called the **Tonic.** A minor third above the tonic characterizes the Minor scale; a major third, the Major.

53. The *Fifth* of the Scale is the **Dominant.**

54. The *Fourth*, the **Sub-Dominant.**

55. The **Key** of a piece of music is the *fundamental tone*, or *one* of the Scale in which it is written, and it is indicated by the signature. (See Art. 41.) It is always *Do*, and is in music "what the foundation is to a house, home to the traveler, or a port to the sailor, from which he takes his departure and to which after his voyage he hopes to return"—the melody always ending with the *Key-note.* The peculiar characteristic of this note Do, in the Major keys, is that above it, successively, are always first two whole tones, then a semi-tone, followed by three whole tones and a semi-tone; then *Do* again, and order of intervals as before. The key of C has no signature. The signatures of the keys that follow are as here shown:

G, one sharp — F♯.
D, two sharps— F♯, C♯.
A, three sharps— F♯, C♯, G♯.
E, four sharps— F♯, C♯, G♯, D♯.
B, five sharps— F♯, C♯, G♯, D♯, A♯.
F♯, six sharps— F♯, C♯, G♯, D♯, A♯, E♯.

F, one flat— B♭.
B♭, two flats— B♭, E♭.
E♭, three flats— B♭, E♭, A♭.
A♭, four flats— B♭, E♭, A♭, D♭.
D♭, five flats— B♭, E♭, A♭, D♭, G♭.
G♭, six flats— B♭, E♭, A♭, D♭, G♭, C♭.

In singing a tune, the first thing to be done is tc find the Key-note as a starting point. The order of the keys in the sharps may very easily be remembered from the initial letters in the sentence, "Good Deeds Are Ever-Blooming Flowers," the last key being F♯ instead of F. The order of the keys in flats is had by reading the sentence backwards, the first key being F, and each of the others adding the flat (♭), as B♭, E♭, A♭, D♭, and G♭. In Minor tunes, the key-note is always a minor third, (three semi-tones), below the place named for *Do* in the above Major keys. That is, the key-note is major C or minor A; G major or E minor; D major or B minor, etc.

"Next letter above last Sharp," is also a simple rule for getting the Key in sharps. One sharp being on F, the next letter above is G, the *key-note;* two sharps, last sharp C, next letter above is D, the *key-note;* and so on. In the flat keys, count four notes *back*, including the note made flat; as B♭, back four notes to F, the *key-note*, and so on.

INTERVALS.

56. An **Interval** is the difference of pitch between any two tones in the scale.

Unisons are of the same pitch. A *Major Second* consists of a step; a *Minor Second* of a half-step. A *Major Third* consists of two steps, a *Minor Third* of a step and a half-step. A *Perfect Fourth* consists of two steps and a half-step; an *Augmented Fourth* of three steps. A *Perfect Fifth* consists of three steps and a half-step; a *Diminished Fifth* of two steps and two half-steps. A *Perfect Sixth* consists of four steps and a half-step; a *Diminished Sixth* of three steps and two half-steps. A *Major Seventh* consists of five steps and a half-step; a *Minor Seventh* of four steps and two half-steps. A *Perfect Octave* consists of five steps and two half-steps. These last named intervals, as they are all found in the Diatonic Scale. Other intervals, called *Chromatic Intervals*, may be formed by the use of sharps and flats. When the lower note of the two representing an interval is placed an octave higher, or the upper one an octave lower, the interval is

said to be *Inverted.* The degrees of an interval are counted upwards, unless the opposite is stated; and the degrees occupied by the notes, as well as the ones between them, are counted.

CHROMATIC SCALE.

57. The **Chromatic Scale** is a regular succession of semi-tones.

58. The tones of the Chromatic Scale are named from the tones of the Diatonic Scale, or the letters of the staff; the intermediate ones taking their names from one or the other of the tones between which they occur, with the addition of the word "sharp" or "flat." Thus, the tone inserted between C and D, when named with respect to Absolute Pitch, is called *C Sharp* or *D Flat;* and with respect to Relative Pitch is called *Sharp One*, or *Flat Two.* This Scale is here given, both Ascending and Descending:

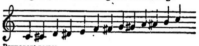

Permanent names,
C, C♯, D, D♯, E, F, F♯, G, G♯, A, A♯, B, C, etc.
Syllable Names,
Do, Di, Re, Ri, Mi, Fa, Fi, Sol, Si, La, Le, Si, Do.
Pronounced,
Do, Dee, Ray, Ree, Mee, Fah, Fee, Sol, See, La, Lay, See, Do.
Numeral names,
1, ♯1, 2, ♯2, 3, 4, ♯4, 5, ♯5, 6, ♯6, 7, 8, etc.

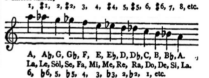

A, A♭, G, G♭, F, E, E♭, D, D♭, C, B, B♭, A.
La, Le, Sol, Se, Fa, Mi, Me, Re, Ra, Do, De, Si, La.
6, ♭6, 5, ♭5, 4, 3, ♭3, 2, ♭2, 1, etc.

THE MINOR SCALE.

59. The **Minor Scale** is a Diatonic Scale, and is named from its third, which is a minor third; the third of the *Major Scale* being a major third. The minor third is a semi-tone lower than a major third.

60. The Minor Scale has various forms. In the **Natural Form** the half-steps occur between two and three, and five and six. Hence, the Natural Minor Scale is formed from the Major Scale, by taking the last two notes above and placing them below.

NATURAL MINOR SCALE.

1, 2, 3, 4, 5, 6, 7, 8.
La, Si, Do, Re, Mi, Fa, Sol, La.

61. The **Harmonic Form** differs from the *Natural* form by the introduction of sharp-seven.

HARMONIC MINOR SCALE.

1, 2, 3, 4, 5, 6, 7, 8.
La, Si, Do, Re, Mi, Fa, Si, La.

62. The **Melodic Form** in ascending has sharp-six and sharp-seven, while it usually descends by the *Natural* form.

63. The Minor Scale, based upon six of the Major Scale, is called its *relative minor;* and the Major Scale, based upon three of the Minor Scale, is called its *relative major.* The signature of a minor piece of music is the same as its relative major, the additional sharps or flats being introduced before the proper notes in the piece. Thus, a minor piece in the key of E has the signature of G major, that is F♯; and D♭ is used instead of D.

64. Transposition is changing from one key to another, that is, moving *Do*, or *one*—the foot of the Tone Ladder—to a higher or lower place on the Staff.

65. The *Transposition of the Scale* is changing it from one. pitch to another—the entire scale being transposed—the intervals between the tones, however, remaining the same. In order to keep the intervals of steps and half-steps in the same order as in the key of C—represented by the white keys of Organ or Piano—it is necessary to use flats or sharps—represented on the key-board by the black keys—at each transposition, according as one or another degree of the staff is made *one* of the Scale.

66. All scales are, in a general sense, alike natural. Whether the key is C, with neither flats or sharps, or E with its four sharps, the singer needs to have no consciousness of the fact. He simply sings the scale, with no change of thought or impression—its intervals being the same in all the keys. It is upon this fact that the Tonic Sol-Fa system is based.

METHOD OF TRANSPOSITION.

67. The Scale may be transposed from one pitch to any other. It is found to be simplest to transpose by *fifths* and *fourths;* that is, to change the key-note so that *five* or *four* of the old scale will become *one* of the new scale.

68. If *one* of the scale is placed on C, the intervals between the tones named by the letters correspond to those of the scale, as will be seen by the following: Intervals marked by a ⌒ are half-steps.

C, D, E, F, G, A, B, C.

1, 2, 3, 4, 5, 6, 7, 8.

The key of C therefore requires no sharps or flats, and is called the Natural key.

69. If, however, any other letter be taken as *one* of the scale, it will be seen that the intervals do not correspond. For example, beginning with G, which is the *fifth* of the key of C:

G, A, B, C, D, E, F, G.

1, 2, 3, 4, 5, 6, 7, 8.

From this it will be seen that if one is placed on G, F, the *fourth* of the key of C is a half-step too low, and hence the intermediate tone between F and G, or F♯, must be taken, thus:

G, A, B, C, D, E, F♯, G.

1, 2, 3, 4, 5, 6, 7, 8.

The signature of the key of G is therefore F♯.

70. Beginning with D, the *fifth* of the key of G, and substituting F♯ for F:

D, E, F♯, G, A, B, C, D.

1, 2, 3, 4, 5, 6, 7, 8.

It will be observed that C, the *fourth* of the key of G, is a half-step too low, and hence the tone a half-step higher, or C♯ must be used, thus:

D, E, F♯, G, A, B, C♯, D.

1, 2, 3, 4, 5, 6, 7, 8.

The signature of key of D is therefore F♯ and C♯.

71. From the above explanations, we may derive the following *Rule for Transposition by Fifths:*

To transpose by *Fifths*, make the fifth of the old scale the key-note of the next scale, and use *sharp-four* in place of four of the old scale. This rule is briefly stated thus: *Sharp-four* transposes a fifth.

72. Again: placing one on F, which is the *fourth* of the key of C:

F, G, A, B, C, D, E, F.

1, 2, 3, 4, 5, 6, 7, 8.

It will be found that B, the *seventh* of the key of C, is a half-step too high, and hence the intermediate tone between B and A, or B♭, must be taken, thus:

F, G, A, B♭, C, D, E, F.

1, 2, 3, 4, 5, 6, 7, 8.

The signature of the key of F is therefore B♭.

73. Beginning with B♭, the *fourth* of key of F,

B♭, C, D, E, F, G, A, B♭.

1, 2, 3, 4, 5, 6, 7, 8.

It will be seen that E, the *seventh* of the key of F, is a half-step too high, and hence the tone a half-step lower, or E♭ must be used, thus:

B♭, C, D, E♭, F, G, A, B♭.

1, 2, 3, 4, 5, 6, 7, 8.

The signature of key of B♭ is therefore B♭ and E♭.

74. By an examination of the above explanations we may derive the following *Rule for Transposition by Fourths:* Make the fourth of the old scale the key-note of the new scale, and use *flat-seven* in place of seven of the old scale. This rule. is briefly stated thus: *Flat-seven* transposes a fourth.

75. In transposing by fifths, those keys are reached whose signatures are one or more sharps; in transposing by fourths, those keys are reached whose signatures are one or more flats.

MELODY. PASSING TONES, Etc.

76. A **Melody** is a single succession of tones.

77. Tones not essentially belonging to a melody, called **Passing Tones**, are often introduced. They are usually represented by small notes.

78. A passing tone that precedes an essential tone on an accented part of a measure is called an **Appoggiatura**; one that follows an essential tone on an unaccented part of a measure, an **After-Tone**.

79. A rapid alternation of a tone with the one next above it is called a **Trill** or **Shake**. It is indicated by *tr.*

80. A tone sung in rapid succession with the tones next above and below it is called a **Turn**. It is indicated by ∾. The Trill and the Turn do not belong to chorus singing.

81. Dots placed across a staff before a bar are called a **Repeat**, and indicate that the preceding passage is to be repeated. The influence of a Repeat extends back to dots placed after a bar; or, if these are omitted, to the beginning.

82. Da Capo, or **D. C.**, indicates a return to the beginning. **Dal Segno**, or **D. S.**, indicates a return to a character called a **Sign**, 𝄋.

83. Fine indicates the place to end after a D. C. or a D. S.

84. The **Hold** or **Pause**, ⌒, signifies that the sound should be prolonged, and the beating suspended until the singer is ready to proceed.

85. If two or more tones of a melody are to be sung to one syllable, the notes representing them are generally connected by a character called a **Slur.** The Slur is also used to indicate a Legato movement.

86. If a syllable is to be sung to a tone represented by two or more notes, these notes are usually connected by a **Tie.** (See Art. 11.)

DYNAMICS: Power of Tones.

87. The power of tones may be indicated by the following Italian words, marks, or abbreviations:

Mezzo, ... m, . . . medium.
Piano, ... p, . . . soft.
Forte, ... f, . . . loud.
Pianissimo, . . pp, . . . very soft.
Fortissimo, . . ff, . . . very loud.
Mezzo Piano. . mp, . . moderately soft.
Mezzo Forte, . mf, . . moderately loud.
Crescendo, . . cres., or ⟨, . gradual increase.
Diminuendo, . dim., or ⟩, . gradual decrease.
Swell, . . ⟨⟩, . increase and decrease.
Sforzando, . ⟨ or sfz, . . an explosive tone, with sudden decrease.

88. The following words and characters are also sometimes used to indicate proper delivery of tones: *Legato,* ⌒, tones smooth and connected. *Staccato,* ❜ ❜ ❜ tones very short and disconnected. *Semi-Staccato,* or *Marcato,* • • • tones moderately short and disconnected.

89. Vocal Utterance, or the Emission of tone, should be instantaneous, decided, and firm; and the tone should be free, open, round, full, pure, and as resonant as possible.

90. A necessary quality of good singing is the proper articulation and pronunciation of the words. Avoid singing a word without properly speaking it; or speaking a word without properly singing it. Do not sing with a too exact, machine-like correctness. Be careful and accurate, but put expression, soul, and intelligent personality into your work.

91. Breath should be taken at such places as will not mar the sense; at pauses and after emphatic words.

MARKS OF EXPRESSION.

92. The following list includes ordinary marks of expression, with certain other terms used in music: *Accelerando,* or *accel.,* accelerate the time, gradually faster and faster; *ad libitum,* or *ad lib.,* at pleasure; *animato,* or *con anima,* animated, with animated expression; *affetuoso,* tender, affecting; *agitato,* with agitation, anxiously; *amoroso* or *con amore,* affectionately, tenderly; *a tempo,* in time; *Bon marcato,* in pointed, well-marked manner; *bis,* twice; *brilliante,* gay, brilliant, sparkling; *brio* or *con brio,* with brilliancy and spirit; *Cantata,* a composition of several movements, comprising airs, recitations and choruses; *coda,* a close, or additional ending of a composition; *con affeto,* with expression; *con dolore,* mournfully, with grief and pathos; *con energia,* with energy; *con espressione,* with expression; *con fuoco,* with ardor, fire; *con grazia,* with grace and elegance; *con moto,* with agitation, emotion; *con spirito,* with spirit, animation; *Declamando, declamato,* in declamatory style; *dolce,* soft, tender, sweet; *doloroso,* tender and pathetic; *Energico,* with energy; *expressivo,* with expression; *Forzando,* with sudden increase of power; *Grave.,* with slow and solemn expression; *Lentando,* gradually slower; *loco,* passage to be played exactly as written in regard to the pitch—it usually occurs after the sign *8va* • • • which means

that the note or passage thus marked has been raised or lowered an octave; *Maestoso,* with dignified, majestic expression; *mesto* or *mestoso,* pensive, sad, mournful; *mezzo,* in medium degree, as *mezzo forte,* rather loud, *mezzo piano,* rather soft; *mezzo voce,* with moderation as to tone; *molto,* much or very, as *molto voce,* with a full voice; *Non,* not; *non troppo,* not too much; *Piu,* more; *piu mosso,* with more motion, faster; *poco,* somewhat, rather, as *poco piano,* somewhat soft; *poco presto,* rather quick; *Rallentando,* (*rallen* or *rall.*) gradually slower and softer; *recitando,* a speaking manner of performance; *recitative,* musical declamation; *rinforzando,* suddenly increasing in power; *ritardando,* (*ritard* or *rit.*) a retarding of the movement; *Sostenuto,* sustained; *sotto,* under, below, as *sotto voce,* with subdued voice; *spirito* or *con spirito,* with spirit, animation; *spiritoso,* with great spirit; *Tutti,* the whole, full chorus; *Vigoroso,* bold, energetic; *veloce,* with rapidity; *vivace,* quick and cheerful; *vivo,* lively, animated; *voici subito,* turn the page quickly.

CHORDS AND HARMONY.

93. A **Chord** is a pleasing combination of tones sounded together.

94. Harmony is a succession of chords, according to the rules of progression and modulation.

95. The **Common Chord** is formed by combining any tone with its third and fifth. If the third of the chord is a Major third, the chord is a *Major chord;* if Minor, it is a *Minor chord.*

96. The chord founded upon the Key-note, or Tonic, is called the *chord of the Tonic;* the chord founded upon the Dominant is called the *chord of the Dominant;* and the chord founded upon the Sub-Dominant is called the *chord of the Sub-Dominant.*

97. The **Chord of the Seventh** is the common chord with the minor-seventh added. This chord is generally founded upon the Dominant. If founded on G, the Dominant of C, it is composed of the tones G, B, D, F.

98. Either the fifth or the octave of a chord may be omitted, but the third must always be present, except in the dominant seventh chord.

99. The different forms of a chord can be made by placing either the key-note, or third, or fifth, in the bass, the first being the first position, the second the second position, and the third the third position of the chord. The positions of the chord of C are:

1st Position.   2d Position.   3d Position.

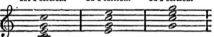

100. The positions of the chord of the dominant seventh are as follows:

1st Position. 2d Position. 3d Position. 4th Position.

The above positions are in the key of C. It will be found to be of advantage for the teacher to explain them in all the keys, and to require pupils to write them, giving the Tonic, Dominant, Sub-Dominant, and Chord of the Seventh, in the different keys. A correct knowledge of the laws of Harmony is essential to the arrangement of music for voices or instruments. As it is not possible to treat this subject at any length in these pages, the student is referred to more extended works for its discussion, and to individual or class training by a competent instructor.

RESPONSIVE SCRIPTURAL READINGS.

NUMBER I.

Leader. O Lord God of Israel, which dwellest between the cherubim, Thou art the God, even Thou alone of all the kingdoms of the earth ; Thou hast made Heaven and earth.

Response. Thou art worthy, O Lord, to receive glory and honor and power : for Thou hast created all things, and for Thy pleasure they are and were created.

L. Seek Him that maketh the seven stars and Orion, and turneth the shadow of death into the morning, and maketh the day dark with night : that calleth for the waters of the sea, and poureth them out upon the face of the earth : the Lord is His name.

R. Thou, even Thou, art Lord alone; Thou hast made Heaven, the Heaven of Heavens with all their host, the earth and all things that are therein, the sea and all that is therein, and thou preservest them all ; and the host of Heaven worshipeth Thee.

Bless the Lord, all His works, in all places of His dominion. Bless the Lord, O my soul.

It is He that has made us, and not we ourselves ; we are His people, and the sheep of His pasture.

Let us now fear the Lord our God ; that giveth rain, both the former and the latter, in his season ; He reserveth unto us the appointed works of the harvest.

The Lord said in His heart, . . . while the earth remaineth, seed-time and harvest, cold and heat, summer and winter, day and night, shall not cease.

He sendeth forth His commandment upon the earth ; His word runneth very swiftly.

He giveth snow like wool ; He scattereth the hoar-frost like ashes.

He casteth forth His ice like morsels ; who can stand before His cold?

He maketh peace in thy borders; and filleth thee with the finest of the wheat.

He causeth the grass to grow for the cattle, and herb for the service of man, that he may bring forth food out of the earth.

That our garners may be full, affording all manner of store.

O give thanks unto the God of gods : for His mercy endureth forever.

O give thanks unto the Lord of lords : for His mercy endureth forever.

To Him who alone doeth great wonders :
For His mercy endureth forever.
To Him that by wisdom made the heavens :
For His mercy endureth forever.
To Him that stretched out the earth above the waters :
For His mercy endureth forever.
To Him that made great lights :
For His mercy endureth forever.
The sun to rule by day :
For His mercy endureth forever.
The moon and stars to rule by night :

For His mercy endureth forever.
Who remembered us in our low estate :
For His mercy endureth forever.
And hath redeemed us from our enemies :
For His mercy endureth forever.
Who giveth food to all flesh :
For His mercy endureth forever.
O give thanks unto the God of Heaven : for His mercy endureth forever.

What shall I render unto the Lord for all His benefits toward me ?

I will take up the cup of salvation, and call upon the name of the Lord.

Lord God, our Father, who art in Heaven.

Hallowed be Thy name ; Thy kingdom come ; Thy will be done on earth as it is in Heaven ; give us this day our daily bread ; and forgive us our trespasses, as we forgive them that trespass against us ; and lead us not into temptation ; but deliver us from evil ; for Thine is the kingdom, and the power, and the glory, forever and ever. Amen.

To do good and to communicate forget not : for with such sacrifices God is well pleased.

Be not weary in well-doing.

Open thine hand wide unto thy brother, to thy poor, and to thy needy, in thy land.

As we have opportunity therefore, let us do good unto all men.

And above all these things, put on charity, which is the bond of perfectness.

So we Thy people, and the sheep of Thy pasture, will give Thee thanks forever.

All Thy works shall praise Thee, O Lord ; and Thy saints shall bless Thee.

Thy saints shall bless Thee forever.

NUMBER II.

Leader. Blessed are the undefiled in the way, who walk in the law of the Lord. Blessed are they that keep His testimonies, and that seek Him with the whole heart.

Response. Oh that my ways were directed to keep Thy statutes ! Then shall I not be ashamed when I have respect unto Thy commandments.

L. My son, forget not my law, but let thine heart keep my commandments ; for length of days, long life and peace shall they add to thee.

R. Order my steps in Thy word ; and let not any iniquity have dominion over me. Make Thy face to shine upon me, and teach me Thy statutes.

The statutes of the Lord are right, rejoicing the heart. The commandment of the Lord is pure, enlightening the eyes. The fear of the Lord is clean, enduring for ever. The judgments of the Lord are true, and righteous altogether.

More to be desired are they than gold, yea, than much fine gold ; sweeter also than honey and the honey-comb.

Moreover by them is Thy servant warned : And in keeping of them there is great reward.

Hold Thou me up, and I shall be safe: And I will have respect unto Thy statutes continually.

Hear, O Israel, the statutes and judgments which I speak in your ears this day, that ye may learn them, and keep, and do them.

Thou shalt have none other gods before Me.

Who is the blessed and only Potentate, the King of kings and Lord of lords.

Thou shalt not make to thyself any graven image, nor the likeness of anything that is in Heaven above, or in the earth beneath, or in the water under the earth. Thou shalt not bow down to them, nor worship them; for I the Lord thy God am a jealous God, visiting the sins of the fathers upon the children, unto the third and fourth generation of them that hate me; and showing mercy unto thousands of them that love me, and keep my commandments.

God is a Spirit: and they that worship Him must worship Him in spirit and in truth.

Thou shalt not take the name of the Lord thy God in vain; for the Lord will not hold him guiltless that taketh His name in vain.

Swear not at all, but let your communication be, Yea, yea; Nay, nay; for whatsoever is more than these cometh of evil.

Remember the Sabbath day to keep it holy. Six days shalt thou labor and do all thy work; but the seventh day is the Sabbath of the Lord thy God: in it thou shalt not do any work; thou, nor thy son, nor thy daughter, thy man-servant, nor thy maid-servant, nor thy cattle, nor the stranger that is within thy gates. For in six days the Lord made Heaven and earth, the sea, and all that in them is, and rested the seventh day; wherefore the Lord blessed the Sabbath day and hallowed it.

It is lawful to do well on the Sabbath day.

Honor thy father and thy mother, that thy days may be long in the land which the Lord thy God giveth thee.

Children, obey your parents in the Lord: for this is right.

Thou shalt not kill.

Love your enemies, bless them that curse you, do good to them that hate you, and pray for them which despitefully use you and persecute you.

Thou shalt not commit adultery.

Know ye not that your body is the temple of the Holy Ghost which is in you . . . if any man defile the temple of God, him will God destroy.

Thou shalt not steal.

Provide things honest in the sight of all men.

Thou shalt not bear false witness against thy neighbor.

Wherefore, putting away lying, speak every man truth with his neighbor; for we are members one of another.

Thou shalt not covet thy neighbor's house, thou shalt not covet thy neighbor's wife, nor his man-servant, nor his maid-servant, nor his ox, nor his ass, nor anything that is thy neighbor's.

Which is the great commandment in the law?

Thou shalt love the Lord thy God with all thy heart, and with all thy soul, and with all thy mind. This is the first and great commandment. And the second is like unto it, Thou shalt love thy neighbor as thyself.

On these two commandments hang all the law and the prophets.

For all the law is fulfilled in one word, even in this, Thou shalt love thy neighbor as thyself.

If a man say, I love God, and hateth his brother, he is a liar: for he that loveth not his brother whom he hath seen, how can he love God whom he hath not seen?

No man hath seen God at any time. If we love one another, God dwelleth in us, and His love is perfected in us.

But whoso hath this world's goods, and seeth his brother have need, and shutteth up his bowels of compassion from him, how dwelleth the love of God in him?

NUMBER III.

TEMPERANCE READING.

Leader. Know ye not that ye are the temple of God?

Response. If any man defile the temple of God, him shall God destroy.

L. For the temple of God is holy, which temple ye are.

R. Ye are not your own; for ye are bought with a price.

Therefore glorify God in your body and in your spirit, which are God's.

Add to your faith virtue; and to virtue knowledge; and to knowledge temperance;

And to temperance patience; and to patience godliness.

Wine is a mocker, strong drink is raging;

And whosoever is deceived thereby is not wise.

Look not thou upon the wine when it is red; when it giveth its color in the cup; when it moveth itself aright.

At the last it biteth like a serpent, and stingeth like an adder.

Be not drunken with wine, wherein is excess; but be filled with the Spirit.

He that loveth pleasure shall be poor; he that loveth wine and oil shall not be rich.

Be not among wine-bibbers; among riotous eaters of flesh.

For the drunkard and the glutton shall come to poverty.

Who hath woe? who hath sorrow?

They that tarry long at the wine; they that go to seek mixed wine.

Who hath contentions? who hath babblings?

They that tarry long at the wine; they that go to seek mixed wine.

Who hath wounds without cause? who hath redness of eyes?

They that tarry long at the wine; they that go to seek mixed wine.

Woe to the crown of pride, to the drunkards of Ephraim, whose glorious beauty is a fading flower, which are on the head of the fat valleys of them that are overcome with wine!

The crown of pride, the drunkards of Ephraim, shall be trodden under foot:

Woe unto them that call evil good, and good evil; that put darkness for light, and light for darkness;

That put bitter for sweet, and sweet for bitter!

Woe unto them that are wise in their own eyes, and prudent in their own sight!

Woe unto them that rise up early in the morning, that they may follow strong drink;

That continue until night, till wine inflame them.

Woe unto him that giveth his neighbor drink,

that putteth the bottle to him, and maketh him drunken also.

Woe unto them that are mighty to drink wine, and men of strength to mingle strong drink.

Finally, my brethren, be strong in the Lord, and in the power of His might.

Put on the whole armor of God, that ye may be able to stand against the wiles of the devil.

For we wrestle not against flesh and blood, but against principalities, against powers, against the rulers of the darkness of this world, against spiritual wickedness in high places.

Wherefore take unto you the whole armor of God, that ye may be able to withstand in the evil day, and having done all, to stand.

Stand, therefore, having your loins girt about with truth, and having on the breastplate of righteousness;

And your feet shod with the preparation of the gospel of peace;

Above all, taking the shield of faith, wherewith ye shall be able to quench the fiery darts of the wicked.

And take the helmet of salvation, and the sword of the Spirit, which is the Word of God:

Praying always with all prayer and supplication in the Spirit.

And watching thereunto with all perseverance and supplication for all saints.

Wherefore let him that thinketh he standeth take heed lest he fall.

Whether therefore ye eat, or drink, or whatsoever ye do, do all to the glory of God.

Now unto Him that is able to keep you from falling, and to present you faultless before the presence of His glory with exceeding joy.

To the only wise God our Saviour, be glory and majesty, dominion and power, both now and ever.

The Lord bless thee, and keep thee:

The Lord make His face to shine upon thee, and be gracious unto thee:

The Lord lift up His countenance upon thee, and give thee peace.

NUMBER IV.

Leader. I will lift up mine eyes unto the hills, from whence cometh my help.

Response. My help cometh from the Lord, which made heaven and earth.

L. He will not suffer thy foot to be moved: He that keepeth thee will not slumber.

R. Behold, He that keepeth Israel shall neither slumber nor sleep.

The Lord is thy keeper: the Lord is thy shade upon thy right hand.

The sun shall not smite thee by day, nor the moon by night.

The Lord shall preserve thee from all evil: He shall preserve thy soul.

The Lord shall preserve thy going out and thy coming in from this time forth, and even for evermore.

I was glad when they said unto me, Let us go into the house of the Lord.

Pray for the peace of Jerusalem: they shall prosper that love Thee.

Peace be within thy walls, and prosperity within thy palaces.

For my brethren and companions' sakes, I will now say, Peace be within thee.

Because of the house of the Lord our God I will seek thy good.

How amiable are thy tabernacles, O Lord of hosts!

My soul longeth, yea, even fainteth for the courts of the Lord: my heart and my flesh crieth out for the living God.

Yea, the sparrow hath found a house, and the swallow a nest for herself, where she may lay her young, even Thine altars, O Lord of hosts, my King and my God.

Blessed are they that dwell in Thy house: they will be still praising Thee.

Blessed is the man whose strength is in Thee; in whose heart are the ways of them.

Who passing through the valley of Baca make it a well; the rain also filleth the pools.

They go from strength to strength, every one of them in Zion appeareth before God.

For a day in thy courts is better than a thousand. I had rather be a doorkeeper in the house of my God, than to dwell in the tents of wickedness.

For the Lord God is a sun and shield: the Lord will give grace and glory: no good thing will be withhold from them that walk uprightly.

O Lord of hosts, blessed is the man that trusteth in Thee.

NUMBER V.

Leader. Blessed is the man that walketh not in the counsel of the ungodly, nor standeth in the way of sinners, nor sitteth in the seat of the scornful.

Response. But his delight is in the law of the Lord: and in his law doth he meditate day and night.

L. And he shall be like a tree planted by the rivers of water, that bringeth forth his fruit in his season; his leaf also shall not wither; and whatsoever he doeth shall prosper.

R. The ungodly are not so: but are like the chaff which the wind driveth away.

Therefore the ungodly shall not stand in the judgment, nor sinners in the congregation of the righteous.

For the Lord knoweth the way of the righteous: but the way of the ungodly shall perish.

Blessed is the man that feareth the Lord, that delighteth greatly in His commandments.

His seed shall be mighty upon earth: the generation of the upright shall be blessed.

Wealth and riches shall be in his house: and his righteousness endureth forever.

Unto the upright there ariseth light in the darkness: he is gracious, and full of compassion, and righteous.

A good man sheweth favor, and lendeth: he will guide his affairs with discretion.

Surely he shall not be moved forever: the righteous shall be in everlasting remembrance.

He shall not be afraid of evil tidings: his heart is fixed, trusting in the Lord.

His heart is established, he shall not be afraid, until he see his desire upon his enemies.

He hath dispersed, he hath given to the poor, his righteousness endureth forever; his horn shall be exalted with honor.

The wicked shall see it, and be grieved; he shall gnash with his teeth, and melt away: the desire of the wicked shall perish.

They that trust in the Lord shall be as Mount Zion, which can not be removed, but abideth forever.

As the mountains are round about Jerusalem, so the Lord is round about His people from henceforth even forever.

For the rod of the wicked shall not rest upon the lot of the righteous; lest the righteous put forth their hands unto iniquity.

Do good, O Lord, unto those that be good, and to them that are upright in their hearts.

As for such as turn aside unto their crooked ways, the Lord shall lead them forth with the workers of iniquity: but peace shall be upon Israel.

The Lord is my shepherd; I shall not want.

He maketh me to lie down in green pastures: He leadeth me beside the still waters.

He restoreth my soul: He leadeth me in the paths of righteousness for His name's sake.

Yea, though I walk through the valley of the shadow of death, I will fear no evil: for Thou art with me; Thy rod and Thy staff they comfort me.

Thou preparest a table before me in the presence of mine enemies: Thou anointest my head with oil; my cup runneth over.

Surely goodness and mercy shall follow me all the days of my life: and I will abide in the house of the Lord forever.

NUMBER VI.

Leader. Praise ye the Lord. Praise ye the Lord from the heavens: praise Him in the heights.

Response. Praise ye Him, all His angels: praise ye Him, all His hosts.

L. Praise ye Him, sun and moon: praise Him, all ye stars of light.

R. Praise Him, ye heavens of heavens, and ye waters that be above the heavens.

Let them praise the name of the Lord: for He commanded, and they were created.

He hath also established them for ever and ever: He hath made a decree which shall not pass.

Praise the Lord from the earth, ye dragons, and all deeps:

Fire and hail; snow and vapor; stormy wind fulfilling His word:

Mountains, and all hills; fruitful trees, and all cedars:

Beasts, and all cattle; creeping things, and flying fowl:

Kings of the earth, and all people; princes, and all judges of the earth:

Both young men, and maidens; old men, and children:

Let them praise the name of the Lord: for His name alone is excellent: His glory is above the earth and heaven.

Praise ye the Lord. Sing unto the Lord a new song, His praise in the congregation of saints.

Let Israel rejoice in Him that made him: let the children of Zion be joyful in their King.

Let them praise His name in the dance: let them sing praises unto Him with the timbrel and harp.

For the Lord taketh pleasure in His people: He will beautify the meek with salvation.

Let the saints be joyful in glory: let them sing aloud upon their beds.

Praise ye the Lord. Praise God in His sanctuary: praise Him in the firmament of His power.

Praise Him for His mighty acts: praise Him according to His excellent greatness.

Praise Him with the sound of the trumpet: praise Him with the psaltery and harp.

Let every thing that hath breath praise the Lord. Praise ye the Lord.

While I live will I praise the Lord: I will sing praises unto my God while I have any being.

Put not your trust in princes, nor in the son of man, in whom there is no help.

His breath goeth forth, he returneth to his earth; in that very day his thoughts perish.

Happy is he that hath the God of Jacob for his help, whose hope is in the Lord his God:

Which made heaven and earth, the sea, and all that therein is: which keepeth truth forever:

Which executeth judgment for the oppressed: which giveth food to the hungry. The Lord looseth the prisoners:

The Lord openeth the eyes of the blind: the Lord raiseth them that are bowed down: the Lord loveth the righteous:

The Lord preserveth the stranger; he relieveth the fatherless and widow: but the way of the wicked he turneth upside down.

The Lord shall reign forever, even thy God, O Zion, unto all generations. Praise ye the Lord.

NUMBER VII.

Leader. By the word of the Lord were the heavens made; and all the host of them by the breath of His mouth.

Response. He gathereth the waters of the sea together as a heap: He layeth up the depth in storehouses.

L. Let all the earth fear the Lord: let all the inhabitants of the world stand in awe of Him.

R. For He spake, and it was done; He commanded, and it stood fast.

The Lord bringeth the counsel of the heathen to nought: He maketh the devices of the people of none effect.

The counsel of the Lord standeth forever, the thoughts of His heart to all generations.

Blessed is the nation whose God is the Lord; and the people whom He hath chosen for His own inheritance.

The Lord looketh from heaven; He beholdeth all the sons of men.

From the place of His habitation He looketh upon all the inhabitants of the earth.

Behold, the eye of the Lord is upon them that fear Him, upon them that hope in His mercy:

To deliver their soul from death, and to keep them alive in famine.

Our soul waiteth for the Lord: He is our help and our shield.

For our heart shall rejoice in Him because we have trusted in His holy name.

Let thy mercy, O Lord, be upon us, according as we hope in Thee.

It is a good thing to give thanks unto the

Lord, and to sing praises unto Thy name, O Most High:

To shew forth Thy loving kindness in the morning, and Thy faithfulness every night.

Upon an instrument of ten strings, and upon the psaltery; upon the harp with a solemn sound.

For Thou, Lord, hast made me glad through Thy work: I will rejoice in the works of Thy hands.

O Lord, how great are Thy works! and Thy thoughts are very deep.

A brutish man knoweth not; neither doth a fool understand this.

When the wicked spring as the grass, and when all the workers of iniquity do flourish; it is that they shall be destroyed forever.

But Thou, Lord, are most high for evermore.

The righteous shall flourish like the palm tree: he shall grow like a cedar in Lebanon.

Those that be planted in the house of the Lord shall flourish in the courts of our God.

They shall still bring forth fruit in old age; they shall be fat and flourishing.

To shew that the Lord is upright: He is my rock, and there is no unrighteousness in Him.

The Lord reigneth, He is clothed with majesty: the Lord is clothed with strength, wherewith He hath girded Himself: the world also is established, that it can not be moved.

Thy throne is established of old: Thou art from everlasting.

The floods have lifted up, O Lord, the floods have lifted up their voice: the floods lift up their waves.

The Lord on high is mightier than the noise of many waters, yea, than the mighty waves of the sea.

Thy testimonies are very sure: holiness becometh Thine house, O Lord, forever.

NUMBER VIII.

Leader. Hear this, all ye people; give ear, all ye inhabitants of the world:

Response. Both low and high, rich and poor, together.

L. My mouth shall speak of wisdom; the meditation of my heart shall be of understanding.

R. I will incline mine ear to a parable: I will open my dark saying upon the harp.

Wherefore should I fear in the days of evil, when the iniquity of my heels shall compass me about?

They that trust in their wealth, and boast themselves in the multitude of their riches;

None of them can by any means redeem his brother, nor give to God a ransom for him:

(For the redemption of their souls is precious, and it ceaseth forever:)

That he should still live forever, and not see corruption.

For He seeth that wise men die, likewise the fool and the brutish person perish, and leave their wealth to others.

Their inward thought is, that their houses shall continue forever, and their dwelling places to all generations; they call their lands after their own names.

Nevertheless man being in honor abideth not: he is like the beasts that perish.

This their way is their folly: yet their posterity approve their sayings.

Like sheep they are laid in the grave; death shall feed on them; and the upright shall have dominion over them in the morning; and their beauty shall consume in the grave from their dwelling.

But God will redeem my soul from the power of the grave: for He shall receive me.

Be not thou afraid when one is made rich, when the glory of his house is increased:

For when he dieth he shall carry nothing away: his glory shall not descend after him.

Though while he lived he blessed his soul, (and men will praise thee, when thou doest well to thyself,)

He shall go to the generation of his fathers: they shall never see light.

Man that is in honor, and understandeth not, is like the beasts that perish.

Man that is born of a woman is of few days, and full of trouble.

He cometh forth like a flower, and is cut down: he fleeth also as a shadow, and continueth not.

And dost Thou open Thine eyes upon such a one, and bringest me into judgment with Thee?

Who can bring a clean thing out of an unclean? not one.

Seeing his days are determined, the number of his months are with Thee, Thou hast appointed his bounds that he can not pass;

Turn from him, that he may rest, till he shall accomplish, as a hireling, his day.

For there is hope of a tree, if it be cut down, that it will sprout again, and that the tender branch thereof will not cease.

Though the root thereof wax old in the earth, and the stock thereof die in the ground;

Yet through the scent of water it will bud, and bring forth boughs like a plant.

But man dieth, and wasteth away: yea, man giveth up the ghost, and where is he?

As the waters fail from the sea, and the flood decayeth and drieth up;

So man lieth down, and riseth not: till the heavens be no more, they shall not awake, nor be raised out of their sleep.

O that thou wouldst hide me in the grave, and Thou wouldst keep me secret, until Thy wrath be past, that Thou wouldst appoint me a set time, and remember me!

If a man die, shall he live again? all the days of my appointed time will I wait, till my change come.

The first man is of the earth, earthy: the second man is the Lord from heaven.

As is the earthy, such are they also that are earthy: and as is the heavenly, such are they also that are heavenly.

And as we have borne the image of the earthy, we shall also bear the image of the heavenly.

Now this I say, brethren, that flesh and blood can not inherit the kingdom of God; neither doth corruption inherit incorruption.

Behold, I shew you a mystery: We shall not all sleep, but we shall all be changed,

In a moment, in the twinkling of an eye, at the last trump: for the trumpet shall sound, and the dead shall be raised incorruptible, and we shall be changed.

For this corruptible must put on incorruption, and this mortal must put on immortality.

So when this corruptible shall have put on incorruption, and this mortal shall have put on immortality, then shall be brought to pass the saying that is written, Death is swallowed up in victory.

O death! where is thy sting? O grave! where is thy victory?

The sting of death is sin; and the strength of sin is the law.

But thanks be to God, which giveth us the victory through our Lord Jesus Christ.

Therefore, my beloved brethren, be ye steadfast, unmovable, always abounding in the work of the Lord, forasmuch as ye know that your labor is not in vain in the Lord.

NUMBER IX.

Leader. Comfort ye, comfort ye my people, saith your God.

Response. Speak ye comfortably to Jerusalem, and cry unto her, that her warfare is accomplished, that her iniquity is pardoned: for she hath received of the Lord's hand double for all her sins.

L. The voice of him that crieth in the wilderness, Prepare ye the way of the Lord, make straight in the desert a highway for our God.

R. Every valley shall be exalted and every mountain and hill shall be made low: and the crooked shall be made straight, and the rough places plain:

And the glory of the Lord shall be revealed, and all flesh shall see it together: for the mouth of the Lord hath spoken it.

The voice said, Cry. And he said, What shall I cry? All flesh is grass, and all the goodliness thereof is as the flower of the field:

The grass withereth, the flower fadeth; because the Spirit of the Lord bloweth upon it: surely the people is grass.

The grass withereth, the flower fadeth: but the word of our God shall stand forever.

O Zion, that bringest good tidings, get thee up into the high mountain; O Jerusalem, that bringest good tidings, lift up thy voice with strength; lift it up, be not afraid; say unto the cities of Judah, Behold your God!

Behold, the Lord God will come with strong hand, and His arm shall rule for Him: behold, His reward is with Him, and His work before Him.

He shall feed His flock like a shepherd: He shall gather the lambs with His arm, and carry them in His bosom, and shall gently lead those that are with young.

Who hath measured the waters in the hollow of His hand, and meted out heaven with the span, and comprehended the dust of the earth in a measure, and weighed the mountains in scales, and the hills in a balance?

Who hath directed the Spirit of the Lord, or being His counselor hath taught Him?

With whom took He counsel, and who instructed Him, and taught Him in the path of judgment, and taught Him knowledge, and shewed to Him the way of understanding?

Behold, the nations are as a drop of a bucket, and are counted as the small dust of the balance: behold, He taketh up the isles as a very little thing.

Why sayest thou, O Jacob, and speakest, O Israel, My way is hid from the Lord, and my judgment is passed over from my God?

Hast thou not known? hast thou not heard, that the everlasting God, the Lord, the Creator of the ends of the earth, fainteth not, neither is weary? there is no searching of His understanding. He giveth power to the faint and to them that have no might He increaseth strength.

Even the youths shall faint and be weary, and the young men shall utterly fall:

But they that wait upon the Lord shall renew their strength; they shall mount up with wings as eagles; they shall run, and not be weary; and they shall walk, and not faint.

NUMBER X.

Leader. The Lord is my light and my salvation; whom shall I fear? The Lord is the strength of my life; of whom shall I be afraid?

Response. When the wicked, even mine enemies and my foes, came upon me to eat up my flesh, they stumbled and fell.

L. Though a host should encamp against me, my heart shall not fear: though war should rise against me, in this I will be confident.

R. One thing have I desired of the Lord, that will I seek after; that I may dwell in the house of the Lord all the days of my life, to behold the beauty of the Lord, and to inquire in His temple.

For in the time of trouble He shall hide me in His pavilion: in the secret of His tabernacle shall He hide me; He shall set me up upon a rock.

Hear, O Lord, when I cry with my voice: have mercy also upon me, and answer me.

When thou saidst, Seek ye my face; my heart said unto Thee, Thy face, Lord, will I seek.

Hide not Thy face far from me; put not Thy servant away in anger: Thou hast been my help; leave me not, neither forsake me, O God of my salvation.

When my father and my mother forsake me, then the Lord will take me up.

Deliver me not over unto the will of mine enemies: for false witnesses are risen up against me, and such as breathe out cruelty.

I had fainted, unless I had believed to see the goodness of the Lord in the land of the living.

Wait on the Lord: be of good courage, and He shall strengthen thine heart: wait, I say, on the Lord.

I cried unto God with my voice, even unto God with my voice; and he gave ear unto me.

In the day of my trouble I sought the Lord; my sore ran in the night, and ceased not: my soul refused to be comforted.

I remembered God, and was troubled: I complained, and my spirit was overwhelmed.

Thou holdest mine eyes waking: I am so troubled that I can not speak.

I have considered the days of old, the years of ancient times.

I call to remembrance my song in the night: I commune with mine own heart: and my spirit made diligent search.

Will the Lord cast off forever? and will He be favorable no more?

Is His mercy clean gone forever? doth His promise fail for evermore?

Hath God forgotten to be gracious? hath He in anger shut up His tender mercies?

And I said, This is my infirmity: but I will remember the years of the right hand of the Most High.

I will remember the works of the Lord: surely I will remember Thy wonders of old.

I will meditate also of all Thy work, and talk of Thy doings.

Thy way, O God, is in the sanctuary: who is so great a God as our God?

Thou art the God that doest wonders: Thou hast declared Thy strength among the people.

Thou hast with thine arm redeemed the people, the sons of Jacob and Joseph.

The waters saw Thee, O God, the waters saw Thee; they were afraid: the depths also were troubled.

The clouds poured out water: the skies sent out a sound: thine arrows also went abroad.

The voice of Thy thunder was in the heaven: the lightnings lightened the world: the earth trembled and shook.

Thy way is in the sea, and Thy path in the great waters, and Thy footsteps are not known.

Thou leddest Thy people like a flock by the hand of Moses and Aaron.

NUMBER XI.

Leader. O give thanks unto the Lord; for He is good: because His mercy endureth forever.

Response. Let Israel now say that His mercy endureth forever.

L. Let the house of Aaron now say, that His mercy endureth forever.

R. Let them now that fear the Lord say, that His mercy endureth forever.

I called upon the Lord in distress: the Lord answered me, and set me in a large place.

The Lord is on my side; I will not fear: what can man do unto me?

It is better to trust in the Lord than to put confidence in man.

It is better to trust in the Lord than to put confidence in princes.

The Lord is my strength and song, and is become my salvation.

The voice of rejoicing and salvation is in the tabernacles of the righteous: the right hand of the Lord doeth valiantly.

The right hand of the Lord is exalted: the right hand of the Lord doeth valiantly.

I shall not die, but live, and declare the works of the Lord.

The Lord hath chastened me sore: but He hath not given me over unto death.

Open to me the gates of righteousness: I will go into them, and I will praise the Lord:

This gate of the Lord, into which the righteous shall enter.

I will praise Thee: for Thou hast heard me, and art become my salvation.

The stone which the builders refused is become the head stone of the corner.

This is the Lord's doing; it is marvelous in our eyes.

This is the day which the Lord hath made; we will rejoice and be glad in it.

Save now, I beseech Thee, O Lord: O Lord, I beseech Thee, send now prosperity.

Blessed be He that cometh in the name of the Lord: we have blessed You out of the house of the Lord.

God is the Lord, which hath shewed us light: bind the sacrifice with cords, even unto the horns of the altar.

Thou art my God, and I will praise Thee: Thou art my God, I will exalt Thee.

O give thanks unto the Lord; for He is good: for His mercy endureth forever.

Give unto the Lord, O ye mighty, give unto the Lord glory and strength.

Give unto the Lord the glory due unto His name; worship the Lord in the beauty of holiness.

The voice of the Lord is upon the waters: the God of glory thundereth: the Lord is upon many waters.

The voice of the Lord is powerful; the voice of the Lord is full of majesty.

The voice of the Lord divideth the flames of fire.

The voice of the Lord shaketh the wilderness: the Lord shaketh the wilderness of Kadesh.

The Lord will give strength unto His people; the Lord will bless His people with peace.

The fool hath said in his heart, There is no God. They are corrupt, they have done abominable works, there is none that doeth good.

The Lord looked down from heaven upon the children of men, to see if there were any that did understand, and seek God.

They are all gone aside, they are altogether become filthy: there is none that doeth good, no, not one.

Have all the workers of iniquity no knowledge? who eat up My people as they eat bread, and call not upon the Lord.

There were they in great fear: for God is in the generation of the righteous.

Ye have shamed the counsel of the poor, because the Lord is his refuge.

O that the salvation of Israel were come out of Zion! when the Lord bringeth back the captivity of His people, Jacob shall rejoice, and Israel shall be glad.

Why standest Thou afar off, O Lord? why hidest Thou Thyself in times of trouble?

The wicked in his pride doth persecute the poor: let them be taken in the devices that they have imagined.

For the wicked boasteth of his heart's desire, and blesseth the covetous, whom the Lord abhorreth.

The wicked, through the pride of his countenance, will not seek after God: God is not in all his thoughts.

His ways are always grievous; Thy judgments are far above out of his sight: as for all his enemies, he puffeth at them.

He hath said in his heart, I shall not be moved: for I shall never be in adversity.

His mouth is full of cursing and deceit and fraud: under his tongue is mischief and vanity.

He sitteth in the lurking places of the villages: in the secret places doth he murder the innocent: his eyes are privily set against the poor.

He lieth in wait secretly as a lion in his den: he lieth in wait to catch the poor: he doth catch the poor, when he draweth him into his net.

He croucheth, and humbleth himself, that the poor may fall by his strong ones.

He hath said in his heart, God hath forgotten: He hideth His face ; He will never see it.

Arise, O Lord ; O God, lift up Thine hand : forget not the humble.

Wherefore doth the wicked contemn God ? he hath said in his heart, Thou wilt not require it.

Thou hast seen it ; for Thou beholdest mischief and spite, to requite it with Thy hand : the poor committeth himself unto Thee ; Thou art the helper of the fatherless.

Break Thou the arm of the wicked and the evil man : seek out his wickedness till Thou find none.

╞ The Lord is King for ever and ever : the heathen are perished out of His land.

Lord, Thou hast heard the desire of the humble : Thou wilt prepare their heart, Thou wilt cause Thine ear to hear :

To judge the fatherless and the oppressed, that the man of the earth may no more oppress.

NUMBER XII.

Leader. Great is the Lord, and greatly to be praised in the city of our God, in the mountain of His holiness.

Response. Beautiful for situation, the joy of the whole earth, is mount Zion, on the sides of the north, the city of the great King.

L. God is known in her palaces for a refuge.

R. For, lo, the kings were assembled, they passed by together.

They saw it, and so they marveled ; they were troubled, and hasted away.

Fear took hold upon them there, and pain, as of a woman in travail.

Thou breakest the ships of Tarshish with an east wind.

As we have heard, so have we seen in the city of the Lord of hosts, in the city of our God : God will establish it forever.

We have thought of thy loving kindness, O God, in the midst of Thy temple.

According to Thy name, O God, so is Thy praise unto the ends of the earth : Thy right hand is full of righteousness.

Let mount Zion rejoice, let the daughters of Judah be glad, because of Thy judgments.

Walk about Zion, and go around about her : tell the towers thereof.

Mark ye well her bulwarks, consider her palaces ; that ye may tell it to the generation following.

For this God is our God for ever and ever : He will be our guide even unto death.

The Lord reigneth ; let the earth rejoice ; let the multitude of the isles be glad thereof.

Clouds and darkness are around about Him : righteousness and judgment are the habitation of His throne.

A fire goeth before Him, and burneth up his enemies round about.

His lightnings enlightened the world : the earth saw and trembled.

The hills melted like wax at the presence of the Lord, at the presence of the Lord of the whole earth.

The heavens declare His righteousness, and all the people see His glory.

Confounded be all they that serve graven images, that boast themselves of idols : worship Him, all ye gods.

Zion, heard, and was glad ; and the daughters of Judah rejoice because of thy judgments, O Lord. For thou, Lord, art high above all the earth : thou art exalted far above all gods.

Ye that love the Lord, hate evil : He preserveth the souls of His saints ; He delivereth them out of the hand of the wicked.

Light is sown for the righteous ; and gladness for the upright in heart.

Rejoice in the Lord, ye righteous ; and give thanks at the remembrance of His holiness.

Make a joyful noise unto the Lord, all ye lands.

Serve the Lord with gladness : come before His presence with singing.

Know ye that the Lord He is God : it is He that hath made us, and not we ourselves ; we are His people, and the sheep of His pasture.

Enter into His gates with thanksgiving, and into His courts with praise ; be thankful unto Him, and bless His name.

For the Lord is good ; His mercy is everlasting ; and His truth endureth to all generations.

O sing unto the Lord a new song ; for He hath done marvelous things : His right hand, and His holy arm, hath gotten Him the victory.

The Lord hath made known His salvation ; His righteousness hath He openly shewed in the sight of the heathen.

He hath remembered His mercy and His truth toward the house of Israel : all the ends of the earth have seen the salvation of our God.

Make a joyful noise unto the Lord, all the earth ; make a loud noise, and rejoice, and sing praise.

Sing unto the Lord with the harp ; with the harp, and the voice of a psalm.

With trumpets and sound of cornet make a joyful noise before the Lord, the King.

Let the sea roar, and the fullness thereof ; the world, and they that dwell therein.

Let the floods clap their hands : let the hills be joyful together

Before the Lord ; for He cometh to judge the earth : with righteousness shall He judge the world, and the people with equity.

NUMBER XIII.

Leader. Bless the Lord, O my soul : and all that is within me, bless His holy name.

Response. Bless the Lord, O my soul, and forget not all His benefits :

L. Who forgiveth all thine iniquities ; who healeth all thy diseases ;

R. Who redeemeth thy life from destruction ; who crowneth thee with loving kindness and tender mercies ;

Who satisfieth thy mouth with good things ; so that thy youth is renewed like the eagle's.

The Lord executeth righteousness and judgment for all that are oppressed.

He made known His ways unto Moses, His acts unto the children of Israel.

The Lord is merciful and gracious, slow to anger, and plenteous in mercy.

He will not always chide : neither will He keep His anger forever.

He hath not dealt with us after our sins ; nor rewarded us according to our iniquities.

For as the heaven is high above the earth, so great is His mercy toward them that fear Him,

As far as the east is from the west, so far hath He removed our transgressions from us.

Like as a father pitieth his children, so the Lord pitieth them that fear Him.

For He knoweth our frame; He remembereth that we are dust.

As for man, his days are as grass : as a flower of the field, so he flourisheth.

For the wind passeth over it, and it is gone; and the place thereof shall know it no more.

But the mercy of the Lord is from everlasting to everlasting upon them that fear Him, and His righteousness unto children's children ;

To such as keep His covenant, and to those that remember His commandments to do them.

The Lord hath prepared His throne in the heavens; and His kingdom ruleth over all.

Bless the Lord, ye His angels, that excel in strength, that do His commandments, hearkening unto the voice of His word.

Bless ye the Lord. all ye His hosts ; ye ministers of His, that do His pleasure.

Bless the Lord, all His works in all places of His dominion : bless the Lord, O my soul.

O Thou that hearest prayer, unto Thee shall all flesh come.

Thou crownest the year with Thy goodness; and Thy paths drop fatness.

They drop upon the pastures of the wilderness : and the little hills rejoice on every side.

The pastures are clothed with flocks; the valleys also are covered over with corn ; they shout for joy, they also sing.

Now know I that the Lord saveth His anointed : He will hear him from His holy heaven with the saving strength of His right hand.

Make a joyful noise unto God, all ye lands : Sing forth the honor of His name : make His praise glorious.

Say unto God, how terrible art Thou in Thy works ! through the greatness of Thy power shall Thine enemies submit themselves unto Thee.

All the earth shall worship Thee, and shall sing unto Thee ; they shall sing to Thy name.

Come and see the works of God : He is terrible in His doing toward the children of men.

He turned the sea into dry land : they went through the flood on foot : there did we rejoice in Him.

He ruleth by His power forever ; His eyes behold the nations : let not the rebellious exalt themselves.

O bless our God, ye people, and make the voice of His praise to be heard :

Which holdeth our soul in life, and suffereth not our feet to be moved.

For thou, O God, hast proved us : Thou hast tried us, as silver is tried.

Thou broughtest us into the net ; Thou laidst affliction upon our loins.

Thou hast caused men to ride over our heads : we went through fire and through water : but Thou broughtest us out into a wealthy place.

I will go into Thy house with burnt offerings : I will pay Thee my vows,

Which my lips have uttered, and my mouth hath spoken, when I was in trouble.

I will offer unto Thee burnt sacrifices of fatlings, with the incense of rams : I will offer bullocks with goats.

Come and hear, all ye that fear God, and I will declare what He hath done for my soul.

Return, O Lord, deliver my soul : O save me for Thy mercies' sake.

For in death there is no remembrance of Thee : in the grave who shall give Thee thanks?

I am weary with my groaning; all the night make I my bed to swim; I water my couch with my tears.

Mine eye is consumed because of grief ; it waxeth old because of all mine enemies.

Depart from me, all ye workers of iniquity ; for the Lord hath heard the voice of my weeping.

The Lord hath heard my supplication ; the Lord will receive my prayer.

Let all mine enemies be ashamed and sore vexed : let them return and be ashamed suddenly.

NUMBER XIV.

Leader. O give thanks unto the Lord ; call upon His name : make known His deeds among the people.

Response. Sing unto Him, sing psalms unto Him : talk ye of all His wondrous works.

L. Glory ye in His holy name : let the heart of them rejoice that seek the Lord.

R. Seek the Lord, and His strength : seek His face evermore.

Remember His marvelous works that He hath done ; His wonders and the judgments of His mouth;

O ye seed of Abraham His servant, ye children of Jacob His chosen.

He is the Lord our God : His judgments are in all the earth.

He hath remembered His covenant forever, the word which He commanded to a thousand generations.

Which covenant He made with Abraham, and His oath unto Isaac ;

And confirmed the same unto Jacob for a law, and to Israel for an everlasting covenant :

Saying, Unto thee will I give the land of Canaan, the lot of your inheritance ;

When they were but a few men in number; yea, very few, and strangers in it.

When they went from one nation to another, from one kingdom to another people ;

He suffered no man to do them wrong ; yea, He reproved kings for their sakes ;

Saying, touch not Mine anointed, and do My prophets no harm.

Moreover He called for a famine upon the land : He brake the whole staff of bread.

He sent a man before them, even Joseph, who was sold for a servant :

Whose feet they hurt with fetters : he was laid in iron :

Until the time that his word came: the word of the Lord tried him.

The king sent and loosed him ; even the ruler of the people, and let him go free.

He made him lord of his house, and ruler of all his substance :

To bind his princes at his pleasure ; and teach his senators wisdom.

Israel also came into Egypt; and Jacob sojourned in the land of Ham.

And He increased His people greatly ; and made them stronger than their enemies.

He turned their heart to hate His people, to deal subtilely with His servants.

He sent Moses His servant; and Aaron whom He had chosen.

They shewed His signs among them, and wonders in the land of Ham.

He sent darkness, and made it dark; and they rebelled not against His word.

He turned their waters into blood, and slew their fish.

Their land brought forth frogs in abundance, in the chambers of their kings.

He spake, and there came divers sort of flies, and lice in all their coasts.

He gave them hail for rain, and flaming fire in their land.

He smote their vines also and their fig-trees; and brake the trees of their coasts.

He spake, and the locust came, and caterpillars, and that without number,

And did eat up all the herbs in their land, and devoured the fruit of their ground.

He smote also all the firstborn in their land, the chief of all their strength.

He brought them forth also with silver and gold: and there was not one feeble person among their tribes.

Egypt was glad when they departed: for the fear of them fell upon them.

He spread a cloud for a covering; and fire to give light in the night.

NUMBER XV.

Leader. When the Lord turned again the captivity of Zion, we were like them that dream.

Response. Then was our mouth filled with laughter, and our tongue with singing: then said they among the heathen, the Lord hath done great things for them.

L. The Lord hath done great things for us, whereof we are glad.

R. Turn again our captivity, O Lord, as the streams in the south.

They that sow in tears shall reap in joy.

He that goeth forth and weepeth, bearing precious seed, shall doubtless come again with rejoicing, bringing his sheaves with him.

Lord, I cry unto Thee: make haste unto me; give ear unto my voice, when I cry unto Thee.

Let my prayer be set forth before Thee as incense; and the lifting up of my hands as the evening sacrifice.

Set a watch, O Lord, before my mouth; keep the door of my lips.

Incline not my heart to any evil thing, to practice wicked works with men that work iniquity: and let me not eat of thei. dainties.

Let the righteous smite me; it shall be a kindness: and let him reprove me; it shall be an excellent oil, which shall not break my head: for yet my prayer also shall be in their calamities.

When their judges are overthrown in stony places, they shall hear my words; for they are sweet.

Our bones are scattered at the grave's mouth, as when one cutteth and cleaveth wood upon the earth.

But mine eyes are unto Thee, O God the Lord: in Thee is my trust; leave not my soul destitute.

I looked on my right hand, and beheld, but there was no man that would know me: refuge failed me; no man cared for my soul.

I cried unto Thee, O Lord: I said, Thou art my refuge and my portion in the land of the living.

Attend unto my cry; for I am brought very low: deliver me from my persecutors; for they are stronger than I.

Bring my soul out of prison, that I may praise Thy name: the righteous shall compass me about: for Thou shalt deal bountifully with me.

NUMBER XVI.

Leader. O come, let us sing unto the Lord: let us make a joyful noise to the Rock of our salvation.

Response. Let us come before His presence with thanksgiving, and make a joyful noise unto Him with psalms.

L. For the Lord is a great God, and a great King above all gods.

R. In His hand are the deep places of the earth: the strength of the hills is His also.

The sea is His, and He made it: and His hands formed the dry land.

O come, let us worship and bow down: let us kneel before the Lord our Maker.

For He is our God; and we are the people of His pasture, and the sheep of His hand.

O sing unto the Lord a new song: sing unto the Lord, all the earth.

Sing unto the Lord, bless His name; show forth His salvation from day to day.

Declare His glory among the heathen, His wonders among all people.

For the Lord is great, and greatly to be praised: He is to be feared above all gods.

For all the gods of the nations are idols: but the Lord made the heavens.

Honor and majesty are before Him: strength and beauty are in His sanctuary.

Give unto the Lord, O ye kindreds of the people, give unto the Lord glory and strength.

Give unto the Lord the glory due unto His name: bring an offering, and come into His courts.

O worship the Lord in the beauty of holiness: fear before Him, all the earth.

Say among the heathen that the Lord reigneth: the world also shall be established that it shall not be moved: He shall judge the people righteously.

Let the heavens rejoice, and let the earth be glad; let the sea roar, and the fullness thereof.

Let the fields be joyful, and all that is therein: then shall all the trees of the wood rejoice before the Lord.

For He cometh, for He cometh to judge the earth: He shall judge the world with righteousness, and the people with His truth.

Praise ye the Lord, for it is good to sing praises unto our God; for it is pleasant; and praise is comely.

The Lord doth build up Jerusalem: He gathereth together the outcasts of Israel.

He healeth the broken in heart, and bindeth up their wounds.

He telleth the number of the stars; He calleth them all by their names.

Great is our Lord, and of great power: His understanding is infinite.

The Lord lifteth up the meek: He casteth the wicked down to the ground.

Sing unto the Lord with thanksgiving; sing praise upon the harp unto our God.

Who covereth the heaven with clouds, who prepareth rain for the earth, who maketh grass to grow upon the mountains.

He giveth to the beast his food, and to the young ravens which cry.

He delighteth not in the strength of the horse: He taketh not pleasure in the legs of a man.

The Lord taketh pleasure in them that fear Him, in those that hope in His mercy.

Praise the Lord, O Jerusalem; praise thy God, O Zion.

For He hath strengthened the bars of thy gates; He hath blessed thy children within thee.

He maketh peace in thy borders, and filleth thee with the finest of the wheat.

He sendeth forth His commandment upon earth: His word runneth very swiftly.

He giveth snow like wool: He scattereth the hoar-frost like ashes.

He casteth forth His ice like morsels: who can stand before His cold?

He sendeth out His word, and melteth them: He causeth His wind to blow, and the waters flow.

He showeth His word unto Jacob, His statutes and His judgments unto Israel.

He hath not dealt so with any nation: and as for His judgments, they have not known them. Praise ye the Lord.

NUMBER XVII.

Leader. Lord, make me to know mine end, and the measure of my days, what it is; that I may know how frail I am.

Response. Behold Thou hast made my days as a hand-breadth; and mine age is as nothing before Thee: verily every man at his best state is altogether vanity.

L. Surely every man walketh in a vain show: surely they are disquieted in vain: he heapeth up riches, and knoweth not who shall gather them.

R. And now, Lord, what wait I for? my hope is in Thee.

Deliver me from all my transgressions: make me not the reproach of the foolish.

Hear my prayer, O Lord, and give ear unto my cry; hold not Thy peace at my tears· for I am a stranger with Thee, and a sojourner, as all my fathers were.

O spare me, that I may recover strength, before I go hence, and be no more.

Lord, Thou hast been our dwelling-place in all generations.

Before the mountains were brought forth, or ever Thou hadst formed the earth and the world, even from everlasting to everlasting, Thou art God.

Thou turnest man to destruction; and sayest, Return, ye children of men.

For a thousand years in Thy sight are but as yesterday when it is past, and as a watch in the night.

Thou carriest them away as with a flood; they are as a sleep: in the morning they are like grass which groweth up.

In the morning it flourisheth, and groweth up; in the evening it is cut down, and withereth.

For we are consumed by Thine anger, and by Thy wrath are we troubled.

Thou hast set our iniquities before Thee, our secret sins in the light of Thy countenance.

For all our days are passed away in Thy wrath: we spend our years as a tale that is told.

The days of our years are threescore years and ten; and if by reason of strength they be fourscore years, yet is their strength labor and sorrow; for it is soon cut off, and we fly away.

Who knoweth the power of Thine anger? even according to Thy fear, so is Thy wrath.

So teach us to number our days, that we may apply our hearts unto wisdom.

Return, O Lord, how long? and let it repent Thee concerning Thy servants.

O satisfy us early with Thy mercy; that we may rejoice and be glad all our days.

Make us glad according to the days wherein Thou hast afflicted us, and the years wherein we have seen evil.

Let Thy work appear unto Thy servants, and Thy glory unto their children.

And let the beauty of the Lord our God be upon us: and establish Thou the work of our hands upon us; yea, the work of our hands, establish Thou it.

NUMBER XVIII.

Leader. God is our refuge and strength, a very present help in trouble.

Response. Therefore will not we fear, though the earth be removed, and though the mountains be carried into the midst of the sea;

L. Though the waters thereof roar and be troubled, though the mountains shake with the swelling thereof.

R. There is a river, the streams whereof shall make glad the city of God, the holy place of the tabernacles of the Most High.

God is in the midst of her; she shall not be moved: God shall help her, and that right early.

The heathen raged, the kingdoms were moved: He uttered his voice, the earth melted.

The Lord of hosts is with us; the God of Jacob is our refuge.

Come, behold the works of the Lord, what desolations He hath made in the earth.

He maketh wars to cease unto the end of the earth; He breaketh the bow, and cutteth the spear in sunder; He burneth the chariot in the fire.

Be still, and know that I am God: I will be exalted among the heathen, I will be exalted in the earth.

The Lord of hosts is with us; the God of Jacob is our refuge.

Be merciful unto me, O God, be merciful unto me: for my soul trusteth in Thee: yea, in the shadow of Thy wings will I make my refuge, until these calamities be overpast.

I will cry unto God most high; unto God that performeth all things for me.

My heart is fixed, O God, my heart is fixed: I will sing and give praise.

Awake up, my glory; awake, psaltery and harp: I myself will awake early.

I will praise Thee, O Lord, among the people: I will sing unto Thee among the nations.

For Thy mercy is great unto the heavens, and Thy truth unto the clouds.

Be Thou exalted, O God, above the heavens; let Thy glory be above all the earth.

The works of the Lord are great, sought out of all them that have pleasure therein.

His work is honorable and glorious: and His righteousness endureth forever.

He hath made His wonderful work to be remembered: the Lord is gracious and full of compassion.

He hath given meat unto them that fear Him: He will ever be mindful of His covenant.

He hath shewed His people the power of His works, that He may give them the heritage of the heathen.

The works of His hands are verity and judgment; all His commandments are sure.

They stand fast for ever and ever, and are done in truth and uprightness.

He sent redemption unto His people: He hath commanded His covenant forever: holy and reverend is His name.

The fear of the Lord is the beginning of wisdom: a good understanding have all they that do His commandments: His praise endureth forever.

NUMBER XIX.

Leader. Lay not up for yourselves treasures upon earth, where moth and rust doth corrupt, and where thieves break through and steal: ·

Response. But lay up for yourselves treasures in heaven, where neither moth nor rust doth corrupt, and where thieves do not break through nor steal:

L. For where your treasure is, there will your heart be also.

R. The light of the body is the eye: if therefore thine eye be single, thy whole body shall be full of light.

But if thine eye be evil, thy whole body shall be full of darkness. If therefore the light that is in thee be darkness, how great is that darkness!

No man can serve two masters: for either he will hate the one, and love the other; or else he will hold to the one, and despise the other. Ye can not serve God and mammon.

Therefore I say unto you, Take no thought for your life, what ye shall eat, or what ye shall drink; nor yet for your body, what ye shall put on. Is not the life more than meat, and the body than raiment?

Behold the fowls of the air: for they sow not, neither do they reap, nor gather into barns; yet your heavenly Father feedeth them. Are ye not much better than they?

Which of you by taking thought can add one cubit unto his stature?

And why take ye thought for raiment? Consider the lilies of the field, how they grow; they toil not, neither do they spin:

And yet I say unto you, That even Solomon in all his glory was not arrayed like one of these.

Wherefore, if God so clothe the grass of the field, which to-day is, and to-morrow is cast into the oven, shall He not much more clothe you, O ye of little faith?

Therefore take no thought, saying, What shall we eat? or, What shall we drink? or, Wherewithal shall we be clothed?

(For after all these things do the Gentiles seek:) for your heavenly Father knoweth that ye have need of all these things.

But seek ye first the kingdom of God, and His righteousness; and all these things shall be added unto you.

Take therefore no thought for the morrow: for the morrow shall take thought for the things of itself. Sufficient unto the day is the evil thereof.

* * * * * *

Blessed are the poor in spirit: for theirs is the kingdom of heaven.

Blessed are they that mourn: for they shall be comforted.

Blessed are the meek: for they shall inherit the earth.

Blessed are they which do hunger and thirst after righteousness: for they shall be filled.

Blessed are the merciful: for they shall obtain mercy.

Blessed are the pure in heart: for they shall see God.

Blessed are the peacemakers: for they shall be called the children of God.

Blessed are they which are persecuted for righteousness' sake: for theirs is the kingdom of heaven.

Blessed are ye, when men shall revile you, and persecute you, and shall say all manner of evil against you falsely, for my sake.

Rejoice, and be exceeding glad: for great is your reward in heaven: for so persecuted they the prophets which were before you.

NUMBER XX.

Leader. I will bless the Lord at all times: His praise shall continually be in my mouth.

Response. My soul shall make her boast in the Lord: the humble shall hear thereof, and be glad.

L. O magnify the Lord with me, and let us exalt His name together.

R. I sought the Lord, and He heard me, and delivered me from all my fears.

They looked unto Him, and were lightened: and their faces were not ashamed.

This poor man cried, and the Lord heard him, and saved him out of all his troubles.

The angel of the Lord encampeth round about them that fear Him, and delivereth them.

O taste and see that the Lord is good: blessed is the man that trusteth in Him.

O fear the Lord, ye His saints: for there is no want to them that fear Him.

The young lions do lack, and suffer hunger: but they that seek the Lord shall not want any good thing.

Come, ye children, hearken unto me: I will teach you the fear of the Lord.

What man is he that desireth life, and loveth many days, that he may see good?

Keep thy tongue from evil, and thy lips that they speak no guile.

Depart from evil, and do good; seek peace, and pursue it.

The eyes of the Lord are upon the righteous, and His ears are open unto their cry.

The righteous cry, and the Lord heareth, and delivereth them out of all their troubles.

The Lord is nigh unto them that are of a broken heart ; and saveth such as be of a contrite spirit.

Many are the afflictions of the righteous : but the Lord delivereth him out of them all.

He keepeth all his bones : not one of them is broken.

Evil shall slay the wicked : and they that hate the righteous shall be desolate.

The Lord redeemeth the soul of His servants : and none of them that trust in Him shall be desolate.

If it had not been the Lord who was on our side, now may Israel say ;

If it had not been the Lord who was on our side, when men rose up against us :

Then they had swallowed us up quick, when their wrath was kindled against us :

Then the waters had overwhelmed us, the stream had gone over our soul :

Then the proud waters had gone over our soul.

Blessed be the Lord, who hath not given us as a prey to their teeth.

Our soul is escaped as a bird out of the snare of the fowlers : the snare is broken, and we are escaped.

Our help is in the name of the Lord, who made heaven and earth.

Out of the depth have I cried unto Thee, O Lord. Lord, hear my voice : let Thine ears be attentive to the voice of my supplications.

If Thou, Lord, shouldest mark iniquities, O Lord, who shall stand ? But there is forgiveness with Thee, that Thou mayest be feared.

I wait for the Lord, my soul doth wait, and in His word do I hope.

My soul waiteth for the Lord more than they that watch for the morning : I say, more than they that watch for the morning.

Let Israel hope in the Lord : for with the Lord there is mercy, and with Him is plenteous redemption.

And He shall redeem Israel from all his sins.

NUMBER XXI.

Leader. Now when Jesus was born in Bethlehem of Judea in the days of Herod the king, behold, there came wise men from the east to Jerusalem,

Response. Saying, where is He that is born King of the Jews? for we have seen His star in the east, and are come to worship Him.

L. When Herod the king had heard these things, he was troubled, and all Jerusalem with him.

R. And when he had gathered all the chief priests and scribes of the people together, he demanded of them where Christ should be born.

And they said unto him, In Bethlehem of Judea ; for thus it is written by the prophet.

And thou Bethlehem, in the land of Juda, art not the least among the princes of Juda : for out of thee shall come a Governor, that shall rule my people Israel.

Then Herod, when he had privily called the wise men, inquired of them diligently what time the star appeared.

And he sent them to Bethlehem, and said,

Go and search diligently for the young child ; and when ye have found Him, bring me word again, that I may come and worship Him also.

When they had heard the king, they departed ; and, lo, the star, which they saw in the east, went before them, till it came and stood over where the young child was.

When they saw the star, they rejoiced with exceeding great joy.

And when they were come into the house, they saw the young child with Mary His mother, and fell down, and worshiped Him : and when they had opened their treasures, they presented unto Him gifts ; gold, and frankincense, and myrrh.

And being warned of God in a dream that they should not return to Herod, they departed into their own country another way.

And when they were departed, behold, the angel of the Lord appeareth to Joseph in a dream, saying, arise, and take the young child and His mother, and flee into Egypt, and be thou there until I bring thee word : for Herod will seek the young child to destroy Him.

When he arose, he took the young child and His mother by night, and departed into Egypt :

And was there until the death of Herod : that it might be fulfilled which was spoken of the Lord by the prophet, saying, out of Egypt have I called my Son.

And there were in the same country shepherds abiding in the field, keeping watch over their flock by night.

And, lo, the angel of the Lord came upon them, and the glory of the Lord shone round about them ; and they were sore afraid.

And the angel said unto them, Fear not : for, behold, I bring you good tidings of great joy, which shall be to all people.

For unto you is born this day in the city of David a Savior, which is Christ the Lord.

And this shall be a sign unto you ; Ye shall find the babe wrapped in swaddling clothes, lying in a manger.

And suddenly there was with the angel a multitude of the heavenly host praising God, and saying,

Glory to God in the highest, and on earth peace, good-will toward men.

For unto us a child is born, unto us a son is given : and the government shall be upon His shoulder : and His name shall be called Wonderful, Counselor, The mighty God, The everlasting Father, The Prince of Peace.

Of the increase of His government and peace there shall be no end, upon the throne of David, and upon His kingdom, to order it, and to establish it with judgment and with justice from henceforth even forever. The zeal of the Lord of hosts will perform this.

In the beginning was the Word, and the Word was with God, and the Word was God.

The same was in the beginning with God.

All things were made by Him ; and without Him was not anything made that was made.

In Him was life ; and the life was the light of men.

And the light shineth in darkness ; and the darkness comprehended it not.

There was a man sent from God, whose name was John.

The same came for a witness, to bear witness

of the Light, that all men through Him might believe.

He was not that Light, but was sent to bear witness of that Light.

That was the true Light, which lighteth every man that cometh into the world.

He was in the world, and the world was made by Him, and the world knew Him not.

He came unto His own, and His own received Him not.

But as many as received Him, to them gave He power to become the sons of God, even to them that believe on His name:

Which were born, not of blood, nor of the will of the flesh, nor of the will of man, but of God.

NUMBER XXII.

Leader. Who hath believed our report? and to whom is the arm of the Lord revealed?

Response. For He shall grow up before Him as a tender plant, and as a root out of dry ground: He hath no form nor comeliness; and when we shall see Him, there is no beauty that we should desire Him.

L. He is despised and rejected of men; a man of sorrows, and acquainted with grief: and we hid as it were our faces from Him; He was despised, and we esteemed Him not.

R. Surely He hath borne our griefs, and carried our sorrows: yet we did esteem Him stricken, smitten of God, and afflicted.

But He was wounded for our transgressions, He was bruised for our iniquities: the chastisement of our peace was upon Him; and with His stripes we are healed.

All we like sheep have gone astray; we have turned every one to His own way; and the Lord hath laid on Him the iniquity of us all.

He was oppressed, and He was afflicted, yet He opened not His mouth: He is brought as a lamb to the slaughter, and as a sheep before her shearers is dumb, so He openeth not His mouth.

And when they had platted a crown of thorns, they put it upon His head, and a reed in His right hand: and they bowed the knee before Him, and mocked Him, saying, Hail, King of the Jews!

And they spit upon Him, and took the reed, and smote Him on the head.

And after that they had mocked Him, they took the robe off from Him, and put His own raiment on Him, and led Him away to crucify Him.

And as they came out, they found a man of Cyrene, Simon by name: him they compelled to bear His cross.

And when they were come unto a place called Golgotha, that is to say, a place of a skull,

They gave Him vinegar to drink mingled with gall: and when He had tasted thereof, He would not drink.

And they crucified Him, and parted His garments, casting lots: that it might be fulfilled which was spoken by the prophet, They parted my garments among them, and upon my vesture did they cast lots.

And sitting down they watched Him there;

And set up over His head His accusation written, This is Jesus the King of the Jews.

Then were there two thieves crucified with Him; one on the right hand, and another on the left.

And they that passed by reviled Him, wagging their heads,

And saying, Thou that destroyest the temple, and buildest it in three days, save Thyself. If Thou be the Son of God, come down from the cross.

Likewise also the chief priests mocking Him, with the scribes and elders, said,

He saved others; Himself He can not save. If He be the King of Israel, let Him now come down from the cross, and we will believe Him.

He trusted in God; let Him deliver Him now, if He will have Him: for He said, I am the Son of God.

The thieves also, which were crucified with Him, cast the same in His teeth.

Now from the sixth hour there was darkness over all the land unto the ninth hour.

And about the ninth hour Jesus cried with a loud voice saying, Eli, Eli, lama sabachthani? that is to say, My God, my God, why hast Thou forsaken Me?

Some of them that stood there, when they heard that, said, This man calleth for Elias.

And straitway one of them ran, and took a sponge, and filled it with vinegar, and put it on a reed, and gave Him to drink.

The rest said, Let be, let us see whether Elias will come to save Him.

Jesus, when He had cried again with a loud voice, yielded up the ghost.

And behold, the veil of the temple was rent in twain from the top to the bottom; and the earth did quake, and the rocks rent;

And the graves were opened; and many bodies of the saints which slept arose,

And came out of the graves after His resurrection, and went into the holy city, and appeared unto many.

The first day of the week cometh Mary Magdalene early, when it was yet dark, unto the sepulchre, and seeth the stone taken away from the sepulchre.

Then she runneth, and cometh to Simon Peter, and to the other disciple, whom Jesus loved, and saith unto them, They have taken away the Lord out of the sepulchre, and we know not where they have laid Him.

Peter therefore went forth, and that other disciple, and came to the sepulchre.

So they ran both together: and the other disciple did outrun Peter, and came first to the sepulchre.

And he stooping down, and looking in, saw the linen clothes lying; yet went he not in.

Then cometh Simon Peter following him, and went into the sepulchre, and seeth the linen clothes lie,

And the napkin, that was about His head, not lying with the linen clothes, but wrapped together in a place by itself.

Then went in also that other disciple, which came first to the sepulchre, and he saw, and believed.

For as yet they knew not the Scripture, that He must rise again from the dead.

Then the disciples went away again unto their own home.

But Mary stood without at the sepulchre weeping: and as she wept, she stooped down, and looked into the sepulchre,

And seeth two angels in white sitting, the one

at the head, and the other at the feet, where the body of Jesus had lain.

And they say unto her, Woman, why weepest thou? She saith unto them, Because they have taken away my Lord, and I know not where they have laid Him.

And when she had thus said, she turned herself back, and saw Jesus standing, and knew not that it was Jesus.

Jesus saith unto her, Woman, why weepest thou? whom seekest thou? She, supposing Him to be the gardener, saith unto Him, Sir, if thou have borne Him hence, tell me where thou hast laid Him, and I will take Him away.

Jesus saith unto her, Mary. She turned herself, and saith unto Him, Rabboni; which is to say, Master.

Jesus saith unto her, Touch Me not; for I am not yet ascended to My Father: but go to My brethren, and say unto them, I ascend unto My Father, and your Father; and to My God, and your God.

Mary Magdalene came and told the disciples that she had seen the Lord, and that He had spoken these things unto her.

NUMBER XXIII.

Leader. And Jesus called a little child unto Him, and set him in the midst of them,

Response. And said, Verily I say unto you, except ye be converted and become as little children, ye shall not enter into the kingdom of heaven.

L. Whosoever therefore shall humble himself as this little child, the same is greatest in the kingdom of heaven.

R. And whoso shall receive one such little child in My name, receiveth Me.

That our sons may be as plants grown up in their youth:

That our daughters may be as corner-stones, polished after the similitude of a palace.

For He hath strengthened the bars of thy gates; He hath blessed thy children within thee.

Honor thy father and thy mother, as the Lord thy God hath commanded thee:

That it may go well with thee, in the land which the Lord thy God giveth thee.

My son, hear the instruction of thy father, and forsake not the law of thy mother.

'For they shall be an ornament of grace unto thy head, and chains about thy neck.

Children, obey your parents in the Lord; for this is right.

Come ye children, hearken unto Me; I will teach you the fear of the Lord.

And these words which I command thee this day, shall be in thine heart;

And thou shalt teach them diligently unto thy children, and shalt talk of them when thou sittest in thine house, and when thou walkest by the way, and when thou liest down, and when thou risest up.

And thou shalt bind them for a sign upon thy hand, and they shall be as frontlets between thine eyes.

Hear, O my son, and receive my sayings; and the years of thy life shall be many.

I have taught thee in the way of wisdom; I have led thee in right paths.

Take fast hold of instruction; let her not go; keep her, for she is thy life.

A wise son maketh a glad father: but a foolish son is the heaviness of his mother.

Train up a child in the way he should go; and when he is old he will not depart from it.

And ye, fathers, provoke not your children to wrath; but bring them up in the nurture and admonition of the Lord.

Only take heed to thyself, and keep thy soul diligently, lest thou forget the things which thine eyes have seen, and lest they depart from thy heart all the days of thy life;

But teach them to thy sons and thy son's sons; that they may learn to fear Me all the days that they shall live upon the earth, and that they may teach their children.

And they brought young children to Him, that He should touch them:

And His disciples rebuked those that brought them. But when Jesus saw it He was much displeased,

And said unto them, Suffer the little children to come unto Me, and forbid them not: for of such is the kingdom of God.

And He took them up in His arms, put His hands upon them, and blessed them.

NUMBER XXIV.

Leader. Though I speak with the tongues of men and of angels, and have not charity; I am become as sounding brass, or a tinkling cymbal.

Response. And though I have the gift of prophecy, and understand all mysteries, and all knowledge; and though I have all faith, so that I could remove mountains, and have not charity, I am nothing.

L. And though I bestow all My goods to feed the poor, and though I give My body to be burned, and have not charity, it profiteth me nothing.

R. Charity suffereth long, and is kind; charity envieth not; charity vaunteth not itself, is not puffed up,

Doth not behave itself unseemly, seeketh not her own, is not easily provoked, thinketh no evil;

Rejoiceth not in iniquity, but rejoiceth in the truth;

Beareth all things, believeth all things, hopeth all things, endureth all things.

Charity never faileth: but whether there be prophecies, they shall fail; whether there be tongues, they shall cease; whether there be knowledge, it shall vanish away.

For we know in part, and we prophecy in part.

But when that which is perfect is come, then that which is in part shall be done away.

When I was a child, I spake as a child, I understood as a child, I thought as a child: but when I became a man, I put away childish things.

For now we see through a glass, darkly; but then face to face: now I know in part; but then shall I know even as also I am known.

And now abideth faith, hope, charity these three; but the greatest of these is charity.

Behold, what manner of love the Father hath bestowed upon us, that we should be called the sons of God: therefore the world knoweth us not, because it knew Him not.

Beloved, now are we the sons of God, and it

doth not yet appear what we shall be: but we know that, when He shall appear, we shall be like Him; for we shall see Him as He is.

And every man that hath this hope in him purifieth himself, even as he is pure.

The ransomed of the Lord shall return, and come to Zion with songs and everlasting joy upon their heads:

They shall obtain joy and gladness, and sorrow and sighing shall flee away.

In Thy presence is fullness of joy: at Thy right hand there are pleasures for evermore.

Eye hath not seen, nor ear heard, neither have entered into the heart of man, the things which God hath prepared for them that love Him.

The gift of God is eternal life, through Jesus Christ our Lord. I shall be satisfied, when I awake, with Thy likeness.

Whosoever committeth sin transgresseth also the law: for sin is the transgression of the law.

And ye know that He was manifested to take away our sins; and in Him is no sin.

Whosoever abideth in Him sinneth not; whosoever sinneth hath not seen Him, neither known Him.

Little children, let no man deceive you: he that doeth righteousness is righteous, even as He is righteous.

He that committeth sin is of the devil; for the devil sinneth from the beginning. For this purpose the Son of God was manifested, that He might destroy the works of the devil.

In this the children of God are manifest, and the children of the devil: whosoever doeth not righteousness is not of God, neither he that loveth not his brother.

For this is the message that ye heard from the beginning, that ye should love one another.

NUMBER XXV.

Leader. My son, forget not my law; but let thine heart keep my commandments:

Response. For length of days, and long life, and peace, shall they add to thee.

L. Let not mercy and truth forsake thee: bind them about thy neck; write them upon the table of thine heart:

R. So shalt thou find favor and good understanding in the sight of God and man.

Trust in the Lord with all thine heart; and lean not unto thine own understanding.

In all thy ways acknowledge Him, and He shall direct thy paths.

Be not wise in thine own eyes: fear the Lord, and depart from evil.

It shall be health to thy navel, and marrow to thy bones.

Honor the Lord with thy substance, and with the first-fruits of all thine increase:

So shall thy barns be filled with plenty, and thy presses shall burst out with new wine.

My son, despise not the chastening of the Lord; neither be weary of His correction:

For whom the Lord loveth He correcteth; even as a father the son in whom he delighteth.

Happy is the man that findeth wisdom, and the man that getteth understanding:

For the merchandise of it is better than the merchandise of silver, and the gain thereof than fine gold.

She is more precious than rubies: and all the things thou canst desire are not to be compared unto her.

Length of days is in her right hand; and in her left riches and honor.

Her ways are ways of pleasantness, and all her paths are peace.

She is a tree of life to them that lay hold upon her: and happy is every one that retaineth her.

The Lord by wisdom hath founded the earth; by understanding hath He established the heavens.

By His knowledge the depths are broken up, and the clouds drop down the dew.

My son, let not them depart from thine eyes: keep sound wisdom and discretion:

So shall they be life unto thy soul, and grace to thy neck.

Then shalt thou walk in thy way safely, and thy foot shall not stumble.

When thou liest down, thou shalt not be afraid: yea, thou shalt lie down, and thy sleep shall be sweet.

Remember now thy Creator in the days of thy youth, while the evil days come not, nor the years draw nigh, when thou shalt say, I have no pleasure in them;

While the sun, or the light, or the moon, or the stars, be not darkened, nor the clouds return after the rain:

In the day when the keepers of the house shall tremble, and the strong men shall bow themselves, and the grinders cease because they are few, and those that look out of the windows be darkened,

And the doors shall be shut in the streets, when the sound of the grinding is low, and He shall rise up at the voice of the bird, and all the daughters of music shall be brought low;

Also when they shall be afraid of that which is high, and fears shall be in the way, and the almond tree shall flourish, and the grasshopper shall be a burden, and desire shall fail: because man goeth to his long home, and the mourners go about the streets:

Or ever the silver cord be loosed, or the golden bowl be broken, or the pitcher be broken at the fountain, or the wheel broken at the cistern.

Then shall the dust return to the earth as it was: and the spirit shall return unto God who gave it.

Vanity of vanities, saith the Preacher; all is vanity.

And moreover, because the Preacher was wise, He still taught the people knowledge; yea, He gave good heed, and sought out, and set in order many proverbs.

The Preacher sought to find out acceptable words: and that which was written was upright, even words of truth.

The words of the wise are as goads, and as nails fastened by the masters of assemblies, which are given from one shepherd.

And further, by these, My son, be admonished: of making many books there is no end; and much study is a weariness of the flesh.

Let us hear the conclusion of the whole matter: fear God, and keep His commandments: for this is the whole duty of man.

For God shall bring every work into judgment, with every secret thing, whether it be good, or whether it be evil.

THE Franklin Square Song Collection, compiled by J. P. McCASKEY, comprises Eight Numbers of 176 pages each. Each book contains 200 favorite songs and hymns with much reading matter relating to music. The page affords so much space that a surprisingly large amount of music is given here in clear type. An old song is often wanted—the figure after each title shows the Number of the Collection in which it is found.

Abide With Me, 1
A Charge to Keep I Have, 5
A Dainty Plant is the Ivy, 8
Adeste Fideles, 6
Adieu, 6
Adieu, My Native Land, 3
A Dollar or Two, 3
Ae Fond Kiss, 8
A Farewell, 4
A Few More Years Shall Roll, 5
After Many Roving Years, 1
Age of Progress, 8
A Glory Gilds the Page, 2
A Greenness Light and, 4
Ah, for Wings to Soar, 3
Ah, I have Sighed to Rest, 3
Ah, So Pure! 3
A Hermit There Was, 5
A Hundred Years to Come, 3
Alas and Did My Saviour, 1
A Last Prayer, 8
Alice Gray, 6
Alice, Where Art Thou? 3
A Life on the Ocean W 3
All Among the Barley,
All Around My Hat, 8
All by the Shady Greenwood, 5
All Glory, Laud and Honor, 6
All Hail the Power, 1
All's Well, 8
All That Glitters is Not Gold, 8
All the Saints Adore Thee, 1
All Things Love Thee, 8
All Together, 1
Alphabet Song, 5
Alpine Horn, 1
A Man's a Man for a' That, 6
American Cradle Song, 3
Amid the Greenwood, 4
A Mighty Fortress, 2 .
Andreas Hofer, 6
An Evening Song, 8
Angelic Songs are Swelling, 1
Angel of Peace, 4
Angels Ever Bright and Fair, 2
Angels from Realms of Glory, 6
Angry Words, 3
Angus Macdonald, 8
Anna Song, 5
Annie Laurie, 1
Annie's Tryst, 6
Answers, 8
Anvil Chorus, 5
A Poor Wayfaring Man,
Araby's Daughter, 5
Arbor Day Song, 8
Are There Tidings? 4
Are Ye Sleepin', Maggie? 5
Arms are Strong and Hearts, 4
Art Thou Weary? 5
As a Little Child, 1
As I'd Nothing Else to Do, 5
A Soldier's Life, 2
A Spring Song, 5,
As the Wind Blows, 8
As with Gladness Men of Old, 7
At Evening Time, 4
At the Ferry, 6
A Thousand Leagues Away, 6
Auf Wiedersehn, 2
Auld Lang Syne, 1
Auld Robin Gray, 3
Aunt Jemima's Plaster, 8
Austrian National Hymn, 3
Autumn Dreaming, 4
Ave Maria (*Gounod*), 7
Ave Maria (*Schubert*), 7
Awake, My Soul, 3, 4
A Warrior Bold, 7
Away! Away! (*Massaniello*), 1
Away Now, Joyful Riding, 4
Away to School, 2
Away to the Mountain, 7
Away with Melancholy, 6
A Wet Sheet, a Flowing Sea, 5
Baby Bye, Here's a Fly, 1
Baby's Skies, 8
Backward, Turn Backward, 4
Baloo, My Wee, Wee Thing, 3
Banks of Allan Water, 6
Banks of the Lee, 8

Barney Buntline, 8
Basseti, 6
Battle Eve, 4
Battle Hymn of Republic, 2
Battle Prayer, 5
Bay of Dublin, 2
Beats There a Heart Sincere, 4
Beautiful Bells, 6
Beautiful Day, 8
Beautiful Faces, 3
Beautiful Minka, 6
Beautiful Rhine, 7
Beautiful Sea, 3
Beautiful Spring Time, 2
Beautiful Venice, 2
Because He Loved You So, 7
Bedouin Love Song, 6
Behold How Brightly, 6
Be Hushed, My Dear, 6
Be Kind to the Loved Ones, 1
Bell is Ringing, 2
Bells of Aberdovey, 7
Bells of Shandon 3
Be Mine, 7
Ben Bolt, 1
Beside a Green Meadow, 8
Beside the Mill, 1
Better Land, 6
Better Wish, 2
Beulah Land, 2
Bibabutzeman, 5
Bid Me Good-Bye, 5
Billy Boy, 3
Birdie in the Cradle, 3
Birdie Sweet, 7
Bird Let Loose, 1
Bird of the Forest, 3
Bird of the Greenwood, 7
Bird of the Wilderness, 8
Birds in the Woodland, 2
Birds in the Night, 5
Bird Song, 1
Blackbird, 6
Bleib Bei Mir, 5
Blessed Country, 6
Blest be the Tie That Binds, 5
Blest Symbol of Blest Name, 3
Bloom On, My Roses, 8
Blossom Time, 1
Blue Alsatian Mountains, 2
Blue Bells of Scotland, 1
Blue Bird, 1
Blue-Eyed Mary, 2
Blue Juniata, 3
Blushing Maple Tree, 6
Boatman's Return, 3
Boat Song, 1
Boatswain's Story, 7
Bohemian Gipsy Song, 7
Bold be Your Stroke, 4
Bonnie Blue Flag, 6
Bonnie Charlie's Now Awa', 1
Bonnie Doon, 1
Bonnie Dundee, 6
Bonnie Hills of Heather, 3
Bonnie Lad and gentle Lassie, 3
Bounding Billows, 2
Bowld Sojer Boy, 7
Brzes o' Balquither, 3
Brzes o' Gleniffer, 7
Brahmin Love Song, 4
Brave Old Oak, 1
Bread of the World, 4
Break, Break, Break, 3
Bread to Pilgrims Given, 6
Breathings of Spring, 2
Breeze from Home, 3
Bridal Chorus (*Lohengrin*), 3
Bride Bells, 3
Bride's Farewell, 8
Brightest and Best, 3
Brightly, 2
Brightly Glows the Morning, 3
Bright, Rosy Morning, 2
Bright Morning, Hail, 4
Bright Star of Hope, 5
Bring Flowers, 4
Broken Ring, 2
Brother and I, 5
Brother so Fine, 6
Buttercup Test, 7
But the Lord is Mindful, 2

Buy My Roses, 7
Buy My Strawberries, 4
By Cool Siloam's Shady Rill, 1
Bye-lo, Baby, Bye, 7
By the Blue Sea, 6
By Quiet Water Gleaming, 4
By the Sad Sea Waves, 2
By the Well Before the Door, 4
Caller Herrin, 3
Call Me Pet Names, 7
Call Me Thine Own, 5
Calm on the Listening Ear, 1
Calm O'er the Ocean Blue, 8
Campbells are Coming, 5
Canadian Boat Song, 4
Carol, Brothers, Carol, 3
Carol, Carol, Christians, 7
Carrier Dove, 2
Castanets are Sounding, 6
Castles in Spain, 6
Cast thy Bread on the Waters, 6
Cast thy Burden on the Lord, 6
Chapel, 2
Cheer, Boys, Cheer, 2
Cheerily, Cheerily, 4
Cheerily the Bugle Sounds, 3
Cherish Faith in one another, 6
Cherish Kindly Feelings, 3,
Cherries are Ripe, 6
Cherries Ripe, 1
Cherry Ripe (*Horn*), 8
Chide Mildly the Erring, 1
Child of Earth, 2
Child of the Regiment, 3
Children of Heavenly King, 4
Children's Hosanna, 6
Children's Kingdom, 6
Child's Hymn, 1
Chime Again, Beautiful Bells, 3
Chime On, Old Bells, 6
Chimes of Zurich, 3
Christ is Born in Bethlehem, 4
Christ is Born, 3, 7
Christmas Bells are Sound'g, 3
Christmas Day, 8
Christmas Hymn, 6, 7
Christmas is Coming, 4
Christmas is Here, 4
Christmas Song, 5
Christmas Tree, 6
Christmas Time is Come, 1
Christ was Born on Xmas day, 1
Clang of the Wooden Shoon, 4
Claudine, 6
Clear the Way, 2
Clochette, 7
Clover So White, 8
Cock Robin and Jenny Wren, 5
Cold Water Song, 4
Columbia, God Preserve, 2
Columbia, Gem of the Ocean, 1
Come Again, 2
Come, All Ye Faithful, 1
Come, all ye Jolly Shepherds, 1
Come and See Me, Mary Ann, 2
Come Watch the Daylight. 7
Come and Worship, 6
Come Away, Lads, to Labor, 6
Come Away to the Fields, 6
Come Back, Sweet May, 3
Come Back to Erin, 5
Come, Boor, Your Little Blue, 5
Come, Cheerful Companions, 2
Come, Come, Come, 1
Come, Come, Quickly Away, 4
Come, Girls, Come, 8
Come, Haste Away, 7
Come, Holy Ghost, 5
Come, Holy Spirit, 1, 4
Come, Humble Sinner, 8
Come, Hunters, Come, 7
Come, Join in Merry Chorus, 5
Come, Join Our Ch'ful Songs, 5
Come, Let us Learn to Sing, 6
Come, Listen, Dear Child, 8
Come, Gallant Soldier, Come, 3
Come, O Come with Me, 2
Come out, 'tis now Sept'ber, 5
Come, Rest in This Bosom, 5
Come, Said Jesus' Voice, 4
Come, Sing That Air Again, 2
Come, Sing This Round, 7

Come, Sing to Me Again, 8
Come, Thou Almighty King, 2, 4
Come, Thou Fount, 3
Come to the Forest, 8
Come to the Home, 3
Come to the Meadows, 5
Come to the Old Oak Tree, 1
Come to the Sea, 4
Come to Spark'l'g Fountain, 3
Come, Trembling Sinner, 4
Come unto Him, 4, 8
Come When the Twilight, 5
Come When Thou Will, 7
Come Where Flowers, 3
Come Where Aspens Quiver, 7
Come Where the Sunlight, 8
Come with the Gypsy Bride, 5
Come with Thy Lute, 2
Come, Ye Disconsolate, 1
Come, Ye Sinners, 4
Come Ye that Love the Lord, 8
Comin' Thro' the Rye, 1
Commit Thy Ways, 7
Confide Ye aye in Providence, 5
Coronation, 2
County Guy, 7
Cousin Jedediah, 7
Crabbed Age and Youth, 8
Cracovian Maid, 5
Cradled All Lowly, 6
Cradle Hymn, 1
Cradle Song, 8
Cradle Song of Soldier's Wife, 3
Cradle Songs, 1, 3
Crown Him with Crowns, 2
Cuckoo, 2, 6
Cuckoo, Welcome thy Song, 1
Cuddle Doon, 5
Cup of Joy, 7
Daddy, 7
Dance of the Fairies, 6
Dance On Forever, 5
Danube River, 2
Darby and Joan, 4
Dark Day of Horror, 6
Darling, Go to Rest, 8
Dawn of Day, 7
Day is Gone, Night is Come, 6
Daylight Closes round us, 8
Dayl't Fades, Even'g Shades, 4
Daylight Slowly Fades, 6
Day of Wonder, 2
Day on the Mountain, 8
Days of Absence, 2
Deadly Cup, 1
Dearest Love, Remember, 5
Dearest Native Land, 6
Dearest Spot, 1
Dear Father, Drink No More, 4
Dear Little Shamrock, 4
Dear Native Home, 5
Dear Santa Claus, 7
Dear Summer Morn, 8
Deck the Hall with Holly, 1
Deep are the Wounds, 4
Departed Days, 5
Departed Days (*Root*), 6
Depth of Mercy, 5
Dermot Astore, 4
Der Rose Sendung, 3
Deserted by Waning Moon, 8
Ding-Dong, 8
Dip, Boys, Dip the Oar, 4
Distant Drum, 4
Distant Shore, 5
Disturb Not His Slumbers, 6
Dolorous Ditty, 8
Don't Kill the Birds, 8
Don't Leave Mother, Tom, 5
Do They Miss Me at Home, 3
Do They Think of Me, 2
Douglas, Tender and True, 2
Down in a Coal Mine, 5
Down in the Neckar Vale, 8
Down the Burn, Davie, 6
Down the Stream Cheerily, 5
Do You Think of the Days, 6
Do You Think of the Days, 8
Draw the Sword, Scotland, 4
Dream Faces, 5
Dreaming Golden Dreams, 7
Dreamland, 5

Dream On, 3
Dream On, Young Hearts, 5
Dreams, 6
Drift, My Bark, 6
Drink to Me Only with Eyes, 7
Dry the Tear for Holy Eva, 7
Dublin Bay, 4
Dunois, the Brave, 6
Ehren on the Rhine, 4
Eiapopeia, My Baby, Sleep, 3
Eileen Achora, 2
Embarrassment, 8
Enchanted Isle, 6
Ere the Twilight Bat, 6
Evangeline, 2
Evening Bells, 6
Eve'g Hymn, Ave Sanctiss., 1
Eve'ng Hymn (Mendelssohn), 3
Evening Hymn (Hatton), 6
Evening Shades are Falling, 8
Even Me, 1
Ever be Happy, 4
Ever of Thee, 2
Ever to the Right, 8
Every Inch a Sailor, 5
Eve's Lamentation, 5
Exile of Erin, 4
Eyes So Blue and Dreaming, 6
Faded Flowers, 6
Fade, Each Earthly Joy, 6
Fading, Still Fading, 3
Faint a Lonely Rose Tree, 7
Faint and Wearily, 8
Faintly as Tolls the Chime, 4
Faintly Flow, Falling River, 3
Fair as the Morning, 1
Fairest Lord Jesus, 4
Fairies' Dance, 7
Fair Land of Hope, 8
Fair Land of Poland, 5
Fair Luna, 6
Fairy Ring, 2
Faithful Johnnie, 3
Faithful Comrade, 8
Faithful Little Bird, 1
Fallen Thy Throne, O Israel, 4
Far Above the Deep Blue Sea, 6
Far Away, 1
Fare Thee Well, 8
Farewell, Ye Streams, 6
Farewell, but Whenever, 8
Farewell Forever, 5
Farewell, Good Night, 8
Farewell, My Lovely Nancy, 8
Farewell, My Peaceful Vale, 5
Farewell, O Farewell to Thee, 5
Farewell, O Joyous Grove, 1
Farewell Those Happy Hours, 5
Farewell to Lochaber, 1
Farewell to My Harp, 5
Farewell to the Woods, 1
Far, Far upon the Sea, 3
Farmer's Boy, 8
Far o'er Hill and Dell, 8
Far o'er the Sea, 7
Father, I Scarcely Dare, 8
Father Joe, 8
Father, on Thee I Call, 5
Father, Whate'er of Earthly, 1
Feast of Roses, 4
Fiddle-de-dee, 5
Fine Old English Gentleman, 5
Fire of Home, 4
First Christmas Gifts, 1
Fisher, if beside that Stream, 7
Fishermen's Chorus, 6
Five O'clock in the Morning, 7
Flag of the Free, 1
Flag of Our Union Forever, 3
Flee as a Bird, 2
Float Away, 4
Floating on the Wind, 3
Flowerets Blooming, 4
Flowers for the Brave, 4
Flowers of May, 7
Flow Gently, Sweet Afton, 2
Flow, Rio Verde, 8
Fly Away, Pretty Moth, 2
Fold Thy Hands, Little One, 8
Follow Me, Full of Glee, 1
Fondest Affections Cling, 4
Foot Traveler, 5
Foresters Bold, 7
Forever and Forever, 1
Forever and Forever, (Tosti), 5
For Full Five Hund'd Years, 7
Forgive, thro' Thy Dear Son, 4

Forsaken Am I, 4
For Tenderness Formed, 7
Fourth of July Hymn, 7
Fox and Goose, 5
Fragrant Air, 6
Freedom's Flag, 1
Free from Slumber, 6
French Cradle Song, 4
French Patriotic Song, 8
Fresh and Strong, 7
Friends of Freedom, 7
Friends We Never Forget, 5
Fritz's Lullaby, 4
From All That Dwell, 7
From City Gate, 6
From Days of Old, 2
From Every Spire, 7
From Every Stormy Wind, 5
From Greenland's Icy, 2
From Morning till Night, 6
From Merry Swiss Home, 8
From the Desert I Come, 6
Full and Harmonious, 3
Full Far Away a City, 1
Funeral Dirge, 4
Gaily Our Boat Glides, 5
Gaily Sings the Lark, 5
Gaily the Troubadour, 1
Gaily Thro' Life Wander, 4
Gascon Vespers, 6
Gaudeamus Igitur, 6
Gentle Annie, 7
Gentle Breezes Sighing, 8
Gentle Ma'den, 7
Gentle Mary, 4
Gentle Waves upon Deep, 8
Gentle Words, 1
Gently Rest; Slumber, 4
Gently Sighs Breeze, 4, 7
Geography Song, 1
Geraldin, 6
German Cradle Song, 2
German Fatherland, 8
German Watchman Song, 3
Girl I Left Behind Me, 2
Give Me Jesus, 3
Give to Winds Thy Fears, 7
Give Us Our Daily Bread, 7
Glad Christmas Bells, 1
Gleam, O Silver Stream, 6
Gliding 'mid the Poor, 8
Gloomy Wintre's Awa', 8
Glorious Things Spoken, 6
Glory and Love, 4
Glory Begun Below, 8
Glory Gilds Sacred Page, 4
God Bless Native Land, 1
God for Us, 6
God Hath Sent His Angels, 5
God Moves in Mysterious, 4
God of Our Fathers, 2
God Preserve the Kaiser, 5
God Rest Ye, 8
God Save Our Czar, 3
Go Down, Moses, 6
Go, Forget Me, 1
Going Home. Heimgang, 3
Going to Market, 5
Golden Days, 4
Golden Rule, 1, 7
Golden Shore, 2
Golden Slumbers Kiss, 2
Golden Stars are Shining, 6
Golden Years Ago, 6
Good-Bye, 2
Good-Bye at the Door, 5
Good-Bye to Summer, 1
Good-Bye, Sweetheart, 6
Good Cheer, 1
Good Night, 1, 2, 4, 5
Good Night, Good M'rn'g, 3
Good Night, Farewell, 7
Good Night, Ladies, 6
Good Shepherd, 5
Go Thou and Dream, 8
Go to Sleep, Lena Darling, 4
Go Where Glory Waits, 3
Grace, a charming sound, 8
Grave of Bonaparte, 5
Grave of Washington, 6
Green Fields of America, 2
Green Grow Rashes O', 4
Greenwood Tree, 4
Groves of Blarney, 4
Guadalquiver, 7
Guardian Angel, 8
Guardian Mother, 7

Guide Me, Great Jehovah, 1, 4
Gum-Tree Canoe, 5
Hail and Farewell, 3
Hail, Beauteous Stranger, 4
Hail Columbia, 1
Hail, Evening Bright, 3
Hail, Thou Glorious Scion, 3
Hail, Thou Long Expected, 7
Hail, Thou Most Sacred One, 1
Hail, Thou Once Despised, 5
Hail to the Brightness, 2
Hail to the Chief, 2
Hail to the Lord's Anointed, 8
Hallelujah Chorus, 5
Happy and Light, 8
Happy and Merry, 7
Happy Are We To-Night, 4
Happy Bayadere, 8
Happy Days Gone By, 2
Happy Greeting to All, 3
Happy Land, 1
Happy Summer, 8
Hare and Hunter, 7
Hark and Hunter, 7
Hark! Hark! My Soul, 1
Hark! Hark! the Lark, 8
Hark! I hear an Angel Sing, 7
Hark! O'er the Stilly Lake, 4
Hark! Ten Thousand Harps, 7
Hark! the Glad Sound, 7
Hark! the Herald Angels, 2, 7
Hark! Those Holy Voices, 6
Hark! 'Tis the Angelus, 3
Hark to the Shrill Trumpet, 6
Hark to the Distant Drum, 4
Hark! What Mystic Sounds, 8
Harp of My Country, 8
Hasten, Sinner, to be Wise, 2
Heartache for Home, 5
Hearts and Homes, 2
Hear the Birds of Summer, 4
Heaven is My Home, 4
Heavily Wears the Day, 4
Heilige Nacht, 7
Heirs of Unending Life, 1
He Giveth His Beloved, 1, 2
He Never Said He Loved, 4
Her Bright Eyes Gleaming, 6
Her Bright Smile, 6
Her Eyes Like Clouded Stars, 8
Herdsman's Mount'n Home, 2
Here Awa', There Awa', 5
Here's a Health to All, 5
Here's the Bower, 8
Here Under the Greenwood, 4
Here we stand, Hand in Hand, 2
Hero's Serenade, 3
He Sailed o'er Ocean Spray, 7
He Was a Punchinello, 4
He Was Born of Low Degree, 8
Highland Mary, 6
Hoe Out Your Row, 2
Ho! Ho! Vacation Days, 1
Holly Wreath, 4
Holy Bible, Book Divine, 2
Holy, Holy, Holy, 1
Holy Spirit, Source of, 8
Home Again, 5
Home, Can I Forget Thee, 6
Home, Fare Thee Well, 5
Home of My Childhood, 5
Home of the Soul, 1
Home's Not Merely, 2
Home So Blest, 8
Home, Sweet Home, 1
Homeward Bound, 3
Honor His Holy Name, 5
Hope Brightly Gleams, 8
Hot Cross Buns, 7
Ho, the Boating, 8
Hours There Were, 6
How Bright and Fair, 5
How Can I Leave Thee, 1
How Dark and Drear, 8
How Fair Art Thou, 5
How Firm a Foundation, 4
How Gaily the Linnet Sings, 7
How Gaily Rows the G'dolier, 7
How Happy is the Child, 1
How Happy We Have Been, 7
How Lovely Thy Note, 8
How Softly are Glancing, 4
How Sweet the Name, 4
How Tedious and Tasteless, 4
How the Wind Blows, 8
Hungarian Cradle Song, 3
Hunter's Farewell, 2
Hunter's Song, 2, 6

Hunting Song, 1
Hurdy-Gurdy, 7
Hush-a-By, Hush-a-By, 6
Hush, My Babe, 1
Hush, My Baby, 1
Hush, My Baby, Sleep, 4
Hush, My Darling, 8
Hush, the Waves are Roll'g, 5
I am Content, 3
I am Dreaming of Thee, 7
I am the Glad New Year, 7
I Built a Bridge of Fancies, 6
I Cannot Sing the Old Songs, 3
I Come from Alabama, 7
I Come, I Come, 4
I Dreamed a Dream, 8
I Dream of All Things Free, 2
I Dream of My Fatherland, 2
I Dreamt I Dwelt in Marble, 2
I'd Offer Thee This Hand, 5
I'd Weep with Thee, 4
"If," 8
I Fain a Winning Tale, 8
If ever I see on Bush or Tree, 4
If I Were a Sunbeam, 8
If Thou Hast Crush'd Flow'r, 4
If Thou Wert by My Side, 2
If You be My May Margaret, 4
I Gave Her a Rose, 5
I Had a Bird, a Little Bird, 1
I Had Four Brothers, 1
I Had Gold, I Had Gems, 7
I Have Come from Mount'ns, 3
I Have Heard Sweet Music, 8
I Heard an Old Farmer, 8
I Heard a Red Robin, 7
I Heard the Wee Bird Sing, 3
I Hear Not a Footfall, 1
I Hear them o'er the Meadow, 6
I Hear Them Tell, 4
I Hear the Robin Sing, 6
I Hear To-night the Bells, 7
I Know a Bank, 6
I Know an Eye so Bright, 5
I'll Do My Duty, 2
I'll Hang My Harp, 5
Ilka Blade of Grass, 5
I Lo'ed Ne'er a Laddie, 3
I'll Sing an Old Ballad, 5
I'll Weep with Thee, 8
I Love Little Pussy, 5
I Love My Love, 6
I Love the Merry Sunshine, 2
I Love the Song of Birds, 1
I Love the Spring, 5
I Love the Summer Time, 3
I Love Thy Kingdom, Lord, 5
I Love to Gaze on Smiling, 4
I Love to Sing, 6
I Love to Tell the Story, 2
I'm Afloat! I'm Afloat! 3
I'm a Merry Gypsy Maid, 6
I'm a Merry Laughing Girl, 6
I'm a Pilgrim, 4
I'm a Shepherd of the Valley, 1
I'm Dreaming Now of Hallie, 6
I Met My Love in a Dream, 8
I'm Glad I am a Farmer, 4
I'm Leaving Thee in Sorrow, 7
I'm Little Robin Redbreast, 7
I'm Not Myself at All, 5
I'm Saddest When I Sing, 6
I'm Sitting on the Stile, 7
I'm Very Fond of a Song, 4
In Car'lina's Clime, 4
In Childhood, with Crown, 6
In Days of Old when Knights, 7
In Excelsis Gloria, 7, 8
In Flakes of a Feathery, 1
In Happy Moments, 3
In Mantua, in Fetters, 6
In Merry Chorus, 5
In My Swift Boat, 6
Ingleside, 1
Innisfail, 4
In Shadowland, 6
Integer Vitæ, 6
In the Gloaming, 4
In the Golden Eventide, 5
In the Land of My Birth, 8
In the Starlight, 2
In the West the sun declining, 1
In the Wild Chamois Track, 1
In this Sheltered Dell, 7
Into the Silent Room, 8
Into the Woods My Master, 6
I Once Had a Comrade, 8
I Remember My Childh, 4

I Remember a Sunny Vale, 5
Irish Emigrant's Lament, 7
I Sat Beneath the Maples, 5
I Saw a Ship a-Sailing, 5
I See My Home in Twilight, 5
Isle of Beauty, 3
I Stood on the Bridge, 3
Italian Cradle Song, 3
It Came upon the Midnight, 6
I Think When I Read that
  Sweet Story of Old, 2
It is Better to Laugh, 3
It was a Breton Village, 6
It was the Noon of Night, 7
I've Been Roaming, 2
I've Been Thinking of Home, 1
I've Come Across the Sea, 5
I've Found a Joy in Sorrow, 3
I've Left Ballymornach, 7
Ivy Green, 8
I Walked and I Walked, 7
I Wandered by the Brookside, 4
I Was a Wandering Sheep, 5
I Was Seated at Thy Feet, 8
I Welcome Thee, 5
I Will be Happy Yet, 3
I Will Lay Me Down, 6
I Worship Thee, Sweet Will, 7
I Would I were a Boy Ag'n, 4, 7
I Would Not Die in Sp'gtime, 7
I Would Not Live Alway, 1
I Would That My Love, 7
Jack and Jill, 3
Jack at Sea, 7
Jamie! Jamie !8
Jamie's on the Stormy Sea, 6
Janet's Choice, 1
Jeannette and Jeannot, 2
Jenny Lind's Bird Song, 5
Jenny Lind's Good Night, 3
Jerusalem, My Happy Home, 1
Jerusalem, the Golden, 1
Jessie, Flower of Dumblane, 5
Jesus is Mine, 6
Jesus, Lover of My Soul, 1, 2
Jesus, My All, to Heaven, 5
Jesus, O'er the Grave, 1
Jesus, the Very Thought, 1
Jock o' Hazeldean, 3
John Anderson, My Jo, 1
John Brown's Body, 1
Johnny Sands, 2
Johnny Schmoker, 8
Jolly Jester, 2
Jolly Old St. Nicholas, 1
Joseph Baxter is My Name, 3
Joyfully, Joyfully, 7
Joy in Sorrow, 3
Joy, Joy, Freedom To-day, 8
Joyous Song, 6
Joys That We've Tasted, 1
Joy to the World, 6
Joy Wait on Thy Morrow, 2
Juanita, 2
Judith ! Our God Alone, 5
Just as I Am, 4
Just Touch the Harp Gently, 7
Kathleen, 7
Kathleen Aroon, 3
Kathleen Mavourneen, 2
Katy Darling, 2
Katy's Letter, 1
Keen Blaws the Wind, 7
Keep a Light Heart, 8
Keller's American Hymn, 4
Kelvin Grove, 5
Kerry Dance, 4
Killarney, 3
Kind Friends, We Meet Again, 8
Kindred Hearts, 2
Kind Words Can Never Die, 1
King of Love, 1
Kiss of a Little Child, 8
Kitty Tyrrell, 3
Laddie, 2
Lady Beatrice's Lament. 6
Land Ahead, 1
Landing of the Pilgrims. 5
Land of Dreams 5
Land of Memory, 1
Land o' the Leal, 1
Land of Our Fathers 8
Land Without a Storm, 6
Lang o' Comin', 6
Larboard Watch, 3
Last Greeting, 3
Last night when all was still, 5

Last Rose of Summer, 1
Laughing Glee, 7
Lavender's Blue, 5
Lead, Kindly Light, 1
Let Erin Remember the Days, 1
Let Me Dream Again, 4
Let Not Grief Annoy, 8
Let Others Dream, 2
Let the Palms Wave, 7
Let Us Sing Merrily, 3
Life Laid Down, 2
Life Let Us Cherish, 1
Light and Rosy thy Slumb'rs, 5
Light in the Window, 2
Light of Other Days, 2
Lightly Row, 1, 4
Like the First Fresh Scent, 8
Linden Tree, 6
Listen to the Mocking Bird, 6
Listen to the Water Mill, 3
List, 'Tis Music Stealing, 3
List to the Convent Bells, 3
Little Bennie Was Our Darl'g, 2
Little Birdie in the Tree, 1
Little Bird on the Green Tree, 2
Little Boy Blue, 6
Little Brother, Darling Boy, 1
Little Cherry Blossom, 2
Little Children, Can you Tell, 7
Little Children's Day, 4
Little Drops of Water, 1
Little Eva, 7
Little Gypsy Jane, 6
Little Lips, 8
Little Maggie May, 3
Little Orphant Annie, 6
Little Sunbeam, 2
Little Tin Soldier, 7
Lochaber No More, 3
Lock! Lock! Ahoy ! 7
Lo, the Heavens Rending, 4
Lone Starry Hours, 8
London Bridge, 5, 6
Longing for Spring, 1
Long, Long Ago, 1
Long, Weary Day, 2
Look in My Face, Dear, 4
Look Not Upon the Wine, 4
Lord, Dismiss Us, 3
Lord, Forever at Thy Side, 3
Lord, in this Thy Mercy's Day, 1
Lord, We Come Before Thee, 4
Lord, with Glowing Heart, 2
Lorena, 7
Lo, the Seal of Death, 5
Lotus Flower, 2
Loud the Sounding Strings, 3
Love and Mirth, 2
Love at Home, 3
Love, Hope, Happiness, 1
Love, I Will Love You Ever, 4
Lovely Mary Donnelly, 7
Lovely May, 4
Lovely Nancy, 8
Lovely Rose, 1
Love Not, 2
Love's Golden Dream, 7
Love Smiles No More, 3
Love's Ritonella, 1
Love's Young Dream, 2
Loving Voices, 4
Low-Backed Car, 4
Lucy's Flittin', 4
Lullaby from Erminie, 5
Lullaby, Lullaby, 6
Lurialine, 4
Maggie's Secret, 7
Maid Elsie Roams, 3
Maiden and Rose, 7
Maid of Llangollen, 2
Maid of the Mill, 6
Majestic Sweetness, 5
Make Me No Gaudy Chaplet, 4
Make the Best of It, 2
Make Your Mark, 2
Maltese Boatman's Song, 6
Mamma's Love, 8
Mandolin Song, 6
Maple from the Wildwood, 3
March, March, 5
Marching Song, 2
March of the Cameron Men, 7
Marseilles Hymn, 1
Mary and Martha, 4
Maryland, My Maryland, 5
Mary Morrison, 5
Mary of Argyle, 2

Mary of the Wild Moor, 7
Mary's Tears, 7
Maxwelton's Braes, 1
May is Here, 4
May Margaret, 4
May Queen, 2
Meek and Lowly, 1
Meet Me by Moonlight, 5
Mellow Horn, 2
Mellow Notes of Horn, 7
Melodies of Many Lands, 1
Men of Harlech, 6
Mermaid's Evening Song, 8
Merrily Every Bosom, 2
Merrily Greet the Morn, 1
Merrily, Merrily Sing, 3
Merry Hours of Youth, 6
Merry May, 7
Merry Swiss Boy, 3
Midnight Moon, 8
'Mid Scenes of Confusion, 5
Midshipmite, 8
'Mid Woods and Forest, 6
Miller of the Dee, 2
Miller's Daughter, 3
Mill May, 1
Mill Wheel, 2
Mine Own, 6
Minstrel Boy, 1
Mistress Santa Claus, 6
Monarch of the Woods, 5
Month of Apple Blossom, 1
Moon is Beaming, 3
Morning Red, 1
Mother, are there Angels, 3
Mother's Wish, 1
Mountain Boy, 5
Mountain Bugle, 3
Mountaineer's Farewell, 3
Mount'n Maid's Invitat'n, 1
Mowers' Song, 1
Murmur, Gentle Lyre, 4
Murmuring Sea, 5
Musical Alphabet, 5
Music at Nightfall, 5
Music Everywhere, 2
Music of Labor, 5
Music on the Waves, .
Must I leave thee, Par'dise, 5
Must I Then Leave, 5
Must Jesus Bear the Cross, 5
My Ain Countrie, 2
My Childhood's Love, 8
My Country, 'Tis of Thee, 1
My Friend is the Man, 8
My Heart and Lute, 4
My Heart is Light, 6
My Heart is Sair, 8
My Heart's in Highlands, 1
My Jamie's o'er the Sea, 6
My Jesus, as Thou Wilt, 4
My Laddie Far Away, 7
My Life is Like the Rose, 7
My Little Valley Home, 8
My Love Beyond the Sea, 8
My Mother Dear, 3
My Mother Loves Me Not, 1
My Mother's Bible, 2
My Mother's Song, 4
My Nannie's Awa', 4
My Native Land, 8
My Own Guiding Star, 7
My Own Native Land, 3
Nancy Lee, 2
National Hymn, 1
Nearer, My God, to Thee, 1, 4
Near the Lake, 1
Neva Boatman's Song, 4
Never Alone, 6
Never is My Heart So Gay, 4
Never Say Fail, 2
New Hail Columbia, 5
Nice Young Girl, 6
Nice Young Man, 6
Nicodemus, the Slave, 3
Night and Day, Love, 7
Night is Fine, 4
Nigh to a Grave, 4
Night Sinks on the Wave, 6
Ninety and Nine, 2
Nobody knows the Tr'ble, 5
None Can Tell, 3
Norah Darling, 8
Norah McShane, 5
Not a Sparrow Falleth, 6
Not for Joseph, 3
Nothing True but Heaven, 7

Not in Halls of Splendor, 8
Now All the Merry Bells, 5
Now Thank We All Our God, 2
Now the Day is Waning, 5
Now the Merry Spring, 6
Now to all a Kind Good-night, 7
Nun Dankett Alle Gott, 2
Nymphs of Air and Sea, 7
O Alien Brothers, 8
O Be Just, 8
O Boatman, Row Me O'er, 6
O Come, All Ye Faithful, 1
O Come, Come Away, 1
O Come, Emmanuel, 6
O Come, Maidens, Come, 4
October Gave a Party, 5
O Could Our Thoughts, 2
O County Guy, 7
Ode for Decoration Day, 8
O Dear Sixpence, 3
O'er the Sea in My Fairy Boat, 3
O Fair Dove, O Fond Dove, 4
Of All the Busy People Round, 5
Oft in Danger, Oft in Woe, 3
Oft in the Stilly Night, 1
Oh, Are Ye Sleepin', Maggie, 5
Oh, Broad Land, 8
Oh, but You've Been Lang, 6
Oh, Dearest Mae, 6
Oh, Don't You Remember, 5
Ohé, Mamma, 6
Oh, for a Thousand Tongues, 5
Oh, for a Heart to Praise, 7
Oh, Gaily thro' Life Wander, 4
Oh, Give Me My Arab Steed, 7
Oh, Gladly We Hail Thee, 1
Oh, Hope, Delusive Dream, 6
Oh, How Cold the Winter, 1
Oh, I Have Had Dreams, 6
Oh, I'm a Happy Creature, 1
Oh, Is It Thus We Part, 7
Oh, Jacob, Get the Cows, 7
Oh, Loved Italia, 8
Oh, Many a Time I'm Sad, 7
Oh, My Bravest and Best, 7
Oh, Pilot, 'tis a Fearful Night, 4
Oh, Sister Dear, 5
Oh, Smile as Thou Wert Wont, 5
Oh, Solemn Hour, 5
Oh, Susanna, 7
Oh, Sweet and Dim the Light, 7
Oh, Take Me Back to Switz'l'd, 2
Oh, Tell Me What it Meaneth, 1
Oh, That I Never More, 4
Oh, the Flowers in Wildwood, 6
Oh, the Lone Starry Hours, 8
Oh, the Sailor Shall Sing, 6
Oh, Touch the Harp, 4
Oh, Touch Those Chords, 4
Oh, 'twas Sweet to Hear Her, 6
Oh Hush Thee, My Baby, 3
Oh, Wert thou in Cauld Blast, 4
Oh, What is the Matter, 4
Oh, Who So Gay and Free, 5
Oh, Why Does the White Man, 7
Oh, Why Left I My Hame, 3
O Jesu, Thou are Standing, 1
O Land of Saints, 1
Old Arm Chair, 3
Old and Young Marie, 7
Old Cottage Clock, 1
Old Easy Chair by the Fire, 8
Old Familiar Place, 1
Old Friends and Old Times, 2
Old Granite State, 3
Old Grimes, 2
Old House at Home, 3, 8
Old Hundred, 1
Old King Cole, 7
Old Oaken Bucket, 1, 4
Old, Old Song, 5
Old Rosin the Bow, 2
Old Santa Claus, 6
Old Santa Claus in Christmas, 7
Old Tubal Cain, 4
O Mary, Call the Cattle Home, 7
O Native Land, 8
Once Again, 3
Once Again, O Blessed Time, 2
Once Again the Flowers, 4
Once in Days of Golden, 4
Once I Saw a Sweetbrier Rose, 1
Once More, My Soul, 7
Once There was a Little Voice, 8
One by One the Sands, 4
One Morning, Oh So Early, 8
One Night Came on 8

One Night When the Wind, 7
One or Two, 5
One Sweetly Solemn Tho't, 7
On Foot I Take My Way, 5
On Long Island's Sea-girt, 6
Only a Gentle Word, 4
Only a Year Ago, 6
Only to See Thee, 8
Only With Thine Eyes, 7
On the Fount of Life, 3
On the Mountains, 5
On Tombigbee River, 5
On to the Field, 8
On We are Floating, 1
On Yonder Rock Reclining, 6
Origin of the Harp, 4
Origin of Yankee Doodle, 1
O Rowan Tree, 6
Orphan Ballad Singers, 8
O Sacred Head, 2
O Sad Were the Hours, 8
O Say, Do You Remember, 7
Ossian's Serenade, 4
O Take Her, but be Faithful, 8
Our Christmas Rose, 8
Our Country's Flag, 1
Our Daily Bread, 7
Our Father in Heaven, 1
Our Fatherland, 1
Our Flag is There, 1
Our Flag O'er Us Waving, 5
Our Home is on the Sea, 5
Our Merry Swiss Home, 8
Our Mother's Way, 8
Our Songs of Joy and Gladn's,8
Our Way Across the Sea, 5
Our Wonderful House, 4
Out in a Beautiful Field, 6
Out of the Window, 1
Over the Dark Blue Sea, 3
Over the Hills and Far Away, 7
Over the Mountain, 6
Over the Mountain Wave, 2
Over There, 2
Over the Sea, 7
Over the Stars There is Rest, 3
Over the Summer Sea, 3
Over the Water to Charlie, 1
Over the Waves We Float, 4
O Ye Tears, 1
Paddle Your Own Canoe, 3
Pagoda Bells, 4
Parting Song at Graduation, 3
Pat Malloy, 7
Peaceful Fold, 5
Peaceful Slumbering, 4
Peace on Earth, 5
Peace to the Brave, 6
Pearl that Worldlings Covet, 2
Perri Merri Dictum, Domine, 1
Pierrot, 3
Pharaoh's Army, 6
Pilot, The, 4
Pity One in Childhood Torn, 8
Pleasure Climbs to Mount'n, 4
Pleyel's Hymn, 2
Polish Maiden Song, 1
Polish May Song, 1
Poor Tho' My Cot May Be, 4
Portuguese Hymn, 4
Postilion, The, 3
Praise Jehovah's Name, 4
Praise to God, 2, 8
Prayer from Freischutz, 1
Press On, Press On, 4
Pretty Pear Tree, 6
Prince Charming, 3
Priory Chimes, 6
Proud and Lowly, 6
Pull Away, Brave Boys, 2
Punchinello, 4
Queen of the Night, 8
Queen's Maries, 6
Quiet,Lord,My Frow'd Heart, 7
Quiet Night, 8
Rainfall Follows the Plow, 2
Rain Upon the Roof, 3
Raise Your Hands, 7
Rataplan, 4
Red, Red Rose, 2
Remember Thy Creator Now,1
Rejoice, Rejoice, 2
Rest for the Weary, 3
Revive Us Again, 7
Ring On, Sweet Angelus, 5
Ring On, Ye Bella, 4
Ring Out, O Bells, 6

Ripe Are the Apples, 6
Ripples Touched by the Moon,8
Rise, Crowned with Light, 2
Rise, Glorious Conqueror, 8
Rise from Thy Mourning, 6
Rise, My Soul, 4
Robert! Robert! 7
Robin Adair, 1
Robin Redbreast, 1, 7
Robinson Crusoe, 1
Robin Song, 7
Rock-a-bye-Baby, in tree-top,3
Rockaway, 6
Rocked in Cradle of the Deep, 2
Rock Me to Sleep, Mother, 4
Roll, Jordan, Roll, 4
Roll On, Silver Moon, 2
Rosalind, 3
Rose-Marie, 7
Rose of Allandale, 1
Rose of Lucerne, 5
Rosin the Bow, 2
Rosy Crown, 2
Round the Corner, 5
Row, Row, Cheerly Row, 2
Row, Row, Homeward, 3
Row, Row, My Boatie, 7
Row Thy Boat Lightly, 5
Row Your Boat, 1
Roy's Wife of Aldivalloch, 4
Rule Britannia, 7
Russian Driver's Song, 2
Russian Hymn, 2
Russian National Hymn, 3
Sabre Song, 1
Sadly Bend the Flowers, 4
Sad Was the Hour, 7
Safe Home at Last, 5
Safely thro' Another Week, 1
Safe Wi'hin the Vail, 1
Sailing, 3
Saints' Sweet Home, 5
Sally in Our Alley, 6
Salute the Happy Morn, 7
Sands of Dee, 1
Santa Lucia, 8
Saved from the Storm, 6
Saviour, to Thy Dear Name, 3
Saviour, Source of Blessing, 3
Savourneen Dheelish, 7
Saw Ye My Saviour, 5
Saw Ye Never in the Twilight, 1
Say, What Shall My Song be, 3
Scarlet Sarafan 2
Scenes That are Brightest, 1
Scotch Cradle Song, 3
Scots, Wha' Hae wi' Wallace, 7
Sea Birds' Song, 2
See, Amid the Winter's Snow, 8
See at Your Feet, 3
See-Saw Waltz Song, 6
See the Happy Kitten, 4
See the Proud Banner, 5
See the Sun's First Gleam, 4
See Where the Rising Sun, 2
Serenade, 7
Serenade of Don Pasquale, 3
Shall We Meet Beyond the, 2
Shamrock of Ireland, 4
She Bloomed with the Roses, 4
Shed Not a Tear, 8
Shells of Ocean, 1
Shepherd Boy, 2
She's All My Fancy Painted, 6
She Sits Alone, 1
She Stands on the Pier, 7
She Wore a Wreath of Roses, 6
Ship of State, 8
Should Auld Acquaintance, 1
Shout the Glad Tidings, 6
Sigh not o'erToil andTrouble,5
Silence, 2
Silently, Silently, 5
Silently Falling Snow, 1
Silent Night! Holy Night! 1
Silver Chimes, 2
Sing Always, 1
Sing a Song of Sixpence, 7
Sing Glad Songs for Him, 4
Singing in the Rain, 1
Singing Thro' the Forest, 5
Sing it Over, 5
Sing, Smile, Slumber, 6
Sing, Sweet Bird, 8
Sing, Thou Merry Bird, 1
Skylark, The, 7
Slave Hymns 4

Sleep, Baby Dear, 5
Sleep, Baby, Sleep, 8
Sleep, Beloved, Sleep, 1
Sleep, Darling, Sleep, 8
Sleep, Gentle Mother, 3
Sleep, My Baby, Sleep, 3
Sleep, My Darling, 8
Slumber Song (Kucken), 2
Smiling Faces, 4
Smiling May, 2
Snow Bird, 1
Soft Music is Stealing, 1
Softly Vernal Breezes, 1
Softly Now the Light, 1, 3
Soldier of the Cross, 8
Soldiers' Chorus (Faust), 4
Soldier's Tear, 3
Some Day, 4
Sometimes I Dream, 5
Somewhere, 6
Song of Arbor Day, 3
Song of Blanche Alpen, 3
Song of Night, 4
Song of Rest, 8
Song of Seven, 2
Song of Sunshine, 7
Song of Temperance, 7
Song of the Angels, 6
Song of the Brook, 2
Song of the Children, 5
Song of the Daisy, 3
Song of the Fisher Boy, 8
Song of the Fowler, 6
Song of the Hop Pickers, 6
Song of the Maple, 3
Song of the May, 5
Songs of Praise, 1
Songs Revealing, 1
Sons of Men, Behold, 1
Sorry Her Lot, 5
So Runs My Dream, 7
So Sweet Her Voice, 7
Sound of Harps Angelical,4
Sound Our Voices, 2
Spanish Serenade, 8
Sparkling and Bright, 1
Speak Gently, 2
Speed Away, 1
Speed, My Bark, 5
Speed Our Republic, 4
Spider and the Fly, 1
Spinning Song, 6
Spinning Was Clochette, 7
Sprig of Shillelah, 7
Spring, Gentle Spring, 2
Spring Returning, 7
Spring Time Once Again, 4
Starlight is Streaming, 3
Star Spangled Banner, 1
Stars Trembling O'er Us, 2
Stay, My Darling, Stay, 5
Steal Away, 2
Still is the Night, 8
Still so Gently Stealing, 5
Still, Still with Thee, 1
Storm (Hullah), 2
Story of the Nightingale, 8
Story of the Shepherd, 7
Strangers Yet, 4
Strawberry Girl, 5
Strike the Cymbal, 3
Strike the Harp Gently, 8
Strong Lads of Labor, 1
Styrian Land, 2
Suabian's Song of Home, 8
Summer Days Coming, 2
Summer Eve is Gone, 8
Summer is Coming, 3
Summer Song, 7
Summer Suns Glowing, 7
Swedish Cradle Song, 5
Sweet and Low, 2
Sweet Bird, Thy Note, 1
Sweet By and By, 5
Sweeter than the Breath, 4
Sweet Evenings Come, 3
Sweet Hour of Prayer, 1
Sweetly Sleep, 4
Sweet Memories of Thee, 4
Sweet My Child, for Thee, 8
Sweet Robin, 8
Sweet Saviour, Bless Us, 1
Sweet Song Bird, 2
Sweet Voices, 6
Sweet Will of God, 7
Swinging 'Neath the Old Apple Tree, 1

Swing, Cradle, Swing, 6
Swiss Girl, 3, 5
Swiss Hunter, 6
Swiss Shepherd's Song, 8
Switzer Boy, 3
Switzer's Farewell, 3
Switzer's Song of Home, 2
Take Back the Heart, 5
Take Me Back to Switzerland,5
Tara's Harp, 1
Tea in the Arbor, 3
Tell Her I Love Her So, 6
Tell Me, Beautiful Maiden, 6
Tempest of the Heart, 6
Tenting on the Old Camp, 6
That Day the World shall see, 2
That Old Waltz by the Linden,5
That Sweet Story of Old, 2
The Anchor's Weighed, 8
The Baden Polka, 2
The Bairnies Cuddle Doon, 5
The Banks of the Lee, 8
The Bells of Aberdovey, 7
The Birds Must Know, 5
The Birds Sleeping Gently, 3
The Blue Alsatian Mount'ns, 2
The Boatman's Return, 3
The Boatswain's Story, 7
The Bowld Sojer Boy, 7
The Brave Old Oak, 2
The Breeze from Home, 3
The Bride Bells, 3
The Bridge, 3
The Bright Stars Fade, 6
The Broken Ring, 2
The Campbells are Coming, 5
The Carrier Dove, 4
The Chapel, 2
The Child of the Regiment, 3
The Chorister, 7
The Christmas Chimes, 8
The Church's One Foundat'n 4
The Corn Song, 7
The Cricket, 8
The Cuckoo, 2
The Danube River, 2
The Dawn is Breaking, 8
The Days of My Youth, 8
The Day Star is Shining, 8
The Dearest Spot, 1
The Dear Little Shamrock, 4
The Departed, 3
The Die is Cast (Pestel), 3
The Distant Drum, 4
The Distant Shore, 5
The Dream is Past, 7
The Evening Bell, 4
The Evening Bells Sound, 8
The Farmer, 1
The Farmer's Boy, 8
The Fire of Home, 4
The Fisher by the Stream, 7
The Flag of Our Union, 3
The Flowers that Bloom, 1
The Forget-Me-Not, 4
The Future Smiles Brightly, 4
The Girl I Left Behind Me, 2
The Golden Shore, 2
The Golden Sun, 3
The Gondolier, 2
The Good Angels, 8
The Good Ship Rode, 7
The Good "Three Bells," 3
The Good Time Coming, 8
The Harp is Now Silent, 8
The Harp that Once Thro', 1
The Heart Bowed Down, 1
The Heart that Knows, 4
The Heart, the Heart, 8
The Heath is All Lonely, 6
The Hero's Serenade, 3
The Hindoo Girl, 8
The Hobby Horse, 1
The Hour of Rest, 7
The Hunter's Song, 2
The Indian Hunter, 7
The Ingleside, 1
The Ivy Green, 8
The Jewish Maiden, 6
The Kerry Dance, 4
The King's Highway, 7
The Lark, 2
The Lark Sings Loud, 8
The Leaves Falling, 3
The Life Laid Down, 2
The Light House, 2
The Light in the Window, 6

The Little Busy Bee, 8
The Little Leaves, 6
The Little Voice, 8
The Long, Weary Day, 2
The Long Years, 1
The Lord into his Garden, 5
The Lord's Prayer, 1
The Loreley, 1
The Low-Backed Car, 4
The Lover's Sigh, 8
The Mahogany Tree, 4
The Maister, 3
The May Queen, 2
The Mellow Horn, 2
The Mercy Seat, 5
The Merry Birds, 8
The Midnight Moon, 8
The Midshipmite, 8
The Miller of the Dee, 2
The Minstrel Boy, 1
The Minstrel's Request, 8
The Monkey's Wedding, 7
The Moon is Beaming, 3
The Morning Light, 4
The Mother's Wish, 1
The Mountain Bugle, 3
The Mourner, 1
The Night is Fine, 4
The Noontide Ray, 3
The Officer's Funeral, 6
The Old Arm Chair, 3
The Old Familiar Place, 1
The Old Lock, 7
The Old Oaken Bucket, 1, 4
The Old Sexton, 4
The Pagoda Bells, 4
The Palms. 7
The Party at the Zoo, 6
The Pe'ril that Worldlings, 2
The Pilot, 1
The Quiet Night, 8
The Red, Red Rose, 2
The River Lee, 3
The River's Message, 8
The Romany Lass, 8
The Rose Bush, 6
The Rose all are Praising, 3
The Rosy Crown, 2
The Rowan Tree, 6
The Scout, 5
The Sea, the Sea, 8
The Sea Gulls, 6
The Seasons, 6
The Singing of Birds, 5
The Sky Lark, 3, 7
The Sleigh Ride, 7
The Slumber Song, 2
The Soldier's Return, 7
The Soldier's Tear, 1
The Sound of Harps, 4
The Spacious Firmament, 3
The Spirit in Our Hearts, 8
The Spring Has Come, 8
The Spring Time of Year, 3
The Standard Fearer, 8
The Star o' Glengary, 7
The Star of Hope, 8
The Styrian Land, 2
The Sun is Low, 7
The Sun o'er Mountain, 7
The Sweet Bird Winging, 7
The Switzer's Farewell, 3
The Tar's Farewell, 6
The Tear, 1
The Teetotalers Coming, 1
The Tempest, 8
The Tempest Rages Wild, 5
The Third Day Was the Marriage Feast, 7
The Tree of Odenwald, 6
The Trees and the Master, 6
The Vacant Chair, 3
The Vesper Bells Ringing, 6
The Vesper Chime, 4
The Voice of Free Grace, 3
The Waefu' Heart, 7
The Watcher, 4
The Water Into Wine, 7
The Water Mill, 3

The Weary Are at Rest, 5
The Wee Bird, 7
The Wife's Welcome, 7
The Wood Horn, 6
The World is Full of Beauty, 4
The Yankee Boy, 7
The Years Creep Slowly By, 7
The Young Indian Maid, 7
Then You'll Remember Me, 2
There Came to the Beach, 4
There is a Bonny Isle, 7
There is a Happy Land, 1
There is a Land, 5
There is Beauty in the Forest, 4
There is Dew for Flow'ret, 5
There's a Dear Little Plant, 4
There's a Good Time Coming, 8
There is a Green Hill far away, 5
There's a Land that is Fairer, 5
There's a Sigh in the Heart, 8
There's a Wedding in Orchard, 1
There's Music in the Air, 1
There's Not a Word, 7
There's Room Enough for All, 4
There Was Little Water Sprite, 4
There Was One Little Jack, 6
They Grew in Beauty, 3
They Sailed Away, 4
This Happy Day 7
This is My Dream, 5
This World a Fleeting Show, 7
Those Endearing Themes, 1
Those Evening Bells, 1, 2
Thou Art Gone from my Gaze, 7
Thou Art My Rose, 6
Thou Art So Near and Yet, 5
Thou Art the Way, 3
Though Lost to Sight, 8
Thoughts of Home, 1
Thoughts of Wonder, 4
Thou'rt Like Unto a Flower, 4
Thou, Thou, Reignest, 7
Thou, Too, Sail On, O Ship, 8
Thou Wilt Never Grow Old, 4
Tho' You Leave Me in Sorr'w, 7
Three Bells, 3
Three Cheers for Olden Time, 4
Three Children Sliding, 2
Three Fishers, 4
Three Kings of Orient, 7
Three Poor Mariners, 7
Thro' the Rustling Woods, 4
Through the Wood, 3
Thy Face is Near, 8
Thy Glory thou didst Manifest, 7
Thy Name the Magic Spell, 2
Thy Voice is Near, 5
Thy Way, Not Mine, O Lord, 3
Time Doth Pass Away, 2
Timothy's Welcome, 6
Tippecanoe and Tyler Too, 6
Tired, So Tired, 7
'Tis Evening Brings My Heart, 7
'Tis God Who Ordains Me, 5
'Tis Lone on the Waters, 2
'Tis Midnight Hour, 6
'Tis Moonlight on the Sea, 4
'Tis Not True, 8
'Tis Years Since Last We Met, 6
Tit Willow, 5
To Alexis I Send Thee, 3
Too Late! Too Late! 5
To Thee, Our Father, 7
To Thy Pastures Fair, 2
Touch Not the Cup, 3
Touch Us Gently, Time, 6
Tramp, Tramp, Tramp, 5
Trancadillo, 4
Traveler's Evening Song, 6
Trip it Lightly, 8
Troika, Russian Driver's Song, 2
True Hearts, 8
True Love Can Ne'er Forget, 2
True Love is Sweet, 5
Try, Try Again, 1
'Twas a Summer's Morning, 5
'Twas in Sunny Rhineland, 7
'Twere Vain to Tell Thee, 6
Twickenham Ferry, 2

Twilight Dews, 4
Twilight is Falling, 1
Twinkle, Twinkle, Little Star, 1
Tyrolese Mountain Song, 7
Uncle Ned, 5
Underneath the May Tree, 1
Under Willow She's Sleeping, 7
Upidee: "Excelsior," 1
Upon the Height I Stood, 3
Up the Hills, 1
Vacant Chair, 3
Verdant Grove, Farewell, 1
Vesper Bell, 2
Vesper Chime, 4
Vesper Hymn, 2
Vine Dresser's Song, 6
Viva L'America, 2
Vive Le Roi, 3
Visions of Morning, 1
Voices All Merry, 6
Waiting for Me, 8
Wake, for the Night is Flying, 2
Wake, Happy Children, 3
Wake, Nicodemus, 3
Waking Flowers, 7
Waking or Sleeping, 3
Wake, Wake the Morning, 1
Wanderer's Farewell, 3
Wandering Willie, 5
Wander Staff, 1
Warren's Address, 2
Watchman, Tell of the Night, 3
Watch on the Rhine, 1
Water Mill, 3
Wear a Bright Smile, 6
We Are All Noddin', 4
We Are Fairies of the Sea, 8
We Are Tenting To-night, 6
Wearing of the Green, 5
Weary, So Weary, 7
We'd Better Bide a Wee, 2
Weep for the Fallen, 1
We Hail Thee, Glad Spring, 8
We Have Been Friends, 1
We Come with Joyful Greet'g, 3
We Have Lived and Loved, 2
We Lay Us Down to Sleep, 1
Welcome, Fair Evening, 6
Welcome, Pretty Primrose, 8
Welcome to Morning, 1
Well-a-Day, Ah, Well-a-Day, 4
We'll Go to the Mountains, 5
We'll Laugh and Sing, 4
We Love to Go Each Day, 6
We May be Happy Yet, 1
We May Rove the Wide World, 1
We Met, 'Twas in a Crowd, 8
We Praise Thee, O God, 7
We Roam Thro' Forest Shades, 3
We Sat by the River, 8
We Speak of Realms of Blest, 6
We Three Kings of Orient, 7
We were Crowded in Cabin, 8
Wha'll Buy Caller Herrin', 3
What a Charm has the Drum, 4
What a Friend in Jesus, 4
What Are Wild Waves Saying, 4
What Can the Matter Be, 1
What Fairy-like Music, 1
What I Love and Hate, 1
What is Home With't Mother, 2
What Means This Glory, 5
What's a' the Steer, Kimmer. 3
What Will You Do, Love, 1
When All the World is Young, 4
When at Twilight So Softly, 6
When His Salvation Bringing, 6
When I Come, 5
When I Remember, 4
When I Was a Beggarly Boy, 6
When I Was a Lad, 1
When Jack is Tall and Twenty, 8
When Little Samuel Woke, 4
When Night Comes O'er, 5
When Other Friends, 5
When Roses Bloom, 6
When St all We Meet Again, 1
When Soft Stars are Peeping, 4

When Stars in Quiet Skies, 1
When Sweet Music, 6
When Bloom is on the Rye, 6
When the Boats Come Home, 1
When the Corn is Waving, 6
When Day with Rosy Light, 1
When the Golden Morn, 4
When the Green Leaves, 2
When the Humid Showers, 3
When the Kye Come Hame, 5
When the Leaves, 3
When Leaves Are Falling, 8
When the Mists Have Rolled, 1
When Morn o'er Mountain, 3
When the Night Wind, 6
When the Soft Twilight, 5
When the Summer Rain, 4
When the Swallow Comes, 6
When Swallows Homew'd fly,
When This Cruel War is Over, 4
When Twilight Dews, 4
When Up the Mountain, 3
When We Arrive at Home, 5
When wild War's deadly blast, 7
When You and I were Young, 8
Where Are Now the Hopes, 4
Where Are the Friends, 2
Where Are Those Dreamers, 8
Where Gadie Rins, 5
Where is German Fath'land, 8
Where Is Now the Merry Party, 1
Where My Home Lies, 7
Where, My Pretty Maid, 3
Where Roses Fair, 8
Where the Aspens Quiver, 7
Where the Faded Flower. 7
Where Warbling Waters, 6
Whether You Whisper Low, 6
Whichever Way the Wind, 3
While Shepherds Watched, 7
While the Days are Going by, 1
While the Morning Bells, 2
While We Shed a Tear, 6
Whistle and Hoe, 2
White Blossoms, 7
Who is he Plants for the Days, 4
Who'll Buy My Posies, 3
Who Rides Yonder, Proud, 7
Who Shall be Fairest, 4
Why Do I Weep for Thee, 7
Why Do Summer Roses Fade, 2
Why Left I My Hame. 3
Why Linger, Mourn'r Mem'ry, 5
Why Weep Ye by the Tide, 3
Wide-Wide-Wene, 5
Will You Go, Lassie, Go, 3
Will You Love Me Then as Now, 8
Winkum, Winkum, 8
With Crown and Sceptre, 6
With Glory Lit the Midnight, 8
With Glowing Heart, 1, 2
Within a Mile of Edinboro, 3
With Joy We Hail, 5
Wonderful Weaver, 6
Won't You Tell Me Why, Robin, 2
Woodman, Spare That Tree, 3
Words, Vain Words, 5
Work and Play, 1
Work, for the Night is Coming, 1
Yankee Boy, 7
Yankee Doodle, 3
Ye Banks an' Braes, 1
Ye Golden Lamps of Heaven, 5
Yeoman's Wedding Song, 6
Ye Sons of France, Awake, 1
Ye Sons of the Nation, 6
Yes, the Die is Cast, 3
Yestreen the Queen, 6
Y'heave Ho, My Lads, 5
You and I, 8
You and Me, 5
You Have Told Me, 8
You Never Miss the Water, 6
Young Agnes, 8
Young Indian Maid, 7
Young May Moon, 5
Your Hand is Cauld as Snaw,
Your Mission, 1
Zephyr of Nightfall, 5

ImTheStory.com

Personalized Classic Books in many genre's

Unique gift for kids, partners, friends, colleagues

Customize:

- Character Names
- Upload your own front/back cover images (optional)
- Inscribe a personal message/dedication on the
  inside page (optional)

Customize many titles Including
- Alice in Wonderland
- Romeo and Juliet
- The Wizard of Oz
- A Christmas Carol
- Dracula
- Dr. Jekyll & Mr. Hyde
- And more...

CPSIA information can be obtained at www.ICGtesting.com
Printed in the USA
LVOW10s1001170115

423272LV00021B/1910/P